CLINICAL GERONTOLOGY

A Guide to Assessment and Intervention

CLINICAL GERONTOLOGY
A Guide to Assessment and Intervention

Edited by
T. L. Brink, PhD

THE HAWORTH PRESS
NEW YORK • LONDON

Clinical Gerontology: A Guide to Assessment and Intervention has also been published as *Clinical Gerontologist,* Volume 5, 1986.

The Haworth Press, Inc., 28 East 22 Street, New York, New York 10010-6194
EUROSPAN/Haworth, 3 Henrietta Street, London WC2E 8LU England

Library of Congress Cataloging in Publication Data
Main entry under title:

Clinical gerontology.

　　"Has also been published as Clinical gerontologist, volume 5, 1986"—T.p. verso.
　　Includes bibliographies and index.
　　1. Geriatric psychiatry—Addresses, essays, lectures. I. Brink, T. L.
[DNLM: 1. Mental Disorders—in old age. 2. Psychotherapy—in old age.
W1 CL71D v. 5 / WT 150 C64035]
RC451.4.A5C525　1986　　618.97'689　　86-240
ISBN 0-86656-536-1

Contents

V. RELATED TOPICS

Preface

This book has also been simultaneously published as several issues of the quarterly journal, *Clinical Gerontologist: The Journal of Aging and Mental Health.* The decision on which topics to cover was based, in part, on considerations of what we have already covered in the journal's first four volumes.

Topics such as reminiscence, behavior modification, and cognitive retraining have been covered by numerous articles and clinical comments. Some previous issues have had comprehensive review articles on topics such as assessment of dementia (II, 4, pp. 3–23), delirium (I, 1, pp. 3–10), antidepressant medications (II, 1, pp. 3–29) and the Luria-Nebraska (I, 2, pp. 3–21). Therefore, these topics are not covered here.

If you are not yet a subscriber to the journal, we hope that this book will convince you that psychogeriatrics is a new and important field which is rapidly advancing its frontiers. *CG* attempts to keep us abreast of changes in the field.

T. L. Brink, PhD

I
ASSESSMENT OF THE GERIATRIC PATIENT

CLINICAL GERONTOLOGY

A Guide to Assessment and Intervention

1/REASONS FOR LOW UTILIZATION OF MENTAL HEALTH SERVICES BY THE ELDERLY

Milton C. Lasoski, PhD

Editor's Introduction

Lasoski presents an impressive analysis of an enduring problem: low elder rates of utilization of mental health services. The problem is not recent; it is more accurate to say that the mental health care of later life did not expand proportionately with the other advances of social services in the 1960s. Even two decades later, the majority of elder Americans in need of mental health care do not receive adequate intervention and treatment.

Lasoski offers an explanation in terms of three types of inter-related barriers to mental health care: professional attitudes, elder attitudes, and practical limitations.

The problem with professional attitudes is, simply stated, that few mental health practitioners have both the competence and commitment to work with the aged. Lasoski cites some problems based upon ignorance or exaggeration: the idea that the psychopathology of the aged is incurable, or that elder rigidity precludes effective change. Lasoski gives some reasons why mental health professionals may be less interested in working with elders, e.g., the lack of status within the profession. (A problem not mentioned in this article would be that of caregiver burnout: many mental health professionals have removed themselves from full-time geriatric work. See *CG*, v. 2, #3, the issue devoted to the topic of burnout.)

Milton C. Lasoski is affiliated with Psychology Dept. 116B, Ft. Lyon, VA Medical Center, Ft. Lyon, CO 81038.

Elder attitudes about mental health are somewhat characteristic of those attitudes of most Americans half a century
ago: mental illness is something to be ashamed of, it is incurable, requires life-long confinement in an institution, etc.
Elders are less likely to recognize a mental disorder (e.g.,
depression) in themselves or others, but are more likely to
ignore it or misinterpret it as a physical (or spiritual) problem, thereby requiring the services of general practice physicians (or clergy). A related problem is the fact that elders
are less likely to use social services in general, due to both a
reluctance to take "charity" and a pessimism about the efficacy of such programs in meeting their needs.

Practical problems revolve around the lack of adequate
reimbursement, transportation, referral, publicity, outreach,
training, research, and organizational responsiveness.

One solution, not mentioned by Lasoski, would be to
recruit more elders into the mental health care delivery
system as professionals or peer volunteers. See *CG*, v. 3,
#2, pp. 71-72.

I must wholeheartedly agree with Lasoski's conclusion:
the best way to increase mental health services utilization is
to develop, implement, and evaluate programs specifically
devised for removing the barriers.

There has been much discussion as to the reasons for the well
documented low utilization rate of outpatient mental health services
by our society's elderly population. Much of the blame has been
credited to the failure to disengage from societally generated stereotypes which has come to be termed as agism (Butler, 1969). The effects of agism have been described as impacting on many different
levels in ways which combine to encourage the placement of low
priority on the provisions of high quality mental health care to our
elderly citizens. There may also be attitudinal barriers on the part of
the elderly which dissuade them from the timely pursuit of the mental health services they need. Which factors are operative and how
they manifest themselves are areas which are just now being uncovered and explored by gerontologists. It is clear from the many
anecdotal reports that the causes of the current low utilization rate
are probably best viewed as manifold and interactive. Yet attempts
to intervene will require a more thorough and scientific analysis and

understanding of how the many factors manifest themselves in the delivery of mental health services to the elderly.

UTILIZATION PATTERNS

Estimates of mental disorders for the elderly repeatedly exceed the point prevalence rate of 10% given for the occurrence of mental problems requiring treatment for the general population (Redick & Taube, 1980; Romaniuk, McAuley, & Arling, 1983). Depending on whether criteria encouraged the reporting of mild, moderate, or severe impairment, ranges of 10-40% of the community elderly have been reported as psychologically impaired (Blazer, 1980; Kay & Bergmann, 1980; Myers, Weissman, Tischler, Holzer, Leaf, Oravschel, Anthony, Boyd, Burke, Kramer, & Stoltzman, 1984; Neugebauer, 1980; Pfeiffer, 1977; Weyerer, 1983). Rates would be higher if the institutionalized elderly population had been surveyed as well. Finkel (1981) summarizes these efforts by concluding that 15-25% of the elderly display significant symptoms of mental illness.

Large numbers of aged community residents receive no formal treatment. Estimates for 1980 (Levenson & Felkins, 1979) suggested that 80% of those elderly needing mental health services would not receive adequate assistance. The underrepresentation of the elderly as service recipients is most glaring in the area of outpatient services. Estimates are that the elderly comprise only 2-3% of the patient loads in private practice and hospital outpatient clinics (Butler & Lewis, 1982). Only 4-5% of the patients at Community Mental Health Centers are 65 years old or older (Knight, 1979; Redick & Taube, 1980).

It is also evident that the community elderly do not receive the frequency of services in proportion to their need. Redick, Kramer, and Taube (1973) reported that, while 29% of patient care episodes in outpatient work are with those under 18, only 2% are with those 65 or older. Moreover, Kahn (1975) reports that services for the elderly may be declining. A gathering of experts (Patterson, 1979) concluded that, despite a legislative mandate, "the Community Mental Health Centers have not been successfully attracting the elderly and little effort has been made to find out why" (p. 23).

Additionally, the mental health care that is provided is generally deficient in quality. For instance, Butler and Lewis (1982) point out that the elderly are seldom seen for active treatment but, rather, are frequently seen only for routine diagnostic evaluations and rapid disposition. These "routine" workups have not only been criticized for leading to premature labeling of many elderly patients as chronic organic brain syndromes (Lieff, 1982), but "disposition" is seldom to facilities where more than superficial attention can be given to psychological needs (Kucharski, Royce, & Schratz, 1979). Outpatient treatment has been criticized for an unjustified overreliance upon drug-only modes of psychotherapy (Ford & Sbordone, 1980; Lowy, 1980). Ronch and Solomon (1978) point to the fact that in many cases prevention of institutionalization has remained the only goal of outpatient service programs, and in so doing underestimates both the needs and capabilities of the community elderly.

PROFESSIONAL BARRIERS

Societal biases against active treatment for the elderly are often cited as underlying the neglect of the mental health needs of this segment of our society. There has been much discussion as to how the failure to disengage from societally generated stereotypes has led to therapeutic nihilism among the majority of mental health professionals (Blank, 1974; Garfinkel, 1975; Romaniuk, 1982). A number of studies have empirically established that such biases are widespread among professionals regardless of discipline (Kosberg & Harris, 1978). When age is the only factor allowed to vary in vignette presentations, professionals repeatedly show prejudices against active treatment of the elderly (Kucharski, Royce, & Schratz, 1979; Ford & Sbordone, 1980). There is little empirical evidence to suggest why some individuals within each profession are able to overcome societal influences.

Those who anecdotally report having overcome their own biases suggest their bases lie in a myriad of faulty premises about the nature of the aged and their mental disorders. The following claims are often listed as probable barriers to treatment:

1. Many problems of the elderly are too readily and wrongly viewed as irreversible symptoms, inevitably linked to the aging process.
2. Practitioners assume the elderly are too resistant to change, while geriatricians report that, just because the elderly stand so near to death, they often are quite capable of showing a surprising degree of psychological flexibility and resourcefulness.

3. Therapists avoid treatment of chronic and other conditions where they believe their skills are either inadequate or too narrow to solve a complex of multiple problems out of their realm of control.
4. The aged may stimulate the therapists' own anxieties and unresolved conflicts about their parental relationships or their own eventual aging, disability, or death.
5. Therapists associate work with the elderly with low professional status due to acceptance of the untested position that one should only offer the elderly supportive, non-confrontational forms of therapy, a second-rate procedure not requiring sophisticated professional skills.
6. Rather than viewing the aging person's remaining years as precious to society because there is so little time to achieve a triumphant closure to one's existence, there is the calculation that so few years can never pay back the therapist's investment in change-oriented treatment.

These attitudes are unfortunate as those clinicians who do work with the elderly report that good therapeutic results are obtained once therapists overcome their resistances to treating the aged. The common theme in the literature describing therapy experiences with the elderly (Brink, 1979; Knight, 1979) is that change and growth have no age limits.

PRACTICAL BARRIERS

Perhaps many of the foregoing professional biases would diminish, if progress were made in dismantling a number of practical barriers to making treatment accessible to the elderly. A number of problems in the current delivery system of mental health services are described below:

Real and Exaggerated Reimbursement Concerns

These often provide the hesitant therapist with excuses not to be involved in geriatric services. Governmental funding policies favor reimbursement for institutional inpatient care over non-medically provided outpatient services (Knight, 1979). Only 1.5% of mental health care expenditures are allocated for community-based services

(Reveron, 1982). Reveron reports that Medicare pays for only 50% of outpatient services with a maximum of $250. This contrasts with 80% coverage for routine ambulatory health care under Medicare-Part B. It has been found that outpatient agencies tend to offer only those services that are reimbursable through Medicare or Medicaid (Patterson, 1979). Outpatient services may not be available because of these funding policies, even when the need is clear.

Recent changes in public funding procedures may lead to a worsening of reimbursement practices for inpatient mental health services as well. The new Diagnostic Related Group formulas for length of stay appear slanted against the less acute psychiatric disorders or those physical disorders with concomitant psychological problems such as depression. Such policies may further encourage rapid disposition to nursing home placements and thereby deny the elderly with more chronic conditions from access to more specialized forms of psychological assistance. Case mix formulas, prevalent in long-term care facilities, base their reimbursement primarily on the level of nursing care needed to maintain the physical requirements of residents. Thus funding for trained psychotherapists and mental health rehabilitation programming would have to be taken out of budgeting for the essential custodial care of residents. In such an atmosphere it is likely that only emergency psychiatric services will be provided. Perhaps funding policies should consider monetarily rewarding programs for success in bringing patients from a more dependent level of care toward the independence needed for community placement. Thus programs would have incentives to add mental health rehabilitative components, and administrators would thus be encouraged to procure services from providers who proved their methods lead to effective results.

Transportation Problems

Older persons are particularly vulnerable to physical mobility difficulties and must often depend on others for vehicular transportation. These transportative difficulties hinder access to specialized services and may encourage irregular attendance once treatment has begun. This is especially true in rural settings (Gaitz, 1974). In a survey of rural elderly, Weyerer (1983) discovered an overreliance on treatment by general practitioners by older people having mental disorders, and concluded that the major reason for the low consultation rate of psychiatrists was the distance from the patient's home to the outpatient treatment facility.

Lack of Referral

More than half of the elderly receive their mental health care from primary care or general practice physicians as opposed to mental health specialists (Butler & Lewis, 1982). Studies on the utilization patterns of people of all ages having mental disorders reveal that as a group they are relatively high users of ambulatory health services, and indeed more than half initially present their psychological problems to primary care providers (Shapiro, Skinner, Kessler, Von Korff, German, Tischler, Leaf, Benham, Cottler, & Regier, 1984). However, the older psychologically impaired patient reportedly receives differential treatment from their family physicians. Stotsky (1972) reports they choose to treat the psychological problems of their elderly patients more frequently without the assistance of mental health specialists. Yet there is no evidence (Weyerer, 1983) to support the view that primary care physicians recognize the mental disorders of their older patients less often than in their younger patients. Perhaps such reluctance reflects the general practitioners' acceptance of stereotypic views of the mentally ill elderly. They may be prone to the overgeneralization of attributing disordered behavior in the elderly to irreversible physical causes. They may simply have a lack of faith that such services are efficacious for patients who reach old age.

Lack of referrals for specialized psychiatric services may also be a function of availability of mental health professionals with the interest and skills to work with this population (Shapiro et al., 1984). Another suggestion for the low referral rate to specialized psychiatric services relates to the intermix of both physical and mental problems which are more frequently and intensely found among the geriatric patient population. Perhaps the concomitant physical needs of their patients impress general practitioners in such a way that they view themselves as having a more vital role where there is real need for their skills to take precedence in patient management. Primary care physicians may thus lack confidence that physical impairments will receive as adequate or aggressive attention if patients pursue specialized mental health treatment outside of their care. Referral may also be dissuaded due to fears of offending family members or having to deal with non-cooperative attitudes.

Lack of Research

Despite the many anecdotal accounts of successful, change-oriented therapy with the elderly, the views of most psychotherapists remain pessimistic. Research findings should be more influential in the promotion of psychotherapy with the elderly. Research is needed to ascertain whether psychological services are being offered in the forms most helpful or attractive to the elderly. For instance, many anecdotal reports have advocated more extensive use of group methods (Lasoski & Thelen, 1984). In comparison to individual psychotherapy, group psychotherapy may be more effective in reducing the older person's sense of social isolation. It provides peer problem solving models, and may provide the consoling knowledge of the universality of their shared aging-related problems. Proponents also advocate its use because of its affordability, perception as a lesser threat to independence, and provision of a suitable replacement for lost natural supports systems. Unfortunately, these hypothesized advantages have as yet to be adequately tested empirically.

While research has clearly established that professionals are not immune from the affects of agism, research is needed into the reasons behind the development of the different types of negative attitudes which affect those who are responsible for the triage, referral, assessment, rehabilitation, care and re-education of older persons and their support systems. If these were understood it might be possible to instill positive professional attitudes. Research is also needed to determine what methods or approaches are efficacious in: (a) screening for those whose attitudes are barriers to effective care, (b) encouraging the formation of helpful attitudes, (c) providing the correct mix of theoretical and practicum experiences which will instill more productive viewpoints among prospective practitioners.

Lack of Training

Gerontologists deem the modification of professional attitudes through supervised training experiences as crucial if health practitioners are to deal effectively with the mental health needs of the elderly. Yet, graduate and professional programs seldom offer adequate theoretical preparation or practicum experiences (Ford & Sbordone, 1980; Ingersoll & Silverman, 1978). Furthermore major teaching medical centers treat proportionately fewer older people than other hospitals, and teaching staff reportedly consider chronic medical illnesses complicated by psychological disorders to be bad teaching cases (Lieff, 1982). Thus a vicious cycle occurs. Lack of interest results in poor training and education, frustrating therapeutic results follow when the problems of the elderly are encountered, negative attitudes toward the treatment of the elderly are thereby reinforced, and this further reduces the desire to use such cases for training purposes. It is not surprising, in light of this, that few practitioners feel comfortable in offering their services to this population.

Unresponsive Organizational Structures

Many of the foregoing issues reflect problems in the mental health system itself. These cannot be corrected by changes in the values and training of professionals alone. A redirection in societal and administrative priorities is necessary. For instance, organizational structures and reimbursement policies may make services inaccessible to the elderly.

Furthermore, inefficient coordination between professions often leads to poor case management and follow-up (Reveron, 1982). Pratt and Kethley (1980) studied the anticipated and actual barriers found by developers of mental health programs for the elderly. Twenty professionals were pretested on several indices of anticipated obstacles and post-tested as to the actual nature of the barriers they encountered. Existence of higher priority program areas and lack of adequate staff background in aging were the two most commonly anticipated obstacles that later materialized. Lack of support from external agencies was less of a problem than anticipated. Organizational bureaucracy issues within their own agency were not anticipated, but in fact became major deterrents to effective program development.

Patterson (1979) presented a systematic evaluation of how community mental health centers encouraged low utilization. They found that some centers discouraged community referrals by leaving the impression ''that the centers did not want to be involved with treating the elderly'' (p. 29). Centers had a direct clinical service focus rather than a more preventative, public health focus. This meant that only those seeking help received attention and no effort

was made to reach others with the same or more severe psychological problems. Outreach programs were deemed necessary if the
centers were to successfully attract elderly patients.

Lack of Publicity and Outreach

Changes in professional attitudes and the development of more efficacious treatment programs may not be sufficient alone to change
utilization patterns given the years of community exposure to past
treatment practices. The elderly must be made aware that meaningful services exist. Fichter and Weyerer (1982) have found that in
comparison to younger age groups, the elderly are less informed
about the availability of mental health services. Lack of information
strongly influences patterns of health agency usage by the elderly
(Snider, 1980). To successfully attract patients, programs may have
to take an active outreach approach. This could entail advertising
programs at activity and housing centers, delivering services at convenient places, and starting preventative programs such as self-help
groups. Outreach may include finding out from the elderly what
type of programs they need and which approaches they would ap-
prove, support, and utilize.

BARRIERS BY THE ELDERLY

Probably, many elderly fail to receive adequate services, not
through any discrimination against older people, but because of
their own prejudiced attitudes toward the seeking of assistance for
psychological disorders. It is, therefore, important to develop an
understanding of the influences of elderly attitudes as they may bear
on preventing fuller usage of existing mental health services.

Little is known about how different age groups differ in their
views of mental health issues. There are some indications that what
differences might exist are a function of social status factors rather
than purely aging effects (Clausen & Huffine, 1975). The structure
of beliefs about aging are common to all adult age groups (Kilty &
Feld, 1976). Attitudes toward the aged are typically negative, with
the aged themselves holding the most negative attitudes. However,
positive stereotypes tend to occur in samples of elderly with high occupational or educational status (Brubaker & Powers, 1976).

Mental health services are seldom elicited as needs by the elderly
in open-ended questionnaires (Coward, 1979). Moreover, Moen

(1978) reports the existence of a "non-acceptor syndrome" among today's aged, where a taboo exists toward programs they perceive as unearned (i.e., requiring income eligibility). This view toward services appears to be a cohort rather than an aging effect. Moen believes that tomorrow's elderly will become more aggressive toward obtaining assistance.

In an effort to compare and examine the perceptions of middle aged and elderly adults toward mental illness and related treatment services, Lasoski (1984) conducted a survey utilizing vignettes representing problems which are particularly common among the elderly. There was a high rate of agreement that all the vignette characters had serious psychological problems. This perception did not differ according to age or sex of respondents.

Opinions were also solicited about the need and usefulness of psychological services. Respondents were asked: (1) whether they thought psychological services could help people their age who go for help, and (2) whether they believe that good counseling would help most people get over their psychological problems. The age groups did not differ in their almost total agreement that such services do help. On the other hand, respondents of both age groups were in general disagreement that medicine alone would help most people in similar situations. Though generalization from this study may be limited due to methodological issues such as the rural nature of the sample, it was evident that age was not a factor in how respondents defined serious psychological problems and their readiness to identify professional mental health services as helpful to the psychologically impaired. The elderly not only accepted the notion of mental health intervention as important, they also wanted these services available for their own age cohort.

Despite their stated intention, one cannot assume that respondents would necessarily recognize such problems in themselves when they occur. Research is needed to discover whether there is an age difference in the point of recognition that one is psychologically distressed. Seeking professional treatment may not be a simple function of one's readiness to see such services as appropriate for a fictionalized character with an easily identifiable mental illness.

Waxman, Carner, and Klein (1984) conducted a survey where "well" elderly were asked to disclose their perception of future service utilization if they were to experience various medical or psychological symptoms. No effort was made to determine whether respondents identified the non-medical symptoms as being severe enough to qualify in their minds as symptoms of mental illness. They found that the percentage who would not seek any help went up as the symptoms became less clearly medical in nature. Moreover, when the sample was asked who they would go to first if they wanted to seek help, over 88% indicated they would go to a general physician. Only about 3.5% indicated they would go first to a mental health professional. It is not clear from this study, however, whether the elderly would have been less apt than younger people to go to a mental health professional if their primary care physician had suggested such a referral to them.

Lasoski (1984) surveyed the type of treatment seen as appropriate for vignette characters once they were identified as having a psychological disorder. Overall 49% of the responses indicated help should be sought on an outpatient basis while 36% indicated care should be given on an inpatient basis. Analyses showed that the elderly respondents were less likely to choose outpatient services than were the middle aged respondents. A second significant finding was that those of all ages who had less prior exposure to psychological services were also more inclined to choose inpatient over outpatient care. This psychological experience factor was suggested as a possible intervening variable as the elderly were less likely to have first hand familiarity with psychological services. It was hypothesized that less knowledge about psychological services and not merely chronological age accounted for the greater selection of inpatient services.

Inpatient treatment may be more threatening to the independence of the elderly than outpatient services. If the elderly are less prone to view outpatient services as a viable mode of treatment, then they may view inpatient treatment as a likely outcome if they seek help for their own psychological problems. It might be more difficult for the elderly to seek professional help when they believe doing so will require hospitalization.

Seeking treatment may not be a simple function of psychological mindedness as family and cultural factors may play a predominant role. There may be generational cohort differences which are influenced more by changes in cultural values than by the aging process (Romaniuk, 1982). These values may determine preferred coping styles, the type of resource (family, clergy, professional) called upon first during crises, and level of trust in motives of governmental agencies or profit making professional enterprises.

A variety of hypotheses have been offered as to how the attitudes of the elderly are responsible for their underutilization of services. Generally, there have been no adequate attempts to measure or investigate these influences in ways which will help to determine the extent of their impact. Anecdotally reported factors are categorized below in the interest of providing the background necessary to stimulate empirical research.

1. *Acceptance of societal biases.* Hagebak and Hagebak (1980) suggest that many elderly believe that everyone eventually becomes senile, and that this may deter them from seeking services that might identify reversible physical or psychological problems. Undoubtedly, many elderly have bought into the prevailing public stereotypes of aging and have become depressed, unmotivated, and apathetic as expected. Their loss of societally accepted roles may lead to feelings of uselessness and low self-esteem, which may convince them that they are no longer worth being helped.

2. *The stigma of mental illness.* Patterson (1979) suggests that the elderly are reluctant to think of themselves as having psychological problems and have to be in a crisis before considering the use of services labelled "mental health." Kahn (1975) notes that, while it may be a status symbol for the young to be in treatment, it is a disgrace for the current elderly generation.

3. *Needs perceived as unmet by available services.* The elderly may appraise services as being inappropriate, or inadequate to help solve their problems. The elderly may only choose to seek assistance when they believe the program will leave their sense of self-reliance intact. Coe (1967) suggests that available services have a custodial bias and unless this situation improves toward more active treatment, the elderly will not regain confidence in health services. The elderly may also be unaware when services encourage active treatment and independence. There is little done to bring this message to them.

4. *Financial reasons.* There may be real or fancied financial reasons for the resistance of the elderly to seek mental health intervention. They may shun expensive services because they fear the treatment will cost them their valued financial self-reliance.

5. *Loss of freedom feared.* The low rate of self-referral may reflect the fear of what may be found wrong and the consequences that could result. Blenkner, Bloom, and Nielsen

(1971) believe that the elderly feel threatened by persons representing the authority of society and suspect that, once released, their power will be used to curtail what freedom of action they have left. Others (Hagebak & Hagebak, 1980; Lasoski, 1984) suggest that the aged's image of mental health services is contrary to the current deinstitutionalization emphasis in vogue today.

Perhaps, too, their fears are justified. The elderly may be suspicious from past dealings where agencies seemed geared toward problem solving by relocating them in institutional settings. Blenker et al. (1971), for instance, found a negative association between the delivery of intensive social services to frail elderly and their survival rate. Clients receiving intensive services had a 37% survival rate over a four-year period (expected simulated standard life rates = 67%), while control clients had a 48% survival rate. The authors concluded that this was in part due to earlier institutionalization of the experimental clients. While stress was relieved for the community agents and collaterals involved, the more intensive services (particularly earlier institutionalization) did not prove to be protective. However, the data do not allow generalization to psychotherapeutic intervention programs. Services were directed to providing environmental supports only.

CONCLUSIONS

Older people receive fewer and poorer quality mental health services, but it is unclear whether this is mainly because they do not want it, or because the health services milieu encourages them to avoid contact. It is probably most productive to view the barriers as interrelated. Present utilization patterns, thus, reflect both the current attitudes of the elderly and the current nature of the health care establishment.

A host of specific reasons have been offered to help understand what prevents the elderly who need psychotherapeutic assistance from obtaining quality services. Unfortunately little empirical data from controlled studies exist to shed light on the existence, extent, and role played by the many commonly assumed hypotheses. There is an obvious need for further research with more meaningful dependent measures, controlled variables, and broader, more representative samples. Research is needed to evaluate the relative contributions of various factors. More importantly research could lead to discoveries relevant to designing programs to maximally attract and benefit the psychologically distressed elderly. For instance, empirical study might demonstrate that rejection of active, non-custodial intervention by the elderly has been exaggerated and reflects the stereotypical myths of society. Providing custodial services because we assume the elderly do not want or cannot handle psychotherapeutic efforts may be a self-fulfilling prophecy that continues to distance professionals and the elderly from each other.

As it is likely that both caregivers and recipients need to re-evaluate their assumptions, intervention should address both levels simultaneously. Re-education that dispels stereotypical biases may be necessary to change the distancing attitudes of both older people and health care providers. Findings from existing studies offer several other promising leads capable of producing a more favorable climate for dismantling system barriers.

Studies repeatedly find that older people often bring their complaints of mental health symptoms to the attention of general practitioners. Thus primary care physicians can play a key role since they are first presented with early signs of psychopathology and also have the elderly patient's confidence (Waxman, Carner, & Klein, 1984). Applied research is needed to find ways of increasing the general practitioner's abilities at early recognition of (a) mental disorders, and (b) the advisability of timely referral to mental health treatment programs.

Closer cooperation is needed by both medical and psychosocial disciplines as the elderly are likely to require active treatment in both spheres. One promising development has been the recent spread of specialized geriatric evaluation and treatment programs (Rubenstein, Rhee, & Kane, 1982). These units use an interdisciplinary team model to do medical, psychosocial, and functional status assessments which lead to multidisciplinary rehabilitative treatment plans. Research has shown that such units can have a considerable impact in lowering mortality, reducing institutional placements and readmissions, and providing ongoing care on a cost-efficient basis (Rubenstein, Josephson, Wieland, English, Sayre, & Kane, 1984). Further extensions of this model into the mental health realm may have the advantage of offering integrative approaches

which take care of the older person's holistic health needs while doing so in a less stigmatized atmosphere.

Educational and outreach programs may ultimately be necessary
for dramatic improvement in utilization patterns. Several implications emerge from existing reports. Chronological age may be less
of a factor than cohort differences in attitudes, values, and belief
systems. Older people's resistance to seeking mental health treatment may be accounted for by: (1) misinformation concerning the
domain of mental health specialists, (2) mistrust of authority and the
consequences that result from seeking treatment, or (3) misprecep-
tion of the efficacy of current treatment modalities. The elderly may
be unaware that, in contrast to just a few decades ago, current trends
are toward outpatient services and treatment aimed at helping people
remain in the community. Furthermore, survey data suggest (Lasoski, 1984) that the public is both supportive and ready for greater efforts at media exposure and outreach programs to insure that the
elderly become aware of current conceptions of available psychological treatment.

Perhaps the best way to test the relative contributions of the
various hypothesized barriers to treatment is to study the effects of
intervention programs aimed at removing the barriers!

REFERENCES

Blank, M. (1974). Raising the age barrier to psychotherapy. *Geriatrics, 29,* 141-148.
Blazer, D. (1980). The epidemiology of mental illness in late life. In E. Busse & D. Blazer
    (Eds.), *Handbook of geriatric psychiatry.* New York: Van Nostrand Reinhold.
Blenkner, M., Bloom, M., & Nielsen, M. (1971). A research and demonstration project of
    protective services. *Social Casework, 52,* 483-499.
Brink, T. (1979). *Geriatric Psychotherapy.* New York: Human Sciences Press.
Brubaker, T., & Powers, E. (1976). The stereotype of "old": A review and alternative ap-
    proach. *Journal of Gerontology, 31,* 441-447.
Butler, R. (1969). Age-ism: Another form of bigotry. *Gerontologist, 9,* 243-246.
Butler, R., & Lewis, M. (1982). *Aging and mental health* (3rd Ed.). St. Louis: C. V. Mosby.
Clausen, J., & Huffine, C. (1975). Sociocultural and social psychological factors affecting
    social responses to mental disorders. *Journal of Health and Social Behavior, 16,*
    405-420.
Coe, R. (1967). Professional perspectives on the aged. *Gerontologist, 7,* 114-119.
Coward, R. (1979). Planning community services for the rural elderly: Implications from re-
    search. *Gerontologist, 19,* 275-282.
Finkel, S. (Ed.). (1981, June). *Task force on the 1981 White House Conference on Aging of
    the American Psychiatric Association.* Washington, D.C.: APA Press.
Fichter, M., & Weyerer, S. (1982, September). *The course of mental illness in a representa-
    tive community sample of elderly people.* Paper presented at the Third European Sympo-
    sium on Social Psychiatry, Helsinki, Finland.

Ford, C., & Shordone, R. (1980). Attitudes of psychiatrists toward elderly patients. *American Journal of Psychiatry, 137,* 571-575.

Gaitz, C. (1974). Barriers to the delivery of psychiatric services to the elderly. *Gerontologist, 14,* 210-214.

Garfinkel, R. (1975). The reluctant therapist. *Gerontologist, 15*(2), 136-137.

Hagebak, J., & Hagebak, B. (1980). Serving the mental health needs of the elderly. *Community Mental Health Journal, 16,* 263-275.

Ingersoll, B., & Silverman, A. (1978). Comparative group psychotherapy for the aged. *Gerontologist, 18,* 201-206.

Kahn, R. (1975). The mental health system and the future aged. *Gerontologist, 15,*(1, Part 2), 24-31.

Kay, D., & Bergmann, K. (1980). Epidemiology of mental disorders among the aged in the community. In J. Birren & R. Sloane (Eds.), *Handbook of mental health and aging.* Englewood Cliffs, NJ: Prentice-Hall, Inc.

Kilty, K., & Feld, A. (1976). Attitudes toward aging and toward the needs of older people. *Journal of Gerontology, 31,* 586-594.

Knight, B. (1979). Psychotherapy and behavior change with the non-institutionalized aged. *International Journal of Aging and Human Development, 9,* 221-236.

Kosberg, J., & Harris, A. (1978). Attitudes toward elderly clients. *Health and Social Work, 3*(3), 67-90.

Kucharski, L., Royce, M., & Schratz, M. (1979). Age bias, referral for psychological assistance, and the private physician. *Journal of Gerontology, 34,* 423-428.

Lasoski, M. (1984). Attitudes of the elderly toward mental health treatment strategies. *Dissertation Abstracts International, 44,* 2248B.

Levenson, A., & Felkins, B. (1979). Prevention of psychiatric recidivism. *Journal of the American Geriatrics Society, 27,* 536-540.

Lasoski, M., & Thelen, M. (1984, July). A review of outpatient group psychotherapy with the elderly. *Psychological Documents, 14,* 7-8.

Lieff, J. (1982). Eight reasons why doctors fear the elderly, chronic illness, and death. *Journal of Transpersonal Psychology, 14,* 47-60.

Lowy, L. (1980). Mental health services in the community. In J. E. Birren & R. B. Sloane (Eds.), *Handbook of mental health and aging.* Englewood Cliffs, NJ: Prentice-Hall, Inc.

Moen, E. (1978). The reluctance of the elderly to accept help. *Social Problems, 25,* 293-303.

Myers, J., Weissman, M., Tischler, G., Holzer, C., Leaf, P., Oravschel, H., Anthony, J., Boyd, J., Burke, J., Kramer, M., & Stoltzman, R. (1984). Six-month prevalence of psychiatric disorders in three communities: 1980-1982. *Archives of General Psychiatry, 41,* 959-967.

Neugebauer, R. (1980). Formulation of hypotheses about the true prevalence of functional and organic psychiatric disorders among the elderly in the United States. In B. P. Dohrenwend, B. S. Dohrenwend, M. Gould, B. Link, R. Neugebauer, & R. Wunsch-Hitzig (Eds.), *Mental illness in the United States: Epidemiological estimates.* New York: Praeger.

Patterson, R. (1979). Community Mental Health Centers: A survey of services for the elderly. In *Issues in mental health and aging: Volume 3—Services.* Washington, D.C.: Government Printing Office.

Pfeiffer, E. (1977). Psychopathology and social pathology. In J. Birren & K. Schaie (Eds.), *Handbook of the psychology of aging.* New York: Van Nostrand Reinhold.

Pratt, C., & Kethley, H. (1980). Anticipated and actual barriers to developing community mental health programs for the elderly. *Community Mental Health Journal, 16,* 205-216.

Redick, R., Kramer, M., & Taube, C. (1973). Epidemiology of mental illness. In E. W. Busse & E. Pfeiffer (Eds.), *Mental illness in later life.* Washington, D.C.: American Psychiatric Association.

Redick, R., & Taube, C. (1980). Demography and mental health care of the aged. In J. E. Birren & R. B. Sloane (Eds.), *Handbook of mental health and aging.* Englewood Cliffs, NJ: Prentice-Hall, Inc.

Reveron, D. (1982). Aged are a mystery to most psychologists, *APA Monitor, 13*(2), 9.

Romaniuk, M. (1982). Community mental health practice and the elderly. *Professional Psychology, 13*(2), 222-228.

Romaniuk, M., McAuley, W., & Arling, G. (1983). An examination of the prevalence of mental disorders among the elderly in the community. *Journal of Abnormal Psychology, 92*, 458-467.

Ronch, J., & Solomon, J. (1978). An outreach and prevention unit in a mental health center serving the elderly. *Hospital and Community Psychiatry, 29*, 710-711.

Rubenstein, L., Josephson, K., Weiland, G., English, P., Sayre, J., & Kane, R. (1984). Effectiveness of a geriatric evaluation unit. *The New England Journal of Medicine, 311*, 1664-1670.

Rubenstein, L., Rhee, L., & Kane, R. (1982). The role of geriatric assessment units in caring for the elderly. *Journal of Gerontology, 37*, 513-521.

Shapiro, S., Skinner, E., Kessler, L., Von Korff, M., German, P., Tischler, G., Leaf, P., Benham, L., Cottler, L., & Regier, D. (1984). Utilization of health and mental health services. Archives of General Psychiatry, 41, 971-978.

Snider, A. (1980). Awareness and use of health services by the elderly. A Canadian study. *Medical Care, 18*, 1177-1182.

Stotsky, B. A. (1972). Social and clinical issues in geriatric psychiatry. *American Journal of Psychiatry, 129*, 117-126.

Waxman, H., Carner, E., & Klein, M. (1984). Underutilization of mental health professionals by community elderly. *Gerontologist, 24*, 23-30.

Weyerer, S. (1983). Mental disorders among the elderly. *Archives of Gerontology and Geriatrics, 2*, 11-22.

Questions

1) To what extent are the mental health attitudes of elders themselves a product of their cohort? In fifty years, will the psychologically aware, graying Baby Boomers be as reluctant to get the mental health care they need?

2) What educational programs might be appropriate to changing the mental health attitudes of today's elders?

3) How can we attract more psychiatrists, psychologists, social workers, nurses, and other counselors into the field of geriatrics?

4) What changes in public policy could remove some of the practical barriers mentioned by Lasoski?

2/SPATIAL COMPETENCE
Assessment of Route-Finding, Route-Learning, and Topographical Memory in Normal Aging

Randy Georgemiller, PhD
Fran Hassan, MA

Editor's Introduction

Too often, clinicians use Mental Status Questionnaire scores as if they were measures of a global measure of mental ability. I have noticed that some patients will do poorly on time-referent items (e.g., "What day of the week is today?") and yet wander about their neighborhoods without getting lost. Spatial competence is an important ability in independent living, and therefore the nature and level of spatial competence must be accurately assessed.

Georgemiller and Hassan present a comprehensive review of this oft neglected topic. There is some degree of loss of spatial competence even among elders without cognitive or sensory impairment. This trend can be found in both community and institutionalized elders. This creeping deficit may underlie the increasingly restricted territorial range found among many elders.

Randy Georgemiller is the Director of the Neuropsychology Laboratory, Lutheran General Hospital. Fran Hassan is a graduate student in the Department of Psychology, University of Health Sciences/Chicago Medical School.

We are grateful to Dr. Iseli Krauss for her assistance with researching the literature in the field of geriatric spatial competence and Ms. Rita Bode for providing manuals from the Science Research Associates, Inc. archives. We thank Dorothy Bissell, Nancy Rivas and Roxanne Ray for their help in preparing this manuscript.

Requests for reprints should be sent to Randy Georgemiller, PhD, Director, Neuropsychology Laboratory (12 West), Lutheran General Hospital, 1775 Dempster Street, Park Ridge, Illinois 60068.

19

The authors complain that most instruments designed to measure spatial competence have not been designed with or for elders. The designs are for testing brain injury or child-hood problems, and the scoring systems may penalize elders for a lack of speed, with the result that such tests may have poor validity for the assessment of spatial compe-tence in elders. On the other hand, direct experimental pro-cedures for assessing elders' route-finding ability lack nor-mative data.

Three specific forms of spatial disorientation are discussed: route-finding, route-learning, and topographical memory. The authors give a behavioral description of, and assess-ment strategies for each.

Other discussions of the assessment of dementia are cov-ered in *CG*, including Filinson's comprehensive review of state-of-the-art techniques (v. 2, #4, pp. 3–23) and reflec-tions on battery selection, administration, and interpreta-tion (v. 3, #2, pp. 23–26, 48–52, 52–54).

INTRODUCTION

Clinicians have long recognized problems of spatial orientation and memory as among the first signs of abnormal conditions such as Alzheimer's Disease and Parkinson's dementia (Lezak, 1983; Pir-ozzolo & Lawson-Kerr, 1980). Consequently, a large body of liter-ature (e.g., Kramer & Jarvick, 1979; Pirozzolo & Lawson-Kerr, 1980; Schaie & Schaie, 1977) is available to assist the psychologist in identifying and assessing these conditions. Until recently, how-ever, much less attention has been paid to the assessment of spatial orientation and abilities in the noncognitively impaired elderly.

Normal Aging and Spatial Abilities

Both the psychometric and environmental literature suggests that spatial abilities undergo decrement during normal aging. In a cross-sectional study, Horn and Cattell (1967) extracted factors from a number of intelligence and cognitive tests given to 297 male subjects between the ages of 14 and 61. They found Gv, a second-order fac-tor measuring general visualization functions, to improve through the 20s and then decline after the age of 28. Horn (1970) stated that visualization abilities plateau between the ages of 20 and 70 and then decline when longitudinal studies are being considered. Similarly, Benton, Eslinger, and Damasio (1981) found that 162 normal elderly subjects between the ages of 65 and 84 performed significantly worse on a measure of short-term visual memory than a normative sample of 60- to 64-year-olds.

Studies of elderly nursing home residents without obvious organic brain syndrome suggest that this population has insufficient knowledge of the environment for orientation and way-finding purposes. In general, knowledge of salient spatial locations declines with old age. When Weber, Brown, and Weldon (1978) asked 20 elderly residents to identify slides of landmarks taken in their nursing home, residents recognized an average of 66% of the landmarks but could correctly locate only 29% of them. In another study (Herman & Bruce, 1981), 34 high-functioning residents were asked to place pictures of landmarks on a schematic map of their nursing home. Residents displayed accurate knowledge of only a small area (the central corridor) of the nursing home environment. Norris and Krauss (1982) have demonstrated a significant ($p < .05$) relationship between the spatial behavior of 20 elderly nursing home residents and the kind of cognitive spatial skills which decline in old age. They found knowledge of and movement in the off-ward environment to be correlated with scores attained by these residents on a task of mental rotation abilities and a task of short-term spatial memory (Stafford, Krauss, Divgi, & Schaie, 1984).

Community-residing elderly demonstrate deficits of spatial recall and locational accuracy when compared to young adults. Perlmutter, Metzger, Nezworski, and Miller (1981) had 32 young adults and 32 elderly adults study three simple maps containing several landmarks and then place the buildings on a blank outline map. The younger adults performed significantly ($p < .001$) better than the elderly in both intentional and incidental memory conditions. In a 1983 study, Light and Zelinski demonstrated similar results. Evans, Brennan, Skorpanich, and Held (1984) found that 47 older adults recalled fewer buildings in their community and located the buildings they did recall less accurately than 72 young adults living in the same community. Finally, despite a wide range in individual performance, Walsh, Krauss, and Regnier (1981) found that the cognitive maps of 101 community-dwelling elderly were generally "limited in scope, disorganized, and minimally complex" (p. 337) when compared to maps drawn by younger persons.

Although subtly at first, problems with spatial competence may lead to reduced use of the environment (Walsh et al., 1981). In the long run, these deficits may contribute to the shrinking territorial range, lowered activity level, and constricted social space character-istic of so many elderly. Early indications of mild spatial incompe-tence may be seen in the community-dwelling older adult who aban-dons prior routines like daily walks in the park, the 70-year-old who discontinues driving despite adequate visual and motor skills, or the retirement home resident who restricts movement within the build-ing to well-learned locations like the bathroom and dining room.

While changes in environmental use patterns by the elderly have traditionally been considered as part of a larger process of disen-gagement (Botwinick, 1978), they can also be viewed as an indica-tion of "behavioral regression"; a return to previous less mature coping strategies (Barker & Barker, 1961). Reduced use of the envi-ronment has implications for both quality of life and environmental competence. In addition, the suggestion has been made (Ordy, Briz-zee, & Beavers, 1980; Norris & Krauss, 1982) that diminished levels of environmental exposure may be causing many elderly to lose cognitive skills that "might have been maintained at higher levels with greater stimulation" (Norris & Krauss, 1982, p. 7). If this is so, it behooves us to find ways of assessing deficits in spatial abilities early enough so that preventative and/or remedial interven-tions may be undertaken. For example, verbal prompts from retire-ment home staff or directional signs on corridor walls may help resi-dents to compensate for way-finding difficulties and therefore enhance their behavioral competence. Impaired recall for routes within the nursing home may be ameliorated by providing the pa-tients with written directions to frequently visited locations.

Assessment Issues

Unfortunately, although a wealth of instruments (Lezak, 1983) have been developed for the assessment of spatial problems, few have been designed with our purpose in mind. Most neuropsycho-logical procedures were devised for use with either brain damaged or younger populations, resulting in a lack of appropriate normative data for the aged, scoring systems which often penalize the elderly for lack of speed, and a lack of correspondence between test results and behavioral competence (Gaitz, 1972). Also psychometric tests pose speed problems, lack appropriate age and sex-normed scores, and present problems of reliability, generalizability across cohorts, and ecological and construct validity. In terms of the latter feature, Ohta and Kirasic (1983) have demonstrated conflicting results between the elderly's performance on paper-and-pencil tests and actual route-finding abilities when assessed by naturalistic means. Experimental procedures, while having greater construct validity, factorial distinctiveness, and ecological relevance, often suffer from lack of adequate normative data or fail to demonstrate acceptable psychometric properties (Schaie & Schaie, 1977). Finally, activities of daily living (ADL) scales touch upon, but do not thoroughly sample, the domain of spatial abilities necessary for environmental competence.

In this paper we focus on three categories of spatial disorientation (Benton, 1969) which seem most relevant to the elderly: defective route-finding ability, defective route-learning ability, and defective topographical memory. For each category, we attempt to describe the particular spatial problem involved, discuss possible cognitive and environmental factors underlying the problem, and suggest ways to assess the problem, both with current techniques and tools yet to be developed.

As Benton (1969, 1982) points out, spatial disorientation is a term that has been employed rather loosely. Persons may appear disoriented as a result of problems with verbal labeling, visual acuity, visual scanning, unilateral neglect, global memory loss, inability to concentrate, or general confusion, as well as true spatial disorientation (Lezak, 1983). Within the category of true spatial disorders, patients may demonstrate reading or counting difficulties, right-left disorientation, or an inability to localize objects in space, as well as the route-finding, route-learning, and topographical memory difficulties most relevant to spatial competence. The reader is referred to Lezak (1983, chapters 12 through 15) for a complete discussion of the assessment of visuospatial, perceptual, and attentional disorders.

DEFECTIVE ROUTE-FINDING ABILITY

Behavioral Description

Persons with this deficit are unable to follow a route or find their way from one location to another, despite preservation of topographical memory and the ability to give accurate verbal descriptions of familiar routes. Benton (1969) refers to route-finding difficulties as primarily "disorders in execution." Constructional deficits almost always accompany route-finding difficulties; patients can neither accurately draw a path they have described nor trace paths through mazes of either the pencil-and-paper or locomotor type. People with route-finding difficulties may demonstrate consistent neglect of left turns or nonsystematic directional confusion at choice points. They will omit crucial turns in the drawing of a route, reverse right and left turns, and render inaccurate representations of the relative lengths of route sections. Route-finding difficulties may be partially explained by age-related decrements in spatial abilities. While there is a wide range of individual and sex differences in visuospatial task performance (Norris & Krauss, 1982), the elderly generally take longer mentally to rotate objects in space and tend to make more egocentric errors in perspective-taking tasks than young adults (Gaylord & Marsh, 1975; Herman & Coyne, 1980; Krauss, Quayhagen, & Schaie, 1980; Schultz & Hoyer, 1976).

Recent research indicates that environmental and task attributes significantly affect the accuracy of the elderly in performing spatial tasks. Evans et al. (1984) found that their sample of 47 community-dwelling elderly were better able to recall and locate building landmarks that had high use-intensity, unique style, and symbolic or historical significance. Easily recalled landmarks also tended to be in naturally landscaped settings or situated on a main street. Ohta and Kirasic (1983) stress the increased spatial abilities of the elderly when tasks are set in familiar or ecologically relevant surroundings such as medical centers, supermarkets, or hometown environments. Finally, Hart and Berzok (1982) point to a use of sequence-ordered mapping strategies which may be substituted for configurational strategies depending upon journey purpose and environmental attributes. For instance, elderly with poor directional sense may conceptualize a trip as a series of bus stops rather than follow a city map.

Assessment Strategies

Assessment of route-finding difficulties has traditionally focused on observation of a patient's behavior in real-life surroundings. For example, the patient is observed as she finds her way from bedroom to bathroom, dining room, or office; it is determined if the patient can travel alone from her home to the clinician's office; and the patient's ability to find her way to neighborhood stores and service facilities is assessed. Since actual observation of the patient is not always feasible, verbal reports from relatives or caretakers, drawings of cognitive maps detailing familiar routes, and paper-and-pencil tracings or routes through mazes or road maps, have also been employed (see Lezak, 1983, pp. 368–371, 539–541). Semmes, Weinstein, Ghent, and Teuber (1955) have developed a procedure for assessing extrapersonal orientation which could become a useful tool if developed as a standardized test. In research with this procedure, 108 male veterans with and without head wounds followed 15 paths, walking between red dots painted on the gray floor of a large laboratory. Subjects followed the paths with the aid of white cardboard maps (30.5 cm square) on which black lines (the paths) were drawn to connect red ink dots. The subjects were instructed to hold the maps in a constant orientation to their bodies, with the southern edge of the maps always nearest to them. The direction North was marked on both the maps and the north wall of the room. While the original study tested route finding via tactual and visual maps, discussion of the tactile procedure is beyond the scope of this paper. However, the tactual paths are included in Figure 1 since they could be adapted to visual way finding evaluation in future research.

This procedure provides a relatively realistic test of wayfinding ability which could be modified and made more naturalistic (e.g., altering the laboratory room setting by using posters or murals; using markers in the hallways of the assessment clinic, nursing home, or other indoor environment). Standardized instructions for performing the task while holding the map in a constant position are provided. We suggest that a second administration procedure which allows the subject to find his way by rotating the map to adjust perspective also be given. Like many experimental procedures, this test currently has no normative or other psychometric data and was not developed specifically for use with the elderly. In addition, those wishing to develop this test in a standardized form would need to demonstrate construct validity by correlating performance on this task with environmental wayfinding tasks of the type described by Ohta and Kirasic (1983).

In an example of one such task, these experimenters led 15 elderly community residents and 15 undergraduates on two routes connecting the lobby and the emergency room of a medical center. After having been led on the routes several times, and drawing the routes after each trip, subjects made a final tour in which part of the first route was blocked off and they had to decide whether to backtrack and use the second route or proceed along a novel route which was a shortcut to the emergency room. Despite the fact that elderly

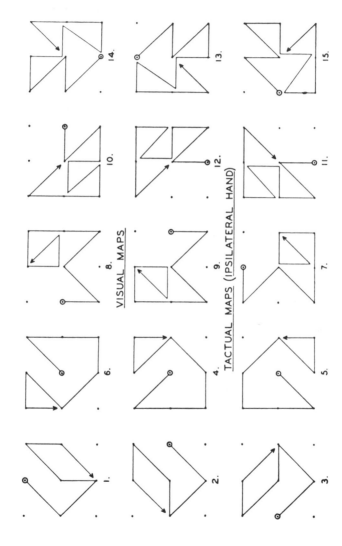

VISUAL MAPS

TACTUAL MAPS (IPSILATERAL HAND)

FIGURE 1. Visual and tactual, maps. Note. From "Spatial Orientation in Man After Cerebral Injury: I. Analyses by Locus of Lesion" by J. Semmes, S. Weinstein, L. Ghent, and H. L. Teuber, 1955, Journal of Psychology, 39, p. 233. Copyright 1955 by the Journal Press. Reprinted by permission.

subjects drew poorer cognitive maps than their younger counter-parts, they were just as successful in devising an appropriate detour. Mental spatial rotations will be considered next. The Primary Mental Abilities Test for Ages 11–17 (PMA), which was originally developed by Thurstone in 1947 has had a long history of use with the elderly (Schaie, 1958; Schaie & Labouvie-Vief, 1974; Schaie & Strother, 1968). The Space subtest consists of 20 items, requiring subjects to mentally rotate a row of figures and then indicate which ones are identical to or a mirror image of the row sample. Norms are based on a sample of more than 40,000 junior high and high school students. Percentile ranks can be arrived at for each age level and the manual (Thurstone, 1958) details factors such as sex differences which affect test performances. Among its advantages, this test comes with a complete manual, including standardized instructions, is self-administered, and possesses an age-fair alternate form, the Adult Mental Abilities Test (AMA), which has recently been reported on by Popkin, Schaie, and Krauss (1983). To our knowledge, correlational data between the AMA and the PMA have not yet been released.

Stafford, Krauss, Divgi, and Schaie (1984) have developed a series of tasks measuring spatial memory and rotational abilities that are easy to administer and which employ pictures of playing cards as familiar, ecologically relevant stimuli. The spatial rotation tasks consist of an array of nine standard playing cards, including twos, threes, and sevens, in three suits. Subjects are asked to imagine the array rotated either 1/4, 1/2, 3/4, 3/8, or one full turn and to reproduce the rotated array with a duplicate set of cards. After completing four rotations, another four rotations are completed with a second set of nine cards of various values, shapes, and suits. A sample of this card array is found in Figure 2. Memory factors are minimized by having the original array remain in view but immovable throughout the task. Scoring for this spatial rotation task is based upon the number of correct rotations. For a combined sample of 58 adults with a mean age of 58.6 years (30–79 years old), the mean score obtained was 4.60 ($SD = 2.74$ out of a possible 8 points. Test-retest reliability was moderate ($r = .76, p < .05$) and scores obtained on the test demonstrated a modest correlation ($r = .40, p < .01$) with performance on the Space subtest of the PMA. Use of the spatial rotation task on additional samples of normal and impaired elderly is advised to complete the normative process and assist clinicians in establishing clinically relevant score cutoffs.

FIGURE 2. Spatial rotation matrix of standard, round and zig-zag cards. *Note.* From *Assessing Cognitive Abilities Across the Adult Lifespan: Validity of Five Novel Tasks* by J. L. Stafford, I. K. Krauss, D. R. Divgi, and K. W. Schaie, 1984, unpublished manuscript. Reprinted by permission.

Finally, some attempt should be made to systematize and assess sequential wayfinding strategies of the type described by Hart and Berzok (1982). It is possible that otherwise oriented, community-dwelling or nursing home elderly with poor spatial configurational skills might prolong competence by being retrained to fall back upon sequential route-finding strategies.

DEFECTIVE ROUTE-LEARNING ABILITIES

Behavioral Description

We use this term to refer to what Benton (1969, p. 217) has characterized as defective short-term memory for spatial location. Patients with this deficit suffer from a failure to learn the spatial arrangement of stimuli even after repeated exposure, or, in milder form, learn new spatial arrangements quite slowly. Lezak (1983, p. 547) points out that this deficit may be so severe that it will take days for an alert and ambulatory patient to learn his way to the ward bathroom. In community-dwelling elderly, relocation to a new apartment building or neighborhood may result in a period of painful reorientation as the normal difficulties of route-learning are complicated by poor spatial memory. In addition, patients affected by this deficit will perform adequately on psychometric tasks of spatial localization, figure copying, or discrimination, but will show significant performance decrement when removal of the stimulus introduces a short-term memory element (Benton, 1969). Krauss et al. (1980) have illustrated this point by administering both sequential and simultaneous versions of tasks requiring mental rotation of shapes and objects to a sample of 48 elderly adults between the ages of 64 and 76. Simultaneous presentation of stimuli facilitated performance while sequential presentation which contained a memory component worsened it.

We realize that short-term memory deficits resulting in defective route-learning often contribute to route finding deficits in real-life situations. However, since short-term memory demands can be minimized by redesigning an environment, therefore, enhancing subsequent route-finding ability (Evans et al., 1984) we believe that route-learning difficulties should be treated separately in discussing spatial competence in the elderly.

Assessment Strategies

In contrast to instruments for assessing route-finding difficulties, several tests exist for the assessment of spatial memory functions.

The Benton Visual Retention Test (BVRT) (Benton, 1974) is designed to assess visual perception, visual memory, and visual constructive abilities. The test can be administered as direct copy, reproduction after 5- or 10-second exposure, or with a 15-second delay after exposure. While this last procedure is still experimental, anecdotal observations suggest that persons with short-term memory problems (Benton, 1974, pp. 72–73) will often perform poorly on this test. Three alternate forms, each containing ten designs with one or more figures per item make up the content of the test. Because of the layout of the test figures, the BVRT is sensitive to unilateral visual neglect as well as memory and constructional problems.

Among the advantages of the BVRT are provision of a manual which includes standardized directions for administration and scoring, a high degree of stability ($r = .85$), and correlation coefficients of between .79 and .84 among the three alternate forms. The copy and two immediate recall versions of the test have been normed on groups of between 103 and 600 subjects. Adult subjects in the norm group were medical patients between the ages of 15 and 64 without known cerebral damage or psychosis. Expected scores are corrected for the effects of age and premorbid IQ, and cutoff scores for the interpretation of acquired cognitive impairment are provided.

The BVRT has been given to several groups of cognitively normal elderly between the ages of 65 and 84 (Benton, Eslinger, & Damasio, 1981). Performance on this test was significantly lower than expected from score extrapolations of the 60- to 64-year-old normative group (Lezak, 1983, p. 449). In addition, Lezak cautions that the BVRT has been found to correlate more highly with tests of visuoconstructive function than with tests of memory. We suggest that this test be used descriptively rather than diagnostically when working with an elderly population.

Stafford et al.'s (1984) Five Novel Tasks includes a simple, ecologically relevant test of memory for spatial designs. In this task, subjects study a fixed matrix of nine playing cards including kings, nines, and fives of hearts, diamonds and spades in three shapes. When the subject feels the matrix is memorized, it is turned face down and the subject tries to replicate the original array with a duplicate set of cards. The test is scored by totaling the number of attributes placed correctly. In the previously mentioned sample of 58, subjects achieved a mean score of 4.90 ($SD = 2.93$). Test-retest reliability was moderate ($r = .73, p < .05$). Scores obtained on the test correlated only .16 ($p < .05$) with the spatial rotation subtest and .29 ($p < .05$) with the PMA spatial relations subtest, thus suggesting the existence of at least two factors important in the assessment of visual spatial competence.

Perlmutter et al. (1981) and Light and Zelinski (1983) have addressed the problem of ecological validity in developing two tasks designed to measure visual memory. In these tasks, elderly subjects were asked to study small maps containing realistic pictures of between 8 and 12 landmarks. Subjects were then tested for either incidental or intentional memory by being asked to remember the structures or to remember both the structures and their locations, filling them in by number on an accompanying outline map. We believe that this procedure can easily be adapted so as to constitute a standardized test. Samples of these maps are given in Figures 3 and 4.

Other naturalistic tests of location memory, while also experimental, hold promise for future development. Accredolo, Pick, and Olson (1975) have developed a location memory test assessing both incidental and intentional memory. In this procedure, subjects are escorted through the hallways of a building and an outdoor environment both with and without landmark features. In the incidental condition, the assessor drops a card or a pencil and asks the subject to pick it up for him. Sometime later in the walk, the subject is asked to return as close as possible to the spot in which the pencil or card was dropped. In the intentional condition, the subject is shown a spot close to or away from a landmark and is asked to remember the location, as he will be required to lead the assessor back to that location at the conclusion of the walk. In addition, the imaginative clinician will think of several other naturalistic ways of assessing spatial memory in the community and nursing home environment, including questioning caretakers about a client's memory for unfamiliar routes.

DEFECTIVE TOPOGRAPHICAL MEMORY

Behavioral Description

This may be described as the inability to recall and describe familiar routes or the spatial characteristics of familiar surroundings. Patients with this disorder usually display loss of former geographical concepts, frequently become lost in their homes or com-

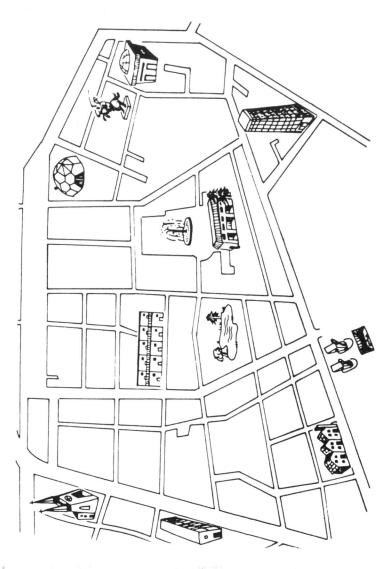

FIGURE 3. Sample map from spatial task. *Note.* From "Spatial and Temporal Memory in 20 and 60 Year Olds" by M. Perlmutter, R. Metzger, T. Nezworski, and K. Miller, 1981, *Journal of Gerontology, 36,* p. 61. Copyright 1981 by the Gerontological Society of America. Reprinted by permission.

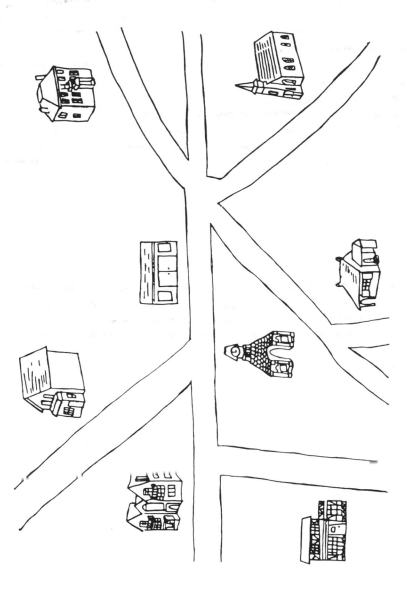

FIGURE 4. 12-structure map. *Note.* From "Memory for Spatial Information in Young and Old Adults" by L. Light and E. Zelinski, 1983, *Developmental Psychology, 19,* p. 903. Copyright 1983 by the American Psychological Association. Reprinted by permission.

munities, and cannot demonstrate an accurate verbal or visual rendering of spatial relationships. Generally, however, route-finding, short-term visual memory, and localization skills remain intact (Benton, 1969), and generalized memory impairment need not accompany this condition (Ratcliff, 1982).

Cognitively, the underlying deficit seems to be "an impairment in revisualization" (Benton, 1969, p. 218) resulting in a failure to retrieve long-established visual memories. Stored information about spatial concepts is no longer available either visually or verbally. While the patient may be able to recite overlearned verbal associations (such as the fact that Miami is in Florida or the sequence of stops on a railroad line), he cannot give directions nor draw or describe the spatial relations between locations. To date, research is lacking on whether environmental factors (such as lack of exposure to an environment due to a decreased activity level) may also play a role in this form of memory deficit.

Assessment Strategies

A quick and convenient method for the assessment of topographical memory loss is to have the patient first verbally describe and then draw routes and spatial arrangements such as the floor plan of their house or ward, a diagram of streets in one's immediate neighborhood, or the route to the nearest grocery store or gas station from one's home. Performance should be evaluated in light of the patient's educational and experiential levels (Benton, 1969; Lezak, 1983). Patterson and Zangwill (1944) had patients draw maps of their city's downtown area while Walsh et al. (1981) had elderly subjects draw "cognitive maps" of their neighborhoods. Maps should be assessed for factors such as accuracy, completeness, and complexity.

Evans et al. (1984) have developed a procedure for assessing location memory for familiar urban landmarks. Twenty-four community dwelling elderly subjects were asked to verbally list all the buildings they remembered within a four square-block downtown area and then place numbers for 13 frequently named buildings on a grid map of the same area in which a central landmark (a well-known park) was provided as a cue. This procedure seems highly adaptable and possesses several clear advantages. Elderly participants do not have a time limit and can ask questions about the tasks whenever necessary. If a subject forgets the name of a building, a brief description of its appearance and location is acceptable. Two scores, one for number of buildings recalled and another for locational accuracy, had high interrater reliability ($r = .90$). However, the complex method used to attain the accuracy scores plus the lack of normative data from a larger sample make individual scores difficult to evaluate. For simplicity sake, it is suggested that the scoring system used by Norris and Krauss (1982), which measures locational accuracy in terms of distance in city blocks between identified and actual locations, be substituted when tasks like this are used for assessment purposes.

Finally, Benton, Levin, and Van Allen (1974) have developed a standardized test of geographic localization which was administered to 84 control patients with physical, noncerebral illness and 50 brain-damaged patients between 20 and 78 years of age. Directions and printed instructions are provided for the administration of three tests which measure verbal association, verbal directions, and map orientation. Scoring directions are clear and easy to follow and level of education (but not age) is taken into account in classifying scores as normal or defective. To our knowledge, information regarding test-retest reliability and construct validity is not available for this measure. Because of the substantial educational level effect and the relatively overlearned nature of this task, behavioral validation of results is suggested. It is possible that a well-educated elderly person may perform adequately or show only mild deficit on this test while doing worse on a test of map knowledge of their neighborhood or nursing home or when being observed naturalistically in familiar surroundings.

CONCLUSION

We realize that our discussion of factors underlying spatial competence is somewhat speculative and that our suggestions for assessment techniques are both incomplete and highly selective. We point to a relative lack of literature specifically addressing the functional spatial capabilities of the elderly and to a need for additional theory-based research in this area. We believe that in order to accurately assess the spatial competence of the elderly, it is necessary to better identify the factors leading to competent spatial behavior or its absence. We agree with Ratcliff (1982) that a true understanding of spatial capabilities will attempt to integrate results from cognitive, developmental, physiological, and psychosocial research as well as traditional neuropsychological literature. Along with Hart and Berzok (1982) and Ohta and Kirasic (1983), we argue that real progress in this area will not be achieved unless research on spatial competence becomes more ecologically grounded. We need to assess the spatial competence of the elderly in settings that are familiar to them and with tasks that are meaningful to them. It is imperative that we standardize these tasks so that they provide meaningful psychometric data. Only in this way can we achieve our stated aim of identifying deficits in spatial competence early enough so that the elderly need not suffer unnecessary cognitive decline and behavioral constriction.

REFERENCES

Accredolo, L. P., Pick, H. L., & Olson, M. G. (1975). Environmental differentiation and familiarity as determinants of children's memory for spatial location. *Developmental Psychology, 495–501.*

Barker, R. G., & Barker, L. S. (1977). The psychological ecology of old people in Midwest, Kansas and Yoredale, Yorkshire. In J. Birren & K. W. Schaie (Eds.), *Handbook of the psychology of aging.* New York: Van Nostrand Reinhold.

Benton, A. L. (1969). Disorders of spatial orientation. In P. J. Vinken & G. W. Bruyn (Eds.) *Handbook of clinical neurology* (Vol. 3): New York: Wiley.

Benton, A. L. (1974). *The Revised Benton Visual Retention Test* (4th ed.). New York: Psychological Corp.

Benton A. L. (1982). Spatial thinking in neurological patients: Historical aspects. In M. Potegal (Ed.), *Spatial abilities.* New York: Academic Press.

Benton, A. L., Eslinger, P. J., & Damasio, A. R. (1981). Normative observations on neuropsychological test performances in old age. *Journal of Clinical Neuropsychology, 3,* 33-42.

Benton, A. L., Levin, H. S., & Van Allen, M. W. (1974). Geographic orientation in patients with unilateral cerebral disease. *Neuropsychologia, 12,* 183-191.

Botwinick J. (1978), *Aging and behavior* (2nd ed.). New York: Springer.

Cooper, L. A. (1975). Mental rotation of random two-dimensional shapes. *Cognitive Psychology, 7,* 20–43.

Evans, G. W., Brennan, P. L., Skorpanich, M. A., & Held, D. (1984). Cognitive mapping and elderly adults: Verbal and location memory for urban landmarks. *Journal of Gerontology, 39,* 452–457.

Gaitz, C. M. (1972). Neuropsychological assessment of cerebral disease. In C. M. Gaitz (Ed.), *Aging and the brain.* New York: Plenum Press.

Gaylord, S. A., & Marsh, G. R. (1975). Age differences in the speed of a spatial cognitive process. *Journal of Gerontology, 30,* 674–678.

Hart, R., & Berzok, M. (1982). Children's strategies for mapping the geographic-scale environment. In M. Potegal (Ed.), *Spatial abilities.* New York: Academic Press.

Herman, J. F., & Bruce, P. R. (1981). Spatial knowledge of ambulatory and wheelchair-confined nursing home residents. *Experimental Aging Research, 7,* 491–496.

Herman, J. F., & Coyne, A. (1980). Mental manipulation of spatial information in young and elderly adults. *Developmental Psychology, 16,* 537-538.

Horn, J. (1970). Organization of data on life span development of human abilities. In L. R. Goulet & P. B. Baltes (Eds.), *Lifespan developmental psychology: Research and theory.* New York: Academic Press.

Horn, J., & Cattell, R. (1967). Age differences in fluid and crystallized intelligence. *Acta Psychologica, 26,* 107–129.

Krauss, I. K., Quayhagen, M., & Schaie, K. W. (1980). Spatial rotation in the elderly: Performance factors. *Journal of Gerontology, 198,* 199–206.

Lezak, M. D. (1983). *Neuropsychological Assessment* (2nd ed.). New York: Oxford University Press.

Light, L., & Zelinski, E. (1983). Memory for spatial information in young and old adults. *Developmental Psychology, 19,* 901–906.

Norris, K. K. A., & Krauss, I. K. (1982, August). *Spatial abilities and environmental knowledge and use in institutionalized elderly.* Paper presented at the Annual Meeting of the American Psychological Association, Washington, D.C.

Ohta, R. J., & Kirasic, K. C. (1983). The investigation of environmental learning in the eldery. In R. Rowles & R. J. Ohta (Eds.), *Aging and milieu: Environmental perspectives on growing old.* New York: Academic Press.

Ordy, J. M., Brizzee, K. R., & Beavers, T. R. (1980). Sensory functions and short term memory in aging. In G. J. Malctta & F. J. Pitozzolo (Eds.), *The aging nervous system.* New York: Praeger.

Patterson, A., & Zangwill, O. L. (1944). Disorders of visual space perception associated with lesions of the right cerebral hemisphere. *Brain, 67,* 331–358.

Perlmutter, M., Metzger, R., Nezworski, T., & Miller, K. (1981). Spatial and temporal memory in 20 and 60 year olds. *Journal of Gerontology, 36,* 59–65.

Pirozzolo, F. J., & Lawson-Kerr, K. (1980). Neuropsychological assessment of dementia. In G. J. Maletta, & F. J. Pirozzolo (Eds.), *The aging nervous system.* New York: Praeger.

Popkin, S. J., Schaie, K. W., & Krauss, I. K. (1983). Age-fair assessment of psychometric intelligence. *Educational Gerontology, 9,* 47–55.

Ratcliff, G. (1982). Disturbances of spatial orientation associated with cerebral lesions. In M. Potegal (Ed.), *Spatial abilities.* New York: Academic Press.

Schaie, K. W. (1958). Rigidity-flexibility and intelligence: A cross-sectional study of the adult life span from 20 to 70. *Psychological Monographs, 72,* (9, Whole No. 609).

Schaie, K. W., & Labouvie-Vief, G. (1974). Generational versus ontogenetic components of change in adult cognitive behavior: A fourteen-year cross-sectional study. *Developmental Psychology, 10,* 305–320.

Schaie, K. W., & Schaie, J. P. (1977). Clinical assessment and aging. In J. Birren & K. W. Schaie (Eds.), *Handbook of the psychology of aging.* New York: Van Nostrand Reinhold.

Schaie, K. W. & Strother, C. R. (1968). A cross-sectional study of age changes in cognitive behavior. *Psychological Bulletin, 70,* 671–680.

Schultz, N. R., & Hoyer, W. J. (1976). Feedback effects on spatial egocentrism in old age. *Journal of Gerontology, 31,* 72–75.

Semmes, J., Weinstein, S., Ghent, L., & Teuber, H. L. (1955). Spatial orientation in man after cerebral injury: I. Analysis by locus of lesion. *Journal of Psychology, 39,* 227–244.

Stafford, J. L., Krauss, I. K., Divgi, D. R., & Schaie, K. W. (1984). *Assessing cognitive abilities across the adult lifespan: Validity of five novel tasks.* Unpublished manuscript, Department of Psychiatry, Massachusetts General Hospital, Boston.

Thurstone, T. G. (1958). *Manual for the SRA Primary Mental Abilities: Ages 11 to 17* (3rd ed.). Chicago: Science Research Associates.

Walsh, D. A., Krauss, I. K., & Regnier, V. A. (1981). Spatial ability, environmental knowledge, and environmental use: The elderly. In L. S. Lieben, A. H. Patterson, & N. Newcombe (Eds.), *Spatial representation and behavior across the life span.* New York: Academic Press.

Weber, R. J., Brown, L. T., & Weldon, J. K. (1978). Cognitive maps of environmental knowledge and preference in nursing home patients. *Experimental Aging Research, 4,* 157–178.

Questions

1) What are the advantages and limitations of using standardized measures of spatial competence as opposed to an experimental observation of the patient's actual performance?

2) Would information resulting fom spatial competence assessment influence a diagnosis of dementia? depression? paranoia?

3) How would information on spatial competence influence decisions regarding institutionalization? rehabilitation?

3/THE HALSTEAD-REITAN NEUROPSYCHOLOGICAL TEST BATTERY AND AGING

Ralph M. Reitan, PhD
Deborah Wolfson, PhD

Editor's Introduction

Reitan and Wolfson have put together a comprehensive review of the use of one of the foremost neuropsychological tests and how it can be used with the aged.

The research reviewed indicates that chronological age, in and of itself, may produce some deterioration similar to that seen in patients with heterogeneous cerebral damage. Moreover, the deficits associated with aging tend to occur on more complex tasks, rather than the simpler ones measured by the Luria-Nebraska. So, if the purpose is to assess the aging effects per se, tests such as the Halstead Impairment Index, Category Test, Tactual Performance-Localization component, and part B of the Trail Making test would be appropriate. If the purpose is to discount effects due principally to aging, the Age-Brain Quotient can be utilized in the interpretation of test scores.

The authors speculate about how neuropsychological testing could be utilized in the rehabilitation of the aged. I agree with their conclusion that rehabilitation programs must be tailored to the specific needs and limitations of the individual patient, and the Halstead-Reitan battery may be one way of initially determining those needs.

Three case studies illustrate the authors' points.

Past *CG* articles have discussd other neuropsychological

The authors are affiliated with the Department of Psychology, University of Arizona, Tucson, AZ 85721.

tests such as the Fuld Object Memory (v. 1, #1, pp. 23–28), the Luria-Nebraska (v. 1, #2, pp. 3–21), and reflexes (v. 3, #2, 19–22). Other articles have discussed the role of neuropsychological testing in light of linguistics (v. 1, #3, pp. 53–79), compared the Halstead-Reitan to CT scans (v. 2, #2, pp. 13–22), and offered hints on increasing the compliance and motivation for neuropsychological testing (v. 3, #3, pp. 40–41).

In order to develop a battery of measurement procedures that is valid and useful in the area of aging, two general criteria must be met: First, formal research studies must be performed to investigate the general and specific relevance of individual variables included in the battery to the effects of aging; and second, for clinical assessment of individual subjects, guidelines based on formal research must be developed in a practical manner. This paper will review evidence regarding each of these two general criteria as it relates to applications of the Halstead-Reitan Battery in the area of clinical gerontology.

REVIEW OF FORMAL RESEARCH STUDIES

Correlation Between Chronological Age and the Halstead Impairment Index

An extensive number of formal research studies using the Halstead-Reitan Battery have been done to assess the effects of aging. In the first of these studies (Reitan, 1955a), the Halstead Impairment Index was evaluated in two groups of persons: the first group (N = 194) had heterogeneous cerebral damage and the second group (N = 133) had no history or present evidence of cerebral disease or damage, even though most of these subjects were hospitalized. Prior research of the Halstead Impairment Index (Halstead, 1947; Reitan, 1955b) had indicated that this measure was more specifically sensitive to the condition of the cerebral cortex than any of the individual measures on which it was based; therefore, the Halstead Impairment Index was selected as a summarical measure of the adequacy of brain function.

In Reitan's 1955 study, each sample of subjects was divided into

5-year age intervals ranging from 15 to 65 years. The test results indicated that, regardless of age, the group with cerebral damage consistently showed significant impairment. For the group with brain damage, a Pearson product-moment coefficient of correlation between chronological age and the Impairment Index was only +0.23. This finding suggested that cerebral damage was a dominating factor in producing significant impairment and that in the presence of such a predominating factor, chronological age was of relatively little significance.

In the group without cerebral damage, rather different results were obtained. Up to 45 years of age, the tests results generally fell within the normal range; but for each 5-year age interval from age 45 to 65 years there was a progressive decrement in adequacy of performance.

These results suggested that the Halstead Impairment Index (a highly sensitive indicator of brain functions) showed that some degree of deterioration of brain functions appeared to begin particularly in the 45 through 49 years age interval. For the group without cerebral disease or damage, the correlation between chronological age and the Halstead Impairment Index was +0.54.

These results, even though based on a cross-sectional research design, represented one of the first findings to suggest that neuropsychological investigation in the area of normal aging had a promising future.

Correlation Between Chronological Age and Wechsler Scales

Reitan (1956) emphasized explicit use of neuropsychological measures when he replicated these initial results and also studied findings based on the Wechsler-Bellevue Scale. The Wechsler-Bellevue Scale was developed to evaluate intelligence of normal subjects. Although sensitive to the effects of cerebral damage, the subtests of the Wechsler Scale are significantly less sensitive to brain dysfunction than the Halstead Impairment Index (Reitan, 1959).

On the Wechsler-Bellevue Scale there was a gradual decline in level of performance with advancing chronological age; but the declining curves were essentially similar in groups both with and without cerebral damage. Correlations between chronological age and the Wechsler-Bellevue Total Score for the brain-damaged and non-brain-damaged groups were .37 and .35, respectively. In this study the comparable correlations between chronological age and the Halstead Impairment Index were .37 for the group with brain lesions and .60 for the group without brain damage. Among subjects whose brain-behavior relationships had not been previously affected by significant cerebral damage, the coefficient of largest magnitude occurred between a sensitive neuropsychological measure (Impairment Index) and chronological age in each of these investigations.

Correlation Between Chronological Age and Selected Tests on the Halstead-Reitan Battery

Many additional studies have explored further details of the relationships between neuropsychological measures from the Halstead-Reitan Battery and chronological age. We will not attempt to review all these studies in detail, but, to identify additional significant points of information, brief reference will be made to some of them.

Reitan (1962) wanted to gain information about the rate of deterioration of various abilities over time in one group of subjects with cerebral damage and another group without such evidence. Adult subjects were divided into four groups: (1) 34 years of age and less; (2) 35 through 44 years; (3) 45 through 54 years; and (4) 55 years and older. In addition to using the Halstead Impairment Index, more detailed neuropsychological information was gained by including other measures shown to be among the most sensitive generally to the effects of cerebral damage. These measures included the Category Test, the Localization component of the Tactual Performance Test, and Part B of the Trail Making Test.

The overall results of this investigation indicated progressive impairment through all four categories of chronological ages. Within each group, it seemed necessary to have a difference of at least 10 chronological years to produce a statistically significant indication of impairment. In terms of total intergroup comparisons, it required about 30 years for the group without cerebral damage to reach the level of deficit demonstrated initially by the group with heterogeneous cerebral damage.

Based on these findings, the general conclusion was that deterioration similar to that seen in persons with heterogeneous cerebral damage may occur as a result of normal aging over approximately a 30-year period in the adult age span (at least in terms of level of performance).

Halstead and his associates (Halstead & Rennick, 1962) were also involved in evaluating the effects of aging, focusing especially on test results of executives and correlating them with company ratings of adequacy of performance. Results on the Halstead-Reitan Battery agreed in general with company ratings, and suggested that preserved integrity of brain functions was a significant factor in executive job performance in the 45–64 year age range.

These results also served as a preliminary basis for estimating what Halstead and Rennick called "biological age." This concept reflected the general relationship between chronological age and adequacy of scores obtained on the Halstead-Reitan Battery. A relatively young person who performed in a manner characteristic of older persons would have a higher biological than chronological age; an older person who performed in a manner similar to younger persons would have a lower biological age than his own chronological age.

Halstead and Rennick did not specify either precise relationships or a manner for computing the "biological age" of the individual person. However, this general concept was related to Halstead's theoretical description of the bases of thinking, imagery and memory (Halstead 1958). In his more theoretical discussions of the individual differences in brain-behavior relationships shown among older persons, Halstead (1958) postulated that these differences were probably due to: "(1) genetic differences in the perfection of systems themselves, resulting in differing rates of production of "incorrect" molecules in ordinary conditions; (2) genetic differences in self-corrective mechanisms involved in the prevention of breakdown during deviations from the ideal steady-state conditions, as in stress; and (3) environmental differences in the amount of interference with the operation of the systems from such factors as disease and injury.

The nature of psychological impairment or deficit in individual subjects, as associated with aging effects, seems to be quite variable. As will be noted in a later section of this paper, the kinds of deficits shown by individuals are closely correlated with the person's clinical problems and self-image, and have definite significance to his/her capabilities of meeting occupational and everyday requirements of living.

Thus, from a clinical point of view, it is apparent that a careful assessment of each individual person is necessary. It appeared likely, though, that certain generalizations about the nature of difficulties shown as a result of aging would occur. One of the old generalizations—that speed of performance was the significant factor in aging effects—was definitely not borne out by our findings. A more pervasive principle of the neuropsychology of aging is that as an individual advances in age, he or she experiences a comparative loss in basic problem-solving and reasoning abilities as related to performances on measures requiring retrieval of stored information.

In an early study, Matthews and Reitan (1963) had postulated a continuum of neuropsychological tests ranging from these involved particularly in abstraction and reasoning to tests heavily dependent upon stored information. Matthews and Reitan applied this conceptualization in an investigation of cognitive functions in the area of mental retardation. Using this same continuum of tests, it was possible to study comparative levels of function of older and younger groups of subjects. The ideas that older persons might be less flexible in their thought processes, have more difficulty solving complex problems for which past experience was of little help, and be comparatively better on tasks for which past information and experience were especially relevant were scarcely new; however, these postulates had not been specifically investigated using tests that had been validated as neuropsychological instruments.

Using this continuum, Fitzhugh, Fitzhugh, and Reitan (1964) performed a study based on 283 patients tested in a state-supported hospital for persons with neurological disorders. The total group was divided at the median age (35.5 years) and results were computed on 22 variables ranging from tasks primarily dependent upon reasoning and logical analysis (without the relevance of past experiences) to tasks directly requiring retrieval of stored information. The results showed quite consistently that (1) the younger group of subjects scored better on the tests requiring problem-solving and (2) the scores of the two groups were not significantly different (and nearly equivalent) on the tests dependent upon stored information. This finding clearly suggested that one of the fundamental neuropsychological deficits associated with aging related to facility performing problem-solving tasks and complex intellectual problems for which past experience was not immediately relevant.

Reed and Reitan (1963a) performed a similar study by comparing persons without evidence of brain damage. Again, the same continuum of tests was analyzed. The results indicated that the younger subjects were clearly superior to older subjects on the tests heavily dependent upon immediate adaptive ability; but the older subjects were slightly superior to the younger subjects on tests judged to be more dependent upon stored memory and experiential background. The consistency of this effect was clearly manifested by a correlational coefficient of 0.77 between the intergroup mean differences and the actual rank-order of the tests along the continuum from basic problem-solving to stored information.

From a clinical point of view, this study indicates again that one of the principal neuropsychological variables is the degree of impairment on immediate and basic problem-solving tasks. Such deficits would appear to fall particularly in adaptive areas requiring abstraction and reasoning, comprehension and solution of complex problems, orientation in time and space in relatively unfamiliar environments, and organizational and categorization abilities, especially those requiring memory skills. There seems to be little question that overall organizational abilities clearly help to facilitate memory and recall.

A more detailed and comprehensive study of neuropsychological deficits was recently performed by Meyerink (1982) using the Halstead-Reitan Battery. Meyerink studied 125 subjects with no past or present evidence of cerebral disease or damage. Each subject was placed into one of five age groups: (1) 20–29 years; (2) 30–39 years; (3) 40–49 years; (4) 50–59 years; and (5) 60–70 years. Each group was composed of 25 subjects with equivalent educational backgrounds. Even though many of the patients had been referred for medical evaluation, each group had similar types of medical complaints.

In data analysis, Meyerink's initial approach was to perform a multivariate analysis of variance comparing the performances of the five age groups, followed by post-hoc testing to specifically identify the pattern of change of each significant variable.

The results indicated that a number of conclusions could be drawn, based on the Halstead-Reitan Battery test results: (1) Tests related to prior learning and retention of longstanding experiences did not show any change across the age groups; (2) Sensory input functions deteriorated slightly with age, but the actual change was quite limited and was demonstrated only on measures using complex stimuli; (3) With advancing age, simple motor functions showed no changes, but complex motor functions which involve reasoning types of performances showed a substantial deterioration; (4) Ability to use language processing skills decreased significantly with age but the actual amount of change was minimal; (5) Substantial loss of complex visual-spatial abilities occurred with advancing age and a particularly striking decrement was demonstrated by the group aged 60–70 years; (6) A very pronounced curve of deterioration of abilities involving abstraction, reasoning, and logical analysis occurred with increasing age and, again, the group in their 60s showed a particularly large decrement.

Based on Meyerink's findings, several generalizations may be made. First, deficits associated with aging tend to occur primarily on complex types of tasks. In this context it is important to note that many of the neuropsychological batteries that have recently been developed (particularly stemming from Luria's approach) emphasize very simple types of performances. In fact, these performances are frequently so simple that they fall essentially into a dichotomous relationship and are judged by whether or not they can be performed successfully. Meyerink attempted to use some such measures in his study but found that they showed very minimal differences between younger and older groups and he dropped a number of variables of this kind because of their limited contribution to the variance associated with chronological age. Thus, it is important for a neuropsychological battery which assesses aging effects to include a number of tests that are relatively complex and sensitive to the general integrity of the cerebral hemispheres. The four most sensitive indicators which should probably be included in any neuropsychological battery of this type are represented in the Halstead-Reitan Battery: the Halstead Impairment Index, Category Test, Tactual Performance Test-Localization component, and Part B of the Trail Making Test. It must also be noted that Meyerink (in accordance with earlier studies by Halstead and his associates as well as Reitan and his associates) confirmed the finding that measures related to abstraction, reasoning and immediate problem-solving skills were most significantly impaired with aging, whereas measures based upon stored information showed relatively little deterioration.

Second, and in contrast with many of the reports in the literature, measures based on simple sensory-perceptual and motor functions were relatively unimpaired in older as compared with younger subjects. Only as motor tasks became complicated and more difficult did the subjects show decrements which corresponded with aging. Again, we must emphasize the importance of general psychological measures, as contrasted with specific measures that correlate with localized deficits, as a basis for evaluating older persons. The types of biological changes that occur with aging are not strictly focal or localized, and measures which relate to specific areas of cerebral cortical function are not among the most useful for evaluating the behavioral effects of aging. However, the overall adaptational potential of more complex tests (such as the Halstead Category Test) are well known and of very special significance in evaluating the subtle but extremely important types of deficits that may occur in older persons.

BIOLOGICAL CHANGES IN THE AGING BRAIN

Biological changes of the brain associated with aging have been identified previously (Bondareff, 1959; Magladery, 1959), but it has been difficult to relate anatomical, physiological, and pharmacological changes specifically to behavioral deficits.

Welford and Birren (1965) have summarized the role of the brain and nervous system in determining the types of psychological changes seen in aging. Much of this evidence strongly suggests that brain changes may be responsible for at least many of the psychological deficits shown by the aged.

In this context it should also be noted that there have been several studies relating to morphological and physiological changes in other organs and systems of the body, and gradually progressive impairment has been associated with the aging process (Shock, 1962). Investigation of morphological and functional changes of the brain has represented an active area of study, and increasingly detailed documentation continues to be published (Cervos-Navarro & Sarkander, 1983; Samuel, Algeri, Gershon, Grimm & Toffano, 1983).

No attempt will be made in this paper to review the types of morphological (principally neuronal loss, senile plaques and neurofibrillary tangles) and neuropathological changes that occur in the aging brain, but the reader should be aware that these types of changes do happen and, in fact, are sometimes difficult to differentiate from the neuropathological changes occurring in conditions such as Alzheimer's disease and the clinical manifestations of cerebral vascular disease. Such pathological changes have been related to dementia (Selkoe, 1978) and would certainly lay a basis for deterioration of higher-level neuropsychological functions dependent upon the integrity of the cerebral cortex. There probably is no possibility of perfectly differentiating the kinds of pathological changes that occur with aging from brain diseases of a vascular or degenerative nature, but in most cases of normal aging one would presume that the neuro-pathological changes are diffusely represented rather than involving focal areas of pathological involvement.

Research Studies Concerned with Age-Related Changes in the Brain

A general approach to the question of the organic basis of brain-related neuropsychological changes may be made by (1) considering the types of tests which demonstrte major age-related changes and (2) comparing age-related neuropsychological changes in persons without evidence of cerebral disease or damage with persons having heterogeneous cerebral disease or damage.

In the first of these approaches Reitan (1957) studied 138 normally functioning male executives and professional persons who ranged in age from 27 to 65 years. The Halstead Category Test and the Verbal and Performance IQ values of the Wechsler-Bellevue Scale were the dependent variables. When the results for these normal subjects were plotted in 5-year intervals from 25 to 55 years and older, each of the three variables showed a progressive degree of decline. The greatest comparative deficits occurred on the Category Test and the Performance IQ; a lesser degree of progressive impairment was shown on the Verbal IQ.

Since the Category Test and Performance IQ have generally been found to be more sensitive to impaired cerebral functions than Verbal IQ, one might presume that at least in part, a brain-related basis was responsible for the age-associated changes. The inferential process used in drawing this conclusion is essentially similar to the findings of principal deficit, reported above, on tests of reasoning, concept formation, and basic problem-solving as compared with measures of stored information, particularly of a verbal nature.

Reed and Reitan (1963b) approached this problem more directly in a study comparing three groups: younger subjects with cerebral damage, younger subjects without cerebral damage, and older subjects who were normal from a neurological point of view. This design permitted the opportunity to identify the effects of cerebral damage in the younger group and discern the effects of aging by comparing the older normal with the younger normal group. The basic problem was to determine differences in these groups and identify any similarities in the pattern of differences.

Each younger group (with and without cerebral damage) had a

mean age of 28 years and an educational level of approximately 12 years. The older normal group had a mean age of 55 years. The results obtained with the Halstead-Reitan Battery indicated that the young control subjects did better than the young brain-damaged subjects, as might well be expected. In addition, the older normal subjects performed more poorly than did the younger normal subjects.

In order to test the critical hypothesis, however, it was necessary to determine whether the tests most sensitive to brain damage also tended to be the tests most sensitive to aging effects. Each of the 31 variables used in this study was ranked according to its comparative sensitivity to (1) brain damage and (2) aging effects. A Spearman rank-difference correlation was computed between these two sets of rank orders and a coefficient of 0.49 was obtained (p < .01). Thus, the results strongly suggested that deterioration of abilities due to brain damage was similar in many respects to the changes associated with aging. From this finding it would appear that at least some of the manifestations of aging, as shown by the Halstead-Reitan Battery, are very probably related to biological changes of the brain.

DEVELOPMENT OF THE BRAIN-AGE QUOTIENT

Reitan (1973) performed another study concerned with developing a rating of neuropsychological aspects of brain functions in accordance with an individual's chronological age. Six tests selected on the basis of their general sensitivity were studied, using a level-of-performance model of brain damage or dysfunction. These six tests were the Category Test, Tactual Performance Test-Total Time, Tactual Performance Test-Localization, Trail Making Test-Part B, and the Block Design and Digit Symbol subtests from the Wechsler Scale.

Results on these tests were obtained from 155 normal subjects ranging in age from 30 to 65 years. Using a T-score transformation, a single score was obtained for each subject by adding the scores of the six individual tests. These resulting scores were plotted in 5-year age intervals from 30–65 years of age.

Interestingly, the youngest group (30–35 years) had the highest mean score and there was a progressive and invariable succession of decrement in each 5-year interval through the 60–65 year group. It may be observed that these data agree with cell counts of neurons that show a highly significant approximately linear neuronal loss between the third and ninth decades which represents a total mean attrition of 50% (Henderson, Tomlinson, & Weightman, 1975; Brody, 1955).

Observing this progressive decline in abilities suggested a situation essentially similar to the progressive increase in absolute level of performance for children, a finding that allowed the computation of the Intelligence Quotient. It appeared possible to use the progressive decline at the other end of the age distribution as a basis for relating absolute performance to chronological age in a statistical manipulation that would produce an IQ type of scale. Reitan performed this manipulation which generated a preliminary set of norms for determining how each individual, based on his/her performance on each of these six tests, would compare to other persons in his/her respective age range.

For example, if a 60-year-old person performed as well as the average 40-year-old, he would earn a score that was well above average. Reitan called this score a Brain-Age Quotient, and converted the data into a distribution that was essentially the same as the IQ distribution with a mean of 100 and a standard deviation of 15. Thus, a person earning a Brain-Age Quotient of 115 would be one standard deviation above the mean in terms of his/her performances with relation to his/her chronological age. Conversely, a person with a Brain-Age Quotient of 85 would be one standard deviation below the expected performance for a person of his/her age.

A measure of this type has all of the disadvantages of any type of average score, but it does provide useful information for assessing the results of individual persons in a clinical context. In fact, this type of objective comparison of brain-related abilities with chronological age may have very significant usefulness in the future, especially considering the urgent need to evaluate the variability among individual older persons. The possible practical applications are essentially unlimited.

APPROACHES TO REMEDIATION
OF NEUROPSYCHOLOGICAL DEFICITS
ASSOCIATED WITH AGING

If neuropsychological functions deteriorate with advancing age because of morphological or pathophysiological changes, it should be possible to design experiments to evaluate the behavioral consequences of such changes. The experimental question would concern the extent to which structural and physiological changes, specified with regard to type, result in neuropsychological deficits.

Not a great deal of work has been done to answer this type of question. Part of the problem has been in obtaining information about morphological and pathophysiological changes in persons who have been evaluated by comprehensive neuropsychological methods such as provided by the Halstead-Reitan Battery. Reitan and Shipley (1963) conducted one investigation of this type by studying the relationship between changes in serum cholesterol levels and neuropsychological measures. The presumption in this study was that if changes in serum cholesterol levels contributed significantly to neuropsychological performances, it should be possible to objectively demonstrate this effect with neuropsychological measurements.

The study included 156 medically healthy men between the ages of 25 and 65 years. In order to measure deviations from fully effective brain-related performances, subjects functioning with a high level of productivity and efficiency were selected principally from management and scientific levels of employment (24.5% of the group held doctoral degrees). Eleven standardized neuropsychological measures were individually administered to each subject. These measures yielded a summary score essentially similar to the Halstead Impairment Index. Each subject first entered a six-month control period during which serum cholesterol levels were monitored in order to be sure of stable baselines (in terms of laboratory procedures as well as serum cholesterol levels within the individual subject). A Pearson-moment correlation of 0.81 was obtained between initial and 6-month serum cholesterol levels. Subjects included in the study were given the battery of 11 tests at the beginning of the study and again 12 months later. During the 12 months between examinations, a considerable number of the subjects showed significant reductions in their serum cholesterol levels; others maintained or even increased their initial levels.

In analyzing the data, it was possible to divide the subjects according to whether or not their serum cholesterol levels had been lowered by 10% or more during the 12-month period between neuropsychological examinations. The results indicated that younger groups of subjects tended to perform significantly better than older groups in absolute level of performance, but the younger groups showed no test-retest changes that could be attributed to changes in their serum cholesterol levels.

However, in subjects aged 40 years or more, a statistically significant difference was present in those subjects that had not lowered serum cholesterol levels compared with subjects who had shown a 10% or more decrease. The older group who had *not* lowered their serum cholesterol levels showed a progressive decrease in each 5-year interval from 40 to 65 years, compared with their original test results. The older group in whom serum cholesterol levels had been lowered, however, tended to hold their own on the retest results.

These results suggest that in men aged 40 years and over, reducing serum cholesterol levels by 10% or more (even when the initial level was not markedly elevated) appears to have a beneficial effect on retaining neuropsychological functions demonstrated to show deterioration with advancing age.

We should note that by themselves, serum cholesterol levels are not a particularly potent determiner of neuropsychological performances. In the same groups of subjects, a comparison between those with initially high serum cholesterol levels and those having much lower levels showed only a trend toward poorer performances in the former group. Based on this finding, one would not judge that serum cholesterol levels have a very strong influence in determining absolute level of neuropsychological performances. However, in a study designed to test the individual subject over a 12-month period, during which serum cholesterol levels were monitored and the subject was his own control, the results did show a statistically significant relationship between degree of reduction of serum cholesterol levels and neuropsychological retest performances.

One would not postulate that serum cholesterol levels are in any sense to be considered as an overall indicator of the physiological correlates of aging. Many factors, such as regulation of diet, exercise, reduction of body weight, discontinuation of practices having adverse influences (excessive smoking, alcohol consumption, etc.) may all be significant factors. Nevertheless, the results using only serum cholesterol levels as an independent variable were very encouraging in the sense that they demonstrated that controlling even this single variable appeared to have some effect in retarding neuropsychological aging.

This particular study by Reitan and Shipley was performed more than 20 years ago and there has been no significant neuropsychological follow-up study since. Such a study would be particularly relevant now, as it could easily be integrated with companion studies oriented toward evaluating cardiovascular or cerebral vascular functions. For current purposes, however, our point is to note that it may be entirely possible to retard the progression of aging effects through manipulation of underlying physiological conditions.

Even more exciting possibilities exist concerning retraining of impaired brain functions in older persons. At the 1983 meeting of the American Psychological Association a symposium entitled, "Innovative Rehabilitational Approaches for the Geriatric Patient" was held and investigators reported definite improvement, both in abilities and emotional status and mood, in older persons who had experienced cognitive training.

Out own contribution to that symposium centered around the use of a detailed and carefully structured brain retraining program called REHABIT (Reitan & Sena, 1983). This program uses extensive and carefully selected training materials organized into five tracks and relative to the higher-level neuropsychological functions of the brain.

Track A includes training material specifically limited to left-hemisphere functions, centering around language, verbal, and symbolic aspects of both a receptive and expressive nature. Track B also includes extensive language and verbal material but selected to involve abstraction, reasoning, and logical analysis within a verbal framework. Track C contains relatively pure abstraction and reasoning materials ranging from simple to complex tasks. The fourth track, Track D, also engages in abstraction and reasoning, but uses right-hemisphere tasks involved in temporal sequential, visual spatial, and manipulatory types of performances. The final track, Track E, encompasses rather pure right-hemisphere types of tasks related to fundamental aspects of perception and manipulation of spatial and temporal relationships. Each track includes an extensive set of training materials, organized from relatively simple to quite complex functions.

The training program for the individual person begins with neuropsychological evaluation and diagnosis. Results of the Halstead-Reitan Battery provide an assessment of the strengths and weaknesses of the older client. As noted earlier in this paper, such an evaluation is necessary because of the variability among individuals, in spite of the fact that aging impairs certain areas of function more than others. Following comprehensive evaluation, a training program is prescribed for the individual. Our experience has suggested that the weaknesses of the subject must be approached directly, rather than

hoping that by training the strong areas, the weak areas will also improve. Hoping that training the strong areas will have a generalized,
overlapping concomitant effect on the weak areas is generally not a
successful approach. Instead, we have made deliberate attempts to
work patiently and supportively with the individual client in the
areas of his or her weaknesses. It is necessary to sustain and maintain the older person's motivation in every way possible, and the intrinsic nature of the tasks included in REHABIT (presented in the
form of games) is of advantage in this respect.

A number of different approaches to brain retraining are being
proposed, some even using video game techniques; but our experience suggests that a tremendously critical initial step is to identify
the patient's areas of weakness to establish a basis for prescribing a
brain training program that meets the needs of the individual.

CLINICAL APPLICATIONS

In discussing clinical application it must first be recognized that
any person, regardless of age, may have any of the problems or deficits that occur in daily life. Thus, one should not assume initially
that older persons have special problems particular to their age
group, even though neuropsychological deficits may occur more
frequently among the aged. A full assessment, including neuropsychological evaluation and careful consideration of the stresses of the
client's environment, may be needed in each instance. It is necessary to be prepared to assess brain-related bases of adjustment problems as well as emotional difficulties and stresses imposed by environmental demands for every client. Thus, the methods of clinical
neuropsychology must be complemented by the usual procedures in
clinical psychology in order to effectively assess and treat the older
person.

As suggested above, awareness of the clinical complexity and
variability of the individual person augments the need for evaluating
both the emotional and neuropsychological aspects of the client. The
geriatric psychologist should be well versed in both areas, and be
especially aware of their complementary aspects. Considering the
clinical questions that arise in gerontology, there is a great need for
neuropsychologists who have a broad range of experience in clinical
interpretation of brain-behavior relationships. The purpose of this
section of the paper will be to provide brief illustrations of some of
the problems with which clinical neuropsychology can be of assistance.

Not uncommonly, older persons have various types of somatic complaints and, in fact, it appears that their emotional stresses are often manifested in symptoms related to bodily dysfunction. Thus, one of the most common clinical problems in gerontology is differentiating between problems that are basically rooted in emotional difficulties of adjustment and behaviors that may genuinely manifest deterioration of cerebral functions. Although this question is often identified as "emotional vs. organic," in many instances the more important problem is to precisely identify the input of problems from each area and the various interactions. In some cases, however, the differentiation may be made quite clearly through neuropsychological examination even though neither the initial complaint of the patient nor the medical examination is able to provide the answer.

Case #1

A 59-year-old woman who had been a very successful physician is an example of the situation described above. This woman had been ill for many years with cardiac disease, hypoglycemia and attacks of brief loss of consciousness. She had been thoroughly examined by an internist who had found a definite physical basis for some of her illnesses but was not able to elicit any positive neurological signs or objective evidence of impaired cerebral functions. However, the patient herself felt that she suffered from significant impairment of brain functions. She had experienced a number of episodes (probably relating to hypoglycemia) during which she lost consciousness for three to ten minutes. About four months prior to being referred for neuropsychological examination, she experienced a significantly more serious episode and was in a state of impaired consciousness for about 12 hours. When questioned directly, the patient said that her memory was failing, she suffered from fatigue, was seriously depressed, and had frequent crying spells. She noted that she had emotional as well as neurological problems, that she had, in her judgment, experienced changes that resulted in rather serious deficits, and was concerned about her ability to continue practicing medicine.

In most instances, a history and list of symptoms of the type described above would probably be found to relate to both emotional and neurological difficulties. In this case, however, the results were quite definite in pointing towards emotional problems of adjustment in a person whose brain-behavior relationships were not only in the normal range but better than those for most persons of her age. She had high I.Q. values (Verbal I.Q.-129; Performance I.Q.-127; and Full Scale I.Q.-129) but this finding is not uncommon even in older persons who have experienced a considerable degree of neuropsychological deficit. The clinical neuropsychologist with experience in gerontology is well aware of the tendency toward retention of I.Q. values even when significant and serious deterioration is shown on measures more sensitive to impaired brain functions.

However, this woman performed relatively well on each of the four most sensitive measures in the Halstead-Reitan Battery: She had an Impairment Index of 0.4, made only 32 errors on the Category Test, required 81 seconds on Part B of the Trail Making Test, and was able to localize 5 of the 10 figures in the Tactual Performance Test. Her degree of alertness was sufficient for her to complete the Seashore Rhythm Test without making a single error. Comparisons of performances on the two sides of the body were essentially within the normal range. There were minor indications of brain-related deficits, but these were entirely overshadowed by the excellent general level of performance.

On the other hand, results on the Minnesota Multiphasic Personality Inventory (MMPI) showed a striking elevation on the first three clinical scales, (Hypochondriasis, Depression and Hysteria) suggesting the presence of significant and even serious emotional problems of adjustment. Thus, in this case, the negative findings on the neuropsychological examination were of great significance in understanding the total problem and directing the course of treatment. The patient did not show significant evidence of neurological deterioration of brain functions and, in fact, her excellent scores on the Halstead-Reitan Battery suggested that this area represented a significant strength for her. Clinical psychological or psychiatric treatment was instituted with good results.

Case #2

The next client to be described also was a physician. The patient, a 67-year-old man, was referred by his neurological surgeon who had found no positive results on physical neurological examination but nevertheless suspected that there might be significant deterioration of abilities dependent upon brain functions. When we asked the patient about his difficulties, he tended to deny any significant problems. He said that other people felt that he had "something of a memory problem'' and that ''they might possibly be right,'' but the patient himself felt that the problem was of little general significance. The patient worked principally as a general surgeon. As noted above, neurological findings, including computed tomography, were essentially negative.

This man also had relatively adequate I.Q. values (Verbal I.Q.-118; Performance I.Q.-115; and Full Scale I.Q.-115), even though the results on individual subtests of the Wechsler Scale suggested that there very probably had been some significant deterioration. For example, his Vocabulary score was 15 whereas his Arithmetic score was 7 and Digit Symbol was 6. On neuropsychological examination the patient demonstrated a great deal of variability in adequacy of performances. He was able to pay excellent attention to specific stimulus material (Seashore Rhythm Test and Speechsounds Perception Test), indicating that when the stimulus material was well defined and he knew exactly what he was supposed to do, the patient was able to perform very well. However, he made 111 errors on the Category Test and, on three trials with the Tactual Performance Test, was able to place only 18 blocks in 45.5 minutes. He also required 178 seconds on Part B of the Trail Making Test.

This man even showed rather specific deficits on certain tasks, significantly distorting the spatial configurations in his attempts to copy a Greek cross and a skeleton key. However, he did not show any striking deficits on measures of finger tapping speed or the Sensory-perceptual Examination. Normal results on these latter measures frequently are consistent with negative findings on the physical neurological examination. The importance of neuropsychological examination, however, is to compare those findings with the physical neurological examination and progress to assessing the significant areas of higher-level psychological functions (central processing).

It was apparent from this man's test results that he was significantly and strikingly impaired in his ability to deal with immediate problem-solving situations. An extremely poor score on the Category Test is often interpreted clinically (and sometimes by the patient) as a manifestation of memory difficulty. However, the problem in this case was much more basic than memory difficulties alone. Prominent deficits occurred in the areas of logical analysis, abstraction, reasoning, and concept formation; quickness and flexibility in thought processes; dealing with simple spatial configurations and relationships; and adaptive psychomotor functions when trying to solve relatively complex problems. It would seem that all of these difficulties would be of definite significance to this man's ability to perform as a general surgeon. Results on the MMPI, however, were well within normal limits.

In cases of this type, the neuropsychological results are somewhat difficult to deal with in terms of clinical application. Probably the best approach is to counsel the patient to begin an organized plan of disengagement from the type of professional activities that he is poorly prepared to handle.

Because of the great variability among individual instances, it is not possible to illustrate the full range of clinical problems among the aged in which neuropsychological examination is of value. However, results using the Halstead-Reitan Battery have been shown to be very useful in persons who actually have the types of physical illnesses commonly seen in a geriatric population. The important point in this respect is that neuropsychological evaluation complements the medical history and examination. In fact, the medical examination often neglects the more significant and meaningful aspects of the illness, which are reflected in impairment of higher-level functions.

Case #3

The next case is one of a 76-year-old woman who had a long history of various types of illnesses. In general, these illnesses did not involve the central nervous system. However, she had suffered from essential hypertension for a considerable period of time and had difficulty controlling her blood pressure. Approximately three years before her referral for neuropsychological examination she had suffered a possible stroke with resulting left-sided weakness. Her internist believed that the patient may have also had a coronary occlusion about two months before the present examination, but he was not sure of this and felt that the patient's difficulties might be related to psychological problems. This patient had been followed by the same group of internists for a considerable period of time, and these physicians felt that there probably had been no significant neuropsychological deterioration because they had not observed any apparent changes clinically. However, the patient was then seen by a neurologist. He found no definite neurological deficits, but recognized that neuropsychological deficits might, nevertheless, be a significant part of the total clinical picture, and referred the patient for neuropsychological testing.

This 76-year-old woman had a 12th grade education, was the wife of a nationally prominent politician and clearly had been relatively capable previously. She still had a Verbal I.Q. of 117, a Performance I.Q. of 126, and a Full Scale I.Q. of 118, even though she showed a striking degree of variability among performances on individual subtests. The four most sensitive indicators in the Halstead-Reitan Battery were all significantly impaired: Impairment Index, 1.0; Category Test, 113 errors; Trail Making Test-Part B, 140 seconds; and Tactual Performance Test-Localization, 1. In addition, the patient showed some definite lateralizing results on comparisons of the two sides of the body; however, the deficits tended to occur on both sides and implied diffuse bilateral rather than focal cerebral damage.

There was no doubt, considering the overall results, that this woman had experienced very striking impairment of higher-level brain functions, even though her I.Q. values were still relatively intact. This type of deterioration is quite difficult to discern on the basis of clinical observation, and must be determined by using explicit procedures such as those included in the Halstead-Reitan Battery. Impairment of this kind is pervasive in its undercutting of self-confidence and insidious in its erosion of efficiency in performance in everyday living. It is not uncommon for persons with such problems to develop significant indications of anxiety and depression. This woman showed distinct and definite evidence of such problems as well as considerable deterioration of adaptive abilities. Although it is often difficult to provide effective treatment for this type of patient, the neuropsychological examination probably represented the first comprehensive statement of the difficulties that this woman was facing. As an increasing number of clinical psychologists and psychiatrists are beginning to recognize, a striking disparity between past abilities and current adaptive capabilities is often present in the aged and the first step in effective counseling and supportive psychotherapy is for the therapist to have a comprehensive understanding of brain-behavior relationships.

CONCLUSION

In brief summary, these three cases illustrate some of the types of problems experienced by the aged and the important contributions that can be made through neuropsychological assessment. As is always true in clinical situations, a broad range of experience and knowledge is necessary to be able to produce effective results. Although many psychologists and psychiatrists are very competent in clinical evaluation of emotional problems of adjustment, another variable that must be assessed is possible deterioration of brain functions and an increasing number of psychologists are developing expertise in this area.

REFERENCES

Bondareff, W. (1959). Morphology of the aging nervous system. In J.E. Birren (Ed.), *Handbook of aging and the individual* (pp. 136–172). Chicago: University of Chicago Press.

Brody, H. (1955). Organization of the cerebral cortex. Vol. III: A study of aging in cerebral cortex. *Journal of Comparative Neurology, 102,* 511–556.

Cervos-Navarro, J., & Sarkander, H.-I. (Eds.). (1983). *Brain aging: neuropathology and neuropharmacology.* (Aging, Vol. 21). New York: Raven Press.

Fitzhugh, K. B., Fitzhugh, L. C., & Reitan, R. M. (1964). Influence of age upon measures of problem solving and experiential background in subjects with long-standing cerebral dysfunction. *Journal of Gerontology, 19,* 132–134.

Halstead, W. C. (1947). *Brain and intelligence: A quantitative study of the frontal lobes.* Chicago: University of Chicago Press.

Halstead, W. C. (1958). Some biopsychology of thinking, imagery and memory. *Perspectives in Biology and Medicine, 1,* 326–341.

Halstead, W. C., & Rennick, P. (1962). Toward a behavioral scale for biological age. In C. Tibbits & W. Donohue (Eds.), *Social and psychological aspects of aging.* New York: Columbia University Press.

Henderson, G., Tomlinson, B. E., & Weightman, D. (1975). Cell counts in the cerebral cortex using a traditional and an automatic method. *Journal of Neurological Sciences, 25,* 129–144.

Magladery, J. W. (1959). Neurophysiology of aging. In J. E. Birren (Ed.), *Handbook of aging and the individual* (pp. 173–186). Chicago: University of Chicago Press.

Matthews, C. G., & Reitan, R. M. (1963). Relationship of differential abstraction ability levels to psychological test performances in mentally retarded subjects. *American Journal of Mental Deficiency, 68,* 235–244.

Meyerink, L. H. (1982). Intellectual functioning: The nature and pattern of change with aging. (Doctoral dissertation, University of Arizona, 1982). *Dissertation Abstracts International.*

Reed, H. B. C., & Reitan, R. M. (1963a). Changes in psychological test performances associated with the normal aging process. *Journal of Gerontology, 18,* 271–274.

Reed, H. B. C., & Reitan, R. M. (1963b). A comparison of the effects of the normal aging process with the effects of organic brain damage on adaptive abilities. *Journal of Gerontology, 18,* 177–179.

Reitan, R. M. (1955a). The distribution according to age of a psychologic measure dependent upon organic brain functions. *Journal of Gerontology, 10,* 338–340.

Reitan, R. M. (1955b). An investigation of the validity of Halstead's measures of biological intelligence. *Archives of Neurology and Psychiatry, 73,* 28–35.

Reitan, R. M. (1956). The relationship of the Halstead Impairment Index and the Wechsler-Bellevue Total Weighted Score to chronological age. *Journal of Gerontology, 4,* 2.

Reitan, R. M. (1957). The comparative significance of qualitative and quantitative psychological changes with brain damage. *Proceedings of the Fifteenth International Congress of Psychology,* 214–215.

Reitan, R. M. (1959). The comparative effects of brain damage on the Halstead Impairment Index and the Wechsler-Bellevue Scale. *Journal of Clinical Psychology, 15,* 281–285.

Reitan, R. M. (1962). The comparative psychological significance of aging in groups with and without organic brain damage. In C. Tibbits & W. Donohue (Eds.), *Social and psychological aspects of aging* (pp. 880–887). New York: Columbia University Press.

Reitan, R. M., & Shipley, R. E. (1963). The relationship of serum cholesterol changes on psychological abilities. *Journal of Gerontology, 18,* 350–356.

Reitan, R. M. (September, 1973). *Behavioral manifestations of impaired brain functions in aging.* Paper presented at the meeting of the American Psychological Association, Montreal, Canada.

Reitan, R. M., & Sena, D. A. (August, 1983). *The efficacy of the REHABIT technique in remediation of brain-injured people.* Paper presented at the meeting of the American Psychological Association, Anaheim, CA.

Samuel, D., Algeri, S., Gershon, S., Grimm, V. E., & Toffano, G. (1983). *Aging of the brain.* (Aging, Vol. 22). New York: Raven Press.

Selkoe, D. J. (1978). Cerebral aging and dementia. In H. R. Tyler & D. M. Dawson (Eds.), *Current neurology* Vol. I (pp. 360–387). Boston: Houghton Mifflin Professional Publishers.

Shock, N. W. (1962). The physiology of aging. *Scientific American, 206,* 100–110.

Welford, A. T., & Birren, J. E. (Eds.). (1965). *Behavior aging and the nervous system.* Springfield, IL: Charles C. Thomas.

Questions

1) What other tests would you see as appropriate in Case #1? What treatment do you think would be most appropriate?

2) What other tests would you see as appropriate in Case #2? What treatment do you think would be most appropriate?

3) What other tests would you see as appropriate in Case #3? What treatment do you think would be most appropriate?

4) Compare the Halstead Reitan battery with the Luria-Nebraska, Stimulus Recognition Test, or Fuld Object Memory Test.

4/THE CLINICAL USE OF PROJECTIVE TECHNIQUES WITH THE AGED
A Critical Review and Synthesis

Bert Hayslip, Jr., PhD
Rodney L. Lowman, PhD

tool used to assess

Editor's Introduction

interpretive

Projective techniques give the clinician a valuable qualitative perspective on assessment. Furthermore, they may be more useful in establishing the rapport and commitment necessary in the therapeutic relationship. Whereas geriatric psychometry as a whole is in need of further research, projective techniques have been the most neglected.

Hayslip and Lowman give an amazingly comprehensive review of what has been done in this area. They begin by suggesting several clinician decisions for which projective data may give valuable input. These techniques can be used to assess competency, need for institutionalization, suicidal risk, aggression, readiness for psychotherapy, etc.

The authors make an essential clarification early in their discussion of the topic: *projective techniques are not "tests," but clinical tools, and greatly dependent upon the practitioner's talent.* This point gives us the proper perspective for subsequent discussions of validity and reliability. The authors then review normative data, validity, reliability and utility, for the Rorschach, Thematic Apperception Test (and two versions designed for elders, the SAT and GAT), Holtzman Inkblot, Figure Drawing, Hand Test, and Sentence Completion.

Bert Hayslip, Jr. and Rodney L. Lowman are with the Department of Psychology, North Texas State University.

The authors strongly recommend that future research attempt to establish the predictive ability of specific test indices (e.g., Exner's depressive and suicidal indicators) with the aged. Also, it would be helpful to compare such techniques to neurological, laboratory and "objective" techniques in terms of accuracy, cost, patient acceptance, etc.

Other, less formalized, projective techniques are not discussed in this chapter. Dream interpretation is discussed by Brink (1977, 1979). The use of the arts in therapy provides a projective tool for assessment as well. Previous issues of *CG* have discussed the use of poetry (v. 3, #3, pp. 89–90), music (v. I, #2, pp. 76–77; v. 3, #2, pp. 40–41), art (v. 1, #4, pp. 82–83; v. 2, #1, pp. 45–53; v. 2, #2, p. 67; v. 2, #3, pp. 98–100; v. 3, #1, pp. 72–73; v. 3, #2, pp. 89–90), movement and dance (v. 3, #3, pp. 46–47), and drama (v. 3, #1, pp. 15–24).

While there is some question about the validity and reliability of these techniques, there is little question that, in the hands of a trained and talented clinician, we have a potent tool for opening up the therapeutic relationship.

INTRODUCTION—WHY PROJECTIVE TECHNIQUES?

While recent gerontological research has concentrated upon either functional assessments or upon objective personality assessment, comparatively little interest has been expressed in projective assessment of personality functioning, particularly for clinical purposes. It is the intent of this paper not only to examine the reasons for this reluctance, but also to evaluate critically the literature on the projective assessment of the aged in light of its clinical utility.

Historically, doubting clinicians and researchers alike have expressed concerns about the reliability and validity of projective techniques (whether used with the young or the aged), and it is clear that an inability to resolve these issues has hindered work in this area (Lanyon, 1984). Before sounding the death knoll prematurely regarding their use we feel it is prudent to discuss several issues regarding the criteria against which projective techniques might be validated with the aged. Specifically, this task can be best understood in light of a clear *a priori* definition of the purposes for which projective techniques might be utilized with the aged. As many (Klopfer & Taubee, 1976; Schaie & Schaie, 1977) have noted, only *after* the purposes for which assessments (projective or otherwise) are conducted have *first* been defined can a clear understanding of its worth with the aged be reached.

While normative data examining age trends do permit one to differentiate older versus younger persons in a general sense (see Panek, Wagner, & Kennedy-Zwergel, 1984), they tell us little regarding the clinical utility of these scales in predicting the older individual's ability to cope with a variety of events that may or may not accompany the aging process (i.e., illness, death, surgery, retirement, relocation/institutionalization).

"Are projectives appropriate to use in clinical practice?" The answer to the question depends on the questions needing to be resolved for a given patient. Typically, clinical questions for which projectives might be useful include:

1. Does the individual require institutionalization?; and alternatively
2. Can the individual care for himself/herself? Can the individual make competent decisions regarding his affairs?;
3. Is the individual depressed, likely to be harmful to self, or likely to commit suicide?;
4. Is the individual organic, mentally disturbed, or both?;
5. Can the person be expected to be aggressive to others?;
6. Can the individual continue in a work role?;
7. What impact have changes in health, or widowhood made on the person?;
8. Is the individual psychotic?; and
9. Is the individual appropriate for psychological intervention?; Has he or she benefited from treatment?

Moreover, such techniques may elucidate the elder's reaction to the loss of cognitive skills accompanying dementia or stroke; these persons may not otherwise be testable. They may also aid in identifying those elderly who are suicidal or near death. An awareness of internal dynamics made possible via the use of projectives would prove invaluable to both family and the older person in facilitating communication and/or handling "unfinished business," or to assist the clinician in working with persons who are dying who are unable to acknowledge their feelings (e.g., anger, despair, helplessness, anxiety, acceptance). Projective techniques are also suited to assessing psychological disengagement particularly for those persons to whom being productive is salient. Likewise, real or imagined changes in body image accompanying illness or surgery might be understood via the use of figure drawings; such information could be utilized to reduce dysfunctional anxiety associated with such changes.

Despite the potential use of projectives with the aged, numerous factors have contributed their underutilization. Anastasi (1976) notes that part of this problem stems from the treatment of projectives as "tests" rather than as clinical techniques to aid the examiner in more fully understanding his client, a talent which is highly dependent upon the skills and experience of the clinician. Given the lack of clinical experience present clinicians are likely to have with elderly clients, the tendency to fall back on elaborate scoring systems (often poorly spelled out and lacking in validity) contributes to the false impression that a given technique can be treated as a test. Klopfer and Taubee (1976) note that the greatest problem with the validity of projective techniques is the lack of appropriate criteria by which to validate them, e.g., using behavioral criteria of ill-defined diagnostic groups for concurrent or predictive purposes. Moreover, for the aged, criteria such as coping behavior that is/is not adaptive are by definition, age/cohort and context specific (Gurland, 1973). Diagnostic categories that are used are often ill defined and misleading in nature (e.g., senile, depressed) or rest upon diagnostic typologies that have yet to be demonstrated to be relevant to aged persons (e.g., DSM-III) (Butler & Lewis, 1981). Kahana (1978) advocates performance on other projectives or dream content as criteria. Blatt (1975) notes the use of inappropriate, unreliable, oversimplified criteria, scoring and administration by unskilled examiners, failures in differentiating short-term vs. long-term prediction, and ignorance of the complexity of behavior in a social context as factors making it difficult to adequately assess the validity of projective techniques based upon existing research. The tremendous heterogeneity among the aged (Maddox & Douglass, 1974), moreover, supports the use of techniques that reflect this variability, and allow the clinician to study aging personality dynamics from an idiographic perspective that techniques emphasizing personality constructs (traits) (which generalize *across* persons *and* situations) cannot represent. For example, considering the dearth of knowledge about individual differences among the aged as mediators of the efficacy of therapy (see Emery & Lesher, 1982), the use of projectives in this manner seems quite promising. A last reason for their underutilization lies in the fact that psychoanalytic theory has fallen into relative disrepute as a framework within which to understand personality/ psychotherapeutic change in the aged (see Brammer, 1984; Kastenbaum, 1978).

Many (see Lawton, Whelihan, & Belsky, 1980) note that projectives are easily administered to elderly persons, are easily understood, and do not require highly sophisticated verbal skills. Moreover, they do not penalize the elder for a lack of testwise skills, and permit the examiner to obtain information about highly personal, painful topics in a manner that allows the elder to "save face," and thus maintain rapport. In this regard, Ferm (1983) has utilized projectives as an adjunct in dealing with a sexually dysfunctional elderly man. Not only are they less susceptible to faking, but also (see Gallagher, Thompson, & Levy, 1980) also enable the clinician to observe the elder's response to unstructured situations, information which may prove especially valuable in understanding the response of older persons with fragile, impoverished internal resources who may prefer to remain in supportive, predictable, highly structured situations in order to survive.

In some cases, projectives do not induce fatigue though they may be contraindicated for elderly who are seriously impaired (Eisdorfer, 1960a, 1963). Thus, their use more often than not avoids the large number of "untestable" persons. Sensory deficits must thus be taken into account not only as possible contraindications for administering projectives, but also as necessitating special care in interpreting results. Eisdorfer (1960a), for example, demonstrated that corrected visual deficits did not result in a Rorschach pattern suggesting increased constriction of personality, while hearing deficits did. However, the measure of constriction was only one variable on the Rorschach and no studies were found studying the results of visual deficits on other Rorschach variables or on the TAT. Surprisingly, almost no research addresses the role of deficiencies in color vision on the Rorschach responses, despite the fact that such functions deteriorate with age (Gilbert, 1957). Kettell (1964), for example, found color vision as measured by the Dovrine Pseudoisochromatic Color Plates and color perception on the Rorschach to decline with age. Similarly, Klopfer (1974) indicated that elderly respondents may report vague percepts on the Rorschach due to visual deficits. Certainly it would appear highly desirable for the clinician routinely to have checked the adequacy of the patient's hearing, vision, and color vision before making a decision to employ projectives and before making interpretative statements about the results of projective testing.

Ames (1960), Ames, Learned, Metraux, & Walker (1954) and Lawton, et al. (1980) have all emphasized the need for flexibility, persistence, and patience in testing the elderly, i.e., explaining in great detail the rationale of each test, breaking the testing sessions into small units, remaining available when self-administered tests are being taken, conducting an inquiry after each card rather than at the end of the Rorschach Test. While there is only prescriptive data available to suggest the usefulness of recommendations such as these for modifying test administration techniques for administering the projectives, it remains to be determined whether such modifications of technique change what the patient reports perceiving. For example, the Exner technique for administering the Rorschach requires a very non-directive method with little encouragement or reaction on the part of the examiner (Exner, 1974, 1985). Research is required to determine whether the suggested more intrusive role for the examiner with the aged results in distortion in what the subject reports seeing. Regarding the TAT, many studies have not even specified the instructions that were used for administration; most that have include standard directions.

Projectives may however, pose some problems for the clinician who must provide feedback about interpretation to unsophisticated, often skeptical elderly persons and/or their families who may feel more comfortable in receiving more straightforward information. Information must thus be presented cautiously and without embellishment in many cases. Where appropriate data exist, this feedback can be provided in normative terms, or with regard to present/future status in coping with the immediate situation.

While previous reviews have concentrated upon the Rorschach and the TAT, our intent is not only to provide an overview of the clinical usefulness of projective techniques with the aged, but also to examine projectives that have been utilized less often (Gerontological/Senior Apperception Tests, Holtzman Inkblot Technique, Hand Test, Figure Drawing and Sentence Completion Techniques) in greater detail. It is to an examination of this literature that we now turn.

NORMATIVE DATA, RELIABILITY AND VALIDITY OF PROJECTIVES TECHNIQUES RORSCHACH

No studies have been reported providing normative data on the Rorschach for large probability samples of the elderly on a national basis similar to those which are now standard practice for intellectual measures; those that have provided such data typically have made use of convenience samples with small *n*'s of questionable representativeness. Moreover, existing studies have often grouped institutionalized with community residing elderly (e.g., Ames, 1960; Klopfer, 1946; Thales, 1952) despite evidence that these two populations are quite different (Light & Amick, 1956; Prados & Fried, 1947). When the two subgroups are differentiated, the resulting sample sizes are often too small to provide much useful information. Thus, conclusions about expected results on the Rorschach among non-institutionalized, community residing older Americans are difficult to draw with any degree of confidence. Further compounding the difficulties, the typical normative study makes use of cross-sectional data (see Panek, Wagner, & Kennedy-Zwergel, 1984), which are confounded by cohort differences (Botwinick, 1984) and variations in intellectual abilities (Eisdorfer, 1963; Reichlin, 1984).

The interpretation of the existing normative literature on the Rorschach has also been made more difficult by the absence, until recently, of a uniform method for collecting and scoring Rorschach data, so that it is questionable whether existing small samples can be combined in meta-analytic procedures. Finally, the age ranges covered have been large and inconsistent from one study to another. For example, Hays (1952) studied older adults aged 50 to 65, while Chesrow, Wosika, and Reinitz (1949) studied patients from 64 to 83 years of age. More recent work on aging suggests that there are distinct subgroups of the elderly, such groupings may more correctly be made on the basis of life events (Smyer, 1984) or ability levels than on age alone (Baltes, Reese, & Nesselroade, 1977).

Despite these serious flaws, the normative studies conducted to date do demonstrate consistency in the reported structural data on the Rorschach, even when differing methods of scoring and administration have been used. Panek, Wagner, and Kennedy-Zwergel (1984) and Reichlin (1984) have provided excellent reviews of this literature which suggests elderly respondents, especially institutionalized ones, generally to be rather emotionally and cognitively restricted, more introversive, decreased in imagination compared to younger adults, and often cut off from meaningful interpersonal relations (e.g., Chesrow, Wosika, & Renitz, 1949; Hays, 1952; Klopfer, 1946; Davidson & Kruglov, 1952). In general, existing literature suggests that there are age differences in response frequency for persons of average and below-average intellectual ability, but not for above average intelligence subjects (Eisdorfer, 1963; Reichlin, 1984). An apparent decrease in human movement responses (M) is also tied to intellect since the frequency of M actually increases in high IQ subjects while decreasing in low and average ones (Caldwell, 1954). Refusals to provide responses also increase with age (Ames, 1960), but the possible moderating effects of intelligence and socioeconomic status (SES) on this variable have apparently not been examined.

Longitudinal studies such as those conducted by Ames and her associates (Ames, 1960; Ames, Metraux, Rodell, & Walker, 1973), few in number and generally employing small sample sizes, have typically confirmed the tendency for the aging process (when the effects of intelligence have not been controlled) to be associated with increasing constriction on the Rorschach, loss of color and movement, lessened form quality, and increased use of F and A as determinants.

Estimates of reliability on the Rorschach have been complicated by the instrument's use to assess change in the elderly. If the instrument is being used to attempt to capture change in personality, it follows that test-retest estimates of reliability may be low if it can be assumed that the person rather than the reaction to the test is what has changed. More recent work on the Rorschach, though not yet extended to the elderly, suggests that some indices are more likely to remain stable while others are sensitive to change (Exner, 1974, 1978) so test-retest reliabilities may in the future be appropriate to report for certain Rorschach variables. Internal estimates of reliability are also inappropriate since each of the Rorschach cards attempts to assess different aspects of personality. While inter-rater reliabilities against the scoring criteria would certainly be appropriate to note, they have typically not been reported in studies on the elderly. Therefore, no conclusions can be drawn at this point about the reliability of the scoring criteria used on the Rorschach in geropsychology studies.

The validity of the Rorschach for use with the elderly fares little better. The evidence has mostly been based on classic approaches to clinical interpretation that have not specifically been validated for the elderly, despite evidence that this may be in error. As Caldwell (1954, p. 319) put it ". . . the assumption is made that the rationale of the test variables does not change with age, and, since different profiles are found at different age levels, these must represent change within the individual." Moreover, existing literature is primarily directed to attempting to establish general profiles of changes associated or expected to occur as part of the process of aging, rather than attempting to validate the instrument as a clinical measure of psychopathology, as it would typically be used in clinical practice. No studies were found, for example, attempting to determine the appropriateness of Exner's (1978, 1985) Suicide Constellation and Depression Index for use with the elderly, despite the fact that depression is the most frequently encountered mental health disorder among the elderly (Breslau & Haug, 1983). At the present time it is simply undetermined whether the Rorschach is valid for such assessment purposes.

THE THEMATIC APPERCEPTION TEST

As with the Rorschach, more studies address the usefulness of the TAT as a measure of general personality changes associated with aging than address its use as a clinical tool for the assessment of psychopathology or other age-relevant problems.

Few normative data on the TAT for the elderly exist, a problem for the use of the TAT with any age group. Establishing TAT norms is complicated by the fact that no commonly accepted scoring criteria exist for the instrument. Typically, clinicians have made use of the TAT in a idiographic, qualitative manner while researchers have scored TAT responses for various needs or personality characteristics using specific and rather narrow scoring criteria (e.g., needs for achievement or power).

Because all of the TAT cards are almost never administered, individual researchers choose cards thought to be useful for their specific purposes. As a result, there is frequently no commonality across studies even in the cards used. For example, Britton and Britton (1972) used cards 7BM, 6BM, and 10; Rosen and Neugarten (1960) used cards 1, 2, 7Bm, 10, and 17Bm (Cumming & Henry,

1961), while Pasewark, Fitzgerald, Dexter, and Cangemi (1976) used cards 3GF, 6BM, 7GF, 10, and 15. Such variability could certainly result in different needs and conflicts being scored as salient, since the cards were designed to elicit different themes (Murray, 1943). Some researchers (e.g., Fink, 1957; Peck, 1960) have not specified in their research reports which TAT cards were used, while others (e.g., Kowal, Kemp, Lakin, & Wilson, 1964; Lieberman & Caplan, 1970; Neugarten & Guttman, 1958; Richardson, 1984-85) used "TAT-like cards", the results of which are of uncertain comparability to the original TAT measures and therefore are not reported here.

While the literature supports the idea that reliability in using the TAT improves when specific scoring criteria are adopted and trained scorers employed (Karon, 1981; Zubin, Eron, & Schumer, 1965), divergence of research purposes across the relatively few studies using the TAT with the elderly make generalizations about the TAT very difficult and normative data virtually non-existent. Estimates of the reliability of the TAT are also complicated by the issues previously discussed on the Rorschach. However, some scoring methods have been developed to score common themes across all TAT cards such as Guttman's (1975) scoring scheme for environmental coping styles. Unfortunately, inter-rater reliability agreement has often not been reported in the literature. Those studies that have done so suggest generally adequate reliability estimates (e.g., Britton, 1963; Pasewark et al., 1976).

Studies using the TAT suffer from similar drawbacks as those with the Rorschach, i.e., small samples, age ranges inconsistent from one study to another, variation in their inclusion of institutionalized or community living subjects. Many of these studies were conducted as part of the Kansas City Study of Adult Life, making use of the same sample or subsections of it (Cumming & Henry, 1961; Guttman, 1964; Lubin, 1964; Peck, 1960; Rosen & Neugarten, 1960; Shukin & Neugarten, 1964). Little cross-validation has occurred.

Scoring systems for the use of the TAT with the elderly cover diverse variables. Guttman (1964, 1975) developed a scoring system for active, passive, and magical methods of attempting to master one's environment. Rosen and Neugarten (1960, 1964) measured four TAT story characteristics thought to measure components of the elderly's energy and connectedness to the environment: introducing additional characters to the story, introducing conflict to the story, characterization of figures as having an active level of energy, and intensity of affect. Their inter-rater reliabilities on 20 of the 144 protocols scored ranged from .68 to .93. Miller and Lieberman (1965) reported scoring criteria for ego energy and ego pathology, and obtained reliabilities in the .70's. The Dana system for perceptual organization and range was adapted by Lieberman, Prock, and Tobin (1968) and by Neugarten and Miller (1964) (see Neugarten, Crotty, & Tobin, 1964) to score TAT protocols of the elderly. Lieberman, Prock, and Tobin also used the TAT to measure ego energy, heterosexual futurity, future events orientation, and interpersonal meaning of others to the respondent. Reported inter-rater reliabilities ranged from .65 to .98. Peck and Berkowitz (1964) combined interview and TAT data to make judgments about seven dimensions of personality adjustment ranging from "cathectic flexibility" to sexual integration. Shukin and Neugarten (1964) scored the TAT responses of 103 respondents for three variables: concern with causality, future versus past orientation, and optimism. Finally, Neugarten, Crotty, and Tobin (1964) used TAT responses along with many other personality variables rated on a clinical interview and projective measures to create typologies of personality among the elderly.

What all these approaches have in common, in addition to their reliance on the same overall data set, is the absence of convincing evidence for the validity of the variables proposed by the authors. While the inter-rater reliabilities were generally (though not always) acceptable, there is scant evidence other than the authors' assertions, that the scales measured what was claimed. External and cross-validation are badly needed.

Although the specific themes scored on the TAT responses were quite varied, the major findings of the cross-sectional and longitudinal research done to date with the TAT are generally suggestive of a movement with increased age toward greater constriction of affect and affection, isolation of self from the external world (Rosen & Neugarten, 1960), particularly among institutionalized subjects (Guttman, 1979), increased passivity, and less tendency to use action or active mastery to handle problems (Cumming & Henry, 1961; Guttman, 1964). Peck (1960), however, found no consistent relationship between aging and decreased mental or emotional flexibility. Britton and Britton (1972), in their longitudinal study of small town elderly, found that a TAT index of adjustment was not a good predictor of social involvement, health changes, activity level or the number of sources of support, though it did relate positively to peer ratings.

Lieberman, Prock, and Tobin (1968) found community residing elderly more mentally active and involved than institutionalized elderly and than persons waiting to enter an institution on five TAT-measured variables. Similarly, Fink (1957) found institutionalized patients to have a greater restriction of interests and more focus on the past than elderly persons who were still residing in the community. Miller and Lieberman (1965) found that neither ego energy or ego pathology as measured by the TAT predicted which elderly institutionalized female patients would best adjust to a forced move to a new institution. Kowal, Kemp, Lakin, and Wilson (1964) found that age was less potent than gender in the propensity to describe characters' problems on TAT-like cards in psychological terms. Kahana and Kahana (1968, 1970) used the TAT as a criterion measure in the examination of whether hospitalized elderly adjusted better to an age-segregated or an age-integrated environment, finding greater affective expressiveness and interaction in the latter setting.

Finally, and very importantly from the perspective of clinical concerns, studies such as those of Cumming and Henry (1961) suggest that there are considerable individual differences within any sample of elderly. Many older persons even among the oldest groups, continue to use pro-active approaches to deal with their environments. Moreover, as Guttman (1975) illustrated in his cross-cultural studies with the TAT, societal and cultural influences can affect the extent to which the elderly are likely to assume active roles rather than passive withdrawal. These findings suggest a greater need to search for individual difference and cultural variables helping to explain the psychology of healthy adjustment among the elderly, not just to focus on allegedly universal processes of aging which presume inevitable decline.

There appears to be no question that the TAT is a potent measure for eliciting thematic concerns of the elderly (Fitzgerald, Pasework, & Fleisher, 1974; Pasework et al., 1976). However, it remains to be determined whether TAT stories of the elderly are good predictors of overall adjustment or of specific forms of psychopathology. Moreover, there have been no studies yet reported examining the effects of sensory deficits on stories elicited or attempting to determine systematically the effects of such variables as intelligence, socioeconomic status, race and sex on TAT stories provided by elderly patients.

DIAGNOSIS OF PSYCHOPATHOLOGY

Rorschach

The primary research concerning the diagnostic efficacy of the Rorschach for different types of psychopathology has been the diagnosis of organic impairment and of depression. However, the diagnostic utility of such Rorschach indicators as Piotrowski's (1936) "organic signs" has certainly been called into question (e.g., Chesrow et al., 1949).

Reichlin's (1984) literature review of the Rorschach's use with the elderly notes the following Rorschach signs as suggestive of deterioration associated with the dementias: poor form quality, decrements in response number, narrowing of the number of determinants and content categories used, increased use of pure form and of animal content, absence of movement, shading and color determinants. Though also reporting similar Rorschach profiles for the organically impaired, Chesrow, Wosika, and Reinitz (1949) found no specific correlation between Rorschach results and a measure of (cognitive) deterioration. While the general findings have been supported by some criterion group studies using Rorschach responses of groups with known neurological impairments (e.g., Dorken & Kral, 1951; Kettell, 1976; Orme, 1958; Singer, 1963), such studies have not ruled out the effects of such variables as sensory deficits. In fact, Oberleder (1967) provided an alternative explanation for each of the alleged Rorschach signs of deterioration with aging. Other suggested signs of organic impairment include perseveration, increased anatomic content, impotence and anxiety (Kettell, 1976; Singer, 1963).

Ames and her associates (Ames, 1960; Ames et al., 1954) divided subjects into normal "presenile" and "senile" groups on the basis of certain Rorschach results. Cognitive impairment was judged related to very high A% and high anatomy responses (or both), very high or very low F + %, low R, little content variety, and certain "qualitative signs" of aging supposedly distinguishable on the basis of their having been or not been present from childhood. Ames' studies suggest that the normal aged (in contrast to those with increased cognitive deterioration) more closely resemble the responses of normal (younger) adults. However, no external criteria were employed to assign cases to degree-of-organicity groupings. While there was a tendency for the more deteriorated groups also to score lower on the Incomplete Man test, the Bender Gestalt, the Monroe Visual Three, and the Color Tree Test (Ames, 1974), clinical use of the Ames et al. "senility indicators" cannot be recommended until cross validation has occurred using appropriate external criteria for establishing the presence of cognitive deterioration.

The signs of depression in Rorschach protocols of the elderly have been claimed not to differ significantly from those of younger adult depressives (Reichlin, 1984), though there are surprisingly few studies to support such a conclusion. Differential diagnosis of depression from cognitive impairments has been addressed by a few studies. Orme (1955) reported that depressed patients had fewer whole responses, more inanimate movement (*m*) responses, more use of form color (FC) responses, and increased anatomy responses. While there is some suggestion that other types of psychopathology may also demonstrate similar signs among the elderly as among younger patients with such disorders (e.g., Muller & LeDinh, 1976; Weilander, 1967), there have been very few studies specifically examining the usefulness of the Rorschach to diagnose psychiatric problems of the elderly other than organicity, and, to a lesser extent, depression.

It also remains to be determined whether many of the variables interpreted as signs of organicity or depression on the Rorschach are reflective of characteristics of the person or are artifacts of sensory impairments or perceptual defenses to what may be perceived as a threatening experience. For example, it is commonly assumed that the low level of color responses in the typical Rorschach protocol of the elderly is due to increased constriction of affect thought to characterize the aging process. However, Gilbert's (1957) study of color perception as a function of age found a clear decrement in the ability to discriminate colors by those 50 and older in every part of the color spectrum, including red. The same finding has been reported by other researchers (e.g., Tiffin & Kuhn, 1942). Oberleder (1967) also makes the case that, far from reflecting psychopathology, the typical Rorschach responses of the elderly may in fact reflect anxiety at taking the test and an attempt to actively control what may be perceived as a threatening experience. These findings strongly suggest the need for great caution in making judgments about depression and withdrawal in the elderly on the basis of Rorschach responses until impairments in the ability to perceive color can be ruled out. Similarly, visual acuity deficits known to occur with aged need to be evaluated more thoroughly than Eisdorfer's (1960) lone study on a single Rorschach variable (rigidity).

These concerns, and the absence of validation of the clinical findings against external criteria, suggest the need for extreme caution in making clinical use of the Rorschach with the elderly. Differential diagnosis and interpretation of Rorschach protocols must take into account the *expected* changes in an elderly record for a person of the patient's intellectual level and socioeconomic status. Given the paucity of research on whether the modern indices of personality and psychological dysfunction also apply to the elderly, clinicians must use the Rorschach very conservatively as the basis for establishing a diagnosis or differentiating between psychotic processes and organicity.   ··

Thematic Apperception Test

While Lawton et al. (1980) claim that the TAT is underutilized in clinical practice and better validated than the Rorschach against clinical criteria, a review of the research literature raises questions about the accuracy of this conclusion. Since the TAT has rarely been validated against specific diagnostic criteria with any age group, it is not surprising that there is virtually no such data specifically for the elderly. While the bulk of the literature to date implies that, with age, respondents become more constricted, more withdrawn, and less interested in external stimuli (especially interpersonal), validation against such criteria as diagnosis of depressive or paranoid personality disorders has not yet occurred.

Variations on the TAT with the Aged: GAT and SAT

On the basis that the TAT did not reflect situations with which older adults could identify, more cohort relevant sets of pictures, depicting aged persons in situations designed to elicit more relevant themes of isolation, loss of physical mobility/sexuality, dependency or ageism (Wolk & Wolk, 1971) were developed. Despite the generally negative tone of most of the situations (all of which are achromatic) depicted in the GAT (Mercer, 1973) the Gerontological Apperception Test (GAT, 14 cards) (Wolk & Wolk, 1971) and the Senior Apperception Test (SAT, 16 pictures) (Bellak, 1975) are purported to represent an improvement upon the TAT. The SAT is perhaps more closely aligned with Murray's TAT, permitting an analysis of needs, press, psychodynamic conflict and defenses. While the authors claim that certain age-relevant themes would be elicited more frequently among the aged with the GAT/SAT than with the TAT, research has yet to confirm this assumption, with the possible exception of physical limitations and isolation from others (Fitzgerald et al., 1974; Pasewark et al., 1976; Rembowski, 1982; Schroth, 1978). The development of more elaborate scoring systems, (in view of the short stories elicited by many aged) may be necessary before their validity can be ascertained, and simple frequency counts of theme content seems to be a rather unsatisfactory way of comparing these techniques in the absence of clinically relevant criteria. Inter-scorer reliabilities are high for both scales, however, though internal consistency estimates are absent and may be inappropriate (see above). While Foote and Kahn (1979) found the SAT to be useful in separating elderly with degrees of cognitive impairment, Traxler, Swiener, and Rogers (1974) did not find the GAT to be able to validly identify aged persons in this regard.

   Research to date clearly does not support the clinical utility of either the GAT or SAT, though the use of more complex, age-relevant scoring systems and validity studies utilizing clinically relevant criteria are necessary before the GAT and the SAT can be fully evaluated.

Holtzman Inkblot Technique

   Oberleder (1967) has recommended the Holtzman Inkblot Technique (HIT) as an alternative to the Rorschach due to its ability to yield more specific information about constructs that may be of importance to the aged, i.e., hostility, anxiety, reality testing and impulse control. Despite Gamble's (1972) suggestion to do so, few have explored the HIT's utility with older age groups. While internal consistency and test-retest estimates of reliabilities are reported for the original standardization samples (Holtzman, Thorpe, Swartz, & Heron, 1961), these have yet to appear with aged subjects. Much of the HIT research with the aged to date has concentrated upon the establishment of age trends (Swartz, Norwood, & Reinehr, 1982; Witzhe, Swartz, & Drew, 1971). These studies are far from normative in their yield due to the small number of subjects ($N = 20$) in the Witzhe et al. (1971) study, the oldest of whom were only aged 61 (range 50–61); only 40 elderly (aged 60–79) were studied in the Swartz et al. (1982) investigation. Due to the small numbers of persons involved, as well as a lack of information about cognitive and/or health status, it is difficult to interpret these data or contrast them with other projective data reporting sex differences (Ames,

Metraux, Rodell, Walker, 1973; Stoner, Panek, & Satterfield, 1982). Most importantly, these data tell us little about the *functional* significance of any age effects (or lack of them) obtained. Perhaps the HIT might be better used to assess the *impact* of such cognitive and/or contextual factors on older persons' emotional state and/or body image rather than to investigate cognitive change (see Kahana, 1978) per se, though validation against more accepted measures of intellectual functioning (i.e., WAIS-R, more specific abilities) would be desirable (see below).

There are limited HIT data regarding the differentiation of normal versus pathological aged, as well as available for institutionalized elderly. Overall and Gorham (1972) found that the HIT successfully differentiated normal aged (55–84) from those with clinically diagnosed chronic organic brain syndrome (OBS). Two discriminant functions were obtained, one differentiating younger and older persons, and one separating those who were organic from the remaining non-organic persons. While Location, Rejection, Animal, Color, Shading and Barrier separated the former groups, Integration, Human, Popular, Movement, Anxiety and Hostility differentiated persons in the latter groups. Sadly, no attempt at interpretation of their findings was made by the authors. These data do suggest older (versus younger) normals to be characterized by less adequate cognitive functioning, a more defended style of dealing with bodily changes and a tendency to structure the environment as a coping mechanism. Those who were organic could be described as more constricted and isolated from others, caused by or a consequence of feelings of anger and vulnerability associated with the loss of cognitive skills. While Overall and Gorham (1972) do provide norms for institutionalized aged, they utilized the group administered version of the HIT. Moreover, they provide no rationale or reliabilities for the clinical diagnosis of OBS.

Hill (1972) does provide normative data for "average" adults (all female) aged 19–65; there appear to be a few aged (an age limit of 63 years) in her samples of chronic schizophrenics, and some middle aged in her neurotic and alcoholic samples (upper limits of 53 and 59 years respectively). However, no specification of elderly performance is made in either case, and no interpretation of HIT variables regarding cognitive or affective status (e.g., intelligence, pathological thinking, anxiety, depression) is made particular to younger versus older persons. As noted above, Overall and Gorham (1972) do provide normative data for institutionalized aged, but comparisons with that for community-living persons (Hayslip, 1982a) are confounded by method of administration.

Hayslip (1982a) has established normative data for community living elderly persons, and a factor analysis of these data yielded seven factors (anxiety over ideational sufficiency, hypochondriasis, feelings about bodily integrity, spontaneous use of intellectual resources, perceptual differentiation, problem solving, organizational ability). These factors are similar in some respects to those identified by Hill (1972) and by Reinehr and Holtzman (1983), principally reflecting a joint emphasis on cognitive processes and their use in dealing with the demands of reality, as well as a concern with physical functioning/bodily integrity. Notably absent in the Hayslip (1982a) data is a factor defining psychopathology (see Swartz et al., 1983), perhaps reflecting the positively biased nature of his sample. Research investigating the validity of HIT scoring criteria thus needs to be conducted (i.e., changes associated with OBS or institutionalization) for aged persons. Likewise, studies extending constructs established in previous research (e.g., body image HIT variables of penetration/barrier), perhaps utilizing factor analytically defined constructs (e.g., Hayslip, 1982a) would be highly desirable. Hayslip (1982a) also found some intra-sample variability by age, sex, and level of education for some HIT variables. As Kahana (1978) has noted, evidence for such inter-individual variability in projective test performance among the aged is essential and may have clinical utility in understanding how different types of older persons represent and/or cope with diverse life events. In addition to within-sample variation across the above dimensions, evidence for the effects of individual differences in verbosity (Hayslip, 1981) and in dimensions of intellectual functioning (Horn, 1978) found to meaningfully describe older versus younger persons (Hayslip, 1982b) has been found. This variation suggested "younger" older adults to be more ideationally sufficient, more concerned with bodily integrity, and more capable of using their intellectual resources to deal with reality. "Older" elderly seemed to be more concerned with conforming to external demands. Older men were more threatened by card content (more card rejections) and expressed sex-related themes more frequently than did women. More highly educated elderly tended to have better reality contact. These data (Hayslip, 1981) also indicated that older persons who produced longer responses to reject fewer cards, but more importantly, produce higher scores for 13 of 21 HIT variables. They thus may verbalize more about concerns over bodily functioning and be more open about efforts to utilize their problem-solving skills to deal with reality-based demands. In a more practical sense, however, more verbose elderly may be more difficult to examine; the HIT can be fatiguing for some aged (it contains 45 cards).

Regarding validity against the criterion of intellectual functioning (Eisdorfer, 1963), Hayslip (1982b) found fluid intelligence (Horn, 1978) to load on a HIT factor defining the "use of cognitive processes that are reality oriented," whereas crystallized ability (Horn, 1978) loaded on a HIT factor defined in the Hayslip (1982a) study as "concern over ideational sufficiency." It thus appears that those aged who are *more* intact are more concerned about the loss of their cognitive skills. Alternatively, the HIT does tap skills that (independent of past experience) enable the older adult to cope with the demands of unstructured, novel situations. While these data are intriguing, they need to be replicated and validated against real-life criteria (see above) (i.e., institutionalization).

HIT reliabilities are yet to be reported, as are relationships with other objective/projective measures, evidence that would more fully establish its construct validity with the aged. Effects of group administration (Holtzman et al., 1961; Swartz & Holtzman, 1963) on performance or studies of the use of a short-form of the HIT with the aged need to be carried out before the HIT can be administered on an efficient basis with the aged. Deficits in Color or in Location with age (see above) might be more easily explained in terms of the loss of visual acuity or color vision (Botwinick, 1984) or in terms of a reduced preference for complexity (Albaugh & Birren, 1977) brought on by environmental sameness. Additionally, research validating constructs such as anxiety/hostility (Fehr, 1976) and guilt (Sison & Fehr, 1981) with younger persons needs to be extended to elderly persons. It must be pointed out that the HIT is *not* the Rorschach (Swartz, Reinehr, & Swartz, 1981) in either an administrative or interpretative sense, and thus research with the HIT must proceed independently, yet directed to those areas of overlap that the two techniques share.

Hand Test

The Hand Test (HT) (Wagner, 1962; Wagner & Wagner, 1981) has been described as a promising projective instrument for use with the aged, being particularly adept at measuring reality contact. It is easily administered with aged persons (each card contains a hand to which the individual responds by describing what the hand might be doing). High test-retest reliabilities have been obtained for institutionalized aged (Stoner & Lundquist, 1980). The HT primarily measures that dimension of personality Wagner (1971, 1976) describes as the "Facade Self," consisting of "learned and readily available attitudes and action tendencies designed to cope with the external world" (Wagner, 1976, p. 247). It is thus well suited to understand the older adult's coping skills as they reflect covert intrapsychic dynamics (termed the "introspective self," see Wagner, 1971, 1976). Data on the Hand Test's validity have been collected by Forman (1979), Panek and Rush (1979), Panek and Hayslip (1980) and by Hayslip and Panek (1982, 1983). Forman (1979) (as cited in Panek et al., 1984) found Hand Test Variables to differentiate community living and institutionalized aged (60% of whom were diagnosed as suffering from some form of functional psychoses and 40% diagnosed as organic). Similar validity regarding the HT withdrawal score was obtained by Panek and Rush (1979). Panek and Hayslip (1980) and Hayslip and Panek (1982) have found a number of Hand Test variables (notably the Withdrawal and Pathology scores) to intercorrelate (p < .05) with Mental Status Questionnaire (MSQ) scores (indexing diffuse organicity) among institutionalized aged. Even slight decrements (as few as 2 of 10 errors on the MSQ) in orientation to time and place were found to be associated with increases in the HT Withdrawal and Pathology scores. Hayslip and Panek (1982) cross-validated these findings utilizing institutionalized aged persons whose degree of cognitive losses (as measured by the MSQ) were more extensive. Substantial covariation among level of organicity and the HT Withdrawal/Pathology scores was observed, independently of age and length of institutionalization. These findings suggest that older person's reactions to progressive degrees of mental impairment are accompanied by degrees of frustration and anxiety; such feelings are often expressed as failures in controlling others or things in the objective environment. They also indicate that some elderly will require more interpersonal/environmental support than others in order to maintain their equilibrium. Hayslip and Panek (1983) have also found such changes (i.e., increased withdrawal) to accompany more dependency (as measured by blindly rated assessments of each individual's self-care skills by the staff) among institutionalized aged.

Such older persons lacked good judgement, were impulsive, and experienced declines in the quantity and quality of their relationships with others. Such changes may be a *response* to lessened self-care associated with cognitive impairment. On the other hand, dependency may be symptomatic of an underlying pathological style of coping established earlier in life. These data tentatively suggest (in view of future validation research) that the Hand Test is not only reliable, but also a valid indicator of variations in personality functioning associated with decreased cognitive functioning and/or increased dependency. While such changes may accompany institutionalization, they need not. They can be brought about by poor health or isolation. Further research with the HT should, however, be carried out in other contexts, particularly in clinical settings with elderly who are pathological, perhaps utilizing other variables (i.e., Acting Out Ratio) that may have implications for the adjustments older persons make in response to widowhood, relocation, or poor health.

Figure Drawing Techniques

Oberleder (1967) recommends the use of figure drawing techniques with the aged, but states that they are of questionable validity, noting Lewisohn's (1964) finding that smaller drawings are indicative of depression. She suggests a parallel between older adults' tendency to make tiny drawings and the prevalence of depression among the aged. Kahana (1978) acknowledges the influence of impaired psychomotor skills (arthritis) and the loss of visual acuity on the quality of productions by aged persons. While some studies (see Lawton et al., 1980; Panek et al., 1984; Schaie & Schaie, 1977) suggest human figure drawings to be a general index of the level of cognitive functioning, others suggest that such drawing techniques adequately measure self concept or body image. Not only are cross sectional findings difficult to evaluate (due to the influence of decreased psychomotor skills/visual acuity, and to the differential clinical significance of drawings for younger versus older persons (see Kahana, 1978; Saurni & Azara, 1977; Wolk, 1972), studies are not comparable due to the use of different instructions (draw self vs. a person), different scoring systems (see Gilbert & Hall, 1962; Machover, 1952) and the recruitment across studies of subjects simultaneously varying in age, health status, and institutional residence. At best they suggest drawings to be a rough screening device

to assess general level of intactness, thus serving as a less threatening indicator of general intelligence than more formal means of assessment, particularly with suspicious, hostile aged persons. While
no external criteria have been utilized in most research to date,
Cumming and Henry (1961) did utilize a measure of ego energy
derived from the TAT to validate the drawings of their older subjects. Lakin (1956) (see Lakin, 1960) found human figure drawings
(being more constricted, shorter, and less adequately centered) to
differentiate older institutionalized aged and preadolescents. No
comparisons with noninstitutionalized aged were made, though
Lakin (1960) did carry out such a comparison, finding institutionalized aged to produce more constricted, less centered, shorter
figures. In contrast, Tuckman, Lorge, and Zeman (1961) found no
institutional effects. While the Lakin (1960) study and an investigation by Apfeldorf, Randolph, and Whitman (1966) (finding less
centeredness among institutionalized aged who used furlough
privileges the least) suggests that centeredness may reflect anxiety
or regression, no independent assessment of these constructs was
ever conducted. Within the above limitations, we might tentatively
conclude that while figure drawing techniques do seem to grossly
estimate level of cognitive functioning (though they may not be the
most efficient way of doing so), and are sensitive to the effects of institutionalization, little evidence of their ability to differentiate
elderly persons who are pathological has come to light. Notable
however, is research by Tuckman et al. (1961), who found DAP
scores not to differentiate institutionalized aged by level of rated
disturbance. While, Gilbert and Hall (1962) however, found a
marked qualitative resemblance between in the drawings of
schizophrenics and normal aged persons, reliable differences in
figure drawing scores (using a modified Goodenough scale) between
schizophrenics and normal individuals (favoring the latter at *every*
age) were obtained. Similarly, Yaguchi (1981) found reliable differences in tree drawings between older schizophrenics, elderly
organics, and aged normal persons, with the drawings of the schizophrenic and organic persons being more constricted, shorter, and
less adequately centered.

Isolated reports of figure drawings' validity regarding a number
of criteria have also been found in the literature. Leiberman (1965)
found the figure drawings of a death-imminent (within 1 year) group
versus a death-delayed group (death a year or more from testing) to
be of less complexity with time. Harrower, Thomas, and Altman

(1975) (while not utilizing aged persons) indicated that the DAP could retrospectively differentiate individuals who had/had not lapsed into poor physical/mental health (i.e., cancer, cardiovascular disorders) over a 20-year period. Kahana (1978) notes two studies by Modell (1951) and by Wolk (1972) utilizing the DAP as a criterion measure in assessing pre- versus post-therapy change (i.e., increases in size, and detail accompanied by improvements in depression, relationships with others, improvements in reality contact). While Gravitz (1969) found no effects of marital status (presumably reflecting psychosexual adequacy) on the quality/choice of sex in older women, older men (regardless of marital status) drew more same sex figures, however. The DAP may be potentially useful for use with sexually dysfunctional older couples in therapy; its use in this regard has yet to be demonstrated, however.

More direct evidence for figure drawings as a reflection of body image in middle aged and elderly persons and in disturbed versus normal aged has been collected by Ames (1974) and by Plutchik, Weiner, and Conte (1971), Plutchik, Conte, and Weiner (1973a, 1973b) and by Plutchik, Conte, Weiner, and Teresi (1978). Ames (1974) found a number of figure drawing scales (to include Gessell Incomplete Man and Color Tree Tests) to differentiate elderly normals, and those of differing levels of cognitive intactness (on the basis of Rorschach performance) (see above), however. In the Plutchik et al. (1978) study, a total of 186 aged individuals (48 normals, 33 geriatric inpatients [primarily with dementia, borderline psychosis] 30 adult schizophrenics, and 75 normal adults) were asked to draw a nude female and a nude male. In the 1971 and 1973 studies, utilizing both younger and older normals and psychiatric patients, psychiatric status, *not* chronological age differentiated the groups along a number of dimensions (anxiety about body image, value attached to one's body parts). Using a 10-point rating scale (assessing various areas of dysfunction) and a twelve point scoring system measuring anxiety/disturbed functioning developed by Koppitz (1968), Plutchik and his colleagues found substantial evidence for increased dysfunction/intellectual impairment with increased age (e.g., lack of sexual differentiation, depression, anxiety). However, while the extent of age effects for those who were disturbed (psychiatric patients) was minimal and no differences were found between normal and adult/elderly psychiatric persons, clear age effects were obtained for normals and reliable differences were found for normal versus psychiatric adults. Thus, while this well-designed study (controlling for socioeconomic/educational differences in subjects, utilizing reliable scoring systems) yields clear developmental trends favoring younger adults, it does not suggest figure drawing techniques to be able to differentiate normal versus impaired elderly. While the authors do not rule out psychomotor disturbances as a causal factor, they do suggest that "the process of aging *per se* has effects on figure drawings that are similar to the effects of mental illness at any age" (p. 74). As noted above, a lack of contact with/isolation from others, produced by malnutrition, ill health, or institutionalization could act in this manner. Despite their failure to differentiate normal versus disturbed aged, studies by Plutchik and his colleagues exemplify the attention to a number of methodological issues that had for the most part, been lacking in figure drawing research with the aged.

Sentence Completion Techniques

While a scoring system that yields high interrater agreement and test-reliability has been developed for the aged (Carp, 1967), little validity work has been completed with the Sentence Completion method using aged samples, with the exception of studies investigating this technique's sensitivity to residential status (institutionalized versus community living). Studies by Shimonaka and Marese (1975), Kahana and Kiyak (1976) and Kahana and Felton (1976) (as cited by Kahana, 1978) indicate that the Sentence Completion Test (Holsopple & Miale, 1954; Rotter & Rafferty, 1950) can reliably discriminate between institutionalized and noninstitutionalized aged, as well as be sensitive to variations in styles (instrumental, intrapsychic, affective, escapist, resigned helplessness) of coping with relocation that (with the exception of an intrapsychic mode of dealing with change) were consistent across time (see Kahana, 1978). Tobin and Leiberman (1977) found sentence completion dimensions of futurity, anxiety and depression to differentiate institutionalized/waiting list aged from community living elderly. Comparisons of studies with the sentence completion method are complicated by the lack of a consistent scoring system; many are poorly described or impossible to locate (see Kahana, 1978). The effects of stem length or directional set (Turbow & Dana, 1981) might be explored with elderly who are especially prone to have difficulty in shifting perceptual set (Botwinick, 1984).

Miscellaneous Techniques

While we have concentrated on the Rorschach, TAT, HIT, Figure Drawing, Sentence Completion techniques and the Hand Test in our examination of the clinical utility of projectives with the aged, scant evidence for the use with the aged of a number of other scales does exist, i.e., Bender-Gestalt, Gooddy's Arrow Drawing Test, Rosenzweig Picture-Frustration Test, and Impulses, Ego, Superego (IES) Test. With the exception of several studies indicating the Bender-Gestalt's ability to be able to differentiate organic and or ill aged from normal aged (see Kahana, 1978; Panek et al., 1984), little, if any research that would permit viable conclusions regarding the clinical utility of these scales exists. The interested reader is referred to Kahana (1978) and Panek et al. (1984).

CLINICAL RESEARCH NEEDS

At this point projectives can neither be accepted or rejected for routine clinical use on the basis of existing literature. Consequently, clinicians must employ considerable caution and conservatism in routinely employing projectives with the elderly until more is conducted. The following would appear to be the most needed tasks for each of the major instruments reviewed in this paper:

(1) Validation of specific projective test indices, especially those with clinical relevance (such as Exner's [1985] Depressive and Suicidal indicators) against relevant clinical criteria.

(2) Comparison of the relative efficacy of projectives and objective personality measures for the important referral questions associated with the elderly. Even if projectives can be demonstrated to be valid for identifying clinical problems, are they the fastest, cheapest, and most valid approach? There are virtually no data yet available on these questions directed specifically to the elderly,

(3) Determination of whether projective psychological tests can be used to differentiate psychopathology which existed prior to the aging process, and which may therefore be relatively resistant to treatment, versus problems which are specific to the aging process.

(4) When criteria such as institutionalization, degree of organicity or depression, or status intellectual are being used, they should be clearly defined, resting on procedures specifically validated for the

aged, and preferably not solely upon expert judgements of such. Rather than be after the fact, such research should be conducted on an *a priori* basis using purposeful samples, rather than samples of convenience.

REFERENCES

Albaugh, P., & Birren, J. (1977). Variables affecting creative contributions across the adult life span. *Human Development, 20,* 240–248.

Ames, L. B. (1960). Age changes in the Rorschach responses of a group of elderly individuals. *The Journal of Genetic Psychology, 97,* 257–285.

Ames, L. B. (1966). Changes in the Rorschach response throughout the human life span. *Genetic Psychology Monographs, 74,* 89–125.

Ames, L. B. (1974). Calibration of aging. *Journal of Personality Assessment, 38,* 507–529.

Ames, L. B., Learned, J., Metraux, R. W., & Walker, R. N. (1954). *Rorschach responses in old age.* New York: Hoeber-Harper.

Ames, L. B., Metraux, R. W., Rodell, J. L., & Walker, R. N. (1973). *Rorschach responses in old age.* New York: Brunner/Mazel.

Anastasi, A. (1976). *Psychological testing.* New York: Macmillan.

Apfeldorf, M., Randolph, J., & Whitman, G. (1966). Figure drawing correlates of furlough utilization in an aged institutionalized population. *Journal of Projective Techniques, 30,* 467–470.

Baltes, P., Reese, H., & Nesseroade, J. (1977). *Life-span developmental psychology: Introduction to research methods.* Belmont, CA: Wadsworth.

Bellak, L. (1975). *The TAT, CAT, and SAT in clinical use.* New York: Grune & Stratton.

Blatt, S. J. (1975). The validity of projective techniques and their research and clinical contribution. *Journal of Personality Assessment, 39,* 327–343.

Botwinick, J. (1966). Cautiousness in advanced age. *Journal of Gerontology, 21,* 347–353.

Botwinick, J. (1984). *Aging and behavior.* New York: Springer.

Brammer, L. (1984). counseling theory and the older adult. *Counseling Psychologist, 12,* 29–37.

Breslau, L., & Haug, M. (1983). *Depression and aging.* New York: Springer.

Butler, R., & Lewis, M. (1981). *Aging and mental health: Positive psychosocial approaches.* St. Louis: Mosby.

Caldwell, B. McD. (1954). The use of the Rorschach in personality research with the aged. *Journal of Gerontology, 9,* 316–323.

Carp, F. (1967). The application of an empirical scoring standard for a sentence completion test administered. *Journal of Gerontology, 22,* 301–307.

Chesrow, E. J., Wosika, P. H., & Renitz, A. H. (1949). A psychometric evaluation of aged white males. *Geriatrics, 4,* 169–177.

Cumming, E., & Henry, W. E. (1961). *Growing old.* New York: Basic Books.

Davidson, H. H., & Kruglov, L. (1952). Personality characteristics of the institutionalized aged. *Journal of Consulting Psychology, 16,* 5–12.

Dorken, H., & Kral, V. A. (1951). Psychological investigation of senile dementia. *Geriatrics, 6,* 151–163.

Eisdorfer, C. (1960a). Developmental level and sensory impairment in the aged. *Journal of Projective Techniques, 24,* 129–132.

Eisdorfer, C. (1960b). Rorschach rigidity and sensory decrement in a senescent population. *Journal of Gerontology, 15,* 188–190.

Eisdorfer, C. (1963). Rorschach performance and intellectual functioning in the aged. *Journal of Gerontology, 18,* 358–363.

Emery, G., & Lesher, E. (1984). Treatment of depression in older adults: Personality considerations. *Psychotherapy: Theory, Research and Practice, 19*, 500–505.

Exner, J. E., Jr. (1974). *The Rorschach. A comprehensive system.* New York: Wiley.

Exner, J. E., Jr. (1978). *The Rorschach: A comprehensive system. Vol. 2: Current and advanced interpretation.* New York: Wiley.

Exner, J. E., Jr. (1985). *A Rorschach workbook for the comprehensive system.* 2nd Ed. Bayville, NY: Rorschach Workshops.

Fehr, L. (1976). Construct validity of the Holtzman Inkblot Technique anxiety and hostility scores. *Journal of Personality Assessment, 40*, 483–486.

Ferm, R. (1983). *Projective techniques as a diagnostic guide in the treatment of the older adult.* Paper presented at the Annual Scientific Meeting of the Gerontological Society. San Francisco, CA.

Fink, H. H. (1957). The relationship of time perspective to age, institutionalization, and activity. *Journal of Gerontology, 12*, 414–417.

Fisher, S. (1970). *Body experience in fantasy and behavior.* New York: Appleton-Century Crofts.

Fitzgerald, B. J., Pasework, R. A., & Fleisher, S. (1974). Responses of an aged population on the Gerontological and Thematic Apperception Tests. *Journal of Personality Assessment, 38*(3), 234–235.

Foote, J., & Kahn, M. (1979). Discriminative effectiveness of the Senior Apperception Test with impaired and nonimpaired elderly persons. *Journal of Personality Assessment, 43*, 360–364.

Forman, E. (1979). *A normative study on a group of adjusted and maladjusted aged using the Hand Test.* Unpublished Master's Thesis. University of Akron.

Gallagher, D., Thompson, L., & Levy, S. (1980). Clinical psychological assessment of older adults. In L. Poon (Ed.), *Aging in the 80's: Psychological issues.* Washington, D.C: American Psychological Association.

Gamble, K. (1972). The Holtzman Inkblot Technique: A review. *Psychological Bulletin, 77*, 172–194.

Gilbert, J. G. (1957). Age changes in color matching. *Journal of Gerontology, 12*, 210–215.

Gilbert, J., & Hall, M. (1962). Changes with age in human figure drawing. *Journal of Gerontology, 17*, 397–404.

Gravitz, M. (1969). Marital status and figure drawing choice in normal older Americans. *Journal of Social Psychology, 77*, 143–144.

Gurland, B. (1973). A broad clinical assessment of psychopathology in the aged. In C. Eisdorfer & M. P. Lawton (Eds.), *The psychology of adult development and aging.* Washington, D.C.: American Psychological Association.

Guttman, D. L. (1964). An exploration of ego configurations in middle and later life. In B. L. Neugarten (Ed.), *Personality in middle and late life. Empirical studies.* New York: Atherton Press.

Guttman, D. (1975). Alternatives to disengagement: The old Maya and the Highland Druze. In J. F. Gubrium (Ed.), *Time, roles, and self in old age.* New York: Human Sciences Press.

Guttman, D. (1979). *The diagnostic use of the TAT with other patients.* Paper presented at the annual conference of the American Psychological Association, 1979.

Harrower, M., Thomas, C., & Altman, A. (1975). Human figure drawings in a prospective study of six disorders: Hypertension, coronary heart disease, malignant tumor, suicide, mental illness, and emotional disturbance. *Journal of Nervous and Mental Disease, 161*, 191–199.

Hays, W. (1952). Age and sex differences on the Rorschach experience balance. *Journal of Abnormal and Social Psychology, 47*, 390–393.

Hayslip, B. (1981). Verbosity and projective test performance in the aged. *Journal of Clinical Psychology, 37*, 662–666.

Hayslip, B. (1982a). The Holtzman Inkblot Technique and aging: Norms and factor structure. *Journal of Personality Assessment, 46*, 248–256.

Hayslip, B. (1982b). *Personality-ability relationships in the aged.* Paper presented at the Annual Scientific Meeting of the Gerontological Society. Boston.

Hayslip, B., & Panek, P. (1982). Construct validation of the Hand Test with older adults: Replication and extension. *Journal of Personality Assessment, 46,* 248–256.

Hayslip B., & Panek, P. (1983). Physical self-maintenance, mental status, and personality in institutionalized elderly adults. *Journal of Clinical Psychology, 39,* 479–485.

Hill, E. F. (1972). *The Holtzman Inkblot Technique: A handbook for clinical application.* San Francisco: Jossey-Bass.

Holsopple, J., & Miale, F. (1954). *Sentence completion—a projective method for the study of personality.* Springfield, IL: C. C. Thomas.

Holtzman, W., Thorpe, J., Swartz, J., & Heron, E. (1961). *Inkblot perception and personality: Holtzman Inkblot Technique.* Austin: University of Texas Press.

Horn, J. L. (1978). Human ability systems. In P. B. Baltes (Ed.), *Life-span development and behavior.* New York: Academic Press.

Kahana, B. (1978). The use of projective techniques in personality assessment of the aged. In M. Storandt, I. Siegler, & M. Elias (Eds.), *The clinical psychology of aging.* New York: Plenum.

Kahana, E., & Felton, B. (1976). *Continuity and change in coping strategies in a longitudinal analysis.* Paper presented at the Annual Scientific Meeting of the Gerontological Society. New York, NY. (abstract).

Kahana, E., & Kahana, B. (1968). Effects of age segregation on affective expression of elderly psychiatric patients. *American Journal of Orthopsychiatry, 38,* 158–165.

Kahana, B., & Kahana, E. (1970). Changes in mental status of elderly patients in age-integrated and age-segregated hospital milieus. *Journal of Abnormal Psychology, 75,* 177–181.

Kahana, B., & Kiyak, A. (1976). *The use of projective tests as an aid to assessing coping behavior and coping styles among the aged.* Paper presented at the Annual Scientific Meeting of the Gerontological Society. New York, NY. (abstract).

Karon, B. (1981). The Thematic Apperception Test. In A. I. Rabin (Ed.), *Assessment with projective techniques.* New York: Springer.

Kastenbaum, R. (1978). Personality theory, therapeutic approaches, and the elderly client. In M. Storandt, I. Siegler, & M. Elias (Eds.), *The clinical psychology of aging.* New York: Plenum.

Kettell, M. E. (1964). *Integrity of ego processes in aged females.* Unpublished Ph.D. dissertation. Boston: Boston University Graduate School, 1964.

Kettell, M. E. (1976). Perceptual and behavioral correlates of "organicity" in old age. *Journal of Geriatric Psychiatry, 9,* 85–87.

Klopfer, W. G. (1946). Personality patterns of old age. *Rorschach Research Exchange, 10,* 145–166.

Klopfer, W. G. (1974). The Rorschach and old age. *Journal of Personality Assessment, 38,* 420–422.

Klopfer, W., & Taubee, E. (1976). Projective techniques. *Annual Review of Psychology, 27,* 543-567.

Koppitz, E. (1968). *Psychological evaluation of children's human figure drawings.* New York: Grune & Stratton.

Kowal, K. A., Kemp, D. E., Lakin, M., & Wilson, S. (1964). Perception of the helping relationship as a function of age. *Journal of Gerontology, 19,* 405–412.

Lakin, M. (1960). Formal characteristics of human figure drawings by institutionalized and non-institutionalized aged. *Journal of Gerontology, 15,* 76–78.

Lanyon, R. (1984). Personality assessment. *Annual Review of Psychology, 35,* 667–701.

Lawton, M. P., Whelihan, W., & Belsky, J. (1980). Personality tests and their uses with older adults. In J. E. Birren & R. B. Sloane (Eds.), *Handbook of mental health and aging.* Englewood Cliffs, NJ: Prentice-Hall.

Leiberman, M. (1965). Psychological correlates of impending death: Some preliminary observations. *Journal of Gerontology, 20,* 182–190.

Leiberman, M. A., & Caplan, A. S. (1970). Distance from death as a variable in the study of aging. *Developmental Psychology, 2,* 71–84.

Leiberman, M. A., Prock, V. N., & Tobin S. S. (1968). Psychological effects of institutionalization. *Journal of Gerontology, 23,* 343–353.

Lewisohn, P. (1964). Relationship between height of figure drawings and depression in psychiatric patients. *Journal of Consulting Psychology, 28,* 380–381.

Light, B. H., & Amick, J. H. (1956). Rorschach responses of normal aged. *Journal of Projective Techniques, 20,* 185–195.

Lubin, M. I. (1964). Addendum to chapter 4. In B. L. Neugarten (Ed.), *Personality in middle and late life. Empirical studies.* New York: Atherton Press.

Machover, K. (1952). *Personality projection in the drawing of the human figure.* Springfield, IL: C. C. Thomas.

Maddox, G., & Douglass, E. (1974). Aging and individual differences: A longitudinal analysis of social psychological and physiological indicators. *Journal of Gerontology, 29,* 555–563.

Mercer, M. (1973). Review of the Gerontological Apperception Test. *Journal of Personality Assessment, 37,* 396–397.

Miller, D., & Leiberman, M. A. (1965). The relationship of affect state and adaptive capacity to reactions to stress. *Journal of Gerontology, 20,* 492–497.

Modell, A. (1951). Changes in human figure drawings by patients who recover from regressed states. *American Journal of Orthopsychiatry, 21,* 584–596.

Muller, C., & LeDinh, T. (1976). Aging of schizophrenic patients as seen through the Rorschach Test. *Acta Psychiatrica Scandinavia, 53,* 161–167.

Murray, H. A. (1943). *Thematic Apperception Test.* Cambridge, MA: Harvard University Press.

Neugarten, B. L., Crotty, W. J., & Tobin, S. S. (1964). Personality types in an aged population. In B. L. Neugarten (Ed.), *Personality in middle and late life. Empirical studies.* New York: Atherton Press.

Neugarten, B., & Guttman, D. (1958). Age-sex roles and personality in middle age: A thematic apperception study. *Psychological Monographs, 72,* 1–33.

Oberleder, M. (1967). Adapting current psychological techniques for use in testing the aged. *The Gerontologist, 7,* 188–191.

Orme, J. E. (1955). Intellectual and Rorschach test performances of a group of senile dementia patients and a group of elderly depressives. *Journal of Mental Science, 202,* 863–870.

Overall, J. E., & Gorham, D. R. (1972). Organicity versus old age in objective and projective test performance. *Journal of Consulting and Clinical Psychology, 39,* 98–105.

Panek, P., & Hayslip, B. (1980). Construct validation of the Hand Test withdrawal score on institutionalized older adults. *Perceptual and Motor Skills, 51,* 595–598.

Panek, P., & Rush, M. (1979). Intellectual and personality differences between community-living and institutionalized older adult females, *Experimental Aging Research, 5,* 239–250.

Panek, P. E., Wagner, E. E., & Kennedy-Zwergel, K. (1984). A review of projective test findings with older adults. *Journal of Personality Assessment, 47,* 562–582.

Pasewark, R. A., Fitzgerald, B. J., Dexter, V., & Cangemi, A. (1976). Responses of adolescent, middle-aged, and aged females on the Gerontological and Thematic Apperception tests. *Journal of Personality Assessment, 40,* 588–591.

Peck, R. F. (1960). Personality factors in adjustment to aging. *Geriatrics, 15,* 124–130.

Peck, R. F., & Berkowitz, H. Personality adjustment in middle age. In B. L. Neugarten (Ed.), *Personality in middle and late life: Empirical studies.* New York: Atherton Press.

Piotrowski, Z. A. (1936). On the Rorschach method and its application in organic disturbances of the central nervous system. *Rorschach Research Exchange, 1,* 23–40.

Plutchik, R., Conte, H., & Weiner, M. (1973a). Studies of body image: II. Dollar values of body parts. Journal of *Gerontology, 28,* 89–91.

Plutchik, R., Conte, H., & Weiner, M. (1973b). Studies of body image: III. Body feelings as measured by the semantic differential technique. *International Journal of Aging and Human Development, 4,* 375–380.

Plutchik, R., Conte, H., Weiner, M., & Teresi, J. (1978). Studies of body image: IV. Figure drawings in normal and abnormal geriatric and nongeriatric groups. *Journal of Gerontology, 33,* 68–75.

Plutchik, R., Weiner, M., & Conte, H. (1971). Studies of body image: I. Body worries and body discomforts. *Journal of Gerontology, 26,* 344–350.

Prados, M., & Fried, E. G. (1947). Personality structure in the older age groups. *Journal of Clinical Psychology, 3,* 113–120.

Reichlin, R. (1984). Current perspectives on Rorschach performance among older adults. *Journal of Personality Assessment, 48,* 71–81.

Rembowski, J. (1982). Elderly people as portrayed through the Gerontological Apperception Test. *Psychogica Wychowawcza, 25,* 51–60. (abstract).

Richardson, V. (1984-85). Projective measurement of adult peer relations as a function of chronological age. *International Journal of Aging and Human Development. 19,* 11–19.

Rosen, J. L., & Neugarten, B. L. (1960). Ego functions in the middle and later years: A thematic apperception study of normal adults. *Journal of Gerontology, 15,* 62–67.

Rosen, J. L., & Neugarten, B. L. (1964). Ego functions in the middle and later years: A thematic apperception study. In B. L. Neugarten (Ed.), *Personality in middle and late life. Empirical studies.* New York: Atherton Press.

Rotter, J., & Rafferty, J. *Manual: Rotter Incomplete Sentences Blank: College Form.* New York: Psychological Corporation.

Saurni, C., & Azara, V. (1977). Developmental analysis of human figure drawings in adolescence, young adulthood and middle age. *Journal of Personality Assessment, 41,* 31–38.

Schaie, K. W., & Schaie, J. P. (1977). Clinical assessment and aging. In J. E. Birren & K. W. Schaie (Eds.), *Handbook of the psychology of aging,* New York: Van Nostrand Reinhold.

Schroth, M. (1978). Sex and generational differences in Senior Apperception Technique projections. *Perceptual and Motor Skills, 47,* 1299–1304.

Shimonaka, Y., & Marese, T. (1975). Self-percepts of the aged: A comparison of SCT responses between groups of different living conditions and different ages. *Japanese Journal of Educational Psychology, 23,* 104–113. (abstract).

Shukin, A., & Neugarten, B. L. (1964). Personality and social interaction. In B. L. Neugarten (Ed.), *Personality in middle and late life. Empirical studies.* New York: Atherton Press.

Singer, M. (1963). Personality measurements in the aged. In J. E. Birren, R. N. Butler, S. W. Greenhouse, L. Sokoloff, & M. R. Yarrow (Eds.), *Human Aging.* Washington, D.C.: National Institute of Mental Health. Public Service publication, No. 986.

Sison, G., & Fehr, L. (1981). A projective analysis of guilt: The Holtzman Inkblot Technique. *Journal of Personality Assessment, 45,* 23–26.

Smyer, M. (1984). Life transitions and aging: Implications for counseling older adults. *Counseling Psychologist, 12,* 17–28.

Stoner, S., & Lundquist, T. (1980). Test-retest reliability of the Hand Test with older adults. *Perceptual and Motor Skills, 50,* 217–218.

Stoner, S., Panek, P., & Satterfield, G. (1982). Age and sex differences on the Hand Test. *Journal of Personality Assessment, 46,* 260–264.

Swartz, J., & Holtzman, W. (1963). Group method of administration of the Holtzman Inkblot Technique. *Journal of Clinical Psychology, 19,* 433–441.

Swartz, J., Norwood, M., & Reinehr, R. (1982). Perceptual-cognitive development of older adults as measured by the Holtzman Inkblot Technique. *Academic Psychology Bulletin, 4,* 17–21.

Swartz, J., Reinehr, R., & Holtzman, W. (1983). Personality development throughout the lifespan. In C. D. Spielberger & J. N. Butcher (Eds.), *Advances in personality assessment: Volume 3.* Hillsdale, NJ: Lawrence Erlbaum.

Swartz, J., Reinehr, R., & Swartz, C. (1981). The Holtzman Inkblot Technique is not the Rorschach: A reply to Lockwood, Roll, and Matthews. *Journal of Personality Assessment, 45,* 582–583.

Thales, M. B. (1952). *The application of three theories of personality to the Rorschach records of seventy-five older persons.* Unpublished Doctoral Dissertation, University of Denver.

Tiffin, J., & Kuhn, N. S. (1942). Color discrimination in industry. *Archives of Opthamology, 28,* 951–959.

Tobin, S., & Leiberman, M. (1977). *Last home for the aged.* San Francisco: Jossey-Bass.

Traxler, A., Sweiner, R., & Rogers, B. (1974). The use of the Gerontological Apperception Test (GAT) with community-dwelling and institutional aged. *The Gerontologist, 14,* 52. (abstract).

Tuckman, J., Lorge, I., & Zeaman, F. D. (1961). The self-image in aging. *Journal of Genetic Psychology, 99,* 317–321.

Turbow, K., & Dana, R. (1981). The effects of stem length and directions on sentence completion test responses. *Journal of Personality Assessment, 45,* 27–32.

Volans, P., & Woods, R. (1983). Why do we assess the aged? *British Journal of Clinical Psychology, 22,* 213–214.

Wagner, E. E. (1962). *The Hand Test: Manual for administration, scoring, and interpretation.* Los Angeles: Western Psychological Services.

Wagner, E. E. (1971). Structural analysis: A theory of personality based on projective techniques. *Journal of Personality Assessment, 35,* 422–435.

Wagner, E. E. (1976). Personality dimensions measured by projective techniques: A formulation based on structural analysis. *Perceptual and Motor Skills, 43,* 247–253.

Wagner, E. E. & Wagner, C. (1981). *The interpretation of projective test data: Theoretical and practical guidelines.* Springfield, IL: C. C. Thomas.

Weilander, D. (1967). Alcoholics and the influence of age on variables of the Structured-Objective Rorschach Test (SORT). *Journal of Psychology, 65,* 57–58.

Witzke, D., Swartz, J., & Drew, C. (1971). Level of perceptual development of normal adults as measured by the Holtzman Inkblot Technique. *Proceedings of the 79th Annual convention of the American Psychological Association, 6,* 609–610.

Wolk, R. L. (1972). Refined projective techniques with the aged. In D. P. Kent, R. Kastenbaum, & S. Sherwood (Eds.), *Research planning and action for the elderly: The power and potential of social science.* New York: Behavioral Publications.

Wolk, R. L., & Wolk, R. B. (1971). *The Gerontological Apperception Test.* New York: Behavioral Publications.

Yaguchi, K. (1981). A study of tree-drawings in aged groups: An examination of formal indices of the drawings. *Journal of Child Development, 17,* 32–34.

Zubin, J., Eron, L. D., & Schumer, F. (1965). *An experimental approach to projective techniques.* New York: John Wiley.

Questions

1) What are some of the inherent advantages and limitations of projective techniques?

2) In which kinds of cases would these techniques be most appropriate? least appropriate?

3) What pattern of responses on several projective tests would we expect for a depressed elder? a demented elder?

4) Discuss the comparative advantages of using the interpretation of the patient's dreams, artwork, or drama as a projective technique.

II
DEPRESSION SCALES
FOR USE
IN LATER LIFE

5/DIRECTIONS FOR CLINICAL-PSYCHOSOCIAL ASSESSMENT OF DEPRESSION IN THE ELDERLY

Jean Addington, PhD
P. S. Fry, PhD

Editor's Introduction

Previous issues of *CG* have discussed the etiology of geriatric depression: the relationship with physical disease (v. 1, #2, pp. 51–58), medical conditions (v. 1, #4, pp. 5–7), family relations (v. 1, #4, pp. 77–78), and diurnal mood fluctuation (v. 2, #2, pp. 55–57).

The topic of assessment of depression was covered by articles emphasizing the problems with family ratings (v. 1, #3, pp. 94–95), the dexamethasone suppression test (v. 2, #2, pp. 3–12; v. 3, #21, pp. 28–36), problems with DSM-III categories (v. 2, #3, pp. 3–13), pseudodementia (v. 2, #3, pp. 60–61; v. 3, #2, pp. 46–48; v. 3, #3, pp. 42–43).

The assessment of geriatric depression remains such a complex corner of the field of assessment that it deserves a special section in this book.

Addington and Fry introduce the section by giving a review of the numerous concerns involved, and emphasizing the need for multidimensional assessment. The key points they make are that accurate assessment is the key to

The authors are affiliated with the Department of Educational Psychology, The University of Calgary.

Requests for reprints should be sent to Jean Addington, Department of Educational Psychology, The University of Calgary, 2500 University Drive N.W., Calgary, Alberta, Canada T2N 1N4.

effective intervention with the aged (and no where is this more true than it is in the case of depression), the tests and symptomatology which are so useful in identifying depression in younger patients simply do not work with elders, the interaction of depression with physical disease (and drugs), and the problem of a differential diagnosis with organic brain syndrome ("pseudodementia").

The authors present three perspectives from which to view depression in later life: the medical model, psychodynamic model, and cognitive-behavioral model, discussing the utility and limitation of each. Even though a given form of therapy and/or model may be in vogue at any given point in time, Addington and Fry's conclusion will probably endure: "using only one method of assessment will probably not suffice, particularly when dealing with the elderly person." Their suggestion, a multidimensional assessment which includes more than mere measures of mental health, is necessary for effective, multidisciplinary intervention to launch a campaign against depression on several fronts.

Assessment can be viewed as a systematic evaluative process that leads to specific judgements about a given person's current and potential level in a variety of settings. These judgements contribute to a decision-making process that can have a significant impact on that person's subsequent life pattern. Psychological assessment should not be equated with procedures of psychometric testing but is better conceptualized as more broadly oriented toward issues of problem solving (Maloney & Ward, 1976).

The purpose of assessment is twofold. First, we want to diagnose the problem, in this case identify the depression, and secondly, having diagnosed depression, we want to assess those aspects of the depression at which the intervention will be aimed.

The assessment of psychopathology has traditionally emphasized identifying underlying syndromes suggested by the presenting symptoms. Classifying systems such as DSM III are useful for outlining broad groups of disorders such as psychotic versus neurotic or grouping together psychological problems in which mood is a factor and also provide an overview of the variety of mental disorders. However, DSM III uses labels that are of little use in planning treatment since, in practice, most schools of psychotherapy do not vary techniques to any great extent according to the psychiatric label.

An alternative method for assessing psychological disorders is to obtain descriptions of the person's problems in as specific detail as possible. By identifying the particular contexts in which problem behaviors are manifested, the practitioner or clinician can develop hypotheses concerning environmental or person variables that are associated with the problem behavior and then intervene to change some aspects of this person-environment interaction.

Recently, a number of investigators have begun to highlight problems encountered in the psychological assessment of the elderly (Crook, 1979). In test construction and psychometric issues, representative problems include poor standardization on elderly subjects, lack of normative data, poor reliability and external validity, absence of ecologically valid measures of functional capacity in the elderly, ambiguous instructions, inappropriate content of items for older persons, and inability of tests to discriminate at lower levels of functioning (Gallagher, Thomson, & Levy, 1980).

Assessment of elderly patients is the critical key in the development of effective mental health programs for the aged. Careless or uninformed diagnosis can lead to inadequate treatment of various problems. The picture is complicated by a tendency to equate processes of normal aging with the effects of disease. Thus, with respect to assessment strategies, emphasis is placed on the need for integrative multidimensional approaches to minimize the likelihood of misdiagnosis when the perspective of only one discipline is considered. There has also been increasing emphasis on determining the strengths and weaknesses of the older person's general psychological organization. These are too often overlooked when the emphasis of assessment is on psychopathology.

Depression constitutes one of the more serious mental health problems for persons over sixty-five. Gurland (1976) presents data from the United States-United Kingdom Cross-National project indicating that only 5% of patients over 65 were diagnosed as depressed by the study psychiatrists; but that many more patients gave themselves high depression ratings on a symptom checklist. It has been suggested that older people may be diagnosed as clinically depressed less frequently because they may be subject to a higher incidence of transient depressive episodes (possibly precipitated by external events). It, also, may be that measures currently used to assess depression in the general population are not suitable for this older age group. It is apparent, therefore, that depression in the elderly is complex, confusing and difficult to diagnose.

It is the purpose of this paper to explore the topic of assessing depression in the elderly. Issues that will be discussed include features of depression; the relationship between depressive symptoms and medical disease; and differential diagnosis. Further, assessment procedures that precede the various modalities of treatment will be compared.

GENERAL FEATURES OF DEPRESSION IN THE ELDERLY

Clinical Symptomatology

Depression in the elderly may resemble the familiar clinical syndrome seen in younger adults. There are unfortunately, few studies that compare depressive symptomatology in the elderly and in younger adults. Overall, agitation is more frequently seen in older patients and retardation more frequently seen in younger patients (Winokur, Morrison, Clancy, & Crowe, 1973). These data, however, are concerned with a separation between patients above and below 40 years of age. Whether this kind of difference would hold true between patients who are above and below 65 is questionable. Chronicity is more frequently seen in older females (over 40) and recurrent episodes are more frequently seen in older males (over 40). Whether patients who were 60 or older would have more chronicity or more episodes compared to patients who are 40–60 is unknown. Epstein (1976) describes older depressed patients as manifesting an atypical pattern, with apathy, listlessness, and a quiet attitude of self-deprecation emphasized more than in the young. Somatic complaints such as insomnia, loss of appetite, other gastrointestinal problems, and headaches also tend to be emphasized more by older depressed patients (Gurland, 1976), while feelings of dysphoria or sadness are reported less. Blazer (1982) compares his study with two other studies of the comparisons of symptoms of elderly and younger adult depressed patients. Worry, feelings of uselessness, sadness, pessimism, fatigue, inability to sleep, and volitional difficulties are relatively common symptoms in the elderly population.

Comparisons of young and old persons with depressive disorders, usually have not taken into account another important factor: whether the symptoms of persons whose disorders are manifested for the first time in late life differ from those of individuals who have had repeated depressive episodes beginning in early or middle adulthood (Zarit, 1980).

In severe cases of depression the clinician should have little difficulty recognizing the disorder. The elderly patient looks sad and may express a sense of helplessness, despair, and worthlessness. Guilt is not usually a serious problem with the elderly but it may exist over real or imagined past failures, errors, or indiscretions. Patients may be agitated, with pacing, hand wringing, and twisting of clothes. Others may be withdrawn, or mute and refuse food or drink. Some very severe cases can take to their bed, be unable to rise, unable to care for body functions, and may be incontinent.

Somatic Symptoms

Delusions of somatic dysfunction may dominate the clinical picture. Such patients may claim that parts of their body are dead, cancerous, or non-functional. Vegetative (somatic) signs of depression are regular components of late life affective illness and at times may be the earliest signals of a depressive disorder. Insomnia, anorexia with weight loss, and fatigue are a familiar triad (Pfeiffer, 1970). Constipation is the most common somatic symptom of depression (Anderson, 1971), although diarrhea has also been noted. Other less severely depressed elderly patients may appear apathetic and expressionless, with poor concentration and attention. Although the elderly are at a stage in life where there is an increase in disease and physical decline and interpretation of these somatic symptoms may be difficult, such complaints should not be automatically dismissed merely as being part of the aging process.

Physical Health

In evaluating a depressed elderly patient the clinician has to decide how much of a physical status evaluation to perform. Patients who seem physically ill or have specific physical complaints should be medically evaluated. Symptoms such as apathy or weight loss that persist as depression lifts should be investigated for a possible physical illness.

THE RELATIONSHIP BETWEEN DEPRESSIVE
SYMPTOMS AND MEDICAL DISEASE

Symptoms of depression are occasionally among the initial pre-senting symptoms of serious medical disease in elderly patients. The differential diagnosis of medically related depression versus the symptoms of depression of a psychogenic origin may be difficult. Apathy, anorexia, insomnia, decreased energy, decreased libido, pain, protean somatic symptoms, and hypochondriasis may be man-ifestations of depression in the elderly as well as parts of a medical disease (Salzman & Shader, 1979). Four aspects of the relationship between depressive symptoms and medical disease shall be dis-cussed, namely: (1) depression as a response to physical illness, (2) masked or atypical depression, (3) diseases that may present with depression, or that may be accompanied by depressive symptoms, (4) effect of drugs.

1. Depression As a Response to Physical Illness

Pfeiffer (1970) suggests that there is a close association between physical illness and depressive reactions in old age. It is thus pos-sible that depression in the elderly may be precipitated by physical illness. Verwoerdt (1981) contends that the severity, duration, and rate of progression of the illness are factors in determining the magnitude of the depessive response of the elderly to their illness. Verwoerdt (1973) suggests other important factors that may affect the severity of the depression: (a) the organ system involved and its role in the maintenance of life; (b) the degree of narcissistic attach-ment to the lost functioning; (c) the ability to maintain a positive body image while acknowledging the loss of parts or functioning.

One of the most common illnesses of old age is cardiovascular disease. Cardiac illness can produce severe depressive illness (Kav-anagh, Shepherd, & Tuk, 1975). Depression appears early in this disease. Fatigue, exhaustion, irritability, anxiety, dependency, aim-lessness, and boredom can set in. This is sometimes falsely attrib-uted to the failing heart. When there is an increase in dependency, further regression, helplessness, and social isolation may ensue (Payne, 1975). Another diagnosis that can lead to depression is cancer. Some of the reaction to cancer results from the loss of cer-tain affected body parts through surgery.

In order to remain in contact with reality, stimulation is required from the environment. Loss of vision and/or hearing may lead to loss of independence, social isolation, and depression. The overall incidence of depression that accompanies medical disease suggests that depression is a relatively frequent companion to such illness in all age groups. However, since the elderly have an increased incidence of medical disease, then it is likely that the incidence of depression will be raised to higher levels in this group.

2. Masked or Atypical Depressions

Although medical illness may present with depression or depressive-like symptoms the reverse is also true. In some cases the use of somatic complaints to communicate affective states represents an active ego-coping mechanism. Many elderly patients with depression present with an aggravation of pre-existing physical illness (Pfeiffer, 1970). A variety of symptoms may be unconsciously used by a patient to mask depression as well as to communicate and ask for help. Gastrointestinal symptoms are the most common. The patient is preoccupied with constipation, flatulence, and abdominal pains (Blazer, 1982). These symptoms may serve to mask affective symptoms particularly in those who, as younger adults, had difficulty acknowledging dysphoria and tended to seek help by making somatic complaints to their general practitioner. Psychoanalytic explanations of this phenomenon are derived from the theory of hypochondriasis. Anger and guilt are turned against the self and can be understood as self-punishment or even partial suicide, when surgery is conducted to relieve symptoms (Salzman & Shader, 1979). Another explanation is that somatic hyperconcern of elderly people may be a consequence of real loss of objects or means of getting external support (Busse, 1975). Failing functioning is a reality in the elderly as are the devastating effects of physical disease and the prospect of death. It may be that for many older people the communication of affective distress may be more threatening than talk of physical illness.

3. Diseases That May Present with Depression

Depression can accompany some physical disorders. It is a common symptom in individuals with organic mental disorders. The nature of this interaction will be discussed later. The prevalence of depression is high in early Parkinson's disease. There does not seem to be a relationship among the degree and prevalence of depression associated with Parkinson's, the patient's age and the severity and duration of the patient's disability. Assnis (1977) suggests that depression may not only be reactive to the disability but may also be biochemically related to the disease. In particular, there is a decreased concentration of serotonin, and its principal metabolite, 5-hydroxyindolacetic acid, in both Parkinsonian patients and depressed patients.

Endocrine abnormalities are often associated with alterations in affective states. In general, both hypo and hyperfunctioning of the various endocrine systems have been implicated in depression. Hypothyroidism is a disease which should be considered in the care of geriatric patients since it is associated with an 80% incidence of depressive symptoms. Addison's disease and Cushing's disease may present as depression although they are less common.

4. Depression As an Effect of Drugs

Drugs, either prescribed by a physician or taken independently, are often responsible for the development of depression, the aggravation of a pre-existing depression on the inducement of depressive-like symptoms such as sedation, apathy, and lethargy. Firstly, the elderly are more likely to be taking drugs for treatment of a medical problem and thus are predisposed to their side effects. Secondly, the elderly are more susceptible to unwanted toxic effects of drugs. This increased susceptibility is the result of a series of naturally occurring morphologic changes. Some examples of depression-inducing drugs are digitalis, antihypertensives, anti-Parkinson drugs, corticosteroids, and anticancer drugs (Blazer, 1982).

In summary, it can be seen that depression can present as a reaction to physical illness; as physical illness; accompanying physical illness; or as a result of chemotherapy. Having recognized depression as a frequent concomitant of physical disorders, increased attention has to be placed on the correct diagnosis of depression in the medically ill. The differential diagnosis of depression in the elderly patient with physical illness is complicated by the individual's response to the illness (Blazer, 1982). After an individual accepts a sick role he or she has a different view of the world. Physical illness may be a more acceptable means of withdrawal than depressive symptoms, especially in the elderly. The presence of a concomitant or precipitating organic disorder, however, should not preclude treatment of depression. Often a very treatable depression exists in the presence of both terminal and non-terminal illness.

DIFFERENTIAL DIAGNOSIS OF DEPRESSION AND DEMENTIA

Perhaps the most difficult task in the differential diagnosis of depression is the distinction from senile dementia. It is estimated that 15% of all elderly persons diagnosed as being depressed show signs of cognitive impairment and other indications of dementia (Salzman & Shader, 1979). The term pseudodementia has been applied to elderly individuals who complain both of depression and of memory and other cognitive problems, but for whom there is no clear evidence of organic brain damage. Post (1962) estimated the incidence of these reversible dementias, or pseudodementias to be between 7% and 19%. It is often difficult to know whether the memory problems are concomitants of depression and/or anxiety or if anxiety and depression are the natural accompaniments of memory loss in the early stages of senile dementia or other forms of organic brain damage.

The ability to distinguish pseudodementia from dementia is not merely of academic interest, but has important implications for treatment and management. It is conceivable that in both groups the anxiety and the depression would respond to treatment with an antidepressant. It is also conceivable that the true dementia group might have a higher susceptibility to the adverse effects of these drugs, especially their anticholinergic effects. The most unfortunate thing that could happen to depressed elderly patients is to be misdiagnosed as senile. Without proper treatment for depression these patients deteriorate radically. The condition can be fatal if left untreated. Treatment of the physical complications followed by treatment for the depressive symptoms may bring about complete recovery.

In the assessment of cognitive impairment most clinicians would probably start with the Wechsler Adult Intelligence Scale (WAIS) although it is unlikely that the WAIS would give any clear indication. In a series of studies Savage, Brittan, Bolten, and Hall (1973) looked at the structure of cognitive functioning in elderly people and attempted to assess the effects of aging and pathology. They concluded that age and diagnosis were affecting different areas of functioning. Changes in general intellectual level and in verbal performance discrepancy appeared to be related more notably to aging than to diagnosis while the reverse was true for intellectual deterioration and verbal learning impairment.

Intellectual deterioration implies more than just differences between individuals in general level of functioning. Some types of tasks will show a greater performance decrement than others; in particular, tasks involving much old "crystallized" ability, such as vocabulary knowledge, will be little affected, while those needing a new problem-solving approach, "fluid ability" will show more effect. Deterioration is thus measurable by indices taking into account differential level of performance on various types of task. Several such measures have been developed that may be derived from the WAIS. It has been suggested that there are similarities in the impairments shown on the WAIS by various types of patients. Whitehead (1973) tested depressives and dements on the WAIS and found that, although the dementing patients scored at a lower level over all, there was no difference in the pattern of subtest scores; both groups tended to have better or worse scores on the same subtests. This study is consistent with the general tendency towards intellectual deterioration: similar tasks show impairments whatever the process involved in causing the decline. Material mainly involving the use of "crystallized" ability is little affected by aging or by pathological processes, but where "fluid" ability is required, impairments will be noted. Overall, the deficit shown in depression is both less severe and more circumscribed than that shown in dementia.

In general, patients with dementia tend to do poorly on tests of learning or memory (Miller, 1980). Erikson and Scott (1977) provide an extensive review of clinical memory tests. The various design copying tests have also been used in the diagnosis of dementia, mainly the *Visual Motor Gestalt Test* and the *Revised Visual Retention Test*. Neuropsychological assessments can also be useful in discriminating dementia from functional disorders. A detailed account can be found in Lezak (1983). At times the depressive pseudodementia may mimic the progressive deterioration that is the hallmark of senile dementia. Zung and Green (1972) also noted that psychomotor slowing or agitation, labile affect, decreased libido, constipation, and paranoid ideation may be features common to both depression and organic brain syndrome. Despite these problems in diagnosis, differences in symptoms have been noted in these two groups of patients. Roth (1955) showed that in 150 patients over age 60, those with affective psychoses had symptoms of depression, retardation, self-reproach, and nihilistic, somatic, or paranoid delusions that occurred with a clearly defined onset and without evidence of progressive deterioration in adjustment prior to the presenting illness. Patients with senile psychosis, on the other hand, were characterized by an insidious onset with progressive failure at work in routine activities, or both. The principal symptoms in these latter patients were confusion with disorientation, intellectual deterioration, impairment of memory, restlessness, and hallucinations.

Gurland, Kuriansky, Sharpe, Simon, Stiller, and Birkett (1978) reported that the depressive group showed more depression, anxiety, somatic complaints, and depersonalization than the organic brain disease group, but showed less impairment on the dimensions of cognitive function such as impaired memory, cortical dysfunction, and disorientation. The organic brain disease group was best separated from the depressives on disorientation. This latter finding suggests that the organic brain disease subjects in Gurland's study were probably a chronic group of fairly deteriorated patients. The absence of depression in these patients by no means rules out the possibility of patients in the earlier stages of senile dementia becoming depressed and anxious when memory and other cognitive problems first become apparent, a view partially supported by others (Kahn, Zarit, Hilbert, & Niederehe, 1975).

Wells (1979) has presented one of the more thorough recent examinations of the problem of pseudodementia. He describes 10 patients with pseudodementia and presents several clinical criteria to help distinguish pseudodementia from dementia: short duration of symptoms; rapid progression; previous psychiatric dysfunction; pervasive affective changes; vociferous and detailed complaints of cognitive impairment; variability of performance; well-preserved attention span, and concentration. McAllister and Price (1980), however, noted that clinical signs and symptoms of an underlying depression are quite atypical and the patients presented a clinical picture of profound progressive cognitive impairment indistinguishable from that typical of diffuse progressive degenerate CNS disease.

It must be noted, however, that in case studies cited a few of the subjects appeared to have a severe depression on top of a dementia. Antidepressant therapy dealt with the depression leaving the patient in a much improved condition, although still showing evidence of dementia (Cavenar, Meiltbie, & Austin, 1979). In some cases testing may be no use and it is necessary to rely on past psychiatric history. The only feature that seemed to differentiate these cases from cases of dementia was that there was a history of depression in the past. Pseudodementia is one of the most important treatable forms that every clinician must consider and rule out.

ASSESSMENT AND MODELS OF PSYCHOPATHOLOGY AS RELATED TO CLINICAL DEPRESSION

The clinician's framework or model of psychopathology is critical because it influences whether he perceives that a person has a problem; whether treatment is likely to be affective if a problem exists; and what type of treatment to use. The means of assessment one uses is dictated by one's beliefs about the nature of psychopathology. The purpose of this section is to review several models of conceptualizing the assessment of depression and their application to the problems of old age.

1. The Medical Model

This model implies that various mental and emotional disturbances are due to structural damage to body organs, especially the brain, or to altered physiological processes such as in disorders of metabolism or endocrine function. In terms of the elderly this model provides an appropriate framework for conceptualizing some common psychiatric problems. Principal among these are the brain disorders.

However, at another level its conceptualizations are inaccurate for the majority of psychological disturbances. Most emotional or behavioral problems do not result from similar etiological factors as do physical illnesses. Another emphasis of this model is that disordered behaviors emanate from within the individual. The consequence of looking for causes within the individual is that critical interpersonal and environmental events that have a profound influence on dysfunctional behaviors may be missed. An overreliance on the medical model can lead to problems in the aged. There is a tendency to see any problem of older persons as due to a vaguely defined internal disorder—the aging process (Zarit, 1980). Aging is incorrectly perceived by many people as involving a gradual deterioration in functioning in all areas. Behaviors of the old are sometimes inappropriately labeled "senile" or "senescent." The extent to which the process of biological aging is implicated in the development of behavioral problems of the elderly is difficult to ascertain accurately. It is likely that the aging process will contribute in varying degrees to the onset of behavioral and affective symptoms, including depressive disorders.

The difficulties and confusion in diagnosing depression in the elderly, in the presence of physical illness has been reviewed. The role of the medical model in assessment of depression is prominent when a differentiation is required among physical illness accompanied by depression, depression as a result of illness; illness or somatic complaints masking depression as well as the differential diagnosis of depression and dementia. Results of such evaluation would have obvious implications for the role of the medical model in the treatment of the depressed elder.

2. Psychodynamic Model

Psychodynamic models of treatment and diagnosis form an important variant of the medical model. Rather than viewing the causes of disorders as medical illness, however, psychodynamic theories stress the importance of early psychological experiences as the roots of symptoms manifested in adulthood. Similar to the medical model, psychodynamic writers emphasize that the symptoms reflect an underlying illness, and that one must treat the deep-seated conflict that lies at the core of the symptoms. Again looking for causes within the individual brings the risk of ignoring critical interpersonal and other environmental effects.

Although the psychodynamic model has its limitations, it is valuable in its conceptualizations of intraindividual variables. The elderly may mask their depression through a variety of ego-defensive mechanisms. They commonly are reluctant to admit depression and use denial, counterphobic defenses, or express depressive symptoms through somatic complaints and hypochondriasis (Salzman & Shader, 1979). Faced with loss, diminished capacity for flexible gratification and withdrawal of supports, a failing self-esteem and a sense of hopelessness may threaten to overwhelm the older person. In order to cope, the ego of the older person may employ a variety of adaptive defense mechanisms that are attempts to reduce the conscious awareness of psychic pain (Salzman & Shader, 1979). Ego defenses that they used when they were younger may still be available and even become exaggerated with age.

Denial is a common mechanism in elderly people and may account for the failure to recognize physical or psychic pathology (Freud, 1946). In its mild form denial can help the elderly person by providing a coping mechanism to deal with some of the tensions and diminishing capacities. However, the denial is maladaptive when it leads to worsening of physical illness, or failure to develop realistic coping mechanisms to deal with changes in later life. According to Salzman and Shader (1979) severe denial can lead to some restriction of the ego so that anything that produces discomfort or painful effect is avoided by an ensuing restriction of awareness. In the majority of elderly people denial is not so severe and is usually incomplete. Certain memories, cognitive abilities, and sensory functions are variably retained while others are excluded from consciousness. This makes evaluation of the elderly person's mental status at times a confusing task.

Freud (1946) described isolation as the intrapsychic splitting of affect from content. It can be an adaptive function by dealing with intolerable affect. But it can be maladaptive by separating the older person from his friends and family affectively. Progressive withdrawal from relationships occurs when affective bonds with these other people are broken. This process is known as disengagement (Cumming & Henry, 1961). The final stage of this process is social isolation culminating in hopelessness and despair. Fry (1984) demonstrated that depression, from a psychodynamic perspective, is closely linked with hopelessness. Due to multiple losses, illness, and social isolation, many elderly report feelings of hopelessness about recovering lost physical and cognitive abilities. Hopelessness is also reported with respect to regaining interpersonal worth and spiritual love and grace, and finally there is a sense of hopelessness about receiving nurturance, respect, or remembrances.

It is interesting to note that hopelessness (as measured by Fry's recently developed Scale of Geriatric Hopelessness) correlated significantly with the elderly subjects' self-reportings of depression and also with the ratings of behavioral depression provided by observers and informants (Fry, 1984).

Somatization is an ego process by which psychic phenomena such as depressive affects are converted into bodily symptoms. In the elderly, somatization, when it is severe, can become hypochondriasis, an obsessive concern and fear of bodily ill-health. In the elderly true illness and bodily dysfunction may form the focus for the development of such a somatic preoccupation. Depression can thus be disguised so that the affects are not openly felt (Salzman & Shader, 1979). Instead the elderly person experiences physical suffering.

Thus, from a psychodynamic point of view in assessing depression, the clinician is concerned with causes lying within the individual and identifying the mechanisms of defense. When the orientation of treatment is psychodynamic, this would be the appropriate method of evaluation.

3. The Cognitive-Behavioral Model

The behavioral model proposes that problem or maladaptive behaviors are governed by similar principles of learning as are other actions. The behavioral approach focuses on the specific maladaptive actions, thoughts, or emotions, and the contexts in which they occur. Treatment is conceived of as providing new learning that competes with the maladaptive behaviors and/or manipulating stimulus cues or reinforcers that are related to the specific problems. From this point of view assessment involves clarifying the presenting problems, obtaining a social history that focuses on the origins of the problem behavior, and identifying relationships in the person's current environment that may be controlling or reinforcing the maladaptive behaviors.

Unlike the medical model there is less difficulty in differentiating normal from abnormal behavior. In the medical model the professional uses relatively unreliable criteria to determine if symptoms suggest an internal conflict or disorder. In contrast a behavioral approach is not concerned with whether an illness is present. The focus is placed instead on the perception of problems in functioning by the individual, or by persons closely associated with the client. When a person is brought to treatment by others, the process of assessment involves determining how each of the involved persons contributes to the problem situation.

A *behavioral assessment* may also indicate functional links between the problems presented by a patient and other behaviors. Depressed persons generally report their low spirits as the principal problem, but recent work has found that depression is related to certain dysfunctional thoughts that lead to overly negative evaluations of one's self (Beck, 1967), and to the failure to engage in activities that one finds pleasurable. This process of identifying functional associations among thoughts, behaviors and mood represents a different process from inferring a disease from overt symptoms. *Activity level* is a particularly good indicator of depression among the elderly, and one that is subject to quantification. Gross measures such as the number of activities attended may be easily documented by activities personnel or family members. These are also ideal measures for assessing the efficacy of treatment as well.

Another array of behaviors which helps signal the presence or absence of depression is the *cognitive component*. In the geriatric patient, expressions of loneliness, worthlessness, and sadness often occur before the more obvious behaviors of avoidance and reduced participation. The assessor should be alert to statements incorporating references to no longer being in control or being under the control of others. These are often the initial signs in a chain which may terminate in passive acceptance and a low level of responsibility (Hussian, 1981).

Three models have been discussed, the medical, the psychodynamic and the cognitive-behavioral. Each of these models has its own theory of the etiology of depression and its own method of intervention. For example, the psychodynamic therapist will be more interested in unearthing the underlying conflict, and evaluating the mechanisms of defense while the cognitive-behaviorist therapist is more concerned with activity schedules and cognitive correlates. No one method of treatment has as yet been shown to be superior in the treatment of depression. However, using only one method of assessment will not suffice, particularly when dealing with the elderly person. Each orientation offers something valuable to a more comprehensive assessment of the aged.

SUMMARY AND CONCLUSIONS

This paper has been concerned with issues in the assessment of depression in the elderly. It is apparent that depression in the elderly is complex, confusing, and difficult to diagnose. One of the problems is that there are few studies comparing depressed younger adults with the depressed aged. The relationship between depressive symptoms and physical disease has been reviewed. It is difficult to differentiate among depression as a response to physical illness, depression presenting with physical illness, and somatization. Another difficult differential diagnosis is between dementia and depression. Rating scales are a common assessment procedure with depressed individuals, but they present difficulties when used with an elderly population. Finally, the effect of a clinician's orientation on his or her assessment has been discussed. Different models of pathology offer different ways of assessment, particularly when treatment is being considered.

In light of the difficulties encountered in assessing depression in the elderly and the shortcomings of many of the techniques, emphasis should be placed on the need for integrative multidimensional approaches to minimize the probability of misdiagnosis when the perspective and tools of only one discipline are used. There has been increasing emphasis on determining the strengths and weaknesses of the older person's general psychological organization.

Multifunctional Assessment

Gerontologically oriented psychologists such as Lawton and his associates organize assessment under the construct of competence, which emphasizes positive aspects of functional capacities (Lawton, 1971). Functional assessment means any systematic attempt to measure objectively the level at which a person is functioning, in any of a variety of areas, e.g., physical health, quality of self-maintenance, quality of role activity, intellectual status, social activity, attitude toward the world and self, and emotional status. These are, however, not all in the domain of mental health. Since the unity of body and mind is nowhere better exemplified than in the aging person, it seems essential to consider every area that may possibly affect the older person's emotional state.

The crucial aspect of the functional assessment of elderly individuals is that they are likely to have a conglomerate of social, physical, and psychological problems. Their status is influenced by many factors and it is sometimes all but impossible to determine which factors are most influential. The functional status of various systems is typically interdependent; physical and psychological functions are often intricately interrelated and are frequently complicated by social factors and cultural attitudes.

Gaitz and Baer (1970) suggest that multifunctional assessments should be multidisciplinary in approach. Such an approach explicitly acknowledges that each participating discipline may uncover impairments, disorders, or problems. The relative importance of the findings is not prejudiced and the risk that only selected diagnostic procedures are administered is averted. The effects of such an assessment based on a multifunctional model may clearly have far-reaching bearing on treatment. One way in which this is manifested is in the better utilization of community resources, which in turn depends partly on the way the team communicates with community agencies and caregivers. If the recommendations of the assessment team are to eventuate in comprehensive care programs, the efforts of multiple caregivers require mobilization. Each caregiver should not only get information relevant to his particular area of competence, but also should understand how his portion is integrated into a total plan.

Multifunctional Assessment Tools

Gurland et al. (1978) designed the *Geriatric Mental Status (GMS)* interview specifically for the differential diagnosis of elderly psychiatric patients. This semistructured interview schedule consists of 500 items pertinent to the individual's psychopathology. There are questions on somatic concerns, cognitive function, affective states, and behavioral symptoms rateable from the interview; results are interpreted in light of additional data obtained on the patient, e.g., medical examination, presentation of sociocultural history, and information about the older person's previous social adjustment. Within mental health systems psychologists seem most likely to provide a systematic evaluation of cognitive, behavioral, and emotional functioning in older adults. They can focus on individual strengths and weaknesses in contrast to the medical model which focuses on disease and pathological processes. This is similar to the model advocated by Lawton (1971) and Gaitz and Baer (1970) emphasizing multifunctional assessment.

In dealing specifically with the assessment of depression, a multifunctional assessment is advocated. A multidimensional evaluation of the potential contribution of a variety of factors that interact and affect an elderly person's current status is valuable. However, to avoid the assessment becoming overly expensive and cumbersome, it may be more practical to use one of the current multidimensional batteries, such as *Older American's Resources Services Questionnaires (OARS)* (Pfeiffer, 1970), or the *Comprehensive Assessment and Referral Evaluation (CARE)* (Gurland et al., 1978). The OARS is an interview with forced choice responses that permits ratings of social resources, economic recources, mental health and physical health. Parts of this technique are designed to be completed by a multidisciplinary team working independently (e.g., a psychiatrist and psychologist). The CARE battery is a new and reliable assessment technique designed to elicit rate of and classify information on the health and social problems of the older person. It helps in determining whether an individual should be referred for services, and can be readministered to measure effectiveness. The interview is so designed that symptoms can be examined in order to determine the nature of the problem; the factors contributing to the symptoms being reported and whether the symptoms have clinical significance. The use of these batteries at the initial screening stage may provide an economical and thorough way to begin the assessment process and to set the stage for later in-depth assessment of specific domains appropriate for a given individual.

At this level of assessment in working with the depressed elderly, a functional behavioral analysis of the problem might be most appropriate (Kanfer & Saslow, 1976). These authors suggest seven major areas: (1) analysis of the problem situation; (2) identifying antecedents and consequences of the problem behavior; (3) the individual's other assets and deficits; (4) an analysis of social relationships; (5) motivational analysis; (6) the relation of the patient to his social, cultural, and physical environment; and (7) a developmental history. These seven areas are elaborated in Kanfer and Saslow (1976), and in Zarit (1980).

The practical applications of instruments such as OARS and CARE may be limited. They are lengthy instruments and may not be suitable for all clinical settings. Thus, despite the obvious necessity for the multifunctional and multidimensional assessment in many clinical settings, it may not be a realistic approach. A medical approach is warranted in many cases, because the older person's depression is caused by or related to the effects of an illness. In any case this possibility must always be considered. But the majority of disorders in old age, however, have no obvious physiological correlates and a behavioral analysis which focuses on such factors as the frequency of occurrence and the antecedents and consequences of problem behaviors is more likely to indicate treatable aspects of the situation. A behavioral method of assessment locates problems in the immediate situational contexts in which they occur, as well as evaluating the person's current social and psychological functioning and developmental history.

REFERENCES

Anderson, W. F. (1971). *Practical management of the elderly.* Oxford: Blackwell.

Assnis, G. (1977). Parkinson's disease depression and ECT: A review and case study. *American Journal of Psychiatry, 134,* 191–199.

Beck, A. T. (1967). *The diagnosis and management of depression.* Philadelphia: University of Pennsylvania.

Blazer, D. G. (1982). *Depression in late life.* St. Louis: C. V. Mosby.

Busse, E. W. (1975). Aging and psychiatric diseases of late life. In M. F. Reiser (Ed.), *American handbook of psychiatry, (Vol. 4).* New York: Basic Books.

Cavenar, J. O., Mciltbie, A. A., & Austin, L. (1979). Depression simulating organic brain disease. *American Journal of Psychiatry, 136,* 521–523.

Crook, T. H. (1979). Psychometric assessment in the elderly. In A. Raskin & L. F. Jarvik (Eds.), *Psychiatric symptoms and cognitive loss in the elderly* (pp. 207–220). New York: John Wiley & Sons.

Cumming, F., & Henry, W. R. (1961). *Growing old. The process of disengagement.* New York: Basic Books.

Epstein, L. J. (1976). Depression in the elderly. *Journal of Gerontology, 31,* 278–282.

Erikson, R. C., & Scott, M. L. (1977). Clinical memory testing: A review. *Psychological Bulletin, 84,* 1130–1149.

Freud, A. (1946). *The ego and mechanisms of defense.* New York: International Universities Press.

Fry, P. S. (1984). The development of a Geriatric Scale of Hopelessness: Implications for counseling and intervention with the depressed elderly. *Journal of Counseling Psychology, 31,* 322–331.

Gaitz, C. M., & Baer, P. E. (1970). Diagnostic assessment of the elderly: A multifunctional model. *The Gerontologist, 1,* 47–52.

Gallagher, D., Thomson, L. W., & Levy, S. M. (1980). Clinical psychological assessment of older adults. In L. W. Poon (Ed.), *Aging in the 1980's* (pp. 19–40). American Psychological Association.

Gurland, B. J. (1976). The comparative frequency of depression in various adult age groups. *Journal of Gerontology, 31,* 283–290.

Gurland, B., Kuriansky, J., Sharpe, L., Simon, R., Stiller, P., & Birkett, P. (1978). The Comprehensive Assessment and Referral Evaluation (CARE)—Rational development and reliability. *International Journal of Aging and Human Development, 8,* 9–42.

Hussian, R. A. (1981). *Geriatric psychology.* New York: Van Nostrand Reinhold.

Kahn, R. L., Zarit, S. H., Hilbert, N. M., & Niederehe, G. (1975). Memory complaint and impairment in the aged. *Archives of General Psychiatry, 32,* 1569–1573.

Kanfer, F. H., & Saslow, G. (1976). Behavior diagnosis. In L. R. Allman & D. T. Jaffe (Eds.), *Readings in abnormal psychology: Contemporary perspectives.* New York: Harper & Row.

Kavanagh, T., Shepherd, R. J., & Tuk, J. A. (1975). Depression after myocardial infarction. *Canadian Medical Association Journal, 113,* 23–27.

Lawton, M. P. (1971). The functional assessment of elderly people. *Journal of the American Geriatrics Society, 19,* 465–481.

Lezak, M. D. (1983). *Neuropsychological assessment.* New York: Oxford University Press.

McAllister, T. W., & Price, T. R. D. (1980). Severe depressive pseudodementia with and without dementia. *American Journal of Psychiatry, 139,* 626–629.

Maloney, M., & Ward, M. P. (1976). *Psychological assessment: A conceptual approach.* New York: Oxford University Press.

Miller, E. (1980). Cognitive assessment of the older adult. In J. E. Birren & R. B. Sloane (Eds.), *Handbook of mental health and aging* (pp. 520–536). Englewood Cliffs, NJ: Prentice.

Payne, E. C. (1975). Depression and suicide. In J. G. Howells (Ed.), *Modern perspectives in the psychiatry of old age* (pp. 290–312). New York: Brunner/Mazel.

Pfeiffer, E. (1970). *Multidimensional functional assessment: The OARS Methodology.* Durham, NC: Duke University, Center of the Study of Aging and Human Development.

Post, F. (1962). *The significance of affective symptoms in old age. Maudsley Monograph 10.* London: Oxford University Press.

Roth, M. (1955). The natural history of mental disorders in old age. *Journal of Mental Science, 101,* 281–301.

Salzman, C., & Shader, R. I. (1979). Clinical evaluation of depression in the elderly. In A. Raskin & L. F. Jarvik (Eds.), *Psychiatric symptoms and cognitive loss in the elderly* (pp. 39–72). New York: John Wiley & Sons.

Savage, R. D., Brittan, P. G., Bolton, N., & Hall, E. H. (1973). *Intellectual functioning in the aged.* London: Methuen.

Verwoerdt, A. (1973). Emotional responses to physical illness. In C. Eisdorfer & W. E. Fann (Eds.), *Psychopharmacology and aging* (pp. 169–181). New York: Plenum.

Verwoerdt, A. (1981). *Clinical geropsychiatry* (2nd ed.). Baltimore: Williams & Wilkins.

Wells, C. W. (1979). Pseudodementia. *American Journal of Psychiatry, 136,* 895–900.

Whitehead, A. (1973). The pattern of Wais, performance in elderly psychiatric patients. *British Journal of Social and Clinical Psychology, 12,* 435–436.

Winokur, G., Morrison, J., Clancy, J., & Crowe, R. (1973). The Iowa 500: Familial and clinical families favour two kinds of depressive illness. *Comprehensive Psychiatry, 14,* 99–107.

Zarit, S. H. (1980). *Aging and mental disorders.* New York: Free Press.

Zung. W. W. K., & Green, R. L. (1972). Detection of affective disorders in the aged. In C. Eisdorfer & W. E. Fann (Eds.), *Psychopharmacology and aging* (pp. 213–224). New York: Plenum.

Questions

1) How might a case of geriatric depression escape detection if assessment is limited to some of the standard techniques employed with younger patients?

2) How does the possible presence of dementia complicate the assessment of dementia?

3) How does the possible presence of physical disease (real or imagined) complicate the assessment of depression?

4) How could a multidisciplinary team make use of the multidimensional assessment that the authors recommend?

6/USE OF THE CENTER FOR EPIDEMIOLOGICAL STUDIES-DEPRESSION SCALE WITH OLDER ADULTS

Lenore Sawyer Radloff
Linda Teri, PhD

Editor's Introduction

Radloff and Teri begin with an excellent, and concise review of the problems of the construction of depression scales, especially scales for the aged. The points discussed also apply to the Zung, Beck, MMPI, and other scales not specifically designed for use with geriatric depression. Perhaps the greatest problem, of any measure of depression, is that "there is no perfect criterion measure of depression."

Note the caveat that the CES-D scale was designed for research (especially epidemiological research) rather than the clinical assessment of individuals. "Scores on the scale should never be used to make clinical decisions about individuals, except for the decision to do further diagnostic assessment." Nevertheless, the sensitivity and specificity of the CES-D compare favorably with scales such as the Beck and Zung.

The authors review validity and reliability, and give several pointers for administration and scoring.

INTRODUCTION

The assessment of depression in older adults is a well recognized diagnostic dilemma (c.f. Post, 1975; Gallagher & Thompson, 1983). Although many factors contribute to the difficulty in diagnos-

---

Lenore Sawyer Radloff is affiliated with the National Institute of Mental Health. Linda Teri is affiliated with the University of Washington.

119

ing depression in older adults, the primary concerns are that the phenomenology of depression may be different in older adults than it is in younger adults and that factors of aging and physical disease may complicate the assessment of depression in older adults. Consequently, should older adults complain of depression symptoms, the practicing clinician needs to determine whether these complaints are natural concomitants of aging, indications of an underlying physical malady, or symptoms of a clinical depression. Accurate diagnosis necessitates a careful interview obtaining information about the presence, severity, and duration of depressive symptoms and the context in which they occur. Clinicians, however, can benefit from using a short, simple screening measure to alert them to the possibility of depressive symptomatology. To be useful for such purposes, a measure must be easy to use, acceptable to most people, reliable (i.e., get consistent results when given twice under the same conditions), valid (i.e., measure what it claims to measure), and provide a cutoff score which identifies as many cases as possible, without too many errors.

The range of concerns in assessing depression in older adults are discussed in greater detail elsewhere in this issue (see also Gallagher & Thompson, 1983; Lewinsohn, Teri, & Hoberman, 1983). This paper will focus on those issues most relevant to the validity of one such measure with older adults, the Center for Epidemiological Studies-Depression Scale (CES-D; Radloff, 1977). This paper will first describe the CES-D's psychometric properties in the general population including, the purposes for which it was originally developed, and then evaluate the evidence about these properties when used with older adults.

THE ORIGINAL DEVELOPMENT OF CES-D SCALE

The CES-D scale was originally developed for a large general population study of depressive symptoms, called the Community Mental Health Assessment (CMHA), in 1971-73 (Comstock & Helsing, 1976; Radloff, 1977). It consists of 20 items that were chosen from other existing depression measures to cover the areas of depressed mood, feelings of guilt and worthlessness, feelings of helplessness and hopelessness, loss of energy, and disturbances of sleep and appetite. (See Table 1 for the items and format of the scale). Four items are worded in the positive direction, to assess positive affect (or the lack of it) as well as to break up the tendency to answer all the questions in the same direction. The scale was designed to measure *current* state and to be responsive to changes over time, so it asks how often each symptom occurred *during the past week.* Each answer is scored from zero (least often for negative items, most often for positive ones). Scores can range from zero to 60, with the higher scores indicating more depressive symptomatology.

Since the CES-D was designed for research, not for clinical purposes, it was not intended as a diagnostic measure. It was developed before the DSM-III criteria (APA, 1980) were available and therefore does not perfectly match those criteria nor does it distinguish sub-types of depression (e.g., bipolar from unipolar, endogenous from reactive, primary from secondary). However, the CES-D items do include most of the important symptoms of depression (except that suicidal items are omitted) along with ratings of frequency/severity. Items are intended to evaluate symptoms of depression, not just general distress.

ACCEPTABILITY AND ADMINISTRATION

The CES-D has been used in many different studies on a variety of types of people. It has been found to be acceptable to people of a wide range of ages (junior high students to those over age 80), education, geographic area (urban and rural U.S., and several foreign countries), and racial, ethnic, and language groups (black, white, Hispanic, Asian, and European).

The scale can be used in personal interviews (e.g., CMHA) or telephone interviews (e.g., Aneshensel, Frerichs, Clark, & Kopenic, 1982) without any special training of experienced lay interviewers. It can also be used as a self-administered "paper-and-pencil" scale, with appropriate cautions. For example, one study (NCHS; Hanes, 1980) found more errors in a self administered format than did the CMIIA surveys using interviewers. The most common error was marking the same answer (usually "never") for every item. It is unlikely that all four of the positive items would be answered the same way as all the negative items if the person was reading carefully and answering honestly. Flagging the positive items or editing the forms on the spot might reduce these problems.

As a rule of thumb, the whole scale should be considered invalid if all items are answered "always" or "never" or if more than five items are left unanswered. If fewer items are missing, a total score can be estimated by finding an item average (the sum of the values of the items answered divided by the number of items answered) and reweighting that average by multiplying by 20. For clinical use, however, missing items could be checked during the discussion of the patient's symptoms.

The scale is short and takes less than five minutes with any method of administration. If it takes much longer, it is likely that the person is having some problems with it. If inadequate reading ability, vision, or hearing is suspected, the items should be read aloud as the respondent follows along and marks the answers. The scale does not require a very high reading or vocabulary level, but probably cannot be used if there is serious cognitive impairment.

Reliability

There are two basic ways to estimate reliability. When measuring something seen as an enduring trait (such as IQ), then high test-retest reliability is necessary to show that the measure will give the same answer at different times. Since the CES-D was designed to measure *current* state (past week), and since depression is expected to be episodic and the symptoms to vary over time, we would not expect very high test-retest reliability. In the CMHA study, the correlations of scores obtained 2, 4, 6, and 8 weeks apart averaged .57, which indicates considerable change in scores over even these brief intervals. Test-retest intervals of 3, 6, and 12 months gave correlations only a little lower. In general, there was no strong trend for the correlations to be higher with shorter intervals, but two weeks was the shortest time tested (Radloff, 1977).

When measuring a variable state, more appropriate measures of reliability are those based on internal consistency, to indicate that the different items of the scale are all measuring the same thing. Two such statistics, the corrected split-halves correlation and coefficient alpha were found to be satisfactorily high (.85 to .92) in the CMHA study (Radloff, 1977). Internal consistency was also tested and found high in age, sex, geographic, and racial/ethnic subgroups of the population (Radloff, 1977; Roberts, 1980).

Factor Structure and Subscales

In a measure with very high internal consistency, analysis for independent factors should be interpreted with caution. However, factor analysis does give some clues about the clustering of subsets of items. In the CMHA data (Radloff, 1977), factor analysis was consistent with the prevalent view of depressive symptomatology, yielding a strong depressed affect factor, a separate positive affect factor, a somatic/vegetative factor, and a weak fourth factor weighted mainly with the two interpersonal items (dislike and unfriendly). Similar factor structure has been found across sex, age, geographic, and racial/ethnic subgroups (Radloff, 1977; Roberts, 1980; Noh, Wood, Turner, Note 3). For some purposes, it is useful to score subscales based on the four factors, using items with the strongest and most consistent loadings. In Table 1, the letter in parentheses after 18 of the 20 items indicates the subscale in which it is scored.

Validity

There are many ways to assess the validity of a measure. Criterion validity is the most obvious: the measure is compared with a criterion which is considered "truth." In the case of depression, "truth" is relative; even a careful, complete clinical evaluation is prone to some error (e.g., what the client reports and how the clinician interprets). Therefore, multiple criteria of "truth" were used: patient status and clinical diagnosis (see also the section in this chapter on "screening"); clinical rating scales; and other previously tested, valid self-report measures of depression. "Discriminant validity" requires the measure to be more closely related to other measures of the same thing (i.e., depressive symptoms) than to measures of related but different things (e.g., general distress), and to be negatively related to opposite things (e.g., positive affect). "Construct validity" is inferred when the measure relates to other constructs as would be predicted by theory.

The CES-D discriminates well between clinical patients and general population samples and discriminates in predictable ways among subgroups of patients. For example, compared with general population average score of about 9, a sample of psychiatric inpatients of mixed diagnoses scored an average of about 24 (Craig & Van Natta, 1976) and a sample of acutely depressed outpatients averaged about 38 (Weissman, Sholomskas, Pottenger, Prusoff, & Locke, 1977). In the latter study, it was found the schizophrenics, alcoholics, and heroin addicts in treatment also had average scores higher than the general population (ranging from 23 for alcoholics to 13 for schizophrenics), but lower than the depressed patients. This is consistent with the finding that a large proportion of patients

Table 1

The CES-D Scale

INSTRUCTIONS FOR QUESTIONS. Below is a list of the ways you might have felt or behaved. Please tell me how often you have felt this way during the past week.

HAND CARD A.

> Rarely or None of the Time (Less than 1 Day)
>
> Some or a Little of the Time (1-2 Days)
>
> Occasionally or a Moderate Amount of Time (3-4 Days)
>
> Most or All of the Time (5-7 Days)

During the past week:

1. I was bothered by things that usually don't bother me. (S)

2. I did not feel like eating; my appetite was poor. (S)

3. I felt that I could not shake off the blues even with help from my family or friends. (D)

4. I felt that I was just as good as other people. (P)

5. I had trouble keeping my mind on what I was doing. (S)

6. I felt depressed. (D)

7. I felt that everything I did was an effort. (S)

8. I felt hopeful about the future. (P)

9. I thought my life had been a failure.

10. I felt fearful.

11. My sleep was restless. (S)

12. I was happy. (P)

13. I talked less than usual.

14. I felt lonely. (D)

15. People were unfriendly. (I)

16. I enjoyed life. (P)

17. I had crying spells. (D)

18. I felt sad. (D)

19. I felt that people disliked me. (I)

20. I could not get "going." (S)

Table 1 continued

Key

The letter in parenthesis
indicates the factor sub-scale
for the item.

D = Depressed affect

P = Positive affect

S = Somatic/vegetative signs

I = Interpersonal distress

with primary diagnoses other than depression were given a secondary diagnosis of depression (from 59% of the alcoholics to 28% of the schizophrenics, Weissman, Pottenger, Kleber, Ruben, & Williams, 1977). In both of these studies, the CES-D correlated well with ratings of severity of depression made by clinicians familiar with the patients. In the latter study, a sample of 35 of the depressed patients was retested with the CES-D after four weeks of treatment; their average score had gone down from 39 to about 21 (Weissman, Prusoff, & Newberry, 1975a).

A study in rural Tennessee (Husaini, Neff, Harrington, Hughes, & Stone, 1980) found an average score of about seven in the general population, compared with about 27 in mixed diagnosis outpatients in the mental health clinic. There were substantial differences among the patients, with those being treated for marital maladjustment scoring highest (average about 35) and alcoholics lowest (about 20). There were significantly higher scores for patients rated by clinicians as having more severe problems, those tested at intake rather than after some treatment and those receiving antidepressant medication.

As evidence of discriminant validity, in the CMHA study (Radloff, 1977), the CES-D correlated most highly and positively with the Bradburn Measure of Negative Affect, moderately positively with the Langner Measure of General Distress (including depression, anxiety and somatic items), and low and negatively with the Bradburn Scale of Positive Affect. In a clinical sample of depressed patients, the CES-D correlated very highly with the Beck Depression Inventory and the Zung Self-rating Depression Scale (Weissman, Prusoff, & Newberry, 1975b) and with the depression sub-scale of the SCL-90 (Weissman et al., 1977).

As evidence of construct validity, the CES-D has been found to relate to other variables as would be expected from a valid measure of depressive symptoms. For example, average CES-D scores were considerably higher for people who answered "yes" to the question, "Did you have an emotional problem for which you felt you needed help?" (average score of 18 for "yes" and 8 for "no," Radloff, 1977). Numerous studies using the CES-D have confirmed the relationship of depression to negative life events, physical illness, gender, socioeconomic status and a variety of specific stressors (see Radloff and Locke [in press] for a review of some of these studies).

USE AS A SCREENING MEASURE

As already mentioned, a useful screening measure must be short, and easy to use. Therefore, it cannot be expected to be perfectly accurate. The degree and kinds of inaccuracies which are acceptable depend on the purposes of the screening. The simplest measures of error are the rates of false positives (classified as a "case" by the screener but not by the criterion diagnostic procedure) and false negatives (true cases missed by the screener). If the screener gives a score and caseness is defined as being above a certain cutoff score, then generally as the cutoff is raised, the false positives will decrease and the false negatives will increase. If it is especially important not to miss any true cases, then a low cutoff would be chosen; the positives would then be given a more complete diagnostic work-up to separate the true from the false positives. It is assumed that there will be almost no true cases among those who were negative on the screener. On the other extreme, if the full diagnostic procedure is very expensive or risky, or if, as is more likely in the mental health field, there is some stigma or resistance involved, then the cutoff would be set high, to minimize false positives. Usually, however, the cutoff is chosen to get the best balance of false positives and negatives.

Of course, this kind of evaluation of a screening measure assumes that the criterion diagnostic procedure is perfectly accurate and assesses the same thing as does the screening measure. In the case of the CES-D, neither of these conditions hold, so the results of studies must be interpreted with caution. Since there is no perfect criterion measure of depression, some of the disagreement with the CES-D could be errors in the criterion rather than in the measure. More importantly, the CES-D was designed as a measure of depressive symptoms, including those due to major depressive disorder, minor depression, secondary depression, situational depressive reaction, and transient mood variations. Therefore, when compared with psychiatric diagnosis of major depression (or even major and minor depression), a large number of false positives would be expected. This is why scores on the scale should never be used to make clinical decisions about individuals except for the decision to do further diagnostic assessment.

The first use of a cutoff score for the CES-D was in the CMHA study. The overall general population average was about 9 (the same as found in most, but not all, such studies since), and the 80th percentile (i.e., about 20% score at and above this point) was 16. This cutoff was used for research purposes, to identify a high scoring group large enough for data analysis. It was interpreted as a high-risk group, but not as a group of clinically depressed people (e.g., see Comstock & Helsing, 1976).

In a clinical sample (Weissman et al., 1977), the cutoff of 16 was found to be satisfactory in discriminating patients rated by clinicians as depressed versus nondepressed on the Raskin Depression Rating Scale. In the rural Tennessee study (Husaini et al., 1980), cutoff scores were developed to discriminate depressed patients from other patients, taking problem severity into account. These cutoffs were then tested for their ability to discriminate within the community sample between those who reported emotional problems and/or felt a need for help. The authors suggest that a CES-D score of 17 or over could be used to designate "possible" cases, with a score of 23 or over for "probable" cases.

In a study in a prepaid medical practice (Hankin & Locke, 1982), patients filled out the CES-D while waiting to see the physician. The physician rated the patient on depressed mood after seeing the patient but without seeing the CES-D scores. Twenty-one percent of the patients scored 16 or above on the CES-D (very similar to the CMHA study), but the physicians judged a very small number of patients to be depressed. The authors interpreted this not as evidence of error in the CES-D, but as evidence of the need for such a screening measure to alert primary care physicians to possible problems which should be further evaluated.

We have identified five studies which compared with CES-D with diagnosis based on a comprehensive, structured diagnostic interview. One in New Haven (Myers & Weissman, 1980) one in Alameda County, California (Roberts & Vernon, 1983) and one in Eugene, Oregon (Teri & Lewinsohn, Note 1) used the Schedule for Affective Disorders and Schizophrenia (SADS; Spitzer, Endicott, & Robins, 1978). One study done in Pittsburgh (Schulberg, Saul, McClelland, Ganguli, Christy, & Frank, in press) and one in Los Angeles, California (Hough, unpublished, cited in Schulberg et al.) used the NIMH Diagnostic Interview Schedule (DIS: Robins, Helzer, Croughan, & Ratcliff, 1981). Using a CES-D score of 16 as a cutoff, and a diagnosis of major depression as criterion, four of the five studies found very few false positives (under 20%) and many false negatives (up to 40%). Only the Pittsburgh study found many false positives and very few false negatives. Differences in the designs of the studies did exist (e.g., different interviews, different intervals between CES-D and interview, different types of samples) but cannot easily be used to explain the different results. The Pittsburgh study was done in a medical setting (both primary care and mental health center) while the other four were interviews in the general community population. It is possible that patients filling out the CES-D while waiting to see a physician might be sensitized to report symptoms, especially in comparison with people being interviewed in the community.

Understanding the nature of the false positives and negatives is probably more important than explaining differences among these studies. A case-by-case analysis of the discrepancies found in the New Haven study (Boyd, Weissman, Thompson, & Myers, 1982) is useful for this purpose. Of the 28 false positives, 15 (36%) had depressive symptoms on the SADS interview but did not meet criteria for major depression because of too few symptoms, too short a duration, absence of functional impairment or exclusion criteria such as bereavement or medical illness. These are, hopefully, the kinds of contextual factors that a clinician would discuss with a patient when interpreting answers to the CES-D scale. Five (12%) of the false positives seemed to be "deniers" on the SADS interview, since the interviewers noted an impression of depression which agreed with the CES-D rather than the SADS. Seven (17%) of the false positives were not depressed according to the SADS nor interviewer observation, but did have other SADS diagnoses. In summary, 81% of the false positives had some confirming evidence of depressive symptoms and another 17% had other psychiatric disorders. Only one person had a high CES-D score with no other sign of problems. This finding was partially confirmed in both the Alameda County and Pittsburgh studies: a substantial proportion of the false positives had some psychiatric diagnosis other than major depression. Confirmation of subcriterion levels of depressive symptoms was not reported in these studies.

Explanations for the high rates of false negatives are more difficult. Here Boyd's analyses are invaluable. Of the eight false negatives (a small number but a large proportion of the true cases in this community sample), three were noted by the interviewer as having serious trouble filling out the CES-D. Four were noted as having a tendency to deny symptoms, even during the SADS interview, probing was necessary to elicit positive responses. One case was explainable only by the interviewer comment, "seems to accept her current depression as transient episode and is sure she will get better." Data of this type are not available from the other studies.

In summary, the CES-D is a good but far from perfect screening measure. False positives can best be reduced by further diagnostic assessment, and many will indicate problems other than major depression. To reduce false negatives, problems with the self-administered format could be alleviated by interviewer assistance. However, it seems that there may be a core of people who will deny symptoms, especially on a structured self-report scale where the interviewer is not free to probe. It is possible, but yet to be verified, that these are people who see their symptoms as transient or unimportant and who would resist treatment if it were suggested. If this is the case, then their loss in screening might be clinically acceptable. For research purposes, however, they would be interesting to study.

USE OF THE CES-D WITH OLDER ADULTS

Fortunately, data are accumulating on the use of the CES-D with older adults. Two types of studies provide most helpful information, those that obtained data on older adults as part of a larger general adult population (for example, those from NCHS: Eaton & Kessler, 1981; Sayetta, 1980 and those from CMHA, Comstock & Helsing, 1976; Radloff, 1983) and those that focused on older adults per se (for example, the Kentucky studies: Himmelfarb & Murrell, 1983; Murrell, Himmelfarb, & Wright, 1983; and the Oregon study, Teri & Lewinsohn, Note 1). While the studies to be discussed are by no means exhaustive of the literature, available, they do represent significant information on the use of the CES-D with older adults and offer direction for practitioners and researchers in the field.

Murrell, Himmelfarb, and Wright (1983) investigated the CES-D in 2,517 community residing adults over 55 years of age. Data were reported for males and females separately. Mean CES-D scores for males was 9 (s.d. = 9) and for females 11; mean scores for both genders increased at age 75. For males, mean scores consistently increased with age; for females, mean scores were highest in the 55 to 59 and 75+ age groups and lowest for the 60 to 75 year olds. Fourteen percent of the males and 18% of the females obtained scores above 20. Age did not influence these percentages for men, although more men over 75 reported high scores than any other age group. Age did influence these findings for women: significantly more of the youngest (55–59) and oldest (75+) women reported high scores. More women over 75 reported high scores than any other age group. The relationship between age, demographic data, and depression was not reported.

Himmelfarb and Murrell (1983) investigated the relationship of five measures of "mental health," including the CES-D. Data were obtained on an inpatient psychiatric sample over the age of 50 (N = 109) and on a community-residing older sample (age, not reported; N = 270). The CES-D correlated significantly with the other measures of "mental health," with coefficients ranging from .59–.77. Mean CES-D scores for the clinical sample were significantly higher than for the community sample, for both men (27.52 vs. 10.24) and women (27.61 vs. 9.98). In addition, the depression scale was one of two measures which successfully differentiated both groups via stepwise discriminant analysis. (The General Well-Being Scale was the other scale.) Using cutoff scores of 16, 20, and 23 on the CES-D, the accuracy for depression diagnosis was 78%, 82%, and 82% respectively. Comparing cutoff scores of 20 and 23, the authors reported that 20 yielded the optimal balance of false positives to false negatives. Finally, subjects between 50 and 65 years of age reported higher CES-D scores than older subjects (mean score of 19.57 vs. 9.40). In summary, the CES-D adequately correlated with other measures of depression, successfully differentiated patient from nonpatient groups and did not increase with increasing age.

Teri and Lewinsohn (Note 1) examined the CES-D in two community-based samples: one aged 18 through 97, with a mean age of 39 and 20% over 55, and one aged 50 through 92, with a mean age 62. The relationship of the CES-D with two other indices of depression, (self-labeling of depressive mood and clinical diagnosis), and symptom pattern change with age were investigated. No significant increase in depression was obtained with advancing age. CES-D scores declined between ages 55 and 74 and after age 75, a modest (but not significant) increase was obtained. This pattern was replicated on each measure of depression. Thus, the CES-D yielded a prevalence pattern consistent to self-labeling of depressive mood and clinical diagnosis.

No significant effect for age was obtained when comparing CES-D scores to clinical diagnosis (based on the SADS-RDC). However, there was a trend for more older subjects with high CES-D scores to be diagnosed depressed. Age was a significant mediator of high CES-D score and self-labeling, however. Among those with high scores, older subjects were significantly less likely to label themselves as depressed.

Gender differences in rates and symptomatology of depression were consistent across the 18-to-97-year age span studied. More females than males were diagnosed depressed and reported higher CES-D scores regardless of age. No one symptom or constellation of symptoms accounted for the depression findings. Contrary to expectations, somatic concerns were not overrepresented among older adults and psychological concerns were not underrepresented.

The clinical implications of these findings are straightforward. First, the CES-D is as good or better a predictor of diagnosis of depression for older adults as it is for younger adults. Second, practitioners do need to assess depressive symptomatology as well as mood. Relying on mere report of depressed mood will underestimate the presence of depression in older adults.

Integrating these studies with each other and other studies tapping older adults, the following psychometric summary can be provided.

Reliability

Reliability coefficients obtained on the CES-D have been high (.85–.91) (Himmelfarb & Murrell, 1983) and factor structures have remained consistent past age 75 (Berkman, Note 2; Teri & Lewinsohn, Note 1). Mean CES-D scores reported across studies were between 8 and 9 for community elderly; with standard deviations averaging around 8.

Validity

Mean CES-D scores reported above are comparable to scores reported on younger samples as reviewed earlier in this paper indicating that CES-D scores are not normatively higher among older adults (see Note 1). Studies that examined the CES-D across a wide age range found that scores were highest in the younger age groups (under 30) and lowest in the middle age group (30-65) (Comstock & Helsing, 1976; Eaton & Kessler, 1981; Frerichs, Ansechensel, & Clark, 1981; Teri & Lewinsohn, Note 1). There was indication of an increase in the very old (over 75) (Murrell et al., 1983; Teri & Lewinsohn, Note 1). The relationship of demographic characteristics (such as gender, socioeconomic status, and marital status) to depression was similarly unaffected by age: women consistently reported higher scores than men and those divorced, widowed, or separated reported higher scores than those currently or never married (Radloff, 1980; Sayetta, 1980; Murrell et al., 1983; Teri & Lewinsohn, Note 1; Goldberg, Van Natta, & Comstock, 1985).

Diagnostic Utility

Himmelfarb and Murrell (1983) obtained an 82% "hit" rate when comparing subjects with high CES-D scores to clinical diagnosis. Teri and Lewinsohn (Note 1) found that older subjects diagnosed depressed were as likely to obtain high CES-D scores as younger subjects. In the case by case analysis by Boyd et al. (1982), decribed earlier, the rates of false positives and false negatives of SADS diagnoses based on the CES-D were unaffected by age. Thus, across these studies, high self-report of depressive symptomatology is as good or better in predicting diagnosis among older adults as it is in younger adults.

Mediating Factors

As already discussed, one of the major concerns in assessing depression in older adults is the influence of health on depression score. Older adults are more likely to be in poor health and poor health is consistently associated with depression. Ergo, the question arises regarding the relationship of these three variables: age, depression, and physical health. A wide range of studies are pertinent here. Focusing on those using the CES-D, depression scores have been found to be more strongly associated to physical heath status than age, per se. Murrell et al. (1983) found a significant relationship between health and depression for both males and females, but this relationship was unaffected by age. Older adults in poor physical health reported more depression than those in good physical health. Teri and Lewinsohn (Note 1) reported a significant relationship between somatic complaints and depression, also unaffected by age. Subjects over 75 years of age reported somewhat more somatic symptoms than younger subjects, but they reported more general symptoms as well. Berkman (Note 1) found adults over 65 reported more somatic complaints but, again they also reported more complaints overall. Finally, Noh, Wood, and Turner (Note 3) found a similar relationship in a disabled sample: CES-D total score and scores on all negative items were higher in the disabled sample than in the general population, but this relationship was unaffected by age.

SUMMARY AND FUTURE FINDINGS

Data that exist thus far indicate that the CES-D is a promising scale for use with older adults. It has yielded consistent results across a varied age range: reliability is high; factor structures are stable; scores and factors are not significantly influenced by age; demographic variables and physical health status do not influence scores differentially across age; the proportions of older individuals diagnosed depressed with high CES-D scores are comparable to younger populations; and, finally, there is no indication that older adults are unable to comprehend or comply with instructions.

Clearly, there are limitations as well. Most of the data available thus far relate to community residing elderly. More is needed on patient and institutionalized populations. We need to know if there are any patient characteristics that preclude use of the CES-D. Obviously, scores obtained by the visually or cognitively impaired elderly would be suspect. One wonders how sensory modifications (such as an audio tape of the items for the visually impaired) would effect intra- and inter-test reliability and validity. In addition, the relationship of CES-D scores to depression indices such as the Geriatric Depression Scale (Yesavage, Brink, Rose, Lum, Huang, Adey, & Leirer, 1983) is yet unknown. Currently, studies are expanding the investigation of the CES-D with older adults. It is being employed in an outpatient geriatric clinic (Teri, personal communication), with elderly arthritis patients (Loring, personal communication), and in a number of other studies with a focus on older adults. Clearly, more information is needed and many questions await future research.

REFERENCE NOTES

1. Teri, L. and Lewinsohn, P.M. (1983). Depression and age: The relationship of age, gender, and method of assessment on the symptom pattern of depression. Unpublished manuscript. University of Oregon.
2. Berkman, L., Berkman, C., Kast, S., Ostfeld, A., Freeman, D., Leo, L., Cornoni-Huntly, J., and Brady, J. (1983). Prevalence of depressive symptoms among the elderly.
3. Noh, S., Wood, D.W., and Turner, R.J. (1984). Depression among the physically disabled: Somatic and psychological contributions. Paper presented at APHA, Anaheim, CA.

REFERENCES

American Psychiatric Association. (1980). *Diagnostic and Statistical Manual of Mental Disorders,* ed 3. Washington DC, American Psychiatric Association.

Aneshensel, C.S., Frerichs, R.R., Clark, V.A., & Kopenic, P.A. (1982). Measuring depression in the community: A comparison of telephone and personal interviews. *Public Opinion Quarterly, 46,* 110–121.

Boyd, J. H., Weissman, M. M., Thompson, W. D., and Myers, J. K. (1982). Screening for depression in a community sample. *Arch Gen Psychiatry, 39,* 1195–1200.

Comstock, G. W., & Helsing, K. J. (1976). Symptoms of depression in two communities. *Psychological Medicine, 6,* 551–563.

Craig, T. J., & Van Natta, P. A. (1976). Recognition of depressed affect in hospitalized psychiatric patients: Staff and patient perceptions. *Dis Nerv Syst, 37,* 561–566.

Eaton, W. W., & Kessler, L. G. (1981). Rates of symptoms of depression in a national sample. *American Journal of Epidemiology, 114,* 538–548.

Endicott, J., & Spitzer, R. L. (1978). A diagnostic interview: The schedule for affective disorders and schizophrenia. *Arch Gen Psychiatry, 35,* 837–844.

Frerichs, R. R., Ansechensel, C. A., & Clark, V. A. (1981). Prevalence of depression in Los Angeles county. *American Journal of Epidemiology, 113,* 691–699.

Gallagher, D., & Thompson, L. (1983). Depression. In P. M. Lewinsohn & L. Teri (Eds.), *Clinical geropsychology.* New York: Pergamon Press.

Goldberg, E., Van Natta, P., & Comstock, G. (1985). Depressive symptom, social networks and social supports of elderly women. *American Journal of Epidemiology, 121,* 448–456.

Hankin, J. R., & Lock, B. Z. (1982). The persistence of depressive symptomatology among prepaid group practice enrollees: An exploratory study. *Am J Pub Health, 72,* 1000–1006.

Himmelfarb, S., & Murrell, S. A. (1983). Reliability and validity of five mental health scales in older person. *Journal of Gerontology, 38,* 333–339.

Husaini, B. A., Neff, J. A., Harrington, J. B., Hughes, M. D., & Stone, R. H. (1980). Depression in rural communities: Validating the CES-D scale. *Journal of Community Psychology, 8,* 137–146.

Lewinsohn, P. M., Teri, L., & Hoperman, H. (1983). Depression: Perspectives on etiology, treatment and life span issues. In M. Rosenbaum & C. Franks (Eds.), *Perspectives on behavior therapy in the eighties.* New York: Springer.

Murrell, S. A., Himmelfarb, S., & Wright, K. (1983). Prevalence of depression and its correlatives in older adults. *American Journal of Epidemiology, 117, 2,* 173–185.

Myers, J. K., & Weissman, M. M. (1980). Use of a self-report symptom scale to detect depression in a community sample. *Am J Psychiatry, 137,* 1081–1084.

National Center for Health Statistics. (1980). Basic data on depressive symptomatology: United States, 1974–75, by R. B. Sayetta and D. P. Johnson. Vital and Health Statistics. Series 11-No.216. DHEW Pub No (PHS) 80-1666. Public Health Service. Washington, D.C.: U.S. GPO.

Post, F. (1975). Dementia, depression and pseudo-dementia. *Psychiatric aspects of neurological disease.* New York: Grune & Stratton.

Radloff, L. S. (1977). The CES-D Scale: A self-report depression scale for research in the general population. *App Psychol Meas, 3,* 385–401.

Radloff, L. S. (1980). Risk factors for depression: What do we learn from them? In D. Belle & S. Salasin (Eds.), *Mental health of women: Fact and fiction* (pp. 93–109). New York: Academic Press.

Radloff, L. S., & Locke, B. Z. (in press). The community mental health survey and the CES-D scale. In M. Weissman, J. Myers, & C. Ross (Eds.), *Community surveys,* New York: Prodist.

Roberts, R. E. (1980). Reliability of the CES-D scale in different ethnic contexts. *Psychiatry Res, 2,* 125–134.

Roberts, R. E., & Vernon, S. W. (1983). The Center for Epidemiological Studies depression scale: Its use in a community sample. *Am J Psychiatry, 140,* 41–46.

Robins, L., Helzer, J., Croughan, J., & Ratcliff, K. (1981). National Institute of Mental Health Diagnostic Interview Schedule. *Arch Gen Psychiatry, 38,* 381–389.

Sayetta, R. B. (1980). *Basic data on depressive symptomatology: United States, 1974–1975.* Washington, DC: DHEW Publication #80-1666.

Schulberg, H. C., Saul, M., McClelland, M., Ganguli, M., Christy, W., & Frank, R. (in press). Assessing depression in primary medical and psychiatric practice. *Arch Gen Psychiatry.*

Spitzer, R. L., Endicott, J., & Robins, E. (1978). Research diagnostic criteria: Rationale and reliability. *Arch Gen Psychiatry, 35,* 773–782.

Weissman, M. M., Pottenger, M., Kleber, H., Ruben, H. L., & Williams, D. (1977). Symptom patterns in primary and secondary depression: A comparison of primary depressives with depressed opiate addicts, alcoholics, and schizophrenics. *Arch Gen Psychiatry, 34,* 854–862.

Weissman, M. M., Prusoff, B. A., & Newberry, P. (1975a). Comparison of the CES-D with standardized depression rating scales at three points in time. Technical Report, Yale University, Contract ASH 74-166, NIMH.

Weissman, M. M., Prusoff, B. A., & Newberry, P. (1975b). Comparison of CES-D Zung Self Rating Depression Scale and Beck Depression Inventory. Progress report, Contract 42-74-83, NIMH.

Weissman, M. M., Sholomskas, D., Pottenger, M., Prusoff, B. A., & Locke, B. Z. (1977). Assessing depressive symptoms in five psychiatric populations: A validation study. *Am J Epidemiol, 106,* 203–214.

Yesavage, J., Brink, T., Rose, T., Lum, O., Huang, O., Adey, V., & Leirer, V. (1983). Development and validation of a geriatric depression screening scale: A preliminary report. *J Psychiatric Res, 7,* 37–49.

Questions

1) What evidence specifically substantiates the authors' claim that the CES-D is as good or better a predictor of diagnosis of depression for older adults as it is for younger adults?

2) Why is the self-report of depression among elders likely to under-report its incidence?

3) Much of the evidence cited by Teri and Lewinsohn, using the CES-D, denies that the aged have higher levels of depression, or that they are more likely to have the somatic symptoms of depression. How could this be reconciled with other research, conducted by other researchers using other scales, which have consistently found increased levels of depression with increased age?

7/USE OF THE ZUNG SELF-RATING DEPRESSION SCALE IN THE ELDERLY

William W. K. Zung, MD
Elizabeth M. Zung, BA

Editor's Introduction

Zung and Zung review a depression scale which has probably received more citations and translations than any
other. The authors' review of the use of that scale with
elders is ideally comprehensive.

On the positive side, the preponderance of the data on the
SDS indicate that:

1. it can be used with (most) aged subjects,
2. its increasing scores in life reflect the opinion of many
   clinicians that vulnerability to depression does increase
   in old age,
3. it can demonstrate statistically significant differences
   between depressed elders and normal elders,
4. it demonstrates a precipitous drop in scores of elders
   who have been treated for depression.

However, the accuracy of the Zung in cases of individual
assessment is suspect. Compared with a clinical interview,
sensitivity of the Zung is only 58% (correct classification =
74%, kappa = .47). Readjustment of scoring may produce
higher sensitivities and correct classification (*CG*, v. 1, #1,
pp. 37–43).

William W. K. Zung and Elizabeth M. Zung are affiliated with Duke University Medical
Center, VA Medical Center, Durham, NC.

Support of this project from the Selma Wolff Research Fund is gratefully acknowledged.

Reprint requests may be addressed to Dr. William Zung, VA Medical Center, Durham,
NC 27705.

137

The primary reasons for problems with the SDS with older patients is the possible presence of vegetative symptoms (e.g., constipation, insomnia) and cognitive loss secondary to dementia.

The need for a rating scale for measuring depressive disorders in the elderly population is demonstrated by the fact that between 5% and 20% of the 20 million Americans 65 years of age and older are estimated to be depressed (Gurland, 1976). Research in problems of mental health in any setting (such as inpatient, outpatient, family practice, nursing home), or with any specific sample population (such as clinical trial of new antidepressant drug in depressed elderly patients, patients undergoing heart surgery, geriatric patients in convalescent homes) cannot be accomplished without some form of controlled comparison. For standardized assessment of symptoms underlying an illness such as depressive disorders, the same instrument should be used in all the studies involved. One approach is to use symptoms to delineate syndromes in studies since they are most easily standardized and measurable.

The Self-rating Depression Scale was first published with the express purpose of constructing a scale for assessing depression in patients which would fulfill the following: it should be all inclusive with respect to symptoms of the illness, it should be short and simple, it should quantitate rather than qualitate, and it should be self-administered and indicate the patient's own response at the time the scale is taken (Zung, 1965). Since its initial publication, it was cited over 335 times by 1979 in the scientific literature (Citation Classic, 1979), translated into 30 languages, and used in national and international studies throughout the world. This report summarizes studies using the Zung Self-rating Depression Scale or SDS in elderly populations.

METHODS

A literature search was made for those publications which specifically cited the SDS in studies in the elderly. Further, reprints from the authors' files provided publications that used the SDS in geriatric settings, but not identified in the literature search. From these, those publications which reported data were reviewed and their results summarized.

RESULTS

Results of studies that generated data that could be summarized in a common tabular form are found in Tables 1 and 2. For those results that do not lend themselves to this format, the results are discussed in the text only.

Table 1. Study population and demographic characteristics of subjects from published results using the Zung Self-rating Depression Scale.

REFERENCE	STUDY POPULATION	N	AGE: RANGE	AGE: MEAN	SEX: M	SEX: F
Zung, 1967	Community normal	169	65-95	77.1	11	158
Zung, 1974	Depressed, out-pt	30	60-79	68.1		
Blumenthal, 1975	Community survey	320	18-65 (20%=60+)		160	160
Heidell, 1975	SCC,nur.hm,hosp-Sen:	60	60+		30	30
	Con:	60	60+		30	30
Shader, 1975	Volunteers, min. dep.	99	65+	70.5	26	73
Matloff, 1977	Multi-service prog.	8		67.9		
	Control	8		69.4		
Murkofsky, 1978	Out-patient	28		71.6	8	20
	Normal	48		70.8	12	36
Elkowitz, 1980	Widow(er)s	49	69-74			
Steuer, 1980	Depressed, out-pt	60	48-79 (75% over 60)	64.5	29	31
Zung, 1980	Depressed, out-pt	16		64.9		
	Demented, out-pt	12		70.1		
	Dep-Dem, out-pt	17		69.5		
	Normal	14		63.4		
Kitchell, 1982	Medical:Depressed	19	60+	66.7	19	
	Non-depressed	23	60+	68.4	21	2
Okimoto, 1982	VA Medical	55	60+	69.4	54	1
Freedman, 1982	General practice	166	60-86		58	108
McGarvey, 1982	Normal:Young-Old	170	58-72	66.7	60	110
	Old-Old	107	73-88	77.9	42	65
Brink, 1982	Depressed	51	"geriatric"			
	Control	20	"elders"			
Yesavage, 1983	VA, county, private	100	55+			
Zung, 1983	Family practice:	1,230	20-64	39	406	824
		307	65-95	72	75	232

Table 2. Study results based on using the Zung Self-rating Depression Scale.

REFERENCE	SDS INDEX MEAN (SD)	DISTRIBUTION 50 50-59 60	SENSI-TIVITY	SPECI-FICITY	VALIDITY/RELIABILITY
Zung, 1967	48.3(10.5) 56% ---44%---				
Zung, 1974	T/Pre:58.3(10.5) Post:48.1(10.0) P/Pre:56.0(10.0) Post:55.7(12.2)				
Blumenthal, 1975		60% 27% 13%			
Heidell, 1975	Mod. sen. higher on SDS than cntrl. No sex, setting diff.				
Shader, 1975	Pre: 46.4				
Matloff, 1977	M/Pre:52.5(8.9) Post:45.5(11.1) C/Pre:47.5(11.1) Post:49.1(10.8)				
Murkofsky, 1978	D: 61.7(14.2) N: 46.6(11.1)				.86(alpha)
Elkowitz, 1980	68.3 ---63%-- 37%				
Steuer, 1980					.19(r,hlth)
Zung, 1980	Dep:62.2(11.9) Dem:50.6(13.8) D&D:53.3(10.8) Nor:35.1(7.3)				
Kitchell, 1982	D: 59.5 ---55%-- 45% C: 46.8		58%	87%	
Okimoto, 1982		24%	82%	87%	.56(kappa)
Freedman, 1982	M: 45.0(11.4) 25% F: 52.3(13.9)				
McGarvey, 1982	Y-O:(35.8)x1.25=44.7 O-O:(38.5)x1.25=48.1				.76(alpha) .59(alpha)
Brink, 1982	C: 35.2(6.6) D: 48.6(10.3)		82%	80%	.79(r,HAMD)
Yesavage, 1983	43.2(11.5) 40% 26% 26%		82%	80%	.87(alpha) .81(sp-hlf) .80(r,HAMD)
Zung, 1983	Y:42.7(10.0) 79% 16% 5% O:42.7(10.4) 79% 14% 7%				

The first studies using the SDS in an elderly population were those published by Zung (1967). The subjects studied were members of community clubs and residents of a local retirement home. These initial results demonstrated that compared to younger normal subjects, a higher percentage of elderly normal subjects scored in the morbidity range (SDS indices of 50 and over) for depressive symptomatology. This observation has been repeated many times since then by numerous investigators, and raises the issue of diagnostic criterion for depression in the elderly.

Since the initial studies, we have administered the SDS to groups of normal control subjects with a combined N of 938. We can see from Table 3 that the mean SDS index is below 40 from age decades 10 through 50. Starting with age decade 60, there is a linear increase of the mean SDS index from 43 to 49.

TABLE 3. Distribution of SDS indices from normal subjects by age in decades.

AGE GROUP	N	MEAN	SD
10-19	374	37.4	7.1
20-29	247	35.6	8.5
30-39	61	32.0	5.9
40-49	48	34.7	8.9
50-59	25	32.1	6.0
60-69	37	43.2	10.6
70-79	81	46.9	9.7
80+	63	49.1	11.1

Morris et al. (1975) gave the SDS as well as the Philadelphia Geriatric Morale Scale, and the Gardner-Hetznecker Sign and Symptom Check List to 89 state mental hospital inpatients, at two different times, with an interval of 15 weeks in between. Their report was based upon the results of various factor analyses that were performed, and which did not correspond with previously identified SDS factors (Guy, 1976). However, according to a review by McNair (1979) no one has ever demonstrated that any SDS factors are more sensitive to change or treatment effect than the total score. Morris et al. reported reliability data and found that the internal consistencies, based on alpha reliability coefficients for the two SDS factors were in the highly satisfactory .80s region, both at time 1 and time 2.

Zung et al. (1974) used the SDS as one of the outcome measures in a clinical trial to evaluate a drug for its potential efficacy as an antidepressant. The Depression Status Inventory (Zung, 1972), which is the interviewer version of the SDS was also used in this study. Results demonstrated the efficacy of the antidepressant drugs evaluated, and the sensitivity of the SDS to change as a result of treatment.

Blumenthal (1975) interviewed 320 subjects with a structural interview that included the SDS. Specific issues raised about the SDS were: (1) Somatic symptoms of the SDS may be a primary measure of the reduced physical endurance and/or medical problems (i.e., cardiovascular disease) that often occur in older age groups, rather than symptoms of depression. (2) Some SDS items are conceived as measuring an optimism index, which may also be age related. She suggests that some symptoms of depression have different meaning for older people than for younger people. Data generated from this study showed that 13% of the population had scores similar to those obtained by patients with diagnosed depressions (SDS of 60 and over), and 27% had scores comparable to a lesser severity of depression (SDS index between 50–59). The author's conclusion was that the extensive usage that the SDS has received makes it an exceedingly valuable instrument, since the usage had generated substantial evidence on the validity of the instrument.

Heidell and Kidd (1975) designed a study to determine the degrees of depression, if present, in individuals over 60 years of age, who are diagnosed as nonsenile or moderately senile. The study was done from subjects from senior citizen centers, convalescent hospitals and nursing homes. The results showed that moderately senile subjects scored significantly higher on the SDS than did the nonsenile subjects, but were not significant for study setting, or for sex.

Shader et al. (1975) used the SDS as well as other measures of mood and memory to investigate the effects of an elixir on minimally depressed subjects. Their initial baseline results are in the summary tables. The authors concluded that although no significant treatment effects were found in their study, the methods of assessment used are readily applicable to elderly people.

Matloff and Lair (1977) compared the effectiveness of a geriatric multi-service program (includes chemotherapy, individual, group, and family therapy, visiting housekeepers and nurses, and an active outreach program) to a traditionally oriented senior center. Results showed that the multi-service program reduced the SDS more effectively than did the control unit. The authors further noted that the mean posttest SDS for the multi-service group of 48.1 very closely approximates the mean SDS index for normal aged reported by Zung (1967).

Murkofsky et al. (1978) pointed out that psychiatric evaluation of the elderly is especially difficult for several reasons, e.g., the presence of organic impairment, the effects of multiple drug therapy, and the tendency to confuse the normal concomitants of aging with neurotic symptoms. The authors administered a battery of assessments designed to assist the psychiatrist in the process of diagnosis, including the SDS. The overall results (including the SDS) showed significant differences between the geriatric patients and the normal senior citizens.

Elkowitz and Virginia et al. (1980) were interested in how the elderly coped with depression, and the pattern and correlates of physical and psychologic complaints. They reported that there is a significant relationship between sex and the expression of feelings of distress, i.e., widows show dejection more freely than do widowers, and that widows scored significantly higher on the SDS than did widowers.

One of the hypotheses Steuer et al. (1980) studied was the relationship between a physical health rating (as performed by a physician) and depression (as measured by the SDS). The authors found that physicians' ratings of health were not significantly related to the total SDS score, thus lessening the concern that health as a confounding variable obscures the measurement of depression in the elderly. In addition, the authors found that in contrast to low associations between somatic illness and the total SDS score, the relationship between the nonsomatic items and total SDS score were significant. Thus, they found that somatic symptoms seemed to contribute less to depression than measures of lack of hope, decreased activity, feelings of uselessness, and problems in decision making. They interpreted their results as contrary to clinical lore which emphasizes somatization as an important aspect of depression in the elderly (Raskin, 1979).

Zung (1980) reported the results of a study which investigated the relationship between depression and dementia. Results using the SDS and DSI showed that depressed patients had the highest mean SDS index, with patients who are both depressed and with dementia to be next, patients with dementia alone third, and normal elderly to be lowest.

Kitchell et al. (1982) as part of an effort to improve detection of depression in geriatric hospitalized medical patients, evaluated the validity of the SDS. Based upon a total sample of 42 subjects, the following were the results of ratings using the Hamilton depression scale (HAMD) and the SDS. On the HAMD, depressed patients had a mean of 14.9, while non-depressed patients had a mean of 6.2. On the SDS, depressed patients had a mean of 59.5, and non-depressed patients a mean of 46.8. Both the HAMD and SDS were significantly different between the two patient groups with $p < .001$.

Further, based upon the psychiatric diagnoses assigned to the patients by the investigators using the APA DSM-III (APA, 1980) diagnostic criteria as an independent measure, the SDS showed the following:

DSM Interview Diagnosis:

SDS	Depressed	Non-depressed	Total
(+)	11	3	14
(−)	8	20	28
Total	19	23	42

Calculations based on these results showed a sensitivity of 11/19 = 58%, specificity of 20/23 = 87%, correct classification of 31/42 = 74%, and a kappa coefficient k of .466 ($p < .01$). The investigators concluded that by using a cut-off index of 60, specificity increased to be most effective as a screening tool for moderately to severely depressed elderly medical inpatients.

Okimoto et al. (1982) compared the SDS ratings with diagnosis assigned by a psychiatrist using DSM-III criteria, who was blind to scale results of patients seen in a geriatric medical clinic of a Veteran Administration medical center. Their results are summarized in Tables 1 and 2. Based on their findings, the authors suggest that the choice of cutoff index score to depend on the purpose for which the depression scales are applied. For screening purposes, one might accept a lower specificity (i.e., a higher false-positive rate) in the first phase of depression detection. On the other hand, for research purposes one might choose a higher cutoff index score in order to ensure greater specificity. Alternatively, one could use a statistical analytic method to improve performance. Differences in scale results achieved by using univariate versus multivariate analyses (factor, discriminant function) on the same data set were demonstrated in a study by Zung and Wonnacott (1970).

The study by Freedman et al. (1982) addresses several major methodologic issues in the assessment of depressive illness among the elderly family practice patients living in the community. These include the selection of screening locale, the definition of depression in the elderly, and the evaluation of age trends within this group. The authors selected to use in their study, the Zung Depression Status Inventory as a compromise between a direct, self-report symptom inventory, and a full-scale psychiatric assessment procedure, which did not fit readily into the demands of a general practice setting. In addition to the results summarized in Tables 1 and 2, the authors found that the ratio of women to men of patients who scored 60 or above on the DSI was 2-1/2 times greater for women. The authors reported an age trend in the DSI scores which was curvilinear, with the peaks nonsynchronous for the two sexes. Women showed peak symptom levels between 65–69 years, and men between 70–74 years. The authors final conclusion was that it was feasible to use the general practitioner's office as a mental health screening locale. The screening procedure can be carried out in a way that does not interfere with office routine, and may actually enhance the effectiveness of the practice.

McGarvey et al. (1982) cited the SDS as a popular instrument for the assessment of clinical depression which has displayed varied consistency in application. The scale typically indicates elevated depression in the elderly as compared to younger populations. One of the purposes of their investigation was to assess the reliability (internal consistency) of the SDS in different age groups. Result of their study with the young-old (58–72 years) and old-old (73–88 years) are summarized in Tables 1 and 2.

One group of investigators developed a new Geriatric Depression Screening (GDS) scale with a total of 30 items (Yesavage et al., 1983). Results of this study generated relevant data with regards to the SDS and its comparison to the interviewer-rated Hamilton rating scale for depression. The correlation between the SDS and HAMD was 0.80. Other relevant data are summarized in Tables 1 and 2. In another study published by the authors of the GDS, additional data relevant to the SDS were provided (Brink et al., 1982). The data demonstrated that all of the scales studied (GDS, SDS, HAMD) were able to distinguish between the depressed aged and the control aged groups.

We have been actively screening patients in family practice settings, and combined the results of two published studies (Zung et al., 1983; Zung and King, 1983) to analyze for age differences in this population of over 1,500 subjects. Results showed no significant differences for the mean SDS index between the young (20–64 years old) and the old (65–95 years old), using a t-test. In addition, the distribution of SDS indices for these two age groups into normal, mild, and severe ratings of depressive symptomatology was not significant, using a chi-square analysis for categorical data. Previous results from these two studies showed that 12–13% of these patients scored 55 or above on the SDS index. Thus in a subject population which is at risk for depression, the previously noted age trends were not present.

DISCUSSION

The Self-rating Depression Scale was constructed on the basis of commonly agreed upon signs and symptoms of a depressive disorder without regards to age. Similarly, the diagnostic criterion for a major depressive disorder in the DSM-III was operationalized, but without regards to age. However, the DSM-III diagnostic criterion does not generate a quantitative score. Since the SDS does provide a measurement by way of an index, the use of a reference value (morbidity cut-off index) as a function of age becomes an issue. One problem in using the scale with geriatric patients is that symptoms identified as depressive in nature may become difficult to distinguish from events of "normal aging." In addition, since the elderly are more prone to have coexisting medical conditions, there is the problem of distinguishing or separating the contribution of symptomatology between depression and the coexisting medical illness. Despite these problems, the results of use of the SDS in several studies agreed with diagnosis made by psychiatric interviews, as demonstrated by its sensitivity, specificity, and kappa values.

As a number of studies have demonstrated, old age is not a homogeneous condition, and there are differences for the various age decades. Data from our normal subjects show that there is a steady level of baseline endorsement of depressive symptomatology until the 60s decade, after which it increases with age. This finding of a higher "baseline" index for normal subjects was reported by a number of investigators in various settings, demonstrating a universally observable phenomenon. Of further interest is the fact that for populations who are at risk for depressive disorders, such as the patients seen in family medicine settings, the mean SDS indices between the young and old were not significantly different. This is similar to our findings in the cross-national studies using the SDS. We found that although the mean SDS indices among different countries from normal subjects were not significantly different, some significant differences were found for some SDS items. However, these item differences (culture-bound) were no longer present when results from depressed patients were tabulated (culture-free). The issue of interpretation of any "laboratory test" result has to be based upon understanding the concept of "normality" and "reference values" which is beyond the scope of this present review.

REFERENCES

American Psychiatric Association: Diagnostic and Statistical Manual of Mental Disorders, 3rd ed., (DSM-III), 1980, Washington, DC.

Blumenthal M: Depressive symptomatology and role function in a general population. Arch Gen Psychiatry, 1975, 32, 985–991.

Brink TL, Yesavage J, Lum O, Heersema P, Adey M, Rose T: Screening tests for geriatric depression. Clin Gerontologist, 1982, 1, 37–43.

Citation Classic: Current Contents, 1979, 7, for: Zung WWK, A self-rating depression scale.

Elkowitz E. & Virginia A: Relationship of depression to physical and psychologic complaints in the widowed elderly. J Am Geriatrics Soc, 1980, 28, 507–510.

Freedman N, Bucci W, Elkowitz E: Depression in a family practice elderly population. J Am Geriatrics Soc, 1982, 30, 372–377.

Gurland B: The comparative frequency of depression in various adult age groups. J Gerontology, 1976, 31, 283–292.

Guy W: ECDEU assessment manual for psychopharmacology, (Rev. ed.) DHEW Publication No. ADM 76-388, 1976, Washington, DC.

Heidell ED & Kidd AH: Depression and senility, 1975, J Clin Psychology, 31, 643–645.

Kitchell M, Barnes R, Veith R, Okimoto J, Raskind M: Screening for depression in hospitalized geriatric medical patients. J Am Geriatric Soc, 1982, 30, 174–177.

McGarvey B, Gallagher D, Thompson L, Zelinski E: Reliability and factor structure of the Zung Self-rating Depression Scale in three age groups. Essence, 1982, 5, 141–151.

McNair D: Self-rating scales for assessing psychopathology in the elderly, in Psychiatric Symptoms and Cognitive Loss in the Elderly: Evaluation and Assessment Techniques, Raskin A & Jarvik L (eds.), 1979, Wiley, New York.

Matloff M & Lair C: Effect of treatment by a geriatric multi-service unit prototype on self-reported clients' depression. Psychological Reports, 1977, 41, 542.

Morris JN, Wolf RS, Klerman LV: Common themes among morale and depression scales. J Gerontology, 1975, 30, 209–215.

Murkofsky C, Conte H, Plutchik R, Karasu T: Clinical utility of a rapid diagnostic test series for elderly psychiatric outpatients. J Amer Geriatrics Soc, 1978, 24, 22–26.

Okimoto J, Barnes R, Veith R, Raskind M, Inui T, Carter W: Screening for depression in geriatric medical patients. Am J Psychiatry, 1982, 139, 799–802, 1982.

Raskin A: Signs and symptoms of psychopathology in the elderly. In: Raskin A & Jarvik L (eds.), Psychiatric Symptoms and Cognitive Loss in the Elderly: Evaluation and Assessment Techniques. Hemisphere Publication, 1979, Washington, DC.

Shader R, Harmatz J, Kochansky G, Cole J: Psychopharmacologic investigations in healthy elderly volunteers: Effects of pipradol-vitamin (Alertonic) elixir and placebo in relation to research design. J Am Geriatrics Soc, 1975, 23, 277–279.

Steuer J, Bank L, Olen E, Jarvik L: Depression, physical health and somatic complaints in the elderly: A study of the Zung Self-rating Depression Scale. J Gerontology, 1980, 35, 683–688.

Yesavage J, Brink TL, Rose T, Lum O, Huang V, Adey M, Leirer VO: Development and validation of a geriatric depression screening scale: A preliminary report. J Psychiatric Res, 1983, 17, 37–49.

Zung WWK: A self-rating depression scale. Arch Gen Psychiatry, 1965, 12, 63–70.

Zung WWK: Depression in the normal aged. Psychosomatics, 1967, 8, 287–292.

Zung WWK & Wonnacott T: Treatment prediction in depression using a self-rating scale. Biol Psychiatry, 1970, 2, 321–329.

Zung WWK: The Depression Status Inventory: An adjunct to the Self-rating Depression Scale. J Clin Psychology, 1972, 28, 539–543.

Zung WWK, Gianturco D, Pfeiffer E, Wang S, Whanger A, Bridge T, Potkin S: Pharmacology of depression in the aged: Evaluation of Gerovital H3 as an antidepressant. Psychosomatics, 1974, 15, 127–131.

Zung WWK: Affective Disorder, in Busse E & Blazer D (eds.), Handbook of Geriatric Psychiatry, 1980, Van Nostrand Reinhold, New York.

Zung WWK, Magill M, Moore J, George T: Recognition and treatment of depression in a family medicine practice. J Clin Psychiatry, 1983, 44, 3–6.

Zung WWK & King R: Identification and treatment of masked depression in a general medical practice. J Clin Psychiatry, 1983, 44, 365–368.

Questions

1) How could we explain the range of correlation coefficients and sensitivity/specificity reported by different investigators in Table 2?

2) For which elders would the Zung SDS probably give the most accurate assessment of depression?

3) What would be the most appropriate use of the Zung SDS with the aged?

8/THE BECK DEPRESSION INVENTORY AND OLDER ADULTS
Review of Its Development and Utility

Dolores Gallagher, PhD

Editor's Introduction

Beck's BDI is probably second only to the Zung in terms of number of citations. Unfortunately, there are much fewer studies that have been done with elders.

Gallagher reviews the use of the BDI with elders, discussing its usage, validity, reliability, factor structure, and utility for screening, research, and symptom monitoring. Specific problems and limitations are emphasized, especially with elders who have limited educational background or cognitive capacity, a social undesirability response set, or numerous somatic complaints.

HISTORICAL DEVELOPMENT

The Beck Depression Inventory (BDI) was published more than 23 years ago by Aaron T. Beck and colleagues at the University of

Dolores Gallagher is affiliated with Stanford University School of Medicine and Geriatric Research, Education and Clinical Center (GRECC), Veterans Administration Medical Center, Palo Alto, CA.

Preparation of this report was supported in part by grant #RO1-MH3716-04 from the National Institute of Mental Health. The author wishes to thank Mr. Troy Schmit for his assistance in conducting the library research for this manuscript.

A comprehensive library search was conducted for the years from 1975 to the present, referencing *Index Medicus, Psychological Abstracts,* and *Citation Index* for that period. From 1974 back to 1961, these sources were searched under the heading of Beck Depression Inventory only. Due to space limitations, all available references could not be included; however, all known studies of the BDI with elders have been included.

Pennsylvania (Beck, Ward, Mendelson, Mock, & Erbaugh, 1961). It was designed to be an inventory (useable for research purposes) that approximated clinical judgments of the intensity of depression. Items were chosen that maximally discriminated depressed from non-depressed patients, and that gave an accurate estimate of the severity of each symptom. The BDI was developed as a standardized, consistent measure that would not be sensitive to the theoretical orientation or idiosyncracies of the person administering it, since all questions would be asked of the patient in exactly the same way. Also, it provides a single numerical score, to facilitate comparison with other quantitative data and to allow statistical manipulation. Details on the construction of the BDI can be found in Beck (1967, pp. 186–207; Beck & Beck, 1972); for our purposes, a brief description follows.

Items Included in the BDI

BDI items were primarily clinically derived, and resulted from Beck's psychotherapeutic work with depressed patients. (See Beck, 1967, pp. 189–193 for description of the patient samples employed to construct the item pool.) Items selected were also consistent with descriptions of depression contained in the psychiatric literature at the time, and reflected prior research by Beck evaluating and discarding other items (e.g., increased dependency) which were low in frequency in patient samples and/or had insufficient theoretical support.

The final inventory consists of 21 categories of symptoms and attitudes; each category describes a specific manifestation of depression (cognitive, behavioral, or vegetative). Originally, each contained four to five self-evaluative statements among which patients chose the one most representative of their feelings. This was modified subsequently; now there are four response choices for all categories, graded from zero (which essentially means the symptom is not there) to 3 (which means it is intensely present). The categories are: mood, pessimism, sense of failure, lack of satisfaction, feelings of guilt, sense of deserving punishment, self-dislike, self-accusations, suicidal wishes, crying spells, irritability, social withdrawal, indecisiveness, distortion of body image, work inhibition, sleep disturbance, fatigability, appetite problems, weight loss, somatic preoccupation, and loss of libido. The entire scale cannot be given here because it is copyrighted; however, below is an example of one category and its response choices.

Self-Accusations:

0   I don't feel that I am any worse than anybody else
1   I am critical of myself for weaknesses or mistakes
2   I blame myself for my faults
3   I blame myself for everything bad that happens

Administration and Scoring of the BDI

Originally, the scale was administered in an interviewer-assisted manner: the interviewer read each group of statements aloud, with patients following along on their own copy. They were instructed to select whichever *one* of the statements best described the way they felt at that time. Instructions have since been modified so that the scale is filled out unassisted by the patient as a self-report measure. Also, patients are told to "read each group of statements carefully, then pick the one statement in each group which best describes the way you have been feeling the *past week, including today!*" (emphasis theirs; see Beck, Rush, Shaw, & Emery, 1979, pp. 398–399 for a copy of the currently used version of the long form BDI and for the address to write to for permission to use this scale).

A total score is obtained by summing the numbers of the choices selected. Various authors have used different cut-off scores to designate severity of depression; Beck indicates that no one set of cut-off scores will serve every purpose. The appropriate scores to use depend on patient characteristics and the purpose for which the inventory is being used in a given study. Nevertheless, the following have become conventionally used by some in the field: 0–9: Normal Range; 10–15: Mild Depression; 16–19: Mild to Moderate Depression; 20–29: Moderate to Severe Depression; 30–63: Severe Depression.

Psychometric Data: Reliability, Validity, and Factor Structure

Much early psychometric work on the BDI was done by Beck himself, and is reported in detail in Beck and Beamesderfer (1974). Reliability and validity studies, along with several factor analyses, are described there. A subsequent review by Mayer (1978) contains additional studies that appeared later. In terms of reliability, both split-half and item-total correlations have been adequate; however, test-retest correlations have been mixed, with some studies reporting adequate stability (e.g., Strober, Green, & Carlson, 1981 with a sample of psychiatrically hospitalized adolescents), and others finding significant change within a short interval in untreated samples (e.g., Hammen, 1980, with a college student sample). Concurrent, discriminative, and construct validity have been demonstrated for the BDI (see Beck & Beamesderfer, 1974; Bumberry, Oliver, & McClure, 1978; Berndt, Petzel, & Kaiser, 1983, and Oliver & Simmons, 1984 for data on concurrent validity; see Beck, 1972 and Lukesch, 1974 on discriminant validity; and Beck & Beck, 1972 for information on construct validity). Essentially, the weight of the evidence supports the conclusion that the BDI has adequate reliability and validity for clinical and research purposes in general adult samples of varying ages.

Reliability and Validity with Elders

Only two studies could be found that address these issues with elder samples. One by Gallagher, Nies, and Thompson (1982) focused on the reliability of the BDI. It compared a patient sample (N = 77) with a comparable group of non-clinical volunteers (N = 82); mean ages were in the late 60s for both groups. The BDI was administered twice to each subject, between 6 and 21 days apart. The test-retest correlation coefficient for the whole sample was .90; coefficient alpha (which measures a scale's internal consistency) was .91 overall; and the split-half index of reliability was .84 for the total sample. Thus, the BDI appears to have adequate reliability for use with the elderly. The second study, by Gallagher, Breckenridge, Steinmetz, and Thompson (1983), assessed the concurrent validity of the BDI by examining the degree of congruence between conventional BDI cutoff scores and selected diagnostic classifications of the Research Diagnostic Criteria (RDC; Spitzer, Endicott, & Robins, 1978) in a sample of 102 elders seeking treatment for depression. It was found that 91% of those scoring at 17 or greater on the BDI were independently diagnosed as being in an episode of Major Depressive Disorder, using the Schedule for Affective Disorders and Schizophrenia interview (SADS; Endicott & Spitzer, 1978) and the RDC classification system. Also, 81% of those scoring 10 or less on the BDI did not meet criteria for any RDC-specified depressive disorder. These findings support the validity of the BDI with elders, and suggest that it is a useful screening instrument for identification of clinically depressed persons over 60 years of age.

Factor Analyses

The major factor analytic studies on the BDT have been done by Cropley and Weckowicz (1966), Giambra (1977), Pichot and Lemperiere (1964) (cited in Beck & Beamesderfer, 1974) and Weckowicz, Muir and Cropley (1967). According to Mayer (1978), all have essentially found three factors (named differently across studies). These are: negative views of self and future; somatic disturbances; and physical withdrawal or retardation (e.g., work inhibition and fatigability). These fairly consistent results suggest that depression is not a unidimensional construct, but rather consists of several components that reflect disturbances in somatic, cognitive, and behavioral areas of daily life. More recent papers on the factor structure of the BDI have focused on specialized populations such as alcoholics (Steer, McElroy, Margo, & Beck, 1982; Steer, McElroy, Margo, & Beck, 1983) and mildly depressed college students (Golin & Hartz, 1979). Only one study could be found that factor analyzed the responses of elders to the BDI. Zemore and Eames (1979) had 79 elders (48 who were residents of homes for the aged, and 31 who were on waiting lists for entrance into these homes) complete the BDI unassisted (when possible). Two primary factors emerged: one that they called a general factor of depression (including somatic and cognitive/behavioral items) and one that consisted primarily of cognitive items (e.g., pessimism, sense of failure, guilt, etc.). These factors accounted for 37% of the total variance. Unfortunately, the nature of the sample used in this study, and its small size, make it very difficult to generalize these results to other groups of elders.

Influence of Extraneous Factors on BDI Scores

Beck and Beamesderfer (1974) investigated the correlation of total BDI scores with background variables including age, sex, and educational level to determine if they systematically biased outcome. They found no significant relationship between BDI scores and age in a sample of 606 patients; however, females obtained significantly higher scores. The latter does not seem to be an artifact since many other studies have found a higher frequency of depressive symptoms in women (cf. Teri, 1982; Hammen & Padesky, 1977). However, the relationship of age to BDI scores is unclear at present; other authors (cf. Zemore & Eames, 1979) have found a significant correlation. Beck and Beamesderfer (1974) also reported that patients with lower levels of education scored higher on the BDI compared to those of higher socioeconomic status. This has been found by others as well; see Hirschfeld and Cross (1982) and Vernon and Roberts (1982) for reviews of various factors affecting rates of depression (although special attention has not been paid to the elderly in this regard.) Beck and Beamesderfer (1974) also questioned whether the validity of the BDI was reduced by the presence of a social desirability response set—meaning patients' tendencies to answer in ways that make them look favorable. They concluded that this was not the case, since correlations between clinicians' ratings and BDI scores have been consistently high, and the BDI has been found to be effective in discriminating between depression and anxiety. However, no formal study of the social desirability value of BDI items has been conducted, and an interesting recent study by King and Buchwald (1982) suggests that further study of the influence of social desirability variables should be undertaken before finally concluding that the BDI is free of such influences.

Other Versions of the BDI

It has been translated into German (see Blaser, Low & Schaublin, 1968; Kammer, 1983); Spanish (see Conde & Useros, 1975; Conde, Esteban & Chamorros, 1976); and French (see Bourque & Beaudette, 1982). There is also a Children's Depression Inventory (Saylor, Finch, Spirito, & Bennett, 1984) that is described as "a downward extension of the BDI" and an abridged version of the full BDI, called the short form BDI (Beck & Beck, 1972).

The short form consists of 13 items that were selected because of high correlations with both clinicans' ratings (r = .61) and with the original long form (r = .96) in a sample of 599 patients. Items reflect the domains of: sadness, pessimism, sense of failure, dissatisfaction, guilt, self-dislike, self-harm, social withdrawal, indecisiveness, negative self-image, work difficulties, fatigability, and appetite problems. As with the long form, each item contains four response choices from which one is selected. However, instructions for the short form say to answer based on how the patient is feeling that particular day (rather than overall feelings for the past week). Also, response choices are arranged in order of decreasing (rather than increasing) severity. The scale normally takes between five and ten minutes to complete, and is fully self-administered. The range of scores for the abridged BDI (reported in Beck & Beamesderfer, 1974) are: 0-4: none or minimal depression; 4-7: mild; 8-15: moderate; and 16 or greater: severe. Other studies (by Beck, Rial, & Rickels, 1974; Gould, 1982; Reynolds & Gould, 1981) have reported high correlations between the long and short forms, and recommend use of the short form when a quick screening tool is needed. However, no comparable studies with the elderly have yet been published.

USES OF THE BDI WITH ELDERS

Published data could be found describing three primary uses of this scale with elder samples: (1) as a screening measure; (2) as an index of pre/post-change in intervention studies; and (3) as an index of fluctuations in specific symptoms during treatment. Other clinical uses of the BDI (e.g., as a predictor variable) have not yet appeared in the gerontological literature. The major uses will be discussed below, followed by mention of some potential problems that may be encountered when using the BDI with elders.

Screening for Depression

As noted earlier, research by Gallagher et al. (1983) found that use of a cut-off score of 17 or greater on the long form BDI was associated with a diagnoseable clinical depression in over 90% of the sample studied. While these results have not yet been replicated, they strongly suggest that the BDI can be appropriately used for screening purposes in outpatients without serious medical problems. The utility of the BDI for depression screening in medically ill patients is currently under investigation in our laboratory (Norris, Gallagher, & Winograd, 1985). Prior work by Schwab and colleagues (Schwab, Bialow, & Holzer, 1967; Schwab, Bialow, Clemmons, Martin, & Holzer, 1967) and by Nielsen and Williams (1980) suggested cutting scores ranging from 10 to 13 on the long form BDI to detect depression in samples of non-aged medically ill patients. Recent work by Yesavage and colleagues (Yesavage, Brink, Rose, Lum, Huang, Adey, & Leirer, 1983) on the development of a new self-report depression scale (called the Geriatric Depression Scale; GDS) is promising in this regard. This measure was constructed to be free of somatic items which may cloud the diagnostic picture in elders—particularly in those with serious medical problems (cf. Salzman & Shader, 1979). In the study by Norris et al. (1985) both the BDI and GDS are being used to tap self-reported depression; results are being compared to those obtained from the SADS/RDC interview and classification system. These findings should shed light on the comparative value of these scales for detection of depression in the aged medically ill.

Finally, the BDI has been found to be very helpful when evaluating bereaved elders, to determine if the depressive symptoms they report are part and parcel of normal grief or are indicative of a clinical level of depression. Research by Gallagher, Breckenridge, Thompson, Dessonville, and Amaral (1982) compared the responses of 77 elder outpatients diagnosed as in an episode of Major Depression with those of 77 elders whose spouses had died within the previous two months, and 82 nondepressed, nonbereaved community residing elders who provided the control sample. Depressives were found to have significantly higher BDI scores than either of the other groups; in addition, the bereaved and depressives could be readily distinguished by the particular items endorsed. Both depressed and bereaved elders reported being tearful, sad, and dissatisfied with themselves. However, the depressives were more pessimistic, felt like personal failures, showed greater self-dissatisfaction, were more irritable, cried more, felt less personally attractive, and had greater fatigue and health concerns than the bereaved. Thus, elder bereaved who report symptoms related to low self-esteem and consistent negative self-evaluation may be burdened with clinical depression as well as grief.

Index of Change

The BDI has been extensively used with younger and middle-aged depressives as a measure of change in intervention studies using either psychotherapy, pharmacotherapy, or both (see Beck et al., 1979; Hollon & Beck, 1978; Rush, 1984; Thompson & Gallagher, in press, for selected reviews of this research). Several recent studies report the BDI to be a sensitive measure of change for older adults participating in various forms of outpatient psychotherapy, although no published research on the impact of pharmacotherapy on the BDI in elder samples was located. Gallagher and Thompson (1982a) found that significant change occurred on both the BDI and Hamilton Rating Scale for Depression (Hamilton, 1967) in a sample

of 30 depressed elder outpatients treated with 16 sessions of individual therapy (either cognitive, behavioral or insight-oriented).
Thompson and Gallagher (1984) reported preliminary data from a
second psychotherapy trial which essentially replicated their earlier
findings. In this study, a waiting list control group was also included;
when assessed after six weeks' wait, those patients had not improved
(on the BDI, Hamilton Scale, or in terms of clinical diagnoses) compared to treated patients who showed significant reduction in their
distress during the first six weeks of therapy. Steuer, Mintz, Hammen, Hill, Jarvik, McCarley, Motoike, and Rosen (1984) compared
the effectiveness of cognitive/behavioral and psychodynamic group
psychotherapies in a sample of 33 outpatient elder depressives.
They found that patients in the cognitive/behavioral groups had
significantly lower scores on the BDI (short form) than did those in
the psychodynamic groups at the completion of treatment. However, since there were no differences between the groups on several
other outcome measures, they suggest that measurement bias should
be considered in interpreting these results. Specifically, since the
short BDI contains many items reflecting negative cognitive appraisals (e.g., self-criticism; future pessimism) and patients in cog-
nitive/behavioral therapy presumably learned how to confront these
negative thoughts, they may have "learned" how to complete the
BDI in a favorable way. Current research in progress in our laboratory (Thompson & Gallagher, 1985) with a sample of 90 elders who
recently completed a psychotherapy trial comparing behavioral,
cognitive, and brief psychodynamic treatments indicates that change
in BDI scores from pre- to post-therapy is highly correlated with extent of change in other measures (e.g., SADS/RDC diagnoses;
Hamilton Rating Scale scores; GDS scores). Thus in our opinion,
the BDI can be viewed as a sensitive and accurate indicator of improvement (or lack thereof) in outcome research with elders.

Index of Symptomatic Change During Treatment

Besides its utility as an outcome measure, the BDI can be very
helpful clinically if it is administered session-by-session, so that
fluctuations in overall distress level (and in distress on specific
items) can be monitored and evaluated by the therapist. In our outcome research, in order to avoid confounding these "intermediate"
results with "final" results, we use the long form BDI in our pre-,
post- and follow-up assessments, and the short form BDI during

treatment. It is completed by patients right before each therapy session, and is reviewed by the therapist in the initial few moments of the session. Both total scores, and scores on specific troublesome items, are examined. For example, one patient may obtain a total score of 9 because of endorsing the "3" level on three specific symptoms week after week; another patient may obtain the same score due to frequent "1s" and "2s" on the scale. These different patterns imply different therapeutic strategies. The patient experiencing repeated intense distress related to a few symptoms needs to begin to see improvement in these particular areas in order to continue to be motivated for therapy. Thus, the therapist in that situation might focus the session on the distressing symptoms, to evaluate them more carefully and plan suitable intervention strategies. Conversely, patients who are generally experiencing milder distress on several symptoms may be more amenable to a less symptom-oriented therapy focus; this allows the therapist more flexibility to work on other important treatment targets (e.g., interpersonal difficulties, coping problems, etc.). Serial use of the BDI has been found to be very acceptable to private practice patients as well, particularly if results are shared with the patient at appropriate intervals. Additional examples of how this method has been used with elders can be found in Gallagher and Thompson (1982b) and Thompson, Davies, Gallagher, and Krantz (this volume).

Potential Problems in Use of the BDI with Elders

There are several considerations that clinicians and researchers should keep in mind in deciding whether or not to use the BDI with the elderly. First, there is the issue of the scale's readibility. Berndt, Schwartz, and Kaiser (1983) found that an eighth grade reading level was required to really understand the items themselves, and the gradations of severity implied in the response choices. This may be a problem for some elders with limited formal education, or with language problems (e.g., if English is not their native tongue). Clearly, cognitively impaired elders have difficulty with this scale (as they do with most others). We have found that the GDS (Yesavage et al., 1983), with its yes/no response choice format, can be completed by elders with minimal education and/or mild cognitive impairments. Thus, when choosing which self-report depression scale to use in a given situation, one should consider the patient's abilities to read and comprehend the material.

A second issue concerns the possible presence of a social desirability response set that may alter the accuracy of self-report data. Harmatz and Shader (1975) found that elders tended to under-report symptomatic distress on a depression rating scale in an effort to "put their best foot forward." Others, working with non-aged samples, have pointed to the opposite phenomenon: namely, that depressives may over-report symptoms due to their generally negative perceptual style (cf. Langevin & Stancer, 1979, who refer to this as a tendency toward social *un*desirability). In our clinical experience we have encountered elders with both types of bias. Under-reporting has been more common in elder males, who may not even wish to admit that they are depressed, while over-reporting has been frequently seen in older women with hystrionic and/or dependent personality characteristics. Of course, such problems are not unique to the BDI; yet further study is needed to evaluated the extent to which these biases confound the usefulness of this measure.

A third issue involves the controversy over the role of somatic complaints in diagnosing depression in the elderly. Since the BDI does have a number of somatic items, this is a relevant concern. Some gerontologists suggest that somatic complaints are not a true indicator of depression because many somatic changes occur normally with age, and many more elders have serious physical problems of some kind (cf. Salzman & Shader, 1979). One study by Dessonville, Gallagher, Thompson, Finnell, and Lewinsohn (1982) studied this issue in some detail by comparing the SADS interview responses of depressed and nondepressed elders in good or poor self-reported physical health. Analyses indicated a strong main effect for diagnosis, with no main effects for health or age, and no significant interactions. Inspection of individual SADS items indicated that for nondepressed elders over 70 who reported their health as poor, it was difficult to interpret the items related to insomnia, hypersomnia, weight loss, weight gain, and somatic anxiety. Supplemental information (e.g., medical history and/or evaluation) seems needed in this instance to determine whether positive symptoms are due primarily to health or age factors rather than to affective status. This same kind of work is needed with the BDI scale; the study in progress by Norris et al. (1985) is addressing this issue, but further research is clearly warranted.

Finally, one might argue that because of the above-mentioned problems, what the field really needs are carefully developed, valid, and reliable *behavioral* measures of depression—either to supplement data obtained from more traditional sources, or to provide significant independent information. Such measures would eliminate concerns about reading and comprehension, would not necessarily be subject to response set bias, and could be free of confusion about the role of somatic complaints. Interesting work in this regard has been done by Lewinsohn (1974) and Malouff (1984). Each has developed reliable rating scales that could be completed by trained observers or peers (e.g., family members or friends). Little application of this method to elders could be found, however.

SUMMARY

In this paper we have reviewed the development and psychometric properties of the BDI, and presented information about several ways it has been useful in research and clinical practice with older adults. We concluded that the BDI is a reliable index of depression in the aged, and that it has good concurrent validity with SADS/RDC diagnoses. Several studies have found the BDI to be a useful screening instrument and a sensitive indicator of elders' change over time in outcome research. It has also been used to monitor change in symptoms and in overall distress during treatment. While some issues need to be considered when evaluating the appropriateness of the BDI for use in a given instance (e.g., patient's reading level, ability to make judgments about intensity of symptoms, and honesty in completing the questionnaire), in general it is a useful tool that has much to recommend it in clinical practice and research with older persons.

REFERENCES

Beck, A. T. (1967). *Depression: Clinical, experimental, and theoretical aspects.* New York: Harper & Row. (Republished as *Depression: Causes and treatment.* Philadelphia: University of Pennsylvania Press, 1972).

Beck, A. T., & Beck, R. W. (1972). Screening depressed patients in family practice. *Postgraduate Medicine, 52,* 81–85.

Beck, A. T., & Beamesderfer, A. (1974). Assessment of depression: The Depression Inventory. In P. Pichot (Ed.), *Psychological measurements in psychopharmacology, Vol. 7: Modern problems in pharmacopsychiatry* (pp 151–169). Basel, Switzerland: Karger.

Beck, A. T., Rial, W. Y., & Rickels, K. (1974). Short form of the Depression Inventory: Crossvalidation. *Psychological Reports, 34,* 1184–1186.

Beck, A. T., Ward, C. H., Mendelson, M., Mock, J. & Erbaugh, J. (1961). An inventory for measuring depression. *Archives of General Psychiatry, 4,* 53–63.

Beck, A. T., Rush, A. J., Shaw, B. F., & Emery, G. (1979). *Cognitive therapy of depression.* New York: Guilford Press.

Berndt, D. J., Petzel, T. P., & Kaiser, C. (1983). Evaluation of a short form of the Multiscore Depression Inventory. *Journal of Consulting and Clinical Psychology, 51,* 790–791.

Berndt, D. J., Schwartz, S. & Kaiser, C. (1983). Readability of self-report depression inventories. *Journal of Consulting and Clinical Psychology, 51,* 627–628.

Blaser, P., Low, D. & Schaublin, A. (1968). The measurement of the depth of depression with a questionnaire. *Psychiatria Clinica, 1*(5), 299–319.

Bourque, P., & Beaudette, D. (1982). Psychometric study of the Beck Depression Inventory in a sample of French-speaking university students. *Canadian Journal of Behavioral Sciences, 14,* 211–218.

Bumberry, W., Oliver, J. M., & McClure, J. (1978). Validation of the Beck Depression Inventory in a university population using psychiatric estimate as criterion. *Journal of Consulting and Clinical Psychology, 46,* 150–155.

Conde, L. V., & Useros, S. E. (1975). Spanish adaptation of Beck evaluation scale for depression. *Revista de Psiquiatria y Psicologia Medica, 12,* 217–236.

Conde, L. V., Esteban, C. T., & Useros, S. E. (1976). Critical review of the Spanish adaptation of the Beck questionnaire. *Revista de Psicologia General y Aplicada, 31,* 469–497.

Cropley, A. J., & Weckowicz, T. E. (1966). The dimensionality of clinical depression. *Australian Journal of Psychology, 18,* 18–25.

Dessonville, C., Gallagher, D., Thompson, L. W., Finnell, K., & Lewinsohn, P. M. (1982). Relation of age and health status of depressive symptoms in normal and depressed older adults. *Essence, 5,* 99–117.

Endicott, J., & Spitzer, R. L. (1978). A diagnostic interview for affective disorders and schizophrenia. *Archives of General Psychiatry, 35,* 837–844.

Gallagher, D., & Thompson, L. W. (1982a). Treatment of Major Depressive Disorder in older adult outpatients with brief psychotherapies. *Psychotherapy: Theory, Research and Practice, 19,* 482–490.

Gallagher, D., & Thompson, L. W. (1982b). Cognitive therapy for depression in the elderly. In L. Breslau & M. Haug (Eds.), *Depression and aging: Causes, care, and consequences* (pp. 186–192). New York: Springer.

Gallagher, D., Nies, G., & Thompson, L. W. (1982). Reliability of the Beck Depression Inventory with older adults. *Journal of Consulting and Clinical Psychology, 50,* 152–153.

Gallagher, D., Breckenridge, J. N., Steinmetz, J., & Thompson, L. W. (1983). The Beck Depression Inventory and Research Diagnostic Criteria: Congruence in an older population. *Journal of Consulting and Clinical Psychology, 51,* 945–946.

Gallagher, D., Breckenridge, J. N., Thompson, L. W., Dessonville, C., & Amaral, P. (1982). Similarities and differences between normal grief and depression in the elderly. *Essence, 5,* 127–140.

Giambra, L. M. (1977). Independent dimensions of depression: A factor analysis of three self-report depression measures. *Journal of Clinical Psychology, 33,* 928–935.

Golin, S., & Hartz, M. A. (1979). A factor analysis of the Beck Depression Inventory in a mildly depressed population. *Journal of Clinical Psychology, 35,* 322–325.

Gould, J. (1982). A psychometic investigation of the standard and short form Beck Depression Inventory. *Psychological Reports, 51,* 1167–1170.

Hamilton, M. (1967). Development of a rating scale for primary depressive illness. *British Journal of Social and Clinical Psychology, 6,* 278–296.

Hammen, C. (1980). Depression in college students: Beyond the Beck Depression Inventory. *Journal of Consulting and Clinical Psychology, 48,* 126–128.

Hammen, C., & Padesky, C. (1977). Sex differences in the expression of depressive responses on the Beck Depression Inventory. *Journal of Abnormal Psychology, 86,* 609–614.

Harmatz, J., & Shader, R. (1975). Psychopharmacologic investigation in healthy elderly volunteers: MMPI Depression Scale. *Journal of the American Geriatrics Society, 23,* 350–354.

Hirschfeld, R. M., & Cross, C. (1982). Epidemiology of affective disorders. *Archives of General Psychiatry, 39,* 35–46.

Hollon, S. D., & Beck, A. T. (1978). Psychotherapy and drug therapy: Comparison and combinations. In S. Garfield & A. E. Bergin (Eds.), *Handbook of psychotherapy and behavior change: An empirical analysis* (2nd ed.) (pp. 437–490). New York: Wiley.

Kammer, D. (1983). A study of the psychometric properties of the German Beck Depression Inventory. *Diagnostica, 29,* 48–60.

King, D. & Buchwald, A. M. (1982). Sex differences in subclinical depression: Administration of the Beck Depression Inventory in public and private disclosure situations. *Journal of Personality and Social Psychology, 42,* 963–969.

Langevin, R., & Stancer, H. (1979). Evidence that depression rating scales primarily measure a social undesirability response set. *Acta Psychiatrica Scandinavica, 59,* 70–79.

Lewinsohn, P. M. (1974). Clinical and theoretical aspects of depression. In K. Calhoun, H. Adams, & K. Mitchell (Eds.), *Innovative treatment methods in psychopathology* (pp. 63–120. New York: Wiley.

Lukesch, H. (1974). Test criteria of the depression inventory of A. T. Beck. *Psychologie und Praxis, 18*(2), 60–78.

Malouff, J. (1984). Development and validation of a behavioral peer-rating measure of depression. *Journal of Consulting and Clinical Psychology, 52,* 1108–1109.

Mayer, J. (1978). Assessment of depression. In P. McReynolds (Ed.), *Advances in psychological assessment* (vol. 4, pp. 358–425). San Francisco: Jossey-Bass.

Nielsen, A. C., & Williams, T. A. (1980). Depression in ambulatory medical patients: Prevalence by self-report questionnaire and recognition by nonpsychiatric physicians. *Archives of General Psychiatry, 37,* 999–1004.

Norris, J., Gallagher, D., & Winograd, C. (1985). The assessment of mood in older adult medical patients: Validity of two screening scales. Unpublished manuscript, GRECC/182 B, Veterans Administration Medical Center, Palo Alto, CA.

Oliver, J. M., & Simmons, M. E. (1984). Depression as measured by the DSM-III and the Beck Depression Inventory in an unselected adult population. *Journal of Consulting and Clinical Psychology, 52,* 892–898.

Pichot, P., & Lamperiere, T. (1964). Analyse factorielle d'un questionnaire d'autoevaluation des symptomes depressifs. Cited in Beck, A. T. & Beamesderfer, A. (1974).

Reynolds, W. M., & Gould, J. (1981). A psychometric investigation of the standard and short form Beck Depression Inventory. *Journal of Consulting and Clinical Psychology, 49,* 306–307.

Rush, A. J. (1984). A phase II study of cognitive therapy of depression. In J. B. W. Williams & R. L. Spitzer (Eds.), *Psychotherapy research: Where are we and where should we go?* (pp. 216–233). New York: Guilford Press.

Salzman, C., & Shader, R. I. (1979). Clinical evaluation of depression in the elderly. In A. Raskin & L. F. Jarvik (Eds.), *Psychiatric symptoms and cognitive loss in the elderly* (pp. 39–72). Washington, D.C.: Hemisphere Publishing Corporation.

Saylor, C. F., Finch, A. J., Spirito, A., & Bennett, B. (1984). The Children's Depression Inventory: A systematic evaluation of psychometric properties. *Journal of Consulting and Clinical Psychology, 52,* 955–967.

Schwab, J. J., Bialow, M. R. & Holzer, C. E. (1967). A comparison of two rating scales for depression. *Journal of Clinical Psychology, 23,* 94–96.

Schwab, J. J., Bialow, M. R., Clemmons, R., Martin, P., & Holzer, C. (1967). The Beck Depression Inventory with medical inpatients. *Acta Psychiatrica Scandinavica, 43,* 255-266.

Spitzer, R. L., Endicott, J., & Robins, E. (1978). Research diagnostic criteria: Rationale and reliability. *Archives of General Psychiatry, 35,* 773–782.

Steer, R. A., McElroy, M., & Beck, A. T. (1982). Structure of depression in alcoholic men: A partial replication. *Psychological Reports, 50,* 723–728.

Steer, R. A., McElroy, M., & Beck, A. T. (1983). Correlates of self-reported and clinically assessed depression in outpatient alcoholics. *Journal of Clinical Psychology, 39,* 144–149.

Steuer, J., Mintz, J., Hammen, C., Hill, M. A., Jarvik, L. J., McCarley, T., Motoike, P. & Rosen, R. (1984). Cognitive-behavioral and psychodynamic group psychotherapy in treatment of geriatric depression. *Journal of Consulting and Clinical Psychology, 52,* 180–189.

Strober, M., Green, J. & Carlson, G. (1981). Utility of the Beck Depression Inventory with psychiatrically hospitalized adolescents. *Journal of Consulting and Clinical Psychology, 49,* 482–483.

Teri, L. (1982). The use of the Beck Depression Inventory with adolescents. *Journal of Abnormal Child Psychology, 10,* 277–284.

Thompson, L. W., & Gallagher, D. (1984). Efficacy of psychotherapy in the treatment of late-life depression. *Advance in Behaviour Research and Therapy, 6,* 127–139.

Thompson, L. W., & Gallagher, D. (1985, August). *Psychotherapy for depressed elders: Outcomes and issues.* Paper presented at the meeting of the American Psychological Association, Los Angeles, CA.

Thompson, L. W., & Gallagher, D. (in press). Treatment of depression in elderly outpatients. In G. Maletta (Ed.), *Advances in neurogerontology Vol. 5: Treatment of the elderly neuropsychiatric patient.* New York: Praeger.

Vernon, S. W., & Roberts, R. E. (1982). Use of the SADS-RDC in a tri-ethnic community survey. *Archives of General Psychiatry, 39,* 47–58.

Weckowicz, T. E., Muir, W., & Cropley, A. J. (1967). A factor analysis of the Beck Inventory of depression. *Journal of Consulting Psychology, 31,* 23–28.

Yesavage, J. A., Brink, T. L., Rose, T. L., Lum, O., Huang, V., Adey, M., & Leirer, V. O. (1983). Development and validation of a geriatric depression screening scale: A preliminary report. *Journal of Psychiatric Research, 17,* 37–49.

Zemore, R., & Eames, N. (1979). Psychic and somatic symptoms of depression among young adults, institutionalized aged and non-institutionalized aged. *Journal of Gerontology, 34,* 716–722.

Questions

1) Compare the Beck to the Zung (and/or the CES-D). Do the similarities outweigh the differences?

2) Do the factor analyses of the BDI tell us more about geriatric depression per se, or the way that the BDI *measures geriatric depression?*

9/GERIATRIC DEPRESSION SCALE (GDS) Recent Evidence and Development of a Shorter Version

Javaid I. Sheikh, MD
Jerome A. Yesavage, MD

Editor's Introduction

Sheikh and Yesavage review the depression scale specifically designed on, with, and for the aged. *CG* has had three previous articles discuss the GDS (v. 1, #1, pp. 37–43; v. 2, #3, pp. 60–61; v. 3, #4, pp. 57–60). The authors of this chapter review the unique features of the GDS (e.g., a yes/no format, no somatic items) and consider the data of other researchers published in other journals. Of special interest is the section on the use of the GDS with special populations (e.g., arthritics, demented) and the development of a shorter form.

It may be premature to tout the superiority of the GDS. Although its utility as a screening device is fairly well established, evidence on its ability to monitor changes in depression during treatment, or over a long period, is still limited.

Javaid I. Sheikh is affiliated with Veterans Administration Medical Center, Palo Alto, CA 94304. Jerome A. Yesavage is affiliated with Department of Psychiatry and Behavioral Sciences, Stanford University School of Medicine, Stanford, CA 94305.

This research was supported by the Medical Research Service of the Veterans Administration, and NIMH grant MH 35182-02. Dr. Sheikh is supported by research training grant MH 16744-04.

165

INTRODUCTION

Depressive disorders are presently the most common psycho-pathologic syndromes afflicting the elderly (Butler & Lewis, 1982). However, in that age group, a very common reason for failure to treat them is a failure of recognition (Gurland, 1982). Considering the fact that the percentage of elderly amongst the general population is increasing rapidly, the need for prompt recognition of symptoms of depression is readily apparent. Development of the GDS (GDS) was a step in this direction. In this article, we provide data on the GDS from recent studies and introduce a shorter version.

BRIEF REVIEW OF VALIDATION STUDIES OF THE GDS

As the GDS was designed specifically for the elderly, its items were developed after careful consideration of unique characteristics of depression in the elderly (Coleman et al., 1981; Jarvik, 1976; Kahn, Zarit, Hilbert, & Niederehe, 1975; Wells, 1979), as well as of other sensitive issues relevant to this age group (Salzman & Shader, 1978). The scale was developed and validated in two phases which have been described in detail elsewhere (Brink, Yesavage, Owen, Heersema, Adey, & Rose, 1982; Yesavage & Brink, 1983) and will be alluded to briefly here for the purpose of providing background information for the reader.

In the first phase, 100 widely varied yes/no questions were selected and tested for their potential for distinguishing elderly depressives from normals.

Of the original 100 items, the 30 with the highest correlaton with depression were chosen for inclusion in the final version of the GDS. A second phase of validation included two of the more established depression measures, the Zung Self Rating Scale for Depression or SDS (Zung, 1965; Biggs, 1978; Hedlund, & Vieweg 1979), and the Hamilton Rating Scale for Depression or HRS-D (Hamilton, 1960, 1967; Carroll, Fielding & Blashki, 1973; Knesevich, Biggs, Clayton & Ziegler, 1977) All three scales were found to be internally consistent, reliable, and valid as depression measuring scales amongst the elderly. Moreover, as a measure of convergent validity, correlations between the scales were also computed and found to be statistically significant at or beyond the .001 level.

Information regarding the sensitivity and specificity of the GDS was provided in a later study (Brink et al., 1982). They found that a cut-off score of 11 on the GDS yielded a 84% sensitivity rate and a 95% specificity rate. A more stringent cut-off score of 14 yielded a slightly lower, 80%, sensitivity rate, but resulted in the complete absence of nondepressed persons being incorrectly classified as depressed, i.e., a 100% specificity rate. Based on these findings Brink et al. (1982) suggested that a score of 0-10 be viewed as within the normal range while a score of 11 or greater taken as a possible indicator of depression.

These findings suggest that the GDS is a promising screen for detecting depression in the elderly. It is also worth mentioning that the various forms of reliability measurements of the GDS have consistently been higher than those found in the HRS-D and SDS (Brink, Curran, Dorr, Janson, McNulty, & Messina, 1985; Yesavage & Brink, 1983).

COMPARISON OF GDS WITH CES-D, HRS-D, & D-CAL

In a recent study conducted at the Department of Psychology, Wake Forest University, Winston-Salem, North Carolina (Best, Davis, Morton, & Romeis, 1984), 334 subjects, male and female, were given four depression scales as part of a general health and attitude survey for adults. The scales included the Hamilton Rating Scale for Depression (HRS-D), the Center for Epidemiological Studies Depression Scale (CES-D), the Depression Adjective Check List (DACL), and the Geriatric Depression Scale (GDS). Almost half of these subjects were taken from a Family Practice Clinic and were randomly selected from patient records. This selection resulted in a younger group, aged from 45 to 60 years with a mean of 52.7, and an older group aged 66 to 87 with a mean of 73.1. The remainder of the subjects (174) were taken from different community settings with an age range of 52 to 98 with a mean of 77.2. An independent measure of depression, the Rockliff Rating Scale of Depression (Best et al., 1984) which is composed of ten rating scales covering common behavioral manifestations of depression, was also included. The researchers expected the Rockliff scaled scores to correlate with the selected measures of depression. Each scale discriminated between depressed and nondepressed subjects. However, the GDS and the HRS-D were the best predictors of major depression among the elderly, while the CES-D and the GDS were the best in the younger subjects. The authors make the following recommendation: "Researchers who are primarily interested in assessing depression in the elderly would be advised to use the GDS, which is not heavily weighted toward health concerns, and which seems to be especially sensitive to the aspects of depression experienced by the older adults." Since the purpose of this study was to evaluate the appropriateness of assessment scales for particular populations, it has important implications for future research in this area.

USE OF THE GDS WITH SPECIAL POPULATIONS

As a large proportion of the elderly suffer from some kind of physical ailment at any given point in time, a geriatric depression scale should be applicable to both the physically well and the ill. Furthermore, it should have the potential for use with select populations in which the aged are more heavily represented, e.g., the cognitively impaired. There is some evidence that the GDS may satisfy these needs. Using data from a study by Gallagher, Slife, and Yesavage (unpublished manuscript), we found that the GDS differentiated depressed from nondepressed elderly subjects suffering from physical illness. These subjects were elderly arthritics who had been given the GDS after having been classified as either depressed or nondepressed based on a comprehensive clinical interview. The mean score of the depressed arthritic subjects (13.1, s. d. = 7.14) was significantly higher than that of the nondepressed subjects (5.10, s.d. = 4.21), t(47) = 4.94, p < .001). These data indicate that the GDS has validity with the physically ill also.

In another study (Yesavage, Rose, & Lapp, 1981), the usefulness of the GDS was tested in a group of elderly subjects undergoing cognitive treatment for senile dementia. These subjects were classified as demented by criteria of Folstein's (1975) Mini-Mental Status exam. The subjects categorized as depressed by a therapist blind to GDS scores received a mean score of 14.72 (s.d. = 6.13) on the GDS versus a mean of only 7.49 (s.d. = 4.26) for nondepressed subjects, t(41) = 4.4, p < .001. However, Brink (1984) has shown that in severe cases of dementia the subjects may fail to comprehend the questions. This suggests that the usefulness of the GDS might be limited to subjects with mild to moderate degree of dementia.

These studies then provide preliminary evidence that the GDS has potential for application with the physically ill as well as the cognitively impaired elderly.

DEVELOPING A SHORTER VERSION OF THE GDS (SHORT FORM)

Much has already been written about unique problems of measuring depression in the elderly (Coleman et al., 1981; Jarvik, 1976; Kahn et al., 1975; Salzman & Shader, 1978; Wells, 1979). In addition, some other nonspecific factors such as fatigue and poor concentration can interfere with such a measurement by making it difficult for the elderly to remain focused while filling out lengthy scales. The GDS was devised to minimize such possibilities. We feel that the ease of administration and the relatively less time required to complete it compared to most other scales are its important advantages. Extending this line of reasoning further, especially to further cut down on time requirement, we recently developed a shorter version of the GDS. We selected 15 questions from the GDS which had the highest correlation with depressive symptoms in our validation studies. These questions were then arranged in a 15-item, one page, easy-to-understand yes/no format (GDS, Short Form, Table 1), similar to the regular version (Long Form) of the GDS. Furthermore, these were ordered so as to maximize the acceptance of the questionnaire. Of the 15 items, 10 indicated the presence of depression when answered positively, while the rest (Nos. 1, 5, 7, 11, 13,) indicated depression when answered negatively. We then conducted a validation study to compare the Long Form of the GDS with the Short Form. Thirty-five elderly subjects were included in this study. They consisted of 18 normal elderly from the community, and 17 elderly patients in a variety of treatment settings for complaints of depression. The latter group of elderly met the DSM-III criteria of either a major depression or a dysthymic disorder. Both male and female subjects were included and all were above 55 years of age. The subjects were given both versions of the GDS, the Long and the Short Form for self-rating of symptoms of depression. Both forms were successful in differentiating depressed from nondepressed subjects with a high correlation (r = .84, p < .001). This initial data suggests that the the Short Form of GDS can also be used successfully as a screening device for depression. We think that it

TABLE 1: GERIATRIC DEPRESSION SCALE (SHORT FORM)

CHOOSE THE BEST ANSWER FOR HOW YOU FELT OVER THE PAST WEEK

1. Are you basically satisfied with your life? ....yes / no

2. Have you dropped many of your activities and interests?   yes / no

3. Do you feel that your life is empty?   yes / no

4. Do you often get bored?   yes / no

5. Are you in good spirits most of the time? ....yes / no

6. Are you afraid that something bad is going to happen to you?   yes / no

7. Do you feel happy most of the time?   yes / no

8. Do you often feel helpless?   yes / no

9. Do you prefer to stay at home, rather than going out   yes / no

    and doing new things?

10. Do you feel you have more problems with memory than most? ....yes / no

11. Do you think it is wonderful to be alive?   yes / no

12. Do you feel pretty worthless the way you are now?   yes / no

13. Do you feel full of energy?   yes / no

14. Do you feel that your situation is hopeless?   yes / no

15. Do you think that most people are better off than you are? ....yes / no

---

should be especially useful for physically ill and demented patients who are likely to feel fatigued and are usually limited in their ability to concentrate for any length of time. (The Short Form takes an average of five to seven minutes to complete.) Further studies with the Short form of GDS are being planned.

Ease of Administration and Other Desirable Characteristics

As described above, ease of administration, and economy of time are among the desirable features for a depression scale for the elderly. In this regard the Short Form of GDS is especially desirable. In both versions of the GDS, however, the items are tailored for use with the elderly. Questions that might increase the defensiveness of subjects or otherwise reduce cooperation and rapport were avoided.

In addition, the yes/no format provides a simpler task for elderly subjects than the response required in some other scales, where the subjects must estimate the frequency of particular symptoms. Not only does the yes/no format undoubtedly shorten the time required for a scale's administration, it may also bolster reliability to the extent additional choices for the individual simply lead to greater errors of measurement rather than heightened sensitivity.

As elsewhere described (Yesavage et al., 1983), the GDS compares very favorably with the observer-rated HRS-D with respect to the task of differentiating between various degrees of depression. This means that the GDS provides a reasonable substitute when economy of administration is an issue. This is not meant to imply that the GDS provides a substitute for the HRS more generally. Given the emphasis on the subjective aspects of depression, the GDS should not be used for purposes of diagnostic classification. It should be followed up by a clinical interview or a measure of endogenous depression such as the HRS-D if significant levels of depressive symptomatology are found and further treatment indicated. It remains to be determined, however, if the GDS may be useful for measuring changes in the severity of depression following treatment.

CONCLUSION

The data cited show that the GDS (both the Long and the Short form) represents a reliable and valid screening device for measuring depression with elderly individuals. The GDS is also sensitive to depression among elderly persons suffering from mild to moderate dementia and physical illness. Furthermore, the Short Form of GDS is particularly useful in situations where economy of time is required. Although not a substitute for observer-rated scales such as the HRS-D or for in-depth interviews, recent data suggest that it might be the self-rating scale of choice for depression in the elderly.

REFERENCES

Best, D. L., Davis, S., Morton, K., & Romeis, J. Measuring Depression in the Elderly: Psychometric and Psychosocial Issues. Presented at the Annual meeting of American Gerontological Association, Houston, October 1984.

Biggs, J. T., Wylie, L. T., Ziegler, & V. E. Validity of the Zung Self-Rating Depression Scale. Br. J. of Psychiat., 1978, 132, 381–385.

Brink, T. L. Limitations of the GDS in cases of pseudodementia. *Clin. Geron.*, 1984, *2*(3), 60–61.

Brink, T. L., Yesavage, J. A., Owen, L., Heersema, P. H., Adey, M., & Rose, T. L. Screening Tests for Geriatric Depression. *Clin. Geron.*, 1982, *1*(1), 37–43.

Brink, T. L., Curran, P., Dorr, M. L., Janson, E., McNulty, U., Messina, M. Geriatric Depression Scale Reliability: Order, Examiner and Reminiscence Effects. *Clin. Geron.*, 1985, *3*(4), 57–59.

Butler, T., & Lewis, M., *Aging and mental health (3rd ed.).* St. Louis: Mosby, 1982.

Carroll, B. J., Fielding, J. M., & Blashki, T. G. Depression Rating Scales: A Critical Review. *Arch. Gen. Psychiat.*, 1973, *28*, 361–366.

Coleman, R. M., et al. Sleep-Wake disorders in the elderly: A polysomnographic analysis. *J. Am. Ger. Soc.*, 1981, *29*, 289–296.

Folstein, M. F., Folstein, S. E., McHugh, P. R.: Mini-Mental State: A Practical Method for Grading the Cognitive State of Patients for the Clinician. *Journal of Psychiatric Research*, 1975, *12*, 189–198.

Gallagher, D., Slife, B., & Yesavage, J. Impact of Physical Health Status on Hamilton Rating Scale Depression Scores. Under editorial review.

Gurland, B. J., & Toner, J. A. Depression in the Elderly: A Review of Recently Published Studies. In Eisdorfer, C. (Ed.), *Annual Review of Gerontology and Geriatrics, vol. 3.* New York: Springer Publishing Co., 1982, 228–265.

Hamilton, M. A Rating Scale for Depression. *J. Neurol. Neurosurg. Psychiat.*, 1960, *23*, 56–62.

Hamilton, M. Development of a Rating Scale for Primary Depressive Illness. *Br. J. of Soc. and Clinical Psychology*, 1967, *6*, 278–296.

Hedlund, J. L., & Vieweg, B. W. The Zung Self-Rating Depression Scale: A Comprehensive Review. *Journal of Operational Psychiatry*, 1979, *10*, 51–64.

Jarvik, L. F. Aging and Depression: Some Unanswered Questions. *J. Gerontol.*, 1976, *31*, 324–326.

Kahn, R. L., Zarit, S. H., Hilbert, N. M., & Niederehe, G. Memory Complaint and Impairment in the Aged: The Effect of Depression and Altered Brain Function. *Archives of Gen. Psychiat.*, 1975, *32*, 1569–1573.

Knesevich, J. W., Biggs, J. T., Clayton, P. J., Ziegler, V. E. Validity of the Hamilton Rating Scale for Depression. *Br. J. of Psychiat.*, 1977, *131*, 49–52.

Salzman, C., & Shader, R. I. Depression in the Elderly: Relationship Between Depression, Psychologic Defense Mechanisms and Physical Illness. *J. Am. Ger. Soc.*, 1978, *26*, 253–259.

Wells, C. E. Pseudodementia. *Am. J. Psychiat.*, 1979, *36*, 895–900.

Yesavage, J., Rose, T. L., & Lapp, D. Validity of the Geriatric Depression Scale in Subjects with Senile Dementia. Clinical Diagnostic and Rehabilitation Unit, Palo Alto Veterans Administration Medical Clinic, Palo Alto, California, 1981.

Yesavage, J., & Brink, T. L. Development and Validation of a Geriatric Depression Screening Scale: A Preliminary Report. *J. Psychiat. Res.*, 1983, *17*, 37–49.

Zung, W. W. K. A Self-Rating Depression Scale. *Archives of Gen. Psychiat.*, 1965, *12*, 63–70.

Zung, W. W. K., & Green, Jr., R. L. Detection of Affective Orders in the Aged. In Eisdorfer, C., Fann, W. E. (Eds.), *Psychopharmacology and Aging.* New York: Plenum Press, 1973, 213–223.

Questions

1) What are the main differences between the GDS and the other tests for depression?

2) What reasons would there be for using any other depression test with the aged?

3) What kinds of research design would be appropriate to further demonstrate the utility of the GDS?

10/A BRIEF MMPI DEPRESSION SCREENING SCALE FOR THE ELDERLY

David M. Dush, PhD
R. R. Hutzell, PhD

Editor's Introduction

Dush and Hutzell also embarked on a quest to find an easily administered, reliable and valid, simple and inoffensive method for measuring depression in the aged. What is unique about their attempt is that they sought to modify the most widely known psychological test in the world, the MMPI. The result is a brief questionnaire, with a yes/no format, specifically designed for the aged.

Note that the criterion for item selection was the correlation with the full-scale score on the MMPI-D scale and not an independent measure of depression.

In many ways, Dush and Hutzell have given a methodological blueprint for researchers seeking to develop shorter scales. However, they have not established the validity of their scale as a clinical measure of depression per se. That remains the task of future research on this scale.

The aged represent a group with characteristically excessive stressors and constrictions in resources. Kramer, Taube, and Redick (1973) estimated that as many as 20% of this group are in need

David M. Dush is affiliated with Midland-Gladwin Community Mental Health Services. R. R. Hutzell is affiliated with Knoxville, Iowa VA Medical Center.

This research was supported in part by the Veterans Administration Western Research & Development Office, Livermore, CA, and presented at the annual meeting of the National Council of Community Mental Health Centers, Washington, D.C., 1985. Reprint requests should be sent to R. R. Hutzell, Psychology Service (116B), VAMC, Knoxville, IA 50138.

of mental health services. Epstein (1976) suggested that affective disorders alone impact between 10% and 65% of older adults in the communities and hospitals. Depression has been viewed as the most common problem among older adults, as implicated by the observation that, while accounting for only about 11% of the population, older adults account for about 25% of reported suicides (Butler & Lewis, 1977). In a study of 176 homebound elderly patients referred for in-home psychiatric evaluation, Levy (1985) found full symptomatology of major depression as the primary diagnosis in 26%. Only primary degenerative dementia was more frequently observed (48%).

At the same time, geriatric individuals remain low utilizers of mental health services, in spite of their frequent contact with potential referral sources such as community agencies and medical facilities. This may reflect in part reluctance to seek help, but apparently not simply a denial or distortion of symptoms. An important part of the problem lies with failure of service providers to recognize or respond to symptomatology patterns suggestive of depressive disorders. For example, Gurland (1976) found that persons over 65 had the highest rates of reported symptoms of depression, yet were *not* highest in prevalence of psychiatric diagnoses of depression.

A contributing factor to the under-diagnosis of depression in the elderly has been the shortcomings of traditional psychological assessment techniques as applied to older persons along numerous psychometric and qualitative dimensions (Gallagher, Thompson, & Levy, 1980). Raskin (1979) concludes that there is little understanding to date of the symptoms of depression in the elderly or of how these differ from the symptoms in younger individuals. Comparing differences between younger versus older adults on conventional psychological tests is not an adequate solution, nor is simply constructing separate norms. Assessment techniques need to be developed or refined via investigations which can detect potentially unique symptom patterns and item interrelationships for older populations.

The present investigation initiated such an effort, focusing specifically on the need for a brief depression screening test. A screening test holds the promise of broad utilization in health and mental health settings to detect and "flag" symptomatology warranting additional and intense assessment to rule out the presence of an affective disorder or mimicking conditions. Several criteria were considered in constructing the test:

a. brevity and ease of administration;
b. reliability and validity;
c. simple, easily understood format;
d. non-threatening, inoffensive item wording;
e. minimal response complexity.

The Geriatric Depression Scale (GDS) (Yesavage, Brink, Rose, Lum, Huang, Adey, & Leirer, 1983) meets several of these criteria, and it was constructed specifically for older adults. It consists of 30 Yes/No self-report items, a length that the present investigation attempted to improve upon further. The Self-Rating Depression Scale (SDS) (Zung, 1965) also has been investigated with older adult samples (Zung, 1967), but requires a Likert-type response to items (a task which can prove difficult for substantial segments of the elderly population). Other common depression tests were found to depart from more than one of the present criteria.

The present study attempted to produce a short form of the Depression (D) scale of the Minnesota Multiphasic Personality Inventory (MMPI) (Hathaway & McKinley, 1943), the most widely used personality test. While various short forms of the MMPI exist, present intentions differed in the focus on (a) minimal brevity for depression screening purposes and, more substantially, (b) item selection from analyses of exclusively older adults representing a variety of psychiatric and medical disorders.

METHODS

Subjects

Subjects were males at an inpatient psychiatric and geriatric facility for veterans. A total of 147 subjects participated in 4 stages of the test development and validation: item selection (N = 61); cross validation (N = 29); reliability and predictive validity (N = 34), and convergent validity (N = 23). Demographic and diagnostic data for all four groups are summarized in Table 1.

Procedure

All MMPI data were collected as part of ongoing assessments conducted for clinical purposes at the facility. For the first two stages of development, the data were extracted from full MMPIs

Table 1

Characteristics of Subject Samples

Sample Characteristic	Subject Group			
	Item selection	Cross validation	Reliability	Convergent validity
Sample size	61	29	34	23
Age				
Mean	67.00	69.20	68.09	61.70
Standard deviation	6.04	4.55	11.35	12.00
Minimum age	60	65	50	52
Diagnosis				
Depression				
Unipolar	4	2	3	1
Bipolar	3	3	1	1
Schizophrenia				
Paranoid	5	4	1	2
Other	19	7	5	3
Alcoholic deterioration	11	2	7	1
Organic[a]	19	11	17	15

[a]Including a wide range of disorders such as head trauma, senile dementia, Alzheimer's Disease, and cerebral arteriosclerosis.

available in the Psychology Service files. Data presented in the reliability and validity studies were used clinically but subjects were additionally advised that the data could be used for research purposes, and data were collected from those who consented to participate after being provided with information about the study.

Item Selection. In the first phase of the study, D scale responses from MMPIs of 61 subjects were analyzed. Individual item responses for all 60 D scale items were correlated with full scale D scores to determine their relative contribution. The objective was to arrive at a brief short form with optimal power in predicting the full D score.

Cross validation. Data from a second sample of 29 subjects were analyzed to attempt to replicate and refine the observations of the item selection stage.

Reliability and predictive validity. The D scale and the non-extracted short form (D_{15}) were administered, twice each to 34 subjects, across four testing dates. Four possible sequences were counterbalanced ($D - D_{15} - D - D_{15}$; $D_{15} - D - D - D_{15}$; $D - D_{15} - D_{15} - D$; $D_{15} - D - D_{15} - D$). The first administration of each test was separated by 1 to 9 days from the second testing (a median of two days). These data were used for two purposes: (a) to provide an estimate of the test-retest reliability of the D_{15}, and (b) to compare the predictive validity of the D_{15} to the D scale, with the criterion behavior being subsequent test performance on the D scale.

Convergent validity. The nature of the D_{15} was investigated further by examining its correlation with six other related scales administered to 23 subjects:

a. the D scale;
b. The Beck Depression Inventory (BDI) (Beck, Ward, Mendelson, Mock, & Erbaugh, 1961);
c. the Life Purpose Questionnaire (LPQ) (Hablas & Hutzell, 1982);
d. the Philadelphia Geriatric Center Morale Scale (PGC) (Lawton, 1975);
e. the Purpose-in-Life (PIL) test (Crumbaugh & Maholick, 1969); and
f. the Self-rating Depression Scale (Zung, 1965).

RESULTS

Item Selection

Point biserial correlations were computed between each D item (True = 0, False = 1) and the total D score. The 20 largest item correlations are presented in Table 2, along with the percentage of True responses for each item. Notably, True responses were favored for all 20 items, although the most skewed item distribution (#205) still evidenced 20% False responses. False implies greater depression in all but one instance. Nonetheless, item wording was not altered, and the criterion for item selection remained strictly em-

Table 2

The Top Twenty Item Correlations

Item number (form R)	Point biserial correlation	Percentage of True responses
8	.66	64
51	.65	74
88	.57	71
242	.58	71
107	.58	74
272	.57	77
207	.55	74
248	.54	63
122	.51	77
18	.49	72
57	.47	69
131	.47	64
130	− .45	64
36	.44	71
46	.43	69
233	.43	66
205	.43	80
160	.39	54
152	.37	75
9	.35	56

pirical—that is, potency in predicting the total D score. A separate investigation would be warranted to determine if rewording the items to counterbalance true/false response biases would improve instrument performance.

Cross Validation

Potential short forms of the 5, 10, 15, and 20 items correlating strongest with the total D score were investigated. The characteristics of each version and its relationship to total D score are summarized in Table 3 for both the initial and cross validation sample. For the initial sample, a five item test performed well ($r = .83$), and no gain in predictive power was realized beyond a length of 10 items. In the cross-validation, however, considerable gain was evident by going to 15 items, while the added benefit of 20 items was relatively small. The 15-item short form (D_{15}) was selected for subsequent study.

Reliability and Predictive Validity

A new sample was administered the D_{15} and the D scale on alternating days, twice, separated by an average of two days. The order of testing proved to have no significant relationship to any of the subsequent correlations and was disregarded. The test-retest correlation for D_{15} was .81 ($p < .001$), which is comparable to the test-retest correlation for the full D scale ($r = .88$, $p < .001$). Predictable variance increased only from 66% to 77% by using the longer,

Table 3

Performance of Four Lengths of Short Forms

	Five items	Ten items	Fifteen items	Twenty items
Item selection sample				
Correlation with full D	.83	.90	.89	.90
Mean	1.51	2.89	4.56	6.25
Standard deviation	1.70	2.88	4.13	5.15
Cross validation sample				
Correlation with full D	.68	.70	.80	.84
Mean	1.83	3.86	5.76	7.72
Standard deviation	1.65	2.59	3.52	4.38

60-item D scale. The adjacent administrations of the D scale and D_{15} again produced agreement on both the first ($r = .71$) and the second ($r = .81$) occasions, even while these were now non-extracted scores separated by one day.

A particularly useful comparison is the relative predictive utility of D_{15} versus the D scale. This was operationalized as the ability of each to predict later behavior—namely, test performance on the second administration of the D scale. The correlation indicating the prediction of the second D scale score from the first D scale score was .88 ($p < .001$). In comparison, the prediction of the second D scale score by the first D_{15} score was $r = .77$ ($p < .001$). Considering the restriction of range from 60 to 15 items, the D_{15} performed quite well.

Linear regression analyses of the cross-validation data were used to provide estimates of D scale T scores from D_{15} raw scores (see Table 4). According to the regression analysis, a D_{15} raw score of 5 or larger corresponds to a predicted D score suggestive of significant clinical depression (T above 70). Thus, on *empirical* grounds, a D_{15} of 5 or larger is suggested as a cutoff for depression screening purposes.

The performance of D_{15} was further evaluated by examining "hits" and "misses" in using the D_{15} to identify subjects who were or were not clinically depressed based upon the full D score. The 34 subjects from the reliability and predictive validity study were used for this analysis. At the first administration of D for this group, 15 (44%) of the subjects evidenced clinical levels of depression (T ranging from 75 to 111, median = 82). Fourteen of these 15 were also identified as depressed by D_{15}, producing a correct classification of 93% and a "false negative" rate of 7%. Four additional subjects were identified as depressed by D_{15}, but not by D. Thus, the cutoff produced a "false positive" for 21% of the 19 subjects who were *not* depressed according to their D score.

The same subjects were readministered the D and D_{15} an average of 2 days later. While there was some shifting of scores, exactly the same rates of classification by D_{15} were observed. Inspection of the present data suggested that it was not possible to further reduce the false negative rate without greatly increasing the false positives.

Convergent Validity

The final group of 23 subjects were administered the D scale, D_{15}, and five other relevant tests in random order. The intercorrela-

Table 4

Predicting Full Scale Scores from the Depression Short Form[a]

Short form score	Predicted T-score for D
15	108
14	105
13	101
12	97
11	94
10	90
9	86
8	83
7	79
6	75
5	72
4	68
3	64
2	61
1	57
0	53

[a]Derived from linear regression analyses on the cross-validation sample.

tions with the D scale and D_{15} are presented in Table 5. The two forms were similarly related to the BDI, LPQ, and PQC, with the relationships to D_{15} being weaker in each case. The two were equally predictive of the PIL. Interestingly, the largest discrepancy occurred with the SDS, which was more closely related to D_{15} than to the D scale. Aside from expectable fluctuations, the more telling observation is that D_{15} mimics the D scale quite closely in its pattern of relationships to conceptually similar tests.

DISCUSSION

Data from the four stages of test construction and preliminary validation suggest that the D_{15} is adequately reliable, is predictive of the

Table 5

Correlations of D and D_{15} with Five Conceptually Related Tests

	BDI	LPQ	PGC	PIL	SDS
Full scale D	.54	-.44	-.73	-.44	.55
D_{15} short form	.41	-.30	-.58	-.44	.75

full D scale, and mimics the D scale closely in its pattern of relationships to other related tests. The low false negative rate (7%) suggests that D_{15} is efficient in detecting those likely to be diagnosed as depressed in more extensive assessments. False positives were more common (21%), but this is less crucial for a screening test. For this purpose, it is preferable to trade-off a higher proportion of false positives who can be ruled out in subsequent, thorough clinical assessments, to minimize the risk of missing those who are truly depressed, lest they fail to receive the needed clinical attention. The D_{15} cannot be viewed as a substitute for the MMPI or other more elaborate assessment procedures, but its brevity, simplicity, and ease of administration and scoring may promise a widely useful screening inventory for research and clinical applications for the elderly.

There are several cautions for further use or study of the D_{15}. Foremost, the generalizability of present findings to females, non-veterans, general medical, or outpatient populations is an empirical question which remains to be addressed. Male veterans in psychiatric facilities doubtless represent a large proportion of patients routinely administered psychological tests, but the prevalence of under-diagnosed depression among the elderly in general argues for a much broader application of screening instruments sensitive to depression in family practice, community service, and medical settings. Further study of the D_{15} with these populations is a clear area of need.

While the D_{15} performed well across four separate samples, these samples were modest in size. Independent replication of present findings is needed to secure its evidence of validity. It may also be helpful to establish normative data for the D_{15} among older adults apart from conventional MMPI norms. Finally, investigations are needed to empirically test the D_{15} or similar instruments for their potential to identify and facilitate treatment of depression of older adults that is otherwise unattended, especially in non-psychiatric settings.

REFERENCES

Beck, A. T., Ward, C. H., Mendelson, M. D., Mock, J. E., & Erbaugh, J. (1961). An inventory for measuring depression. *Archives of General Psychiatry, 4,* 561-571.

Butler, R. N., & Lewis, M. (1977). *Aging and mental health.* St. Louis: Mosby.

Crumbaugh, J. C., & Maholick, L. T. (1969). *Manual of instructions for the Purpose in Life test.* Munster: Psychometric Affiliates.

Epstein, L. J. (1976). Symposium on age differentiation in depressive illness: Depression in the elderly. *Journal of Gerontology, 31,* 278-282.

Gallagher, D., Thompson, L. W., & Levy, S. M. (1980). Clinical psychological assessment of older adults. In L. W. Poon (Ed.), *Aging in the 1980's: Psychological issues* (pp. 19-40). Washington, D.C.: American Psychological Association.

Gurland, B. J. (1976). The comparative frequency of depression in various age groups. *Journal of Gerontology, 31,* 283-292.

Hablas, R., & Hutzell, R. R. (1982). The Life Purpose Questionnaire: An alternative to the Purpose-in-Life Test for geriatric, neuropsychiatric patients. In S. A. Wawrytko (Ed.), *First analecta frankliana* (pp. 211-215). Berkeley: Strawberry Hill Press.

Hathaway, S. R., & McKinley, J. C. (1943). *The Minnesota Multiphasic Personality Inventory manual.* Minneapolis: University of Minnesota Press.

Kramer, M., Taube, C. A., & Redick, R. W. (1973). Patterns of use of psychiatric facilities by the aged: Past, present, and future. In C. Eisdorfer & M. P. Lawton (Eds.), *The psychology of adult development and aging.* Washington, D.C.: American Psychological Association.

Lawton, M. P. (1975). The Philadelphia Geriatric Center Morale Scale: A revision. *Journal of Gerontology, 30,* 85-89.

Levy, M. T. (1985). Psychiatric Assessment of elderly patients in the home: A survey of 176 cases. *Journal of the American Geriatrics Society, 33,* 9-12.

Raskin, A. (1979). Signs and symptoms of psychopathology in the elderly. In A. Raskin & L. Jarvik (Eds.), *Psychiatric symptoms and cognitive loss in the elderly* (pp. 3-18). Washington, D.C.: Hemisphere.

Yesavage, J. A., Brink, T. L., Rose, T. L., Lum, O., Huang, V., Adcy, M., & Leirer, V. O. (1983). Development and validation of a geriatric depression screening scale: A preliminary report. *Journal of Psychiatric Research, 17,* 37-49.

Zung, W. W. K. (1965). A self-rating depression scale. *Archives of General Psychiatry, 12,* 63-70.

Zung, W. W. K. (1967). Depression in the normal aged. *Psychosomatics, 8,* 287-292.

Questions

1) Why are the MMPI scales not usually accepted as valid measures of psychopathology in later life?

2) How could we explain the data reported in Table 5: the D15 has a correlation of .75 with the Zung, but only .41 with the Beck?

11/ASSESSMENT OF MOOD AND AFFECT IN THE ELDERLY
The Depression Adjective Check List and the Multiple Affect Adjective Check List

Bernard Lubin, PhD
Christine M. Rinck, PhD

Editor's Introduction

Lubin and Rinck review two adjective checklists, the DACL and MAACL. These tests have several advantages. One is that such checklists of several dozen items are usually quicker and easier than tests comprised of an equal number of questions or statements. Another advantage is that these tests can be given in a "state" or "trait" format. Yet another feature is that the MAACL can be used to measure affects such as hostility, anxiety, and sensation seeking in addition to depression.

Unfortunately, the authors have not presented any comparisons between these checklists and other depression scales or clinical measures used with the aged

There is a strong need for reliable, valid, brief, easy to administer, and easily tolerated assessment procedures with older patients. Reliability and validity are important considerations regardless of the age of the patient group, but brevity of instruments and acceptance of the assessment procedure are particularly important when working with the elderly. Although it is probably accurate to attrib-

Bernard Lubin and Christine M. Rinck are affiliated with the University of Missouri—Kansas City.

187

ute some of the underuse of mental health resources to lack of public education (Waxman, Carver, & Klein, 1984) and to the sensitivity of the elderly to negative attitudes toward them by some caregivers (Levin & Levin, 1980; Lubin & Brady, in press), easy fatigability and wish for privacy (Harmatz & Shader, 1975), also are important to consider. Many clinicians have worked with elderly patients who have expressed irritation at procedures that take a long time to administer and are invasion of privacy (Harmatz & Shader, 1975).

Even normal aging with the inevitable physical health problems and loss of close friends and family members is for many people accompanied by increases in depressive mood and affect (Levitt, Lubin, & Brooks, 1983). For a significant proportion of the elderly population, anxiety, depression, and irritation, unfortunately, are severe enough to require professional attention (Smyer & Pruchno, 1984).

The Depression Adjective Check List (DACL) (Lubin, 1981) was developed to measure depressive mood. It consists of two sets of adjectives (Set 1 = forms A, B, C, D, each with 32 non-recurring adjectives, and Set 2 = forms E, F, G, each with 32 non-recurring adjectives) to which the patient responds by checking every adjective that describes how they feel, either "now-today" (state version) or "in general" (trait version). The lists within each set are equivalent, thus, interchangeable. Ordinarily only one list would be given at each session. About two minutes are required to complete each list on the average. Norms for the elderly on the state version are available (Lubin & Levitt, 1979) and norms for the trait version are being developed. Session by session depressive mood scores can be plotted for each patient on the Affect Chart. Patients completing the DACL have indicated that they felt as if someone had asked them "how do you feel?" in an interview.

The Multiple Affect Adjective Check List (MAACL) (Zuckerman & Lubin, 1985) like the DACL, measures depressive mood, but in addition, contains scales for anxiety, hostility, positive affect, and sensation seeking. Also, two composite scores can be computed: (1) DYS = the sum of the anxiety, depression, and hostility scores, and (2) PASS = the sum of the positive affect and sensation seeking scores. The MAACL consists of one sheet on which there are 132 adjectives from which all of the above scores (anxiety, depression, hostility, positive affect, sensation seeking, DYS, and PASS) are derived. Again, studies indicate acceptable levels of reliability and validity (Zuckerman & Lubin, in press). National norms on the trait version ("how you generally feel") are available for an elderly sample, and norms on the state version for this aged sample are being developed.

As the positive affect scale is orthogonal to the anxiety, depression and hostility scales, the MAACL can be used to assess possible concurrent changes in positive and negative affect without the necessity of making inferences from one to the other. The MAACL requires about five minutes to complete, on the average.

The separate state ("today") and trait ("in general") forms of the DACL and MAACL help to offset the growing criticism of several life satisfaction, happiness, and morale type instruments used with the elderly that the time span seems to be ignored (Horley, 1984). With the DACL and MAACL, in addition to either the "today" or "in general" focus, the time span can be altered as needed, e.g., "during the past week", "during the past month", etc.

Occasions arise when it might be advisable to assess mood in older persons who have such impairments as functional illiteracy, visual defect, or inability to write from such causes as arthritis, etc. The reading level of the DACL has been determined to be at the seventh grade level (Lubin, 1981). An advantage of the DACL is that it can be administered orally by an examiner if such a need is present, for it has been determined that there is no difference in mean scores when DACLs were administered in the standard manner, i.e., self-administration, and when they are read orally to the same subjects by an examiner (Lubin, Marone, & Nathan, 1978).

Both instruments, the DACL and the MAACL, have been used in a large variety of clinical, experimental, and epidemiological studies. *Science Citation Index* and *Social Science Citation Index* contain approximately 325 references to the DACL and 800 references to the MAACL. Both instruments would seem to be very useful in any setting in which it is advisable to assess the mood of elderly people. The situations are seemingly unlimited. A few examples are: general clinical assessment, evaluation of medication, assessment before and after institutionalization, evaluation of psychotherapeutic interventions, evaluation of the effects of relaxation exercise programs, etc.

Readers who have access to a large elderly population and would like to collaborate on future studies using the DACL and/or the MAACL, please write to the senior author. Copies of the forms, scoring keys and manual are available from EdITS, Inc., P.O. Box 7234, San Diego, CA 92107.

REFERENCES

Harmatz, J. S., & Shader, R. I. (1975). Psychopharmacologic investigations in healthy elderly volunteers—MMPI depression scale. *Journal of the American Geriatrics Society, 23,* 350-354.

Horley, J. (1984). Life satisfaction, happiness, and morale: Two problems with the use of subjective well-being indicators. *Gerontologist, 24,* 124-127.

Levin, J., & Levin, W. C. (1980). Blaming the aged. In J. Levin and W. C. Levin (Eds.), *Ageism: Prejudice and discrimination against the elderly.* Belmont, CA: Wadsworth.

Levitt, E. E., Lubin, B., & Brooks, J. (1983). *Depression: Concepts, controversies, and some new facts.* Second Edition. Hillside, NJ: Lawrence Erlbaum.

Lubin, B. (1981). *Depression Adjective Check Lists: Manual.* Second Edition. San Diego, CA: EdITS.

Lubin, B., & Brady, K. (in press). Training in geropsychology at the doctoral level: 1984. *Journal of Social and Clinical Psychology.*

Lubin, B., & Levitt, E. E. (1979). Norms for the Depression Adjective Check Lists: Age group and sex. *Journal of Consulting and Clinical Psychology, 47,* 192.

Lubin, B., Marone, J. G., & Nathan, R. (1978). A comparison of self-administered and examiner-administered Depression Adjective Check Lists. *Journal of Consulting and Clinical Psychology, 36,* 339-343.

Smyer, M. A., & Pruchno, R. A. (1984). Service use and mental impairment among the elderly: Arguments for consultation and education. *Professional Psychology: Research and Practice, 15,* 528-537.

Waxman, H. M., Carver, E. A., & Klein, M. (1984). Underutilization of mental health professionals by community elderly. *Gerontologist, 24,* 23-30.

Zuckerman, M., & Lubin, B. (in press). *Multiple Affect Adjective Check Lists: Manual.* Second Edition. San Diego, CA: EdITS.

Questions

1) How could we explain the comparatively low mean depression scores for the aged give in Table 1?

2) How could we explain the comparatively low standard deviations for the aged given in Table 1?

3) How useful would the data in Table 1 be for determining if a given individual is depressed? or if he/she is responding to treatment?

Table 1

DACL (E) Means and Standard Deviations For Various Age Groups

	MALES						FEMALES						CONBINED					
Ages	18-22	23-30	31-40	41-50	51-60	61-up	18-22	23-30	31-40	41-50	51-60	61-up	18-22	23-30	31-40	41-50	51-60	61-up
Mean	8.55	7.95	7.8	8.03	8.25	8.13	8.34	8.35	8.70	8.77	8.37	8.32	8.44	8.16	8.31	8.42	8.56	8.22
Standard Deviation	7.70	4.68	4.3	4.17	4.40	4.43	4.70	4.00	4.28	4.50	4.22	3.87	6.22	4.34	4.33	4.36	4.32	4.16
N	125	257	257	258	240	306	152	282	293	293	238	300	277	539	550	551	478	606

12/ASSESSMENT OF PESSIMISM AND DESPAIR IN THE ELDERLY
A Geriatric Scale of Hopelessness

P. S. Fry, PhD

Editor's Introduction

Fry's scale focuses on a specific component of depression: hopelessness. For several reasons, this may be an extremely appropriate focus. First, consider the fact that the vegetative symptoms may lose their diagnostic specificity in later life. Second, one highly effective treatment for depression is cognitive therapy, which should have its main impact on ideation such as hopelessness.

The author explains the rationale behind the scale, scoring norms, factor analysis, reliability, and validity. The preference for an oral administration and a yes/no response format are consistent with a vast body of experience in geriatric assessment.

Notice that the GHS was constructed in the same way as the GDS, by correlating each item to the total score, thus coming up with a uni-factorial scale.

There is a strong need for a brief and easy-to-administer scale for the assessment of pessimism and cognitions of hopelessness in elderly clients. Recently, an increasing concern has been expressed

P. S. Fry is affiliated with The University of Calgary, Calgary, Alberta, Canada.

Requests for reprints or other correspondence may be sent to P. S. Fry, Department of Educational Psychology, The University of Calgary, 2500 University Drive, N.W., Calgary, Alberta, Canada, T2N 1N4.

about the assessment of hopelessness because of its assumed relationship with depression and suicide attempts, in many inpatient and outpatient elderly. Studies examining the incidence and etiology of suicide (Barraclough, 1971; Grollman, 1971; Resnick & Cantor, 1970) have noted that feelings of sheer hopelessness and pessimism about personal worth and prospects for the future are often strong motives for the development of suicidal ideation and intent in many elderly. These studies have drawn attention to the high degree of futility, anomie, and loss of meaning about life which exists in the elderly. Such pessimism has been attributed to prevailing conditions of loneliness, isolation, and rejection which are often associated with the process of aging and which, in the culmination period of the life span, give rise to a high incidence of depression and depressive disorders. Therefore, the elderly's feelings of pessimism and hopelessness are very important to consider in any program of social intervention, psychotherapy, medication, or surgery.

Although it is probably accurate to attribute some of the underuse of mental health resources to lack of public education (Waxman, Carver, & Klein, 1984) and to the sensitivity of the elderly to negative attitudes of the caregivers toward them (Levin & Levin, 1980), another more recent and feasible explanation is presented by Fry (1983) who argues that many elderly "give up" because of their feelings of hopelessness and pessimistic beliefs that not even professionals can help them in the resolution of their problems (Fry, 1982). Even normal aging with inevitable concomitants of physical illness, bereavement, financial and social losses, is for many elderly, accompanied by increases in pessimism and hopelessness (Butler, 1975; Levitt, Lubin, & Brooks, 1983; Osgood, 1982). For a significant proportion of the elderly population, however, feelings of pessimism and hopelessness often leading to depression and suicide attempts, are severe enough to require professional attention (Smyer & Pruchno, 1984).

In recent years, the relationship between hopelessness and depression has been the focus of a number of studies with adults (see, for example, Beck, 1972; Minkoff, Bergman, Beck, & Beck, 1973; Beck, Weissman, Lester, & Trexler, 1974).

These studies address the need for clinicians and mental health practitioners working with elderly clients, to give increasing attention to the task of developing diagnostic measures for the understanding and assessment of hopelessness themes and cognitions of the elderly. Thus more specific knowledge concerning the elderly's negative expectancies about the self and the future is required. Also necessary is an identification of the affective, cognitive, and motivational components of these negative expectancies. Thus, a Geriatric Hopelessness Scale (GHS) (Fry, 1984) was developed in response to the practitioner's need for such a diagnostic measure. The GHS is modeled after the Beck et al. scale (Beck, Weissman, Lester, & Trexler, 1974) used with adults. As in the Beck et al. scale, hopelessness is defined as negative expectancies toward oneself, the world, and the future. Based on the assumption that the elderly's themes of pessimism and hopelessness are distinctly different from those of other age groups, the content items of the scale were drawn from interview data with 138 elderly subjects.

This newly developed scale has been standardized on a large sample of nonpsychiatric, subclinical elderly subjects unselected for the severity of their depression. These subjects reported a wide spectrum of pessimistic feelings ranging from episodic expressions of hopelessness such as "I've had a hopeless feeling all day today" to "my whole life is futile and there is no way in which anyone can help me."

Overall, therefore, the scale has been validated on community samples and should be differentiated from earlier scales of hopelessness that have used psychiatrically impaired patients selected by the DSM-III criteria.

A major objective of the scale development was the identification of overt and covert themes of hopelessness in the elderly and the assessment of the degree of hopelessness. The scale has 30 items that refer to the affective, motivational, and cognitive components of hopelessness in the subject. There are 15 items that, if marked "true," denote high hopelessness in the subject, and 15 other items that, if marked "false," denote low hopelessness in the subjects (see Table 1).

The scale which has a self-rating format can be administered in oral or written form. If administered in oral format, the elderly subject must be instructed to give a clear "true" or "false" response. Most elderly subjects in Fry's (1984) sample, expressed a preference for giving oral responses to the items.

Although the direction of responding (true-false) to an item on the hopelessness scale varies, the scale is scored so that the higher the score (0–30), the greater the hopelessness or frequency of negative

Table 1

The Geriatric Hopelessness Scale: Items, Scoring Key, and Item-Total Score Product Moment
Correlations

Item	Item-total score correlation
True	
1. If I allow myself to feel hopeful again, I'll probably be letting myself in for a lot more hurt in the future	.59**
3. I might as well give up because I can't make things better for myself or others	.62**
5. All I can see ahead of me is more grief and sadness	.64**
7. What's the point of trying; I don't think I can ever get back my energy and strength	.49*
9. I will always be old and useless	.67**
11. I don't think God will ever forgive me for my useless life on earth	.49*
13. All I fear is God's punishment for my sins	.39*
15. There is no point in hoping that I will meet my loved ones after I die	.37
17. The notion of ever being happy again is unclear and confusing to me	.54**
19. There is no point in hoping that any one here will remember me after I am gone	.71**
21. There is no use in trying to get something I want because I'll be too tired and old to enjoy it if I get it	.57**
23. I've never had much luck in the past, and there's no reason to think I will now that I'm old and tired	.44*
25. I cannot believe that anyone would take an interest in me now that I have little to say that is interesting to others	.62**
27. The future seems very confusing to me	.41*
29. I see no reason why anybody would notice me	.56**
False	
2. I have faith that things will become better for me	.57**
4. Although things are going badly, I know that they won't be bad all of the time	.61**
6. I believe that my days of grief and sadness are behind me	.62**
8. These days there are many different foods and medicine to restore my energy	.39*

Table 1 continued

Item	Item-total score correlation

False

10. Even as an elderly person, I can be useful and helpful to others .68***

12. I believe that God is kind and merciful towards older people .39*

14. I believe that God in His mercy will forgive me for all my sins .39*

16. I believe that after I die I will see my loved one in God's care .38*

18. I believe that we all deserve the best of of life, regardless of age .44*

20. I believe that my family and friends will miss me after I'm gone .44*

22. Although I'm getting older, I have enough time and energy to finish
    the things I really want to do .56**

24. I think I can make myself interesting and attractive to others .31

26. The future is full of peace and hope .34

28. I will get more good things in life than most other persons my age .39*

30. I believe my life has a definite purpose and that everyday I am
    getting closer to achieving it .36

Note. Hopelessness levels: Scores 1-10 = Low; 11-18 = Moderate; 20-30 = High. The answer "True" on the true items and the answer "False" on the false items yielded a higher hopelessness score for the respondent.

*p < .05. **p < .01. ***p < .001.

expectancies for the self or for the future. Using distribution scores on the GHS obtained from community-based subjects between the ages of 65 and 80 years, Fry (1984) has suggested natural cut-off points for three distinct levels of geriatric hopelessness:

1. Scores 0 to 10 denote low hopelessness with few signs of pessimism among normal elderly;
2. Scores 11 to 19 denote moderate levels of hopelessness in elderly subjects who may be indicating a need for help and moral support; and
3. Scores 20 to 30 denote high hopelessness in elderly subjects who are feeling clinically despaired and may need prompt professional help.

RELIABILITY AND VALIDITY OF THE GHS

In order to evaluate the subjects' responses to the GHS, several correlational statistics were computed. Internal consistency of the scale (measured by Cronbach's (1951) coefficient alpha) was .69 ($p < .01$). The Spearman-Brown split-half reliability measure yielded a correlation of .73. Both these procedures indicate an acceptable level of the internal consistency of the scale. The individual item-total score correlations (see Table 1) show moderate to high-range correlations for 26 of the 30 items (overall average $r = .57$, $p < .01$).

Pearson product moment correlations indicated that in the total sample, subjects' age and depression scores correlated significantly with hopelessness ($r = .42$ and $r = .57$, respectively).

The validity of the GHS was evaluated by examining the relationship between the Geriatric Hopelessness Scale (GHS) and the Geriatric Depression Scale (GDS) developed by Brink, Yesavage, Lum, Heersema, Adey, & Rose (1982), and between the GHS and Observer Ratings of Behavioral Depression (RBD). As expected, GHS scores correlated significantly and positively with scores on the GDS (.49) and RBD (.29).

Also, as expected, hopelessness scores on the GHS correlated negatively with positive self-esteem scores on the Tennessee Self-Concept Scale (Fitts, 1965). As noted, the correlational pattern of hopelessness, depression, and self-esteem is consistent with the correlational pattern that has been evidenced in earlier studies of adult hopelessness (see: Wetzel, Margulies, Davis, & Karam, 1980; Minkoff, Bergman, Beck, & Beck, 1973).

Since today's elderly cohorts are not seen to be highly educated, reliability in terms of subjects' comprehension of the items was an important consideration. To ensure item comprehension among the elderly respondents, the readability and comprehension of the items was assessed in a group of junior high school students. This assessment guaranteed that the reading level of the scale items corresponded to that of persons approximately 14 to 16 years or older, and that the scale would be fully comprehensible to the elderly, regardless of their educational level (Fry, 1984).

The 30 items included in the GHS self-rating scale were selected for their relevance to an elderly population from a larger pool of 52 items (32 items that represented thoughts of pessimism about the future, and 20 that represented thoughts of pessimism concerning the present). Factor analysis of the total pool of 52 items yielded four major themes of hopelessness in the elderly: *Factor 1:* A sense of hopelessness about recovering lost physical and cognitive abilities. This factor included concerns about poor concentration, easy fatigability, and decreasing ability to enjoy anything. *Factor 2:* A sense of hopelessness about recovering lost personal and interpersonal worth and attractiveness. This factor included concerns about being useless, dull, physically unattractive, and generally worthless. *Factor 3:* A sense of hopelessness about recovering spiritual faith and receiving spiritual grace. This factor included concerns about obtaining God's forgiveness and love, and hopelessness about the value of prayer; and *Factor 4:* A sense of hopelessness about recovering lost nurturance and respect. This factor included concerns about being remembered after death and being worthy of others' love and respect.

All the factors had factor loadings ranging between .68 and .76.

Thus one of the additional advantages of using the GHS is that it can help in the identification of major themes of hopelessness in the individual's profile. Depending upon the particular theme of hopelessness, the clinician or practitioner could determine whether the most effective help can be given to the elderly client by a family member, clergyman or minister, a medical practitioner, or any other caregiver.

The scale requires only 5 minutes to complete, on an average, and is therefore especially useful with elderly subjects who complain about fatigability during testing.

Clinicians whose practice includes a significant number of elderly patients, and mental health practitioners who need a short, portable, valid, and reliable instrument to screen hopelessness are encouraged to use the GHS for further validity and reliability studies. Compared to the Beck et al. (1974) Hopelessness Scale, it has the advantage of being validated within an elderly population. It has a simple, easily understood format and an ability to discriminate between elderly who are mildly pessimistic about themselves and their world from those who are severely pessimistic and who need prompt professional help in the resolution of their problems. The instrument would be very useful in any setting in which it is advisable to assess pessimistic moods and beliefs of elderly persons. The situations are seemingly unlimited in both clinical and nonclinical settings. A few examples are: evaluation of chronically ill elderly; evaluation of medication, and the impact of a regimen of psychotherapy; assessment of the impact of social support; assessment before and after hospitalization; evaluation of depression as related to hopelessness; and evaluation of the effects of life-review therapy (Butler, 1963). Further validation studies on samples of institutionalized elderly are in progress. The GHS has also been compared with the Beck Hopelessness Scale for Adults in a sample of elderly who attempted suicide, and both measures have been found to be internally consistent.

Practitioners or clinicians who have access to a large elderly clientele and would like to collaborate on future studies using the Geriatric Hopelessness Scale along with existing scales of depression are urged to write to the author.

REFERENCES

Beck, A. T. (1972). *Depression: Causes and treatment.* Philadelphia: University of Pennsylvania Press.

Beck, A. T., Weissman, A., Lester, D., & Trexler, P. (1974). The measurement of pessimism: The hopelessness scale. *Journal of Consulting and Clinical Psychology, 42,* 861–865.

Brink, T. L., Yesavage, J. A., Lum, O., Heersema, P., Adey, M., & Rose, T. L. (1982). Screening test for geriatric depression. *Clinical Gerontologist, 1,* 37–43.

Butler, R. N. (1963). The life review: An interpretation of reminiscence in the aged. *Psychiatry, 26,* 65–76.

Butler, R. N. (1975). Psychotherapy in old age. In S. Arieti (Ed.), *American Handbook of Psychiatry* (Vol. 5, pp. 807–828). New York: Basic Books.

Cronbach, L. J. (1951). Coefficient alpha and the internal structure of tests. *Psychometrika, 16,* 297–334.

Fitts, W. H. (1965). *Manual: Tennessee Self-Concept Scale.* Nashville, TN: Counselor Recordings and Tests.

Fry, P. S. (1984). The development of a Geriatric Scale of Hopelessness: Implications for counseling and intervention with the depressed elderly. *Journal of Counseling Psychology, 31,* 322–331.

Fry, P. S. (1983). Structured and unstructured reminiscence training and depression in the elderly. *Clinical Gerontologist, 1,* 15–37.

Fry, P. S. (1982, July). *Social, affective and cognitive mediators of depression in the elderly.* Paper presented at the Twentieth International Congress of Applied Psychology, Edinburgh, Scotland.

Grollman, E. A. (1971). *Suicide: Prevention, intervention, and postvention.* Boston: Beacon Press.

Levin, J., & Levin, W. C. (1980). Blaming the aged. In J. Levin and W. C. Levin (Eds.), *Ageism: Prejudice and discrimination against the elderly.* Belmont, CA: Wadsworth.

Levitt, E. E., Lubin, B., & Brooks, J. (1983). *Depression: Concepts, controversies, and some new facts.* Second Edition. Hillside, NJ: Lawrence Erlbaum.

Minkoff, K., Bergman, E., Beck, A. T., & Beck, R. (1973). Hopelessness, depression, and attempted suicide. *American Journal of Psychiatry, 130,* 455–459.

Osgood, N. J. (1982). Suicide in the elderly. *Post-graduate Medicine, 72,* 123–130.

Resnick, H. L., & Cantor, J. M. (1970). Suicide and aging. *Journal of American Geriatric Society, 18,* 152–158.

Silverman, P. (1977). Widowhood and preventive intervention. In S. H. Zarit (Ed.), *Readings in aging and death: Contemporary perspectives.* New York: Harper & Row.

Smyer, M. A., & Pruchno, R. A. (1984). Service use and mental impairment among the elderly: Arguments for consultation and education. *Professional Psychology: Research and Practice, 15,* 528–537.

Waxman, H. M., Carver, E. A., & Klein, M. (1984). Underutilization of mental health professionals by community elderly. *Gerontologist, 24,* 23–30.

Wetzel, R. D., Margulies, T., Davis, R., & Karam, E. (1980). Hopelessness, depression, and suicide intent. *Journal of Clinical Psychiatry, 41,* 159–160.

Questions

1) How could clinicians use the GHS as a supplement to the other depression scales?

2) Which of the GDS items are similar to the GHS?

III
THERAPY IN LATER LIFE

13/PSYCHODYNAMIC THERAPY WITH THE AGED
A Review

Nancy A. Newton, PhD
Diane Brauer, ACSW
David L. Gutmann, PhD
Jerome Grunes, MD

Editor's Introduction

Seven years ago, I discounted the utility of psycho-analytic therapy with the aged (Brink, 1979). I am most pleased to admit that the talents and patience of a number of therapists have proved me wrong. I still maintain that strict Freudian techniques are not appropriate for the majority of the aged, and Erikson's theories do not translate well into concrete applications, but modified psychoanalytic perspectives are being used to do some very effective and exciting things in geriatrics.

Newton, Brauer, Gutmann, and Grunes begin with a theoretical review of psychodynamic perspectives potentially relevant to aging (e.g., neo-Freudian, developmental, self-psychology). The single unifying feature is the emphasis on the development of intrapsychic processes (e.g., libido). Each individual fashions different means of managing sexual and aggressive impulses. Although these personality structures are established fairly early in life, the stresses encountered in later life can impair the internal controls that have functioned so well for so long. The authors attempt to describe the potential impact of aging in terms of

The authors are affiliated with Northwestern University Medical School, Chicago, Illinois.

The authors express appreciation to Ms. Deborah Jackson for her assistance in preparing this chapter for publication.

205

an increased focus on the Self, a redistribution of the libido, and regression.

Psychodynamic therapy with elders centers around the importance of developing insight, especially awareness of intrapsychic processes. The authors concede that many elders are not appropriate candidates for such therapy. If there is severe regression or a lack of "psychological mindedness" then the objectives of insight, modification of personality structure, and fashioning more mature coping mechanisms are less attainable.

The fundamental modifications of psychodynamic therapy include an awareness of the importance of the role of the therapist, who must project more empathy and symbolic giving than traditional Analytic Neutrality would allow. The therapist's role must be more active, less formal. Greater flexibility must be employed in issues of scheduling and termination.

Transference and countertransference can take on several different scenarios, dependent upon variables such as the patient's "secret inner age" and societal prejudices.

The authors present the case of a self-reliant, suicidal 64-year-old divorced woman. In depth therapy and that TAT yielded a picture of nurturing as overcompensation for dependency, intellectualization, and sublimation. A combination of supportive and insight techniques were used.

Although *CG* has published little on psychodynamic therapy per se (e.g., v. #3, pp. 48–50), some of the techniques used in psychodynamic therapy have been discussed quite frequently (e.g., reminiscence: v. 1, #2, pp. 59–67, 76–79; v. 1, #3, pp. 15–43; v. 2, #4, pp. 37–49).

Psychodynamically oriented clinicians have contributed to our understanding of psychological processes of aging and to the development of psychotherapeutic approaches to elderly patients. This chapter will describe their contributions in both of these areas. In order to provide a framework for conceptualizing psychodynamic psychotherapy with the elderly, the effects of aging on psychological development and on intrapsychic processes will be discussed. The remainder of the chapter will describe psychotherapeutic process and technique with the elderly patient from a psychodynamic perspective.

THEORETICAL FRAMEWORK FOR PSYCHOTHERAPY
WITH THE ELDERLY

Psychodynamic theorists have viewed aging from a variety of perspectives, applying specific models and concepts from the broad framework of psychodynamic theory. For example, developmentally oriented theorists (Erikson, 1982; Gutmann, 1981; Hildebrand, 1982) have emphasized the unique psychological tasks encountered and resolutions achieved in late life. Self-psychologists (Kohut, 1972; Lazarus, 1980; Meissner, 1976) have focused on the influence of aging on the development of self. More traditionally oriented analytic clinicians (Berezin, 1963; Cath, 1965; Levin, 1965) have discussed the potential impact of aging on intrapsychic processes, such as the functioning of the ego, regulation of internal drives, and maintenance of libido equilibrium.

Despite differences in focus, these clinicians generally share certain assumptions regarding personality functioning that shape their conceptions of aging. Psychodynamic theory is unique in its emphasis on the contribution of internal, intrapsychic forces to the aging process. Although knowledge about the pervasive, external stressors of aging is important, understanding of these external events cannot fully explain their selective impact on the individual aging person. Knowledge about the intrapsychic processes which shape each individual's way of adapting and finding restitution is seen as essential to an understanding and appreciation of the uniqueness of each older person (Berezin, 1963). Intrapsychic factors are also viewed as crucial in understanding the differences between people who continue to function well in late life and those elderly who enter treatment for the first time with newly emerging psychological symptoms.

Psychodynamic conceptualizations of the aging process also assume that late life changes develop out of, and are mediated by, successful or maladaptive resolution of developmental issues specific to earlier periods of the life span. The individual enters late life with a personality structure that reflects a long history of life experiences. Idiosyncratic means of managing internal sexual and aggressive impulses and of coping with external stresses have been established, a well-engrained sense of self has been formed and shaped, providing an internalized representation that guides behavior and experiences, and child, adolescence, and adulthood disappointments and traumas have marked the individual with particular areas of psychological strength and weakness. In late life, the adult confronts age-correlated events (retirement, physical changes and illness, loss through death of friends and family) and internal psychological changes that can re-evoke long-unresolved but defended against internal conflicts, undermine the sense of self, and increase demands on ego resources and defense mechanisms thus requiring a new level of integration and development or resulting in depression, anxiety, or psychotic disturbance.

With these general assumptions as a framework, the following sections provide a brief overview of specific contributions to the understanding of the psychology of aging from the perspective of self-psychology, developmental theorists and analytically oriented clinicians.

Self-Psychology Perspectives on Aging

As a result of childhood, adolescent, and adulthood experiences, each individual develops and psychologically invests in a sense of self. The self may be defined as an experienced constancy formed in early childhood that constitutes a coherent, vital core of personality. Even for people whose investment in the self is healthy and whose self-image is realistic, age-correlated experiences, such as declines in physical and mental effectiveness, restrictions in economic resources and social roles, and diminished genital sexuality and physical attractiveness can attack the essential sense of self and undermine self-esteem regulating systems.

Some theorists (Kohut, 1972; Lazarus, 1980; Meissner, 1976) have suggested that these challenges to the sense of self and the accompanying assaults on self-esteem constitute the essential problem of aging. The magnitude of an elderly person's reactions to a particular loss is dependent, to some degree, on the extent of psychological investment in the lost function. For example, for the aged person whose self-esteem depended on intellectual achievement, failing memory may provoke anger, rage, and depression. Kohut (1972) cites the example of the aging person who, because of brain injury, is unable to solve simple problems. He becomes enraged over the fact that "he is not in control of his own thought processes, of a function which people consider to be most intimately their own, i.e., as a part of the self" (p. 383).

Confronted with an assault to the sense of self, the older person attempts to find restitution. At times, these attempts to adapt may appear psychopathological. For example, regression within the self sector of the personality may serve adaptive functions by preserving one's self-esteem and warding off feelings of emptiness and fragmentation. The retired industrialist whose self-esteem rested upon financial successes may brag exhibitionistically about past accomplishments as a way of compensating for current feelings of diminished self-esteem. The tendency of older persons to reminisce about the past may serve not only to perserve a sense of continuity with the past but also, from the perspective of self psychology, to recreate a time when they felt worthwhile, vital, and competent.

For the individual whose sense of self is fragile, with self-esteem based on illusions of omnipotence and on roles and relationships which served to gratify narcissistic needs, assaults of aging present even greater challenges. When loss of roles and shifts in interpersonal relationships undermine these illusions and disrupt need gratification, alienation from self and others can result. In such people, narcissistic loss can result in compensatory reactions, such as pronounced jealousy, envy of the young, rigid adherence to the no-longer gratifying but previously effective behavior patterns, excessive entitlement, and adherence to an illusion of self-sufficiency (Kernberg, 1977; Levin, 1977).

Developmental Perspectives on Aging

Throughout life, each individual is involved in an ongoing process of confronting both age/stage-expectable challenges and idiosyncratic crises. At each period he can master the challenge, adapting to new demands, integrating the self-awareness gained and thus furthering psychological growth. At the opposite extreme, inability to master the challenge can so strain defensive coping mechanisms that internal conflict and psychological regression result. Late life is no exception to this ongoing process. Aging specifically challenges the individual's capacity for achieving and maintaining intimacy and balanced autonomy, for integrating newly emerging aspects of the self, and for resolving issues related to ego integrity.

Intimacy and Autonomy

Aging can present new challenges to the individual's functioning within interpersonal relationships. The exit of children from the home and retirement serves to diminish the strict instrumental roles within marital relationships, increasing the need and potential for relationships based on companionship and affection. Not only are there external changes, aging people also increasingly emphasize the importance of the affectional, nurturant components of relationships (Roberts, 1979-80). As a result, long-standing problems in intimacy that were avoided during the hectic years of career-building and child-rearing can emerge with renewed force (Hildebrand, 1982; King, 1980).

Aging can also result in crisis in people who have never established an appropriately balanced sense of personal autonomy. Early life experiences which have led to a basic sense of mistrust of others and over reliance on self-sufficiency can make the person ill-prepared to cope with the forced dependency that can accompany physical disability. At the other extreme, older people who have never established a sense of personal autonomy and who have overly relied on others to meet stong dependency needs can also experience acute distress when those others are no longer available. For example, elderly who avoided early adulthood issues of autonomy by establishing enmeshed, symbiotic marital relationships may, when widowed, directly face fears of aloneness and personal inadequacy for the first time.

Emergence of Other Aspects of Self

Late life changes in societal roles and family relationships and the exit of children from the home also may lead to the emergence of other aspects of the self, including long dormant inner potentials (Gutmann, 1981). Older men, who were formerly preoccupied with production and competition during the achievement, career-oriented period of adulthood are confronted with previously repressed and thus newly emerging needs to nurture and desires for intimacy. During this same developmental phase, women become more aware of previously submerged strivings to be assertive and to live out their own needs. The woman's strivings, which had previously been lived out vicariously during the parental years through the husband's career achievements, are now expressed more directly. As a result, some women tend to seek out a new career or other new directions providing self-gratification and fulfillment.

Adults who are threatened by the occurrence of these normal psychological changes and/or whose marriage cannot sustain these changes, may be more vulnerable to developing emotional problems for the first time in middle or late life. (Gutmann, Griffin, & Grunes, 1982). For example, depressive disorders in men may be precipitated during mid-life when their lifelong dependency needs can no longer be defended against by counterdependent lifestyles or by projection of these needs onto maternal figures (e.g., the wife). Increased awareness of their own capacity for affection and previously submerged wishes for nurturance and sensuality not only threatens their lifelong adjustment but simultaneous assertiveness and aggressivity in their wives make the wives less available as nurturing objects and for the husband's projection of dystonic dependency needs.

Shift from Active to Passive Mastery

Another aspect of the developmental changes that may occur in the post-parental period is the shift in ego mastery styles (Gutmann, 1964). Men become less oriented toward coping with stress by producing changes in the environment or in the stressful situation itself and more oriented toward accommodating themselves to the environment. As a result, adjustment is increasingly achieved through changes in perceptions of the self in relationship to the environment. In the Kansas City Studies of Adult Life, Gutmann (1964) found that the majority of men aged forty to forty-nine assumed a stance of active mastery. That is, these men viewed their environment as one that rewards boldness and risk taking and themselves as capable of meeting those opportunities. Their energies and attention were focused on interaction with the external world, and it was to that realm that they looked for justification, challenge, and stimulation.

In contrast, men in the older age groups tended to view the world as complex and dangerous and themselves as accommodating and conforming to outer world demands. As a result, men in the older age groups tended to maintain homeostasis via passive or magical mastery. Men taking a passive mastery stance withdrew from active engagement with the external world and disengaged themselves from feelings and excitement. Rather than achieving objectives through reshaping the environment, these men reshaped themselves to conform to external demands or their own superego strictures. Finally older men relying on magical mastery to achieve adjustment altered the world by perceptual fiat. That is, they seemed to operate on the principle that "wishing will make it so" (Gutmann, 1964).

Ego Integrity

Even in very advanced age and as death approaches, potential for psychological development can continue, although the focus of development shifts. Erikson (1963) has framed this last development stage in terms of ego integrity. Achieving ego integrity involves the emotional integration of life experiences and an acceptance of life as it has been lived. This process involves acceptance that all of one's earlier goals and dreams may not be accomplished, a re-evaluation and reconceptualization of earlier life experiences in light of later ones, and a revision of one's sense of self in a way that is compatible with those experiences. Erikson (1963) believes that developing a sense of ego integrity allows one to "defend the dignity of his own life style against all physical and economic threats" (p. 268) and to face death without despair. This process represents growth and maturation for it allows the elderly individual the opportunity to use a full lifetime of experience to come to terms with the self and world. At the same time, for the elderly person whose regrets about his life are strong, who has never come to terms with inadequacy and failure, and whose idealized life plan has never been integrated with reality, achievement of integrity can be a difficult process, accompanied by bitterness and despair.

Effects of Aging on Psychological Functioning

Whether or not one is able to master the psychological challenges presented by late life reflects a number of factors: maturity of ego functions, nature of personality structure, capacity for interpersonal relationships, tolerance for anxiety and tension, and the ability to synthesize past and present within the current situation (Berezin, 1972; Cath, 1965). Many psychodynamic theorists have suggested that aging can impact on these psychological processes that mediate healthy psychological functioning. Examples of these potential age-related changes are increased focus on the self, redistribution of libido, and psychological regression.

Increased Focus on the Self

Many theorists have reported that frequently with aging there is a shift away from preoccupation with the outer world and toward an inner world orientation. This increased focus on the self can take many forms, including increased preoccupation with inner life, decreased emotional investment in the environment and in others, constriction in the ability to integrate complex impinging stimuli, and greater concern about satisfaction of one's own needs (Neugarten, 1964). Elderly adults increasingly focus on health and bodily functions, inner affective experiences, and past life reminiscences. This increased focus on the self can lead to heightened self-awareness. For some people such self-awareness can facilitate expression of creative impulses. At the same, depression can result from the individual's confrontation with aspects of himself about which he feels shame and despair. As available psychological energy becomes more limited with aging, this increased narrowing of psychic focus to the self may also have adaptive value in that it ensures survival by utilizing remaining energy to meet one's essential needs.

An example of this process is the phenomenon of "exclusion of stimuli" (Weinberg, 1975). Because aging curtails one's capacity to deal with a complex multitude of stimuli, superfluous details of everyday life are less attended to while more attention is given to information that is most pertinent and psychologically relevant to the individual. "Exclusion of stimuli" is reflected in the tendency of many older people who do not hear well to hear "what they should not hear" when issues pertaining to their well-being are discussed. For example, elderly people with hearing deficits may become surprisingly attentive when their adult children talk in hushed voices about nursing home placement.

Redistribution of Libido

Levin (1965) has suggested that losses of late life may necessitate shifting of available psychological energy (or libido) from the lost function into other areas, thus sublimating narcissistic needs in age-appropriate ways. For example, investment in the next generation, increased commitment to society and to larger value systems and use of reminiscence to draw upon the past as a source of gratification can serve as ways to redirect the older person's psychological investment from lost areas to new sources of gratification. Levin also described the problems that can arise in the elderly person's attempts to re-establish libido equilibrium. The older person may be psychologically unable to shift investment into available, potentially gratifying relationships or interests if he remains too strongly attached to the irretrievable object, if all energy is withdrawn from others and invested in the self or in the past, if others also withdraw investment from the aged person, or if denial and resistance to the shift is strong.

In addition to establishing new sources of psychological gratification, the older person must also be able to modify the idealized self and superego expectations in line with the reality of his past and present life, to restructure value systems in line with obtainable qualities (i.e., move from valuing achievement to emphasizing integrity, kindness), and to incorporate a positive sense of aging into the self-concept.

Regression

Many theorists, particularly clinicians who have observed the functioning of the psychologically and physically frail elderly, have discussed the relationship between psychological regression and age (Berezin, 1963; Linden, 1963; Modell, 1970). The term "regression" refers to several phenomena, including the increased dominance of unconscious forces accompanying turning in of libido, the reinstatement of earlier developmental stages and the emergence of more primitive defense mechanisms (Modell, 1970). Although psychological regression accompanies severe psychopathology at any age, some clinicians (Berezin, 1963; Zarsky & Blau, 1970) have suggested that it is more likely to occur in late-life and, at times, may serve adaptive functions for the elderly.

Several age-related factors may interrelate to increase the likelihood of regression. The stresses and losses that sometimes accompany the aging process may cause the aging ego to withdraw from the stimulation of the external milieu, resulting in greater dominance of unconscious forces (Linden, 1963). Simultaneous decline in the integrative, synthetic capacities of the ego compounds the forcefulness of these unconscious drives. As the more mature defensive operations developed in adulthood become less effective, more direct emergence of unconscious drives may occur along with reliance on more primitive defense mechanisms. The elderly person's acceptance and tolerance of these regressive forces may have adaptive value, in that it enables the self to obtain gratification for primitive dependency needs not previously permitted by the superego or ego (Zarsky & Blau, 1970).

A related factor potentially leading to regressive phenomena in late life is the diminution of genital sexuality and re-emergence of more primitive, pregenital oral and anal impulses. While some theorists have emphasized the regressive meanings of this shift (Berezin, 1963), it also may enable the development of an age-appropriate "omnisexuality" in which genital and pregenital modalities are integrated (Gutmann, 1981).

Whether or not regression is a pathological phenomenon is dependent upon the extent to which the unconscious mainstream of psychological activity has been dominated by serious, unresolved problems originating in childhood and the integrity and effectiveness of the defensive barriers against primitive drives that were developed during adulthood (Linden, 1963). In the psychologically healthy older individual, regression can result in access to long-hidden and submerged creative aspects of the self and provide new opportunities to resolve earlier life conflicts.

Not only does the older adult who is experiencing regression provide a valuable arena for the study of unconscious material (Zarsky & Blau, 1970), psychotherapy may be shaped by the nature of regressive phenomena. For example, helping the patient to accept regressive changes may play an important role in successful aging (Berezin, 1963). The therapist's support of healthier, more mature defenses enables the patient to cope with the re-emergence of primitive drives and impulses. If regression is conceived only as an irreversible, inevitable process of aging, it can cause the therapist to have negative expectations regarding treatment of the elderly. Zinberg (1964) has argued that regression, rather than hindering treatment, may actually facilitate a more direct emergence of unconscious material and thus easier access to the patient's basic problems. More recently, Levin (1970) has proposed that maladaptive regression can be reversed through effective clarifications and interpretations and by encouraging patients' efforts to carry out more adaptive behaviors.

PSYCHODYNAMIC PSYCHOTHERAPY WITH THE ELDERLY

The elderly are no exception to the adage that treatment issues and objectives are shaped by the challenges and stresses of the particular phase of the life cycle the patient is attempting to navigate. Many themes that emerge in treatment, such as grief and restitution for loss of loved ones, fear of physical illness and disability, fears and anxiety regarding death, and guilt and despair over the past (Blank, 1974) tend to occur much more frequently with the elderly. On the other hand, desire to change previous life patterns and to get a second chance or a new start (Butler & Lewis, 1977) emerge in older as well as younger patients, although the limited life span remaining may serve to heighten the intensity of these desires, thus increasing motivation for treatment.

As Alexander and French (1946) suggest, treatment objectives for older people may be different from those of younger patients. While the latter have greater opportunity to bring about actual changes in their life situation, older patients may be more open to processes of introspection, in touch with feelings, thoughts and unconscious drives, and motivated to make internal changes. In choosing a psychotherapeutic approach, the important factors to consider are not only the present situation, but also the patient's physical condition, life-style, previous adaptation, personality style, and character traits (Weinberg, 1975).

Many psychodynamic and psychoanalytic therapists have long advocated the use of supportive treatment approaches with the elderly and have provided case material that exemplifies the effectiveness of these techniques (Alexander, 1944; Fenichel, 1949; Grotjahn, 1955; Kaufman, 1940; Meerloo, 1953; Pfeiffer & Busse, 1973; Wayne, 1953; Weinberg, 1975). Within supportive psychotherapy, the therapist can enable the older patient to maintain his/her current level of functioning or reestablish his/her premorbid level of functioning by compensating for failing ego functions and shoring up stressed defense mechanisms, thus enabling the patient to more adequately contain primitive impulses and gratify needs. By providing mirroring and reconfirmation of the patient's strengths in the face of the patient's awareness of declines, the therapist can enable the patient to re-establish a sense of self-continuity and build self-esteem. The therapist may also be called upon to serve as a less critical superego for the overly self-demeaning and critical patient (Meerloo, 1961).

Although the value of supportive psychotherapeutic techniques with depleted, psychological regressed elderly patients has long been accepted, recent case reports illustrate the effectiveness of insight-oriented psychotherapy with psychologically healthier aging persons. In these treatments there is generally very little difference in therapeutic approach and treatment objectives between younger and older adults (daSilva, 1967; Myers, 1984; Sandler, 1978; Segal, 1958). For example, criteria for selecting insight-oriented therapy for the younger adult are applicable to the older patient (Cath, 1982) and include factors such as the patient's diagnosis, personality structure, cognitive resources, "psychological mindedness" and capacity for introspection, and ability to establish a therapeutic alliance. Treatment objectives, including achievement of insight, modification of personality structure, and development of more mature defense mechanisms, are equally applicable to older and younger adults in insight-oriented psychotherapy.

Whether or not age in and of itself serves to impact on the likelihood of the older patient fulfilling the criteria for insight-oriented psychotherapy has been long-debated (Abraham, 1919; Freud, 1905). For example, some theorists have suggested that aging may serve to facilitate amenability to psychotherapy by increasing interest in and tolerance for self-examination. A long life of experience may enable the adult to more easily confront unpleasant truths about himself. Similarly, the narcissistic grandiosity of youth is likely to have been tempered by aging and experience. As Grotjahn (1951) suggests: "Some lessons against which younger people rebel bitterly do not antagonize older people as much. Lifelong struggle is sometimes a good preparation for psychotherapy; it loosens the ground and shatters character defenses" (p. 309). Psychotherapy may also be facilitated by qualities that may accompany aging such as increased capacity to delay gratification and acceptance of the pain that is necessary to achieve gains (Weinberg, 1970).

Modifications in psychodynamic therapeutic techniques with the elderly patient has focused on two general areas—the relationship between the therapist and the older patient and modifications in the framework and process of psychotherapy.

PATIENT-THERAPIST RELATIONSHIP

For many isolated older people, who are bereft of previously sustaining relationships and who have difficulty investing in new ones, the impact of the therapist can be dramatic. The therapist's role as an empathic, trustworthy listener can, in and of itself, serve as a stabilizing influence. Viewing the patient, despite his limitations, as effective and as his "old self", can re-establish self-continuity. By substituting for the losses the patient has sustained, "symbolic giving" can provide gratification for psychological neediness and thus help contain the patient's dependency needs (Pfeiffer & Busse, 1973). If the therapist serves to neutralize nihilistic thoughts and feelings about aging, patients may use the therapist for emotional refueling to restore psychic equilibrium (Cath, 1967). In their study of the process and outcome of brief psychotherapy with the elderly, Lazarus et al. (1984) found that patients identified with their therapist's respectful, empathic and understanding attitude, and tended to experience what their therapists said as reaffirming their view of themselves as competent.

The individual's capacity to establish relationships, including a therapeutic alliance, may be influenced by aging. Older people who have experienced multiple losses with subsequent decathexis from the world may be reluctant to engage. Such patients may have become "misers" of their affections, with fear that their feelings will not be returned (Busse, Barnes, Silverman, Thaler, & Frost, 1955). As a result, they may frequently test the therapist's commitment and trustworthiness. The patient whose negative attitudes about aging and fears about dying are expressed through rage, hostility, and envy of the young may be particularly difficult to engage, particularly if these attitudes are so rigidly held that they persist despite interpretation.

Many modifications in psychotherapeutic technique are directed at building the alliance with the older patient, for example by maintaining a less formal relationship with the patient (Knight, 1979) and assuming an active stance in addressing concrete patient concerns. At the same time, the patient should not be allowed to fall into a dysfunctionally passive dependency on the therapist, but instead encouraged to perceive himself as an active participant in solving problems (Wayne, 1953). Greater flexibility may also be required in dealing with termination issues. For many elderly patients, continued contact with the therapist on a limited, infrequent basis may be more appropriate than a final termination, particularly for patients who have few other relationships.

Understanding transference reactions, the unconscious process wherein the therapist is distorted in ways reflective of the patient's relationships with significant others, can also be invaluable (King, 1980). The kinds of transference relationships that develop, as well as the way in which the relationship is managed in therapy, may differ from younger patients. Whereas unresolved issues with parental figures are likely to be the focus of transference reactions in the younger adult, the older person has a much longer history of many significant relationships, particularly with spouse and children, that may also influence the nature of the transference.

The nature of the transference is also affected by the patient's "secret inner age" (Berezin, 1972). Although to the young therapist, the older patient clearly appears elderly, the older patient's inner sense of self may be that of a much younger person than his chronological age suggests. For example, the person with a life-long hysterical character disorder reflecting unresolved oedipal issues may develop amorous and dependent feelings toward the therapist. Such transference reactions may, however, be particularly threatening to the younger therapist who is uncomfortable with the elderly person's sexual fantasies, perhaps because of unconscious prohibitions and taboos regarding sexual activity in an older person.

The patient's "secret inner age" may also be a factor in the development of a "peer" transference in which the therapist is "transformed into a trusted symbol of the patient's spouse, business associate, or roommate" (Hiatt, 1971, p. 595). Hiatt suggests that this type of transference, in which the patient looks to the therapist for help with decision-making and for sharing of experiences, is unusual in other age groups.

Another factor influencing the type of transference relationship is the extent to which the patient feels overwhelmed by loss and stress. The frail older person confronted with life threatening assaults may perceive the therapist as a strong, powerful parental figure whose protection and power he courts (Goldfarb & Sheps, 1954). In such a relationship, the patient may attribute to his therapist idealized, almost god-like powers, and he may seek to ally himself with this powerful figure. Goldfarb and his colleagues (Goldfarb, 1955; Goldfarb, 1956; Aronson, 1958), working with brain-damaged nursing home patients, suggest that if the frail patient can believe that he has some control and mastery over the perceived powerful parental figure, the transference relationship can serve to re-establish the patient's self-esteem and sense of mastery over a world he has perceived as threatening and uncaring.

Another type of transference relationship frequently encountered with the older patient is one in which the therapist is perceived as the patient's son, son-in-law, or grandson. In an attempt to deny unacceptable dependency needs, the patient may assume the role of the therapist's teacher or mentor (Hiatt, 1971). Grotjahn (1955) has focused on one particular aspect of this type of transference which he labels the "reverse oedipal constellation." When the patient was a young adult, he had to resolve conscious and unconscious feelings of envy, hostility, and fear toward parental figures; similar feelings may now emerge in relation to younger adults who are now perceived in the more powerful role. The transference relationship can provide an opportunity for the older patient to work through these feelings of envy and rage towards the adult child. Grotjahn suggests that this can provide the patient with the opportunity "to analyze in the transference relationship the Oedipus complex, but this time in reverse. The father should not submit to the son, nor should he kill him like the father of Oedipus tried to do. The father should realize that his life may be continued in the son" (1955, p. 423).

Countertransference

The reluctance of many mental health professionals to treat older patients and pessimism regarding their responsiveness to psychotherapy may be reflective of the negative countertransference feelings aroused by the elderly. Because these countertransference reactions are shaped by social-cultural values, prejudices, and stereotypes, as well as unconscious remnants of the therapist's early parental interactions, countertransference feelings aroused by older adults can be powerful and strongly engrained.

The therapist views the older patient through a filter that is colored by his own fears about aging and agedness as well as by his particular early life experiences with parents and grandparents. For example, inability to accept the older adult's sexuality may reflect not only generalized discomfort with fantasies about parental sex, but also unresolved Oedipal fears and fantasies. Unconscious anger and unresolved feelings of revenge against parents because of the therapist's previous submissive childhood stance can be acted out against the aging patient (Grotjahn, 1955). On the other hand, idealization of the elderly can serve as a defense against that unconscious rage, resulting in an inappropriate need to see the patient as strong and/or causing the therapist to assume an overly protective, infantilizing stance toward the patient.

The particular nature of the patient-therapist relationship is likely to arouse specific countertransference feelings. The elderly patient can present a vivid, and sometimes painful image of the aging process, thus forcing the therapist to confront his own feelings about aging and death. Just as the therapist's sense of personal omnipotence may be assaulted, so may his narcissistic investment in his powers as a therapist. Working with the elderly person who is facing death or disability may be frustrating and undermine the therapist's feelings of competency and potency. The therapist may find it difficult to invest in the frail elderly patient, for fear that the patient may die during the course of treatment. Or, the therapist may be frightened by the dependency and strong therapeutic bond that may form with the lonely, frightened, or depressed older person who has little opportunity for developing alternative attachments (Zinberg, 1964).

These countertransference feelings may obstruct the therapeutic process and elderly patients may be astute at detecting them. As Hiatt (1971) suggests, "the older patient has spent a lifetime sizing up other persons. Many can spot a 'phony' and it is useless to play games with them" (p. 597).

Framework and Processes of Psychotherapy

In contrast to younger patients, greater flexibility may be required in psychotherapy with the elderly. This applies to the structure of psychotherapy (for example, the frequency and duration of sessions, degree of contact with family members and collateral community agencies) and to the psychotherapeutic process. Because the older patient is increasingly vulnerable to destabilizing external crisis, during some periods the therapist's primary function may be to shore up defenses and gratify dependency needs while during other periods the patient may be open to introspection and eager for increased self-awareness.

Frequently, the older patient enters treatment during a time of psychological crisis. Defense mechanisms are stressed and thus ineffective, self-esteem is low, and the patient may be in a state of despair. As a result, a long initial period of treatment in which mirroring of the patient's strengths, encouragement of adaptive, self-enhancing behaviors, and opportunity for ventilation of affect may be required before the patient will be psychologically available for more insight-oriented psychotherapy. Thus, sometimes the older patient's capacity for introspection and increased self-understanding cannot be accurately assessed until this initial treatment phase has been completed.

Flexibility in approach is also essential when treating different patients, even when the goal of the therapeutic intervention is similar. For example symbolic replacement of the patient's losses may call for the therapist to take a sympathetic, TLC approach with one patient while such an approach might be disastrous with the next patient (Finkel, 1982).

Many clinicans (Pfeiffer & Busse, 1973; Wayne, 1953; Weinberg, 1975; Yesavage & Karasu, 1982) have stressed the need for the therapist to take a more active stance in treating the elderly patient. The older patient, who may be more accommodating, more unfamiliar with psychotherapy, and more intimidated by this process than the younger patient, may be more likely to look to the therapist for direction (Abraham, 1953). The therapist may need to assume greater initiative in probing and identifying areas of conflict and treatment goals (Pfeiffer & Busse, 1973).

The educational component of psychotherapy may also be of importance in the treatment of the elderly patient. For example, interpretations may take on a more educational cast. Providing information about the aging process can reassure the patient as to the normality of his internal reactions to aging and external stresses.

Reminiscence

Life review appears to be a naturally occurring phenomenon in the aged and many clinicians (Butler & Lewis, 1977; Grunes, 1981; Kaminsky, 1984) have stressed the use and value of the reminiscence process in psychotherapy with the elderly. In order to enable the older patient to remember clearly and use this remembering process therapeutically, the therapist must be empathic and nonjudgmental, allow himself to perceive the patient as he existed in the past as well as the present, and actively work with the patient to recover memories (Grunes, 1981). Engaging in an active reminiscence process can serve many functions for the elderly patient. Reinvestment in the self and experiences of the past can re-establish a sense of self-worth and self-continuity as well as compensate for the less gratifying present. Discharge of affect associated with past painful experiences can enable the patient to master the past and thus more freely face the present and future. The process of putting one's life in order and gaining perspective on oneself and one's life's experiences contributes to preparatory processes for death.

A related phenomenon that can be facilitated by psychotherapy is the mourning-liberation process (Pollock, 1981). By enabling the patient to mourn lost, unobtainable, or never obtained parts of the self, unfulfilled hopes and aspirations, and lost relationships, liberation from the past can occur. This process can enable the patient to better face the reality of the present, thus allowing the development of new relationships, interests, and activities.

CASE EXAMPLE OF PSYCHODYNAMIC TREATMENT WITH THE ELDERLY

Mrs. G. illustrates the role played by late life stresses in pressing for the "playing through the chorus again of one's earlier problems" (Hiatt, 1971, p. 591). Previously adaptable resolutions to issues such as automony and achievement of environmental mastery may now be challenged in new ways. For example, many people who experience traumatic losses, or deprivations in childhood are able, in adulthood, to develop life structures which enable them to compensate for or meet their needs, thus avoiding felt psychological distress. At the same time, when these external structures break down in late life, these people are vulnerable to the emergence of underlying, still primitive and never integrated, psychological needs that have been successfully defended against previously. In Mrs. G., age-expectable late life stresses (physical illness) highlighted long-standing conflicts regarding issues of dependency and undermined the effectiveness of immature, but previously effective, coping mechanisms.

Mrs. G. was a 64-year-old divorced woman who was referred for psychiatric treatment during a medical hospitalization after she revealed an elaborate, well-planned, suicide plan. She reported to her physician that following the upcoming holidays, she planned to travel to Bermuda where she lived in the past, overdose on some of her many medications, and die on the beach. Friends, who knew of this plan, had agreed to care for her dog; and her only child had agreed to dispose of her ashes as she wished. Mrs. G. reported that she no longer wished to live because the quality of her life had declined due to health and financial problems. Although presented as a rational decision, Mrs. G's suicidal ideation appeared inappropriate. Her medical problems were serious, but her functioning was in most ways unaffected and her physician felt that improved self-care could at least stabilize her physical condition. Thus, the issue facing the therapist was to understand the meaning of Mrs. G's behavior in such a way as to determine treatment interventions.

At her first outpatient psychotherapy session, Mrs. G. appeared a lively, energetic woman who quickly took command of the interview, vehemently attacking the psychiatrist who had interviewed her during her hospitalization and recommended psychiatric treatment. She reported a generally successful and fulfilling adult life prior to onset of major medical problems. She had been a successful business woman, who had enjoyed her work, travelled widely, and lived abroad for periods of time. Although she only had a high school education, she was well-read and well-informed, interested in the arts and community activities. She had many friends, but had focused her attentions on "wanderers." These were generally homeless young people with whom she had played a charismatic-mentoring role. Mrs. G. reported less success in maintaining long-term relationships with men. Her marriage had been brief, and Mrs. G. reported that although she had been sexually active she had always chosen "bad" men.

Thus Mrs. G. presents herself as an active, commanding woman who invests tremendous energy in coping with the demands of life. External frustrations are to her exciting challenges. She is clearly comfortable with a caretaking role towards others, but much less at ease in relationships that demand trust and caretaking from others. However, there was also a rigidity and fragility about her self-presentation. She worked hard to convey herself as in charge.

It is not surprising then that Mrs. G.'s memories of her early life revealed another side to this complex woman, confirming not only the rigid, well-engrained nature of Mrs. G.'s self-reliance but also the early roots of her inability to trust and rely on others. Her father had been killed when she was 3, leading her mother to place Mrs. G. and her two siblings in an orphanage. The orphanage was so poorly run that both of Mrs. G.'s siblings soon died. Mrs. G.'s own survival was dependent on her strength and wiliness in fighting for self-preservation—a skill that had remained her strength throughout adulthood as long as the fight was against external obstacles.

Psychological testing indicated that underlying this "survivor" stance were prevalent longings for nurturance and caretaking, organized and expressed on a very primitive oral level. The extent and primitiveness of this needfulness is so frightening to Mrs. G. that she cannot allow herself to directly experience it. For example, in responding to a TAT stimulus that depicts an adult woman and a girl sitting on a couch, Mrs. G. said:

> A mother reading to her child. But I'm not in it, I walked past on a dark street and caught a glimpse of it, of this happening.

The girl saw it and that's what turned her head toward the window. She saw me walk by and look in . . . Strange this has no meaning—I guess because my mother never read to me. Didn't have a chance to. This is alien to me. I'm outside looking through the window, glancing through the window and moving on because it has no meaning. The girl looked out and saw me and it registered momentarily and then she turned back and paid attention to what her mother was reading and I kept walking in the dark. You know I always wanted a pair of slippers like that when I was a kid. Never got them. (laughed) We had the hand-me-down slippers and clothes and everything at the orphanage and you never got new ones. I didn't even get hand-me-downs like that. I always wanted them. (laughed)

Although never able to integrate these needs for nurturance in a mature way or to resolve the issues of basic trust remaining from very early deprivation, Mrs. G. was able to cope effectively as an adult by: (1) establishing a life structure that enabled her to maintain an overcoping, counterdependent stance; (2) meeting her nurturance needs through incorporation of food and of men in purely sexual relationships; (3) using a strong, rigid, intellectualized system of justification to avoid acknowledging her longings; and (4) sublimation of her sadness and despair through poetry.

When confronted with physical disability that signalled her body's failure and prevented maintenance of this lifestyle, Mrs. G. approached this trauma by again attempting to gain control and take charge through a dramatic, well-articulated suicide plan. At the same time, the conflicts revolving around her strong desire for nurturance and long-standing mistrust of others came closer to the surface, making it difficult for this plan in and of itself to prevent emergence of depression, sadness, and anxicty. The challenges of late lifc have led to direct emergence of unresolved earlier life issues and long-standing conflicts.

The treatment of Mrs. G. illustrates the multidimensional nature of the psychotherapeutic process with the older patient. Despite her initial rage at referral for psychiatric treatment, Mrs. G. was also aware of and frightened by desires for interpersonal closeness. Thus, she was able to ally with a therapist who both provided emotional support and conveyed respect for Mrs. G.'s need for control and autonomy. Within this relationship, feelings of despair that had been masked by her superficially commanding stance were gradually expressed, with appropriate mourning of the many losses in her life.

Both supportive and insight-oriented approaches have been interwoven into the treatment process. Encouragement of her coping efforts, viewing Mrs. G. as a talented and special person, and sharing her life experiences have enabled her to more effectively use her psychological strengths to gain a sense of mastery over the current life stresses and regain a sense of her own value despite her physical illness. At the same time, long-standing personality conflicts have been gradually confronted. For example, reminiscence about her childhood, interpretation of dreams, and exploration of strongly ambivalent feelings toward her still-living mother have enabled Mrs. G. to come to terms with that relationship, and thus with herself, in a more mature way.

CONCLUSIONS

The older patient frequently enters psychotherapy in a state of despair, reflecting difficulty in confronting age-related external stresses and in integrating internal changes. Psychodynamic theory provides a unique understanding of the intrapsychic life of this patient, the complex interweaving of internal and external factors, and the individual patient's particular psychological strengths and weaknesses. This framework can provide a deeper understanding of the patient's symptoms and seemingly pathological behavior, thus facilitating the development of an appropriate treatment approach.

For many elderly patients, insight-oriented psychotherapy provides the opportunity to meaningfully integrate a lifetime of experience while fostering self-understanding and resolution of old and new conflicts. This process can open new avenues for personal growth and development, even in the very last years of life. For many other elderly patients, supportive psychotherapy can shore up stressed defenses and coping mechanisms and re-establish a sense of self-worth and measure of control over their environment. In other situations, environmental manipulation that is based on a thoughtful understanding of the person's needs can serve to temper a crisis confronting both the patient and his family. It is this understanding of the uniqueness of each individual, respect for the diversity that exists between older people and emphasis on the importance of therapeutic flexibility that is the focus of psychodynamic thought and its particular contribution to the aging process.

REFERENCES

Abraham, K. (1953). *The applicability of psychoanalytic treatment to patients at an advanced age.* (In selected papers). New York: Basic Books.

Alexander, F. G. (1944). The indications for psychoanalytic therapy. *Bulletin of the New York Academy of Medicine, 20,* 319–344.

Alexander, F. G., & French, T. M. (1946). *Psychoanalytic therapy: Principles and applications.* New York: Ronald Press.

Aronson, M. J. (1958). Psychotherapy in a home for the aged. *Archives of Neurology and Psychiatry, 79,* 671–674.

Atkin, S. (1940). Discussion: Old age and aging: The psychoanalytic point of view. *American Journal of Orthopsychiatry, 10,* 73–84.

Berezin, M. A. (1963). Some intrapsychic aspects of aging. In N. E. Zinberg & I. Kaufman (Eds.), *Normal psychology of the aging process.* New York: International Universities Press.

Berezin, M. A. (1972). Psychodynamic considerations of aging and the aged: An overview. *American Journal of Psychiatry, 128,* 1483–1491.

Blank, M. L. (1974). Raising the age barrier to psychotherapy. *Geriatrics, 29,* 141–148.

Blau, D., & Berezin, M. A. (1982). Neuroses and character disorders. *Journal of Geriatric Psychiatry, 15,* 55–97.

Busse, E., Barnes, R. H., Silverman, A. J., Thaler, M., & Frost, L. L. (1955). Studies of the processes of aging. X: The strengths and weaknesses of psychic functioning in the aged. *American Journal of Psychiatry, 111,* 896–901.

Butler, R., & Lewis, M. I. (1977). *Aging and mental health: Positive psychological approaches.* 2nd Ed. St. Louis: Mosby.

Cath, S. H. (1965). Some dynamics of middle and later years: A study in depletion and restitution. In M. A. Berezin & S. H. Cath (Eds.), *Geriatric psychiatry: Grief, loss and emotional disorders in the aging process.* New York: International Universities Press.

Cath, S. (1966). Beyond depression—The depleted state: A study in ego psychology in the aged. *Canadian Psychiatric Association Journal, 2,* 329–339.

Cath, S. H. (1967). Persistence of early emotional problems in a seventy-year-old woman: Discussion. *Journal of Geriatric Psychiatry, 1,* 67–71.

Cath, S. H. (1976). Functional disorders. In L. Bellak & T. B. Karasu (Eds.), *Geriatric psychiatry: A handbook for psychiatry and primary care physicians,* New York: Grune & Stratton.

Cath, S. H. (1982). Psychoanalysis and psychoanalytic psychotherapy of the older patient. *Journal of Geriatric Psychiatry, 15,* 43–53.

DaSilva, G. (1967). The loneliness and death of an old man: Three years' psychotherapy of an eighty-one year old depressed patient. *Journal of Geriatric Psychiatry, 1,* 5–27.

Erikson, E. H. (1963). *Childhood and society.* New York: W. W. Norton.

Erikson, E. H. (1982). *The life cycle completed.* New York: W. W. Norton & Co.

Fenichel, O, (1945). *The psychoanalytic theory of neurosis.* New York: W. W. Norton.

Finkel, S. (1982). Psychotherapy in the elderly. In C. Eisdorfer & W. E. Fann (Eds.) *Treatment of psychopathology in the aging.* New York: Springer Publishing Co.

Freud, S. (1905). On psycho-therapy. In *Standard Edition,* 7:257–268.

Goldfarb, A. I. (1955). Psychotherapy of aged persons. IV: One aspect of the psychodynamics of the therapeutic situation with aged patients. *Psychoanalytic Review, 42,* 180–187.

Goldfarb, A. I. (1956). Psychotherapy of the aged: The use and value of an adaptational frame of reference. *Psychoanalytic Review, 43,* 68–81.

Goldfarb, A. I., & Sheps, J. (1954). Psychotherapy of the aged. III: Brief therapy of interrelated psychological and somatic disorders. *Psychosomatic Medicine, 16,* 200–219.

Grotjahn, M. (1951). Some analytic observations about the process of growing old. *Psychoanalysis and the Social Sciences, 3,* 301–312.

Grotjahn, M. (1955). Analytic psychotherapy with the elderly. *Psychoanalytic Review, 42,* 419–427.

Grunes, J. (1981). Reminiscences, regression and empathy—A psychotherapeutic approach to the impaired elderly. In S. I. Greenspan & G. H. Pollock (Eds.), *The course of life: Psychoanalytic contributions toward understanding personality development. Vol. III: Adulthood and the aging process.* Washington, D.C.: Government Printing Office.

Gutmann, D. (1964). An exploration of ego configurations in middle and later life. In B. L. Neugarten (Ed.), *Personality in middle and late life.* New York: Atherton Press.

Gutmann, D. (1981). Psychoanalysis and aging: A developmental view, In S. I. Greenspan & G. H. Pollock (Eds.), *The course of life: Psychoanalytic contributions toward understanding personality development. Vol. III: Adulthood and the aging process.* Washington, D.C.: U.S. Government Printing Office.

Gutmann, D. L., Griffin, B., & Grunes, J. (1982). Developmental contributions to the late-onset affective disorder. In O. B. Brim & P. B. Balters (Eds.), *Life-span development and behavior, Vol. 4.* New York: Academic Press, Inc.

Hiatt, H. (1971). Dynamic psychotherapy with the aging patient. *American Journal of Psychotherapy, 25,* 591–600.

Hildebrand, H. P. (1982). Psychotherapy with older patients. *British Journal of Medical Psychology, 55,* 19–28.

Kaufman, M. R. (1940). Old age and aging. The psychoanalytic point of view. *American Journal of Orthopsychiatry, 10,* 73–84.

Kaminsky, M. (ed.). (1984). *The uses of reminiscence: New ways of working with older adults.* New York: The Haworth Press.

Kernberg, O. (1977). Normal psychology of the aging process-revisited. II. Discussion. *Journal of Geriatric Psychiatry, 10,* 27–45.

King, P. (1980). The life cycle as indicated by the nature of the transference in the psychoanalysis of the middle-aged and the elderly. *International Journal of Psycho-Analysis, 61,* 153–160.

Knight, B. (1979). Psychotherapy and behavior change with the non-institutionalized aged. *International Journal of Aging and Human Development, 9,* 221–236.

Kohut, H. (1972). Thoughts on narcissism and narcissistic rage. *Psychoanalytic Study of the Child, 27,* 360–400.

Lazarus, L. W. (1980). Self psychology and psychotherapy with the elderly: Theory and practice. *Journal of Geriatric Psychiatry, 13,* 69–88.

Lazarus, L. W., Groves, L., Newton, N., et al. (1984). Brief psychotherapy with the elderly: A review and preliminary study of process and outcome. In L. W. Lazarus (Ed.), *Clinical approaches to psychotherapy with the elderly.* Washington, D.C.: American Psychiatric Press, Inc.

Levin, S. (1965). Some comments on the distribution of narcissistic and object libido in the aged. *International Journal of Psychoanalysis, 46,* 200–208.

Levin, S. (1970). The understanding and management of narcissistic regression and dependency in an elderly woman observed over an extended period of time. Discussion. *Journal of Geriatric Psychiatry, 3,* 177–180.

Levin, S. (1977). Normal psychology of the aging process revisited-II. *Journal of Geriatric Psychiatry, 10,* 3–7.

Linden, M. E. (1963). Regression and recession in the psychoses of the aging. In M. A. Berezin & S. H. Cath (Eds.), *Normal psychology of the aging process.* New York: International Universities Press, Inc.

Meerloo, J. A. M. (1953). Contributions of psychoanalysis to the problems of the aged. In M. Heimann (Ed.), *Psychoanalysis and social work.* New York: International Universities Press.

Meerloo, J. M. (1961). Modes of psychotherapy in the aged. *Journal of the American Geriatrics Society, 9,* 225–234.

Meissner, W. W. (1976). Normal psychology of the aging process revisited-I: Discussion. *Journal of Geriatric Psychiatry, 9,* 151–159.

Modell, A. H. (1970). Aging and psychoanalytic theories of regression. *Journal of Geriatric Psychiatry, 3,* 139–146.

Myers, W. A. (1984). *Dynamic therapy of the older patient.* New York: Jason Aronson, Inc.

Neugarten, B. L. (1964). *Personality in middle and late life: Empirical studies.* New York: Atherton Press.

Pfeiffer, E., & Busse, E. W. (1973). Mental disorders in later life—Affective disorders; paranoid, neurotic, and situational reactions. In E. W. Busse, & E. Pfeiffer (Eds.), *Mental illness in later life.* Washington, D.C.: American Psychiatric Association.

Pollock. G. H. (1981). Aging or aged: Development or pathology. In S. I. Greenspan & G. H. Pollock (Eds.), *The course of life: Psychoanalytic contributions toward understanding personality development. Vol. III: Adulthood and the aging process.* Washington, D.C.: U.S. Government Printing Office.

Roberts, W. L. (1979-80). Significant elements in the relationship of long married couples. *International Journal of Aging and Human Development, 10,* 165–172.

Sandler, A. M. (1978). Psychoanalysis in later life. Problems in the psychoanalysis of an aging narcissistic patient. *Journal of Geriatric Psychiatry, 11,* 5–36.

Savitsky, E., & Goldstein, R. (1983). Psychotherapy of the elderly. *Journal of Geriatric Psychiatry 16,* 39–85.

Segal, H. (1958). Fear of death. Notes on the analysis of an old man. *International Journal of Psycho-Analysis, 39,* 178–181.

Wayne, G. J. (1953). Modified psychoanalytic therapy in senescence. *Psychoanalytic Review, 40,* 99–116.

Weinberg, G. (1970). *The action approach.* New York: New American Library.

Weinberg, J. (1975). Geriatric Psychiatry. In A. M. Freedman, H. L. Kaplan, & B. J. Sadock (Eds.), *Comprehensive textbook of psychiatry,* 2nd ed., vol. 2. Baltimore: Williams and Wilkins.

Yesavage, J. A. & Karasu, T. B. (1982). Psychotherapy with elderly patients. *American Journal of Psychotherapy, 36,* 41–55.

Zarsky, E. L. & Blau, D. (1970). The understanding and management of narcissistic regression and dependency in an elderly woman observed over an extended period of time. *Journal of Geriatric Psychiatry, 3,* 160–176.

Zinberg, N. W. (1964). Psychoanalytic consideration of aging. *Journal of the American Psychoanalytic Association, 12,* 151–159.

Questions

1) What kinds of patients would probably do well in Psychodynamic Therapy? Who would be inappropriate candidates?

2) What additional testing could have been applied in the case of Mrs. G.?

3) How would psychodynamic therapy handle a patient who was severely depressed? demented? paranoid? hypochondriacal?

4) What specific parts of psychodynamic theory and therapy would behaviorists be most likely to disagree with?

14/APPLICATION OF GESTALT THERAPY TO GROUP WORK WITH THE AGED

Shraga Serok, PhD

Editor's Introduction

Gestalt therapy came into vogue in the 1960s as one of many "humanistic" schools. Serok reviews the theoretical perspective of Gestalt: immediate and wholistic perception, the organization and interdependency and interaction of the elements of a process, and the need to overcome alienation and achieve closure.

The losses of later life cause certain issues to emerge from the background: e.g., physical health, reduced interpersonal contacts. Furthermore, organic brain syndromes can impede the formation of meaningful perceptions and integrations.

Serok presents suggestions for prophylactic measures and group therapy. Elders must be taken away from their dwelling on the past and fear of the future via a direct experience of the present. The use of techniques such as visualization and role play are discussed.

The topics of reality orientation (*CG*, v. 2, #3, p. 96; v. 3, #2, pp. 11–17), yoga (v. 1, #4, pp. 89–90; v. 3, #4, pp. 45–52), sex therapy (v. 2, #1, 31–44; v. 2, #4, pp. 25–35) and sensory training (v. 1, #2, pp. 81–83) may be applicable here as specific techniques for getting patients "in touch with the here and now."

Shraga Serok is Lecturer, School of Social Work and Department of Psychotherapy, Tel Aviv University, Israel.

231

INTRODUCTION

Gestalt therapy includes work with the individual, family, group, and organization. This is a very intensive form of treatment, as intervention is inclusive of all levels of human expression—intellect, affect, and physical being. Because of the use of body language and various other modes of non-verbal communication, this method facilitates working with a population such as the aged in which verbal expression is extremely difficult. As a therapeutic method Gestalt therapy can be used efficiently in all areas of emotional disturbance or difficulty, especially post-traumatic neuroses, psychosomatic disturbances, depressions, mourning, and bereavement. Due to the frequency which these may be experienced by elderly persons, we believe Gestalt to be a most effective psychotherapeutic approach with this age group.

We begin with a presentation of selected theoretical concepts of Gestalt therapy which relate to the elderly and the process of change they are experiencing. Application of these concepts in work with the elderly betters our understanding of the aging process. A means of preventative intervention and a therapeutic model, including various applicable exercises for group work with the aged, will also be described.

As a life philosophy, the Gestalt method emphasizes the self and the development of one's individuality, clarity in communication, interpersonal contact, and interaction with others.

Gestalt is now widely applied in the fields of education and teaching and yet no publications exist on the application of Gestalt in work with the aged. The need for such elucidation arose as the result of numerous professional discussions and exchanges with colleagues. We shall relate to the topic of Gestalt and the aged in an attempt to respond to this need.

RELEVANT THEORETICAL CONCEPTS

Gestalt therapy is based on three sources: (1) Gestalt psychology; (2) Existentialism; (3) Organistic theories (Fagan & Shepherd, 1970). Relevant to our presentation is the integration of Gestalt Psychology and Existentialism.

Gestalt Psychology deals primarily with perception, stating that an object is perceived as a whole and not as individual, isolated elements. The process of perception allows these elements to integrate according to specific laws, such as similarity of form, direction of movement, distance, and so forth. Only after these elements have been organized into a whole do they express an entire meaning. In other words, the whole is always more than the sum of its parts. For example, in music the tones of a melody must have a certain rhythm and order; only when this order is complete, do we hear a melody or sense a harmony. Another example involves a picture. The parts of the picture, as such, may not express a great deal; once all the parts have found their place, the meaning of the picture becomes clear. After we have perceived the picture (the Gestalt), we should be able to view it separately from the background against which it rests, thus emphasizing the difference between figure and background. In other words, there is a specific interaction between the figure and the background, and the clarity of the figure is greater when differentiation between the two is more intensely defined. Background, moreover, plays an important role even when we are interested only in the figure.

The elements which form the Gestalt are divided into two classifications: (1) primary elements and (2) secondary elements. The term primary elements refers to those elements which are absolutely essential for the expression of the whole, for example, the basic outline of the body. These are the basic components which render the most information and by which the meaning of the whole emerges. Secondary elements are those components which add information to the form, which complete the shape of the figure, and emphasize the vividness of the form against the background. The Gestalt attains full expression once the secondary elements appear, but it is possible, of course, for it to appear without them. In this case, the Gestalt would be understood in a very basic and constricted manner. For instance, in a portrait, beauty marks, facial expressions, as well as details of the surrounding elements, do not appear to be initially related to the focus of the picture. The secondary elements belong to the background and they provide additional information which may be eliminated. When assimilated into the primary elements, however, they enhance and widen the meaning of the Gestalt.

Let us now examine these concepts as they appear in behavior. A "need," as a Gestalt, is composed of elements which reach maximum meaning only when they are organized into a whole. The dynamics involved in creating a need are similar to those involved in creating the wholeness of the Gestalt. For this reason, "need" and "Gestalt" may be interchanged when describing human behavior in Gestalt terms. Need is composed of physiological, emotional, and environmental components and may be divided into primary and secondary elements.

The process of creating a need can be explained in Gestalt terms: our behavior is in a continuous process of need satisfaction as we interact with the environment. This becomes a sequence of activities, since the second activity (need satisfaction) appeared only after the first has been completed. The hierarchy created by needs is subjective, and its order is dependent upon the individual's preferences. A need, as has been previously stated, is composed of elements which are in the process of being organized; because the organism is focused upon this need, it separates itself from other needs and becomes the figure. The other needs recede to the background. Once this first need emerges vividly, it is satisfied. As a result, the need disintegrates, is assimilated into the background, and the succeeding need emerges. Perls (1973) describes this process as Gestalt (need) formation and Gestalt (need) distraction. The emergency of a need, its recession into the background is often a combined and inseparable process. This process occurs during interaction with one's environment, thereby enabling the person to continue developing as an individual within the context of the environment.

An example of this process is "hunger," whose primary elements are pangs of hunger and the swallowing of food. Sexual relations, as another example, includes the primary elements of physiological arousal, a partner, intercourse, and orgasm. Without these components, the need will not develop, nor will it be satisfied and therefore recede. The secondary elements in these cases are those components of behavior which enhance the experience and increase its impact. The need, per se, can be satisfied without these components. In the first example, these secondary components might be the food, its preparation, the manner and place in which it is served, and the concentration on the eating process. In the second example, dating, foreplay, and emotional interaction, may be included. While often important, they are not essential satisfaction of the need. An analogy can be drawn between describing a picture by using only the primary elements, and satisfying human needs by relating only to their primary elements. In both cases, secondary elements provide more vivid expression, "color," and enhancement of the content.

We live in an age of alienation, over-automatization, and pressured achievement orientation. Under these circumstances we have little unplanned time. This situation encourages behavior based only on primary elements, demanding achievement of necessary and basic functioning in a minimum time. Secondary elements are repressed because they are "time wasting" and lacking in importance. This, we believe, is an unhealthy application of the concept of efficiency to the field of behavior.

To fully understand the satisfaction of needs it is essential to briefly present the Gestalt concept of "tendency for closure" and "unfinished business" (Perls, 1969). This concept is based on the premise that in the process of perception we tend to complete any form if we have enough information leading in a clear direction toward that completion. A circle which is missing a part will be perceived as a whole, in spite of the fact that it is lacking a part. However, unclear or confused situation is created when there is not sufficient information, or when an obstruction to the completion process exists. Such a situation consumes energy. As long as it remains unresolved, perception is difficult and the flow of experience is blocked.

In behavior, a need will be satisfied only when this process completes itself. It will then recede and be assimilated into the ground. If the need attains complete expression, and the elements are organized in the correct direction, then the need will be completed and satisfied. When there is interference in the process (especially fear, shock, conflict, and so forth) the experience will remain unfulfilled, or "unfinished," and stagnation will often occur. Such an occurrence prevents the satisfaction of a need, requires tremendous energy, and, in general, negatively affects behavior. Indirect proof of this concept can be found in the "Zeigarnick effect" (Fagan & Shepherd, 1970). This classic experiment proves that unfinished tasks are remembered for a longer period of time than tasks which have been completed.

Satisfying needs only with primary elements may not be sufficient to allow for "closure" and may, in fact, create an inviting situation for "unfinished business."

APPLICATION OF THEORETICAL CONCEPTS
TO WORK WITH THE AGED

This section will focus on a description of man's behavior in old age in terms of the theory delineated above. Those psychophysical changes in behavior which occur in the elderly affect the individuals' interaction with the environment. This is usually a gradual process beginning at various periods of one's life, and reflecting individual personality differences. That is to say, the onset of these changes and their form of expression differ from one individual to another. These changes, however, are definitely concentrated in the final period in man's life.

Interaction between figure and ground, in terms of what emerges as figure and what remains as ground, shifts with age. The importance of events differs with physiological, emotional, and social changes. For example, concern with health issues becomes a "figural" object in old age, because of numerous possible illnesses and the realistic fear of death. For a younger person, this will usually remain in the background. In other words, as the individual ages, this matter moves from background to foreground, gains in importance and affects overall behavior.

Among the elderly these changes in interaction between foreground and background find expression in all areas, including mental and emotional functioning, thought process, outlook, and value systems. Very often these changes radically alter the philosophy of life as the individual ages. This difference between youth and old age may, in part, explain the generation gap between these two groups.

The intensity of expression of one's needs during youth is no doubt much stronger than in old age. This intensity emerges from primary elements. If we continue with our previous examples, hunger and sexual relations, we see that when the intensity of the primary elements is quite strong, the need emerges quickly and satisfaction is found quickly. A young man feels hunger and wants to eat quickly. Similarly, his sexual urge is so strong that once a partner appears there is usually no need for secondary elements to increase the intensity of the need. In old age, the primary elements are weakened and the satisfaction of the need becomes more dependent upon secondary elements. Hunger is not always strong, and therefore the varieties of food, the manner in which it is served, the eating conditions, etc., will be integral in the emergency, satisfaction, recession, and appropriate reappearance of the need. The elderly can most definitely function sexually. They do, however, require many more secondary elements of the need to become aroused and to achieve satisfaction. To a great extent, the physical ability of the elderly to function sexually depends upon secondary elements. At this point in their lives, appearance of a partner is not sufficient. Interpersonal relationships, and possibly courtship, have become so centrally important that without them the aged may have difficulty functioning. In old age the secondary elements of behavior play a very crucial role. In reaching efficient functioning, certainly more so than during youth. Parts of the primary elements tend to weaken and recede into the ground, while secondary elements become more dominant and evolve into figure.

The concept of primary and secondary elements may also be applied to other areas of life patterns, for example, aspirations, interpersonal behavior, and family relationships. In these areas, the primary elements will appear as basic expressions of the subject, the concrete definition of the goal, the most efficient performance and so forth. Secondary elements are found in informal interpersonal relationships, in emotional content, and in various peripheral activities.

It is hypothesized that due to the changes which occur in old age, a much greater sensitivity to secondary elements appears, and their existence is fundamental to the functioning of the elderly individual. It is also felt that a certain amount of dependence upon secondary elements exists at this stage of life.

Behavior which might have been described earlier in the life cycle as spontaneous and flowing slows down in old age. Expression is often not complete and, in more severe cases, may appear only in parts or may break down into its elements. Unnecessary and disorganized expressions and movements appear. This is disturbing to the clarity of expression and the understanding of the meaning. Senses begin to weaken, memory functions with difficulty, and reaction time lengthens. Sclerotic processes in the brain, which occur frequently, render thought processes difficult. Bits of information which are necessary to complete a thought cannot be organized quickly enough, or parts necessary to the expression of a complete thought cannot be recalled. Many times the meaning of the expression is so changed or disrupted, that it cannot be understood (Busse, 1963; Davis, 1981).

Phenomenologically, this situation may be described as a process in which the organization of the parts into a whole is slowed down, the process of organization and order is disrupted, and expression becomes difficult and unclear. At times, unrelated irrelevant parts enter the content and the meaning of the expression becomes even more unclear or may change completely.

In old age the tendency to complete the missing parts lessens. Much more information is necessary for the organization of the whole and for the completion of the missing parts. In addition, due to their overall greater sensitivity, "unfinished business" from the past is now more problematic and a source of great disturbance to the elderly.

PREVENTATIVE INTERVENTION

Interaction between primary and secondary elements tends to become altered in old age, resulting in a change in daily attitudes and activities. A philosophy of life should be developed which emphasizes the use of "secondary elements" in behavior throughout the life cycle. An individual must exercise greater effort to cope with the problems implicit in time limitations and to value the secondary needs in everyday life. As a person reaches old age and the aging person will be better able to utilize, enjoy, and profit from these secondary processes when satisfying his personal needs.

This enjoyment, based on the "use of secondary elements," may find its expression when listening to music, discussing a theoretical presentation, enjoying work as a laborer, feeling the words of a prayer, or in any other daily event. This increases our understanding that a life-style which will provide a human being with satisfaction, is one in which an individual learns to place his needs in a heirarchy and then to concentrate his energy around a dominant need. Such a life-style encourages the individual to realize the importance of discovering the secondary elements in his behavior and to assimilate them in interaction with his environment, even if these elements seem extraneous. One of the principles of this philosophy of life is that the time saved by over-efficiency diminishes the pleasure of everyday living and increases the difficulties in future functioning. In other words, "the gain may turn into a loss." When an individual paces his life according to his ability to interact with his environment, and also exercises patience with the difference between himself and others, he will discover and increase enjoyment in his day to day activities.

This philosophy of life is of secondary importance during one's youth or middle age. It is emphasized, for this reason, as a preventative intervention during the earlier periods of life and not once functioning decreases, or after one's first heart attack. The individual must be helped to realize the importance of such a life-style. Suitable conditions should be created to help the individual learn methods of changing his philosophy of life, thereby changing concrete behavior in accordance with this concept. In the social atmosphere of today's world, such changes occur slowly. Preventative intervention, therefore, must occur over a period of time, and must be based on proper learning methods.

A MODEL OF GROUP WORK WITH THE AGED

Gestalt therapy emphasizes experiences and experiments focused in the "here and now." Any means by which a person is able to express himself may be utilized as a therapeutic tool. Elements found in the physical environment (e.g., room, light, furniture, temperature) and in the human environment (participants, clothing, body language, verbal communication, etc.) may be included in the experience of the present. Zinker (1977) defines this as the "phenomenological here and now," whereby all present elements may serve as part of the therapeutic manipulation.

One can experience only in the present. The past can be remembered, and the future anticipated but experience occurs only at a given moment in the present. All factors involved in the event, even if passive, are part of this experience. If one were aware of all the components in the experience, its intensity would increase and the present would become of primary importance. It is known that the elderly tend to remember the past and to fear the future. Such a situation interferes with the awareness of the present and minimizes the experience of the "here and now." It is recommended, therefore, that when treating the aged, the present be: (1) emphasized and (2) pleasurable. Activity should be created which emphasizes all of the phenomenology of the environment. In this manner the "here and now" experience will expand; its intensity will increase and assume primary importance. It is also possible that a clearer distinction could be achieved among the three dimensions of time—past, present, and future. This is important as it seems to be essential in old age.

The elderly should be taught to identify the secondary elements in their behavior, to understand their relevance, and to utilize them. It is important to convince the elderly to act slowly, to take breaks, and to pay attention to all stages in each activity, including those which may seem unimportant. It is also helpful to convince them that this form of functioning is not a weakness, but in fact, an enrichment of all processes. It heightens pleasure, along with facilitating changeover from one activity to the next. The elderly usually have more leisure time, and this is a positive factor in proceeding in the style of life herein described. It must be explained that, despite its appearance, this is the opposite of wasting time.

This process can be effectively applied in the area of sexual relations. The aging individual must learn that any type of interpersonal relationship, including courtship, foreplay, and contact, which does not result in the sexual act, should not be considered a failure or weakness. Such behavior at times may lead to sexual consumation, but usually provides pleasurable activity in and of itself. The secondary elements, per se, become the important and pleasurable elements.

Based on this precept a group work program for the elderly should include consistent and gradual ordering of activities based on the needs of the aged, as they express them, and not as the therapist perceives them. These activities should include maximum secondary elements, should be concentrated as much as possible on one topic, and should finish in a clear-cut manner. The second activity begins only after the first has been completed.

The above model for group work relates to both interpersonal and intrapersonal activities and focuses on thought organization, awareness, and communication. This model is designed for group process in which participants initiate activities. By working together, the group is able to organize the information in a more effective manner. Learning may be either active or passive. The group therapist should utilize exercises and games in order to clarify the process, and bring enjoyment to it. The goal is to arrive at group interaction which concentrates on concrete events, and utilizes all of the elements in the environment at the given time. The participants will be assisted in the reorganization of the elements in the immediate environment through their thoughts, senses, and emotions. It is assumed that experiments with the reorganization of environmental patterns will enable the participants to better integrate their thoughts, perceptions, and activities. Over time the participants should become capable of generalizing these new abilities to situations outside of the therapeutic setting.

DETAILED EXAMPLES OF GROUP WORK
APPLICATION IN THERAPY

Therapeutically it is possible to help aging persons develop the ability to identify and use the secondary elements in their lives through activities which focus on thought processes, organization of elements, and self-awareness.

During therapy participants learn through thought processes to identify the organization of immediate, concrete, environmental elements, repeat the pattern from memory, and then create a similar pattern and perceive its structural meaning. An example of a suitable exercise would be for the participants (with open or closed eyes) to check recall of the seating arrangement of the group, details of clothing, particulars of the room and so forth. A variation of this exercise involves a game of demonstration, or impersonation, in which one or more participants pantomime an expression, or idea, and the others voluntarily imitate the behavior. In this exercise, the participants study individual differences in performance, their own process of mime, and the means they employ to repeat the original performance as accurately as possible (expression, retention, and organization of elements).

In the area of logical organization of elements, a game of syllogisms can be effective. This exercise involves the inference of logically valid conclusions implied by two premises, such as (1) "all people wearing dresses in this room are women"; (2) "I am wearing a dress," therefore (conclusion), "I am a woman."

Working within the realm of self-awareness, we suggest various exercises focusing separately on each of its three aspects (physical, emotional, and cognitive). An exercise in physical awareness may be developed as follows: participants are required first to concentrate on various organs of their body, to then estimate their size, and finally to examine the comparison between the estimates and reality. Another exercise first involves standing in a circle and concentrating on the self without touching anyone else, and then reaching out, touching others, and feeling the difference. It would be possible also to physically approach a group of people, feel their closeness, and then move away. Another exercise is one in which there are two participants, one being the inviter and the other the invited. The inviter uses a specific signal signifying an invitation to approach him to the point at which he feels comfortable at that moment. If the invited feels that this point is too close, he may signal a refusal. In this manner both participants discover the points at which they feel comfortable. The players may then exchange roles.

The emotional aspect of awareness may be exemplified through an exercise wherein one person demonstrates an emotion (e.g., fear, joy, anger) and another person mimics that emotion. This may lead the latter to discover the external expression of the displayed emotion, and to recognize the internal feeling which may subsequently occur. This follows the theoretical assumption that various parts related to the whole may complement each other and result in a complete expression.

The cognitive aspect of awareness will be expressed in each of the experiments, but may be emphasized through the development of specific exercises. These exercises will enable the individual to clearly recognize, combine and integrate various elements into a whole. This occurs as a result of the process of reaching conclusions, including coping with doubts when they arise, of attaining intellectual control for isolating irrelevant factors, and finally of differentiating among the past, present and future.

Each Gestalt exercise must be relevant to the participants and should arise from a particular "here and now" situation. Because of this, the exercises should not be planned prior to the session. It is preferable for the group therapist to create the exercises according to the needs and type of the participants using personal intuition and creativity, and, of course, suggestions from the participants themselves.

Generally speaking, we would like to emphasize the point that group activity should encourage the participants' spontaneous expression. Many repressed secondary elements are found in spontaneous expression, and this type of activity stimulates their "arousal" and expression.

SUMMARY

The changes occurring among the elderly is a natural process involving such responses as weakening, slowing down, difficulty in functioning, and heightened sensitivity. In more severe cases disorganized thinking and inappropriate expression may be found. We have presented a theoretical formulation which applies Gestalt theory to the field of work with the aged. The ideas were developed to facilitate application of the theory to preventative intervention and group therapy with the aged.

Our purpose has been to suggest another point of view for understanding the aging process. We suggest helping the elderly individual to understand the various elements which comprise this process of change. We must then teach him or her to adjust to the changes, and to enjoy them to their maximum. We believe that Gestalt therapy brings a special contribution to this area.

REFERENCES

Busse, W. "Psychological and Physical Factors," in *Social Group Work with Older People.* A seminar on social group work with older people published by National Association of Social Workers, New York, 1963, pp. 21–33.

David, H. R. (ed.) *Aging: Prospects and Issues.* Chapters 1–4, third edition, The University of Southern California Press, C. L., 1981.

Fagan, J. & Shepherd, I. L. *Gestalt Therapy Now.* Harper & Row, New York, 1970.

Perls, F. *Gestalt Therapy Verbatim,* Real People Press, New York, 1969.

Perls, F. *The Gestalt Approach and Eyewitness to Therapy,* Science and Behavior Books, New York, 1973.

Zinker, J. *Creative Process in Gestalt Therapy,* Brunner/Mazel, New York, 1977.

Questions

1) Discuss the possible role of art, music, and movement in bringing patients into an immediate experience of the ''here and now.''

2) What kinds of patients would probably do well in Gestalt Therapy? Who would be inappropriate candidates?

3) Is there a role for reminiscence in Gestalt Therapy?

4) Is there a role for assessment in Gestalt Therapy?

5) Is there a role for medication in Gestalt Therapy?

6) How does Serok's application of Gestalt to geriatric groups differ from most Gestalt therapy with younger patients?

15/COGNITIVE THERAPY WITH OLDER ADULTS

Larry W. Thompson, PhD
Ruth Davies, MS
Dolores Gallagher, PhD
Susan E. Krantz, PhD

Editor's Introduction

Cognitive therapy has been a major topic in *CG* (v. 1, #3, pp. 45–52; v. 2, #3, pp. 15–23; v. 3, #3, p. 44–45) and recent books on geriatric psychotherapy (see reviews: v. 1, #4, pp. 83–84; v. 2, #3, pp. 92–96; v. 3, #3, pp. 67–68).

Thompson, Davies, Gallagher, and Krantz have given us an authoritative and comprehensive review of this topic. Beginning with a review of Beck's perspective on depression (cognitive triad, schema, errors), critical therapeutic ingredients (collaboration, time limitation, target problems, homework, feedback), the stages of therapy, and empirical research on the efficacy of this approach.

The authors focus on several special issues peculiar to the geriatric application of cognitive therapy: expectations and realities, learning and memory, focusing attention and therapist views. The result is a list of helpful hints for the therapist.

Four case studies go through a range of clinical problems and special considerations which may be encountered in cognitive therapy with the aged.

The authors are affiliated with the Center for the Study of Psychotherapy and Aging and Geriatric Research, Education & Clinical Center, Veterans Administration Medical Center, Palo Alto, CA.

Preparation of this manuscript was supported in part by grant #R01-MH37196-04 from the National Institute of Mental Health to the first author.

Aaron Beck's cognitive model of depression rests on three concepts: (1) the cognitive triad, (2) schemas, and (3) cognitive errors (Beck, Rush, Shaw, & Emery, 1979). The cognitive triad refers to the depressed person's negative view of himself, his experiences, and his future. These negative thought patterns are viewed as a major influence on the affective and behavioral symptoms observed in depressed individuals. Beck uses the concept of schema to explain the way negative views are maintained even when they are no longer consistent with the evidence in an individual's life. Schemas are more stable organizational patterns of thoughts that make up the basic framework a person uses to interpret situations. When schemas contain negative ideas, the individual will consistently show a negative bias to his interpretations. The more active these negative schemas become, the less able is the depressed person to detect any systematic errors in thinking.

The schemas of a depressed person are more likely to incorporate an identifiable pattern of cognitive biases than those of a nondepressed person. These include arbitrary inference (drawing a conclusion in the absence of evidence), selective abstraction (focusing on specific details while ignoring other relevant features of the situation), overgeneralization (assuming the outcome of one incident will occur in all situations), magnification and minimization (distorting the importance or significance of a single event), personalization (assuming automatically that external events relate to oneself), and "all-or-none" thinking (categorizing continuous experiences as dichotomous extremes, such as good or bad, loved or hated). The persistent use of any or all of these systematic errors in cognition helps generate and sustain the depressed person's negative view of self, world, and others, which, in turn, leads to depressed mood and behaviors. The purpose of cognitive therapy is to identify these patterns and to teach depressed clients the skills needed to achieve a more balanced and accurate view of their situation.

CRITICAL THERAPEUTIC INGREDIENTS

For purposes of evaluating the skill level of cognitive therapists, Young & Beck (1980) have identified a number of the important ingredients of cognitive therapy. First of all, cognitive therapy is a collaborative treatment. The collaborative stance of a therapist helps to minimize conflicts and misunderstandings which might hinder the application of cognitive techniques. As cognitive therapy is time limited (generally 15 to 20 sessions), pacing and the efficient use of time are important within the session and in the course of treatment. To insure that the most pertinent problems are covered, an agenda is set at the beginning of each session. This involves pinpointing target problems and mapping out the session's course. The selection of target problems should reflect the therapist's long-range strategy for change. This strategy is developed within the first few sessions and incorporates both the client's goals for treatment and the therapist's broader conceptualization of the issues involved.

Once target problems have been defined, the bulk of the therapist's efforts are then focused on elicitation of automatic thoughts and the selection of appropriate interventions. Automatic thoughts can be elicited through the use of inductive questioning, imagery, role-playing, and through daily recording exercises. With skill, a therapist can probe thoughts to uncover the underlying assumptions. These supporting beliefs then become a focus of treatment as the therapy moves from symptomatic relief to initiating long-term change.

The cognitive therapist has a variety of techniques available to bring about change within the session. These methods are applied within a framework drawing upon the scientific method, in which each dysfunctional thought or belief is formulated as a hypothesis and compared to information from the environment. Actual experiments can be designed, or alternate views can be elicited through inductive questioning and examining both sides of the issue. Sometimes operationalizing a negative idea helps to focus the client and point out a belief's fundamental irrationality. Reattributing the causes of the problem or generating alternative solutions can be effective ways to broaden a client's perspective and sense of control. When appropriate, cognitive therapists often apply behavioral change strategies, such as scheduling activities or focusing on increasing perceived pleasure and mastery. The behavioral strategies are used to provide evidence relevant to testing particular beliefs. When negative beliefs are at least partially realistic, therapy includes problem solving to alter the situation or to discover ways to obtain satisfaction.

Most often, the success of an intervention will rely on how well it is followed up with an appropriate homework assignment. Cognitive therapy is based on the active transfer of learning to the client's outside life, and relevant homework is a crucial feature of this process. Generally, homework in cognitive therapy will follow logically from the problems addressed in the session. Assignments are designed with the client's input. The homework itself is often a means for eliciting the client's thoughts about the process of psychotherapy.

Feedback is also a vital component of successful cognitive therapy. The therapist is continually checking that the client understands the formulations and interventions. In this way the client is made a partner of the collaborative team and is actively involved in defining and revising the course of treatment. Feedback in cognitive treatment extends to the evaluation of each session and of the therapeutic relationship itself. This maximizes client satisfaction and reduces the chance of developing unrecognized transference issues which might hamper short-term treatment.

A time-limited format is another of cognitive therapy's hallmark features. Cognitive therapy does not aim to change the client, per se; rather, its purpose is to teach clients techniques for changing thought and behavior patterns that they can generalize to other aspects of their lives. Unlike psychodynamic therapy, the content of cognitive treatment is focused on "here and now" issues. Therefore, cognitive therapy rarely lasts more than 15 to 20 sessions (Beck et al., 1979).

THE THERAPEUTIC RELATIONSHIP

Although the emphasis of cognitive therapy is on techniques for changing dysfunctional thoughts, the quality of the therapeutic relationship is vital for supporting a successful treatment program. The therapist must carefully engage and monitor the client's participation and collaboration. As in any therapy, the "non-specific" therapeutic factors, such as warmth, concern, and confidence build and enhance the collaborative stance of therapy. In cognitive treatment the therapist's understanding of the client is critical to insure that interventions are directed at issues central to the client's depressive symptoms. Knowledge of the techniques can never be a substitute for an accurate understanding of the client and his or her problems.

Stages of Treatment

Initial sessions focus on defining target complaints and introducing the client to the cognitive model of treatment. In the depressed client, target complaints often are poorly defined or so global that it may be difficult to devlop an effective treatment program. A good starting point in therapy is to help the client define his complaints as solvable problems, in order then to select target goals for therapy.

If suicidal thoughts or wishes are prevalent, they must be given priority. Thoughts of hopelessness and despair can be appropriately handled within the empirical cognitive approach, supplemented with behavioral contracting, to instill a sense of purpose and commitment. As with any part of cognitive treatment, the strategy is to help the client become aware of the inconsistencies within his beliefs. In suicidal clients, the exploration of their feelings of hopelessness serves both to help them look at contradictory information, as well as simultaneously to engage them in the empirical review process. This may involve looking for alternatives to dying, evaluating the pros and cons of thinking so absolutely, and labeling the all-or-none pattern of thinking which typically lets suicide seem an appropriate option.

In order to maximize the opportunities for change to occur, clients must understand the actions required of them and the rationale for treatment. Consequently, the first session of treatment may focus on teaching the client the relationship between thoughts, moods, and behavior. Next, the client may need to learn the basic skills of self-observation, thought monitoring, and how to identify automatic thoughts. This may start in the first session by having the client practice identifying thoughts about beginning therapy or about an event that was encountered recently. The client is encouraged to notice the connection between the thoughts expressed and the subsequent mood. Skills are further developed by homework which emphasizes recording thoughts in "depressing" situations during the week or by tracking the occurrence of a particularly frequent negative thought.

Once the client understands the cognitive model and the actions that are required, and once target goals have been defined, treatment of specific complaints can occur. During this stage of treatment, clients are also helped to monitor their cognitions about therapy itself. It is unlikely that they hold realistic views of their ability to initiate self-change. Clients tend to attribute progress to external sources, such as reactions of family or neighbors or therapist's skill. Such views can be identified and labeled as hypotheses for therapy and they can be tested for their accuracy. The more successfully clients relate their progress to skills they are acquiring, the more potential there is for generalization of treatment effects and for the long-term maintenance of gains.

As therapy progresses and the initial depressive symptoms lessen, clients can begin to focus on the faulty assumptions that predispose and maintain their depressive cognitive schema. They need to learn to identify their own assumptions in order to make the learning process plausible. In working through the initial symptoms of depression, clients have reported their automatic thoughts about different issues. The therapist then uses these to draw inferences about the assumptions which underlie a number of different thoughts and which provide a common thread weaving them together. The type of thinking errors the client consistently makes, the continual use of certain words or labels and the terms the client uses to describe situations can all assist the therapist in locating the implicit assumptions making up the cognitive schema. Once one of these assumptions is identified, the therapist can use pointed questioning or challenging statements to lead clients to define the relief more clearly. For example, an automatic thought like "my husband probably hates me because I don't cook dinners" could be supported by the belief that "people are valued only for what they do," or that "imperfect people won't be liked." A recurrent theme in the assumptions of depressed clients is that of ideal standards or "I shoulds." Having a number of these ideal standards in their view of the world leads to feelings of inadequacy, discouragement, and frustration. Related to these are assumptions of poor self-worth and external control. Ideal standards are generally absolute and are applied to appropriate and inappropriate situations alike.

Rather than trying to reason the client out of such beliefs, the cognitive therapist can approach the "I should" as a testable hypothesis. The client is encouraged to state the standard and define the anticipated consequences if the standard is or is not followed. Following evaluation, the hypothesis can be tested out. A careful review of the positive and negative consequences will probably not result in the belief being totally discarded, but clients often soften their views as a result of this process, and begin to seriously recognize the existence of alternative choices.

There are usually a number of other dysfunctional cognitions readily identifiable in the thinking patterns of depressed clients. Most all have the effect of restricting the client's alternatives and limiting capacities for adaptive, rational evaluation. Consequently, cognitive therapists find that they repeatedly go over the same basic assumptions as they try to get the client to view yet one more situation from a more rational perspective. This kind of repetition helps clients to generalize newly learned cognitive principles to a variety of situations. At times, however, clients do not seem to be able to apply what they have learned about their dysfunctional assumptions to related situations (e.g., someone who has made progress in handling difficulties within the family may seem at a loss in applying this information to the employment arena). This may reflect continuing cognitive rigidity, or it may be a clue that the client is not sufficiently involved in the collaborative aspects of treatment.

There are several techniques for handling a lack of progress in therapy. Sometimes labeling the particularly dysfunctional pattern and then having the client monitor its repeated occurrence will encourage the client to take additional responsibility in initiating a change. Taking a somewhat paradoxical position can at times provide a useful challenge to a particularly resistant thought pattern, though care must be taken to maintain the collaborative relationship. Examining the advantages and disadvantages of holding on to a particular dysfunctional belief often will reveal ways in which the client is deriving benefit from maintaining an otherwise negative and potentially destructive thought pattern. Clarification of these issues in treatment sets the stage for a more objective and rational problem solving approach to modifying the cognitive patterns. For example, the tendency to look at situations dichotomously simplifies the evaluation process (only one of two alternatives can apply). On the other hand, such a view puts immense pressure on the client to achieve whatever is seen as the only acceptable choice. Spelling out the pros and cons of such a belief helps the client see that he or she is already making a choice by continuing to hold on to the dysfunctional pattern of thought. In this way "resistance to change" becomes one more valid hypothesis subject to cognitive therapy's empirical review.

During the latter phases of treatment, the client should be playing an increasingly active role in setting the agenda of sessions and choosing strategies. This policy helps counter the client's tendency to mystify the therapeutic process. A continual emphasis on the acquired skills as being the active ingredients of treatment lessens the client's dependency on the therapist's actions and prepares the client for the eventual termination of therapy and the maintenance of progress.

Even so, it is not uncommon to encounter dysfunctional beliefs about the lasting effect of therapy. Clients may be concerned that they will not be "cured" when termination comes, that change will not occur without the therapist, or that their depression will return when therapy ends. The therapist can point out the unrealistic thinking in the "cured versus sick" dichotomy and can stress the importance of skill acquisition in therapy, without needing to have total mastery. On the second issue, the therapist can point out examples where clients have handled their problems on their own (i.e., through completion of a specific homework assignment), and can then ask the client to identify and challenge thoughts about the therapist's magical powers.

Fears of a relapse can be handled several ways. A mild depression can be discussed as actually useful to the client, for it would provide a chance to practice the skills learned in therapy. A more direct approach would be to have the client think as many negative thoughts as possible in the sessions or for homework and then practice replacing them with a more balanced point of view. By monitoring changes in mood during the exercise, clients demonstrate their ability to handle depressive feelings. Another way to approach the client's fear of relapse is to challenge newly learned skills. If the therapist plays the devil's advocate with the client's original automatic assumptions and thoughts, the client may demonstrate new abilities to respond to these thoughts, with accompanying reflection on the progress that has been made.

The therapist may schedule a few booster sessions spaced four to six weeks apart as a final encouragement. This enables the client to polish plans for maintaining gains that were acquired in the last few sessions. Booster sessions also serve to modulate the shock of termination and decrease clients' concerns about failing that might contribute to an eventual relapse.

EVIDENCE FOR THE EFFECTIVENESS
OF COGNITIVE THERAPY

Numerous studies have been conducted in the past 10 years on cognitive therapy as a specific treatment for depressive disorders. In the first part of this section, we will review those done with non-aged samples. In the latter part, we will focus on research with patients over 60.

Research on Cognitive Therapy with Adults

Several early studies that used college student volunteers or clinic patients are reviewed in Beck et al. (1979, pp. 394–395). The first major study of the impact of cognitive therapy compared cognitive therapy to imipramine in the treatment of 41 depressed outpatients. Results indicated that nearly four-fifths of the patients treated with cognitive therapy "showed marked improvement or complete remission of symptoms" compared with just over one-third of those treated with imipramine (Rush, Beck, Kovacs, & Hollon, 1977). When this sample was followed up one year later, the advantage for cognitive therapy still obtained (Kovacs, Rush, Beck & Hollon, 1981). Blackburn and colleagues compared the effects of cognitive therapy alone, a choice of antidepressant medications (amitriptyline or clomipramine) without psychotherapy, and a combination of cognitive therapy and antidepressants. Patients were referred from two distinct sources: general practice and an outpatient hospital clinic. Patients referred from general practice responded equally well to cognitive therapy alone and to the combination treatment, while patients in the clinic benefited most from the combined condition (compared to either therapy or medication alone). The hospital outpatients had been depressed longer but even when duration was controlled for, the same results were obtained (Blackburn, Bishop, Glen, Whalley, & Christie, 1981).

Murphy and colleagues compared cognitive therapy alone against three other conditions: cognitive therapy plus desipramine, desipramine alone, and cognitive therapy plus a placebo drug. They found no significant differences between conditions at the end of treatment for degree of change on common measures of depressive symptomatology (Murphy, Simons, Wetzel, & Lustman, 1984). They interpreted these results to indicate that *either* cognitive therapy *or* antidepressant drug treatment can be effective in treating patients with primary, unipolar depression of moderate intensity. They also concluded that combining cognitive therapy with an antidepressant medication did not lead to greater positive change. Beck and his colleagues also recently completed another study comparing cognitive therapy alone with cognitive therapy plus amitriptyline with 33 depressed outpatients (Beck, Hollon, Young, Bedrosian & Budenz (1985). Both groups showed statistically significant and clinically meaningful decreases in depressive symptoms, but no differences were found between the conditions in magnitude of change. Patients were followed for one year after termination, and a trend was noted suggesting greater stability of gains for those who initially received the combined treatment. However, many of them had more therapy during the follow-up period, so that trend is difficult to interpret.

In summary, cognitive therapy alone and cognitive therapy combined with a tricyclic antidepressant were roughly equivalent in three of four samples compared, with only the hospital outpatient sample of Blackburn et al. evidencing superiority for the combined approach. Earlier work of Rush et al. (1977) also suggested that cognitive therapy alone is equal to, if not superior to, pharmacotherapy alone.

A major study now in progress is the collaborative research program on depression (funded by the National Institute of Mental Health) about which much will be written in the years to come. The latter is described in detail in Elkin, Parloff, Hadley, and Autry (1985); briefly, the study involves three research sites using identical protocols and examining the comparative efficacy of cognitive/behavior therapy, interpersonal therapy, imipramine plus clinical management (referring to the patient having regularly scheduled appointments to talk briefly with the psychiatrist, as well as to receive the current medications), and placebo plus clinical management. Over 200 patients will be treated in this study by the time it is fully completed in 1986. Elkin et al. indicate that these particular psychotherapies were chosen because they were developed specifically to treat depression, have been standardized in such a fashion that they can be transmitted to other clinicians through available manuals, and a body of research data exists to support the efficacy of each. Thus, cognitive therapy will be receiving considerable national attention as the results of the NIMH collaborative study become available; those data may suggest future directions for work with elders (although, unfortunately, the maximum upper age for inclusion in the Collaborative study is 60).

Research with Older Adults

Research on cognitive therapy with elders has primarily been conducted by three independent groups of investigators: our own work has focused on cognitive therapy done on a one-to-one basis, while the work of Jarvik and colleagues at UCLA have examined pharmacological treatment and cognitive/behavioral therapy done in a group format, and Beutler and associates at the University of Arizona have focused exclusively on group cognitive therapy.

The work of Beutler and colleagues is still in progress; no data have yet been published on the effectiveness of group cognitive therapy with their outpatient samples of elder depressives. However, they have published a practitioner-oriented manual about how to do group cognitive therapy with elders (Yost, Beutler, Corbishley, & Allender, 1985), and it is likely that outcome data will be forthcoming in the near future.

Jarvik and colleagues compared two parallel studies of geriatric outpatients who were diagnosed as Major Depressive disorder. In the first, patients were treated with one of two tricyclic antidepressants (imipramine and doxepin) or with a placebo. In the second, patients were assigned to groups receiving either psychodynamic therapy or cognitive/behavioral therapy. The authors point out that in neither study was assignment of patients to conditions done in a strictly random manner (Jarvik, Mintz, Steuer, & Gerner, 1982, p. 714). Results of the first study (N = 32) indicated that, after 26 weeks of treatment, patients receiving either of the two active drugs improved to a significantly greater degree than those receiving the placebo. Results of the second study indicated that most patients receiving group psychotherapy (of either type) showed some improvement on the Hamilton Rating Scale for Depression (Hamilton, 1967), but only three patients out of 26 (12%) had clear remissions of their depressive disorder as compared to 45% for the drug group. Differences between psychotherapy groups were not significant.

A second paper by this group focused more on the group therapy conditions (Steuer, Mintz, Hammen, Hill, Jarvik, McCarley, Motoike, & Rosen, 1984). Only 20 of 33 patients completed the nine-month course of therapy with approximately equal numbers of dropouts from each condition. Of these 20, 16 (80%) showed some improvement and 8 (40%) went into remission, based on their Hamilton scores. Patients in the cognitive/behavior treatment had lower scores on the Beck Depression Inventory (BDI) (Beck, Ward, Mendelson, Mock & Erbaugh, 1961) than patients in the psychodynamic treatment. However, other outcome measures did not show group differences. They suggested that patients may "learn" to complete the BDI in a favorable way as a result of being in cognitive/behavioral treatment. The short BDI contains many items reflecting negative cognitive appraisals (such as self-criticism and pessimism about the future); patients in cognitive/behavioral therapy learn how to confront such negativistic cognitions, so they suggested that the possibility of measurement bias should be considered in interpreting their results. Their final conclusion was that

". . . it might be reasonable to suspect that the therapy experience was beneficial and may provide an intervention option for older persons who are physically ill and unable to take antidepressant medications" (1984, p. 188).

The picture is considerably clearer with regard to the positive impact of individual cognitive therapy. In a first effort Gallagher & Thompson (1982) randomly assigned 38 elderly patients, who were diagnosed as being in a current episode of Major Depressive Disorder, to either cognitive therapy (following Beck et al., 1979), behavioral therapy (modeled after Lewinsohn, 1974), or brief relational/insight psychotherapy (derived from Bellak & Small, 1965). Therapy lasted for 16 individual sessions over a 12-week period. Substantial improvement was seen in all three treatments from pre- to post-measures on both the Hamilton Rating Scale for Depression and the BDI. There were no differences among the three groups in this comparison. However, during follow-up evaluations a differential effect was evident; patients in both the Cognitive and Behavioral conditions maintained gains in therapy far more effectively than patients in the insight-oriented relational therapy. At the final one-year follow-up, 27 clients were assessed by an independent clinical evaluator who determined that in both the cognitive and behavioral conditions, only one of the nine clients interviewed was diagnosed as currently being in a new episode of major depression (11%), while four clients from the insight-oriented condition had relapsed (44%). This clinical interview also revealed that approximately two-thirds of those who had received cognitive or behavioral treatment were still using specific skills learned in therapy to help them cope with potentially depressogenic situations that had occurred over time; in contrast, only one-third of those treated with relational/insight therapy reported using knowledge or skills acquired in therapy to help them cope.

Individual difference variables were also examined, and patients who met Research Diagnostic Criteria (RDC) (Spitzer, Endicott & Robins, 1978) for endogenous subtype of major depression responded less well to psychotherapy than those who were not classified as endogenous subtype. Because of the small sample size, we could not examine this effect within each modality; however, across modalities, the effect was clear. Only one-third of the endogenous (N = 5/15) could be classified as "responders" (i.e., long form BDI score of 10 or less); in contrast, four-fifths of the nonendogenous (N = 12/15) had reached this criterion ($p = .012$ using

Fisher's exact probability test). Similar results obtained on the Hamilton Rating Scale for Depression. At the final evaluation (one year post-treatment), of the 12 nonendogenous patients available to be interviewed, none had relapsed into a new major episode; of the 15 endogenous patients interviewed, seven had relapsed (Gallagher & Thompson 1983b).

A larger follow-up study is currently underway, in which patients are randomly assigned to either cognitive therapy, behavioral therapy, brief psychodynamic therapy (Horowitz, 1976), or to a six-week delayed treatment/wait list condition. Preliminary results (Thompson & Gallagher, 1984) have revealed that at six weeks into treatment the first 37 patients were significantly improved over ten patients assigned to the delayed treatment control condition. These findings argue against the effects of spontaneous remission or remission evoked by research procedures other than the therapy itself (e.g., repeated assessment interviews). At the post-therapy evaluation point 21 of the 37 patients were in full remission (according to an independent evaluator's clinical assessment of symptoms and levels of distress). An additional seven patients showed substantial improvement, with only a few symptoms remaining and 24% were still clinically depressed. Comparisons among the three active therapy conditions at post on the Hamilton Rating Scale and the BDI indicated significant change across time, but no significant group by time interactions. Available follow-up data indicate that those who reached a remitted status and remained that way for at least two months had very little relapse over a one-year period (9%); in contrast, those who were unable to maintain themselves for two months without getting depressed again had a higher relapse rate in the remainder of the year (approximately 24%). Again, this was irrespective of treatment modality employed.

With respect to predictor variables, 42% of those with endogenous features were still clinically depressed at post, while only about 16% of the nonendogenous were so classified. This supports our previous findings. Also consistent with the earlier work were the data obtained on use of coping skills after therapy was completed. Those who made use of coping skills acquired in therapy were generally able to avoid relapse.

Taken together, these findings support the conclusion that cognitive therapy, engaged in on a one-to-one basis, is efficacious in the treatment of clinically depressed older adults. While it is unclear whether cognitive therapy is superior or essentially equivalent to other forms of psychotherapy and/or pharmacotherapy, the evidence is accumulating that it is a useful clinical approach that holds considerable promise for the future.

SPECIAL ISSUES IN COGNITIVE THERAPY WITH OLDER ADULTS

There are a number of differences between older and younger clients that warrant consideration and inclusion in the therapeutic process if this approach is to be maximally effective with elders.

Expectations and Realities

Older adults are more likely to have sensory and perceptual problems, a slowing of cognitive processing, and decreased ability to retain new information. They might also have divergent and somewhat negative expectations of the therapy experience. These features are important considerations for most forms of psychotherapy with older clients, and in some instances may discourage therapists from initiating treatment. However, we feel that cognitive therapy techniques are especially well-suited for dealing with many of the issues specific to the treatment of older adults. For example, emphasizing repeated summarization of materials covered and soliciting feedback from the client to assure that both therapist and client understand and agree on points of importance being covered are two procedures that help compensate for comprehension and retention problems.

When doing cognitive therapy with older adults, therapists need to be sensitive to the level of therapeutic sophistication of each client treated. Particularly in medical settings, older clients may think of psychotherapy as one more form of medical treatment, and may be prepared to play the passive role of patient waiting to be "cured" by the physician. Alternatively, they may view psychotherapy as a long-term process of personality adjustment and may expect the more dynamic process of free association to be the major vehicle of change. Either of these views can seriously inhibit the establishment of the collaborative relationship, making successful treatment difficult to achieve.

Another area for misconceptions is clients' beliefs about the origins of their depression. Older adults often consider their depressive symptoms, such as physical fatigue, sleep difficulty, appetite disturbance, decreased concentration, and indecisiveness, as due to some biological problem that requires a medical approach, or they may view them as normal concomitants of the aging process and therefore irreversible. Irreversible life changes, such as the death of a spouse or the loss of a job, are often seen as the single major cause of dysphoria in the elderly. These attributions are sometimes so strong that elders believe that nothing can relieve their distress except a return to the earlier situation. Since this is impossible, some think that no manner of options or internal resources will be of any use. Some elders begin treatment with a strongly held belief that they are "too old to change"—perhaps even endorsing the notion that "you can't teach an old dog new tricks." It is generally helpful to tackle such views head-on, by offering the client a balanced presentation of the fact that cognitive therapy may be difficult (for the reasons outlined above), but it is certainly not beyond the grasp of most elders. It is also good to reframe the task of cognitive therapy as helping the client to learn new things about how thoughts influence mood, and to ask the client directly if he or she thinks they have the capacity to learn anything new. If clients continue to believe their depressive symptoms are inevitable or are dependent upon external situations over which they have no control, change in these areas is highly unlikely.

The cognitive therapist can minimize later problems in treatment by carefully assessing clients' original beliefs about therapy and their expectations for how change will occur. The therapist then can tailor the explanation of the cognitive approach to make it maximally relevant to that particular client's needs. For example, clients who believe their depression is biologically driven can be asked to view therapy as an experiment in which this idea will be tested (in a variety of ways) and either supported or refuted. This approach (rather than trying to convince clients their idea is incorrect) communicates respect for a differing opinion and also explains how therapy will proceed—that is, in a collaborative way, with both participants investigating the veracity of commonly held beliefs.

The older adult's expectations for the *process* of treatment also rarely follow those of the therapy-wise counselor. Consequently, it becomes very important for the therapist to make clear the "rules of the game" before starting cognitive therapy. The therapist should detail the active nature of cognitive therapy, the expectation of collaboration, the importance of regular completion of homework assignments, and the structured format of the sessions. In addition, it is helpful to be aware that certain actions in therapy—like challenging another's opinion, interrupting conversation or giving constructive criticism—may be considered socially rude and inappropriate by the older client. It is best to handle these issues at the start of treatment by labeling them as potential problems and agreeing with the client to exempt therapy from the rules of other more formal social interactions.

Learning and Memory

The successful application of cognitive therapy involves the client's assimilation of a good deal of new material. There is considerable documentation for the decline in an older person's ability to learn new information (Botwinick, in press). Both the ability to absorb new information and the ability to recall new information after a delay become impaired as a person's age progresses. Sensory deficits will compound the problem. The issue of how to cope with learning and memory deficits becomes very important when designing treatments for older adults.

Physical adjustments like bright lighting, low background noise, and being seated in close proximity to the client can help compensate for many sensory problems. Having the older client "take notes" and write out important points during therapy sessions generally improves the client's absorbtion of new material. Helping clients provide labels for complex concepts is also helpful. These labels can be used in the sessions and in homework assignments to help the client recall new ideas.

The major points in each therapy session should be repeated over and over again—by therapist *and* client. This approach fits in well in cognitive therapy, where frequent summarizing of session progress is the norm. With older adults it is also very important to point out the therapeutic process as it is occurring, so that the "zig-zag" course of change can be tracked, remembered, and understood. Homework can be designed to reinforce this understanding. For example, at our Center we frequently make two simultaneous audiotape recordings of therapy sessions, and give one to the client to review during the week. Notes are to be made about *how* change occurred in that session, and what the blocks were to further change. This "working over" of the therapeutic material promotes more elaborate associative connections, thus enhancing the elder client's capacity for recall in situations outside the therapy hour.

Modification of termination procedures can also be used to enhance clients' retention of therapeutic material. Clients can be encouraged to maintain a cumulative "Survival Guide"—a record of helpful techniques discovered during the course of therapy to be consulted after termination. Abrupt termination does not appear to be as effective with older adults as is a more gradual tapering off of treatment (Gallagher & Thompson, 1983a). Final sessions may be spaced over several weeks, with each session focusing on summarizing the techniques learned and reviewing the success or failure of their application during the intervening time.

Focusing Attention

Older clients often have difficulty focusing their attention on a single therapeutic issue. Many are distracted by tangential associations as they go through their homework, or describe an incident that occurred (e.g., giving too many details about an event and "losing" the main point). Consequently, it is left up to the therapist to track what is said and to keep the session thematically relevant. This can prove to be somewhat exasperating for therapists who resent having their role include being a conversation monitor! Cognitive therapists deal directly with this issue in session through several means: clients are first told about the pattern; then they are asked to try to "catch" themselves as they see it occurring; some are asked (as a specific homework assignment) to notice their "wandering" when listening to a session tape; others find that an agreed-upon verbal or nonverbal cue of some sort from the therapist is needed to focus attention. For example, therapists may lift a finger or tap the client's shoulder to get attention, or they may simply question how the material relates to the agenda set for that session.

Therapists' Views

Much of the success of cognitive therapy depends on the effectiveness of the collaborative relationship. If the therapist has views that run counter to the establishment of a strong working relationship, therapy may never succeed. Thus it is worthwhile for clinicians to examine their own potential biases by taking stock of their views about growing old and their prior experiences with older adults. For example, if a therapist's primary experience with older adults is in a hospital or long-term care setting, the view may be held that older adults are typically quite frail with serious physical and mental problems that will only continue to worsen over time. Consequently, the therapist may have very limited expectations for the usefulness of doing psychotherapy with this group. This could lead to therapeutic apathy ("what's the point of putting in a lot of effort if Mr. X. is going to die soon anyway?) which usually is communicated (directly or indirectly) to the client involved.

Another obvious bias involves accepting the media's portrayal of old age as an essentially negative experience. It is possible that older adults' uncomplimentary views of themselves are at least partially formed in an effort to cope with society's negative view of the aging process (Emery, 1981). Therapists accepting this position may find themselves feeling sorry for the "awful experiences" that their client is facing. Though well meaning, this kind of commiseration is just as effective in blocking therapeutic progress as either apathy or lowered expectations. The client will not be effectively challenged in treatment, goals are likely to be scaled down, and little new learning will occur. Therapists can counteract these views by spending some time in settings where healthy, active, positive aging is occurring so that information can be obtained about the variety of ways in which people age, and the wide range of individual differences can be appreciated.

CLINICAL CASE EXAMPLES

We would like to begin this section by discussing a patient for whom some modifications in the application of cognitive therapy were required, although in general his course of treatment and follow-up was straightforward. We will then present three patients for whom the standard application of cognitive therapy had varying degrees of success, and close this chapter by discussing several factors that may influence the course and outcome of cognitive therapy with elders.

The Case of Mr. D.

Mr. D. is an 83-year-old white widower who retired from his occupation as a contractor at the age of 66. His wife died two years later. After undergoing a year-long bereavement, he made a good adjustment to living alone, and he continued to live in the family home for the next 13 years. At about age 80 he began to have difficulty with hearing and vision, and by the middle of the 82nd year he was also showing signs of forgetfulness accompanied at times by mild confusion and psychological distress. He became concerned about his ability to manage his affairs, and often was extremely worried about what would become of him in the future. After discussing this with his nearby son and daughter-in-law, it was decided that he would move into their spare room. Shortly after this he became depressed and anxious. At times his distress became so intense that it was disruptive to the family. His condition continued to worsen, and at the families request he agreed to seek help.

Special Considerations

There were a number of factors to be considered in treating Mr. D. with cognitive therapy. First, he was experiencing sensory deficits serious enough to interfere with independent living. This imposed limits on the use of many behavioral procedures to enhance feelings of competence and mastery, as well as being a continual and gruesome reminder of the reality of his predicament. Second, there was evidence of cognitive slowing which was aggravated by his psychological distress. This meant that therapeutic information had to be presented slowly and repeated often in order for him to assimilate it. Third, the idea of psychotherapy was completely novel to him, and considerable education into the role of patient was required.

Early Phase of Therapy

Therapy began by discussing Mr. D.'s current complaints, and then targeting several for him to work on. Three target complaints were selected: first, to reduce his awful feeling of hopelessness about himself; second, to help him learn to control his feelings of being overwhelmed; and finally, to help him stop feeling that he was a failure. When the cognitive therapy model was presented, Mr. D. seemed disappointed and confused because he was expecting to be given something that would solve his problems. The idea of entering into a collaborative relationship where he would be expected to evaluate his opinions about himself seemed futile to him. However, after three sessions had been devoted to discussing the model and its potential application to his problems, he developed some understanding of how therapy would proceed, and agreed to note the kinds of thoughts that occurred at times when he became blue or anxious. Reviewing the thoughts that accompanied his initial disappointment in therapy was helpful to illustrate how a cognitive approach might be used in other situations. By this time it was also evident that Mr. D. had difficulty staying on a given topic in the sessions. Because of this, "rules" were established that gave the therapist permission to interrupt whenever his conversation wandered.

Virtually all of the thoughts reported centered around the theme of feeling worthless because of a lack of accomplishment, and a fear of being unable to handle even simple activities that come up during the day. Having him complete an Activities Schedule was helpful in that it provided objective evidence that indeed he *was* carrying out some activities around the house, and that unusual things occasionally happened which he was unable to take care of. This set the stage for getting him to question the evidence for his thoughts. This took several sessions in which the therapist worked almost exclusively with this strategy.

Middle Phase of Therapy

As he mastered this technique of questioning the evidence for his conclusions about himself, other cognitive techniques were introduced (one at a time) and practiced in session using role plays. By this time, Mr. D. was becoming increasingly flexible in dealing with constructs, and was even able to participate in some reverse role-play situations. He began to have some success in identifying dysfunctional thoughts as they occurred, and in developing more adaptive counteractive thoughts. Although he perceived that this was somewhat helpful to him, he basically saw it as a game in which he was "fooling" himself into thinking things were better than they were. The underlying theme that emerged focused on his lack of contribution to his family or his friends. Therefore, his life no longer had any meaning or purpose, and it was only a matter of time before he would be placed in a home for "worthless" persons.

Two approaches were used to help Mr. D. deal with this pessimistic view. The first built on the fact that his friends still came to visit him. The therapist encouraged him to entertain the idea that they may be coming because they enjoyed being with him, and may actually be benefitting from these visits in other ways as well. This fostered an investigative effort on his part to learn the ways in which his friends benefitted from their time with him. It turns out that several told him he was good to talk to, partly because he listened to them closely. Mr. D. had to struggle against the idea that he still wasn't worth anything because he wasn't *doing* anything for them except listening—this did not represent a service, to him. The therapist pointed out that active listening could in fact be a service for some people with few other friends to talk to.

The second approach focused on helping Mr. D. view himself as a model to help others cope with problems they may encounter as they become older. This was introduced in the following manner:

Therapist. "You say you're worthless, and why is that?"

Mr. D. "Because I'm not doing anything for anybody. My life has no meaning."

Therapist. "Well, let's see if there are some ways you might be doing things for people that you might not realize. You once told me, but it's slipped my mind. How old is your son now?"

Mr. D. "Why, he's 57."

Therapist. "And what are the ages of his children?"

Mr. D. "Well, the oldest is 23; the middle one is 20, and the baby is still at home. I believe she's 17. She's in her last year of school."

Therapist. "OK. Now let's imagine for a moment what things are going to be like 20 years or so from now. Where will you be then?"

Mr. D. "Well, if the good Lord is willing, I'll be gone." (Note: Mr. D. had frequently discussed death wishes prior to this time, but had no intention of acting on them.)

Therapist. "OK. Now how old will your son be, and what do you think he'll be doing?"

Mr. D. "He'd be about my age now, and I don't know but I hope he'd be living at home with Mary."

Therapist. "Well let's hope that's the case. Now do you suppose that they might be experiencing any of the problems that you're having now?"

Mr. D. "Well, I sure hope not, but I can allow that they might be having some problems. I know Mary's not too healthy now. She's overweight, and that's not good, and Edward is complaining of his arthritis."

Therapist. "Well, suppose for a moment that they start having more problems with their health or with other things that come up. What is a likely thing that they might say at a time like that?"

Mr. D. "Well, they might say—What are we to do! What are we to do! We've got to get some help.—I don't know. I guess something like that."

Therapist. "I think you're right, but they might say something else too. When someone says—What are we to do!—what is a logical thing that they might do next?" (Long pause and Mr. D. seems puzzled.) "Well, OK. I don't think I'm making my point very clear here. When we get into stressful situations that are perplexing, and we don't know what to do, often times we begin to look for *models* to help us know how to handle the problem. You're going through a stage of life now that all of us (sooner or later) will have to go through, and none of us know quite what to expect or quite how to deal with it. And so in a sense, you are serving as a model for your family and freinds in how to deal with the problems that come up as we age. Now, do you suppose there is a possibility that your son, and Mary too, might be asking the question—I wonder what Dad would do if he were here?"

Mr. D. "Oh, I see what you mean. Well yes. You know, now that you mention it, I can remember asking myself the same thing about what my Dad would do about something."

Therapist. "It's sort of like being a teacher."

Mr. D. "I never thought of it that way."

This seemed to be a pivotal point in therapy, as Mr. D. accepted the idea that his life still did have purpose as a teacher and role model for others who would encounter similar problems.

Strategies for dealing with stressful situations then began to focus on the use of self-talk. Several sessions were devoted to learning to detect quickly the feeling of being worthless that would well up in him in personal or family crisis situations, and immediately begin to counteract this with thoughts like: "I am worth something; I can handle this without becoming upset, and this will help others learn to do the same." While this didn't always work, it was a conceptual framework that more often than not enabled him to assume a problem-solving posture rather than being overwhelmed by the crisis. It also enabled him to see that in many things the family and his friends did seek out his opinion, and this was extremely gratifying.

Later Phase of Therapy

By this time Mr. D. had accepted the value of discussing problems with others, and getting their help in solving them. He was able to implement this in his relationships with friends so termination was not a serious problem for him. The last three sessions of the 20 session therapy were used to review the specific skills he had learned for identifying and checking his dysfunctional thoughts, and to prepare for potentially depressogenic situations in the future. The therapist raised situations that might occur, and together they practiced how Mr. D. would handle them. Termination was completed gradually with three "booster sessions" spaced six weeks apart at the end to help him review and correct problems in thinking that occurred in between appointments. Throughout these final sessions, the emphasis was on repetition in order to assure that the concepts were highly overlearned, almost to the point of being automatic.

The Case of Mrs. A.

Mrs. A. is a 66-year-old widow with minor health problems who began therapy with a diagnosis of Major Depressive Disorder with strong endogenous features. In addition, she was assessed as having both Dependent and Compulsive personality disorders. Mrs. A. felt guilt about her treatment of her father in his final years. He wanted Mrs. A. to visit more often than her typical frequency of two to three times per month. Mrs. A. also felt very guilty about their last conversation: her father called to complain about a new physical discomfort and Mrs. A. abruptly told him to go to the emergency room (as was his practice). He followed her advice, was hospitalized, and died eight hours later. Mrs. A. did not learn of her father's hospitalization until she was informed of his death.

Treatment consisted of two related approaches. First, to soften Mrs. A's harsh judgements of herself, the therapist encouraged Mrs. A. to review the factors that worked against frequent visits to her father. Significant obstacles included ongoing unpleasantness between father and daughter, the need for Mrs. A. to care for her husband during his recovery from a stroke, her concern that her husband might have another stroke (which prompted her to be closer by her husband—her father lived about 15 miles away), and finally, her desire for time with her family and for herself. Mrs. A. understood that these factors were barriers to frequent visits, but she could not accept that these obstacles were legitimate. She felt that to use her new awareness of these barriers to feel better would be to rationalize away a deserved punishment; she felt that she must "do penance."

The next thrust, then, was to question the appropriate duration of the "sentence" for her "wrong-doing." Unfortunately, Mrs. A.

was unwilling to put any time limit on her self-imposed sentence, or to entertain more adaptive ways of "doing penance." At termination she remained clinically depressed and was referred for additional treatment. Factors associated with her lack of significant change will be discussed later in this section.

The Case of Mrs. B.

Mrs. B. is a 62-year-old widow in good health (her main physical problem was mild asthma) who began treatment with a diagnosis of Major Depression with some endogenous features, along with features of a Dependent Personality disorder. Mrs. B. experienced guilt about how she handled her role as primary caregiver for her husband before he died, and how she was currently handling her role as caregiver for her 90-year-old father. The guilt concerned her beliefs that: (1) she was not doing enough for the ill relative and was thereby contributing to his deterioration, and (2) she should be more emotionally supportive of the ill person. For example, she felt guilty because she became angry at her father for not performing the self-care tasks that he could still perform. Treatment focused on her feelings about her father, primarily because it was a current concern. Mrs. B.'s father, who lived with her, was confined to a wheelchair. He had occasional memory lapses and required assistance with eating, bathing, and managing his catheter. He was just beginning to be incontinent.

One of the cognitive errors that seemed to underlie the guilt was Mrs. B.'s "rule" that family members should always be glad to take care of each other. It was not acceptable to grimace internally when performing tasks that few people enjoy, such as handling another's catheter. She was unaware that caregiving is typically very stressful or that resentment and anger are common reactions to this stress. Nor could she permit herself to view her own needs as important when her father's plight was so unfortunate.

Treatment was a combination of the following interventions: first, information was provided about common caregiver emotions; second, she was helped to assess the influences in her own background which would make resentment an expected result; and third, she was encouraged to re-examine the acceptability and desirability of "taking care of the caregiver." The common goals in each of these approaches was for Mrs. B. to be less harsh in her judgements of herself.

Information about caregiver reactions was provided by means of an article describing the stresses and emotions of caregivers (Crossman & Kaljain, 1984) in which the therapist underlined pertinent sections, and by related questioning to encourage Mrs. B. to re-examine her beliefs about the ways that people react to long-term adversities. These interventions were each only partially successful, but seemed to have an additive effect. It was also suggested that she consider joining a support group for caregivers, but she did not follow through on this idea during the course of her individual therapy.

The second approach to Mrs. B.'s harsh judgements of herself was to trace the pressures developing throughout her life which possibly influenced her current reactions. It was expected that she would feel less guilty if she could attribute her reactions at least in part to situational factors, rather than exclusively to internal short-comings. It turned out that even as a child, she was expected to take care of others and rarely received care from others. Her caregiving activities increased sharply when her husband fell ill. After he died, she hoped that she could finally live for herself. This hope was dashed when it soon became necessary to become her father's care-giver. Mrs. B. began to understand her resentment and anger as "rebellion" against the demands on her, rather than as reflecting her "lazy" or "selfish" personality traits.

Finally, she was asked to examine the acceptability and desirability of taking care of herself. Mrs. B. initially believed that attention to care for the self was selfish. She seemed to think that taking care of herself meant not taking care of others, which was unacceptable. Data in support of a contrary view were gathered by examining the positive consequences of a previous issue worked with in therapy when Mrs. B. stopped leaping up instantly to take care of her grandchildren but instead allowed her daughter-in-law to proceed at her own slower pace. All benefitted from the lessening of tension between the adults and from Mrs. B.'s more positive mood as she felt less burdened. Thus, she was helped to generalize what was learned about the value of reducing her own stress level and was able to begin to view a respect for her own needs more positively. She ended therapy with a more balanced view of how to manage taking care of herself *and* others.

Overall, then, these approaches were helpful. At termination, Mrs. B. reported being somewhat more relaxed in her demands on herself, and therefore experienced less guilt because she committed fewer "wrong-doings." She also reported that she became angry at her father less frequently and less intensely. Although she still had sufficient symptoms remaining to be diagnosed as Minor Depressive Disorder, there had been meaningful reduction in her level of distress in a number of important areas.

The Case of Mrs. C.

Mrs. C. is a 67-year-old widow with a significant health problem—a rare neuromuscular disorder—who began treatment with a diagnosis of Major Depressive Disorder, no endogenous features, and no evidence of a concurrent personality disorder of any type. Mrs. C. felt a deep guilt about her godmother and godfather, a couple in their mid-90's. They had raised her from the time she was orphaned at age 14, and so she felt eternally indebted. She felt the pressure of time in her ongoing struggle to re-pay her debts to them because the couple was so advanced in years. Her "re-payment" took two forms: she expected herself to visit often, and to reduce their long-standing conflicts with their own children. However, visits became increasingly difficult in recent years because of her neurological disorder.

Treatment for her guilt about the first problem consisted of weighing the desirability of more frequent visits against the considerable discomfort of traveling and the added risk to her health when pushing her body beyond its limits. When asked to prioritize the importance of her health and the importance of visiting, she concluded that her health was her first priority. This process of prioritizing helped to dissipate her guilt about this issue. Her guilty feelings at being unable to resolve her surrogate parents' family problems was rooted in the unrealistic notion that well-meaning but uninvited third parties can somehow improve others' relationships. This notion was questioned through a review of her stepbrothers' attempts to achieve the same goal. They were also unsuccessful, and so she concluded that such efforts were generally unlikely to succeed. She no longer felt responsible, and did not feel it was her fault that family relationships did not improve.

Mrs. C.'s problems with guilt required only the straightforward application of standard cognitive therapy techniques. By the conclusion of therapy, she was diagnosed as no longer depressed and this situation has been maintained through the three months of follow-up for which we now have data.

FACTORS ASSOCIATED WITH DIFFERENTIAL TREATMENT OUTCOME

At least five factors can be explored for their relationship to therapeutic outcome in each of the cases described earlier; they also have been associated with treatment responsiveness for other cases treated at our Center. These are: (1) initial intensity of depressed mood, (2) presence of endogenous depressive features, (3) presence of a personality disorder in addition to the depression, (4) depth of emotional bonds with others, and (5) style of working in therapy.

Initial Intensity of Depressed Mood

Figure 1 depicts scores at various time points on the short form of the Beck Depression Inventory (Beck & Beck, 1972) for three of the cases discussed. This measure is completed by the patient before each therapy session, and information is used to evaluate progress over time. As indicated in Figure 1, there was some trend towards a link between pre- and post-treatment intensity of depression. Mrs. C., who was initially in the "moderate" range on this measure terminated with a nondepressed mood and few features of the depressive syndrome. Mrs. A. and Mrs. B., by contrast, both started within the severe range. Mrs. A. showed little improvement; Mrs. B.'s depression had lessened to a moderate level.

If pre-treatment intensity of depressed mood does, indeed, help predict the outcome, why might this be so? Mrs. A., with the initially severe mood disturbance, was focused almost entirely on her misery and could rarely switch to a more constructive focus. Mrs. C., on the other hand, was able to participate actively and collaboratively in her treatment. It may be that pharmacotherapy, for example, if initiated first, would have reduced Mrs. A.'s symptomatic distress so that she could have more effectively participated in cognitive therapy.

Endogeneity

Endogeneity refers to a subtype of Major Depressive Disorder that is characterized by a particular set of symptoms. The cardinal features are lack of reactivity to pleasant events or experiences and pervasive loss of interest or pleasure in all or almost all usual activities. Other typical features include: distinct quality of mood (i.e.,

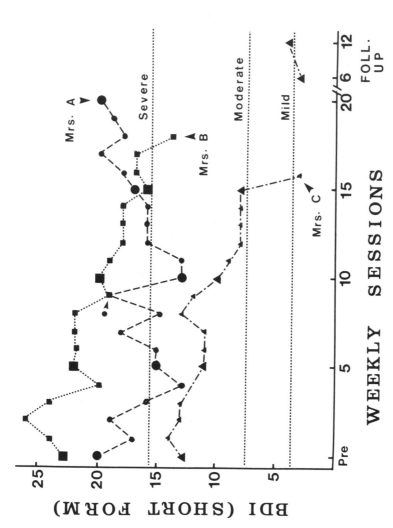

FIGURE 1. Changes in BDI scores (short form) furing the course of Cognitive Therapy for three elderly patients. Followup data were also available for Mrs. C. at six and twelve weeks and for Mrs. B. at six weeks. Dotted lines reflect approximate cut-offs for none, mild, moderate, and severe levels of depression.

mood is described as distinctly different from what one would feel following the death of a loved one), depression which is regularly worse in the morning, early morning awakening (at least two hours before usual time), psychomotor retardation or agitation, weight loss, and excessive or inappropriate guilt (DSM-III, 1980, p. 215). At least four of the above symptoms are required for a diagnosis of endogeneity. Accurately identifying this subtype can be important for decision-making about what type of treatment to employ. It has been speculated that endogenous depressives are not as likely to fully benefit from psychotherapy alone (Bielski & Friedel, 1976) but rather should be treated with medication because of the possibility that a biochemical substrate underlies this form of depression.

Overall, our data have indicated that elders with endogenous features do not respond as well to psychotherapy alone as do those without such features, but the results of other studies on this question are mixed (Persons & Burns, 1985). Outcomes for the four cases reported earlier was consistent with the hypothesized connection between endogeneity and response to therapy: the depression of the nonendogenous cases, Mr. D. and Mrs. C., remitted, while the depression of those with endogenous features was alleviated partially (Mrs. B.) or not at all (Mrs. A.). However, a note of caution is in order here to remind us that no single predictor will be accurate in all individual cases, nor can we generalize from these few cases to all elders.

Personality Disorders

According to the DSM-III (American Psychiatric Association, 1980), a "personality disorder" refers to a personality trait which is inflexible, maladaptive, or causes distress or impairment in social or occupational roles. In other words, the enduring style of thinking and interacting with the environment is dysfunctional. It may be speculated that the treatment of a depression which is superimposed on a personality disorder is more difficult than treatment in the absence of a personality disorder. The added difficulties probably stem from many factors, including the barriers of a rigid style that block experimentation with new thoughts or behaviors, the confirmation of depressive beliefs by feedback from social or occupational environments that have had problematic transactions with the patient (Krantz, in press), and a greater likelihood of strains in the therapy relationship.

As indicated earlier, an independent evaluator judged that Mrs. A. had both Dependent and Compulsive personality disorders, Mrs. B. had a few features of the Dependent personality disorder but did not meet the full set of criteria for the disorder, and both Mrs. C. and Mr. D. showed no evidence of any personality disorder. It is noteworthy that the outcome for each of these patients was consistent with the notion that depression superimposed on a personality disorder is more difficult to treat. The following discussion focuses on Mrs. A.'s Dependent personality disorder because it was evidenced very clearly in the cognitive therapy work.

Mrs. A. avoided making decisions and believed that any decision would be bad simply because she was the one to make it. When her husband was alive, he reportedly had make all the decisions in the family; they invariably turned out to be "right" in her view simply because it was he who made them. She also avoided other types of thinking because she perceived thinking as aversive and beyond her abilities. She explained that her parents always coddled her and never pushed her to master a challenge. For example, they allowed her to stop piano lessons after the second lesson because she found it too difficult. These past experiences left her ill-suited for cognitive therapy. Cognitive therapy presumes that the client can focus attention on the problem at hand, monitor and critically evaluate his/her thoughts, and generate alternatives (of course, these prerequisites are shared by most types of brief psychotherapy). Not surprisingly, Mrs. A. was certain that she did not have, and could not learn, the skills necessary for more adaptive independent functioning.

Another feature of her dependent personality was that Mrs. A. wanted to have someone else take care of the burdens of daily living for her. Ordinary tasks, such as finding a plumber for household repairs, elicited great distress.

Mrs. A. also said that while her husband was alive, he gave her frequent compliments and reassurances. This input had been the main source of her good feelings about herself, which shielded her from her own self-doubts. Since his death, she was alone with a very long-standing negative self-image.

By contrast, Mrs. C. was able to rely on herself to think through her psychological concerns and problems in daily living. Although she initially doubted her adequacy, she at least assumed that these responsibilities were her own. Therefore, the active role of the patient in cognitive therapy meshed with her own perspective on how problems should be tackled.

Social-Emotional Bonds

Were the emotional ties of these patients with friends and relatives related to the outcome of therapy? Recent work on predictors of outcome in the treatment of alcoholics (Bromet & Moos, 1977) indicates that those with better social resources benefit more from treatment than do alcoholics with less solid social networks. This same pattern was observed among the patients discussed here: Mrs. A., who did not benefit greatly from cognitive therapy, had an emotionally impoverished social network and lived alone; Mrs. B., who eliminated many (but not all) depressive symptoms, had no friends but lived with family; and Mrs. C. and Mr. D., who conquered their depressions, enjoyed excellent relationships with their children and close bonds with several friends. The simple frequency of social activities or the number of casual friends seemed relatively unimportant; rather, it was the depth of the bonds with others which seemed to covary with outcome.

To illustrate, Mrs. A. played bridge with others several times per week and attended occasional social functions. She had at least one woman whom she considered to be a friend, but this woman was not perceived as a confidante or a strong source of emotional support. Rather, she longed for her younger brother to fill these needs, but reported that he actively avoided this role. In Mrs. A.'s mind, a satisfying relationship meant having a devoted husband or brother to take care of her. Since neither were possible, she experienced considerable self-imposed aloneness. Mrs. A. did not agree with the therapist's efforts toward deepening her ties with friends because she equated closeness with others with frequent crying on their shoulders. By contrast, the social network of Mrs. C. was very fulfilling. Her adult children were in frequent contact, and seemed to enjoy her company. They also made it clear that they would provide the necessary care if her health deteriorated. She also had several close friends. Their presence helped her to cope with the loss of pleasurable activities in recent years, due to medical problems, because other shared pleasures remained.

In summary, these case examples were presented to illustrate differences in the extent to which alterations or expansions of "standard" cognitive therapy may be required for particular elders, given the nature of their problems and the presence or absence of certain characteristics at the start of therapy. It is clear that the less straightforward cases required a larger number and more variety in the selection of techniques. These cases may also require more time in treatment than is usual (Young, 1984).

In this section we have also examined a variety of factors that appear to be related to differential outcome. However, we caution the reader that these are several among many variables that may affect outcome. We have not yet completed our analyses of how these factors (either alone or in combination) correlate with treatment success in our full sample. Nevertheless, we hope that presentation of this material will encourage the reader to think about the kind of patients for whom cognitive therapy seems most appropriate, and to conduct further research and clinical investigations on this question in the future. As pointed out recently by numerous proponents of cognitive therapy (cf. Emery, 1981; Rush & Watkins, 1981), it is very important to continue our efforts to adapt cognitive therapy to those presenting special challenges.

CONCLUSIONS

Currently, very few controlled outcome studies are being done evaluating the efficacy of cognitive therapy with elders. To our knowledge, research is currently being conducted at the Depression Research Unit at Yale, at UCLA and the Veterans Administration in West Los Angeles, CA., and at the University of Arizona (on group cognitive therapy with the elderly). This is only a beginning, particularly when one considers variations in samples, procedures, dependent measures used to evaluate impact, therapist characteristics, and a whole host of other variables that will differ by site.

Preliminary findings suggest that while the majority of elders treated with cognitive therapy do respond favorably in 16–20 individual sessions, there clearly are *some* elders for whom this approach does not appear to be helpful. Thus, of critical importance is the ability to develop profiles that distinguish these two groups reliably.

Other major issues in need of serious exploration include: (1) indications for lengthening the course of treatment (would some patients respond eventually, if more therapy were given?); (2) indications for when pharmacotherapy would be a useful component of the treatment program (would very severely depressed elders benefit from an antidepressant medication trial, so that when symptomatic distress is alleviated they are more amenable to cognitive therapy, or would some patients benefit from a combined approach?);

(3) need to study carefully the therapeutic process of change. (We do not know what the "critical ingredients" are that really affect change in cognitive therapy. Are the specific techniques of primary importance? What is the contribution of the therapeutic relationship to outcome? Are there documentable "turning points" in cognitive therapy? Do most patients attribute change to the particular approach, or to the particular therapist with whom they have worked?) These and other questions require careful process research—a skill that has been highly developed in the field of psychotherapy research in general (cf. Rice & Greenberg, 1984) but has received virtually no attention in the aging literature.

Finally, we believe that another very important area of inquiry concerns the maintenance of treatment gains after formal therapy is completed—referred to by some as "relapse prevention." While it is well-known that affective disorders tend to reoccur throughout the early and middle adult years, we do not know the extent to which elder depressives suffer relapse, nor do we have, at present, any systematic approaches for relapse prevention that are tailored to elders' special needs. For example, we have described the value of planned booster sessions for many of our patients; should a "walk-in group" be available for those who complete therapy but feel a new depression coming on? Would telephone therapy, and/or periodic telephone contacts, be of value to the more frail elderly, for whom getting around can be a real problem? It seems to us that serious study of the factors promoting relapse prevention could lead to a great savings in cost and in emotional wear and tear for future generations of elders.

REFERENCES

American Psychiatric Association. (1980), *Diagnostic and statistical manual of mental disorders* (3rd ed.). Washington, DC: Author

Beck, A. T. & Beck, R. W. (1972). Screening depressed patients in family practice. *Postgraduate Medicine, 52,* 81–85.

Beck, A. T., Rush, J. A., Shaw, B. F., & Emergy, G. (1979). *Cognitive therapy of depression.* New York: Guilford Press.

Beck, A. T., Hollon, S., Young, J., Bedrosian, R., & Budenz, D. (1985). Treatment of depression with cognitive therapy and amitriptyline. *Archives of General Psychiatry, 42,* 142–148.

Beck, A. T., Ward, C., Mendelson, M., Mock, J. E., & Erbaugh, J. (1961). An inventory for measuring depression. *Archives of General Psychiatry, 4,* 561–571.

Bellak, L., & Small, L. (1965). *Emergency psychotherapy and brief psychotherapy.* New York: Grune & Stratton.

Biekski, R. J., & Friedel, R. O. (1976). Prediction of tricyclic antidepressant response: A critical review. *Archives of General Psychiatry, 33,* 1479–1489.

Blackburn, I. M., Bishop, S., Glen, A., Whalley, L. J., & Christie, J. (1981). The efficacy of cognitive therapy in depression: A treatment trial using cognitive therapy and pharmacotherapy, each alone and in combination. *British Journal of Psychiatry, 139,* 181–189.

Botwinick, J. (in press). *Aging and behavior* (3rd ed.). New York: Springer Publishing Co.

Bromet, E., & Moos, R. (1977). Environmental resources and post-treatment functioning of alcoholic patients. *Journal of Health and Social Behavior, 18,* 326–338.

Crossman, L., & Kaljian, D. (1984). The family: Cornerstone of care. *Generations, 3,* 44–46.

Emery, G. (1981). Cognitive therapy with the elderly. In G. Emery, S. D. Hollon, & R. C. Bedrosian (Eds.), *New directions in cognitive therapy* (pp. 84–98). New York: Guilford Press.

Gallagher, D., & Thompson, L. W. (1982). Treatment of major depressive disorder in older adult outpatients with brief psychotherapies. *Psychotherapy: Theory, Research and Practice, 19,* 482–490.

Gallagher, D., & Thompson, L. W. (1983a). Cognitive therapy for depression in the elderly: A promising model for treatment and research. In L. D. Breslau & M. Haug (Eds.), *Depression and aging: Causes, care and consequences* (pp. 168–192). New York: Springer Publishing Co.

Gallagher, D., & Thompson, L. W. (1983b). Effectiveness of psychotherapy for both endogenous and nonendogenous depression in older adult outpatients. *Journal of Gerontology, 38,* 707–712.

Hamilton, M. (1967). Development of rating scale for primary depressive disorder. *British Journal of Social and Clinical Psychology, 6,* 278–296.

Horowitz, M. J. (1976). *Stress response syndrome.* New York: Jason Aaronson.

Jarvik, L. F., Mintz, J., Steuer, J., & Gerner, R. (1982). Treating geriatric depression: A 26-week interim analysis. *Journal of the American Geriatrics Society, 30,* 713–717.

Kiesler, D. (1966). Some myths of psychotherapy research and the search for a paradigm. *Psychological Bulletin, 65,* 110–136.

Kovacs, M., Rush, A. J., Beck, A. T., & Hollon, S. (1981). Depressed outpatients treated with cognitive therapy or pharmacotherapy. *Archives of General Psychiatry, 38,* 33–39.

Krantz, S. E. (in press). When negative cognitions reflect negative realities. *Cognitive Therapy and Research.*

Lewinsohn, P. M. (1974). A behavioral approach to depression. In R. Friedman, & M. Katz (Eds.), *The psychology of depression* (pp. 157–176). New York: V. H. Winston & Co.

Murphy, G. E., Simons, A. D., Wetzel, R., & Lustman, P. (1984). Cognitive therapy and pharmacotherapy, singly and together in the treatment of depression. *Archives of General Psychiatry, 41,* 33–41.

Persons, J. B., & Burns, D. (1985). *Outcome of cognitive therapy in unselected private patients.* Unpublished manuscript.

Rice, L. N., & Greenberg, L. S. (Eds.)(1984). *Patterns of change.* New York: Guilford Press.

Rush, A. J., & Watkins, J. (1981). Cognitive therapy with psychologically naive depressed outpatients. In G. Emery, S. D. Hollon, & R. C. Bedrosian (Eds.), *New directions in cognitive therapy* (pp. 5–28). New York: Guilford Press.

Rush, A. J., Beck, A., Kovacs, M. & Hollon, S. (1977). Comparative efficacy of cognitive therapy and pharmacotherapy in the treatment of depressed outpatients. *Cognitive Therapy and Research, 1,* 17–37.

Spitzer, R., Endicott, J., & Robins, E. (1978). Research diagnostic criteria: Rationale and reliability. *Archives of General Psychiatry, 35,* 773–782.

Steuer, J., Mintz, J., Hammen, C., Hill, M. A., Jarvik, L. F., McCarley, T., Motoike, P., & Rosen, R. (1984). Cognitive-behavioral and psychodynamic group psychotherapy in treatment of geriatric depression. *Journal of Consulting and Clinical Psychology, 52,* 180–189.

Thompson, L. W., & Gallagher, D. (1984). Efficacy of psychotherapy in the treatment of late-life depression. *Advances in Behavior Research and Therapy, 6,* 127–139.

Weissman, M. M. (1979). The psychological treatment of depression: Evidence for the efficacy of psychotherapy alone, in comparison with, and in combination with pharmacotherapy. *Archives of General Psychiatry, 36,* 1261–1269.

Yost, E., Beutler, L. E., Corbishley, A., & Allender, J. (1985). *Group cognitive therapy: A treatment method for the depressed elderly.* New York: Pergamon.

Young, J. (1984, November). *Cognitive therapy with personality disorders and difficult patients.* Paper presented at the annual meeting of the Association for the Advancement of Behavior Therapy, Philadelphia, Pennsylvania.

Young, J., & Beck, A. T. (1980). *Cognitive therapy rating manual.* Unpublished manuscript, Center for Cognitive Therapy, University of Pennsylvania, Philadelphia, PA.

Questions

1) Are cognitive techniques compatible with psychodynamic? behavioral? Gestalt? and/or pharmacological interventions?

2) What is the role of assessment in cognitive therapy?

3) What kinds of patients would be poor candidates for a cognitive approach?

16/GROUP THERAPY WITH COGNITIVELY IMPAIRED OLDER ADULTS

Michael J. Gilewski, PhD

Editor's Introduction

Group therapy has been a major topic in *CG* (v. 1, #1, pp. 51–58; v. 1, #3, pp. 81–90; v. 1, #4, pp. 19–30; v. 2, #2, pp. 23–37; v. 2, #3, pp. 25–38; v. 2, #4, pp. 37–49) and recent books (see reviews: v. 2, #4, pp. 85–87; v. 3, #3, pp. 73–74). Gilewski's chapter has a specific focus: group therapy with dementia patients. After reviewing the relevant literature, he provides specific critiques (inconsistencies of nosology, institutionalization policies, therapeutic modality, and research methodology).

Nevertheless, Gilewski is able to identify some trends: group therapy is effective with this population. Specifically, improved morale (staff as well as patient), symptom reduction, and increased discharge rates.

Techniques for group therapy are reviewed.

This chapter reviews techniques of group therapy employed with cognitively impaired older adults. First, I review much of the literature on psychotherapy with this population. Actually, the literature on psychotherapy is very sparse. I do not address more programmatic treatments such as milieu therapy and reality orientation. Nor do I cover therapies that are not traditionally considered psychological, such as music and art therapy, although such therapies are used quite frequently and may be effective with

Michael J. Gilewski is affiliated with Veterans Administration Outpatient Clinic, Los Angeles, CA.

281

cognitively impaired elderly adults. I also do not address family treatment, which is covered in the next section. Second, I critique the literature in a general way. Finally, I summarize the techniques that are applicable to group therapy with demented and other cognitively impaired older adults.

EARLY STUDIES

The literature on group therapy with cognitively impaired elderly is trimodal over time. There are several classic studies from the early '50s, some in the late '60s and early '70s, and a growing number published in the past few years. Silver (1950) is generally cited as the earliest publication on group work with "senile" older adults. Seventeen female patients met twice weekly for an hour of group therapy. Each patient was diagnosed senile psychotic. Silver refers to all the patients as organic, and they probably would have been classified as chronic brain syndrome in the first edition of the Diagnostic and Statistical Manual (DSM). The primary recurrent issue in the group led by a psychiatrist was the desire to return home. Other topic areas included physical complaints, "the good old days," money, loneliness, fantasies, and perceived rejection by the family. Refreshments were served about 20 minutes into the session to maintain attention, and music was often employed as an adjunct activity. All patients also received 300 mg of nicotinic acid per day to improve cognitive functioning. The group was judged effective because it led to more careful diagnosis of physical ailments, improved staff morale, relieved family distress over institutionalization, and nurses reported improved behavior in the patients.

Linden (1953) reported on group therapy with a mixture of functional and organic "senile" patients. Meetings were held with 51 women, mean age of 70, for in one-hour sessions, twice a week. The group met for more than two years, and the average number of sessions attended by any individual was 81. The group was led by male and female cotherapists. Linden (1954) suggested the dual leadership was critical to the group's success, because the male-female team stimulated greater resocialization for these regressed and dependent patients. Single leadership at an earlier phase in the group's development did not appear to be as effective. The group began as a traditional psychodynamic group using free association and mutual interpretations. As the group developed, the leaders found it more effective to call on as many members as possible or having members volunteer for 10–20 minute presentations to the group on topics of group or seasonal interest. The psychiatrist and nurse who ran the group rated individuals on improvement from none to much. Overall, 90% of those who were later discharged home or placed elsewhere had shown moderate to much improvement, three times the discharge rate over non-group participants. These members were on the whole more active in group than those who were not discharged. On the other hand, only 32% of those who remained institutionalized demonstrated at least moderate improvement. Thus, higher functioning patients benefitted most from the group.

Rechtschaffen, Atkinson, and Freeman (1954) included group therapy in a more comprehensive programmatic treatment for geropsychiatric patients. Group topics ranged from insight-oriented discussions to talks on hunting and fishing. The discharge rate increased more than 300 times that of the year prior to the program. Qualitative behavioral improvement was also noted for many patients. Wolff (1957) describes a program conducting small groups of four male and four female geropsychiatric patients. The group leader predominantly used passive listening. Most of the patients with definite improvement were paradoxically the most organic ones. Many of these individuals were discharged home or to nursing homes.

LATER STUDIES

Wolk and Goldfarb (1967) report one of the few experimental studies in this area. They randomly selected 50 patients over age 65 from a psychiatric hospital. Approximately half were long-term hospital patients, and about half, recent admissions. Both groups consisted of individuals from various diagnostic categories, but the majority of the long-term group were schizophrenic, and the majority of the other group, chronic brain syndrome (CBS). Approximately half of each group received weekly group psychotherapy in 1.5-hour sessions for 50 weeks. Scores on the Mental Status Questionnaire were approximately equal across all groups, suggesting relatively equal cognitive-impairment at baseline. Group therapy was not insight oriented. Rather the focus was on discussion of interpersonal problems, feelings, and immediate interpersonal relationships. All subjects took the House-Tree-Person (H-T-P) test prior to therapy and the 35 who completed therapy were tested again after therapy. Judgments of severity of depression, anxiety, self-concept, and interpersonal relationship problems from the H-T-P by two psychologists indicated improvement for both treatment groups, but not for controls. Change was generally mild in the recent admissions group (mostly CBS), but moderate to significant positive change dominated the long-term hospital group. Signs of organic mental impairment on the H-T-P in the long-term treatment group also decreased significantly. This study indicates that therapy has positive effects on cognitive impairment and other problems secondary to institutionalization.

Bowers, Anderson, Blomeier, and Pelz (1967) conducted three remotivation therapy groups for 47 individuals from a geriatic facility ranging in age from 62 to 96, with a mean for each group about 80 years. Means scores on a motor design reproduction test were below average for the age group, indicating cognitive impairment. Group sessions led by two ministerial interns and a member of the Recreation Therapy department were conducted twice weekly in 40-minute sessions. Initially and after six months, group leaders rated individuals with a scale measuring in-group behavior and one measuring general social functioning. Two groups with the greatest overall impairment on the design test were passive at first and focused on past reminiscence. As therapy progressed, individuals became more active and present oriented. A third group, the least impaired, avoided "therapy" and focused on projects and activities. All groups evidenced improvement in both in-group and social behavior over six months. Brain impairment did not mean a poor prognosis. One difficulty with this study is that remotivation therapy for these authors, although having the same goal of renewed interest in one's present life and surroundings, did not follow the traditional steps of remotivation therapy (cf. Barnes, Sack, & Shore, 1973; Dennis, 1978). According to the guidelines laid down by the American Psychiatric Association and Smith, Kline, and French's Remotivation Project, each meeting consists of the following components: (a) creating a climate of acceptance, (b) setting up a bridge to reality, (c) sharing the world we live in, (d) appreciating the world, and (e) maintaining the climate of acceptance. It is unclear what the remotivation therapy actually was for Bowers et al., because they did not describe the therapy in detail, nor did they cite sources which would have detailed the procedure.

Oberleder (1970) employed crisis-oriented, short-term group therapy with 12 patients in a state hospital. All patients were diagnosed with senile psychosis with or without arteriosclerosis. Wechsler Adult Intelligence Scale (WAIS) verbal scores ranged at baseline from 73 to 132 with a mean of 100. The study reported six months of weekly therapy. Therapy identified the crisis preceding hospitalization and dealt with senile symptoms of memory loss and confusion as ego-preserving defenses against reality. Often unresolved conflicts from middle-age underlay the "senility." Progress and planning conferences were held with patients during the therapy period, and for all patients at the end of six months, discharge was a possibility. Five actually left the hospital to return to their families or independent living and one died.

Manaster (1972) describes the progression of a group for extremely regressed geriatric patients. The group size was between 10 and 15 persons, and sessions initially lasted about 15 minutes, then later between 30–40 minutes. Group members sat around a square table and refreshments were served. The group began with individuals identifying themselves. Initially, the leader had to be fairly directive in group. As the group progressed, introductions became more spontaneous, and members became more active, sharing in one another's problems and using the group to air criticism about staff, families, etc. Attention span of individuals also increased as the group progressed. Eventually, stronger bonds were formed between members. Recurrent themes in the group discussion were the debilitating effects of aging, memory problems, belief in God, family, and early successes and failures. Manaster cites two benefits of therapy: increased involvement in other ward activities and increased sense of perceived control for the residents.

Ernst and his colleagues (Ernst, Beran, Badash, Kosovsky, & Kleinhauz, 1977) identified six patients with moderate to severe chronic brain syndrome and provided bi-weekly sensory stimulation and group therapy sessions for three months. The aim of group therapy was to reduce social isolation. Groups consisted of getting to know one another, reality orientation discussions, physical exercise, and refreshments, all in addition to the sensory stimulation exercises. Four of six patients had pre-post reductions on the Mental Status Questionnaire, while five had the same or fewer errors on the Face-Hand test post-treatment. Only one patient, though, reported fewer emotional complaints after therapy. In fact, two individuals reported more complaints at post-treatment than pre-treatment. This may indicate increased awareness by these two individuals as a result of therapy. Although the study lacks a sufficient sample size for adequate generalization, the trends indicate such therapy helped the majority of patients.

Burnside (1978b) describes work with three nurse-led groups. The first met 30 minutes weekly for seven months. All seven women members had cerebral arteriosclerosis, six having psychiatric problems, and one with organic brain syndrome (OBS). Patients came from a locked ward of a psychiatric facility. Topics of group discussion included feelings about being women, clothes, and the "prisoner's life" they led. Some sessions included drawing pictures, and refreshments were served at the end of each group. Improved behavior and social grace were noted because of group participation. A second group of six residents of an extended care facility included four individuals with chronic brain syndrome (CBS). The group discussed specific topics, reminisced, and did artwork, the latter being the most effective intervention. A final group of six CBS patients from a locked facility met weekly for 30–60 minute sessions. Group activities included exercise, music, socialization, and discussion. All patients in these groups were clearly mentally impaired, but the psychological nature appeared only one aspect of therapy. The groups were considered successful, but Burnside did not document how success was measured apart from mere clinical judgment.

RECENT STUDIES

Dye (Dye & Erber, 1981; Dye & Richards, 1980) reports on 52 newly admitted nursing home residents who participated in either a resident-only counseling group or a family counseling group or served as control subjects without counseling. Both groups meet twice a week for seven sessions following a structured format. The term *workshop* was used to characterize the sessions to overcome resistance generated by terms such as *counseling* or *therapy*. Each group was led by two clinical psychologists. The resident groups of 3–7 participants focused on adjustment to the institution, and the family groups of 3–5 families focused on similar issues, but emphasized the sharing of thoughts and feelings between family members. After an initial introductory session, sessions 2–4 focused on feelings about being placed in the nursing home. Sessions 5 and 6 focused on solving problems in the nursing home, and the last session served as a wrap-up. All subjects were tested with a battery of psychological tests before treatment, four weeks later (at the end of treatment for the experimental group), and six months after baseline. Subjects varied in level of cognitive impairment, but overall the groups did not differ on any baseline score. The resident-only group seemed to do best on the outcome measures. At Time 2 (immediate post-test) they had significantly less trait anxiety and more internal locus of control than did controls. The family group did not differ from the controls. At six months after baseline, the resident group experienced more agitation, but a lower self-health rating than controls. The authors could not explain why only trait, not state, anxiety differed at Time 2, nor why the results observed at Time 2 did not carry over to Time 3. Thus, although this study is methodologically one of the better ones in the literature and counseling did benefit the residents, the observed results are hard to interpret.

Johnson, Sandel, and Margolis (1982) share their experience with therapy groups for nursing home residents. They incorporated drama and movement into traditional group therapy. Groups met one hour weekly and consisted of 6 to 12 patients. Group leaders first established a safe and stable environment. Then reminiscences were encouraged. As therapy progressed, there was a shift to more here-and-now issues and patients were confronted with their mental and physical limitations, impending death, and other important issues in the present. Movement therapy served to focus attention and drama was used to link past and present by re-enacting past events. Johnson et al. do not discuss the effectiveness of their treatment.

Welden and Yesavage (1982) matched 25 pairs of individuals on age and degree of impairment. All individuals were classified as senile dementia of the Alzheimer's or multi-infarct type according to the DSM-III. An experimental group met for hourly sessions three times a week for three months. In the sessions, individuals learned progressive muscle relaxation, self-hypnosis, shifting attention while relaxing, and mental imagery techniques. Control subjects received the same number of sessions, but discussed current events over refreshments. Experimental subjects improved on all subscales of the Stockton State Hospital Geropsychiatric Profile (SSHGP) compared to control. The total SSHGP score decreased from 507 to 399 pre- to post-treatment for the experimental group, while their was a nonsignificant increase observed for the control subjects

Zarit, Zarit, and Reever (1982) randomly assigned 35 cognitively impaired adults, mean age of 74, to one of three conditions in a memory training study: didactic training on the use of mental imagery, problem solving of situations caused by memory loss, and waiting-list control. Treatment groups met twice weekly in 1.5-hour sessions for seven sessions. Groups consisted of 3–4 participants and their primary caregivers. Each participant made two or more errors on the Mental Status Questionnaire or had a positive Face-Hand Test. Memory tests were administered pre-, mid-, and post-treatment. Because of tremendous intra- and inter-individual variability, results were combined into categories. Both treatment groups demonstrated more improvement than controls on recall tests, but the groups did not differ in recognition. Another result was increased depression as measured by the Zung in both treatment groups, but not the controls. Thus, memory training may have led to improved cognitive functioning, but there was a concomitant deterioration in affective state.

Although not technically psychotherapy, Carroll and Gray (1983) conducted a pilot study examining the effect of integrating three cognitively impaired persons with three more alert individuals in a therapeutic meal group. Through behavioral mapping of group sessions, there was an increase in frequency of appropriate behavior for the impaired individuals from 67 to 93%, but little change in affect balance. They did not report any adverse effect for the more intact individuals.

Finally, Foster and Foster (1983) surveyed 20 therapists conducting group therapy with elderly adults in ambulatory or residential settings. Mild dementia was frequent in the groups, although severe dementia was avoided. In reviewing the distinctive features of these groups compared to those with younger adults, 85% of the therapists said they were active and directive. Ninety percent were emotionally expressive, and many employed physical touching. Therapists were also more flexible with techniques, employing such things as food and contact outside of group sessions. Participants were considered less willing to engage themselves in the group, and when they did, they were more polite than experienced in groups with primarily younger adults. Goals of the groups included decrease in symptoms, adjustment to real-world problems, improved interpersonal functioning, hope for change, and increased rate of discharge. All therapists preferred higher functioning patients. Attendance rates were 89% for the ambulatory groups, and 67% for the residential ones. Ninety-five percent of the groups became cohesive. For residential groups, cohesion took an average of 2.6 months to attain. For ambulatory groups, cohesion rate was bimodal. Seven therapists reported cohesion in a mean of 1.9 months, and the remainder of the therapists reported taking 10.1 sessions. The principle themes of group discussion were losses, hope versus despair, and loneliness. Although the groups were not predominantly for cognitively impaired individuals, such elderly adults were included in therapy, and thus, the findings may be relevant to work with the impaired.

CRITIQUE OF THE LITERATURE

For a literature spanning 35 years, reports on the use of group therapy with cognitively impaired older adults are rare. Even with the few studies that have been published, results are hard to generalize for several reasons. First, is the diagnostic issue. The early literature is almost exclusively on therapy with individuals diagnosed senile psychotic. Later literature often refers to chronic brain syndrome, while the most recent literature consists of therapy with senile dementia patients. Diagnostic techniques have become considerably more sophisticated in recent years, making for more homogeneous diagnostic groups. Currently, cognitive impairment is often equated with dementia, ignoring various types of deliria and pseudodcmentias which can produce cognitive deficits. Although the majority of individuals in the groups reviewed are cognitively impaired, the diagnostic source of the impairment varies considerably and makes generalization of results difficult.

Related to diagnostic difficulties is the nature of the cognitively impaired population. The impaired elderly used to be locked up with chronic psychiatric patients in state hospitals. The most recent literature focuses on a nursing home population. The present trend is toward outpatient facilities such as day care programs. For instance, 75% of Foster and Foster's (1983) groups were in ambulatory settings. The group therapy literature has rarely focused only on the cognitively impaired person. The impaired individuals are lumped together in therapy with other individuals in an institution or program. The older literature clearly consists of organic and functional psychiatric patients. The more recent literature includes various nursing home residents, namely demented persons and the medically frail. Groups are therefore difficult to compare across time and settings.

We cannot readily determine the effectiveness of group therapy with the cognitively impaired aged also because of the nature of the therapies provided. Out of the entire literature no two therapy groups were alike. In fact, most are eclectic, a mélange of various therapies, some not even psychological. Only in the cases of Welden and Yesavage (1982) and Zarit et al. (1982) do we see pure treatment modalities. Even in Welden and Yesavage, several different methods of relaxation were taught. The Zarit study was also more experimental than therapeutic in design, and thus not a realistic form of therapy.

A final problem is the lack of methodological rigor. Few studies have adequate outcome measures. Most studies are simply clinical descriptions of a treatment (e.g., Manaster, 1972; Silver, 1950). For others, the only objective measure is discharge rate (e.g., Oberleder, 1970; Rechtschaffen et al., 1954). Other studies employ ratings and behavioral observations, often made by group leaders (e.g., Linden, 1953; Bowers et al., 1967). Although easy to obtain, leader ratings are also often biased. Only four studies actually used objective psychological tests to evaluate treatment effectiveness, and all demonstrated some decrease in cognitive impairment (Ernst et al., 1977; Welden & Yesavage, 1982; Wolk & Goldfarb, 1967; Zarit et al., 1982). Finally, only 4 of 20 studies reviewed employ control groups (Dye & Erber, 1981; Welden & Yesavage, 1982; Wolk & Goldfarb, 1967; Zarit et al., 1982). Overall, the methodological rigor is clearly lacking in this literature.

Due to these problems—the limited literature, the diagnostic problem, the nature of the impaired population, the diversity of treatment approaches, the lack of outcome measures, and poor experimental design—nothing conclusive can be offered about the effectiveness of group therapy with cognitively impaired older adults. However, some trends do arise. First, almost every study claims some success. Even though these claims are suspect because of methodological problems, no completely negative results on group therapy with impaired elderly have been reported. Unfortunately, negative studies are often not published. Studies discussing effectiveness admit group therapy does not help everyone, but all studies include individuals that appear to benefit from therapy. Poor evidence though it may be, there is a consistent trend towards the efficacy of group therapy with the cognitively impaired elderly.

Levy, Derogatis, Gallagher, and Gatz (1980) point out that no long-term benefit has been observed in treatment of the brain-damaged elderly. One reason is the absence of any long-term follow-up to begin with. Only Dye and Erber (1981) carry out a follow-up to six months, the longest post-treatment follow-up. In their study, benefits were observed at six months, but immediate post-treatment benefits did not carry over to six months. Also their results are hard to interpret. Therapy with this population thus serves to maintain functioning and reduce symptoms rather than have any curative properties. The aim of treatment is to optimize present functioning. What happens when treatment is discontinued and what gains the cognitively impaired person actually maintains would be a definite contribution to the literature.

The most frequently reported benefits of therapy are improved patient and staff morale and improved cognitive and behavior functioning for patients. Discharge rates from psychiatric institutions also have been improved. Wolk and Goldfarb's (1967) controlled study indicates that the main benefits of therapy are a reduction in the negative effects of institutionalization. Long-term psychiatric patients in their study benefitted more than newly admitted patients. Also there was a significant reduction in cognitive-impairment in these non-organic patients. Improved cognitive functioning also appears to hold true for noninstitutionalized patients (e.g., Zarit et al., 1982).

Another indication of the effectiveness of group therapy is the development of group process. Cohesion increases over time as the group moves through transitions to a working stage. Several reports illustrate this trend (Bowers et al., 1967; Johnson et al., 1982; Linden, 1953; Manaster, 1972). As the group progresses, it becomes more independent of the leader and the focus shifts from discussion of topics of interest to problem-solving and other indications of care for one another in group. The shift may also be categorized as one from then-and-there to here-and-now.

Two studies provide a negative consequence of improved cognitive functioning with group therapy of impaired elderly adults. Ernst et al. (1977) and Zarit et al. (1982) both report increased emotional complaints and dysphoria as a consequence of treatment. For Ernst et al., this was for 2 of 6 patients. These results are consistent with Oberleder's (1970) view that senile symptoms serve as a defense against a painful reality. If treatment is to break down the defense, there is a need to deal with the subsequent emotional reaction. Thus, therapy may potentially be harmful to those impaired persons who do not develop alternative defense mechanisms. This observation requires further study.

TECHNIQUES OF GROUP THERAPY

The characteristics of group therapy with the cognitively impaired elderly vary considerably. Sessions last between 15 minutes (Manaster, 1972) and 1.5 hours (Wolk & Goldfarb, 1967; Zarit et al., 1982). Leadership may be single (e.g., Silver, 1950) and has been as many as three (Bowers et al., 1967). Linden (1954) argues for a male-female team from a psychodynamic point of view. The team serves a parental function in the resocialization process. No study clearly reports focusing on process issues, such as a group commenting on an individual's interpersonal style. Wolk and Gold-farb (1967) may come close by referring to "current interpersonal issues." Rather, most groups are content focused, and the content of sessions varies greatly. Many groups begin with introductions of members (e.g., Ernst et al., 1977; Manaster, 1972), and a number employ refreshments at each meeting (e.g., Manaster, 1972; Silver, 1950). Some use reality orientation techniques (e.g., Ernst et al., 1977) remotivation (e.g., Bowers et al., 1967), and reminiscence (e.g., Rechtschaffen et al., 1954). Barnes et al. (1973) and Burn-side's edition (1978a) describe these and other techniques in detail. Other techniques in the group therapy literature combined psycho-therapy with non-psychological ones such as movement and drama (Johnson et al., 1982) and sensory stimulation (Ernst et al., 1977). Burnside (1978b) lists many of these activities. Some groups are very structured in content (e.g., Dye & Erber, 1981; Zarit et al., 1982), but these are from the more experimental of the studies. The more traditional psychotherapeutic techniques such as problem-solving, catharsis, sharing feelings, etc., occur after a group has become somewhat cohesive (e.g., Johnson et al., 1982; Manaster, 1972), and some techniques such as free association do not seem to work (Linden, 1953).

I have not reviewed the group therapy literature with elderly individuals who are not cognitively impaired. Nursing home residents would contain some cognitively impaired individuals, and groups conducted in such facilities might be heterogeneous in impairment level. Busch (1984) identifies themes of group therapy with nursing home patients. He focuses specifically on how selected studies employ Brink's (1979) themes of social interaction, reality orientation, life review, and remotivation. Because the groups often include some impaired individuals, the studies in Busch's review may provide some ideas relevant to treatment of the cognitively impaired.

Other techniques may be borrowed from individual and other forms of treatment of the impaired elderly. Butler and Lewis (1982) suggest psychotherapy should focus on affective issues, such as helping the individual experience warmth and maintain self-esteem. Zarit (1980) identifies some of the psychological concomitants of organic brain disease, some of which is treatable through psychotherapy: denial, withdrawal, depression, paranoid thoughts, and increased dependency on others. He suggests that therapy should be more supportive and less focused on behavior change and adaptation. Goldfarb and Turner (1953) discuss the use of brief individual psychotherapy for brain-damaged adults. Sessions last for perhaps 15 minutes, and therapy would continue for a limited number of sessions (an average of eight in their study). Their assumption is that the therapist is viewed as an all-powerful parental figure, and the goal of therapy is to let the patient draw power from the therapist toward his or her own well-being and needs. Such minimal intervention might also be relevant to groups of impaired elderly adults.

Lazarus and Weinberg (1980) apply Kohut's (1971) self theory to the brain-damaged patient. An impaired individual is not in control of his or her thought processes, and therefore relies on more primitive defenses such as denial, projection, and withdrawal. As defenses fail, there is fragmentation and discohesiveness of self. Paranoia in such patients is just a projection of loss of competence and body intactness onto others. "I lost my memory for where I put my glasses" becomes "they took my glasses." The therapist should help the patient: (a) work through grief and mourn losses, (b) find realistic substitutes for source of gratification, and (c) revise former goals in accordance with diminished capabilities. The therapist should also be attentive to the attribution of feelings of hopelessness and inferiority placed by the patient to him or her. The therapist is often viewed by the patient as all-powerful and a parental figure, and may be seen as rejecting and critical. The therapist can serve this function for the patient, increasing his or her sense of security. Lazarus and Weinberg's suggestions are not contrary to the aim of brief therapy as described by Goldfarb and Turner (1953). Although therapy following the Kohutian framework is usually individual, Harwood (1983) has outlined suggestions for conducting group therapy using this model.

Yesavage and Karasu (1982) suggest cognitive retraining with those with mild dementia. In addition to memory improvement skills, this would include anxiety reduction techniques such as relaxation and centering techniques to heighten awareness and reduce the effects of interference in learning. Thought-stopping could help deal with negative cognitive sets and expectations. Yesavage, Westphal, and Rush (1981) employed administration of dihydroergotoxine mesylate (Hydergine) with either supportive counseling or cognitive retraining or therapy + a placebo. Medication was given at 3 mg/day for 12 weeks, and individual therapy consisted of 5 one-hour sessions over the same 12 weeks. Subjects had moderate impairment based on the Sandoz Clinical Assessment-Geriatric (SCAG), but there were no group differences at baseline. Therapy alone yielded 8% improvement on the Buschke selective-reminding task, which is consistent with a practice effect. The drug + minimal supervision yielded 17% improvement; the drug + supportive therapy, 40% improvement; and the drug + cognitive retraining, 59% improvement. There were no differences between therapy groups on SCAG behavioral and depression scales. Thus, dihydroergotoxine mesylate interacted with individual therapy to improve memory functioning in cognitively impaired patients.

CONCLUSION

The literature on group psychotherapy with cognitively impaired older adults is very sparse. Although nothing conclusive about effectiveness can be stated, a variety of techniques have been used. The most apparent effectiveness in group therapy is a reduction in the negative effects of institutionalization. These include improved behavior, decreased impairment, affective change, and increased rate of discharge from institutions. Effectiveness has not been documented at follow-up, and therapy, if anything, probably serves a maintenance function.

REFERENCES

Barnes, E. K., Sack, A., & Shore, H. (1973). Guidelines to treatment approaches: Modalities and methods for use with the aged. *Gerontologist, 13*, 513–527.

Bowers, M. B., Anderson, G. K., Blomeier, E. C., & Pelz, K. (1967). Brain syndrome and behavior in geriatric remotivation groups. *Journal of Gerontology, 22*, 348–352.

Brink, T. L. (1979). *Geriatric psychotherapy.* New York: Human Sciences Press.

Burnside, I. M. (Ed., 1978a). *Working with the elderly: Group processes and techniques.* North Scituate, MA: Duxbury.

Burnside, I. M. (1978b). Group work with the mentally impaired elderly. In I. M. Burnside (Ed.), *Working with the elderly: Group processes and techniques* (pp. 173–205). North Scituate, MA: Duxbury.

Busch, C. D. (1984). Common themes in group psychotherapy with older adult nursing home residents: A review of selected literature. *Clinical Gerontologist, 2*(3), 25–38.

Butler, R. N., & Lewis, M. I. (1982). *Aging and mental health* (3rd ed.). St. Louis: C. V. Mosby.

Carroll, K., & Gray, K. (1983). How to integrate the cognitively impaired in group activities. *Clinical Gerontologist, 1*(4), 19–30.

Dennis, H. (1978). Remotivation therapy groups. In I. M. Burnside (Ed.), *Working with the elderly: Group processes and techniques* (pp. 219–235). North Scituate, MA: Duxbury.

Dye, C. J., & Erber, J. T. (1981). Two group procedures for the treatment of nursing home patients. *Gerontologist, 21*, 539–544.

Dye, C. J., & Richards, C. C. (1980). Facilitating the transition to nursing homes. In S. S. Sargent (Ed.), *Nontraditional therapy and counseling with the aging* (pp. 100–115). New York: Springer.

Ernst, P., Beran, B., Badash, D., Kosovsky, R., & Kleinhauz, M. (1977). Treatment of the aged mentally ill: Further unmasking of the effects of a diagnosis of chronic brain syndrome. *Journal of the American Geriatrics Society, 25*, 466–469.

Foster, J. R., & Foster, R. P. (1983). Group psychotherapy with the old and aged. In H. I. Kaplan & B. J. Saddock (Eds.), *Comprehensive group psychotherapy* (2nd ed., pp. 269–278). Baltimore: Williams & Wilkins.

Goldfarb, A. I., & Turner, H. (1953). Psychotherapy of aged persons: II. Utilization and effectiveness of "brief" therapy. *American Journal of Psychiatry, 109*, 916–921.

Harwood, I. H. (1983). The application of self-psychology concepts to group psychotherapy. *International Journal of Group Psychotherapy, 33*, 469–487.

Johnson, D. R., Sandel, S. L., & Margolis, M. B. (1982). Principles of group treatment in a nursing home. *Journal of Long-Term Care Administration, 10*(4), 19–24.

Kohut, H. (1971). *The analysis of the self.* New York: International Universities Press.

Lazarus, L. W., & Weinberg, J. (1980). Treatment in the ambulatory care setting. In E. W. Busse & D. G. Blazer (Eds.), *Handbook of geriatric psychiatry* (pp. 427–452). New York: Van Nostrand Reinhold.

Levy, S. M., Derogatis, L. R., Gallagher, D., & Gatz, M. (1980). Intervention with older adults and the evaluation of outcome. In L. W. Poon (Ed.), *Aging in the 1980s: Psychological issues* (pp. 41–61). Washington, DC: American Psychological Association.

Linden, M. E. (1953). Group psychotherapy with institutionalized senile women: Study in gerontologic human relations. *International Journal of Group Psychotherapy, 3*, 150–170.

Linden, M. E. (1954). The significance of dual leadership in gerontologic group psychotherapy: Studies in gerontologic human relations III. *International Journal of Group Psychotherapy, 4*, 262–273.

Manaster, A. (1972). Therapy with the "senile" geriatric patient. *International Journal of Group Psychotherapy, 22*, 250–257.

Oberleder, M. (1970). Crisis therapy in mental breakdown of the aging. *Gerontologist, 10*, 111–114.

Rechtschaffen, A., Atkinson, S., & Freeman, J. G. (1954). An intensive treatment program for state hospital geriatric patients. *Geriatrics, 9*, 28–34.

Silver, A. (1950). Group psychotherapy with senile psychotic patients. *Geriatrics, 5*, 147–150.

Welden, S., & Yesavage, J. A. (1982). Behavioral improvement with relaxation training in senile dementia. *Clinical Gerontologist, 1*(1), 45–49.

Wolff, K. (1957). Group psychotherapy with geriatric patients in a mental hospital. *Journal of the American Geriatrics Society, 5*, 13–19.

Wolk, R. L., & Goldfarb, A. I. (1967). The response to group psychotherapy of aged recent admissions compared with long-term mental hospital patients. *American Journal of Psychiatry, 123*, 1251–1257.

Yesavage, J. A., & Karasu, T. B. (1982). Psychotherapy and elderly patients. *American Journal of Psychotherapy, 36*, 41–55.

Yesavage, J. A., Westphal, J., & Rush, L. (1981). Senile dementia: Combined pharmacologic and psychologic treatment. *Journal of the American Geriatrics Society, 29*, 164–171.

Zarit, S. H. (1980). *Aging and mental disorders.* New York: Free Press.

Zarit, S. H., Zarit, J. M., & Reever, K. E. (1982). Memory training for severe memory loss: Effects on senile dementia patients and their families. *Gerontologist, 22*, 373–377.

Questions

1) Are group techniques compatible with psychodynamic? behavioral? Gestalt?

2) What is the role of assessment in group therapy?

3) What kinds of patients would be poor candidates for groups?

17/LITHIUM GROUPS AND ELDERLY BIPOLAR OUTPATIENTS

George A. Foelker, Jr., PhD
Victor Molinari, PhD
Jane J. Marmion, ACSW, ACP
Ranjit C. Chacko, MD

Editor's Introduction

The use of lithium in elder patients has been discussed in two articles in *CG* (v. 3, #1, pp. 47–60). The chapter by Foelker, Molinari, Marmion, and Chacko is interesting primarily as an application of group therapy techniques to a disorder that requires a primary pharmacological treatment.

Bipolar disorders do occur in elders, although the prevalence is much lower than that of unipolar reactive depression, dementia, paranoia, or hypochondriasis. Lithium is the treatment of choice, indeed, it may be the only effective treatment in some cases. The dual problem with all lithium patients is compliance and toxicity. (Medication compliance is discussed in a previous *CG* issue: v. 3, #3, pp. 17–22, 40–41.)

Groups for lithium patients not only serve as an adjunctive therapy with supportive and socializing elements, but gives practitioners an opportunity to monitor for compliance and side-effects.

The authors describe (with case studies) their program as part of the efforts of a multidisciplinary mental health care team. (For more on these teams, see *CG*, v. 2, #3,

Dr. Foelker is Coordinator of Geriatric Services, Dallas County Mental Health Center, 3214 Bowen Street, #111, Dallas, TX 75204.
The junior authors are affiliated with Baylor College of Medicine, Community and Social Psychiatry Programs, and Mental Health and Mental Retardation Authority, Houston, Texas.

pp. 47–54, 64–74; v. 3, #2, pp. 38–40; v. 3, #3, pp. 23–34.)

Lithium therapy for the management of bipolar disorder in the elderly is a relatively recent development (Foster, Gershell, & Goldfarb, 1977). Since 1967, the literature has focused on two important issues: the prevalence of bipolar disorder in the elderly, and treatment with lithium salts (cf., Foster & Rosenthal, 1980; Molinari, Chacko, & Rosenberg, 1983). In contrast, very little attention has been paid to the issues of how effective lithium programs are developed and implemented, particularly in outpatient settings. The purpose of this article is to report on an ambulatory geriatric clinic that uses a multidisciplinary treatment approach in serving the bipolar outpatient.

Recent research at psychiatric inpatient facilities found 5.8% (Stevick, 1980) and 9.0% (Spar, Ford, & Liston, 1979) of the elderly patients carried a diagnosis of bipolar disorder. Shulman and Post's (1980) retrospective study of 67 elderly bipolar inpatients found that the mean age of onset of mania was 60. Molinari et al. (1983) evaluated the prevalence of bipolar disorder in an outpatient geriatric clinic and noted that 8% of the elderly patients met the DSM III criteria for bipolar disorder. The mean age for the first manic episode was 55.

Although early comments on the use of lithium with bipolar patients indicated that efficacy of lithium was inversely related to age (Van der Velde, 1970), Foster and Rosenthal (1980) report that in their 12 years of clinical experience using lithium, it was as effective with the elderly as it was with young bipolar patients. Indeed, in Shulman and Post's (1980) study of 67 elderly bipolar inpatients, 24 out of 27 patients who were treated with lithium carbonate responded favorably. More recently, Schaffer and Garvey (1984) evaluated the use of lithium carbonate among 14 inpatients aged 65 to 77, who were in the manic phase of a bipolar affective disorder. Of the 14 patients, 11 responded well to treatment and ten did so within two weeks of reaching the targeted blood levels of 0.5 to 0.8 mEq/1.

A major concern of lithium treatment is the risk of patients developing lithium toxicity (Roose, Bone, Haidorfer, Dunner, & Fieve, 1979; Smith & Helms, 1982). Moreover, this toxicity may occur in the elderly at serum levels within or moderately above the accepted therapeutic range for adults. As Molinari et al. (1983) and Schaffer and Garvey (1984) emphasized, though, elderly patients can be treated effectively with lower serum levels than younger bipolar patients. This may help reduce the incidence risk of elderly patients developing toxicity. Even so, the risk is present. Schaffer and Garvey (1984) found that 2 of their 14 patients developed toxicity with blood levels of lithium of 0.5 to 0.8 mEq/1. Haddad and Miksic (1984) found persistent side effects in elderly dementia patients treated with lithium when blood levels were only 0.25–0.50 mEq/1. In summary, the literature to date suggests that lithium therapy with elderly bipolar patients may be a viable option in providing effective prophylaxis, but that the drug therapy must be closely monitored.

Besides monitoring patients for toxic side effects, effective treatment of the bipolar elderly must also include attention to the potential for noncompliance. Shakir, Volkmar, Bacon, and Pfefferbaum (1979) assert that the most common reason for lithium maintenance failure is discontinuation of the drug. Noncompliance or misuse by bipolar patients may occur for a variety of reasons, including memory problems, denial of illness, and physical problems. These concerns are noted to occur more frequently in elderly bipolar patients than younger ones, making the elderly patients somewhat more at risk for noncompliance. Thus, effective lithium treatment must not only include close monitoring of physical health, but also track the patient's compliance with the recommended treatment.

Elderly bipolar patients, like other patients, often have a combination of psychological, psychiatric, and social problems. For instance, the mood swings typical of bipolar patients often cause marital problems, interpersonal tensions, and financial difficulties. A comprehensive treatment plan would make drug therapy part of an array of therapeutic interventions that address these various problems. Unfortunately, biopsychosocial models for the management of elderly bipolar outpatients are not mentioned in the literature in large part because lithium treatment for the elderly is a relatively recent development. In addition, elderly patients generally are less likely to be served by outpatient mental health facilities and are given fewer services when they are seen as patients (Zarit, 1980). Volkmar, Bacon, Shakir, and Pfefferbaum (1981) point out that many clinicians have been discouraged from using psychotherapeutic approaches with bipolar patients in general, relying exclusively on lithium prophylaxis as the maor treatment modality.

An effective model for treating elderly bipolar patients therefore must include a component for providing psychotherapy when needed. As Zarit (1980) emphasizes, the feeling of support, that the therapist and patient are working together towards mutually agreed upon goals, is required for effective treatment and plays a central role in therapy with older patients. The therapeutic alliance helps the patient become invested in the management of his or her own lithium treatment. In addition, psychotherapy can provide a focus on current dynamic or interpersonal problems that limit or interfere with one's potential.

A combined medication and group therapy program can provide the forum for monitoring side effects, increasing compliance, and offering support. As a medication group, members are presented with information and discuss the illness and its symptomatology, the therapeutic effects of lithium, its possible side effects, and compliance issues. Through group discussion, a therapeutic group process may develop and become an important component of lithium management. Group therapy for older persons also has great potential for offering supportive and socialization experiences. Three of Yalom's (1975) curative factors in groups (imparting of information, installation of hope, group cohesiveness) may be particularly relevant for the elderly. In addition, groups with specific goals have been effective (Zarit, 1980). Unfortunately, there is virtually no literature on group psychotherapy as an adjunct to the treatment of the elderly bipolar outpatient. One study of mixed-age bipolar inpatients does suggest, though, that group psychotherapy would be effective.

Volkmar et al. (1981) reported positive results from combining physical monitoring with group therapy for bipolar inpatients aged 18-63. Using a psychiatrist and a social worker as co-therapists, the group addressed not only lithium related issues, but other problems that affected individuals or the group as a whole. The authors' previous research concluded that group psychotherapy combined with physical monitoring may serve as a simple, efficient, and highly cost effective service for lithium maintenance treatment (Shakir et al., 1979). The conjoint use of group psychotherapy and physical monitoring with elderly bipolar patients is not merely a matter of applying the same techniques to a different age group, because elderly patients have special needs. How those issues are addressed in the group setting will be discussed in more detail in another section.

In outpatient settings, community based social services are needed to complement the biological (lithium monitoring) and psychological (supportive therapy) aspects of treatment. For example, support services such as transportation, economic, or housing assistance may be needed. Mobility issues in particular are more likely to occur with elderly patients. To effectively develop and implement such a comprehensive program, services within the outpatient setting must be coordinated and assistance provided in obtaining them. Such coordination and service brokerage functions can best be provided by a case management system (Johnson & Rubin, 1983; Miller, 1979). The case manager links the patient to service delivery, is responsible for ensuring that the patient's treatment plan is implemented, and remains in contact with the patient on an ongoing basis. A lithium group for elderly bipolar outpatients which utilizes a multidisciplinary team approach will now be described.

PROGRAM DESCRIPTION

The setting is a geriatric unit within a community mental health center in Houston, Texas, which provides services to patients ranging in age from 55 to 90. Patients who are served by this clinic experience the gamut of psychosocial and psychiatric problems (Chacko, Molinari, Marmion, Adams, & Moffic, 1984). The assessment services are provided by a multidisciplinary team comprised of a psychiatrist, psychologist, social worker, nurse, and intake workers. This team conducts intake staffings on new patients, where a provisional diagnosis is made. Patients accepted for clinic services are assigned to a treatment team that consists of a psychiatrist and a casemanager. The latter is responsible for coordination of treatment recommendations.

A group approach to lithium prophylaxis was initiated in the clinic after it became apparent that a significant number of elderly patients had a bipolar disorder. When the group was originally formed, it was recognized that inclusion in group would have to take into account the special factors associated with the elderly status of these bipolar patients. The major criterion for inclusion was motivation on the part of the patient to participate in a monthly group therapy program. It has been noted that elderly bipolar patients are more inclined than younger ones to deny the nature of their disorder. Thus, recruitment of elderly patients began with their acknowledgement of an affective problem and interest in regularly scheduled appointments.

Other criteria for group membership needed to be addressed by the multidisciplinary team. Since the elderly outpatients were deemed more likely than younger ones to have limited financial resources and be dependent on transportation by others, the team and the patients assessed the likelihood of making frequent appointments at set times. The team also assessed the ability of the prospective elderly patient to profit from group interaction. Close attention was thereby paid to patient variables, such as verbal abilities, psychological mindedness, presence of organicity, and hearing problems.

The lithium group is currently composed of seven bipolar patients, ages 58 to 70, stabilized on lithium. The group is conducted by a psychiatrist and a social worker and meets once a month for an hour. Following each session, patients are seen by the clinic nurse for laboratory monitoring, blood pressure, and weight checks.

The group leaders have both individual and shared roles. The psychiatrist encourages discussion from patients about symptomatology and medication issues, such as side effects. At that time medication is prescribed and the need for further medical or laboratory investigations is determined. Serum lithium levels are done at every appointment initially, but later are repeated once every three months. Baseline laboratory studies include renal function studies (BUN, urine specific gravity, serum electrolytes, urinalysis), thyroid function tests (T3, T4, T7, and TSH), CBC, and EKG. Since most elderly patients suffer from chronic physical problems (Jarvik & Perl, 1981), the psychiatrist notes physical symptoms and, when necessary, refers the patients to see their primary care physician. The role of providing medical assessment and liaison is particularly important for elderly patients, since physical conditions such as hypertension, diabetes, and thyroid dysfunction can complicate lithium therapy. In addition, antihypertensive agents and steroid medications frequently affect the course of affective disorder.

The psychiatrist's attention to somatic complaints is also more important for elderly bipolar patients than younger ones. The elderly often tend to deny the emotional nature of their symptoms, and instead somaticize their affective problems. By having a psychiatrist address these somatic complaints, less resistance may be encountered in discussions about affective issues. Another factor more prevalent with elderly group members is that their physical problems can increase the absentee rate and narrow the focus from psychological issues to strictly physical concerns. These problems can slow down or interrupt the group process. By having a medical professional co-lead the group and recognize the impact of these issues, the group members, in turn, can have a forum to share those problems, receive support, and discuss a wider range of their problems.

The social worker performs an important liaison role in the group and helps the group focus attention on various psychosocial issues. When more intensive exploration of such issues is needed, the social worker will refer the patients to their respective case managers. Another part of the liaison role is to notify the casemanager when the patient misses the group appointment, so that follow-up is done. Coordination and documentation is an additional responsibility of the social worker, and includes completion of chart work, laboratory request forms, appointment slips, and reminder notices.

The psychiatrist and social worker both function as facilitators, by enabling patients to talk about current stressors or mood states which affect their functioning. For example, changes in employment, income, health, or living situation, as well as the loss of friends or family members can produce significant stress. These stressors, and medication problems, can lead to mood changes. The facilitators aid the group process by reverting these issues to the group. The group members are encouraged to give feedback, relate individual issues to their own experiences, and offer emotional support. The following brief report is an example of how the therapists and group members work together.

> Mr. N., age 69, is currently a member of the lithium group. At age 54, following episodes of depression and mania with prominent grandiosity, he was placed on lithium by a private psychiatrist and has been stabilized on the medication for the past 15 years. While hospitalized in 1983 for an unrelated problem, he was seen by a psychiatrist for consultation on his medication. The hospital discharge plan included referral to the geriatric clinic for continuing lithium management. Following the subsequent intake staffing, Mr. N. was assigned to the lithium group. Through group participation, Mr. N. developed trust and rapport with other members.

> Mr. N. recently experienced a reactive depression. The situation involved being involuntarily taken off his regular security job and put "on call" by his company. His reactions included a dysphoric mood, sleep disturbance, and loss of interest in his primary hobby, playing the accordion. Mr. N. discussed his job change at the group meeting. The group pro-

cess helped him put his feelings into words. In relating their experiences with mood change to Mr. N., the group members spoke of the importance of talking about problems. It was through the group's encouragement and emotional support that Mr. N. decided to make an appointment with his clinic therapist. In four sessions that were held, individual supportive psychotherapy was used to provide encouragement, which facilitated problem solving and verbalizing feelings. By the next monthly lithum group, Mr. N. shared with the members positive changes regarding the problem he had previously presented. For example, his mood was improved, he was more tolerant of his job change, and he had returned to playing the accordion.

Another important and shared co-therapist role is enhancing treatment compliance. Although estimates are that 20 percent to 50 percent of lithium patients experience difficulties with adhering to treatment regimens, no proven effective interventions have been designed to specifically enhance lithium compliance (Cochran, 1984). Cochran's (1984) study did show promising results from using a cognitive-behavioral intervention to increase compliance in individual outpatients on lithium. Consistent with her model, compliance in the lithium group here is viewed to include both the patients' beliefs and their actions involving lithium use. To promote compliance, the group treatment is designed to impact the patients' belief systems, enhance outcome expectations, and promote self-efficacy (Bandura, 1977). The procedures involve educational instruction, skills development, group modeling, and compliance monitoring. Seltzer, Roncari, and Garfinkel (1980) pointed out that 23% of patients in their study were unaware of the rationale for medication and that noncompliance was correlated with lack of knowledge about the purposes of medication. To minimize those effects, the current lithium group engages in discussions about the relationship between establishing and maintaining therapeutic blood levels of lithium and the control of symptomatology. The patients' expectations of symptom control are developed by emphasizing that acute problems with manic symptoms can be prevented or minimized by adherence to recommended treatment. Patients are encouraged to view taking lithium as a way of gaining personal control over their disorder. The group format allows patients to view other members doing well and hear how they have managed to follow treatment procedures, encouraging them to model their compliant behavior.

Group process is used to develop a norm that patients will comply with treatment and interact with others to solve problems that interfere with compliance. Patients are taught skills to monitor themselves for the early emergence of side effects or bipolar symptoms. The co-therapists share these monitoring roles, and provide feedback to the group about attendance, group participation, and follow through on recommendations. Thus, working together, the co-therapists and the group members address a variety of beliefs and actions that together maximize the usefulness of lithium therapy. The following case illustrates some of these principles.

Mrs. R., age 62, has had psychiatric treatment including hospitalizations over the last 15 years for problems associated with manic behavior and disordered thinking. Due to denial of the severity of her problems and disbelief in the efficacy of her medication, Mrs. R. had not been able to achieve stability. Following her last hospitalization in 1983, Mrs. R. was referred to Mid-City's Geriatric Clinic. To address her diagnosis of bipolar disorder with psychotic features, her treatment plan included individual and marital therapy, Prolixin deconate, and lithium managed through the lithium group.

Since denial of her bipolar symptomatology and non-compliance with medications were problems in the past, Mrs. R.'s placement in the lithium group was used as a means to offer educational information, group feedback, and group support to alter her beliefs and become invested in her treatment plan. She attended regularly, receiving both acceptance into the group and direct support from members. Through therapy outside group and through the group process she was able to engage others in discussing how she felt about her problems. She was able to interact with others with similar problems to learn how they had changed their views about the efficacy of lithium treatment. Through emotional support and encouragement from the group members, Mrs. R. developed a trusting relationship with them and her co-therapists. In time she came to believe in and adhere to psychiatric treatment as a viable way to control her symptoms and achieve mental stability. She has remained relatively stable and out of the hospital now for over one year.

SUMMARY

This paper has reviewed the existing literature on the management of elderly bipolar outpatients, and described a community based program that has been specially designed to meet the diverse needs of this patient population. This increasing awareness of the prevalence of bipolar disorder in the elderly and the effective utilization of lithium salts as a prophylactic treatment modality has brought about a renewed appreciation of the complexity of service delivery that is required to manage geriatric outpatients. Elderly bipolar outpatients, like their younger counterparts, tend to require close monitoring for compliance with prescribed treatment. However, elderly patient populations are more likely to have, in addition: (a) physical conditions that complicate lithium treatment, (b) nonpsychotropic medications that can affect the course of their affective disorder, (c) memory and concentration deficits that affect compliance with the daily medication regimen, and (d) complex psychosocial stressors involved with aging, such as loss of significant relationships, decreased income, deteriorating health, and loneliness.

The program that has been described to address these multiple and often interrelated needs is multidisciplinary in nature, with a strong psychotherapeutic mode of intervention. Active coordination and linkage to service providers and other agencies is a major component of the program, and is enacted by using a case management system. No known studies have focused on the issue of compliance in elderly bipolar outpatients. The group format described here is ideal for research on this issue, and indeed a follow up study on this topic is being planned. Outcome evaluations of such a biopsychosocial program need to be done, especially in comparing it to more traditional models of service delivery. Such studies would be a much needed addition to the existing body of literature.

REFERENCES

Bandura, A. (1977). Self efficacy: Toward a unifying theory of behavior change. *Psychological Review, 84*, 191-215.

Chacko, R. C., Molinari, V. A., Marmion, J., Adams, G. L., & Moffic, psychiatric patient. *Clinical Gerontologist, 2*, 3-14.

Cochran, S. D. (1984). Preventing medical noncompliance in the outpatient treatment of bipolar affective disorders. *Journal of Consulting and Clinical Psychology, 52*, 873-878.

Foster, J. R., Gershell, W. J., & Goldfarb, A. I. (1977). Lithium treatment in the elderly: Clinical usage. *Journal of Gerontology, 32*, 299-302.

Foster, J. R., & Rosenthal, J. S. (1980). Lithium treatment of the elderly. In F. N. Johnson. (Ed.), *Handbook of lithium therapy* (pp. 414–420). Baltimore: Univ. Park Press.

Haddad, L. B., & Miksic, S. (1984). Clinical use of lithium with geriatric patients: Interpretations from single subject designs. *Clinical Gerontologist, 3,* 47–55.

Jarvik, L. F., & Perl, M. (1981). Overview of physiologic dysfunction and the production of psychiatric problems in the elderly. In A. Levenson & R. C. W. Hall (Eds.), *Psychiatric management of physical disease in the elderly.* New York: Raven Press.

Johnson, P. J., & Rubin, A. (1983). Case management in mental health: A social work domain? *Social Work,* Jan-Feb, 49–55.

Miller, G. E. (1979, September). *Case management: The essential service.* Keynote address, conference on case management, Waterville Valley, N.H.

Molinari, V. A., Chacko, R. C., & Rosenberg, S. D. (1983). Bipolar disorder in the elderly. *Journal of Psychiatric Treatment and Evaluation, 5,* 325–330.

Roose, S. P., Bone, S., Haidorfer, C., Dunner, D. L., & Fieve, R. R. (1979). Lithium treatment in older patients. *American Journal of Psychiatry, 136,* 843–844.

Seltzer, A., Roncari, I., & Garfinkel, P. (1980). Effect of patient education on medication compliance. *Canadian Journal of Psychiatry, 25,* 638–645.

Schaffer, C. B., & Garvey, M. J. (1984). Use of lithium in acutely manic elderly patients. *Clinical Gerontologist, 3,* 58–60.

Shakir, S. A., Volkmar, F. R., Bacon, S., & Pfefferbaum, A. (1979). Group psychotherapy as an adjunct to lithium maintenance. *American Journal of Psychiatry, 136,* 455–456.

Shulman, K., & Post, F. (1980). Bipolar affective disorder in old age. *British Journal of Psychiatry, 136,* 26–32.

Smith, R. E., & Helms, P. M. (1982). Adverse effects of lithium therapy in the acutely ill elderly patients. *Journal of Clinical Psychiatry, 43,* 94–99.

Spar, J. E., Ford, V. C., & Liston, E. H. (1979). Bipolar affective disorder in aged patients. *Journal of Clinical Psychiatry, 40,* 504–507.

Stevick, C. P. (1980). Some demographic and diagnostic characteristics of a geriatric population in a state geriatric facility. *Journal of the American Geriatrics Society, 28,* 426–429.

Van der Velde, C. C. (1970). Effectiveness of lithium carbonate in the treatment of manic-depressive illness. *American Journal of Psychiatry, 127,* 345–351.

Volkmar, F. R., Bacon, S., Shakir, S. A., & Pfefferbaum, A. (1981). Group therapy in the management of manic-depressive illness. *American Journal of Psychotherapy, 35,* 226–234.

Yalom, I. D. (1975). *The theory and practice of group psychotherapy.* New York: Basic Books.

Zarit, S. H. (1980). *Aging and mental disorders.* New York: Free Press.

Questions

1) Could group techniques be used with other medications in order to monitor compliance and side effects?

2) What group therapy techniques would be most appropriate in such medication groups?

3) How could a multidisciplinary team be used to manage a different psychopathology of later life?

18/PET-FACILITATED THERAPIES
A Review of the Literature and Clinical Implementation Considerations

Clark M. Brickel, PhD

Editor's Introduction

The use of live animals and plush toys has been discussed in *CG* previously (v. 2, #4, pp. 72–76). Brickel's comprehensive review describes the range and benefits (physical as well as psychological) of pet-facilitated therapy, anecdotal and empirical data, and a comparison of therapist-facilitated versus therapist-absent human-pet interactions. Brickel emphasizes flexibility and practicality in offering hints to practitioners.

Pet-facilitated therapy refers to integrating animals into client-directed, therapeutic activities. Within the last few years such animal usage has gained increasing attention within the therapeutic community. A variety of animals have been used with varying success in treating clientele from, for example, psychiatric and geriatric settings. But just as not all pets are the same, pet-facilitated therapies are not all the same, and the reader should be aware of the differences.

Clark M. Brickel is affiliated with the University of Southern California and The Los Angeles Society of the Prevention of Cruelty to Animals.

Inquiries should be directed to the author in care of the LA/SPCA, 5026 W. Jefferson Blvd., Los Angeles, CA 90016.

THE PET-FACILITATED THERAPIES

Actually it would be preferable to call this section "animal-facilitated therapies" since some animals involved in therapeutic transactions have not been pets at all. For example, dolphins have been used in obtaining responses from autistic children (Smith, 1983). Nevertheless the term "pet-facilitated therapy" has been coined, and its definition stretched, to include any animal other than *Homo sapiens*. So be it.

Today the general field of pet-facilitated therapy can be categorized into three types: milieu therapy, physical rehabilitation, and pet-facilitated psychotherapy. These categorizations do not have well-defined boundaries, and may overlap.

Of these three pet therapies, milieu therapy is the kind most commonly employed. In this endeavor animals are simply brought into contact with people (or vice versa). This action is remedial in that a substantial change has occurred in the client's immediate environment via the animal introduction. Implicit in such activity is the hypothesis that animals and animal-related interactions are intrinsically therapeutic. Typically with this form of therapy change comes about over a period of time. However, dramatic changes in behavior are often immediately noticeable.

Physical rehabilitation can be a peripheral benefit of milieu programs, since clients are called upon to perform activities on the animal's behalf such as walking, feeding, or grooming. Persons who ordinarily experience difficulty in carrying out such tasks are motivated to do them for the pet, and the health value of such responsibilities, which call upon fine and gross muscle movement, cannot be underestimated. Physical rehabilitation programs are also specialized, as when mentally or physically disabled persons are enrolled in equestrian programs demanding of motor skills and muscular coordination (see DePauw, 1984, for a brief critique of such programs). A bonus to such programs is that participants enjoy them, and may be more inclined to participate in them than in conventional rehabilitation programs.

Pet-facilitated psychotherapy (PFP) is literally translated. In this category of pet therapy an animal is used by a clinician or paraprofessional to enhance the usual therapeutic curriculum. Here the animal mediates therapy under the guidance of the human therapist. The animal may help to:

— act as a link between therapist and client;
— draw out verbal and emotional responsiveness;
— facilitate social interaction for the client;
— provide a tactile source of comfort;
— build upon the client's inner resources;
— generally enhance the client's quality of life.

The totality of this PFP schema relies directly upon the remarkable ability animals have to draw out responses in people. It is up to the human therapist to capitalize upon this ability.

I. REVIEW OF THE LITERATURE

Examination of the literature on the pet therapies breaks down into two categories: Anecdotal literature based upon the clinical experience of the author; descriptive surveys and studies of a more experimental nature. Before examining these areas a quick book review is in order. These works present rationales for the pet therapies, evidence of effectiveness, and in some cases guidelines for use.

Levinson (1969, 1972) presents two benchmark texts on PFP, the latter giving more attention to working with older populations. Both the edited works of Anderson (1975) and Fogle (1981) represent basic texts on the human-animal bond, and until recently stood alone in examining it from a variety of perspectives. This standing changed with the publication of Katcher and Beck (1983) and Anderson, Hart, and Hart (1984), two books presenting studies on pet therapy and thoughtful discussion on our relationships with animals. White and Watson (1983) produced a popular book delivering a good over view of the field. Cusack and Smith (1984) offer a more advanced text entitled *Pets and the Elderly* written for the geriatric practitioner. These authors also have a work entitled *Using Pets in Clinical Psychotherapy* in preparation.

Two books which have been referenced as texts on pet therapy, but actually devote limited space to the subjects, are presented by Bustad (1980) and Corson and Corson (1980). Finally Arkow (1984) has an edited text covering aspects of the human-animal bond and pet therapy that merits attention, and Sussman (1985) has an edited work covering the salience of pets to families.

Anecdotal Literature

An important early writer on the relationship between animals and humans is Heiman (1956, 1965), probably the first contemporary therapist to practice "zoo therapy," where pets were prescribed for patient treatment. Working from a psychoanalytical background, Heiman contends that pets are symbolically important to their owners, meeting unconscious psychological needs by representing parents, children, or significant others.

Rynearson (1978) agrees with Heiman as to the symbolic importance of pets, but dwells more on attachment needs. Rynearson also points out that undue amounts of affection towards pets may reflect pathology, and discussion of negative person-pet relations is also reflected in the work of Keddie (1977), Ryder (1973), Szasz (1968), and Voith (1981).

Dramatic examples of negative animal-related circumstances do not represent the normal mode of pet involvement. However, they powerfully underline the emotional significance of animals. While pointing out the negative potential of person-pet relationships, the above writers still indicate that pets are important to people due to a pet's affinity for attachment and display of unconditional love.

Feldman (1977) asserts that pets play basic therapeutic roles, where they enhance self-esteem and identity, facilitate interpersonal interaction, act as companions, and enrich personal development. According to Mugford (1980), companionship is the factor through which pets meet the social needs of their owners.

Usually every area of endeavor has one person who stands above the norm in terms of contributions made, and Levinson (1969, 1972) stands alone in pioneering the pet therapies (for a fuller listing of Levinson's work the reader is referred to Brickel, 1980-81). Levinson points out that pets become assets in those vulnerable stages of life—youth and old age—which have become precarious due to one-parent households and the loss of the extended family. In old age pets serve as emotional anchors, or life reinforcements, for persons whose external world is in transition due to the loss of family, friends, and economic responsibility.

Theory

Most forms of psychotherapeutic application are firmly grounded in theory. Such is not the case with PFP although we can extract a distinct theoretical direction. As we have seen, most clinical writers show a psychoanalytical orientation in discussing how pets influence people. Attention is paid to the symbolic qualities of animals, and how using such symbolism enables working out psychodynamic conflict. Levinson (1972) embraces this orientation, taking it one step further in his neoanalytical theory that people have an innate need for affiliating with animals. Hence in one bold, insightful step Levinson introduces the idea that pets are intrinsically therapeutic, and affiliation with animals is a necessity.

Conflicting with an affiliative-need assumption is the harsh fact that people continually insist on pushing whole species of animals to the brink of extinction, and too often, over the edge of its unforgiving precipice. It would be more correct to state that man selects, as a consequence of learning, those animals with whom he will affiliate, and further learns to satisfy emotional needs through preselected animals. Therefore learning theory is presented as another side of the theoretical coin, to explain human-animal relations (Brickel, 1985), and the mechanism of PFP (Brickel, 1982).

Studies on the Pet Therapies

Research on pet-facilitated therapy is split along two major avenues of inquiry. The first, concerned with the health correlates of pet ownership asks "Are pets intrinsically therapeutic?" The second avenue explores the benefits of animals as therapeutic adjuncts, asking "Will pets help in psychotherapy?"

It will be obvious to the clinician that pet therapies (rather than pet therapy) more accurately describe the field, since implementation qualitatively differs according to degree of clinician involvement. A therapist who simply advises a client to obtain a pet does not use the same paradigm as therapists who actively integrate animals into therapeutic strategies. Therefore it seems mandatory to parcel out milieu therapy and PFP from a generic "pet-facilitated therapy."

Even though only PFP is concerned with treatment application, studies on the health benefits of pet ownership which do not include practitioner involvement are commonly presented as pet therapy. To avoid confusion studies covered here are presented along a continuum of therapist participation, and are further broken down into physiological and psychological benefits. Physical rehabilitation programs will not be covered.

Pet Ownership

These studies investigate the health status correlates of pet owner-ship. Positive findings support the stance that pets are intrinsically therapeutic. No therapist involvement has been indicated in these studies.

Physiological Benefits. The most well known studies of this type are those done by Friedmann, Thomas, Noctor, and Katcher (1978) and Friedmann, Katcher, Lynch, and Thomas (1980). These re-searchers studied the survival rates of 92 persons treated for myo-cardial infarction and angina pectoris. The average patient's age was 58 with a total range of 37-79 years. A one-year follow up on mortality comparisons indicated that significantly more survivors owned pets, and this finding held true even when the researchers controlled for pets (dogs) with whom exercise might be a factor. A discriminant analysis of physiological severity and pet ownership on patient survival indicated that ownership was significant in predict-ing survival. No replications of this study have been reported.

Psychological Benefits. Ory and Goldberg (1983) investigated factors related to subjective well-being in elderly women. Struc-tured interviews were carried out with 1,073 women aged 65–75. Bivariate analysis revealed a significant relationship between demographic, health, and social factors and avowed happiness. Pet ownership was found to independently predict happiness after con-trolling for all other variables, but contributed little to the cumulative variance of the equation. A test of interactions showed that pet ownership and happiness was a function of socioeconomic status, with greater happiness among subjects of high status.

Robb (1983) interviewed 37 elderly veterans on psychosocial and health-related variables, finding that morale was higher among pet owners. In a replication Robb and Stegman (1983) examined morale and perceived locus of control in 56 elderly veterans, but no signifi-cant differences were found between owners and nonowners. The authors indicate that this weakens a simplistic cause-effect relation-ship between pet ownership and health. A simple cause-effect rela-tionship is also questioned by Lawton, Moss, and Moles (1984). These researchers reexamined a survey ($N = 3,996$) of elderly per-sons and found no association between pet ownership and well-being or health. These studies suggest that pet-owning health benefits may depend upon situational and personal characteristics.

Evidence of the apparent complexity of the human-animal bond is manifest in mixed research findings. In a comprehensive report, Lago, Connell, and Knight (1983) indicate that pets had no apparent impact on the physical health, mortality, social activity, and well-being of 55 elderly subjects. However, it was mentioned that had several case studies been included, striking pre-post differences would have been found as a result of pet ownership.

In another report (Connell & Lago, 1984), a favorable attitude toward a pet was found predictive of perceived happiness. This is congruent with a study by Kidd and Feldman (1981) where results showed that pet owners were significantly more ". . . self-sufficient, dependable, helpful, optimistic, and self-confident" than nonowning cohorts.

Pet Introduction (No Therapist Participation)

In these studies the researcher or therapist merely introduces an animal. When present, the therapist is a passive spectator giving little or no direction.

Physiological Benefits. In a pilot study Katcher, Friedmann, Beck, and Lynch (1983) monitored the blood pressure of subjects across several conditions: reading, baseline (no activity), watching a blank wall and watching tropical fish. In this young population both hypertensives and normotensives displayed lowest blood pressures in the fish condition. This data however was not subjected to statistical analysis. In a semicontrolled replication and extension, Katcher, Segal and Beck (1984) assigned 42 dental patients about to undergo an extraction to several conditions, one of which was contemplating an aquarium. There was a nonsignificant trend towards greater relaxation in this condition.

In another study examining blood pressure and heart rate, Friedmann, Katcher, Thomas, Lynch, and Messent (1983) assigned children to rest or read conditions, comparing physiological responses when a dog was present or absent. Despite interactions, the presence of a pet was associated with lower blood pressure. Baun, Bergstrom, Langston, and Thomas (1984) followed this line of examination with young adults who read quietly, petted a strange dog, or petted their own dog. Petting an owned dog was again associated with blood pressure reduction.

Psychological Benefits. One of the most frequently cited articles in the literature is the pilot work of Mugford and M'Comisky (1975). These researchers placed pet birds, plants, or nothing in the homes of 19 elderly persons. The individuals given birds showed marked, positive attitude changes towards themselves and others. Interviews with pet owners showed that they developed strong emotional bonds to their pets, and that the animals acted as "social lubricants" in generating attention and conversation from others.

Pet Introduction (Therapist Directed)

These studies differ from the preceding in that some degree of therapist direction takes place in the client-pet interaction; articles here are representative of PFP. No studies revealing physiological benefit could be found.

Psychological Benefits. A classic study of the efficacy of using pets in therapy is provided by Corson, Corson, and Gwynne (1975a); Corson, Corson, Gwynne, and Arnold (1975b, 1977). Dogs and cats were introduced to 30 recalcitrant psychiatric inpatients who ". . . had failed to respond favorably to traditional forms of therapy (individual and group psychotherapy, pharmacotherapy, ECT, occupational and recreational therapy)." Rating scales evaluated social contacts, behavioral improvement, verbal interaction, and other psychological factors, and were supplemented with videotape recordings. Two persons rejected their pets. The remaining 28 displayed marked improvements on both clinical and observational measures.

Two replications of the Corson et al. work have been performed, and in both cases results have supported the utility of PFP. In a nursing home study (Corson & Corson, 1978) the animals proved effective as socializing agents, with one person speaking his first words in 26 years. Andrysco (1981, 1982) replicated the Corson study in another nursing home and found that residents having access to pets displayed improvements in self-care, involvement, socialization, and verbal communication.

Robb, Boyd, and Pristash (1980) observed the effects of a puppy on the behavior of elderly male veterans. In comparison to other stimuli the animal condition yielded demonstrably higher frequencies of social behavior. It was noted that "Two clients who routinely uttered repetitive, monotonous, illogical and undirected statements stopped their remarks in the presence of the puppy."

Thompson, Kennedy, and Igou (1983) worked with 20 chronic psychiatric inpatients, one-half of which were assigned to PFP sessions over six weeks. When level of impairment was taken into account it was disclosed that treated individuals with intermediate impairment levels improved more than their control counterparts. Hendy (1984) examined the effects of various presentations (no pets, toy pets, videotaped pets, and live pets) on the social and health activities of 13 elderly patients. The live-pet condition generated significantly greater amounts of smiling and alertness.

A pet dog was integrated into therapy sessions for depressed, but otherwise well-oriented, elderly nursing home inpatients (Brickel, 1984a, 1984b). Pre-post results were compared with a no-treatment control and a conventional psychotherapy group. Both treatment groups showed reductions of depression, but the reduction for the PFP group was almost twice that of the conventional group.

Dogs seem to be the animal of choice for PFP, but their use is not a necessity. Brickel (1979) surveyed nursing staff who kept cat mascots for a total-care geriatric population. The animals were said to increase patient responsiveness, enhance the ward milieu, and provide reality therapy. Doyle (1975) introduced a rabbit to six chronic psychiatric inpatients. Less regressed patients used the animal as a medium for social interaction. More regressed persons tried incorporating the animal's presence into their personalized reality, and used it as a bridge to external reality.

As shown by Jendro, Watson, and Quigley (1984), positive results are not always forthcoming. These researchers attempted to determine if PFP had an impact on the psychosocial behavior of 22 chronic inpatients with OBS and chronic schizophrenia. PFP sessions were held for one hour a week over five weeks. Statistical analyses revealed no differences between pre-post treatments. In explanation, the authors note that PFP sessions may not have been long enough, or performed frequently enough, to affect a regressed population where "A few patients had to be shown how to pet the puppies."

Summary and Conclusions

Early writers on the theme of pets in therapy came from an analytical orientation. These clinicians were the first to recognize the adjunctive value of animals, and their works provide a basic rationale explaining why pets can be therapeutic. This rationale continues to dominate thinking about the pet therapies, although alternative theoretical explanations (e.g., learning theory) are slowly being introduced, and should enrich future discussion.

The finding of positive but nonsignificant trends in studies on psychological benefits of pet ownership seems to reflect the complexity of the person-pet bond, indicating that meaningful variables have not yet been satisfactorily identified or isolated. Most studies require replication.

Case studies on PFP show excellent potential. When complemented by experimental endeavors, PFP displays even greater promise. It is worthwhile to recall that many PFP studies enlisted elderly inpatients with severe chronic psychiatric disability.

Such populations are difficult to work with, and unfortunately, are perceived by some professionals as refractory due to their chronically unresponsive nature. Stabilization of symptomatology by pharmaceutical means is often the only therapy such persons receive. If PFP displayed only small, idiosyncratic gains with such patients the technique would be auspicious. But PFP has shown significant gains on behavioral and clinical indices with such patients.

We need have no problem with the fact that some studies on PFP incur methodological weaknesses. Many studies on conventional therapeutic application are not textbook perfect, and imperfection should be expected in a relatively unexplored area like PFP. As this research area develops we can expect replication and expansion of the data base. This will enhance the technique's validity and applicability with both the well elderly, and diagnosed elderly subpopulations.

II. CLINICAL IMPLEMENTATION CONSIDERATIONS

We have covered, in the literature review, the available studies examining advantages of animals in therapeutic efforts. The clinical gerontologist wishing to implement PFP faces what constitutes a bewildering array of decisions, for the therapist will be concerned with matching desirable pets (dogs, cats, rabbits, etc.) with specific client populations (well and fragile elderly, those psychiatrically diagnosed). Where then do we start when we are concerned with clinical application?

Some general guidelines have been suggested for pet therapy programs (e.g., Arkow, 1980; Barnett & Quigley, 1984; Cusack & Smith, 1984; Lee, Zeglan, Ryan, & Hines, 1983). And Levinson (1972) should be highlighted for his clinical insights. This section is written exclusively for the practitioner wishing to implement PFP with the elderly. A synopsis of facts will clear the way for initial preparation:

1. PFP is a nonstandardized technique. There are no strict guidelines to follow, so the gerontologist should not fear incorrect application. A "right way" has yet to be established; studies reporting harmful effects have yet to be reported.
2. PFP should be guided by common sense.
3. Selecting the appropriate pet means that client, staff, therapist, and environmental needs are all taken into consideration.
4. PFP, like all the pet therapies, is adjunctive. It is not meant to constitute an exclusive therapeutic modality, although it sometimes does, and in individual cases has been extremely effective. PFP should supplement—not substitute for—the practitioner.
5. The strength of PFP resides in the ability of animals to: (a) draw out emotional and behavioral responses; (b) provide a distraction from dysfunctional cognitive and psychic distress; (c) enhance or establish inner strengths. It is up to the therapist to exploit these abilities for the client's benefit.

Further examination of PFP yields three participants, each of which deserve individual consideration: the therapist, the patient, and the pet.

The Therapist

Therapists engaging PFP must genuinely enjoy animals, for despite its potential, PFP will not work well in the hands of a reluctant practitioner. The technique is demanding in that the requirements of responsible pet ownership must be met In addition to ongoing responsibilities. The animal will be adjunctive to the mainstream therapy involved, but because the pet is a sentient organism it cannot be put away like a book. If the practitioner regularly attends meetings, performs research, or is involved in other activities where a pet's company is inappropriate, a backup person must be found who can reliably care for the pet.

The therapist should be creative. With creativity pets can be integrated into any theoretical rationale, be it behavioral (pets as reinforcements), psychoanalytical (for symbolic content), reality therapy (fostering responsibility) or another school of thought. Since the pet will occasionally refuse participation, patience and flexibility are also needed. And of course the health of the therapist is a consideration in terms of allergies or phobias. If the reader finds the prospect of PFP aversive the technique is contraindicated.

Basic Approach

It is suggested that animals be introduced into therapeutic contexts unobtrusively, especially when working with patients in institutional settings. Rather than implying that a pet would be "good" for a patient, a better tactic employs statements such as "I recently obtained a pet and need to get it used to people; will you help me?", or "We thought it would be nice to have a mascot around here. Any ideas on where we should keep it?" Such conduct lends itself to soliciting client feelings, and it is this writer's opinion that whenever possible, the elderly client be enabled to participate in therapeutic decision-making processes.

Once the animal is placed the therapist controls and directs activity of benefit to the client. A depressed, withdrawn patient might be asked to hold or watch the pet briefly. A noncommunicative person might be drawn out verbally or emotionally by bringing attention to the pet, or placing it gently in the person's lap. In one-on-one situations, the pet is allowed to present a distraction when threatening issues are being dealt with, and can offer affectionate, tactile comfort. Client-pet interactions are observed for information on how the individual interacts with others. Opportunities to use the pet as a social catalyst, where others are drawn into the person's social network, are encouraged.

It is understood that this basic approach is a sketch of how the practitioner might apply PFP. It is open for modification and improvement. By allowing the animal to take an active—but directed—part in therapeutic procedures, the practitioner is afforded a multitude of opportunities to aid clients.

The Patient

Perhaps in ten years researchers will detail pet typologies suitable for diagnostic nomenclatures in a future *Diagnostic and Statistical Manual of Mental Disorders*. Current recommendations of this nature are precocious, and so discussion of the patient shall be limited to general criteria used for client selection and consideration.

The following criteria are suggested for assessing client suitability. Rule out persons with histories of acting out in a manner dangerous to themselves or others, who are on any immunosuppressive regimen, have animal allergies or phobias (antiphobic treatment using animals is desensitization, not PFP), or who have exhibited behavior indicative of sadism or cruelty. Patient screening includes an interview regarding history of pet-keeping which probes for interest in animals. Recalling that pets represent a major responsibility, this process is crucial if a home pet is recommended, for an affectionate companion pet will be considered a burden by a compliant but unenthusiastic client.

Severely psychiatrically disabled do not present as much of a problem as could be anticipated. We have seen several studies (Brickel, 1979; Corson & Corson, 1978; Robb et al., 1980) where pets have been used with such persons with no negative consequences. If doubts about patient suitability remain a stuffed toy animal may be presented (and there is some evidence that this activity is therapeutic—see Francis & Baly, 1984).

In working with the physically disabled, take care that the pet generates no discomfort for the client. Persons may allow the animal to lick their face, and there is no harm in this. See that no traces of animal hair linger on the patient which could cause irritation. Cats which have been declawed are forever more indoor cats, so if declawing is performed permanent house arrangements must be made for the animal. In all cases where mental or physical impairment is severe, close supervision is called for which protects patient and pet. This supervision, coupled with provisions for the patient's comfort (e. g., a towel to protect clothing or bedding) insures an enjoyable experience.

The Pet

Just as it is misleading to identify diagnostic types of patients amenable to PFP, it is also misleading to suggest specific types (dogs vs. cats) or breeds (terriers vs. beagles) of pets best suited for this work. There is too much individual variation to generalize. We are again faced with the question of where to start.

If we start with the client, initiation of a pet search includes building an animal profile suited to the client's preferences. Similar profiles can be generated for the therapist working with the animal, and for the environment where the animal will reside.

Limiting discussion to dogs and cats, the desirable animal for older people will, in general, be well socialized to people and animals, housebroken, nondestructive, trained (or trainable), in good health, neutered, of small to medium size, short-coated, of good disposition, low to moderately active (avoid hyperactive animals), and promiscuously affectionate. This global description is admittedly an idealized one, but many animals *will* be available which meet most criteria. It is incumbent upon the clinician to get familiar with a variety of animals and their characteristics. With study and consultation from individuals who work with animals, the clinician will soon become adept at selecting suitable pets for the elderly.

A cautionary note for the clinician: one does not have to be an "animal lover" to impulsively adopt an appealing animal which, over time, proves to be an unsatisfactory therapy pet. Prior to any search, the reader is best prepared by resolving not to choose an animal until some arbitrary number have been observed.

Pets for Community-Residing Elderly

There are several considerations for pets in the person's home. The patient must be oriented well enough to meet the reponsibilities of pet ownership. Here pet choice is largely dictated by degree of responsibility the client can capably handle. In general, the smaller the pet the less responsibility, with fish representing the easiest pets to maintain. Responsibility however does not diminish in terms of importance. Pets must be well taken care of for both therapeutic and humane reasons. A sick, injured, or dying animal is counter-therapeutic—unless the animal comes into the person's care in such status, and the client undertakes efforts to heal the animal. Allowing an animal to be passively abused is unethical, for the therapist ultimately shares responsibility for both patient and pet.

Judgments must also be made on the client's physical condition and ensuing pet responsibilities. This presents only minor problems with ambulatory patients. Wheelchair-bound persons long ago proved their independence, and should have no problems in pet-keeping, but this, as in all cases, is judged on an individual basis. Ideally other people will share the home and assume responsibility when needed. Neighbors can be solicited for their aid, and this has the distinct advantage of helping patients build and maintain social support networks.

Another consideration is economic. Can a pet be afforded? Pensioners and those living on disability have fixed incomes, and we must avoid the imposition of an economic burden. If economics are a factor, contact animal-oriented agencies who might subsidize pets costs and provide volunteers to aid the placement.

Pets in Institutional Settings

Institutional settings have the great advantage that, on occasions when patients are unable to care for pets, alternate care-givers are available. Many nursing homes are set up so that small pets (birds, hamsters, hermit crabs) are easily integrated into group or individual rooms. Larger animals entail more responsibility and room. If the setting cannot sustain any number of larger animals a mascot presents a desirable alternative.

Young vs. Old Animals

Younger animals are superbly charming, but require greater responsibility. They need to be housebroken, and cause physical discomforts when teething or clawing. A young animal may also, during its development, bond to one person to the exclusion of others.

Older animals can be as playful as younger ones. They are trainable, and in many cases already housebroken. Furthermore their social characteristics are less likely to change, and their size (and propensity to eat) is already established.

Negative Staff Reactions

Introducing an animal into an institutional setting, particularly a hospital setting, draws mixed reactions. Some hospital staff will resist changes that clash with a commonly perceived notion of the medical model. That is, to conservative medical personnel pets may represent behaviorally unpredictable, disease spreading vectors complete with legal quandaries. The presence of pets in such facilities can subsequently threaten personnel responsible for the ongoing quality and delivery of medical services (Brickel, 1983).

Advocates of animal placement should request permission for pets only where appropriate. Pets do not belong in intensive care units, but in wards where physical recovery is not an issue, and the psychological status of patients is no threat to others. Many wards that serve the elderly, in both general and psychiatric hospitals, meet such criteria.

Nevertheless many staff will object to animals, and where such persons are a majority their wishes cannot be ignored. If, as is usually the case, staff reactions are mixed, controversy can be settled by obtaining a select number of staff who volunteer responsibility for the pet. This diminishes the most common negative anticipation of overburdened staff—an "additional responsibility." Forethought regarding the animal, its maintenance, and contingencies starts well before the actual placement. With adequate planning resistant staff will become ardent supporters of the animal.

Positive Staff Reactions

While research studies have yet to be performed establishing a strong, reliable correlation between liking for people and animals, reality dictates that this will often be the case.

Staff may not only be encouraged about patient progress when they observe patient reactions to pets, staff may also feel better about working in a less antiseptic, more natural environment. Staff will also enjoy the presence of animals; this writer has visited several settings where the animal's bedding was in the nursing station. Petting, playing, or observing an animal presents relaxing interludes for staff, and may eventually be shown to enhance staff morale and effectiveness.

Since ultimate responsibility for maintaining a mascot will fall upon staff, they should help establish preliminary criteria for the animal. Discussion should focus upon global characteristics (age, size, sex, type) instead of interbreed debate (boxer vs. terrier). Discussion is overshadowed by consideration of what pet best fits into the environment. At least one person per shift is responsible for the animal. The pet may be exposed to patients via "rounds," or can be placed in a conspicuous, supervised area such as a dayroom or patio.

Special Considerations for the Pet

Therapy animals are working animals, and breaks are in order to prevent fatigue. Mascots must have access to areas where they can relax, unbothered by others. Constant touching and handling of an animal will stress it, so behavioral and physiological changes must be monitored. If fatigue in a pet is apparent, remove it to a rest area and let the patients know why—they will be concerned.

Animals, like people, can become institutionalized when they spend most of their life in a specialized setting. It is undesirable to allow therapy animals to reach such a state because there will come times when the pet has to venture outside for veterinary checks or other visitations. Allow persons—both patients and staff—to take the pet home overnight or for weekends. This expands the pet's ability to adapt to new environments while enriching its socialization.

Another consideration is feeding. Therapy animals risk the danger of obesity because patients, staff , and visitors enjoy feeding them. This becomes a health risk for the pet, given the number of people it will be exposed to. Rules need to be established for the pet's food intake. One person can be given the task, or the task can be rotated. The giving of treats can itself be a task for the more impaired client.

A Final Note on Attachment

Attachment indicates that an emotional linkage has been established between people and pets, and this is something to be fostered. However two types of attachment are undesirable.

The first type is pathological attachment to the animal, where the patient experiences inappropriate distress regarding separation from the animal, and withdraws from people to companion the animal. While rare, the therapist must watch for this and work for its prevention, using the pet to expand the patient's social network.

The second type of attachment to be avoided occurs where the therapist uses an animal adjunctively, taking it around to different patients. A dog may form an exclusive attachment to the therapist in such a situation, and consequently will not interact well with other persons. This can be avoided by rotating responsibility for the pet among staff and patients whenever possible. If efforts to change the animal fail, the therapist has the option of adopting it or finding it a home.

Summary

The contents of this section attempted to outline areas of consideration for the practitioner interested in PFP. All suggestions mentioned are amenable to modification, and the therapist initiating PFP should not hesitate developing a style of personal choice. It is this writer's hope that other practitioners will be encouraged to apply the technique and document their results.

Pet animals do not represent a panacea for mental or physical impairment. But they do represent an adjunctive technique of potential benefit to elderly clientele. And we are obligated to pursue all therapeutic avenues of potential benefit. Pets will not be suitable for every client, but for those clients that respond well to animals, the results can be outstanding. Such endeavors show a mutual respect for people and animals, and are luminescent examples of the human-animal bond at its apex.

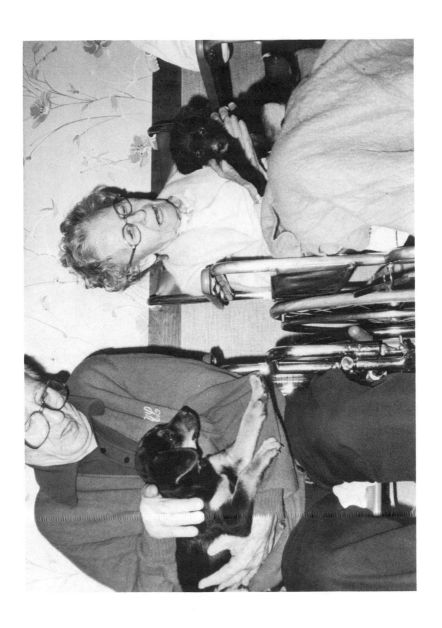

REFERENCES

Anderson, R. K., Hart, B., & Hart, L. (Eds.), (1984). *The pet connection*. University of
    Minnesota Press: CENSHARE.
Anderson, R. S. (Ed.) (1975). *Pet animals and society*. London: Balliere-Tindall.

Andrysco, R. M. (1981). *Pet-facilitated therapy in a retirement nursing care community.* Paper presented at the First International Conference on the Human/Companion Animal Bond. Philadelphia, October (unpublished).

Andrysco, R. M. (1982). *A study of ethologic and therapeutic factors of pet-facilitated therapy in a retirement-nursing community.* Unpublished doctoral dissertation, Ohio State University.

Arkow, P. (1980). *"Pet therapy": A study of the use of companion animals in selected therapies,* 2nd Edition. Colorado: The Humane Society of the Pikes Peak Region, P. O. Box 187, Colorado Springs, CO.

Arkow, P. (Ed.), (1984). *Dynamic relationships in practice: Animals in the helping professions.* California: The Latham Foundation.

Barnett, J. C., & Quigley, J. (1984). Animals in long-term care facilities: A framework for program planning. *The Journal of Long-Term Care Administration,* Winter, 1–7.

Baun, M. M., Bergstrom, N., Langston, N. F., & Thomas, L. (1984). Physiological effects of petting dogs: Influences of attachment. In R. K. Anderson et al. (Eds.), *The pet connection.* University of Minnesota Press: CENSHARE.

Brickel, C. M. (1979). The therapeutic roles of cat mascots with a hospital-based geriatric population: A staff survey. *The Gerontologist, 19,* 368–372.

Brickel, C. M. (1980–81). A review of the roles of pet animals in psychotherapy and with the elderly. *International Journal of Aging and Human Development, 12,* 119–128.

Brickel, C. M. (1982). Pet-facilitated psychotherapy: A theoretical explanation via attention shifts. *Psychological Reports, 50,* 71–74.

Brickel, C. M. (1983). *The institutional bite: Resistance to pets in hospital settings and strategies for change.* Paper presented at the 1983 Conferences on the Human-Animal Bond, University of Minnesota, June (unpublished).

Brickel, C. M. (1984a). Depression in the nursing home: A pilot study using pet-facilitated psychotherapy. In R. K. Anderson et al. (Eds.), *The pet connection.* University of Minnesota: CENSHARE.

Brickel, C. M. (1984b). The clinical use of pets with the aged. *Clinical Gerontologist, 2,* 72–75.

Brickel, C. M. (1985). Initiation and maintenance of the human-animal bond: Familial roles from a learning perspective. In M. Sussman (Ed.), *Pets and the Family.* New York: The Haworth Press.

Bustad, L. (1980). *Animals, aging, and the aged.* Minneapolis: University of Minnesota Press.

Connell, C. M., & Lago, D. J. (1984). Favorable attitudes toward pets and happiness among the elderly. In R. K. Anderson et al. (Eds.), *The pet connection.* University of Minnesota: CENSHARE.

Corson, S. A., & Corson, E. (1978). Pets as mediators of therapy in custodial institutions and the aged. In J. H. Masserman (Ed.), *Current Psychiatric Therapies* (Vol. 18). New York: Grune & Stratton.

Corson, S. A., & Corson, E. (Eds.), (1980). *Ethology and nonverbal communication in mental health.* Oxford: Pergamon Press.

Corson, S. A., Corson, E., & Gwynne, P. H. (1975a). Pet-facilitated psychotherapy. In R. S. Anderson (Ed.), *Pet animals and society.* London: Bailliere Tindall.

Corson, S. A., Corson, E., Gwynne, P. H., & Arnold, L. E. (1975b). Pet-facilitated psychotherapy in a hospital setting. *Current Psychiatric Therapies, 15,* 277–286.

Corson, S. A., Corson, E., Gwynne, P. H., & Arnold, L. E. (1977). Pet dogs as nonverbal communication links in hospital psychiatry. *Comprehensive Psychiatry, 18,* 61–72.

Cusack, O., & Smith, E. (1984). *Pets and the elderly.* New York: The Haworth Press.

Cusack, O., & Smith, E. (in preparation). *Using pets in clinical psychotherapy.* New York: The Haworth Press.

DePauw, K. P. (1984). Therapeutic horseback riding in Europe and America. In R. K. Anderson et al. (Eds.), *The pet connection.* University of Minnesota: CENSHARE.

Doyle, M. C. (1975). Rabbit—Therapeutic prescription. *Perspectives in Psychiatric Care, 13,* 79–82.

Feldman, B. M. (1977). Why people own pets: Pet owner psychology and the delinquent owner. *Animal Regulation Studies, 1,* 87–94.

Fogle, B. (Ed.), (1981). *Interrelations between people and pets.* Illinois: Charles C Thomas.

Francis, G. M., & Baly, A. J. (1984). Plush animals as therapy in a nursing home. *Clinical Gerontologist, 2,* 75–76.

Friedmann, E., Thomas, S., Noctor, M., & Katcher, A. H. (1978). Pet ownership and coronary heart disease patient survival. *Circulation, 58,* 168 (supplement).

Friedmann, E., Katcher, A. H., Lynch, J. J., & Thomas, S. (1980). Animal companions and one-year survival of patients after discharge from a coronary care unit. *Public Health Reports, 95,* 307–312.

Friedmann, E., Katcher, A. H., Thomas, S., Lynch, J. J., & Messent, P. (1983). Social interaction and blood pressure: Influence of animal companions. *Journal of Nervous and Mental Disease, 171,* 461–465.

Heiman, M. (1956). The relationship between man and dog. *Psychoanalytic Quarterly, 25,* 568–585.

Heiman, M. (1965). Psychoanalytic observations on the relationship of pet and man. *Veterinary Medicine/Small Animal Clinician, 60,* 713–718.

Hendy, H. M. (1984). Effects of pets on the sociability and health activities of nursing home residents. In R. K. Anderson et al. (Eds.), *The pet connection.* University of Minnesota: CENSHARE.

Jendro, C., Watson, C., & Quigley, J. (1984). The effects of pets on the chronically-ill elderly. In R. K. Anderson et al. (Eds.), *The pet connection.* University of Minnesota: CENSHARE.

Katcher, A. H., & Beck, A. M. (Eds.), (1983). *New perspectives on our lives with companion animals.* Pennsylvania: University of Pennsylvania Press.

Katcher, A. H., Friedmann, E., Beck, A. M., & Lynch, J. J. (1983). Looking, talking, and blood pressure: The physiological consequences of interaction with the living environment. In A. H. Katcher & A. M. Beck (Eds.), *New perspectives on our lives with companion animals.* Pennsylvania: University of Pennsylvania Press.

Katcher, A. H., Segal, H., & Beck, A. M. (1984). Contemplation of an aquarium for the reduction of anxiety. In R. K. Anderson et al. (Ed.), *The pet connection.* University of Minnesota Press: CENSHARE.

Keddie, K. M. (1977). Pathological mourning after the death of a domestic pet. *British Journal of Psychiatry, 131,* 21–25.

Kidd, A. H., & Feldman, B. M. (1981). Pet ownership and self-perceptions of older people. *Psychological Reports, 48,* 867–875.

Lago, D., Connell, C. M., & Knight, B. (1983). PACT (People and animals coming together): A companion animal program. In M. A. Smyer & M. Gatz (Eds.), *Mental health and aging: Programs and Evaluations,* Beverly Hills, CA. Sage Publications.

Lawton, M. P. Moss, M., & Moles, E. (1984). Pet ownership: A research note. *The Gerontologist, 24,* 208–210.

Lee, R. L., Zeglen, M. E., Ryan, T., & Hines, L. M. (1983). Guidelines: Animals in nursing homes. *California Veterinarian* (Supplement), *3,* 1a–43a.

Levinson, B. M. (1969). *Pet-oriented child psychotherapy.* Illinois: Charles C Thomas.

Levinson, B. M. (1972). *Pets and human development.* Illinois: Charles C Thomas.

Mugford, R. A. (1980). The social significance of pet ownership. In S. A. Corson & E. Corson (Eds.), *Ethology and nonverbal communication in mental health.* Oxford: Pergamon Press.

Mugford, R. A. & M'Comisky, J. (1975). Some recent work on the value of cage birds with old people. In R. S. Anderson (Ed.), *Pet animals and human development.* London: Bailliere Tindall.

Ory, M. G., & Goldberg, E. L. (1983). Pet possession and life satisfaction in elderly women. In A. H. Katcher & A. M. Beck (Eds.), *New perspectives on our lives with companion animals*. Philadelphia: University of Pennsylvania Press.

Robb, S. S. (1983). Health status correlates of pet-human association in a health-impaired population. In A. H. Katcher & A. M. Beck (Eds.), *New perspectives on our lives with companion animals*. Philadelphia: University of Pennsylvania Press.

Robb, S. S., Boyd, M., & Pristash, C. L. (1980). A wine bottle, plant, and puppy: Catalysts for social behavior. *Journal of Gerontological Nursing, 6,* 721–728.

Robb, S. S., & Stegman, C. E. (1983). Companion animals and elderly people: A challenge for evaluators of social support. *The Gerontologist, 23,* 277–282.

Ryder, R. D. (1973). Pets in man's search for sanity. *Journal of Small Animal Practice, 14,* 657–668.

Rynearson, E. K. (1978). Humans and pets and attachment. *British Journal of Psychiatry, 133,* 550–555.

Smith, B. A. (1983). Project inreach: A program to explore the ability of Atlantic Bottlenose dolphins to elicit communication responses from autistic children. In A. H. Katcher & A. M. Beck (Eds.), *New perspectives on our lives with companion animals*. Philadelphia: University of Pennsylvania Press.

Sussman, M. (Ed.), (1985). *Pets and the family*. New York: The Haworth Press.

Szasz, K. (1968). *Petishism: Pets and their people in the Western world*. New York: Holt, Rinehart & Winston.

Thompson, M., Kennedy, R. W., & Igou, S. (1983). Pets as socializing agents with chronic psychiatric patients: An initial study. In A. H. Katcher & A. M. Beck (Eds.), *New perspectives on our lives with companion animals*. Philadelphia: University of Pennsylvania Press.

Voith, V. (1981). Attachment between people and their pets: Behavior problems. In B. Fogle (Ed.), *Interrelationships between people and pets*. Illinois: Charles C Thomas.

White, B., & Watson, T. (1983). *Pet love: How pets take care of us*. New York: William Morrow.

Questions

1) Is pet facilitated therapy compatible with other interventions?

2) What is the role of assessment here?

3) What kinds of patients would be poor candidates for pet therapy?

IV
FAMILY THERAPY

19/THE FUNCTIONAL-AGE MODEL OF INTERGENERATIONAL THERAPY
A Social Casework Model

Roberta Greene, ACSW, PhD

Editor's Introduction

The family has recently become the focus in so much of geriatric therapy. *CG* has reviewed a number of new books in this area (v. 1, #2, p. 88; v. 1, #3, pp. 104–106; v. 1, #4, pp. 88–89; v. 2, #2, pp. 70–71; v. 2, #4, pp. 88–89; v. 3, #1, pp. 86–87). *CG* has published articles and clinical comments concerned with issues such as the role of the family in assessment (v. 2, #1, pp. 61–62; v. 1, #3, pp. 94–95) and depression (v. 1, #4, pp. 77–78). In addition to the multigenerational approach, *CG* has looked at the aging marital system (v. 3, #3, pp. 3–15) and the *ersatz* families constructed by patient-patient and patient-staff interactions in institutions (v. 3, #2, pp. 5–10).

Greene develops the functional-age model of intergenerational therapy. The origin of this model is in the psychosocial casework method, which focuses on the individual as enmeshed in various social/interpersonal systems. There is emphasis not only on the interdependence of individuals within a family system, but also on the biological and psychological and social elements of an individual's functional capacities.

Roberta Greene, is Senior Staff Associate for Family Practice, National Association of Social Workers, 7981 Eastern Ave., Silver Spring, MD 20910.

Perhaps the most innovative feature of this model is that the family is not seen as a static context, but as a dynamic system which is impacted by both maturational tasks and contingencies.

This article presents a casework model of biopsychosocial variables for intergenerational family treatment for use by professionals interested in gerontology and family therapy. It suggests innovative diagnostic and treatment modalities for problem-solving in crisis situations arising around family adjustment to the changing needs of its aging members.

INTRODUCTION

During the same period that interest in the aged and the aging process was advancing, the attention of the scientific and practice communities also turned to the family. In the 1950s, as social scientists grew more curious about interpersonal relationships and how individuals interact, the family became an obvious arena for intensified study, resulting in a burgeoning of information related to family functioning. Gerontologists also contributed to this information explosion, and were among the first to call attention to shifts in the U.S. social structure, to study the effects of these changes on intergenerational family relationships, and to challenge the myth of family abandonment of the aged.

The family, as a treatment unit, however, was originally defined in terms of the nuclear family, namely the recognized relationship between a husband, wife and their minor children; the grandparental generation was largely ignored (Spark & Brody, 1972). Pessimistic views of the later stages of life prevailed with most older persons being pictured as isolated or rejected by their families (Butler, 1982; Walsh, 1980).

Throughout the sixties and seventies, research documented the strong positive ties between older people and their relatives. As interactional patterns were studied, it became clear that the family has been and continues to be the major source of care and support for the elderly (Brody, 1981; Brody, Poulshock & Masciocchi, 1978). Most older people, four-fifths of all people over sixty-five years of age, do have children. In fact, it is rare to find an older adult who really has no "family" whether it be a brother, sister, or "adopted kin" (Butler, 1982). These family members exchange visits and services, help each other at times of illness, and generally maintain viable ties.

Those personality theorists who addressed the intergenerational nature of family dynamics have also pointed out that there is a major connecting link between the generations based on loyalty, reciprocity and indebtedness which can be found to some degree in all families (Bowen, 1971; Erikson, 1950; Boszormenyi-Nagy & Spark, 1973). Erikson, one of the few life-cycle personality theorists, was perhaps the first to stress the intergenerational nature of family dynamics; Bowen (1971) proposed that people in each generation are healthier and more productive when viable emotional contact between generations is maintained; Boszormenyi-Nagy and Spark suggested that each family develops its unique code and system of exchange and that it is important to explore this in therapy.

Despite the overwhelming evidence of positive interaction among different generations of family members and the need to address this in therapy, many practitioners have not integrated this knowledge into their current practice. As a result, intergenerational forms of family treatment are just in their infancy. A review of this form of treatment reveals that, while there are diverse family-focused services and programs, there are very few holistic practice models (see Eyde & Rich, 1983; Silverstone & Burack-Weiss, 1983). The goal of closing the gap between theory and practice is a difficult one to achieve and has been seen as one of the mental health challenges of the eighties (Eyde & Rich, 1983). This process involves the integration of up-to-date knowledge of human behavior and the adaptation of existing methods and techniques. The Functional-Age Model for Intergenerational Family Treatment is an attempt to provide such a synthesis.

THEORETICAL BACKGROUND

The Functional-Age Model of Intergenerational Therapy addresses the interplay between the older person's biopsychosocial functioning and the adaptive capacity of the family. The concepts that constitute it are an outgrowth of the psychosocial casework method which strikes a middle ground between intrapersonal and interpersonal relationships. The psychosocial method focuses on the individual in conjunction with the various social systems of which he/she is a part, and therefore is believed to be well suited to understanding elderly clients and their families in a variety of life circumstances.

The psychosocial approach, as an eclectic method, has experienced several alterations as it has expanded to meet new needs. Geriatric social work, as developed in this Model, required two major changes in emphasis. The first relates to the causal nature of the elderly person's functioning by addressing the biological factors related to the aging process. (The core of the Model is a composite of biopsychosocial variables which constitute the person's functional age.) The second relates to the critical role that families play in the lives of older people. The mutual interdependence among family members, and the dynamic development of family structure and organization throughout the various life stages are concepts that provide an important base for this treatment method. In short, the central concepts of the Model were selected to provide a framework and method for assessment and treatment of an older adult within a family context.

THE FUNCTIONAL-AGE MODEL
OF INTERGENERATIONAL FAMILY TREATMENT

The Functional-Age Model of Intergenerational Family Therapy is an innovative view of treatment that can be used wherever an older adult is part of the family constellation. As an intergenerational treatment approach, concerned with *both* the elderly person's functional capacity *and* his/her family system, it requires that the therapist play a central role in processing and integrating diagnostic information in *each* sphere in order to arrive at family-centered interventions.

The Functional-Aged Intergenerational Treatment Model suggests that clients come for help because they are in a state of crisis. In simplest terms, crisis is a period of disequilibrium; a time of heightened vulnerability and threat (Rappaport, 1962). This definition presupposes that individuals and family systems strive to maintain a state of balance through their characteristic adaptive and problem-solving activities. When these adaptive patterns are no longer adequate to meet current demands, functioning breaks down.

The family system, characterized by its high level of interdependence and interrelatedness as compared with other social systems, is particularly vulnerable to disruption when new developmental demands threaten to disrupt the adaptation previously achieved. This can occur during transition points in the family's developmental cycle such as marriage, birth, death and when the family is faced with a biopsychosocial crisis in one of its members. Because of the family's interdependent structure, the practitioner can expect that a change in the functioning, behavior, or role of one member will cause change(s) throughout the group and that the family may come into treatment at such times.

In short, it can be said that the older person and his/her family members constitute a mutually dependent unit with interdependent pasts and futures, and that assessment and treatment must take this into account. Family crisis situations, arising out of developmental issues and/or the changing biopsychosocial needs of an aging family member, are thought to be best resolved through family-focused diagnostic and treatment modalities. In using the Model, the clinician should be prepared to complete a dual prong assessment in which he/she gathers and evaluates biopsychosocial data about the older adult, but also assesses the family unit. The ability to simultaneously evaluate the older adult and his/her place in the family unit is at the heart of the intergenerational treatment model.

The diagnostic elements of the Model are visually represented in Figures I and II.* As can be seen in Figure I, the functional age of the older person becomes the central focus of concern when families in crisis seek help. The Model suggests that presenting problem(s) involving an older adult often revolve around a diminution in the functional capacity of the older relative, and that a decrease in this capacity can take place in any of the three spheres of aging: the biological, the psychological and/or the socio cultural.

Biological decrements may be caused by such factors as the onset of a disease, a stroke or hip fracture. Decreases in psychological functioning may be brought about by a change of residence, an illness, the death of a spouse, or the onset of organic brain disease. A diminution in social skills may be precipitated by inaccessibility to transportation or fear of incontinence. To assess an elderly person's functional age, a clinician must first have a realistic understanding of all these areas of functioning. One area must not be viewed in

---

*Model developed with Dr. Jirina Polivka.

Figure I
THE FUNCTIONAL-AGE MODEL OF
INTERGENERATIONAL FAMILY TREATMENT*

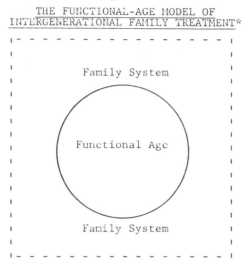

Figure II
The Family as a System

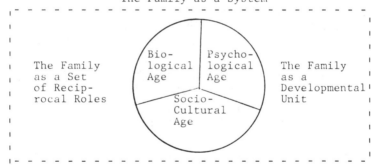

isolation; an individual's functioning in any one area affects all other areas.

"Functional skills are those attributes that are instrumental in meeting environmental demands" (Eyde & Rich, 1983, p. 63). It is not the particular diseases of old age itself but the effects of these conditions upon mental and physical functioning that can affect the ability of older adults to perform certain daily tasks. Those factors

---

*Model developed by Greene and Polivka.

which are found to interfere most with activities of daily living are the ones most likely to have contributed to the crisis situations. The Functional-Age Model also proposes that functional age is best evaluated in relation to the client's functioning within the family system. The caseworker's assessment skills are used to simultaneously evaluate the complex interaction between the changes in the older person's functional abilities and the family's adaptational capacity. When either factor is taxed to the extent that the needs of any individual family member cannot be met, a (social) service agency may be brought into the picture. An assessment of the individual from a family perspective allows the practitioner and family to better understand the structure of life and daily living habits of the older adult, and to arrive at appropriate treatment strategies.

> The older adult who has recently broken a hip may make "excessive" demands on his youngest son. The mildly confused mother may be viewed by her "anxious" daughter as an "appropriate" candidate for nursing home placement. The hospitalized stroke victim may be visited daily for many hours by a "concerned" daughter.

Family problems such as these do not stem solely from either a diminution in the older adult's functional capacity or from a decline in the family's adaptational ability. A complete diagnostic picture requires an understanding of both.

Figure II shows those properties of the family group which are to be evaluated in order to arrive at a family-centered treatment plan. As can be seen, the family unit is considered a social system and its developmental patterns are reflected in family roles. A social system is a grouping of persons in a definite sphere who interact and influence each other. All social systems have their own particular order, structure or organization. The practitioner who recognizes the family as a social system keeps in mind that the family consists of individual members who together form a group. The perspective of the family as a system necessitates that the therapist assess the life of the group and treat the family as an organizational structure that is a functioning whole.

Family functioning is not static. It develops over time as a "result of significant changes in formal family organization and changes in the number, age and composition of the generations" (Eyde & Rich, 1983, p. 11). The family is "re-formed" by the effects of shifting

membership and the changing status of all members in relationship
to one another (Carter & McGoldrick, 1980).

> The newly widowed grandmother moves into the oldest son's
> household "upsetting the routine." The recently retired
> grandfather becomes a "depressed shut-in" refusing to leave
> the home. The newly retired grandmother moves to Florida,
> "abandoning" her daughter and handicapped grandchild.

Throughout the life cycle, the family must learn to cope with
maturational tasks and demands that require changes in its internal
organization.

> Each stage in the life cycle of the family is characterized by an
> average expectable family crisis brought about by the con-
> vergence of bio-psychosocial processes which create phase-
> specific family tasks to be confronted, undertaken, and com-
> pleted. These family tasks reflect the assumption that
> developmental tasks of individual family members have an
> overriding influence or effect on the nature of family life at a
> given time and represent family themes that apply to family
> members as individuals as well as a group. (Rhodes, 1980,
> p. 31)

The dynamic nature of the family life cycle is an important element included in the Functional-Age Model. Family developmental
theory offers the clinician the perspective that each family member
is influenced by, and in turn shapes, the other member's development.

The concept of role provides the practitioners with a vehicle for
examining and defining communication and interaction between
family members. A role in any social structure carries with it expectations of behaviors that are defined and sanctioned by the society.
Translating the concept of role into family terms would mean that
there is a division of labor within the family group and that each
member would be "expected" to behave in a prescribed pattern in a
given situation. Family roles also define certain rights and obliga-
tions for the members. Role changes and transitions in old age are
inevitable and may create alterations in feelings of self-worth and
well-being for the older adult (Bengston & Treas, 1980). As a

result, there can be changes throughout the family system. The Functional-Age Model of Intergenerational Therapy suggests that role expectations are an important aspect in defining interaction between generations. The social worker who understands how these expectations enter into family functioning is better equipped to be of help to the client system in meeting these life transitions.

APPLYING THE MODEL

Most elderly clients come to the attention of an agency at a time of crisis. At that time, the question "who is the client?" must be asked. The crisis is not only a crisis for the individual alone but one for the entire family. Consequently, assessment and treatment must take into account not only the elderly person's biopsychosocial needs, but also the family's adapting and coping capacity. Caseworkers who pursue a family-centered approach to casework with older adults are flexible and modify techniques to fit the client system. For example, they may decide to interview the elderly person alone and/or with his/her family in the home as well as in the office. It is essential, however, that the caseworker *perceive* and *define* the older person's problem(s) in *family terms*. Thinking in intergenerational family terms means that the therapist has considered the family, among other things, as a source of knowledge about the patterns of change that has occurred in their older member.

Families are the silent, unknowing biographers, indirectly recording life events, successful adaptation, and failures of all family members. Their shared experiences provide them the ability to view complementary quirks and habits of older members with a tolerance and humor unmatched by professional outsiders. Their intense motivation, love, and concern fuels their help seeking and advocacy when others are giving up. With this sense of continuity, families become the most knowledgeable observers of change. Complex and subtle changes associated with normal or pathological aging are sensed by observant family members. (Eyde & Rich, 1983, p. 45)

Thinking in intergenerational terms also means that the caseworker has considered the family group as a care-giving resource. Family members are often available, and can be called upon to work with the caseworker on behalf of the older person. Clients rarely experience their problems as located in the total family. It is the therapist who communicates this orientation and helps each family member see "the problem" as a "family problem." By asking to meet with the whole family, the practitioner creates the opportunity for members to communicate and listen to each other, and challenges the family's capacities for decision-making and change (Stamm, 1972). However, the caseworker first must be convinced of the value of this approach and impart it to the family.

"Please join us at our first meeting. We'd like your point of view."

"Your input will be valuable to the family."

"I'd like to hear from everyone in the family."

"In my experience, I have found it most helpful to hear from everyone."

"Can you meet with us at least one time to give us your ideas?"

Relatives who call social service agencies to refer their older parent or to seek community resources can be engaged in the helping process. A family member may be able to care for an older relative at home with the assistance of support services such as a homemaker, meals on wheels or respite care. In those situations where this is not possible or necessary, a family member may act as case manager by planning, arranging, and/or maintaining services for the elderly relative. In the process of working out these arrangements, the caseworker becomes aware of the unique dynamics that characterize that client system. This information about the family can then be used in selecting appropriate interventive techniques.

The family, however, is more than a source of information or care-giving resource. It is an important treatment unit. There are many benefits to be gained from conducting a family group interview. Such interviews can help the worker not only understand each family member in terms of his/her own personality, but also in terms of his/her relationship to other family members. Family transactions and alignments among members can be observed in the "here and now." Family interviews can also assist the family in learning about their patterns of communication and interaction. This gives them the chance to direct their energies to a combined resolution of the problem (Wynne, 1971).

In summary, geriatric social workers have a major responsibility for assessing and treating the older person's family group and addressing family needs. They need to be professionally prepared to understand both the complexity of biopsychosocial functioning of the aged person, as well as its impact on family functioning. As family therapists, they should be well-equipped to understand intergenerational relationships, and the structural changes brought about by a biopsychosocial crisis in any one of its members. The functional age model for intergenerational treatment offers a framework for assessment and treatment of the older adult within a family context. It provides a tool for the simultaneous assessment of the biopsychosocial functioning of an older adult and of the life of the family group. The Model offers the practitioner the means of bridging the gap between an adequate understanding of the older person and a sufficient knowledge of the family as a unit. This integrated assessment process directs the therapist in engaging the family and in selecting family-focused treatment modalities.

REFERENCES

Bengston, V. & Treas, J. (1980). The changing context of mental health and aging. In J. E. Birren & R. B. Sloan (Eds.), *Handbook of mental health and aging* pp. 400–428. Englewood Cliffs, NJ: Prentice-Hall.

Boszormenyi-Nagy, I. & Spark, G. (1973). *Invisible loyalties.* New York: Harper and Row.

Bowen, M. (1971). Aging: A symposium. *The Georgetown Medical Bulletin, 30* (3), 4–27.

Brody, E. (1981). Women in the middle and family help to older people.'' *The Gerontologist, 21,* 471–480.

Brody, S., Poulshock, W., & Masciocchi, C. (1978). The family caring unit: A major consideration in the long-term support system. *The Gerontologist, 18,* 556–561.

Butler, R. N., & Lewis, M. (1982). *Aging and mental health.* St. Louis, MO: C. V. Mosby Co.

Carter, E., & McGoldrick, M. (1980). The family life cycle and family therapy. In E. Carter & M. McGoldrick (Eds.), *The family life cycle: A framework for family therapy.* New York: Gardner Press.

Erikson, E. (1950). *Childhood and society.* New York: W. W. Norton.

Eyde, D., & Rich, J. (1983). *Psychological distress in aging: A family management model.* Rockville, MD: Aspen Publications.

Rappaport, R. (1963). Normal crisis, family structure and mental health. *Family Process, 2(1),* 68–80.

Rhodes, S. (1980). A developmental approach to the life cycle of the family. In M. Bloom (Ed.), *Life span development.* New York: Macmillan.

Silverstone, B., & Burack-Weiss, A. (1982). The social work function in nursing homes and home care. *Journal of Gerontological Social Work, 5(1/2),* 7–33.

Spark, G., & Brody, E. (1972). The aged are family members. In C. Sager & H. Kaplan (Eds.), *Progress in group and family therapy,* pp. 712–725. New York: Brunner/Mazel.

Stamm, I. (1972). Family therapy. In F. Hollis (Ed.), *Casework: A psychosocial therapy.* New York: Random House.

Walsh, F. (1980). The family in later life. In E. A. Carter & M. McGoldrick (Eds.), *The family life cycle.* New York: Gardner Press.

Wynne, L. (1971). Some guidelines for exploratory conjoint family therapy. In J. Haley (Ed.), *Changing families.* New York: Grune & Stratton.

Questions

1) Mental health researchers prefer to think of four kinds of causes of psychopathology:

a) *primary* causes, which are essential for the development of the disorder,

b) *predisposing* causes, which pave the way for future disorder, by making the individual more susceptible,

c) *precipitating* causes, which occur just prior to onset, and trigger the disorder,

d) *perpetuating* causes, which keep the disorder going, or at least make matters worse, after onset.

In which ways would family dynamics be the "cause" of senile confusion? depression? paranoia? hypochondriasis?

2) What would be the role of other family members in helping to manage senile confusion? depression? paranoia? hypochondriasis?

20/THE TECHNIQUES AND CONTEXTS OF MULTIGENERATIONAL THERAPY

Michael Duffy, PhD

Editor's Introduction

Duffy picks up where Greene leaves off and builds an even more persuasive case for family therapy in geriatrics. He moves from the theoretical to the practical, considering such difficulties as scheduling multigenerational sessions to every member's convenience, and reflections on just who is the client.

He then describes some very specific techniques for (or modified forms of) multigenerational therapy: letters, taped sessions, phone calls, home visits, extended sessions. Also considered are the role of the therapist as consultant and the role of community support programs. A paraphrase of his advice would run something like: ''be creative, match the tools to the task.''

Previous articles and clinical comments in *CG* have discussed techniques such as family based management of disturbing behaviors (v. 1, #1, pp. 69–86) and life review (v. 1, #2, pp. 59–67).

At this time, the idea of doing multigenerational therapy has more adherents than practitioners. Individual, and even family, therapists

Michael Duffy is Associate Professor, Counseling Psychology Program, Department of Educational Psychology; Member, Center for Health Systems and Technology, College of Medicine, Texas A&M University. Address correspondence to: Michael Duffy, PhD, Department of Educational Psychology, Texas A&M University, College Station, TX 78743.

347

continue to focus on the nuclear family and act as if extended family members—older parents, grandparents, aunts and uncles, and parents-in-law—do not exist or are relatively insignificant in the dynamics of the family. There is a growing recognition, however, particularly on the part of clinical gerontologists, that this larger network is intimately involved in family processes and support systems. Therapists who work exclusively either with older persons or younger family members run the real risk of operating "in the dark"; their understanding of the family system is liable to be incomplete and their interventions less effective.

THE CASE FOR MULTIGENERATIONAL THERAPY

In a real sense the rationale for multigenerational therapy lies in the phenomenal developments over the past two decades in the fields of family research and family therapy. The original clinical focus on the individual and his or her problem has given way to a more contextual view of pathology. This viewpoint rightly characterizes a problem as an expression of the system in which it exists; in a concrete sense, problems are best understood and treated, at least in part, as expressions of difficulties within the family. Thus therapists routinely see the need to work with the more complex sets of interactions within the family system. The problem is that this family "system" is frequently limited to the nuclear family, with little real awareness of the impact of the larger extended kin network. It is relatively rare to find therapists holding conjoint family sessions which include, for example, older parents or grandparents. In the reverse situation, however, gerontologists increasingly recognize the need to include the younger family in the treatment of their geriatric patients.

This neglect of extended family members in therapy could have some justification if one held the view that the kinship network has only minimal dynamic impact on the nuclear family. This has, in fact, been a pervasive viewpoint since the 1940s when, based on work-related mobility and urban-to-rural migration patterns, the traditional, caring extended family was seen to be in decline (Parsons, 1949). More recent developments, however, have shown this to be largely a misconception. Physical distance and limited access, when present, do not necessarily imply a lack of emotional cohesion among family members. Current research suggests that extended families are adapting to new circumstances (Uzoka, 1979) and, thanks to telephone, automobile, and airplane, are managing to maintain interaction which are as vital (and problematic!) as ever. Interestingly, while the size of the nuclear family has been shrinking, the size of the extended family—the number of coexisting generations is increasing. It is common these days to have four- and even five-generation families due to better health and increased longevity (Riley, 1983; Duffy, 1984). These changes present challenges to the understanding and inventiveness of contemporary therapists.

In addition to these issues, there are other reasons which may encourage therapists to "overlook" the extended family. The systemic view of the family, while being a very significant contribution, has inadvertently led to a common misconception in practice—that systemic interventions necessarily involve the *physical* presence of family members in conjoint therapy. So, extended family members must be present in the therapy room (often impossible) to be successfully included in therapy. This very restrictive and "literal" view of a system has led therapists to be unaware of and unable to capitalize on the reciprocal effects of therapy on family members with whom they have no direct contact. Fortunately, this view is less rigidly held today, to the extent that even nuclear family therapists will often judge that *physical* conjoint therapy is sometimes contraindicated. In turn, this opens the door for a more inventive involvement of the extended family in therapy.

Another constraint on multigenerational therapy is its "inconvenience." The traditional therapy format—weekly, 50-minutes, in-office—is as restrictive on intergenerational therapy as it is convenient for therapists and for reimbursement procedures. This is especially true in the private practice context where the profit incentive cannot be dismissed. It is appealing, however, to explore ways which are both practical and also allow therapists to understand and utilize the complexity of interactions within extended family systems.

What follows is a review of a limited literature discussing what professionals are *doing* in multigenerational therapy, with an emphasis on techniques and strategies. It becomes quickly apparent that creative *contextual arrangements* are as strategically important as therapeutic techniques in the conduct of multigenerational therapy. Multigenerational therapists are distinct from conventional family therapists less by their use of specific techniques than by their viewpoint on the family and the contexts in which they operate. These innovative contextual arrangements, then, will provide the framework for this article and for the various therapeutic techniques discussed.

CONTEXTUAL ARRANGEMENTS AND STRATEGIES

Therapists who work with the extended family system as an integral and necessary part of treating the individual or his or her nuclear family unit are faced with a reorientation of their approach to therapy. First of all there is a need to consider who is the "client" of multigenerational therapy? A predominant alliance with one family member or set of family members implicitly denies the right of other members to be "heard" or understood. Quite apart from the ethical problem this raises, such therapist bias clearly jeopardizes the effectiveness of interventions (Boszormenyi-Nagy, 1974). While from a contractual and financial viewpoint any person may be the client, from an ethical and even functional point of view, the therapist must be thinking of the *whole family as client.*

From this basis, extended family therapists find themselves at odds with traditional weekly, in office therapy formats. This constriction has led many therapists to develop creative contextual arrangements which, while remaining realistic in terms of time limitations and effort, are more sensitively attuned to the needs of multigenerational therapy. This discussion will first address individual family level strategies and then a series of programmatic strategies designed to provide community-level prevention and support for families experiencing predictable crises. These strategies represent both the clinical experience of this author and other multigenerational therapists.

A series of approaches have been found useful for including extended family in therapy in those frequent situations where actual conjoint family sessions are not feasible or desirable.

Letters and Audio-Letters

Experience illustrates that it is commonplace for adult children to struggle with unresolved issues with parents well into their 30s and 40s. These "left-over" issues often restrict the autonomy and power of adult children and invariably affect marital and working relationships to some extent, at least (Spark, 1974). While it may modify the intensity of feelings, geographic separation is often a block (sometimes welcome!) to their resolution. In these cases I have worked with clients to compose a written expression and communication of their feelings (Duffy, 1984). This is a gradual process in which the therapist "reacts" to the initial letter from an understanding of the parent position, and the client is invited to rewrite or reframe their message. In a sense, this therapist-client interaction "replays" more effectively the parent-client interaction and allows the adult child to appreciate parental dilemmas. Revisions of the letter moves from being mere *expressions* of feelings—which can exacerbate the conflict—to being a *communication* of feeling—which allows the parent to respond effectively. Curiously, when this process is complete and a "final" letter is composed, there may be a less urgent need to send it since the adult child has reached a new understanding of the parental relationship and has been able to reframe negative experiences (Cohn & Talmadge, 1976; Zerin, 1983). Another benefit of written communication is that it can allow the clear communications of feelings uninterrupted by the prevailing patterns of misunderstanding and conflict that impede face-to-face interactions. Clearly, written communications can also be used to effect even when family members have regular physical contact.

In a variation on this technique, Williamson (1982a) suggests the use of audiotaped letters which are similarly gradually revised before sending to parents, using the first person singular and imagining a face-to-face conversation. Using a strategic approach, the client is instructed to inform the parents that he/she is thinking of some changes in their relationship, but that this will not happen until it is good for everyone. In this way the client is "serving notice of an idea being flirted with," while being aware of the ". . . dangers of impulsive change" (p. 27). In this creative way, the very indirectness of the audiotape becomes a powerful vehicle for triggering a change of balance of the family system.

Phone Calls

When the basis for clearer communication with family members is emerging—perhaps through letters—guided phone calls can be helpful. The client can explain the process of therapy and describe the therapist who thus gradually becomes a significant—and often controversial—factor in the life of the family. Since these phone calls can (with permission) be audiotaped, the therapist has the advantage of actually experiencing the issues and dynamics of the family and their patterns of interaction without having to resort to "second guessing," however accurate. This can save much time in developing a sensitive understanding of the family and can quickly become a vehicle for therapeutic suggestions and interventions. Williamson (1982a) suggests that initial phone conversations might focus on asking questions and seeking important information on family heritage and the client's early history, sharing impressions and reminiscences. This can lead, in turn, to direct communication on disappointments, regrets and other unspoken feelings.

As an alternative to the review of audio-recordings there is no reason why the therapist cannot join the family in a live telephone conversation at the time of the therapy session. On many occasions I have effectively conducted therapy via telephone, and when present with the client in talking to family members the use of a speaker/ receiver unit can create a conversational atmosphere and ease the discomfort of using a conventional telephone receiver. Also, the technology of conference calls is almost universally available so that family members in several different locations can be simultaneously involved in the conversation. I have conducted interviews and "attended" meetings using both telephone and live video conferences and found the atmosphere natural and the technology nonintrusive. While these methods for doing multigenerational therapy may have some qualitative limitations they are certainly preferable to excluding extended family members.

In-Office Sessions

While intergenerational conjoint sessions may not always be possible or even preferable, they can provide a unique opportunity for the therapist. Dealing with family members from several generations in one room, however, requires a self-assurance and mature authority on the part of the therapist that probably discourages many professionals. Therapists, too, are family members in their own world and can feel overpowered by the presence of older parents and even grandparents of the client. This can lead therapists to assume an overly "reverent and respectful" posture which neutralizes their effectiveness. And, in other scenario, the therapist may identify with the younger family members and assume an equally ineffective "oppositional" posture. If the therapist, on the other hand, can be relatively free of personal or professional adequacy concerns, he/she can enter the family system with enough perspective to evaluate the family processes—including the way the family is dealing with the therapist. In the situation where older parents are invited to join in ongoing therapy with a younger client it has been suggested (Williamson, 1982a) that their involvement and cooperation be elicited by the therapist's overt identification and emotional support of the older generations. I believe, however, that this approach, if purely "strategic" in purpose, is usually transparent and can generate rather than alleviate opposition. It is much better for the therapist to signal his/her "multi-directional partiality"—as opposed to "impartiality"—(Boszormenyi-Nagy, 1974) in the directness and fairness of interactions with each individual family member. In a sense, the therapist's task is to convey the view that clients are not just "parents" and "children" but *persons* who, as such, bear responsibility for their lives and the success of therapy (Williamson, 1981, 1982b). Thus older family members are gently but firmly prohibited from the often subtle role of "co-therapists." This can be achieved quite quickly by simply turning the focus of the session on the older parent or grandparent and implicitly making it clear that they too are your clients.

Framo (1981; Barker, 1983; Beck, 1982), through his "family-of-origin" sessions, based on Bowen's concepts (1978) is perhaps the best known exponent of multigenerational therapy. While doing marital or family therapy, Framo sets up a special session where older parents are invited to discuss issues related to family of origin experiences. There is, however, an implicit and potentially unfortunate element in Framo's approach that is captured in the title of his article "Family of origin as a therapeutic resource for adults in marital and family therapy" (1976). There is a distinct danger that the extended family serves primarily as a *resource* for the adult client rather than being an integral part of the client system. This functional and exclusionary role for extended family members can jeopardize both their real involvement and possible gains to the family as a whole (Duffy, 1982).

> . . . the essence of intergenerational family therapy lies in an ethical or justice orientation. In contrast to individual therapy, it does not offer exclusive alliance with any member at the expense of its concern for other family members of the same relationship system. (Boszormenyi-Nagy, 1974, p. 267)

Clearly, multigenerational conjoint sessions must treat the whole family as client and, whenever necessary, I make this explicit in my own practice. The tendency to treat older family members as an adjunct "therapeutic resource" also stems from an over-preoccupation with "differentiation" as a major goal of multigenerational therapy (Leader, 1978; Haas, 1968; Williamson, 1981, 1982a, 1982b). Thus, the main function of the involvement of older parents in therapy is to help dissolve the parent-child developmental roles. This is often clearly an important therapeutic issue; it should not, however, dominate the process to such an extent that older parents and grandparents are dismissed when no longer "needed." Relationships between extended family members change but continue and the reciprocal influence always remains an issue in family therapy.

Time-Extended Sessions

Whenever extended family members are available for periodic in-office, conjoint therapy, many therapists find it effective to hold longer sessions lasting from 3-7 hours. A variation which I have found useful is to hold 1 to 1-1/2 hour sessions on three consecutive days which allow the family to do some informal "processing" of therapeutic material in the intervening times. This latter approach can be less exhausting and easier to schedule; it is also less troublesome for financial reimbursement since many insurance companies restrict coverage to a single therapy session within a 24-hour period. Breslow and Horn (1977) report on a variety of other time arrangements such as marathon weekends for groups of families and up to 4 consecutive day-long sessions.

The reasons for these types of time arrangements are both practical and strategic. When older or extended family members live at a distance their occasional visits become opportunities for conjoint multigenerational therapy. Similarly, therapists based in university communities have this same opportunity when parents visit town. Therapists can capitalize on these opportunities if they are willing to be flexible; a longer conjoint session or several sessions on these occasions can save a great deal of time and avoid that lack of understanding of the client's world that can so often create an impasse in therapy.

Even within ongoing weekly therapy, time-extended sessions can also serve strategic purposes in the process of therapy. Breslow and Horn (1977) see time as a factor in recognizing and interrupting unproductive interaction patterns early in therapy. Later in therapy, important issues, such as expression of key emotions or confronting conflict, can be avoided by "running out the clock"—a pattern made less easy when time can be extended. Even a single extra session within a short interval, say Friday night and Monday morning in connection with a family visit, can allow the therapist to reevaluate, continue and often bring some closure to a family dispute. It is important on these occasions for the therapist to avoid feeling rushed and distracted from calm concentration.

Home Visits

While there may be a legitimate concern to insure professionalism, there is no reason to hold all family sessions in the office. I have always found families open to meeting in their homes and this is particularly appreciated when sickness or handicap prevents an older family member from coming to the office. If the family represents a context for the individual, so too the home gives important contextual clues about the family. Relationship with pets, assignment of roles and tasks, decor and orderliness, preferential seating, provision for privacy and interaction, quiet or boisterous interaction, mutual respect and deference, the frequency and quality of family meals, the prominence of "spectator" (TV) versus "participatory" (piano) entertainment—these all contribute to a rich perceptual gestalt of the daily life of the family. I do not believe that in-office therapy is an unreal or artificial setting—to a shrewd observer, "role-playing" is fairly transparent and provides useful information in its own right. Occasional therapy sessions in the family home, however, provide insight, depth and clarification to diagnostic impressions. It is likely, in fact, that formal evaluation procedures—for example, with the elderly—could be better completed in the home context (Watson, Rupckyl, Lazarus, Kupferer, Barry & Force, 1984; Steinglass, 1979). And the home is perhaps a better setting than the office to complete more informal evaluation of the family system itself such as structured reminiscence and genograms (Quinn & Keller, 1981), and projective techniques such as family drawings, family sculpting, life review (Greene, 1983; Westcott, 1983) and the "family floor plan" exercise (Coppersmith, 1980). The most immediate benefit of conducting evaluations in the home is that it is more likely that all family members will be present.

Speck (1964) points out the usefulness of home sessions to engage members of the family who are typically absent from sessions in the office. Since "the absent member" usually serves some dynamic function in the family, his/her presence—even if unwilling and brief—allows the therapist some glimpse of this person's role and the opportunity to "tempt" him/her into therapy. Home sessions also permit the therapist to include young children and notice even their "off-stage" behaviors—sometimes a difficulty even in a large and well-equipped office. Speck (1964) also found that family secrets are more easily uncovered in the home setting along with the realization that even young family members are not as naive about the "secret" as parents would like to believe. And the revelation of the secret is often met with a relief that is surprising to the family.

During home visits, perhaps more than any other context, the therapist has to be clear about role and authority. The family may, either through courtesy or avoidance of anxiety, draw the therapist away from a therapeutic role. I believe that the "conventional wisdom" prohibiting the therapists from all "social" contact with cients is overly rigid and unthinking—these judgments are best made individually on the basis of the dynamics of each relationship. What is important professionally is for therapists to be very aware of their changing roles within the family and to avoid situations which are both diversionary and draining (Laskin, 1968). Many therapists have found, however, that well-timed social and informal contacts with families help them to "join" the family quickly and discover a great deal about typical interactions.

Audiotaped Sessions

When family members cannot (or will not) attend therapy sessions it can be very useful to send them audiotaped recordings—with the knowledge and consent of participants. In this way the therapist and family members can "speak to" absent members. I have found this very effective in drawing the interest and attendance of sibling, parents and "oppositional" adolescents I wanted to involve in therapy sessions. On one occasion I sent two "messages" on the audiotape to a 14-year-old boy who was refusing to attend sessions. The first message was that I understood that he was feeling very "left-out" of his divorced family after the departure of his mother and because of the close relationship of his father and older sister—his only sibling. The second message (probably un-necessary) was that I would like him to attend. He attended the next session and became an active participant, making the point that, "I listened to the tape." Family members, even when absent, are inherently interested in what is transpiring in family therapy and therapists will soon detect signals indicating their involvement—opposition, curiosity, mood changes, or sabotage attempts. At this point a communication channel has opened and the therapist can use this to send strategic messages. Videotape recordings provide an excellent vehicle for this communication. In general I lean toward using very little pressure to draw absent family members into therapy, relying mainly on their inherent (if denied) interest to attract them. In some cases it will even be appropriate to use a paradoxical approach, suggesting, for example, that you appreciate the absent member's reticence and agree that it may be better for them not to attend at the moment.

The therapist can also ask the family to audiotape some of their discussions at home (Laskin, 1968). In this way the therapist can better appreciate the interactive style of family conflicts especially when retrospective reports are typically remote and detached. Clients can be instructed to have a tape recorder available and record any conflict that occurs during the week. Or, in a more structured way, the family can be given a homework assignment to choose a time when they can sit down together and discuss a problem or reach a decision which is related to the ongoing issues in therapy.

In addition to work with individual families, some therapists—especially those working in social agencies—may choose to adopt a series of community-level approaches to work with multigenerational family problems. These methods will be most appealing to therapists with a community mental health orientation—adopted as an alternative to the limitations inherent in work with individual families. Community mental health (in its pure form) attempts to develop system-level interventions to address social and mental health problems endemic in communities, as opposed to individual family systems (Iscoe & Harris, 1984). The methods which follow are characteristic of this approach in working with intergenerational problems.

Consultant Roles

The admission of older persons into nursing homes often has considerable impact on their families. As with younger persons, institutionalization alters the functioning of the family and family members often behave in confusing and unaccountable ways. It is not unusual for the family to register their ambivalent feeling in a hostile, critical attitude to nursing home staff, interference and even outright neglect of the resident. Residents, on the other hand, often manifest their dissatisfaction or grief through a series of symptoms such as depression, acting out, physical illness, anger and non-cooperative behavior. When one appreciates the devastating loss of autonomy involved in institutionalization—especially after a lifeline of adult freedoms—these reactions become more understandable. The net result of these situations, however, is a frequent adversarial relationship between families and nursing homes (Duffy & Shuttlesworth, 1985) which leaves all parties dissatisfied and largely unaware of complex changes that are occurring in families.

In this context the family therapist who has developed a good relationship with the nursing home can act in a very effective consultant role to nursing home staff. These family crises are predictable and preventive strategies can be suggested to offset their effects. Rather than intervening with individual families, the therapist can, for example, consult with administrators in developing admission and information procedures (Brandwein & Posttoff, 1977) which are more sensitively attuned to family needs. One critical area is the need for an explicit discussion of mutual expectations of family and nursing home in the assignment of responsibilities for the care of the resident (Shuttlesworth, Rubin, & Duffy, 1982). Many families will welcome a clear contractual agreement as to their responsibilities; a structured caregiving role can quiet their often displaced anxiety over placing their relative in a nursing home.

Another consultant role for the multigenerational family therapist is to help in the development of orientation and support programs for the families of newly admitted residents. While framed in an "educational" format (Silverman, Kahn, & Anderson, 1977; Brandwein, 1977), these support groups can help families identify and cope with their confusing feelings and behaviors associated with institutionalization of their relative. Grievances and fears can be explored in a non-defensive manner. The therapist, with his/her knowledge of family process, might initially lead these groups, perhaps with volunteers or staff coleaders who are trained to lead future programs. It is my belief that some such orientation program should be required as part of the overall admission process since many families tend to deny that they are troubled. On one occasion a

45-year-old bachelor son who had declined voluntary participation in our program because "he didn't need it," was later found to have been admitted for inpatient psychiatric care. Family orientation programs will not be adequate for seriously disturbed families but they can pinpoint the need for referral in these cases and often head off crisis episodes.

Community Support Programs

Families are affected by the onset of aging and increased dependency of their members even when actual institutionalization is not involved. Middle generation women particularly seem to bear the burden of supporting a family which is enlarged due to the survival of older members as well as the continued dependence of younger members. A great deal of attention has been recently given to this phenomenon of the "generation in the middle." Women especially continue to play the "kinkeeping" role of maintaining extended family ties while their available time and energy is limited by their increasing involvement in work and professional roles. This theme is seen frequently in the work of therapists as they work with families to adjust the emotional and financial burdens of caring for older relatives. Several family support group models are available including the University of Michigan's program, "As Parents Grow Older." The stress on families can be even more severe when the older person is the victim of an irreversible organic disorder such as Alzheimer's Disease. As the awareness of this disorder and its effects of family life increases numerous Alzheimer's support groups are springing up (Steuer & Clark, 1982).

Another promising approach to providing services to families is the "network" method (Cutler & Madore, 1980). Project LINC (Living Independently through Neighborhood Cooperation) (Pynoos, Hade-Kaplan, & Fleisher, 1984), for example, forms intergenerational helping networks in city neighborhoods. Participants from various age groups exchange services such as transportation, telephone reassurance, child care, vacation assistance, assisting the homebound, through a central bank." These approaches can also be useful to the therapist working with the individual family; the natural network of extended family, friends, neighbors, schools, religious institutions can be cooperatively joined to help solve family problems (Cutler & Madore, 1980) or manage family crises (Garrison, 1974).

CONCLUSION

This article has discussed a variety of contextual arrangements, techniques and approaches designed to facilitate the process of multigenerational therapy. The hallmark of these approaches is their inventiveness and creativity in confronting the practical and conceptual challenges presented by including the extended family in therapy. Multigenerational therapy, however, is more similar than dissimilar to conventional family therapy and owes its very existence to a logical extension of the principles of family therapy developed in recent decades. And many of the strategies discussed here could well be applied to the general practice of family therapy. Multigenerational therapy simply reflects the recognition that "grandparents are family members too" and should be accounted for even in understanding nuclear family processes.

Therapists interested in including the extended family should not be dissuaded by the misconception that multigenerational therapy requires a complete new set of therapeutic skills. They should also be aware that multigenerational approaches will be very much the business of therapists in the future. Unlike many social phenomena and problems which are time limited and reversible, increased longevity and sheer demographics insure that the extended family system is here to stay!

REFERENCES

Baker, P. E. (1983). Framo's method of integration of family of origin with couple's therapy: A follow-up study of an intergenerational approach. (Doctoral dissertation, Temple University, 1982.) *Dissertation Abstracts International, 44*(1), 295B.

Beck, R. L. (1982). Process and content in the family-of-origin groups. *International Journal of Group Psychotherapy, 32*(2), 233–244.

Boszormenyi-Nagy, I. (1974). Ethical and practical implications of intergenerational family therapy. *Psychotherapy and Psychosomatics, 24*(4-6), 261–268.

Bowen, M. (1978). A family concept of schizophrenia. In *Family Therapy in Clinical Practice.* New York: Aronson.

Brandwein, C. (1977). A therapeutic and didactic model of intervention with adult children of aged parents. *Gerontologist, 17*(5, II), 42.

Breslow, D. B., & Horn, B. G. (1977). Time-extended family interviewing. *Family Process, 16*(1), 97–103.

Cohn, C. K., & Talmadge, S. M. (1976). Extended family presents. *Family Therapy, 3*(3), 235–244.

Coppersmith, E. (1980). The family floor plan: A tool for training, assessment and intervention in family therapy. *Journal of Marital and Family Therapy, 6*(2), 141–145.

Cutler, D. L., & Madore, E. (1980). Community-family network therapy in a rural setting. *Community Mental Health Journal, 16*(2), 144–155.

Duffy, M. (1982). Divorce and the dynamics of the family kinship system. *Journal of Divorce, 5*(1/2), 3–18.

Duffy, M. (1984). Aging and the family: Intergenerational psychodynamics. *Psychotherapy: Theory, Research and Practice, 21*(3), 342–346.

Duffy, M., & Shuttlesworth, G. E. (In press). The resident's family: Adversary or advocate in long-term care. *Journal of Long Term Care Administration.*

Framo, J. (1976). Family of origin as a therapeutic resource for adults in marital and family therapy: You can and should go home again. *Family Process, 15,* 193–210.

Framo, J. (1981). Integration of family therapy with sessions with family of origin. In A. S. Gurman & D. P. Kinskern (Eds.), *Handbook of family therapy.* New York: Brunner/Mazel.

Garrison, J. (1974). Network techniques: Case studies in the screening-linking-planning conference method. *Family Process, 13,* 337–353.

Green, R. R. (1983). Life review: A technique for clarifying family roles in adulthood. *Clinical Gerontologist, 1*(2), 59–67.

Haas, W. (1968). The intergenerational encounter: A method in treatment. *Social Work, 13*(3), 91–101.

Iscoe, I., & Harris, L. C. (1984). Social and community interventions. *Ann. Rev. Psychol., 35,* 333–60.

Laskin, E. R. (1968). Breaking down the walls. *Family Process, 7*(1), 118–125.

Leader, A. L. (1978). Intergenerational separation anxiety in family therapy. *Social Casework, 59*(3), 138–144.

Parsons, T. (1949). The social structure of the family. In R. N. Anshen (Ed.), *The family: Its functions and destiny.* New York: Harper.

Pynoos, J., Hade-Kaplan, B., & Fleisher, D. (1984). Intergenerational neighborhood networks: A basis for aiding the frail elderly. *The Gerontologist, 24*(3), 233–237.

Quinn, W. H., & Keller, J. F. (1981). A family therapy model for preserving independence in older person: Utilization of the family of procreation. *American Journal of Family Therapy, 9*(1), 79–84.

Riley, M. H. (1983). The family in an aging society: A matrix of latent relationships. *Journal of Family Issues, 4*(3), 439–454.

Shuttlesworth, G. E., Rubin, A., & Duffy, M. (1982). Families versus institutions: Incongruent role expectations in the nursing home. *The Gerontologist, 22*(2), 200–208.

Silverman, A. G., Kahn, B. H., & Anderson, G. (1977). A model for working with multigenerational families. *Social Casework, 58*(3), 131–135.

Silverman, A. G., Brahce, C. I., & Zielnicki, C. (1981). *As parents grow older.* Ann Arbor: University of Michigan Institute of Gerontology.

Spark, G. M. (1974). Grandparents and intergenerational family therapy. *Family Process, 13*(2), 225–237.

Speck, R. V. (1964). Family therapy in the home. *Journal of Marriage and the Family, 26*(1), 72–76.

Steinglass, P. (1979). The home observation assessment method (HOAM): Real-time naturalistic observation of families in their homes. *Family Process, 18,* 337–354.

Steuer, J. L., & Clark, E. O. (1982). Family support groups within a research project on dementia. *Clinical Gerontologist, 1*(1), 87–95.

Uzoka, A. F. (1979). The myth of the nuclear family: Historical background and clinical implications. *American Psychologist, 34,* 1095–1106.

Wasson, W., Ripeckyj, A., Lazarus, L. W., Kupferer, S., Barry, S., & Force, F. (1984). Home evaluation of psychiatrically impaired elderly: Process and outcome. *The Gerontologist, 24*(3), 238–242.

Westcott, N. A. (1983). Application of the structured life-review technique in counseling elders. *Personnel and Guidance Journal, 62*(3), 180–181.

Williamson, D. S. (1981). Personality authority via termination of the intergenerational hierarchical boundary: A "new" stage in the family life cycle. *Journal of Marital and Family Therapy, 7*(4), 441–452.

Williamson, D. S. (1982a). Personal authority via termination of the intergenerational hierarchical boundary: Part II—The consultation process and the therapeutic method. *Journal of Marital and Family Therapy, 8*(2), 23–37.

Williamson, D.S. (1982b). Personal authority in family experience via termination of the intergenerational hierarchical boundary: Part III—Personal authority defined, and the power of play in the change process. *Journal of Marital and Family Therapy, 8*(3), 309–324.

Zerin, E. (1983). Finishing unfinished business: Applications of the drama triangle to marital therapy. *Transactional Analysis Journal, 13*(3), 155–157.

Questions

1) Describe a case (actual or fictitious) of a mental health problem in later life. Describe in detail the family constraints, then decide which techniques of multigenerational therapy would be most appropriate.

2) What are your constraints, as a therapist, that would preclude you from offering some of the techniques of therapy cited by Duffy?

21/UNDERSTANDING THE FAMILY COPING WITH ALZHEIMER'S DISEASE
An Application of Theory to Intervention

Robert A. Famighetti, MA

Editor's Introduction

Famighetti looks at a specific problem which many families face: the progressive mental deterioration of a member. The resulting "multiple-crisis syndrome" is understood via the frameworks of the Double ABC-X crisis model and family development theory.

Just as individuals go through stages, adjusting to both epigenetic needs and unanticipated crises, so families must cope with the challenges of formation, childbearing, childrearing, teenagers, the empty nest, retirement, and death/disability. In order to see how the family fares in each stage, we must consider both the nature of the challenge and how the family's coping mechanisms respond to the challenge (i.e., are they strengthened or weakened?). How the crisis affects the family is dependent not only upon the crisis, but how the family sees it, and what the family does about it.

The onset of a dementing illness such as Alzheimer's is not only a problem, but a family role changer: who will be the caregiver? the one to handle the finances? Spouses,

Robert A. Famighetti is Assistant Professor, and Director of Gerontology, Kean College of New Jersey, Morris Avenue, Union, NJ 07083.

The author would like to thank Dr. Robert S. Pickett, Department of Child, Family and Community Studies, Syracuse University, for his guidance and encouragement in the development of this paper.

363

children, and patients must adjust to these role changes, or else unresolved family tensions pile up and exacerbate the primary problem of the disease. Famighetti attempts to chart family coping in phases: pre-crisis, diagnosis, exhaustion, consolidation, adjustment.

CG has previously carried clinical comments discussing the concept and measurement of family burden brought about in cases of dementia. (See v. 1, #4, pp. 75–76; v. 3, #2, pp. 37–38.)

INTRODUCTION AND PURPOSE

It is a fact that an increasing number of the American population is growing old (U.S. Census, 1980). It is also well known that the majority of elderly Americans are in good health and enjoy a fairly comfortable old age (Atchley, 1983). However, some three to four million elderly people suffer from some form of senile dementia. Today, increasing attention is being given to a form of senility known as Alzheimer's disease (Mace & Rabins, 1981). This particular form of senility affects some one million people though not exclusively the chronologically old. It is a form of debilitation that has profound effects on both family members and community support networks (Mace & Rabins, 1981; Sands & Suzuki, 1983).

This paper will attempt to understand the "multiple-crisis syndrome" of Alzheimer's disease and how it affects family coping. This paper is the result of two years of qualitative interviews with families participating in Alzheimer's disease family self-help support groups in New Jersey. The paper attempts to utilize the theoretical frameworks of the Double ABC-X crisis model (McCubbin & Patterson, 1982) and family developmental theory (Duvall & Hill, 1948) to understanding chronic illness and a family's coping ability over time. The paper will discuss the consequences of Alzheimer's disease for the family life cycle, and offer suggestions for clinicians about intervention strategies for use with families.

THE FAMILY DEVELOPMENTAL THEORY

Formulated by Evelyn Duvall and Reuben Hill (1948), the developmental approach views family life as divided into a series of stages. Stages are defined as periods of relative structural stability which are qualitatively and quantitatively distinct from a previous level of family functioning. The developmental approach emphasizes the interrelatedness of parts which exist in the family configuration. A new stage of family development occurs with the addition of family positions through birth and the loss of position through death or the launching of family members at the end of the parenting stage. New stages also result from specific role content changes, as with a mother's entrance to the job market. Thus, the family developmental approach enables one to anticipate normative stressors which accompany "growing up" families at the beginning of the family life and "breaking up" families toward the end of the cycle (Hill & Mattessich, 1979).

Unique to the family developmental approach is the capacity to put its concepts to work over the history of family formation, expansion, contraction, and dissolution. To illustrate this progressive nature of the theory from "establishment" to "dissolution," Duvall's (1977) description of the normal characteristics of the family life cycle clarify the stage-concept formula inherent in the theory. Each stage described carries with it certain developmental tasks which must be completed to satisfy the biological cultural and personal needs of all family members. Duvall's description is based upon the age of the oldest child in the family.

A Simple Model of the Family Life Cycle*

Stage 1. *Beginning Families* (couples married 0-10 years without children).
Stage 2. *Early Childbearing* (oldest child under 12).
Stage 3. *Families with Preschoolers* (oldest child over 5 and under 10),
Stage 4. *Families with Teenagers* (oldest child over 12 and living at home).
Stage 5. *Family as Launching Center* (oldest child gone to youngest child living at home).
Stage 6. *Families of Middle Years* (empty nest to retirement).
Stage 7. *Families in Retirement* (one spouse retired to onset of disability).
Stage 8. *Families in Old Age* (one spouse disabled to death of one spouse).

---

*Adapted from Rollins and Feldman (1970).

A primary strength of the family developmental approach is the theory that permits families to be viewed as growing, changing systems over the family life cycle. It is the only theoretical approach that tracks family developmental issues over time and synchronize these family developments with individual developmental issues. The perspective has been fruitful in understanding particular stressors in relation to specific family stages, such as those associated with the childbearing and parenthood and retirement family stages (Blenker, 1965; Deutscher, 1968; Neugarten & Hagestad, 1976).

THE DOUBLE ABC-X MODEL

The research findings of McCubbin (1975, 1976) on families faced with a prolonged war-induced separation suggest that the original ABC-X model (Hill, 1949) might be strengthened by the addition of post-crisis variables. These post-crisis variables could aid in predicting which families are better able to recover and achieve satisfactory adaptations to stress. The Double ABC-X Model proposed by McCubbin and Patterson (1982) expands on the original crisis model in examining post-crisis variables which influence a family's ability to achieve adaptation. This Double ABC-X model is depicted in Chart 1a. The post-crisis variables to be defined include the following:

The Double A Variable. There appears to be at least two sets of stressors impacting on the family system in a crisis situation. The first is the initial stressor event (the A factor in the pre-crisis stage) which plays a role in moving the family to the crisis state (depicted by the X in Chart 1a). The second stressor is the "pile-up" of family changes resulting from family transitions, role ambiguity, additional normative life events, changes resulting from early efforts at coping and the social ambiguity stressors may bring.

The Double B Variable. This variable refers to new and existing family resources, and appears to be of two types. The first type of resources are the defensive mechanisms readily available to the family to resist the stressor and reduce major disruption in the family. The second type of family resources are those adaptive mechanisms which are strengthened or developed in response to the initial crisis. These adaptive resources refer to four variables: prior experience with coping, family supports, duration of stress, and collective social supports.

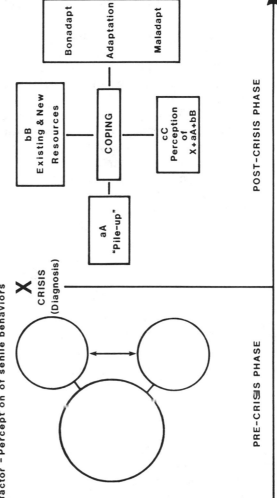

Chart 1a

The Double ABCX Model
ALZHEIMER APPLICATION

B factor – Coping mechanisms of family
Financial / Human resources

C factor – Perception of senile behaviors

X
CRISIS
(Diagnosis)

aA
"Pile-up"

bB
Existing & New
Resources

COPING

cC
Perception
of
X + aA + bB

Bonadapt

Adaptation

Maladapt

PRE-CRISIS PHASE

POST-CRISIS PHASE

TIME FRAME

367

The Double C Variable. This variable refers to the family's perception of the crisis. Family perception appears to have two different forms. A pre-crisis perception and a post-crisis perception. The pre-crisis perception, referred to in Hill's original model as the C factor, is the meaning attached to the event itself and its impact on the family system. The second is the family's perception of the crisis which involves change in the family unit precipitated by the stressor and the pile-up effects of the event over time. The family's post-crisis perception involves, perhaps, a redefinition of the crisis by their family and the family's meaning attached to the crisis (i.e., God's doing, punishment, life-cross) as reported by McCubbin (1979).

Coping, as seen in Chart 1a, refers to the active coping behaviors of family members to manage crisis. Coping behaviors emerge out of the interaction between family resources and family perception. Thus, the concept of family adaptation is introduced to explain family behavior in response to crisis. Adaptation involves the processes of compromise and the achievement of a level of functioning which preserves family unity and enhances the family system. Chart 1a outlines the basic variables of this model.

A THEORETICAL APPLICATION
TO ALZHEIMER'S DISEASE

Family developmental theory has essentially incorporated structural models of adjustment to stress. The theory posits a period of disorganization while the family restructures. This period of family restructuring is followed by a new level of equilibrium (Hill, 1949). The new level of family functioning may be at a higher or lower level of adjustment than prior to the stressful event. Researchers (Rapoport, 1964; McCubbin & Patterson, 1982) have used the model of family stress as proposed by Hill in explicating more precisely the family's efforts at recovery to crisis. These efforts have viewed certain normative and non-normative life crises using a family developmental approach. The application of these theoretical models to the non-normative stress of Alzheimer's disease has not been undertaken. Such an effort at application is provided.

Utilizing a family life cycle framework, the relational and role changes experienced by the Alzheimer family can be grouped into four major categories:

1. The Relationship Between Husband and Wife Changes

Certain tasks, such as household budgeting or doing the laundry, must be taken over by the well spouse. Besides facing the slow deterioration of one's spouse, the spouse also needs to learn new tasks and responsibilities. In addition to having to do the job, the realization that you must take this task away from your spouse may symbolize the stress that such changes have taken place. Also, what happens when the well spouse becomes ill or can no longer provide the constant attention and care. This issue raises the concept of "pile-up" effects as they occur in families of Alzheimer's victims. Little empirical research has been gathered on "pile-up" effects, but the work of Geismar and his colleagues (1972) has assessed multi-problem families. A conclusion from this exploratory research indicates that a family which is already struggling with other life changes, such as major role transitions, may lack the resources to cope with any additional change such as illness or depression of the primary caretaker.

The concept of "pile-up" (Hill & Joy, 1980) is crucial in understanding a family's response to a non-normative stressor. In the case of Alzheimer's disease, the family life cycle stage will determine a family's response pattern and ability to deal with the "pile-up" effects such a disease will bring. For example, whether an Alzheimer family is at the "expansion" or "contraction" stage of the family life cycle will be a determinant in the family supports available to buffer the effects of "pile-up," or the personal fortitude to withstand the stress of prolonged caregiving (Mace & Rabins, 1981; Geismar et al., 1972; Zarit, 1980).

2. The Relationship of a Parent with Alzheimer's Disease and Adult Children Change

The care of an elderly parent is a particularly stressful role for the adult caregiver (Cicirelli, 1981; Troll et al., 1979). The adult child often becomes the primary caregiver or financial provider. This "role reversal" can be a difficult, unwanted, stressful and, in fact, never-ending role. This caregiving role often becomes even more time-consuming and stressful when caring for an Alzheimer parent (Mace & Rabins, 1981; Zarit, 1980).

The work of Zarit (1980) on variables contributing to feelings of burden of caregivers of elderly persons with senile dementia concluded that of the factors considered, "only the frequency of family visits and support had a significant effect upon the degree of caregivers feelings of burden." The "buffering" effect of strong family supports, shared responsibility and role reallocation contribute to a family's ability to cope with the stress of caring for an Alzheimer's victim. The availability of and accessibility to these buffers may be limited depending on the caregiving family's stage in the family life cycle.

3. The Alzheimer Victim Must Adjust to Changing Roles in the Family

Early on in the disease, the Alzheimer victim senses his or her inability. The victim feels stressed. The victim is, however, unable to cope effectively as the disease progresses over time. This makes for greater demands on the family for understanding and meaningful intervention.

This aspect of the disease is indicative of what Hill describes as "internal family resources and supports." The family is seen as a resource exchange network, as well as a family support network. Troll et al. (1979) posit that families in later life may have limited access to these internal family supports as well as the external supports provided by the social community.

The work of Lopata (1971) on coping with widowhood and Neugarten's (1968) work on personality in later life posit perhaps another view to the relational changes in the Alzheimer family. It may be that an older spouse's ability to cope with the stress of caregiving may be enhanced by a lifetime of coping with family stress. The adult children in the family utilize the coping skills acquired within the family. Thus, there may be some support to what Hill (1979) describes as the "crisis-proof family."

4. As the Roles of the Sick Family Member Change, the Expectations of Each Family Member on the Other Is Altered

Relationships and expectations of family members are often based on family roles that have been established over many years. This consistency of role expectations and performance leads to an established pattern of family interaction and behavior (Olson & Mc-

Cubbin, 1982). Change in these expected roles may lead to conflict, misunderstanding, and stress. This period of family role reorganization and family expectation can be most stressful (McCubbin et al., 1982). Mace and Rabins (1981) emphasize the regenerative power of the disease to bring families together with a renewed or newly found sense of purpose. This "regenerative power" is witnessed in observing Alzheimer families in support group networks. It is often at this point in a family's role reorganization that families seek out the assistance of the formal support network. According to McCubbin's model of family stress, this support is sought because the family is at a heightened period of stress requiring restructuring (McCubbin et al., 1980).

Longitudinal observations of families faced with a prolonged war-induced separation (McCubbin & Metres, 1974; McCubbin et al., 1976) revealed that these families changed over time in response to the crisis. The family's ability to adjust to the stress of caring for an Alzheimer family member seems contingent on several processes of adaptation outlined by McCubbin and associates (1980) and seen in the Double ABC-X model. McCubbin has classified three stages of family adaptation referred to as resistance, restructuring, and consolidation. These three stages aid in understanding a family's response pattern and coping ability to a non-normative stress, such as Alzheimer's disease. Thus, a theoretical framework of a family's crisis response and adaptation to an Alzheimer family member will form the next section of this paper.

THE FAMILY'S ADJUSTMENT
TO ALZHEIMER'S DISEASE

McCubbin's work on family response patterns to war-induced separation and reunion attempted to clarify the processes families engage in to achieve adaptation (McCubbin et al., 1980). Adaptation and adjustment are key terms operationalized in the McCubbin model. He attempts to examine the processual nature of family behavior over time to achieve adaptation in the face of multiple, ever changing demands. The concept of "multiple crisis syndrome" is a significant factor in the case of Alzheimer's disease. This concept becomes obvious in field observations of Alzheimer's families in support groups.

Four variables have been observed to have an effect on a family's ability to achieve adaptation. These variables are:

1. The family's prior experience with stressful situations. How successful has the family's experience with shared responsibility and altered role allocation been in meeting the increased demands of the Alzheimer patient?
2. The accessibility of family members to meet the increasing needs of the Alzheimer victim. How many family members are available to share in the responsibilities of caregiving and how effective is this network at providing the needed respite in caregiving chores?
3. The duration of the disease is another important variable in understanding a family's adjustment to this stress. While research findings support the fact that families do "come together" during times of crisis (Lopata, 1971; Cicirelli, 1981), it is not clear just how long a family can cope with the unexpected demands of this chronic illness without some major alteration in the family system.
4. Perhaps the most important variable in an Alzheimer family's adaptation response is the availability of formal and informal support networks. Today, an increasing and responsive network of informal self-help and formal support networks have grown to provide services to families in crisis. How effective these supports are seems less critical than how accessible these services are to the Alzheimer family. It is suggested that these four variables influence a family's ability to achieve adaptation in meeting the crisis situation. The theoretical framework provided by Hill (1949), McCubbin et al. (1980), and Olson and McCubbin (1981) permits an application of this theoretical approach to the particular stress of Alzheimer's disease.

THE MULTIPLE-CRISIS SYNDROME OF ALZHEIMER'S DISEASE

The Pre-Crisis Phase

When a family is confronted with a stressor event, a set of demands is placed upon the family. The family attempts to make adjustments in their patterns of interaction, with minimal change or disruption of the family's established patterns of behavior. These efforts have been described as family resistance (McCubbin, 1980). In the case of Alzheimer's disease, these pre-crisis demands include:

1. The diagnosis of the disease itself, and the hardships directly associated with this early stage of the disease. These hardships might include a realignment of household tasks and responsibilities, the care of the Alzheimer patient, and increased financial strain due to medical expenses and perhaps loss of primary income.
2. The psychological demands placed on the family may limit their ability to deal effectively with the erratic and oftentimes bizarre behavior of the Alzheimer patient. This set of psychological demands moves the family to the crisis stage (depicted by the X in Chart 1a), more quickly perhaps, because the family is no longer able to resist the stressor.
3. Prior strains already present in the family system may be exacerbated by the disease and affect the entire family system. According to McCubbin's theoretical model, the family usually attempts to make adjustments in family patterns of interaction and household management. These efforts at adjustment, utilizing existing resources are an attempt by the family to establish adjustment without disruption to the family's established patterns. This early resistance to change, as defined by McCubbin and Patterson (1982), is depicted in Chart 1b, and explained by Stage 1.

The Diagnosis and Early Progress of the Disease

This early stage of the disease signals the first in a series of "multiple crises" to the Alzheimer's family. The family's prior strains and existing demands will impact on the perceived stress in the model. The important variable, however, seems to be existing personal resources as a measure of a family's coping strategy. Information seeking yet denial of the crisis characterize this stage.

The resistance response begins with the family's awareness of the increased demands which the disease will bring, and the extensive hardships caused by the disease. The family's definition of the crisis results in some decision about managing the problem—visiting nurse, homemaker services, medical day care, companion service,

Chart 1b

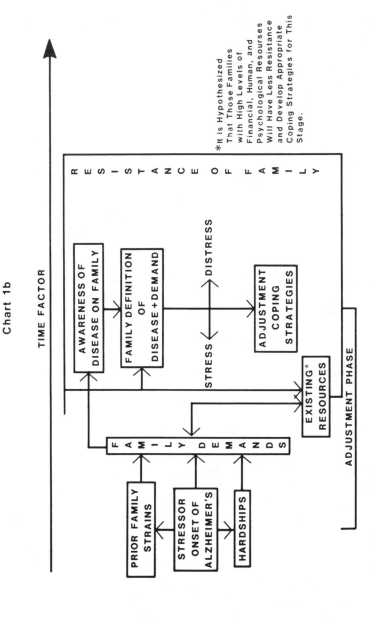

RESISTANCE OF FAMILY

*It is Hypothesized That Those Families with High Levels of Financial, Human, and Psychological Resources Will Have Less Resistance and Develop Appropriate Coping Strategies for This Stage.

TIME FACTOR

AWARENESS OF DISEASE ON FAMILY

FAMILY DEFINITION OF DISEASE + DEMAND

DISTRESS

STRESS

ADJUSTMENT COPING STRATEGIES

EXISTING* RESOURCES

FAMILY DEMANDS

PRIOR FAMILY STRAINS

STRESSOR ONSET OF ALZHEIMER'S

HARDSHIPS

ADJUSTMENT PHASE

STAGE I: THE DIAGNOSIS AND EARLY PROGRESS OF DISEASE

or perhaps even institutionalization. In the case of Alzheimer's disease it is probable that the family's definition of the event is inaccurate or inappropriate at this early stage. As the disease progresses, however, and the strain of related family hardships becomes more severe, the family's definition will be redefined. An agreed upon family definition will be made in large measure by how much accurate information the family has about Alzheimer's disease.

Families faced with the crisis of Alzheimer's disease also struggle with excessive demands of financial and human resources. Case histories show families under severe financial strain. A depression permeates the entire family system because of what may be labeled "anticipatory grief" of the eventual demise of the Alzheimer family member. Families coping with Alzheimer's disease, however, come to realize that in order to restore some functional stability and/or improve family satisfaction, they need to make changes in their existing structure. Such changes may include modifications in established roles, family goals, or patterns of interactions. This need to make structural change in the family calls for the process of accommodation in contrast to a strategy of assimilation often utilized during the pre-crisis phase.

Exhaustion Stage

This stage is described in Chart 1c. It describes the necessary ingredients to move a family from the exhaustion stage to the point of family restructuring. This stage is characterized by the family's new definition of the crisis and their gradual acceptance of the terminality of the disease. Family restructuring and role reallocation, a primary goal of this stage, takes place in a more cohesive fashion at this point in time. This stage is also characterized by an active search for information and support networks by at least one family member. These processual outcomes are the result of what McCubbin (1982) labels family "internal exhaustion." This realization that the family's coping system is no longer able to meet the family's demand for cohesion and consistency that the family moves toward restructuring. What appears to emerge is an awareness by one or more family members that their existing structure and established modes of interaction are not adequate to meet these ever increasing demands. Thus, restructuring of the family's internal capabilities is required. Families which successfully restructure their system through implementation of structural changes employ "adaptive coping mechanisms." These coping strategies are designed to keep

CHART 1c

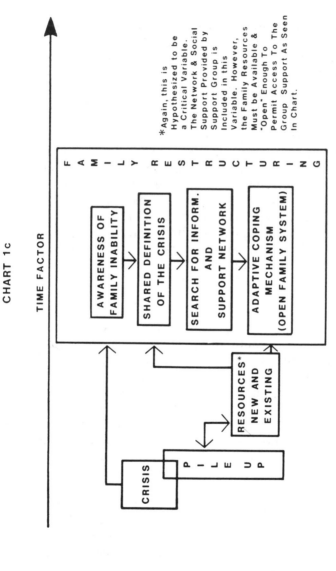

TIME FACTOR

AWARENESS OF
FAMILY INABILITY

SHARED DEFINITION
OF THE CRISIS

SEARCH FOR INFORM.
AND
SUPPORT NETWORK

ADAPTIVE COPING
MECHANISM
(OPEN FAMILY SYSTEM)

FAMILY RESTRUCTURING

*Again, this is
Hypothesized to be
a Critical Variable.
The Network & Social
Support Provided by
Support Group is
Included in this
Variable. However,
the Family Resources
Must be Available &
"Open" Enough To
Permit Access To The
Group Support As Seen
In Chart.

RESOURCES*
NEW AND
EXISTING

CRISIS

PILE UP

STAGE 2: PILE UP DEMANDS ON FAMILY SYSTEM TO NEEDS OF VICTIM
EXHAUSTION STAGE TO RESTRUCTURING

the family functioning together as a unit, to maintain member esteem, and family morale.

Once the family has successfully initiated these changes and the system has restructured itself in some meaningful way, the family moves into what McCubbin (1982) terms a second level of accommodation with efforts to consolidate and mold the family system into a coherent unit. An effort is made to develop a shared family awareness about the "goodness of fit" between the family's newly instituted structural change and the family's established patterns of behavior and structure (see Hansen & Johnson, 1979).

To cite an example of this process, McCubbin's (1975) study of prolonged war-induced separation and the unpredictable outcome of return, found that families sought to "close-out" the missing family member's role in an effort to reorganize. Case histories of Alzheimer families also show this process as a necessary outcome to reorganizing the family unit.

Family Consolidation

If the family has adopted a functional coping strategy in Stage 2, this third stage characterizes a relative stability in family functioning. The reality of institutionalizing the Alzheimer member characterizes this stage, shown in Chart 1d. The reality of institutional placement often becomes clear in the light of additional pile-up effects from constant 24-hour care of the patient. A major factor in the family's decision to institutionalize is the health of the caretaker.

Having achieved this awareness, the family works to identify and initiate concomitant changes in the family system so that the family's new orientation will be coordinated, stable, and congruent. For example, in the case of Mrs. M., the traumatic realization that Mr. M. could no longer provide the kind of care needed by Mrs. M. without severe physical and psychological harm to the rest of the family; she was institutionalized. The institutionalization prompted a new, but less severe, crisis on the family. In order for this particular family to survive, they spent more time together and found new roles to replace the ones subsumed in the care of the patient. The primary caregiver took a more active interest in outside relationships with old friends and became re-involved with former organizations. At the same time, a great deal of day time hours were spent at the nursing home visiting with his spouse. The family unit

Chart 1d

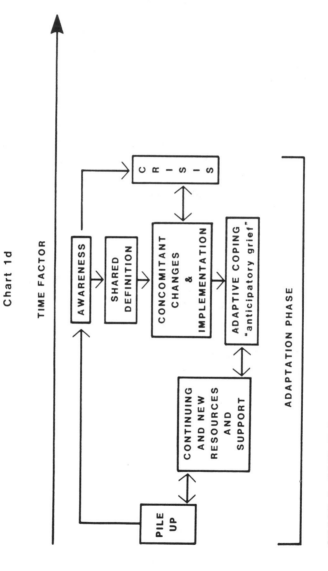

TIME FACTOR

AWARENESS

SHARED DEFINITION

CONCOMITANT CHANGES & IMPLEMENTATION

C R I S I S

ADAPTIVE COPING "anticipatory grief"

CONTINUING AND NEW RESOURCES AND SUPPORT

PILE UP

ADAPTATION PHASE

STAGE 3: FAMILY CONSOLIDATION TO INSTITUTIONALIZATION OF ALZHEIMER MEMBER

378

has, to some extent, dealt with anticipatory grief and separation, and has found itself functioning in the most stable manner since the onset of the illness eight years ago.

The family, in an interaction between existing coping strategies and family resources, was able to achieve consolidation of family member interests and the placement of the Alzheimer patient in an institution. The crisis of institutional placement was not very severe for this family because of the combined effects of family member awareness, shared definition, and limited resources to provide ongoing care. This ability to cope with the placement helped move the family to the final stage of adjustment.

Family Adjustment

The final stage is family adjustment. It is depicted in Chart 1e. This stage is characterized by a family's resolution of the crisis precipitated by the institutional placement of the family member. Even after the placement of the patient, family members often deal with a continuing series of crises requiring continued family restructuring and adjustment. Some examples of post-institutional crisis might be: the institution's unwillingness to keep the resident after the first year, thus placing the family in a serious legal and financial crisis duing the second year after placement. Illness of the Alzheimer's patient may require hospitalization of the patient in a medical facility unwilling or ill-equipped to deal with such patients. Families need to cope with new forms of institutionalization under such conditions, and often contend with hospital administrators and doctors performing various "tests" on the patient without any family member's consent.

Case histories of Alzheimer's families clearly indicate support to the construct of this "multiple-crisis syndrome" of chronic dementia. The Double ABC-X model and other new theoretical perspectives emerging from developmental psychology and family history offer a solid foundation for continued research in this area of family stress-theory building.

THE NON-NORMATIVE STRESS OF ALZHEIMER'S DISEASE AND CONSEQUENCES FOR FAMILY LIFE

In assessing how families go about changing their structure to reflect changes in membership, family needs and expectations from external social networks, the application of Alzheimer's disease is a

Chart 1e

TIME FACTOR

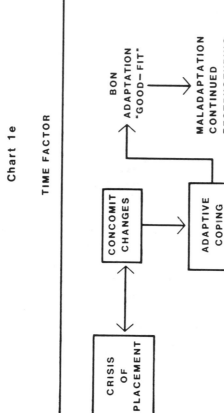

STAGE 4: FAMILY COPING AND ADJUSTMENT

useful example. The disease, and the family's consequent coping mechanisms, provides an opportunity for integrating principles of family stress and family developmental theories prominent in the field of family studies (Mederer & Hill, 1983). Among the consequences this disease has for the field of family studies are:

1. The disease process provides a useful paradigm for applying the theoretical principles of McCubbin's Double ABC-X Model of family stress. It illustrates the "destructuring" and "restructuring" stages of a family's response to severe stress over time. The McCubbin model, however, also refers to "stages" as points of equilibrium and disequilibrium, with resolution indicated by movement to a new stage. This model heightens to a new level of description the stage-discreet model of family developmental theory. The Double ABC-X model does not adequately attend to continual changes at all levels of family functioning. This is due in part because of its inherent dependency on a problem-solving framework (Klein et al., 1978). Despite these shortcomings, the Double ABC-X Model and the resultant family adjustment process is most useful tool for understanding the family dynamics of an Alzheimer's family.

2. Klein et al. (1978) note the differences between the stage-discreet model, characteristic of Duvall's family developmental stages, and the stage transitional model, characteristic of Rapoport's (1964) work. The stage discreet model ignores the question of how families move from one stage of development to the next. On the other hand, the transitional model ignores possible differences before and after the transition is made, such as with the transition of marriage. They (Klein et al., 1978), therefore, propose a merger of the two models. This makes family developmental theory a stage-transitional branching process. The initial concept for such a model was the game tree model of Magrabi and Marshall (1965).

   This proposed stage-transitional branching model offers a synthesis of much of the family developmental, family stress and critical transition theories. It offers a theoretically promising alternative by which to assess change in families over time. Unfortunately, there have been few attempts to test the model empirically. While the model offers a linkage of family developmental, family stress and transition theories to analyze family stress, few methodological instruments permit its application.

3. It is assumed that Alzheimer's disease is a consequence of old age. This is not the case. The disease has an unpredictable life span and etiology, affecting those in middle age as well as those seemingly more susceptible to "senility." Precisely because of the disease's unanticipated and prolonged stress, the family developmental approach is an appropriate model for understanding the disease and intervention.

Carter and McGoldrick (1980) have emphasized the value of the family developmental theory in intervention strategies for families experiencing stress at a particular life cycle stage. The patterns of a family's response are influenced by the family's current family developmental stage. The response pattern of a family in the launching stage, for example, would differ from the response of a family in an earlier or later stage of the family life cycle. Although no empirical evidence is available to substantiate this point, a number of related factors lend support. For instance, the "pile-up" effect of other stress-producing demands, and the family's previous stress history would all be qualitatively and quantitatively different at various stages of the family life cycle. The case of Mrs. T. provides illustration. The family is in the retirement stage of the family life cycle. They lack the financial and human resources to cope with the 24-hour care of the Alzheimer patient. This retirement-stage family has contracted its members. There are few, if any, family supports outside the immediate household. At this particular stage of the family cycle, the spouse may have few options but to rely on formal governmental intervention. The family developmental theory also helps to understand the reluctance of other family members to lend support to the care of an aged parent. For example, in the case of Mrs. T., her children are at the childbearing stage of their own families. The increased demand for support by an aged parent on their adult children is a major determinant in the family's "pile-up" effects. This increased need for care and support by adult children to an aged parent is a recent focus of much family literature (see Troll et al., 1979; Cicirelli, 1981; Troll & Bengtson, 1978). Thus, the family developmental and family stress theories are useful and productive ways to view this demographically induced phenomenon.

It is suggested that these related theoretical frameworks be utilized more frequently in examining what is traditionally known as family stress research. The benefits of applying these other theoretical approaches to family stress research are many. For one, the Double ABC-X Model is an appropriate and useful design to understand a family's response and adjustment to stress. The family developmental theory applied to a family dealing with stress would help predict how successful their adjustment by knowing the consequences and demands of their current stage of the family life cycle.

In conclusion, this paper has provided a theoretical framework to view the non-normative stress of Alzheimer's disease and its consequences for family life. The paper has defined the family developmental theory and related perspectives emerging from developmental psychology, and outlined the redeeming qualities of each by which to view family stress. The application of these theories to the particular case of Alzheimer disease provides a useful and productive linkage of the prominent theories of the family field. The model also provides a useful paradigm for understanding families in the stress of caring for an Alzheimer family member. It also generates a useful intervention model for practitioners and family scholars.

REFERENCES

Atchley, R. *Social Forces in Later Life* (3rd Edition). Belmont, CA: Wadsworth Co., 1983.

Blenkner, M. "Social Work and Family Relationships in Later Life." In E. Shanas and C. Streib (Eds.), *Social Structure and the Family*. New York: Prentice-Hall, 1965.

Cicirelli, V. *Helping Elderly Parents: Role of Adult Children*. Boston, MA: Auburn House, 1981.

Carter, E. & M. McGoldrick. *The Family Life Cycle: A Framework for Family Therapy*. New York: Gardner Press, 1980.

Deutscher, I. "The Quality of Postparental Life." In B. Neugarten (Ed.), *Middle Age and Aging*. Chicago: University of Chicago, 1968.

Duvall, E. & R. Hill. *Report of the Committee on the Dynamics of Family Interaction*. Washington, D.C.: National Conference on Family Life, 1910.

_____ *Family Development*. Philadelphia, PA: Lippincott, 1977.

Geismar, L. et al. *Early Supports of Family Life: A Social Work Experiment*. NJ: Scarecrow Press, 1972.

Hansen, D. & V. Johnson. "Rethinking Family Stress Theory: Definitional Aspects." In W. Burr et al. (Eds.), *Contemporary Theories About the Family* (Volume 1). New York: Free Press, 1979.

Hanson, S. "A Family Life Cycle Approach to the Socioeconomic Attainment of Working Women." *Journal of Marriage and the Family*, 1983, *45*(2), 323–339.

Hill, R. *Families Under Stress*. New York: Harper & Row, 1949.

_____ & C. Joy. Operationalizing the Concept of Critical Transitions to Generate Phases of Family Development. Unpublished paper, 1980.

_____ & P. Mattessich. "Family Development Theory and Life Span Development." In P. Baltes (Ed.), *Life Span Development and Behavior* (Volume 2). New York: Academic Press, 1979.

Klein, D. et al. Family Chronogram Analysis: Toward the Development of New Tools for Assessing the Life Cycle of Families. Unpublished paper. University of Notre Dame, 1978.

Lapota, H. "Widows as a Minority Group." *The Gerontologist,* 1971, *11*(1), 67–77.

LaRossa, R. *Conflict and Power in Marriage: Expecting the First Marriage.* Beverly Hills: Sage, 1977.

Lerner, R. & G. Spanier (Eds.). *Child Influences on Marital and Family Interaction: A Life Span Perspective.* New York: Academic Press, 1978.

Mace, N. L. & P. V. Rabins. *The 36 Hour Day: A Family Guide to Caring for Persons with Alzheimer's Disease.* Baltimore, MD: Johns Hopkins University Press, 1981.

Magrabi, F. & W. Marshall. "Family Developmental Tasks: A Research Model." *Journal of Marriage and the Family,* 1965, *27*, 454–461.

McCubbin, H. "Integrating Coping Behavior in Family Stress Theory." *Journal of Marriage and the Family,* 1979, *41*, 237–244.

_____ & P. Metres. "Maintaining Hope: The Dilemma of Parents of Sons Missing in Action." In H. McCubbin et al. (Eds.), *Family Separation and Reunion.* Washington, D.C.: U.S. Government Printing Office, 1974, 169–178.

_____ et al. "The Returned Prisoner of War: Factors of Family Reintegration." *Journal of Marriage and the Family,* 1975, *37*, 471–478.

_____ et al. "Coping Repertoires of Families Adapting to Prolonged War-induced Separations." *Journal of Marriage and the Family,* 1976, *38*, 461–471.

_____ et al. "Family Stress and Coping: A Decade Review." *Journal of Marriage and the Family,* 1980, *42*(4), 855–871.

_____ & J. M. Patterson. The Family Adjustment and Adaptation Response in the Family Stress Process. Unpublished paper, 1982.

_____ et al. "Families of Prisoners of War and Servicemen Missing in Action." *Journal of Social Issues,* 1975, 31, 95–100.

Mederer, H. & R. Hill. "Critical Transitions Over the Family Life Span: Theory and Research." *Marriage and Family Review,* 1983, *6*(1), 39–60.

Neugarten, B. N. (Ed.). *Middle Age and Aging.* Chicago: University of Chicago Press, 1968.

_____ & G. Hagestad. "Age and the Life Course." In R. Binstock and E. Shanes (Eds.), *Handbook of Aging and Social Sciences.* New York: Van Nostrand Reinhold, 1976.

Olson, D. H. & B. McCubbin. "Circumplex Model of Marital and Family Systems: Applications to Family Stress and Crisis Intervention." In H. I. McCubbin et al. (Eds.), *Family Stress, Coping and Social Support.* Springfield, IL: Charles Thomas, 1982.

Rapoport, R. "The Transition from Engagement to Marriage." *Acta Sociologica,* 1964, *8*, 36–55.

Sands, D. & T. Suzuki. "Adult Day Care for Alzheimer's Patients and Their Families." *The Gerontologist,* 1983, *23*(1), 21–24.

Troll, L. & V. Bengtson. "Generations in the Family." In W. Burr et al., *Contemporary Theories About the Family.* New York: Free Press, 1978.

_____ et al. *Families in Later Life.* Belmont, CA: Wadsworth Co., 1979.

U.S. Bureau of the Census. *Current Population Reports.* Series P025, No. 870, 1980.

Zarit, S. et al. "Relatives of the Impaired Elderly: Correlates of Feelings of Burden." *The Gerontologist,* 1980, *20*(6), 649–654.

Questions

1) What factors make it more likely that a family will successfully adjust to the stresses of dementia?

2) What factors might intervene and prevent a family from progressing through the stages outlined? skip a stage?

22/SUPPORT GROUPS FOR MALE CAREGIVERS OF ALZHEIMER'S PATIENTS

Helen Davies, RN, MS
J. Michael Priddy, MS
Jared R. Tinklenberg, MD

Editor's Introduction

Davies, Priddy, and Tinklenberg discuss a specific technique (support groups) for dealing with an oft neglected subgroup of dementia families (male caregivers). The authors get down to such nuts-and-bolts as recruitment, format, and group cohesion. The group members are profiled both demographically and also with a series of representative case profiles. Some of the themes emerging in the group were caregiver pride, the decision for institutionalization, and needs for validation, information, networks, and physical care. The authors declare that their pilot program was a success and advise small groups that meet bi-weekly, reduced structure in later sessions, provision of information, encouragement of networking, and sensitivity to group dynamics.

Other CG issues have discussed therapy for dementia caregivers both for their support (v. 1, #1, pp. 87–95; v. 2, #3, pp. 15–23; v. 3, #4, pp. 17–34) and for their role in helping the patients (v. 1, #4, pp. 53–67; v. 3, #2, pp. 11–17).

Helen Davies is affiliated with the Gero-Psychiatric Rehabilitation Unit, Psychiatry Service (116A3) Veterans Administration Medical Center, Palo Alto, CA 94304. J. Michael Priddy is affiliated with the Center for the Study of Psychotherapy and Aging (182C) Veterans Administration Medical Center, Palo Alto, CA 94304. Jared R. Tinklenberg is affiliated with the Department of Psychiatry and Behavioral Sciences, Stanford University School of Medicine, Stanford, CA 94305.

385

Support groups for relatives of impaired elderly have proven to be an effective intervention for the relief of caregiver burden (Barnes, Raskind, Scott, & Murphy, 1981; Hausman, 1979; Zarit, Reeves, & Bach-Peterson, 1980). The rapid growth of such grassroots organizations as the Alzheimer's Disease and Related Disorders Association (ADRDA) shows the benefit of informational and social support programs for care providers. Over the last several years, various models have been proposed and tested for caregiver groups, from large gatherings for the provision of information to small, therapeutically oriented groups.

As knowledge about caregivers expands, it becomes increasingly important to examine why and for whom support groups are effective. In other words, now that the benefit of group interventions has been established, researchers and clinicians can begin to examine which types of support groups are most effective for which care providers.

Recent research has investigated sex differences in the perception of and reaction to caregiving (Fitting, 1984; Todd, Zarit, & Zarit, 1984). This article describes a pilot intervention for male caregivers; as an adjunct to a large research center on Alzheimer's disease at the VA Medical Center in Palo Alto, CA, short-term support groups for male spouses of Alzheimer's patients were offered. The idea for all-male groups was indirectly initiated by the men themselves. Several male caregivers who attended a monthly information and discussion group for research participants and their families reported finding the large group overwhelming. They also felt that issues specific to their situations were frequently not discussed. As a result, we established small discussion groups for male caregivers; each will be described, common issues will be highlighted with illustrations from the groups, and recommendations based upon our experiences will be offered.

THE GROUPS

Recruitment Issues

Initially, despite the dissatisfaction expressed regarding the large information and discussion groups, recruitment for the small groups for men was quite difficult. A direct approach was only partially successful. The concept of a small therapeutic group aroused a sense of skepticism in many of the male caregivers. A second recruitment strategy proved more effective. Rather than being offered a support group, the men were told that volunteers were needed to pilot a new intervention for male caregivers, and that they would be able as participants, to provide us with feedback concerning the relevance of the concepts presented and interventions tested in the new groups. Given this spirit of a cooperative venture, recruitment was easier and the men were willing to give both positive and negative feedback about their experiences.

Format

Two six-week support groups were conducted. Both met weekly for 90 minutes, and were cofacilitated by male and female group leaders. The first group, cofacilitated by a male doctoral candidate in counseling psychology and a female post-doctoral trainee in clinical psychology offered a moderately structured program to assist in the development and use of problem solving skills. A second group, co-facilitated by the male doctoral candidate and a female clinical nurse specialist in psychiatry, was conducted as a more traditional discussion group. Six men attended the first group, and five the second. At the conclusion of this second group, there was an interest expressed by members of each group in continuing to meet; a "graduate's group," was formed incorporating input from participants regarding the first two programs. This group continues to meet regularly on a monthly basis, with seven of the original eleven caregivers active.

Demographic Characteristics

The average age of the caregivers who participated in the first two groups was 71.3 years, with a range of 63–83; the length of marriage ranged from 22 to 51 years, with a mean of 39.7 years. One care provider lived in a senior housing community; all others owned their own homes. Participants were well educated (mean = 15.4 years education); all but one were retired. Most had held managerial or other white-collar jobs.

Two members had learned of their wives' diagnosis in the weeks preceding the group; the others had been caregivers for at least two years, frequently much longer. Only three of the eleven reported receiving any in-home help with care provision. The Beck Depression Inventory was administered prior to the group, and, with one exception, participants scored in the nondepressed range; the group mean on the 23-item scale was 5.4.

The average age of the patient was 67.1 years; symptoms were first noticed an average of 4.2 years ago, and the diagnosis of Alzheimer's was made an average of 3.7 years ago.

Group Issues

In conducting the structured problem-solving group, it soon became apparent that there was a clear need among the members to have social interaction with other male caregivers, to validate caregiver experiences, and to share information. As group cohesion developed, an increasing amount of time was set aside for interpersonal exchange. Most men seemed to have evolved an effective problem-solving style, and were more interested in the interpersonal aspects of the group than in the development of new problem-solving methodologies. In the second group, as well as in the monthly "graduate's group," this process of personal sharing with other male caregivers had been given primary emphasis.

The following case illustrations are indicative of some of the specific caregiver issues that came up in the groups, and of the various coping styles employed by the men in handling them.

THE PARTICIPANTS

The New Caregiver

As mentioned, two of our participants had learned of their wife's diagnosis in the weeks immediately preceding the group. Special issues arose for each of these new caregivers. Mr. C., in the most structured condition, was a very shy individual who was initially reluctant to take part in group discussions. The sharing of experiences by the other group members, many of whom had been caregivers for years and whose wives were in advanced stages of the disease, were quite upsetting to him; his distress was manifested by nonverbal indications of anxiety, and in a desire for more factual information from the leaders. The group facilitators attempted to reassure Mr. C. that not every patient developed every symptom, and to alert the other group members to their impact on a new caregiver. Mr. C. eventually became more comfortable with the group process and discussed his feelings more freely; in addition, he

was offered individual supportive counseling. He has not participated in the follow-up sessions.

Mr. H., on the other hand, was one of the most outgoing of our
participants, and one of the few men to have an extended support
network outside of the group. He was aware of his sadness; his
wife's decline represented a potential social, as well as personal
loss. Like Mr. C., he had a strong reaction to hearing about the day-
to-day lives of the veteran caregivers; again, the facilitators made
clear that he should not see each event as an inevitable part of his
future. Mr. H. responded to the group in a positive manner, stating
that he felt better being aware of what lay in store for him, rather
than facing the unkown.

Unfortunately, Mr. H. and Mr. C. were never in the same group.
Their specific concerns, however, alerted us to the special problems
and potential dangers of incorporating new caregivers into a group
of care providers for advanced patients. If enough caregivers for
newly diagnosed patients are available, a special educational program to address their concerns would be appropriate.

The Younger Caregiver

Our youngest caregiver, Mr. B., age 63, also had specific concerns. As the only participant still employed, the demands on his
time were more pressing. In addition, he was the most verbal concerning the loss of a sexual partner, and in general expressed more
anger and frustration than most of the older members. He was less
resigned to his fate than were other participants; his reaction may be
seen as an example of an "off-time" life event (Schlossberg, 1981),
in which an occurrence is perceived as more stressful if it occurs
outside of the normal developmental sequence. While none of our
caregivers expected their wives to develop Alzheimer's, the older
participants seemed more able to accept their spouses' decline.

The Depressed Caregiver

Mr. M. was the only participant to self-report a significant
amount of depression on the prescreening measures, and his
depressive affect was readily apparent throughout the group. His interactive style conveyed a strong sense of dysphoria and hopelessness; the group responded with a series of specific suggestions to
help Mr. M. find more time for pleasurable activities, but Mr. M.

rejected most suggestions. The group as a rule did not deal directly with Mr. M.'s affect, although his depressive tone usually cast a pall of sadness over the group.

Eventually, Mr. M. was started on medication for depression, and seen individually. Despite his negative group style, he has attended every group session of the graduate's group.

Other group members were much less willing to discuss their sadness openly and scored in the nondepressed range on the pre-screening instrument, but it was our clinical judgment that several of the men were masking a significant degree of depression. Other data (Todd, Zarit, & Zarit, 1984) indicate that male caregivers report less "burden" than do women care providers; our experience has been that this is a result of a decreased willingness to disclose negative affect, rather than a lessened experience of distress. As our groups gradually became more cohesive, discussion of affective issues became somewhat more common, although several men who seemed to be clearly saddened by their wives' decline restricted their discussion to factual day-to-day concerns.

GROUP THEMES

Caregiver Pride

Many members of the groups expressed pride in doing the best possible job with difficult situations. Rarely was there any sense of guilt, or a feeling that they were not doing all that they could. In particular, several caregivers prided themselves in having taken on new roles; learning to cook for example, or shopping for women's clothes. Rather than looking outside of the caregiver situation for satisfaction, several of the men seemed more interested in doing the best possible job within the caregiving context. One caregiver expanded this involvement by devoting much of his spare time to ADRDA, and took pride in being able to provide information to other care providers. The men who showed the most caregiver pride saw their role as a difficult assignment, and were determined to put forth their best effort in the face of extreme difficulty.

The Caregiver at the Time of Institutionalization

Two care providers, during the course of our project, have made the decision to institutionalize their spouses. In both cases, this decision came as a surprise to the group. Although both patients were presenting severe management problems, the preparation for the decision was for both men a solitary one. Mr. S., the oldest caregiver in the program, went about the decision in a resigned, businesslike manner, and never discussed the emotional impact of the decision. The group was supportive of his decision, and asked factual questions about the search for a nursing home, but was willing to allow Mr. S. to deal privately with an issue that he seemed to prefer not to discuss.

Mr. J., on the other hand, had appeared for several weeks to be at a critical point as a care provider; he was having to provide almost minute-to-minute supervision for his very agitated spouse, and seemed to be close to the point of physical and emotional exhaustion. The group as a whole was much more involved in Mr. J.'s experience; perhaps because several members identified with Mr. J., the reaction to the decision to place Ms. J. was one of caution. One group member went so far as to discuss his plans to keep his wife home until her death. Clearly, Mr. J.'s choice had posed a threat to the other men's coping styles, which frequently precluded looking very far into the future.

These case vignettes are illustrative of specific group issues. In looking at the broader perspective, four basic themes become apparent:

1. The Need for Validation

Men in the group had had limited contact with other male care providers, and were quite interested in sharing experiences. While many were members of other support groups, they felt a greater freedom to discuss caregiver issues with other men, and defined the caregiving experience as different for men and women. This process of validating the universality of the experience is a fundamental curative factor in groups (Yalom, 1975), and as reported by several group members, was a major "selling point" for the all-male group.

2. The Need for Information

The basic approach to caregiving exhibited by most men in the groups could best be described as stoic-intellectual. There was a constant pull for more information on Alzheimer's, and members frequently asked if a given patient behavior was "normal" or "expected." Information of the most interest related to day-to-day problem management, rather than to affect-laden issues such as institutional placement or caregiver stress. Members sought out the group leaders as authorities on caregiver issues, and frequently seemed to be in search of definitive answers to their concerns.

3. Social Network Issues

In our group, there was a great deal of concern about family acceptance of the illness, and some sense of family support, but very little indication of nonfamily friendships, and a general sense of limited social support. One man directly acknowledged that he had "burned all his bridges" when he became a full-time caregiver. The groups provided a vehicle for male caregivers to develop a sense of comradeship and to expand their limited social support systems.

4. Concern with Physical Care

The men seemed to have a greater concern with physical issues of care provision than did female caregivers, and were also less willing to discuss the affective component of having a spouse with Alzheimer's disease. Bathing, feeding, and dressing issues were frequent topics; the men saw women caregivers as having had practice, as mothers, in these areas. In this domain in particular the men seemed to benefit from a sense of validation through shared experience.

In summary, the primary needs of the male caregivers were for a forum for sharing experiences, the opportunity to confirm that they were not alone in attempting to cope as men with these issues, and a chance to ask specific questions about the disease process. At one point one of the leaders commented on the relative lack of verbalized affective expression in the group, and one caregiver attributed it to the cohort effect: "When you were raised during the Depression like we were, you learned to accept your lot in life and do what had to be done without complaint." Attention to the nonverbal expression of affect on the group, such as a muted group tone or occasional tearfulness, revealed that the affect was indeed present, and that the men were employing communication and coping styles most familiar and comfortable to them.

RECOMMENDATIONS

Based on our experience, male caregiver groups provide a viable means of offering support to this subset of caregiver population and we recommend their implementation by organizations or agencies having a sufficiently large number of interested male caregivers and appropriately trained staff. With the caveat that our experience is based on a small number of caregivers we offer in addition the following specific suggestions.

1. *Offer the group as an adjunct to a larger, co-educational information and support activity.* Our group was a "spin off" of the monthly support and education group for research participants and their families, and most of the men continued to attend the large group as well.

2. *Keep the men's group small, and with a limited influx of new members.* Group cohesion developed rather slowly, however, when at the conclusion of our six-week groups, the men were given the options of discontinuing or merging with female groups, they voted to continue to meet separately. The sense of intimacy in the small group setting (5-7 members), the comradeship available in an all-male setting, and the safety of knowing all of the other members were all cited as making the group valuable. Larger groups, co-educational groups, and groups with a constant turnover of members, on the other hand, were identified as limiting the male caregiver's ability to feel free to share and connect with others.

3. *Meet bi-weekly.* Caregivers, almost by definition, have difficulty finding the time to attend activities without their spouses. Our weekly sessions proved to be a strain on the schedules of several of our members. At the other extreme, monthly meetings endanger the sense of continuity necessary for optimum group cohesion, and require a greater percentage of group time for an updating of the month's events in each caregiver's situation. Meeting every other week would offer the best compromise.

4. *Use a low to moderate level of structure.* The men in our program were more interested in the process of validating their experiences through talking with other male caregivers than with a psychoeducational program to teach specific problem-solving strategies. Most seemed to see themselves as natural copers and problem solvers, and frequently this did indeed seem to be the case. Abstract concepts and hypothetical examples were of less interest than

discussions of the members actual problems. Some initial structure to facilitate sharing may be needed, especially for men without prior group experience or clear expectation of the group; we found an initial "check-in" time to be helpful, in which each member related the events of the week, any specific issues of concern, and was asked to discuss his reactions to these issues. Once the group develops a sense of identity and cohesion, however, this structure can be phased out. As stated, direct expression of affect created more discomfort; an alternative suggestion would be to structure a manner of promoting the expression of feelings, perhaps through an exercise in identifying feelings (Alpaugh & Haney, 1978). Basically, however, the primary goal should be to give group members an opportunity to share experiences and realize that they are not alone in their reactions to being care providers.

5. *Be prepared to provide information.* We found the male caregivers to be interested in learning more about the disease and its progression; leaders should be ready to either answer questions or to refer caregivers to the appropriate sources. Facilitators should be aware that caregiver discussion groups can be fertile ground for the spread of misinformation, especially concerning legal and financial issues.

6. *Be sensitive to group dynamics.* At times, the men were unaware of their impact on other members. As mentioned, our project included two men who had learned very recently of their wives' diagnosis. At times, the amount of information obtained from the group both directly and through listening to caregiver stories, was overwhelming for these individuals. Also, the men's relative inattention to affect led to occasional insensitive statements, such as the comments made following Mr. J.'s decision to institutionalize his wife. These problems were a function of group naiveté, and not at all intentional; nevertheless, leaders need to monitor the impact of these occasional statements and address them when appropriate.

7. *Encourage networking.* We observed that the men were less likely to be part of a social network than female caregivers. The sense of sharing experiences and support, however, seemed at least equally valuable to the men. Male care providers seemed to benefit from networking with each other, but were less likely to do so spontaneously than their female counterparts. Even in session, the men, at least initially, preferred to direct comments and questions to the leaders rather than to each other. With encouragement, however, the men have formed initial contacts. Some structure, such as pro-

viding group rosters and having members call each other as reminders of upcoming meetings, has proved helpful.

8. *Check with the group concerning their perception of the process.* As a result of our recruitment techniques, the men were very aware of the experimental nature of the experience; we asked frequently for their reaction to various group leadership styles and their perceived needs from the group. The men responded quite positively to having a sense of being able to shape the group to meet their needs; this was particularly true when the graduates of the two six-week groups were merged, and the group format was completely open to negotiation.

Clearly, these recommendations are preliminary. Our experience, however, indicates that support groups for male caregivers do meet a specific need, and we feel that research and the development of more clinical experience in this area will prove beneficial. At this point, the desire of the male caregivers to continue the men's group is our strongest indicator of its value.

REFERENCES

Alpaugh P, Haney M. *Counseling the older adult.* Los Angeles: Andrus Gerontology Center, 1978.

Barnes, RF, Raskind MA, Scott M, Murphy C. Problems of families caring for Alzheimer's patients: Use of a support group. *Journal of the American Geriatrics Society,* 29:80–85, 1981.

Fitting M. Caregivers of dementia patients: A comparison of men and women. Paper presented at the 37th Annual Gerontological Society of American Meeting, San Antonio, Texas, 1984.

Hausman CP. Short-term counseling groups for people with elderly parents. *Gerontologist,* 19:102–107, 1979.

Schlossberg NK. A model for analyzing human adaptation to transition. *The Counseling Psychologist,* 9:2–18, 1981.

Todd, PA, Zarit JM, Zarit SH. Differences over time between men and women caregivers. Paper presented at the 37th annual meeting Gerontological Society of America, San Antonio, Texas, 1984.

Zarit SH, Reeves K, Bach-Peterson J. Relatives of the impaired elderly: Correlates of feelings of burden. *Gerontologist,* 20:649–655, 1980.

Questions

1) What are some other caregiver groups that may need special consideration?

2) What differences would there be in a group specifically designed for caregivers of depressed spouses? hypochondriacal parents?

V
RELATED TOPICS

23/LATER LIFE PERSONALITY MODEL
Diagnosis and Treatment

Lee Hyer, EdD
William R. Harrison, MS

Editor's Introduction

There is a maxim to which medicine frequently returns: it is not adequate to figure out what kind of disease a patient has; we must figure out what kind of patient has the disease.

A theme running through the previous chapters has been that these assessment and treatment techniques must be employed flexibly, being intricately tied to the needs of the situation. What works with one patient may not work with another.

Hyer and Harrison give us a useful tool in deciding what to do when, and with whom. They begin by reviewing the literature within geriatric psychotherapy, and then they describe Millon's typology. There are eight personality types, based upon a four-by-two interaction of sources from which rewards are sought (from self, from others, from both self and others, or from neither source) and instrumental style (active or passive). These pure types cannot be found in living patients, rather "they are heuristic crutches to provide clinical structure." The Millon Clinical Multiaxial Inventory has scales which can assess the goodness of fit between a patient and the eight personality styles. A significant contribution of this chapter is the provision of late life norms for the MCMI.

Lee Hyer is affiliated with Augusta VA Medical Center and Medical College of Georgia. William R. Harrison is affiliated with Augusta VA Medical Center.

The authors present four cases which illustrate the interaction of personality style, psychometric data (IQ, MMPI, BDI, STA), and background in the decision about appropriate intervention.

One of the most important topic areas of aging is personality. Despite the fact that there is no consensus about the range or essential nature of the subject matter and there exists a "crisis of paradigms" in personality theory (Neugarten, 1977), there is remarkable consistency or trait stability across time (Botwinick, 1973; Brim, 1974; Costa & McRae, 1977; George, 1978; Gutmann, 1975; Kalish, 1969; Neugarten, 1964; Thomae, 1980). "Ontogenetic stability" (Kahana, 1983) is the norm. Neugarten (1977), Siegler (1980), and Thomae (1980), among others, have outlined multiple dimensions (e.g., egocentrism, introversion, locus of control, etc.) along which personality in older age has been assessed. While some results have been equivocal, longitudinal data point most clearly to consistency (Siegler, 1980).

In addition to trait consistency, personality is also a reliable predictor of adaptation or coping style (Neugarten, 1977). It is reasonably established that the relationship between personality and adaptation changes at successive adulthood periods. As a result, personality dimensions and adaptational styles which are activated at one time are not the same as those activated at other times. This is a result of both development and situational factors. Research findings, however, generally support the principle that later life adaptation is foremost a function of particular personality types. In most schemas of later life personality (e.g., Block, 1971; Maas & Kypers, 1975; Neugarten, 1974; Reichard, Livson, & Peterson, 1962; among others), four to eight personality types are represented and "predictive" of adaptation in any of a variety of settings or traits measured. Clearly, situational factors assert an influence, but personality coherence and continuity of individual differences remain robust (Siegler, 1980). As Neugarten (1973) says, personality type is *the* pivotal factor in predicting which individuals will age successfully.

In clinical areas, very little has been devoted to personality in later life. It is commonly reported that the age period of 25–44 is optimal for personality diagnosis (Verwoerdt, 1980). In an epidemiological survey of nine community studies on the incidence of personality disorders, Simon (1980) showed that between 2 and 12% of older adults had such a diagnosis. There have been no detailed studies of the effects of aging on personality disorders (or vice versa) that have been present since adolescence or early adulthood (Simon, 1980).

This area, however, is not without clinical speculation. Verwoerdt (1977, 1980) suggests that "high energy" personality types (e.g., obsessive, compulsive, or narcissistic) result in problems with age, whereas with "lower energy" personality types (e.g., passive-dependent, schizoid), the reverse is true. The construct personality also is mentioned as an exaggerated or catastrophized component of behavior when an organic brain syndrome is present (Sloan, 1980). In addition, speculation exists among some of the better theorists of later life functioning (Lazarus, Gutman, Grune, Ripeckj, Groves, Newton, Frankel, Havasy-Galloway, 1982), as well as with some of the more validated psychotherapy research (Gallagher & Thompson, 1984), that personality is a central construct in treatment.

Few formal studies, then, have addressed personality as an influence on pathology or as a disorder in later life. In fact, it is unclear if personality style becomes more or less a "disorder" with age. What appears reasonable to infer from aging and personality literature is that personality patterns remain basically consistent, yet highly individualistic across time and assert a substantial influence on later life pathology. This condition, it is believed, exists independent of whether a person possesses a DSM-III, Axis II diagnosis or not (DSM-III, American Psychiatric Association, 1980).

MILLON MODEL

Perhaps the most influential model of pathological personality in the last decade has been that proposed by Millon (1969, 1981). This model served as a guide for DSM-III character disorders and the importance of Axis-II. It has also been an invaluable guide to clinicians in diagnostic and treatment formulation. Basically, this model posits a schema of psychopathology that holds personality as the central concept. Personality is defined as . . .

a   complex   pattern   of   deeply   embedded   psychological characteristics that are largely unconscious, cannot be eradicated easily, and express themselves automatically in most every facet of functioning. Intrinsic and pervasive, these traits form a complicated matrix of biological disposition and experiential learnings and now comprise the individual's distinctive pattern of perceiving, feeling, thinking, and coping. (Millon, 1969, p. 221)

There are eight basic types of personalities based on reward-seeking (none or negative, others, self, *and* both others and self) and instrumental style (active/passive). (The eight types are listed in Table 1.) These personality styles represent a typology where centrality or relative dominance of key traits exists. In essence, this is a social or interactional schema that exists on a continuum of normal autonomous functioning to more pathological functioning based on adaptive inflexibility, the fostering of vicious circles, and tenuous stability. In addition, three more severe personality types are psychological extensions or exaggerations of the basic eight personalities. These are schizotypal, borderline, and paranoid. All eleven personalities are represented in the DSM-III.

It is recognized that there is a controversy regarding situational consistency versus situational-specific behavior. In regard to correlational studies, there is a general finding of low cross-situational consistency with respect to personality and social measures that increases for measures across similar situations (Magnusson, Gerzen, & Ayman, 1968) for longitudinal studies (Block, 1977), and for selected types of variables, especially cognitive ones (Mischel, 1969). Based on these studies and personality trait stability (Levy, 1983), "relative" consistency or "coherence" is held. This position assumes that the rank order of individuals for specific behaviors is stable or that behavior is predictable and coherent but not necessarily consistent in an absolute sense. Emphasis is on the person's pattern of stable and changing behavior across a variety of situations. And, whether the traits at issue are of sufficient intensity and visibility to warrant a DSM-III diagnosis is moot. Millon (1969) argues for a continuum of personality—mild, moderate, severe. It is in this sense that personality is considered here; namely people retain consistent types over time that may or may not become more defined or rigid, and may or may not require a DSM-III, Axis II designation. Personality patterns become rigid or entrenched based on the criteria noted above of adapted inflexibility, the fostering of

Table 1.

Later Life Personality Model

Core Personality (DSM-III)	Modal Styles

	Core Personality (DSM-III)	Modal Styles
1.	Passive Detached (Schizoid)	Affectivity deficit Mild cognitive slippage Interpersonal indifference Behavioral apathy Perceptual insensitivity
2.	Active Detached (Avoidant)	Affective dysphoria Mild cognitive interference Alienated self-image Aversive interpersonal behavior Perceptual hypersensitivity
3.	Passive Dependent (Dependent)	Pacific temperment Interpersonal submissiveness Inadequate self-image Pollyanna cognitive style Initiative deficit
4.	Active Dependent (Histronic)	Fickle affectivity Sociable self-image Interpersonal seductiveness Cognitive dissociation Immature stimulus-seeking
5.	Passive Independent (Narcissisic)	Inflated self-image Interpersonal exploitiveness Cognitive expansiveness Impetulate temperment Deficient social conscience
6.	Active Independent (Antisocial)	Hostile affectivity Assertive self-image Interpersonal vindictiveness Hyperthymic fearlessness Malevolent projection
7.	Passive Ambivalent (Compulsive)	Restrained affectivity Conscientious self-image Interpersonal respectfulness Cognitive constriction Behavioral rigidity
8.	Active Ambivalent (Passive Aggressive/ Borderline)	Labile affectivity Behavioral contrariness Discontented self-image Deficient regulatory controls Interpersonal ambivalence

Self-Perpetuation	Reactance	Aging Precipatants
1. 1. Impassive and cognitively insensitive behavior 2. Diminished perceptual awareness 3. Infrequent social activities	L	Over/under stimulation Depersonalization

Table 1. (cont.)

Assessment		
Self-Perpetuation	Reactance	Aging Precipatants
2. 1. Restricted social experiences 2. Fearful and suspicious behavior 3. Perceptual hypersensitivity 4. Intentional cognitive interference	H	Avoidance gives way to anxiety, somatiform, depressive, obsessive disorders
3. 1. Self-deprecation 2. Avoidance of competence activities 3. Plaintive social behavior	L	Loss/separation fear Excess responsibility
4. 1. Exteroceptive preoccupation 2. Repression 3. Fleeting social attachments	(H) L	Lack of support High energy defenses faulter
5. 1. Illusion of competence 2. Lack of self-controls 3. Social alienation	H	Narcissistic aging insult Exploitation fails Retirement/role jolt
6. 1. Perceptual and cognitive distortion 2. Demeaning affection and cooperative behavior 3. Creative of realistic antagonisms	H	High energy defenses faulter Retirement/role jolt Aging pressures to perform
7. 1. Cognitive and behavioral rigidity 2. Self-criticism and guit 3. Pursuit of rules and regulations	L > H	Stress/excessive demands Perfection goals not accomplished Aggressive drives disruptive
8. 1. Erratic and negativistic behavior 2. Anticipation of disappointment 3. Recreate disillusioning experiences 4. Repetition compulsion	H	Excessive anxiety Buildup of caotic life demands

Treatment		
Health Care Provider Strategies	Short-term Therapeutic Strategies	Long-term Rx Considerations
1. Provide clear directions Reward compliance	Counter withdrawal Skills training Coping skills	Explore/reduce detachment Reduce self-defeating behavior
2. Establish rapport Minimize fears	Trust building Reduce anxiety Modeling	Insight into interpersonal fears

Table 1. (cont.)

Health Care Provider Strategies	Short-term Therapeutic Strategies	Long-term Rx Considerations
3. Careful history and probing Establish independence	Skills training/problems Assertive training Reward autonomy	Explore/reduce abandonment/ separation fears
4. Monitor compliance Health care contract	Alleviate initial panic Control self-defeating behavior Provide consistency	Identity building
5. Give information/ allow control Establish rules	Reward empathy/altruism Strengthen capacity to handle weakness Values clarification	Explore/reduce attachment/closeness fears Build sharing/
6. Allow control/give information Monitor compliance Health care contract	Trust building Reframe problems Build listening skills /empathy skills	interpersonal comfort
7. Lifestyle change focus Use structure/ logical plans	Insight for ambivalent style Permission to relax standards Emotional understanding	Explore/reduce separation/atta- chment conflict Provide insight
8. Matter-of-fact attitude Contract/monitor compliance	Respect resistance Provide consistency Establish controls /identify problem areas	into sources of ambivalent conflict

vicious circles and tenuous stability. Personality type, however, always asserts an influence on behavior.

PSYCHOGERIATRIC MODEL

Based on this schema, a model of personality for later life problem is presented (Table 1). This model has six categories based on the core personality types. Following the Millon Model, it posits that older age problems can best be understood and treated with personality as *the* central issue. This is intended as a working paradigm from which diagnostic formulations and treatment focus can take form. This model also is an extension of Beutler's (1983) eclectic schema of treatment. Beutler holds that individuals can best be conceptualized by their core conflict (Millon Model), symptom type, instrumental style, and reactance type. These constructs are social and interpersonally based. Based on an understanding of these issues, an individual can be offered a set treatment plan.

The older age model begins with a basic understanding of personality. The first three columns represent the personality type, its operative dynamic and interpersonal features, and its self-perpetuation components. While it is beyond the scope of this article to explicate fully these personality types, a brief description is given. These are also "anchored" to the DSM-III. Detached personality patterns are long-standing styles that seek withdrawal from social settings either because of a lack of rewards or validation in life (schizoid), or a surfeit of negative experiences (avoidant). One withdraws for reasons of a lack of drives and blandness (schizoid), the other because of a negative self-image and hyperalertness (avoidant). Dependent personalities, on the other hand, rely on others for support either because of strong attachment needs, often due to abandonment (passive-dependent), or needs related to acceptance received by marketing oneself in social situations (histrionic). Independent personalities are substantially different from these types. They gather rewards from self, either from a genuine sense of excessive self-evaluation (narcissism) or as a counterphobic defense against anticipated punishment (antisocial). Lastly, ambivalent personalities represent a melding of the dependent and independent personality types. They are indecisive about sources of reward, self or others. They appear conforming but with considerable inner turmoil (compulsive), or they openly vacillate and appear chaotic (passive aggressive/borderline).

These eight personality types do not exist in any pure form. They are heuristic crutches to provide clinical structure. In most cases, a person has a mixture of two or more types. In addition, there are three more "severe" variants; schizotypical, borderline, and paranoid. These are adequately described in both Millon (1981) and the DSM-III. They are not outlined here because they represent psychological extensions of the eight basic types. Accordingly, the clinician's first task is to understand and isolate the basic personality type(s) and then consider it (these) in relation to the more severe variants. Schizotypal personalities are decompensatory patterns of the detached types; borderline personalities, the dependent and ambivalent types; and paranoid personalities, the independent and ambivalent types. Each personality style is ultimately unique, representing a biopsychosocial amalgamation of parts that come to life clinically in a particular personality type.

Reactance and aging precipitants complete the assessment portion of this model. Reactance is an important construct related to each personality. It represents the individual's investment in personal control and freedom. It refers to an individual's unwillingness to comply with extended constraints. Low reactant people allow for greater therapeutic control; highly reactant people, less. Some personality styles give the illusion of internal control but actually are dependent on the external situation (active dependent), or, depending on the nature of their conflict or current situational state, could be either high or low reactant people (passive ambivalent). Finally, aging precipitants represent typical older age related problems that are normative for older age, but, when they occur, potentiate problems for a specific personality type.

The treatment section of the model provides for a therapeutic focus. This section outlines clinical considerations for strategies or interventions to be given in health care settings, as well as in therapy. Therapeutic considerations are divided into "mid-level" strategies and longer term treatment issues. Obviously, flexibility and clinical common sense are appropriate here.

These personality types are measured by the Millon Clinical Multiaxial Inventory (MCMI; Millon, 1983). The MCMI is a 175-item self-rating personality scale "anchored" to Axis-II of the DSM-III. It measures 20 separate pathological dimensions, divided into two general areas, personality and symptom disorders. There are eight basic personality structures, as well as three others that possess a greater level of severity. There are nine symptom scales, six "lower level" and three "severe level" scales. The MCMI is distinctive from others in three major ways. It utilizes actuarial base rate data derived from prevalence data instead of normalized scores. This allows for a more refined representation of problem areas. Second, this scale possesses good psychometric components; representative comparison samples, successive validation procedures (including cross validation), and adequate reliability and norms. Finally, this scale is one of the very few based on theory. Consequently, decision rules regarding personality and syndrome combinations are a mix of actuarial and theoretical formulations.

A review of 60 cases is given in Table 2. Subjects were psychiatric admissions to a psychogeriatric unit in a medical center. They were given the MCMI. A base rate of 75 or greater represents "presence" of a personality style and a base rate of 85 or better indicates "prominence" (the probable existence of a personality style). As can be seen, older psychiatric patients possess a greater amount of dependent styles. This is followed by the detached styles. This is not surprising as the incidence of the dependent and avoidant personalities are highest among the populations as a whole. With age, there appears to be a "mellowing" of higher energy personality types. The higher intensity styles (histrionic, narcissistic, and antisocial) are lowest. Where the focus is the frequency of key base rates of presence (75) and prominence (85), dependent and avoidant personality types are also most frequently found for older people.

The MCMI consists of 20 base rate scores; eight basic personality types, three severe level personality types, six mild symptom disorders (Anxiety (A), Somatoform (H), Hypomanic (N), Dysthmic (D), Alcohol Abuse (B), Drug Abuse (T) and three severe symptoms disorders Psychotic Thinking (SS), Psychotic Depression (CC), Psychotic Delusions (PP). (For purposes of scoring, each of these four areas is separated by a double line (//), and each measure is given a base rate score. Base rates greater than 84 are designated by xx, those between 74 and 84 by x, those between 60 and 74 by +, and those between 45 and 59 by . ')

CASES

Four cases are provided, one from each of the global interpersonal styles. These cases are taken from the data given in Table 1. For brevity, one paragraph is devoted to a brief history and clinical symptoms, one for psychological data (based on a screening battery), one for the MCMI clinical description, and one for treatment.

Detached Case

Mr. D. is a 64-year-old white male who is currently hospitalized due to anxiety, vague feelings of depression, as well as an inability to get along with people. Occasionally, this has resulted in altercations with both family and friends. He had experienced one previous psychiatric hospital episode when he was 40 and another at age 56 for similar reasons. Despite only two previous hospitalizations, he has had a disruptive life. He has been married three times and has two children, both of whom are distanced from him. Currently, he lives with his wife of 10 years and entertains hopes of a better life.

Table 2.

Averages and Base Rates

of Later Life Personality Styles

Personality Style	X	(SD)	Base Rate >75*	>85*
Schizoid	69.3	(23)	2	4
Avoidant	72.5	(25)	0	15
Dependent	76.1	(22)	3	23
Histrionic	42.9	(20)	0	0
Narcissistic	49.4	(19)	2	1
Antisocial	51.2	(21)	3	0
Comulsive	53.4	(19)	0	4
Passive Aggressive	65.6	(29)	1	7
Schizotypal	62.7	(14)		
Borderline	63.6	(15)		
Paranoid	66.4	(16)		

* These represent single cases; that is, they represent the highest base rate for a particular person.

In 1980 at the age of 60 he retired from work, having labored as an electrician for many years. On occasion he would abuse alcohol, which would eventually lead to trouble in his life. It appears safe to say that Mr. D. feels at odds with himself and people and is unable to find direction for himself.

Psychological tests:

Verbal Intelligence: low average
Non-Verbal Intelligence: above average
Beck Depression Inventory (21): 17 (mild depression)
State-Trait Anxiety: State (85); Trait (90)
MMPI: 78* 49″ 206′ 135 (F ′KL⁻)
MCMI: 2** 83* 1__75__ + 4′6 // B* // AD**B* // −

The MCMI pictures an avoidant personality with passive/aggressive and dependent features. The central issue here is one of a person desiring detachment from others and fearing independence. Every venture toward others or independence is feared, as he perceives potential punishment or pain. He is in considerable inner turmoil and fears any effort toward independence will end in failure. This tension with people has resulted in a chronic resentment, sometimes an open petulance and passive/aggressive quality. The dependency security he seeks is seriously jeopardized under these circumstances. A vicious circle results. This patient's discontentment, outbursts, and moodiness evoke negative reactions. These rebuffs only serve to reinforce his withdrawal. Conflict and anxiety increase. Self-doubts prevent self-initiated actions. He feels chronically misunderstood, unappreciated and has a negative self-image. Depression and anxious wariness are not soothed by his lonely efforts. Psychological feelings of uselessness and unworthiness are never far from his experiences. His hypersensitive stance both guards against and "pulls" ridicule. Cognitive disruption sometimes develops. Alcohol abuse also does not help.

Treatment for this man will not be an easy affair. According to the model, initial therapeutic efforts are best directed toward trust building and anxiety reduction. As a highly reactant patient, strategies are made to allow this man control and to give him a sense of direction and assistance. The therapist should act as a model of consistency. This is especially valuable for anxiety related or failure anticipated events. This man has led a "quietly chaotic" life with negative goals and interpersonal fears. These issues can be explained and discussed. The patient, therefore, is provided with a "working model" of himself and his behavior and consequent actions can become "understandable." Hopefully, with time, he will be able to relax his defenses, to appreciate his life style, and to alter his life course.

Dependent Case

Mrs. W. is a 74-year-old white woman who was admitted to a psychiatric unit for the first time at the age of 72. Two years ago her husband died. As yet, she has been unable to grieve. The last two years of her life have been a "nightmare." She notes that she simply "can't seem to get going." At present, she lives with her oldest daughter, is inactive, feels anxious, and is often cross. In addition, she is losing weight and has trouble maintaining sleep. She had been married for 48 years and raised five children. Five years ago her oldest son died of a heart attack. Mrs. W. reacted poorly to this death also. Throughout her life, she has been a housewife and family centered. Her husband's death was a loss she did not expect nor cope with.

Psychological testing:

Verbal Intelligence: below average
Non-Verbal Intelligence: below average

Beck Depression Inventory (21): 26 (moderate depression)
State-Trait Anxiety: State (88); Trait (70)
MMPI: 27" 1' 3<u>67</u> − 490/ (F"L−K/)
MCMI: 3** 7** 2' + 4 6' 58 // B* // ADS** // CC*

This MCMI profile is one characterized by a submissively dependent, self-effacing female. Her pattern is one of dependence on
others for guidance and security. She assumes a passive/compliant
role in relationships and is especially vulnerable to separation or
losses. However, resentment is often felt toward those upon whom
she is dependent. Not surprisingly, she is unable to express this. In-
security and fears of abandonment underline what appear on the surface as a quiet, submissive, and benign attitude toward problems. It
is evident, too, that she is most anxious, depressed and given to
somatic concerns. These symptoms cause her considerable distress
and result in weakness and fatigue. She is unable to stand on her
own feet, feels chronically insecure and scared, and has become
more and more depressed. This has taken the form of agitation,
hopeless resignation and fear of the future. Depending on her beliefs, her energy level, and her environmental situation, suicide may
be a major problem. Any intrapsychic support or stability received
from her compulsive defenses (passive ambivalent) appears to have
weakened. At present she feels out of control.

Therapeutically, this female requires considerable assistance. Immediate concerns are those of symptom reduction. This appears to
be best facilitated by therapeutic control, frequent visits, environmental management, and structure. Once this is in place, grief counseling and problem-solving therapies can be applied. As time
passes, she is likely to become dependent on therapy, requiring considerable patience by the therapist. Later therapeutic strategies of
problem-solving, systematic rewards for autonomous behavior, and
skill training procedures can be given. Hopefully, a more stable
identity can be established and independent related activities activated.

Independent Case

Mr. R. has had problems most of his adult life. He is an independent 68-year-old white male who is excessively aggressive and often
appears to have little control or tact with people. He feels, in addition, chronically misunderstood and abused. His life has been one of

confusion and disruption. He has been married three times, all end-
ing in failure. Currently, he is living alone. He abuses alcohol and
appears unapproachable regarding this problem. He has even been
incarcerated on a few occasions as a result of this. He has also been
psychiatrically hospitalized due to his acting-out style on many occasions. Recently, he has appeared more depressed and irritable. His
current hospitalization is a result of apparent suicidal gesture, a mixture of medication and alcohol.

Psychological testing:

> Verbal Intelligence: above average
> Non-Verbal Intelligence: average
> Beck Depression Inventory (21): 18 (mild depression)
> State-Trait Anxiety: State (75%); Trait (50%)
> MMPI: 2871* 34″ 56′9−0 (F″L−K)
> MCMI: 6** 832* + 547′ // PB* // D<u>NB</u>**A* // −

The MCMI points to a long-standing behavior problem, one of
acting-out and conflict. This is a hostile, distrustful male who often
appears to have a chip-on-the-shoulder attitude. His central fear
concerns feelings of weakness or being ineffectual in some respect.
These are to be avoided at all costs. Spurned by repeated rejection
and driven by a need for power, his aggression and conflict-filled
character has developed. As a small part of him also desires to relate
better to his environment in a less hard-boiled and more rational
way, he is able to "connect" with people and maintain short-lived
harmony. Increasingly, however, symptoms of acting-out and inner
fear became manifest. In later life, however, depression, anxiety,
and substance abuse have been problems. Depression, in particular,
is of concern. With age he appears not to have been able to titrate his
aggressive style with the energy level required. One can speculate
also that his high energy personality style has interacted poorly with
aging issues. The result has been depression. His dysphoric mood
and an acting-out style are ever-ready components of passive or active suicidal activity.

Strangely, this may be one of the few occasions that efforts at
meaningful treatment can be applied. As he feels psychic pain and
"appreciates" his age and his long-term problems, he appears to be
more accepting of therapy. According to the model, a therapeutic
focus of trust building (given him respect and control), of thera-

peutic reframing, and of teaching him human skills such as listening and empathy are appropriate. Longer term treatment goals involve those related to rejection and commitment fears, as well as issues related to attachment.

Ambivalent Case

Mr. A. is a 72-year-old white male who has lived in one area and worked at one business his entire life. He is a perfectionist man who ran his own grocery business and worked hard until two years ago when he retired at the insistence of his family. Hopefully, this would allow him time to enjoy life better. He has been married for 43 years, has three grown children, and from all indications has been successful. He was in the service for four years, 1940–1943, and was wounded in action (shrapnel in leg). He relates that he has never had problems but at various times would feel very "stressed" and "victimized." He also noted that he was chronically unsure of himself and insecure about his business, despite success. After retirement, Mr. A. attempted to restructure his life. However, he became increasingly anxious and guarded. Mrs. A. noted that this has become a problem, and the family is very concerned about him.

Psychological testing:

Verbal Intelligence: average
Non-Verbal Intelligence: average
Beck Depression Inventory (21): 4 (no depression)
State-Trait Anxiety: State (75%); Trait (60%)
MMPI: 731' 2 − 689/540 (K−LF/)
MCMI: 7** − * 23 + PP** // 845' 16 // P* // A*H* //

The MCMI is most distinctive because of Mr. A.'s compulsive personality features. This is characteristic of an overly controlled, defensive male who has a restrictive perfectionistic, compliant lifestyle at the expense of affectivity and relaxation. Paranoid personality features are also noted. This component appears reflective of increasing suspiciousness, irritability, obsessive ideation, and defensiveness in an already established personality of conflicted conformity. It appears that this man has always been serious and rarely lets his defenses down. He is vigilantly alert to avoid social transgressions that may provoke problems. He is an inhibited person who avoids situations that are too loosely structured or place him at risk. Increasingly, one can speculate that he has had to guard against the tendency to be argumentative, resentful, and critical of others. It is noteworthy, too, that he is highly anxious and given to somatization. This can only be disconcerting as he must increase his defenses to handle this agitation and feelings of unexplained physical problems or fatigue. Finally, since chronic ambivalence is ever-present, he is perpetually caught between his desire to let loose and discharge hostility and a constant fear that such expressions will only result in rejection.

According to the model it is important therapeutically to respect Mr. A.'s inner turmoil and conflict and to allow him the feeling of safety. Appropriate initial therapeutic strategies are to reduce symptoms of anxiety and allow later therapeutic time for character problems. As a person with adequate cognitive skills, as well as a good psychiatric history, it would be appropriate over time to give him insight into his passive ambivalent character and the conflict-laden problems and defensive armor that are unresolved. The relaxation of self-standards and permission to alter self-goals are very much in order, but will require time. As Mr. A. responds more comfortably in therapy, more affect laden and conflict areas can be pursued. It is believed that this combination will respect Mr. A.'s psychic structure and facilitate growth.

CONCLUSION

Personality is a central dimension along which the clinician can understand problems and provide treatment. To date, it has not been adequately explored as it applies to later life problems. The use of the Millon model (MCMI) and the psychiatric schema in this study provide needed information and structure for treatment to occur.

REFERENCES

American Psychiatric Association. (1980). *Diagnostic and statistical manual of mental disorders (3rd Edition)*. Washington, D.C.: Author.
Beutler, L. (1983). *Eclectic psychotherapy: A systematic approach*. New York: Pergamon Press.
Block, J. (1971). *Lives through time*. Berkeley, CA: Bancroft.

Block, J. (1977). Advancing the psychology of personality: Paradiagnostic shift or improving the quality of research. In D. Magnusson & N. Endler (Eds.), *Personality at the crossroads: Current issues in international psychiatry.* Hillside, NJ: Erlbaum.

Botwinick, J. (1973). *Aging and behaving: A comprehensive integration of research findings.* New York: Springer.

Brim, O. (1974). *Selected theories of the male mid-life crises: A comparative analysis.* Paper presented at the 82nd Annual Meeting of the American Psychological Association, New Orleans.

Costa, P., & McCrae, R. (1978). Objective personality assessment. In N. Storandt, I. Siegler, & N. Elias (Eds.), *The clinical psychology of aging.* New York: Plenum Press.

Gallagher, D., & Thompson, L. (1983, August). Psychotherapy research with elders: Strengths and limitations of clinical trials. Paper presented at the 91st Annual Meeting of the American Psychological Association, Anaheim, CA.

George, L. (1978). The impact of personality and social status factors upon levels of activity and psychological well-being. *Journal of Gerontology, 33,* 840–847.

Gutmann, D. (1975). Parenthood: Key to the comparative psychology of the left cycle. In N. Datan & L. Gunsberg (Eds.), *Life span developmental psychology: Normative life crises.* New York: Academic Press.

Kalish, R. (1969). The dependencies of old people. *Occasional papers in gerontology; No. 6.* Ann Arbor: Institute of Gerontology, University of Michigan—Wayne State University.

Lazarus, L., Gutmann, D., Grune, J., Ripeckyj, A., Groves, L., Newton, N., Frankel, R., & Havasy-Galloway, S. (1982, November). Paper presented at the 35th Annual Meeting of the Gerontological Society, Boston.

Magnusson, D., Gerzen, M., & Nyman, B. (1969). The generality of behavioral data: I. Generalization from observation on one occasion. *Multivariate Behavioral Research, 4,* 29–42.

Maas, H., & Kypers, J. (1974). *From thirty to seventy.* San Francisco: Jossey-Bass.

Millon, T. (1983). *Millon Clinical Multiaxial Inventory.* Minneapolis: Interpretative Scoring Systems.

Millon, T. (1981). *Disorders of personality.* DSM-III, Axis II. New York: Wiley.

Millon, T. (1969). *Modern psychopathology.* Philadelphia: Saunders.

Mischel, W. (1969). Continuity and change in personality. *American Psychologist, 24,* 1012–1018.

Neugarten, B. (1977). Personality and aging. In J. Birren & K. Schaie (Eds.), *Handbook of the psychology of aging.* New York: Van Nostrand Reinhold, 626–644.

Neugarten, B. (1976). Adaptation and life cycle. *The Counseling Psychologist, 6,* 16–18.

Neugarten, B. (1974, September). Age groups in American society and the rise of the young-old. *The Annals of the American Academy of Political Social Science, 415,* 187–198.

Neugarten, B. (1973). Patterns of aging: Past, present and future. *Social Science Review, 47*(4), 571–580.

Reichard, S., Livson, F., & Peterson, P. (1962). *Aging and personality.* New York: Wiley.

Siegler, I. (1980). The psychology of adult development. In R. Busse & D. Blazer (Eds.), *Handbook of geriatric psychiatry* (pp. 169–222). New York: Van Nostrand Reinhold.

Simon, A. (1980). The neuroses, personality disorders, alcoholism, drug abuse and misuse, and crime in the aged. In J. Birren & R. Sloan (Eds.), *Handbook of mental health and aging.* Englewood Cliffs, NJ: Prentice-Hall.

Sloan, R. (1980). Organic brain syndrome. In J. Birren & R. Sloan (Eds.), *Handbook of mental health and aging.* Englewood Cliffs, NJ: Prentice-Hall.

Thomae, H. (1980). Personality and adjustment to aging. In J. Birren & R. Sloan (Eds.), *Handbook of mental health and aging.* Englewood Cliffs, NJ: Prentice-Hall.

Verwoerdt, A. (1980). Anxiety, disassociative and personality disorders in the elderly. In E. Busse & D. Blazer (Eds.), *Handbook of geriatric psychiatry* (pp. 368–380). New York: Van Nostrand Reinhold.

Verwoerdt, A. (1976). *Clinical geropsychiatric.* Baltimore: Williams & Wilkins.

Questions

1) What are the key differences between Millon's personality theory and those of Freud, Jung, Maslow, Erikson, etc.?

2) How would depression present differently in different personality styles?

3) Is there a Millon type for whom cognitive therapy, psychoanalysis, or Gestalt would be most appropriate?

24/POST-TRAUMATIC STRESS DISORDER
Hidden Syndrome in Elders

Beverly L. Nichols, PsyD
Ruth Czirr, PhD

Editor's Introduction

Another way to approach the question of how to decide what treatment to employ for which patient is to look at special groups that are particularly at risk, or who have special needs (e.g., elder latino women, discussed in v. 1, #1, pp. 51–58).

Nichols and Czirr examine an unseen group numbering over ten million, indeed involving half the U.S. males over age 55: military veterans. The author reviews Post-Traumatic Stress Disorder (PTSD): symptoms, course, factors producing susceptibility, presentation of delayed reactions in older veterans. Here the shocking conclusion is that the disorder is more widespread than previously imagined, and its symptoms are frequently misdiagnosed as (or at least ignored in light of) something else: schizophrenia, alcoholism, antisocial personality disorder, depression.

Nichols and Czirr recommend thorough testing involving MMPI and Rorschach, a lengthy observation of behavior, and a sensitivity to affective tone during reminiscence of

The authors are affiliated with Veterans Administration Medical Center, Palo Alto, California.

Harold R. Dickman of Oregon State University and Robert A. Zeiss and Juliet W. Dantin of the Palo Alto V.A. Medical Center are acknowledged for their collaboration in the ongoing treatment and research on PTSD in older veterans.

Preparation of this review was supported in part by NIMH grant MH 37196 to Larry W. Thompson at the Center for the Study of Psychotherapy and Aging.

417

military life. Treatment plans must be individualized, combining behavioral, family, abreactive, and pharmacological
approaches in addition to individual and group psychotherapy. Specific tools (e.g., photographs) are suggested, and
an illustrative case study is provided. The important thing is
that the patient must develop trust in a caring, nonjudging
therapist. Counselors must be aware of countertransference processes and the emotional drain on themselves.

Harry, age 62, presents at the Medical Clinic asking for pills for
his stomach ulcer. His worried wife says he hasn't slept well for
years, and lately has been worse: several times a night he wakes in a
cold sweat, jumps out of bed and paces. He's irritable, tense, over-
reacts to any noise, and is drinking too much. With questioning he
admits to symptoms of depression and anxiety which have worsened
since retirement.

What diagnoses come to mind? Clinicians who didn't consider
Post-Traumatic Stress Disorder as one underlying cause may have
missed the client's primary problem.

Post-Traumatic Stress Disorder (PTSD) is a syndrome of responses to a life-threatening stressor such as combat, rape, car acci-
dents with serious injury, large fires, bombings, torture, or kidnap-
ping. More common events such as divorce, bereavement, or
business failure do not qualify (American Psychiatric Association,
1980); the stressors typically involve intense fear of death and a
sense of loss of control. Persons developing PTSD keep re-experi-
encing the trauma in intrusive memories, nightmares, or flashbacks.
(Flashbacks are hallucinatory experiences in which the person feels
as if the event is actually happening again. These can last for seconds or days, and can vividly involve all five senses.) The patient
tends to withdraw from the external world, with loss of interest in
activities and constricted affect. At the same time there is heightened arousal, including hypervigilance, poor concentration and insomnia. DSM-III criteria are shown in Table 1.

AGING VETERANS AND WAR STRESS

Gerontologists should be aware of PTSD as a massive wave of
veterans reach their 60s. Over 11 million men now over 55—nearly
half of the men in that age group—served in World War II or Korea,

Table 1

DIAGNOSTIC CRITERIA FOR POST-TRAUMATIC STRESS DISORDER

A. Existence of a recognizable stressor that would evoke significant symptoms of distress in almost everyone.

B. Reexperiencing of the trauma as evidenced by at least one of the following:

   1. Recurrent and intrusive recollections of the event

   2. Recurrent dreams of the event

   3. Sudden acting or feeling as if the traumatic event were reoccurring, because of an association with an environmental or ideational stimulus

C. Numbing of responsiveness to or reduced involvement with the external world, beginning after the trauma, as shown by at least one of the following:

   1. Markedly diminished interest in one or more significant activities

   2. Feeling of detachment or estrangement from others

   3. Constricted affect

D. At least two of the following symptoms, not present before the trauma:

   1. Hyperalertness or exaggerated startle response

   2. Sleep disturbance

   3. Guilt about surviving when others have not, or about behavior required for survival

   4. Memory impairment or trouble concentrating

   5. Avoidance of activities that arouse recollection of the traumatic event

   6. Intensification of symptoms by exposure to events that symbolize or resemble the traumatic event

Note. From Diagnostic and statistical manual of mental disorders (p. 238) by the American Psychiatric Association, 1980, Washington, DC: Author.

and 1 in 200 was a prisoner of war (POW). In the year 2000, 2/3 of U.S. men over 65 will be wartime veterans. (These figures do not include captured civilians, nurses, holocaust survivors and displaced persons, or elders who suffered catastrophic stress in civilian life.)

Not all persons at risk develop PTSD. Longer exposure or more severe stressors are correlated with the development and intensity of long-term symptoms (Klonoff, McDougall, Clark, Kramer, & Horgan,1976). All combat soldiers endured fear of death. Many were wounded, witnessed the death of friends, or fought with inadequate supplies. Women veterans can also be affected. Vietnam-era nurses describe guilt, flashbacks, and difficulty adjusting to civilian life.

Witnessing the mutilation of young bodies, failing to stem the constant dying, and emotionally supporting the critically injured all added to their stress (Van Devanter, 1983).

Prisoners of war had very different stress levels depending on where and when they were captured. Those captured in Europe by the Germans had inadequate food and shelter, but most received comparatively humane treatment. However, those interned by the Japanese in the Pacific were brutally and unpredictably abused. The profound psychological impact of being a POW is difficult to imagine. POWs describe a devastating loss of identity and of their familiar world, accompanied by helplessness and an intense and constant fear of death. The POW developed a pervasive insulation from his feelings, which were too painful or dangerous to allow. Clinicians treating ex-POWs should always assess for PTSD. Since POWs' stress was extreme and protracted, it is not surprising that in preliminary surveys between 30% and 60% of World War II and Korean POWs have PTSD *now* (Holmstrom, Waid, & Sexhauer, 1984; Sexauer, Holmstrom, Shaw, & Waid, 1985).

THE COURSE OF PTSD

The passage of time can either relieve or intensify PTSD. In a clinical survey of World War II and Korean POWS, 22% had continuous symptoms; 17% had symptoms which gradually disappeared; 36% has their first symptoms emerge years later; and 20% showed symptoms after combat which disappeared but re-emerged after several years (Zeiss, Dickman, & Nichols, 1985).

Exacerbation of PTSD has been related to aging. Life changes and losses can reactivate symptoms (Archibald & Tuddenham, 1965). Awareness of death, bereavement, and physical disabilities are common both to war and to aging. During one of the first author's therapy groups for elders with PTSD one group member died, another moved into a nursing home, and nearly all were aware of recent physical or emotional losses. These stresses strongly elicited wartime memories of death, physical injury, and lack of control.

Older veterans served when this syndrome was not seen as a stress disorder, and contemporary theories added to their burden. The diagnosis of "war neurosis" assumed personality problems which were merely exacerbated by combat (Figley, 1978). Emphasizing weakness of character made veterans ashamed of stress-related symptoms and many avoided discussing them. Not until the 1970s did theories begin to shift away from emphasis on underlying personality and toward a recognition that extreme stress evokes symptoms in most people. Many older veterans retain prejudices against admitting war-related problems. Many espouse what could be called a "John Wayne" model, and use avoidant and suppressive techniques rather than sharing memories and feelings which were frightening and painful. Real or expected negative reactions of others can be a further deterrent. For these reasons many older veterans may have PTSD symptoms that have never been reported.

DIAGNOSIS

Individuals differ widely in the clinical picture presented and differential diagnosis can be quite difficult, particularly in elders. Schizophrenia, anxiety and depressive reactions, and personality disorders can show symptoms similar to PTSD. On the other hand, many combat veterans who have some nightmares or a startle response do not seem to have PTSD (Hendin, Haas, Singer, Gold, Trigos, & Ulman, 1983).

Symptoms of chronic PTSD were found by Chodoff (1963) in concentration camp survivors after 15 years: (a) irritability, restlessness, and a startle reaction, often worse at night and accompanied by insomnia and nightmares; (b) anxiety, psychosomatic complaints, a phobia of being alone, or obsessive rumination about camp experiences; (c) depression, which tended to dominate in older persons; (d) seclusiveness, apathy, dependency, and feelings of inadequacy, or suspicious, hostile, paranoid reactions. The stress syndrome often persists as chronic hypervigilance: the patient feels tense and anxious, is overstimulated by noise or crowds, and wakes at the slightest noise. Headaches, vertigo, blackouts, depression, and diffuse anxiety were associated with this hyperalertness in a study of veterans 15 years after World War II (Archibald, Long, Miller, & Tuddenham, 1962).

The differential diagnosis in cases of PTSD can be challenging. Rather than emphasizing strict differential diagnosis, Sierles, Chen, McFarland, and Taylor (1983) recommend diagnosing and treating additional disorders when warranted. Among 25 hospitalized veterans (primarily from the Vietnam era) with a diagnosis of PTSD

they found 84% met criteria for at least one other diagnosis (c.f. Atkinson, Henderson, Sparr, & Deale, 1982). But some clinical guidelines are available to help distinguish PTSD from overlapping diagnostic categories.

Schizophrenia

PTSD can be misdiagnosed as schizophrenia because blunted affect, visual and auditory hallucinations, isolation, and disorganized
behavior may be prominent (Van Putten & Emory, 1973). This differential diagnosis can be puzzling, and some patients may have
both disorders. Age at onset, family and personal history, and psychological testing can help make the diagnosis. Table 2 summarizes
several helpful clinical cues. In particular, PTSD patients have
flashbacks directly connected with remembered events while schizophrenic hallucinations are not scenes from one's past (Hogben &
Cornfield, 1981). And among four Vietnam veterans misdiagnosed
as schizophrenic, all experienced transient psychotic states but none
had a thought disorder and all had affect appropriate to the thought
content (Van Putten & Emory, 1973).

Table 2

DIFFERENTIAL DIAGNOSIS BETWEEN PTSD AND SCHIZOPHRENIA

Schizophrenia	PTSD
Inappropriate affect	Affect appropriate to thought content
Flat affect	Constricted affect alternating with anxious affect, with potential for explosive rage reactions
Hallucinations, not reality based	Flashbacks related to actual traumatic events
Disorganized behavior	Acting as if the traumatic event were recurring, which may lead
Illogical thinking	to bizarre behavior
Voices "inside head"	Screams, cries for help, name called, tending to "come from outside head"

Note. Based on Walker, J. I., & Cavenar, J. O. (1982). Vietnam
veterans: Their problems continue. Journal of Nervous and Mental
Diseases, 170, p. 176.

Alcoholism

Veterans who use alcohol to offset the restlessness, insomnia, and intrusive memories of PTSD may become alcoholic, and for them alcohol treatment alone may be insufficient. In fact, eliminating alcohol can exacerbate the PTSD symptoms, which may be confused with alcohol withdrawal. Alcohol can mask stress response symptoms, but a military history and assessment of whether alcohol is used in response to PTSD symptoms can reveal underlying PTSD (Carter, 1982; Lacoursiere, Godfrey, & Ruby, 1980).

Antisocial Personality Disorder

Impulsive and violent behavior and interpersonal problems are typical of both PTSD and antisocial personality disorder. Since the latter is diagnosed only if there was poor adjustment prior to age 15, history differentiates these disorders (APA, 1980); but veterans or camp survivors who were in their teens when the stress occurred may require careful questioning.

Depressive Disorders

While rage and antisocial characteristics have been associated with Vietnam veterans (Brende, 1983; Zarcone, Scott, & Kauvar, 1977), older patients seem more vulnerable to depression, anxiety, and guilt (Chodoff, 1963). Depression can be easily missed in older males who are hesitant to complain of subjective symptoms. On the other hand, it can be overdiagnosed on the basis of physical complaints that are clearly related to depression in younger persons but may be due to aging or physical illness in elders. Careful probing can usually differentiate these conditions (see Czirr & Gallagher, 1984, for detailed guidelines for diagnostic interviewing of depressed elders). Of course, patients may suffer a major depression along with PTSD.

Psychological Testing

Tests such as the Geriatric Depression Scale and State-Trait Anxiety Inventories may help monitor the depression and anxiety of PTSD. The Impact of Event Scale specifically assesses symptoms experienced as a result of a traumatic event (Horowitz & Wilner, 1980). Standard psychological tests may be useful in diagnosis.

Among Vietnam veterans with PTSD, MMPI protocols had mean T scores above 70 on F, 1, 2, 3, 4, 6, 7, 8, with high points on scales 2 and 8. These men appeared more disturbed on all of these scales than a group of noncombat psychiatric inpatients (Fairbank, Keane, & Malloy, 1983). The Rorschach test may help differentiate psychotic conditions from PTSD. While PTSD patients often show depressive indications and color stress (see Weiner, 1966, pp. 190–192), form level is generally good and bizarre responses tend to be related to actual experiences, such as "body parts," or "explosions." On the other hand, confabulation and poor form level on content unrelated to combat are more indicative of thought disorder (Koller, 1985).

Test results may seem dramatic and should be interpreted cautiously since very few data are available for this group. There is a danger of overpathologizing patients when interpreting results, when in fact they may respond well to therapy. Taken alone, extreme scores (such as MMPI T scores over 100) do not imply a need for drastic measures such as major tranquilizers or locked wards unless another diagnosis can be supported or there are immediate concerns about the patient's danger to self or others (Koller, 1985).

THE CLINICAL INTERVIEW

A clear diagnosis of PTSD is not always possible in a single interview; longer observation may be needed. Clinicians should also realize that discussion of the veteran's experiences can be quite upsetting, and arrange ongoing treatment as the painful and often long-hidden story emerges. In our experience it has been rare for these men to volunteer information about stressors, so one usually needs to ask about military experience. Establishing rapport is essential. Remember that the veteran may believe that any sequela from the war brand him as weak or crazy. Empathic comments and brief educational remarks about PTSD can normalize his experience. As the veteran becomes comfortable the clinician can explore the combat and/or POW experience, the duration and severity of stress, the frequency and intrusiveness of memories, and whether the veteran has talked about the experiences. Assessment of functioning prior to combat should include adjustment to school and relationships with friends and family as a child and teenager. Contacts with family can often provide information about changes over time or about behavioral symptoms.

Be alert to the patient's affective tone. Is the account given easily and comfortably, or with distress, anxiety and avoidance? Physiological arousal has been linked to combat-related cues. Signs such as perspiration, muscle tension, agitation, and clammy hands may be key diagnostic features (Foy, Sipprelle, Rueger, & Carroll, 1984). Patients may have a far-away look as they access powerful eidetic imagery of traumatic events.

TREATMENT

Most clinical data come from studies of Vietnam veterans, with a few studies of veterans with more chronic reactions. Although research is needed to establish the efficacy of these methods with older veterans, these techniques are outlined as the only available guidelines. Treatment plans should be individualized. Some veterans benefit from a brief, strictly combat-oriented treatment. However, if symptoms have become enmeshed in many parts of their lives, extensive therapy may be needed in addition to treatment of the combat trauma.

Behavior Therapy

Behavior therapists generally treat anxiety reactions with exposure techniques. These techniques involve systematic presentation of anxiety-producing trauma-related stimuli. A patient might watch videotapes of combat, listen to war sounds, and talk in detail about scenes which are most painful. This may be done gradually in conjunction with relaxation techniques, as in systematic desensitization (Kipper, 1977; Schindler, 1980), or rapidly and intensively as in flooding (Black & Keane, 1982, Fairbank & Keane, 1982; Fairbank, Gross, & Keane, 1983).

Family Therapy

Some families perpetuate PTSD by refusing to listen to the veteran's painful memories or by discouraging any expression of emotion. Other families may encourage inappropriate and violent behavior. These patterns may arise from rigid expectations and family roles, or from lack of understanding of PTSD. Family therapy and spouses' groups can provide support for family members and facilitate communication (Figley & Sprenkle, 1978; Stanton & Figley, 1978; C. M. Williams, 1980).

Abreaction with Drugs or Hypnosis

Drugs such as sodium pentothal have been used to help patients recover suppressed material. Significant underlying pathology is sometimes found during drug interviews which was not apparent during the initial evaluation (Zarcone, Scott, & Kauver, 1977). Drug interviews were a common treatment during World War II, and veterans from that era may expect or fear such treatment now. Hypnosis and meditation techniques have been also been useful in uncovering intense feelings of fear and rage (Brende & Benedict, 1980; Spiegel, 1981).

Medications

Yost (1980) discourages drug treatment of PTSD, suggesting medication only for significant anxiety, depression, or psychosis. Successes with tricyclic antidepressants (Friedman, 1981) and MAO inhibitors (Hogben & Cornfield, 1981) have been reported. Of course, extra care is needed when prescribing these medications for elders; see Strauss & Solomon (1983) for guidelines.

Individual Psychotherapy

Horowitz (1974) presents a rationale for treating stress response syndromes with crisis-oriented individual psychodynamic therapy. The goal of this therapy is to help the patient modulate extremes of flooding and denial. Extreme denial prevents the client from conceptually or emotionally processing the event, while the other extreme of intrusive and repetitive memories can lead to panic states and secondary avoidance maneuvers. Therapy helps the client process painful content at an emotionally tolerable pace. Completion of treatment involves finding new meanings relevant to the traumatic event.

Brende and Benedict (1980) used psychodynamic and hypnotic techniques in three phases. First, *stabilization of functioning,* in which the client begins to express the guilt and rage of the experience and uses support to deal with current pressures and crises. Second, *uncovering traumatic experiences,* in which the client faces helplessness, abandonment, distrust, rage, and guilt. Finally, *re-integration,* in which the client integrates dissociated feelings by reexperiencing and processing the event.

Group Therapy

This is probably the treatment of choice for PTSD (T. Williams, 1980). Like individual therapy, group treatment builds trust, allows expression of affect and memories, and integrates compartmental-ized material. But groups also seem to reduce mistrust, stigmatiza-tion, and the fear of mental illness as men are exposed to others with similar problems. Coping skills are shared among group members, and a sense of community helps break down isolation and facilitate sharing of emotions and recollections (T. Williams, 1980). Unfor-tunately, except for large Veterans Administration facilities, clinics may never see enough older patients to create a group.

The first author and colleagues have conducted three such groups for elders. After initial hesitancy, trust developed quickly and the men began to share memories and feelings. Experiences of feeling helpless in the face of death seemed most stressful and also most related to nightmares and flashbacks. The previously isolated men became cohesive and arranged social contacts outside the group time. During the last phase of the group past and present issues were integrated, including family stress, illness, retirement, financial problems, and approaching death.

These older veterans did not show the dramatic improvement sometimes seen in Vietnam veterans. They may describe partial amelioration of symptoms such as nightmares and startle responses. Many saw treatment as useful, particularly in understanding PTSD, discovering that they were not alone, and realizing they were not losing their minds. This seemed to enable them to cope with their symptoms and with current stress.

Treatment Commonalities

Most treatments have several aspects in common. The client must develop trust that the therapist understands the problem, will not judge, and can be helpful. Only then is the client safe to become ful-ly aware of many suppressed details and of associated affect. Symp-toms often intensify as this painful content is brought to the surface. The client slowly develops a more adaptive perspective on the experience. Behavior therapy places little emphasis on the latter aspect, but even these clients learn that the event can be remembered with less anxiety. Other models emphasize processing and integrating the trauma. Clients overcome the need to avoid memories of the traumatic event and assign new meanings to their history. Termination provides a final opportunity to integrate feelings about loss.

Therapist Reactions

Working with these veterans can arouse strong reactions. Listening to stories of torture and death can be emotionally draining, and dealing with symptoms such as suspiciousness, anger, and passivity call upon many resources. Therapists must confront their attitudes to war, aggression, and death to work effectively with these clients. Countertransference responses can be overwhelming. Ideally, groups should be led by co-therapists (Walker & Nash, 1981), and individual therapists should arrange time with a consultant to process their reactions. Clinicians who are uncomfortable with emotionally laden content are likely to collude with clients in avoiding essential data (Boman, 1982), leading to misdiagnosis and inappropriate treatment.

Use of Contemporary Images

Photographs on common themes can be a useful tool in therapy, prompting group discussion or individual reflection. Many evocative photographs of World War II are readily available. For example, we have used images of a draft induction physical, a soldier saying goodbye to his toddler, combat, prison camps, and a reunion scene to evoke patient responses. See Table 3 for sources.

Organizations for Information or Referral

VA medical services are available to most veterans over 65, since eligibility rules are less stringent for elders. Under Public Law 97-37 ex-POW's are also eligible for special medical and disability benefits. Some VA's have specific experience with elders with PTSD, but all should be cognizant of PTSD in Vietnam veterans and should be able to provide some assistance. Most local employment offices have a veterans' counselor who is familiar with VA re-

Table 3

KEY RESOURCES FOR CLINICIANS

Bailey, R. H. (1981). Prisoners of war. Vol. 30 in C. Osborne &
    S. Cotler (Eds.), World War II. Alexandria, VA: Time-Life.
    (Heavily illustrated survey with 150-item bibliography.
    37-volume series is an excellent layperson's history.)

Evaluation and change (1980). Special Issue: Services for
    victims, survivors.
    (Articles on reactions to various extreme stressors, and
    resources for treatment. Available from 501 South Park Avenue,
    Minneapolis, MN 55415.)

Figley, C.R., (Ed.). (1978). Stress disorders among Vietnam
    veterans: Theory, research and treatment. New York:
    Brunner/Mazel.
    (General overview of combat-related PTSD.)

LIFE: The first decade 1936-1945. (1979). Boston: New York
    Graphic Society.
    (70 pages of evocative photos from World War II.)

Manchester, W. (1979). Goodbye darkness. New York: Little, Brown.
    (Intense first-person account of the WWII Pacific theatre.)

Sherman, D. (1978). LIFE goes to war: A pictorial history of
    World War II. New York: Wallaby.

Williams, T., (Ed.) (1980). Post-traumatic stress disorders of
    the Vietnam veteran. Cincinnati: Disabled American Veterans.
    (Quick reference on PTSD. Available from DAV representatives.)

sources. A national network of the ex-POWs, active in lobbying and providing information and emotional support for POWs, can be located through local Veterans of Foreign Wars (VFW) or Disabled American Veterans (DAV) posts or representatives.

CASE STUDY

John, age 63, came to a VA psychiatric clinic at his wife's insistence. He reported that he had become more depressed, irritable, and apathetic in recent months, with poor sleep, lack of appetite, weight loss, marital discord, and lack of sexual desire. He expressed feeling nervous and depressed since he was in the service, when he was hospitalized for a ''nervous breakdown.''

John was admitted to a psychiatric ward with a diagnosis of Major Depressive Disorder and treated with tricyclic antidepressants. At discharge a month later he was sleeping better but seemed otherwise unchanged. Psychotic features were noted including hearing people laughing and calling his name, seeing his dead father, and avoiding people because of suspicions they were trying to harm him. He had attacked his wife twice in fits of explosive anger and she was threatening to leave unless he controlled himself.

Referred for individual psychotherapy, he dated his violence and hallucinations to experiences as a POW and began to relate details of his 42 months in Japanese camps. Captured at 18, he had been beaten and starved. He had weighed as little as 85 pounds, and had been dumped in the horrific "Zero Ward" where the dying were housed. He felt great guilt over what he had done to survive, such as eating insects and rats and taking clothes from a corpse. After liberation he was hospitalized for several months, but soon married and began work as a housepainter. The marriage was stormy and he had trouble keeping a job. He would get into fights, walk off the job, or be fired. He used alcohol heavily for a few years to avoid memories, but in later years strenuous physical activity served the same function. Although his family had been unstable during his childhood, he had no pre-war history of antisocial behavior. He related shame at his capture, guilt at his survival, and anger about many injustices.

After several weeks of evaluation an Axis II diagnosis of Paranoid Personality Disorder was added. Goals of treatment were to ameliorate depression and to express anger without violence. John declined medications and marital therapy. He had almost never talked about his captivity, and he needed a great deal of support early in therapy. As his trust increased it became clear that his experiences had many lingering effects. He often dreamed about the Bataan Death March, and most nights he deliberately slept only three hours to minimize dreaming. Flashbacks still occurred, as when hearing Chinese spoken behind him in a checkout line triggered a flashback of being surrounded and beaten by Japanese guards. He bolted for the street in terror, and took days to recover from this panic attack. He heard voices every few days, calling his name as the guards had. But in spite of these symptoms no evidence of thought disorder was ever found.

His diagnosis was modified to Chronic Depression, Passive-Dependent Personality Disorder, and PTSD. As he recalled increasingly vivid details he was taught relaxation techniques to help him manage his anxiety and insomnia. At the same time he hesitantly joined a group of older PTSD patients. He befriended a man who had also been a prisoner of the Japanese. The two spent time together and shared some experiences privately. Both gradually spoke more in the group, and John's affect brightened.

A surgery, his mother's death, and a change of therapists exacerbated his symptoms during treatment. Three years after his hospitalization he still has periods of anxiety and depression, as well as symptoms of PTSD. He does have periods of good mood, no longer talks of suicide, sleeps longer, and has fewer nightmares. He has made a few friends and has a part-time job. As he has gained control of his outbursts and became more communicative, he and his wife seem to have had fewer conflicts. He no longer is afraid of losing his mind, as he was when the POW experiences were his secret burden.

CONCLUSIONS

PTSD is easily misdiagnosed. This is a condition which many may have seen in their clients without knowing it. A significant fraction of U.S. elders have been exposed to stressors sufficient to trigger PTSD, and losses and stresses of aging may exacerbate or reactivate earlier stress responses. Clinicians should be alert to this possibility, especially when assessing anxiety or depression, since older clients will rarely raise the issue of a traumatic past.

This article has focused on aging veterans, clearly a group at risk. But the clinician should remember that other groups have also experienced stress sufficient to lead to PTSD, including wartime nurses, victims of rape, assault, or catastrophic accident, and concentration camp survivors. Research is needed to determine the extent of this problem in elders and to determine how this cohort may differ from Vietnam veterans, from whom most existing data arc drawn. Despite these limitations, this survey of PTSD in elders should prove useful to the clinician in integrating this stress disorder into the client's treatment plan.

REFERENCES

American Psychiatric Association. (1980). *Diagnostic and statistical manual of mental disorders* (3rd ed.). Washington, DC: Author.

Archibald, H. C., & Tuddenham, R. D. (1965). Persistent stress reaction after combat: A 20-year follow-up. *Archives of General Psychiatry, 12,* 475–481.

Archibald, H. C., Long, D. M., Miller, C., & Tuddenham, R. D. (1962). Gross stress reaction in combat: A 15-year follow-up. *American Journal of Psychiatry, 119,* 317–322.

Atkinson, R. M., Henderson, R. G., Sparr, L. F., & Deale, S. (1982). Assessment of Viet Nam veterans for posttraumatic stress disorder in Veterans Administration disability claims. *American Journal of Psychiatry, 139,* 1118–1121.

Black, J. L., & Keane, T. M. (1982). Implosive therapy in the treatment of combat related fears in a World War II veteran. *Journal of Behavior Therapy & Experimental Psychiatry, 13,* 163–165.

Boman, B. (1982). Review: The Vietnam veteran ten years on. *Australian and New Zealand Journal of Psychiatry, 16,* 107–127.

Brende, J. O. (1983). A psychodynamic view of character pathology in Vietnam combat veterans. *Bulletin of the Menninger Clinic, 47*(3), 193–216.

Brende, J. O., & Benedict, B. D. (1980). The Vietnam combat delayed stress response: Hypnotherapy of "dissociative symptoms." *The American Journal of Clinical Hypnosis, 23,* 34–40.

Carter, J. H. (1982). Alcoholism in black Vietnam veterans: Symptoms of posttraumatic stress disorder. *Journal of the National Medical Association, 74,* 655–660.

Chodoff, P. (1963). Late effects of the concentration camp syndrome. *Archives of General Psychiatry, 8,* 323–333.

Czirr, R., & Gallagher, D. (1984). Assessing depression in older adults. In P. A. Keller & L. G. Ritt (Eds.), *Innovations in clinical practice: A source book* (pp. 100–116). Sarasota, FL: Professional Resource Exchange.

Fairbank, J. A., Gross, R. T., & Keane, T. M. (1983). Treatment of posttraumatic stress disorder: Evaluating outcome with a behavioral code. *Behavior Modification, 7,* 557–568.

Fairbank, J. A., & Keane, T. M. (1982). Flooding for combat-related stress disorders: Assessment of anxiety reduction across traumatic memories. *Behavior Therapy, 13,* 499–510.

Fairbank, J. A., Keane, T. M., & Malloy, P. F. (1983). Some preliminary data on the psychological characteristics of Vietnam veterans with posttraumatic stress disorders. *Journal of Consulting and Clinical Psychology, 51,* 912–919.

Figley, C. R. (1978). Introduction. In C. R. Figley (Ed.), *Stress disorders among Vietnam veterans* (pp. xiii–xxvi). New York: Brunner/Mazel.

Figley, C. R., & Sprenkle, D. H. (1978). Delayed stress response syndrome: Family therapy indications. *Journal of Marital and Family Therapy, 4*(3), 53–60.

Foy, D. W., Sipprelle, R. C., Rueger, D. B., & Carroll, E. M. (1984). Etiology of posttraumatic stress disorder in Vietnam veterans: Analysis of premilitary, military, and combat exposure influences. *Journal of Consulting and Clinical Psychology, 52,* 79–87.

Friedman, M. J. (1981). Post-Vietnam syndrome: Recognition and management. *Psychosomatics, 22,* 931–943.

Hendin, H., Haas, A. P., Singer, P., Gold, F., Trigos, G. G., & Ulman, R. B. (1983). Evaluation of posttraumatic stress in Vietnam veterans. *Journal of Psychiatric Treatment and Evaluation, 5,* 303–307.

Hogben, G. L., & Cornfield, R. B. (1981). Treatment of traumatic war neurosis with phenelzine. *Archives of General Psychiatry, 38,* 440–445.

Holmstrom, V., Waid, L. R., & Sexhauer, J. D. (1984, August). *Post-traumatic stress 40 years later: Survivors of Japanese prison camps.* Symposium presented at the Annual Convention of the American Psychological Association, Toronto, Canada.

Horowitz, M. (1974). Stress response syndromes: Character style and dynamic psychotherapy. *Archives of General Psychiatry, 31,* 768–781.

Horowitz, M. J., & Wilner, N. (1980). Life events, stress and coping. In L. W. Poon (Ed.), *Aging in the 1980s* (pp. 363–374). Washington, DC: American Psychological Association.

Kipper, D. A. (1977). Behavior therapy for fears brought on by war experiences. *Journal of Consulting and Clinical Psychology, 45,* 216–221.

Klonoff, H., McDougall, G., Clark, C., Kramer, P., & Horgan, J. (1976). The neuropsychological, psychiatric, and physical effects of prolonged and severe stress: 30 years later. *The Journal of Nervous and Mental Disease, 163,* 246–252.

Koller, P. (1985). Personal communication. VA Medical Center, Psychology Service (116B), Palo Alto, California 94304.

Lacoursiere, R. B., Godfrey, K. E., & Ruby, L. M. (1980). Traumatic neurosis in the etiology of alcoholism: Viet Nam combat and other trauma. *American Journal of Psychiatry, 137,* 966–968.

Schindler, F. E. (1980). Treatment by systematic desensitization of a recurring nightmare of a real life trauma. *Journal of Behavior Therapy & Experimental Psychiatry, 11,* 53–54.

Sexauer, J. D., Holmstrom, U. L., Shaw, D. L., & Waid, L. R. (1985, August). *World War II American POW's: Captivity-related stressors and present day symptomatology.* Paper presented at the Annual Convention of the American Psychological Association, Los Angeles, California.

Sierles, F. S., Chen, J. J., McFarland, R. E., & Taylor, M. A. (1983). Posttraumatic stress disorder and concurrent psychiatric illness: A preliminary report. *American Journal of Psychiatry, 140,* 1177–1179.

Spiegel, D. (1981). Vietnam grief work using hypnosis. *The American Journal of Clinical Hypnosis, 24,* 33–40.

Stanton, M. D., & Figley, C. R. (1978). Treating the Vietnam veteran within the family system. In C. R. Figley (Ed.), *Stress disorders among Vietnam veterans* (pp. 281–289). New York: Brunner/Mazel.

Strauss, D., & Solomon, K. (1983). Psychopharmacologic intervention for depression in the elderly. *Clinical Gerontologist, 2,* 3–29.

Van Devanter, L. (1983). *Home before morning.* New York: Warner.

Van Putten, T., & Emory, W. H. (1973). Traumatic neuroses in Vietnam returnees: A forgotten diagnosis? *Archives of General Psychiatry, 29,* 695–698.

Walker, J. I., & Nash, J. L. (1981). Group therapy in the treatment of Vietnam combat veterans. *International Journal of Group Psychotherapy, 31,* 379–389.

Weiner, I. (1966). *Psychodiagnosis in schizophrenia.* New York: Wiley.

Williams, C. M. (1980). The "veteran system" with a focus on women partners: Theoretical considerations, problems, and treatment strategies. In T. Williams (Ed.), *Post-traumatic stress disorders of the Vietnam veteran.* Cincinnati: Disabled American Veterans.

Williams, T. (1980). A preferred model for development of interventions for psychological readjustment of Vietnam veterans: Group treatment. In T. Williams (Ed.), *Post-traumatic stress disorders of the Vietnam veteran.* Cincinnati: Disabled American Veterans.

Yost, J. (1980). The psychopharmacologic treatment of the delayed stress syndrome in Vietnam veterans. In T. Williams (Ed.), *Post-traumatic stress disorders of the Vietnam veteran* (pp. 125–130). Cincinnati: Disabled American Veterans.

Zarcone, V. P., Jr., Scott, N. R., & Kauver, K. (1977). Psychiatric problems of Vietnam veterans: Clinical study of hospital patients. *Comprehensive Psychiatry, 18,* 41–53.

Zeiss, R. A., Dickman, H. R., & Nichols, B. L. (1985, August). *Post traumatic stress disorder in former prisoners of war: Incidence and correlates.* Paper presented at the Annual Convention of the American Psychological Association, Los Angeles, California.

Questions

1) Is PTSD the primary syndrome, of which depression and alcoholism are mere manifestations?

2) What groups, other than military veterans might have some susceptibility to PTSD?

25/ASSESSMENT AND MANAGEMENT OF CHRONIC PAIN IN THE ELDERLY

William E. Haley, PhD
Jeffrey J. Dolce, PhD

Editor's Introduction

Elders are susceptible to falls, arthritis, and other conditions which can lead to chronic pain. Haley and Dolce review some models of pain, then discuss principles of assessment. Of particular importance is the admonition to carefully document what medications the patient uses, and what environmental factors may reinforce pain/wellness behaviors.

Management of pain should be comprehensive, operating at all levels, and dealing with all relevant factors. The authors emphasize the importance of an approach which gets the patient in an active frame of mind. Pharmacological, electrical, cognitive, behavioral, and environmental approaches are reviewed.

AN OVERVIEW

Pain is among the most common clinical complaints presented by older patients. The elderly are at the highest risk for a number of

William E. Haley is currently an Assistant Professor in the Department of Psychology, and an Associate Scholar in the Center for Aging, at the University of Alabama at Birmingham, Birmingham, AL 35294. Dr. Haley is a former faculty member of the Clinical Pain Service at the University of Washington (Seattle) School of Medicine. Jeffrey J. Dolce is Assistant Professor, Division of General and Preventive Medicine at the University of Alabama at Birmingham. Mr. Dolce acknowledges the contributions of the staff at the Pain Management Center at Brookwood Medical Center in Birmingham, Alabama, where he worked as a graduate assistant.

435

common chronic diseases which often lead to pain, especially arthritic disorders, cardiovascular disease, osteoporosis, and cancer
(Rowe & Besdine, 1982). Less common painful disorders, such as
trigeminal neuralgia and post-herpetic neuralgia, are also of increased incidence in the elderly (Butler & Gastel, 1979). Injuries
such as falls and hip fractures are similarly common problems in the
elderly which may lead to chronic pain (Rubenstein & Robbins,
1984). Thus the elderly are at greater risk for experiencing many
painful disorders.

Haley (1983) found that nursing home staff rated pain as the second most common complaint among their elderly patients. Unfortunately, it is difficult to accurately estimate the frequency of chronic pain problems in the elderly because pain can be caused by so
many different disorders, and because not all elderly patients with a
given disease are troubled by pain. For example, up to half of all
myocardial infarctions in the elderly occur without pain (Butler &
Gastel, 1979). Crook, Rideout, and Browne (1984) found that over
25% of a community sample of individuals over age 60 reported being troubled by persistent pain. Rates for individuals under 60 were
less than half of this percentage. While the exact prevalence of pain
in the elderly is not clear, the data suggest that pain is a major concern for the elderly and that it occurs in the elderly at a higher rate
than in younger individuals.

These findings are particularly startling when one considers that
some researchers have reported that pain sensitivity decreases with
aging (Belleville, Forrest, Miller, & Brown, 1971; Kenshalow,
1977). Biological and psychological changes such as increased sto-
icism have been suggested as possible causes for these findings
(Clark & Mehl, 1971). This phenomenon, however, has most recently been questioned due to methodological issues (Harkins,
Kwentus, & Price, 1984).

Pain is of great concern not only because of its possible relation to
serious disease, but also because of its relation to suffering, and impact on the quality of life. Pain, even in the absence of life-threatening disease, can become the focus of every moment in the patient's
day, and sap patients' enjoyment of life. Pain also produces disability, interfering with patients' ability to carry out their usual activities.

There have been significant advances in recent years in the conceptualization of pain, and an explosion of new techniques for pain
management. Knowledge of these advances in pain management is

essential to clinicians working with the elderly, given the frequency of pain as a major problem.

PERSPECTIVES AND MODELS OF PAIN

Traditionally, pain has been viewed as a direct result of stimulation of peripheral pain receptors which send a message through specific neural pathways to specific pain centers in the brain. These "specificity theories," however, are generally acknowledged as too narrow to account for all the observed phenomena of pain. In recent years pain has been recognized to be a complex combination of sensory, affective, cognitive, and behavioral components (Melzack & Wall, 1983; Wisenburg, 1977). Melzack and Wall's (1983) gate control theory is the most widely cited and accepted model of this complex system. Their model proposes that pain perception can be modulated at numerous points in the central nervous system, including the spinal cord level, as well as through the effects of higher order cognitive processes.

Loeser (1980) has presented a scheme which is less elegant in its specification of the physiological mechanisms of pain perception, but which has important clinical implications. Loeser distinguishes between *nociception, pain, suffering,* and *pain behavior.* Clinical pain is viewed as a complex combination of these four components. Nociception refers to the afferent impulses produced by stimulation of certain specialized nerve fibers. In this model, pain is viewed as the individual's perception of the presence of, nature of, and intensity of, a noxious stimulus. Pain is thus a subjective experience, the presence and degree of which can only be inferred by clinicians from the patient's report and behaviors. Suffering is the negative affective response of anxiety, depression, or distress generated by pain, stress, and other unpleasant situations. Different types of suffering such as depression may interact with and exacerbate the negative affective state related to pain. Pain behavior is the occurrence of behavior which is understood by others to communicate the presence of nociception, including complaints of pain, grimacing, limping, inactivity, or taking pain medications. Pain behavior also includes the disability that is often associated with pain.

Contrary to both common lay and clinical views, the correspondence between these aspects of pain is highly variable (Melzack & Wall, 1983). Some patients report high levels of pain in the absence of diagnosed organic disorder (nociception), and some individuals who have undergone severe injuries or with severe medical problems report little or no pain. Some patients with high levels of pain become miserable and depressed (suffering), while others show few such problems. Finally, pain behavior (complaints, disability) may be minimal in patients with severe disorders (e.g., cancer), but flourish in patients who appear medically to have recovered from mild injuries. The clinical team must assess, and manage, all four of these components if the patient's overall quality of life is to be maximized. Effective assessment and treatment can improve one or more of these four dimensions.

An important conceptual distinction for the clinician assessing and managing pain problems is between *acute* and *chronic* pain with a further distinction being made between *benign* and *malignant* chronic pain. As reviewed in detail by Fordyce (1976), acute pain is conventionally defined as pain of less than 6 months duration, and is typically related to readily observable causes which produce nociception. Acute pain serves a valuable function as a signal of disease or warning to cease a harmful activity. Acute pain is typically managed successfully by the traditional medical system, through interventions aimed at treating the underlying disease and/or by blocking nociception. A disease model in which pain is seen as the result only of nociception produced by a pathological process is typically appropriate for these acute pain problems.

Chronic benign pain presents a dramatically different picture than acute pain. There may be little or no medically apparent nociception, as in pain which persists after the healing of an injury. Pain may no longer serve a useful "warning" function in chronic illness. Patients and health care providers tend to persist in the beliefs and behaviors which are appropriate for acute illness. With such patients, treatment aimed at eliminating nociception may provide little or no change in the pain disorder.

Even surgeries which sever presumably afflicted nerves commonly lead to only temporary relief of chronic benign pain syndromes (Melzack & Wall, 1983). In chronic pain syndromes, such factors as family reinforcement, deconditioning, muscle tension, and life-style changes may be critical variables. Treatment of chronic pain syndromes must then focus on management of pain, suffering, and disability. A shift from an acute illness, "cure" approached to a coping, rehabilitative approach must be made if treatment of the chronic pain patient is to be successful.

In chronic malignant pain (related to an ongoing metastic disease process, e.g., cancer) elements of both acute pain and chronic benign pain are evident. The goal of treatment may be managing or controlling, rather than eliminating, the patient's pain, suffering, and disability. Treatment directed at decreasing nociception, where possible, will be an important component of treatment. Progressive, malignant pain also produces unique psychological stressors (e.g., an unpredictable course, fear of disability and mortality) which need to be addressed. In the case of chronic malignant pain, as in chronic benign pain, the link between different aspects of clinical pain is highly variable.

Crue (1983) has also described another class of clinical pain which he refers to as recurrent acute pain syndromes. In these disorders (such as migraine headaches or rheumatoid arthritis), pain occurs intermittently over an extended period of time. These disorders combine elements of acute pain (e.g., flareups associated with changes in a disease or physical process), and chronic pain (e.g., their persistent nature).

In the remainder of this paper the clinical assessment and management of chronic pain will be reviewed. Because of limitations of space, descriptions of specific techniques will be brief, with references for the interested reader.

ASSESSMENT

Basic Principles

The assessment of chronic pain is a challenging task that is frequently hindered by the tendency to view it as a single disorder, or from a single disciplinary perspective. In acute care medicine, or traditional mental health practice, patients are seen by an individual practitioner, occasionally with input from specialized consultants. By the time that patients with chronic pain syndromes are referred to pain clinics, the inadequacy of these typical approaches is readily apparent. Patients have been seen by numerous medical specialists who attempt to assess the problem by finding an undetected disease process which explains the patient's symptoms. If they fail to account for the pain problem on the basis of disease, mental health consultation is often based on the suspicion that the pain is "all in the head," "psychogenic," or "imaginary." The typical mental health consultation may reveal psychosocial problems such as depression or family conflict, but may also fail to appreciate the special problems of the chronic illness. As a result, patients with chronic pain become desperate for a cure, and are at risk for unnecessary invasive procedures, e.g., surgery.

It is rare for any one professional to have access to all of the varied assessments the patient has gone through, or to have the necessary knowledge to integrate the biomedical and psychosocial data on the patient. A multidisciplinary team approach is now recognized as the ideal means of assessing chronic pain problems. Patients and their medical records are given detailed scrutiny by a team including varying combinations of: physicians, psychologists, nurses, physical therapists, occupational therapists, rehabilitation counselors, and social workers. The variables assessed are noted in the sections below. Most important is that these professionals meet as a team and pool their knowledge to allow for a comprehensive picture of the patient's pain problem. Failure to consider all relevant factors in a case may decrease the possibility of significant reductions in pain and may predispose treatment to failure.

Development of appropriate rapport, and a workable orientation toward assessment, is essential with such patients. They may be suspicious of medical and psychological personnel, because they have been unsuccessful in obtaining pain relief in past interactions with health professionals. It is important to communicate both a recognition of the patient's experience of pain, and concern for the patient's suffering. Assessment should include not only direct, detailed examinations of the patient but a close examination of how their lifestyles impact on the experience of pain.

Thus, information about the pain syndrome should come from multiple sources. Medical records should be reviewed in detail, family members should be interviewed, and pain diaries, with self-monitoring of activity, pain levels, and medication intake, should be completed. Direct observations of the patient and what he/she *does* during interviews, and baseline assessments of functioning in physical and occupational therapies is essential.

Medical/Physical Status

An emphasis on thorough medical evaluation is especially important in the elderly patient. Older individuals are likely to present with a complex picture, with multiple chronic illnesses (Rowe & Besdine, 1982). It should be strongly emphasized that evidence of the effect of behavioral/psychological factors on pain does not rule out organic illness. For example, patients with cancer have been found to show dramatic responses to placebos (Shapiro & Morris, 1978).

The role of medical evaluation in the assessment of chronic pain is to determine the extent that organic pathology producing nociception is contributing to the pain problem (i.e., malignant, acute, or recurrent acute). In addition, medical assessment should thoroughly evaluate the patient's general medical status to uncover any problems which may complicate, or contradict, various aspects of a comprehensive treatment approach. The physician should specify the patient's physical limitations, and the extent of deconditioning.

Patients' Experience of Pain

Detailed inquiry about the patient's experience of pain is essential in establishing the clinician as someone who cares and can be trusted. Pain may be described as highly localized to one area of the body, or vague and widespread in distribution. Careful interviews, and pain diaries, will tell the clinician whether certain activities or social stressors are closely linked to increases in pain. The clinician should assess both factors which increase and decrease pain. Clinicians should be alert for increases in pain which are inconsistent with a purely medical/physical explanation. For example, one patient's back pain was described as worsened only by activities such as lifting. Examination of pain diaries revealed that her pain ratings did not change with housework, but increased daily around 5 p.m. when her husband came home from work.

The quality of pain can also be described in vastly different terms. Pain may be described as dull, aching, throbbing, burning etc. The McGill Pain Questionnaire (McLzack, 1975) includes 78 different pain descriptors, and provides a useful method of assessing patient's subjective experience of pain to supplement their descriptions during interviews. In many cases where the elimination of all pain is not possible, reduction in the aversiveness of the pain perception is a worthwhile treatment goal.

Medications and Patients' Methods of Pain Relief

A complete assessment of all types and amounts of medications being utilized by the elderly patient is essential. Older patients are likely to be on multiple medications, which increase the likelihood of harmful drug interactions which occur frequently in the elderly (Berlinger & Spector, 1984). Medications also need to be examined due to the high frequency of habituation and addiction among chronic pain patients (Evans, 1981). It should be emphasized that addiction is a risk even for patients with no history of drug abuse.

Patients may fail to report all medications, either because of poor recall, or an attempt to maintain control of their favored medicines. One useful technique is to ask older patients to bring all of their medications to the clinic in a shopping bag, for a thorough review. Analysis of blood and urine samples may also detect unreported medications. Use of pain diary forms, on which patients write down the times and doses of all medications, may also be informative.

In addition, patients often utilize methods which are not standard medical practice to manage their pain. They may visit chiropractors, get backrubs from their families, apply heat or cold, or use mechanical aids. These techniques should be assessed in order to control any practices which are actually counter-productive for the patient. Patients with chronic pain are also at risk to be bilked by "quack" or "fad" treatments, and re-education may protect them.

Behavioral Functioning

As described above, pain behavior is an important aspect of clinical pain. The types of pain behaviors which occur can be assessed by direct observation of the patient, while resting and active. Interviews with family members, asking how they can tell when the patient is in pain, and when such behaviors are most common, provides important information. Besides pain behavior, "well behavior" and current and past activity levels, should be assessed. Physical and occupational therapy assessments can provide specific examples of patient's behavioral capacities and limitations, such as how long the patient can sit or stand, the distance they can walk, or the amount of weight they can lift. It is often apparent that patients have become excessively disabled, or more impaired than necessary, because of inactivity and deconditioning.

It is important to carefully explore the areas of leisure activities, family interaction, marital and sexual relationships, activity levels, activity of daily living (ADLs), and where applicable, vocational activities. These healthy behaviors are often markedly, and unnecessarily reduced in chronic pain patients.

Changes in income, housing, etc., which often accompany retirement can also affect the patient by adding additional stress to an already unpleasant situation. In summary, a very complete evaluation of the patient's total life situation is needed to effectively target all the factors contributing to their distress and suffering. The evaluation should aim to reveal specific "well behaviors" or activities which can later be targeted for re-activation, and specific pain behaviors which may later be decreased.

Operant Reinforcement Factors

Pain behaviors and well behaviors may be affected by operant reinforcement variables (Fordyce, 1976). Assessment should include interviews with both the patient and a family member, and should note what consequences occur when the patient shows "well behavior" and "pain behavior." Problems occur when pain behavior results in positive or negative reinforcement, and well behavior is either ignored or punished. The clinician should be especially suspicious of operant factors when patients are selectively inactive (e.g., can sit for two hours at a movie but only ten minutes when in-laws visit), or when pain behavior increases in certain situations (e.g., the presence of a spouse).

One case which illustrates the effects of positive reinforcement of pain behavior was a 71-year-old widowed female with a one-year history of chronic low back pain secondary to muscular strain. Medical evaluation failed to reveal any significant organic disease at the time of evaluation. The original soft tissue damage, by all objective findings, had healed. A closer examination of her family and social life revealed that she had been widowed approximately one year prior to the onset of pain. Her social activities had greatly diminished since the death of her husband; however, with the injury to her back, contact with her family increased. Her daughter and two sons would frequently visit to see if she needed anything. Her children were also noted to drop whatever they were doing and rush over to attend to her needs whenever she phoned and expressed increased problems with pain. Thus the increased attention she received for expressing pain resulted in a gradual escalation of the frequency and severity of her pain problem despite adequate healing of the original injury.

Similarly, the avoidance of aversive events can reinforce pain behavior and distress. Most pain patients report experiencing increased pain with activity and are, therefore, likely to reduce their activity level. Activity avoidance is reinforced to the extent to which rest from these activities diminishes pain. In addition, reduced activity levels may be maintained due to the fear and anxiety related to the consequences of an activity. If such activities are avoided, then fear is reduced and the continued avoidance of that activity is strengthened.

Medication regimes which are request-contingent (i.e., p.r.n.) rather than time-contingent are particularly likely to increase pain behaviors by mandating that pain be displayed as an antecedent event to the reinforcing consequences of using a medication (Fordyce, 1976). Such findings have important treatment implications considering that the majority of narcotic analgesics used to control pain for hospitalized low back pain patients are given on a request-contingent basis (Dolce, Doleys, Raczynski, & Crocker, 1985).

A broad variety of other operant reinforcement factors have been found to influence pain behavior, including financial compensation, avoidance of work, household responsibilities, and/or sexual activity. Conditioned pain behaviors may exist with any chronic illness if they occur for sufficient time in environments that are favorable to conditioning. Assessment of operant variables will aid the clinician in targeting changes in the pattern of reinforcement which maybe impacting on the pain problem, especially within the family.

Affective Responses, Cognitions, and Illness Beliefs

Affective reactions and the cognitive styles of patients may contribute to the distress and suffering experienced by the patient. Depression is highly prevalent among elderly individuals, and especially likely to be associated with chronic illness (Gurland & Cross, 1982). Depression and chronic pain often interact in a vicious cycle, in which pain exacerbates depression, and depression increases the suffering and misery of the patients' pain. Fear, uncertainty, and feeling a lack of control can also exacerbate pain and suffering through anxiety (Turk & Rennert, 1981).

Assessment should seek to identify the extent to which depression and anxiety are present, and whether increases or decreases in emotional reactions alter the patient's experience of pain. Chronic pain patients tend to emphasize somatic aspects of depression, such as changes in sleep and appetite, and to minimize changes in mood (Katon & Kleinman, 1982). Depression is often "masked" by these complaints, and goes undetected (Blumer & Heilbronn, 1982).

Assessment of the patient's cognitive styles for dealing with pain may reveal ineffective coping techniques (Turk, Meichenbaum, & Genest, 1983; Keefe, 1982). Patients may have erroneous but persistent illness beliefs which must be addressed. For example, most patients believe that, if pain is severe, there must be an equally severe organic disease process causing the pain. In fact, medically benign processes (e.g., muscle tension) can produce severe pain (Kraus, 1965).

Patients' illness beliefs may also affect their disability and activity. Patients may believe that activity will foster disability, as in the patient who feared that exercise would "grind down" her vertebrae, and put her in a wheelchair.

Somatic preoccupation, and how attention and distraction affect the patient's pain and pain behavior similarly need to be assessed. Chronic illness commonly leads to increases in patients' attention to physical sensations, because of concern about monitoring their disease, inactivity, social isolation, and increased introspection (Turk & Rennert, 1981; Skelton & Pennebaker, 1982). Attentional processes are closely related to pain tolerance (McCaul & Malott, 1984). Clinically, it is not uncommon to observe increased pain behavior (grimacing, squirming) when topics related to pain are discussed in interview.

Muscle Tension

Problems such as muscle tension can be an important component of chronic pain disorders (Wolf, Basmajian, Russe, & Kutner, 1979; Dolce & Raczynski, in press). Muscle tension can either add to the pain and discomfort of a co-existing disorder, such as arthritis (Acterberg-Lawlis, 1982), or may be a source of nociception in its own right, as in myofascial pain disorders. Psychophysiological assessment—especially electromyelogram (EMG) assessment—can aid in determining the role of autonomic arousal and neuromuscular activity. Such assessments can document specific muscle sites which are excessively tense, and provide guidance for subsequent relaxation and/or biofeedback training.

Neuropsychological Functioning

Cognitive impairment is often seen in chronic pain patients of all ages (McNairy, Maruta, Ivnik, Swanson, & Ilstrup, 1984). Elderly chronic pain patients commonly report increased forgetfulness, difficulty with concentration, and/or occasional periods of confusion. The presence and extent of cognitive impairment needs to be carefully assessed through neuropsychological testing. If memory is impaired, the patient may not be a reliable source of information about the history of his/her pain problem, medication use, etc. In such situations, a reliable informant needs to be involved to obtain the details needed to make behavioral treatment possible. Memory and concentration problems can also create difficulties with the patient's ability to benefit from a complex treatment program.

Cognitive impairment may also create a situation which can foster the acquisition of pain behaviors (Fordyce, 1978). One patient, a 69-year-old female, reported severe limitations in her homemaking activities due to pain. She could no longer cook, clean, get out to buy groceries, or run errands. These activities had been taken over by her husband. Both she and her husband noted her mild forgetfulness but also attributed this to her pain. On neuropsychological assessment, marked impairment in recent memory, sequential processing of information, and new learning were observed, of sufficient severity to suggest a dementing illness. On careful examination, it was revealed that the cognitive deficits were the underlying causes of her decreased activity; however, the pain had served as a convenient way of avoiding the acknowledgement of these deficits, thus creating a situation where her pain complaints were reinforced.

TREATMENT

Basic Principles

The success of treating chronic pain, as previously discussed, relies on a thorough assessment of all the factors that contribute to the patient's suffering and disability. Treatment should proceed at each level to deal with all relevant factors. A multidisciplinary team approach is, again, the preferred mode. Each discipline should be well versed in the learning phenomena associated with pain and should apply this knowledge in eliminating pain behaviors and instilling healthy and fulfilling behavior.

Patients must be given a rationale for treatment and understand that management of their pain disorder will entail more than being a passive recipient of medical efforts to reduce nociception. They must further understand that changes in their thinking, activities, physical conditioning, and re-examination of family processes and goals will help them to cope with the multiple aspects of their pain problems. Education about the nature of their limitations, and the treatment team's assessment of their capabilities, may be important. Education of both patients, and their families, is needed. The establishment of clear-cut goals for treatment in the eyes of the patient and staff is also extremely important in the rehabilitation process. In general, the goals of treatment should be to increase independence, level of functioning, and self-control. The complete elimination of pain, however, is typically not a realistic goal. Instead, treatment should focus on teaching the patients to manage their pain effectively so that it no longer interferes as much with their lives.

Many patients are reluctant to give up the search for a single medical cure for their pain. Unless they agree to cooperate with a comprehensive strategy, they are likely to be noncompliant and to do poorly in treatment. Because of the importance of interdisciplinary, specialized assessment and treatment, chronic pain patients are often treated in special pain clinics. These programs are accustomed to the special problems of coordinating the different aspects of treatment of clinical pain. Hospice programs are another major resource in pain management of patients with terminal illness, especially cancer. Comprehensive pain management may also be successfully managed in other settings in which multidisciplinary consultation is available.

Medical Treatment

Ideally, medical intervention is aimed at eliminating or modifying ongoing nociception. Urban (1982) reviews some of the promising medical methods to alter nociception, such as nerve blocks and transcutaneous nerve stimulation, or TENS. He notes however, that modification of nociception is typically either impossible or incomplete in patients with chronic pain. Medical treatment should entail close supervision of patients during treatment for medical complications and the management of any concomitant illnesses or recurrent acute pain problems. While pain complaints should not be reinforced, a system for monitoring these complaints is necessary, since even chronic pain patients are susceptible to new acute injuries. New complaints, however, should be handled as unobtrusively and matter-of-factly as possible.

Medication Adjustments

For patients with chronic benign pain, a common objective is to gradually reduce, and eventually eliminate, the use of narcotic analgesics and sedatives in a manner that breaks up the conditioned pattern of medication utilization. The pain cocktail has become the standard technique to reduce and control these medications. Fordyce (1976) describes this procedure in detail. Initially, the patient should be instructed to take their medications on a p.r.n., or a request-contingent basis, as they normally would for a three to four day baseline period. The types and amounts of medication should be carefully recorded during the baseline phase. At the end of the baseline phase, medication administration is shifted over to the staff, and the active ingredients are placed in a cocktail or masking vehicle, which is administered orally. The cocktail is then given on a time-contingent basis with enough medication to match the level utilized during the baseline. The active ingredients are then faded slowly over the course of treatment. The patient is informed prior to the start of this phase that medications will be gradually withdrawn but that he/she will be unaware when actual reductions are made.

It is especially important when altering medications in the elderly to closely monitor them for side effects and to fade medications very gradually. For example, the 71-year-old widowed female previously discussed, experienced severe side effects from medication withdrawal. The patient was discovered one evening to be wandering the hospital hallways, completely disoriented and experiencing marked confusion. Her medications were increased to the initial doses and her symptoms of delirium abated. Successful withdrawal from narcotics without further incidence was then achieved with a slower fading schedule.

During fading with the cocktail, the patient may continue to take other medications not related to their pain condition (i.e., antihypertensive medications, hormones), but should be monitored. Tricyclic antidepressants are also often added because of their beneficial effects on depressive symptomatology. Tricyclics also appear to have analgesic effects in chronic pain patients (Pfeiffer, 1984). Sleep problems which are frequently encountered in chronic pain patients (Wittig, Zorick, Blumer, Heilbronn, & Roth, 1982) also often improve with antidepressant treatment.

Patients with pain associated with progressive, terminal illness have different medication requirements. With such patients, medication addiction is not the primary clinical concern. Relief of pain is the essential goal. The special medication strategies used in cancer and other terminal illness are described in several recent reviews (Payne & Foley, 1984; McGivney & Crooks, 1984). It is note-worthy that Payne and Foley (1984) describe the inclusion of behav-ioral approaches to pain control as "probably the most important advance" in the care of patients with cancer pain (p. 181). Putting medications on a time-contingent, rather than a PRN or pain-contin-gent schedule, has also been recommended for cancer patients, with the goal of preventing pain rather than merely reacting to pain (Car-ron, 1984).

Patients with recurrent acute disorders, such as arthritis, may use medications which either directly affect the disease process, or reduce inflammation and other consequences of the disease. As with chronic benign pain patients, use of narcotics and sedatives are inef-fective and potentially harmful with long-term use and should be carefully monitored if used to control acute flareups. Brooks, Kean, Kassam, and Buchanon (1984) provide a concise review of the use of medications in managing arthritis.

Enhancing Behavioral Functioning

Exercise programs have become a crucial aspect of many pain management programs (Doliber, 1984). Their success in the man-agement of pain appears to be derived from increases in physical conditioning, deconditioning the fears of being active, and pro-viding behavior that is generally incompatible with pain behavior. Muscle weakness and tendon tightness are often seen which contrib-ute, in part, to limited activity. As previously noted, many patients are also fearful of returning to normal activities. Exercise programs are useful for both correcting physical limitations and desensitizing the patient to the fears of being active.

In particular, exercise quota systems have been demonstrated to be an effective means of increasing exercise tolerance and condi-tioning among chronic pain patients (Doleys, Crocker, & Patton, 1982; Fordyce, 1976). Quota systems are characterized by setting specific exercise quotas or goals that the patient is to achieve. As with medication, a baseline phase is utilized where the patient is in-structed to exercise, with an exercise prescribed by a physical thera-pist and/or physician, until weakness, fatigue, or pain causes them to stop. Once a stable baseline level of exercise has been established, the exercises are placed on quotas, and are then gradually raised over the course of treatment. Exercises to be increased are tailored to the individual patient's goals and physical limitations. Because quotas are increased gradually, a therapeutically safe increase in activity level is achieved, which inhibits patients' overexertion on days when they feel good and facilitates performance on problematic days.

Often it is necessary to reassure these patients that these activities are not harmful to their health but will improve it. As part of increasing activities, patients may need education about body mechanics, training in ADL performance with a given disability, or use of functional aids such as splints or walkers.

Besides improving exercise capacity, the patient should be assisted in planning and carrying out increased activity in real-life settings. In particular, programming pleasurable activities which will be reinforcing to the patient, and maintained after treatment are primary goals of treatment. Ideally, patients should be encouraged to increase formerly enjoyable hobbies and activities whenever possible. In other cases, patients may need to consider alternatives to prior activities, such as volunteer work.

Modification of Operant Reinforcement Factors

The objective here is to alter the lifestyle patterns of patients away from that of the chronically disabled. This may entail opening new leisure outlets, changes in vocation, working through retirement issues, and altering patterns of family interaction. In general, it is necessary to establish meaningful activities for each patient. Activities that are rewarding are necessary if healthy behavior is to be reinforced. Team members should be trained to ignore pain behaviors (limping, posturing, verbal complaints) while observing their occurrence during interactions with patients so as to not inadvertently reinforce their occurrence. In addition, staff must catch the patient expressing healthy behaviors (normal gait, smiling, exercising, etc.) and reinforce these behaviors. In addition, each patient's family also needs to be educated to the basic conditioning factors that may occur within a family. Education should specifically point out family patterns of reinforcement for sick behavior and actively teach how to reward well behavior.

For example, the family of the 71-year-old widowed woman described above had to learn to attend to the patient at times other than when she complained of pain. They learned not to ask her about her pain, and not to visit more frequently if she showed pain behavior.

Management of Affective Responses, Cognitions, and Illness Beliefs

Treatment here is tailored to the patient's individual problems and is aimed at teaching more effective coping responses to the affective reaction associated with chronic pain. Many components of treatment are useful in dealing with depression. Antidepressant medication, engagement in pleasurable activities, and challenging patients' depressogenic cognitions may be important.

Teaching cognitive coping skills for the management of pain is also a promising technique. Cognitive coping strategies, such as distraction to aversive stimulation have been studied in the laboratory by a variety of investigators and appear helpful (McCaul & Malott, 1984; Turk et al., 1983).

In addition a variety of studies have shown that cognitive coping techniques (Rybstein-Blinchik, 1979; Varni, 1981) and hypnosis (Hilgard & Hilgard, 1975), can enhance patients' ability to cope with clinical pain. A sense of personal control and the use of ''coping,'' rather than ''catastrophizing'' cognitions appears important in determining an individual's ability to tolerate pain (Turk et al., 1983; Spano, Radtke-Bodorik, Ferguson, & Jones, 1979).

Management of Tension

Relaxation training is beneficial for managing anxiety, excessive muscular tension, sleep problems, and as a coping technique for decreasing the perception of pain (Sanders, 1983). Biofeedback training may also be of benefit for reducing tension, posturing, and muscular-retraining (Dolce & Raczynski, in press; Wolf, Nacht, & Kelley, 1982). At present, data suggest that relaxation training, a relatively simple and inexpensive procedure, is as effective as more sophisticated and expensive biofeedback procedures (Turner & Chapman, 1982a).

Effectiveness of Comprehensive Pain Management Programs

While pain clinics, pain management programs, and hospices leave have become increasingly popular, there is little well-controlled research evaluating the effectiveness of such programs. There are also little or no data available on whether older patients differ from younger patients in their response to such programs. In the only study known to the authors specifically focusing on the response of elderly patients to behavioral pain management, Miller and LeLieuvre (1982) found that four nursing home residents were able to reduce medication intake, pain behavior, and self-reported pain after a short-term program.

The existing data suggest that a number of comprehensive pain management programs are successful in decreasing patients' reported levels of pain, increasing activity levels, and decreasing their reliance on narcotic pain medications (Sere & Newman, 1976; Turner & Chapman, 1982b). However, it is unclear how long-lasting such changes are (Aronoff, Evans, & Enders, 1983; Latimer, 1982). The areas of enhancing generalization of treatment, and relapse prevention, are in need of development (Dolce, 1984). This is especially important because chronic pain disorders are often a lifelong challenge to the patient's ability to cope and maintain the advances made in treatment.

It is also difficult, if not impossible, to evaluate the contribution of different components of these pain management programs to successful treatment. Even if a given pain program is found to be effective, it is difficult to evaluate the relative impact of such components as exercise, family counselling, and medication adjustments. Placebo effects are also likely to be important components of any effective treatment (Shapiro & Morris, 1978).

SUMMARY AND CONCLUSIONS

From the above review, it is apparent that chronic pain is a major clinical problem in the elderly. Clinicians have developed packages of treatments which address pain at multiple levels. However, the application of these approaches to the elderly has been incomplete for a number of reasons. First, the most commonly studied patients in this area have been those with trauma-induced injury with little or no evidence for continued nociception. The difference between management of patients like those from patients with an ongoing metastic and recurrent acute disease processes, who have well-documented, ongoing nociception is unclear. Older patients are far more likely to suffer from these chronic illnesses.

There are little data on several fundamental problems in aging and pain. Although there is some indication that pain sensitivity decreases with aging, this phenomenon has been questioned and deserves further attention. There are also no data known to the authors comparing the efficacy of pain-management procedures with elderly and younger patients. Some age-related differences in coping with pain might be expected, given that health expectations change with aging (Lazarus & Delongis, 1983). Certainly, chronic pain deserves the special attention of clinicians and researchers hoping to improve the quality of life among the elderly.

REFERENCES

Achterberg-Lawlis, J. (1982). The psychological dimensions of arthritis. *Journal of Consulting and Clinical Psychology, 50*(6), 984–992.

Aronoff, G. M., Evans, W. O., & Enders, P. O. (1983). A review of follow-up studies of multidisciplinary pain units. *Pain, 16,* 1–11.

Berlinger, W. G., & Spector, R. (1984). Adverse drug reactions in the elderly. *Geriatrics, 39,* 45–58.

Blumer, D., & Heilbronn, M. (1982). Chronic pain as a variant of depressive disease: The pain prone disorder. *Journal of Nervous and Mental Disease, 170,* 381–406.

Brooks, P. M., Keen, W. F., Kassam, Y., & Buchanon, W. W. (1984). Problems of antiarthritic therapy in the elderly. *Journal of the American Geriatrics Society, 32*(3), 229–234.

Butler, R. N., & Gastel, B. (1979). Care of the aged: Perspectives on pain and discomfort. In L. Nge & J. J. Bonica (Eds.), *Pain, discomfort, and humanitarian care.* New York: Elsevier.

Carron, H. (1984). Rational management of cancer pain. *Urban Health, 5,* 36–38.

Crook, J., Rideout, E., & Browne, G. (1984). The prevalence of pain complaints in a general population. *Pain, 18,* 199–314.

Crue, B. L. (1983). The peripheralist and centralist views of chronic pain. *Seminars in Neurology, 3,* 331–339.

Dolce, J. J. (1984). Pain management: A reaffirmation. *The Behavior Therapist, 7,* 38 & 50.

Dolce, J. J., Doleys, D. M., Raczynski, J. M., & Crocker, M. F. (1985). Narcotic utilization for back pain patients housed in private and semi-private rooms. *Addictive Behaviors, 10,* 91–95.

Dolce, J. J., & Raczynski, J. M. (in press). Neuromuscular activity and electromyography in painful backs: Psychological and biomechanical models in assessment and treatment. *Psychological Bulletin.*

Doleys, D. M., Crocker, M. F., & Patton, D. (1982). Response of patients with chronic pain to exercise quotas. *Physical Therapy, 62,* 1111–1114.

Doliber, C. M. (1984). Role of the physical therapist at pain treatment centers. *Physical Therapy, 64,* 905–909.

Evans, P. J. D. (1981). Narcotic addiction in patients with chronic pain. *Anaesthesia, 36,* 597–602.

Fordyce, W. E. (1978). Evaluating and managing chronic pain. *Geriatrics,* 59–62.

Fordyce, W. E. (1976). *Behavioral methods in chronic pain and illness.* St. Louis: C. V. Mosby.

Fordyce, W. E., Shelton, J. L., & Dundore, D. E. (1982). The modification of avoidance learning pain behaviors. *Journal of Behavioral Medicine, 5,* 405–415.

Gurland, B. J., & Cross, P. S. (1982). Epidemiology of psychopathology in old age. *Psychiatric Clinics of North America, 5*(1), 11–26.

Haley, W. E. (1983). Priorities for behavioral intervention with nursing home residents: Nursing staff's perspective. *International Journal of Behavioral Geriatrics, 1*(4), 47–51.

Harkins, S. W., Kwentus, J., & Price, D. D. (1984). Pain and the elderly. In C. Benedetti (Ed.), *Advances in pain therapy and research: vol. 7* (pp. 103–121). New York: Raven Press.

Hilgard, E. K., & Hilgard, J. K. (1975). *Hypnosis in the relief of pain.* Los Altos, CA: William Kaufman, Inc.

Katon, W., & Kleinman, A. (1982). Depression and somatization: A review. Part I. *American Journal of Medicine, 72,* 127–135.

Keefe, F. J. (1982). Behavioral assessment and treatment of chronic pain: Current status and future directions. *Journal of Consulting and Clinical Psychology, 50,* 896–911.

Kraus, H. (1965). *Backache, stress and tension: Cause, prevention and treatment.* New York: Simon and Schuster.

Latimer, P. (1982). External contingency management for chronic pain: Critical review of the evidence. *American Journal of Psychiatry, 139,* 1308–1312.

Lazarus, R. S., & Delongis, A. (1983). Psychological stress and coping in aging. *American Psychologist, 38*(3), 245–254.

Loeser, J. D. (1980). Perspectives on pain. *Proceedings of the First World Conference on Clinical Pharmacology and Therapeutics,* pp. 313–316. London: Macmillan.

McCaul, K. D., & Malott, J. M. (1984). Distraction and coping with pain. *Psychological Bulletin, 95*(3), 516–533.

Melzack, R. (1975). The McGill Pain Questionnaire: Major properties and scoring methods. *Pain, 1,* 277–299.

Melzack, R., & Wall, P. D. (1983). *The challenge of pain.* New York: Basic Books.

McGivney, W. T., & Crooks, G. M. (1984). The care of patients with severe chronic pain in terminal illness. *Journal of the American Medical Association, 251*(9), 1182–1188.

McNairy, S. L., Maruta, T., Ivnik, R. J., Swanson, D. W., & Ilstrup, D. M. (1984). Prescription medication dependence and neuropsychological function. *Pain, 18,* 169–177.

Miller, R. B., & LeLieuvre, R. B. (1982). A method to reduce chronic pain in elderly nursing home residents. *The Gerontologist, 22*(3), 314–317.

Payne, R., & Foley, K. M. (1984). Advances in the management of cancer pain. *Cancer Treatment Reports, 68*(1), 173–183.

Pfeiffer, R. F. (1984). Drugs for pain in the elderly. *Geriatrics, 37,* 67–76.

Rowe, J. W., & Besdine, R. W. (Eds.). (1982). *Health and disease in old age.* Boston: Little, Brown & Co.

Rubenstein, L. Z., & Robbins, A. S. (1984). Fall in the elderly: A clinical perspective. *Geriatrics, 39,* 67–78.

Rybstein-Blinchik, E. (1979). Effects of different cognitive strategies on chronic pain experience. *Journal of Behavioral Medicine, 2*(1), 93–101.

Seres, J. L., & Newman, R. I. (1976). Results of treatment of chronic low back pain at the Portland Pain Center. *Journal of Neurosurgery, 45,* 32–36.

Shapiro, A. K., & Morris, L. A. (1978). The placebo effect in medical and psychological therapies. In S. L. Garfield & A. E. Bergin (Eds.), *Handbook of psychiatherapy and behavior change: An empirical analysis* (pp. 369–410). New York: John Wiley.

Skelton, J. A., & Pennebaker, J. W. (1982). The psychology of physical symptoms and sensations. In G. S. Sanders & J. Suls (Eds.), *Social psychology of health and illness* (pp. 99–128). Hillsdale, NJ: Lawrence Erlbaum.

Spanos, N. P., Radtke-Bodorik, H. L., Ferguson, J. D., & Jones, B. (1979). The effects of hypnotic susceptibility, suggestions for analgesia, and the utilization of cognitive strategies on the reduction of pain. *Journal of Abnormal Psychology, 88,* 282–292.

Turk, D. C., & Rennert, K. S. (1981). Pain and the terminally-ill cancer patient: A cognitive-social learning approach. In H. Sobel (Ed.), *Behavior therapy in terminal care: A humanistic approach* (pp. 95–124). Cambridge, MA: Ballinger.

Turk, D. C., Meichenbaum, D., & Genest, M. (1983). *Pain and behavioral medicine: A cognitive-behavioral perspective.* New York: Guilford.

Turner, J. A., & Chapman, C. R. (1982a). Psychological interventions for chronic pain: A critical review. I. Relaxation training and biofeedback. *Pain, 12,* 1–21.

Turner, J. A., & Chapman, C. R. (1982b). Psychological interventions for chronic pain: A critical review. II. Operant conditioning, hypnosis, and cognitive-behavioral therapy. *Pain, 12,* 23–46.

Urban, B. J. (1982). Therapeutic aspects in chronic pain: Modulation of nociception, alleviation of suffering, and behavioral analysis. *Behavior Therapy, 13,* 430–437.

Varni, J. W. (1981). Self-regulation techniques in the management of chronic arthritic pain in hemophilia. *Behavior Therapy, 12,* 185–194.

Wisenburg, M. (1977). Pain and pain control. *Psychological Bulletin, 84,* 1008–1044.

Wittig, R. M., Zorick, F. J., Blumer, D., Heilbronn, M., & Roth, T., (1982). Disturbed sleep in patients complaining of chronic pain. *The Journal of Nervous and Mental Disease, 170,* 429–431.

Wolf, S. L., Nacht, M., & Kelly, J. L. (1982). EMG feedback training during dynamic movement for low back pain patients. *Behavior Therapy, 13,* 395–406.

Wolf, S. L., Basmajian, J. V., Russe, C. T. C., & Kutner, M. (1979). Normative data on low back mobility and activity levels: Implications for neuromuscular reeducation. *American Journal of Physical Medicine, 58,* 217–229.

Questions

1) To what extent could the exaggeration of pain be due to personality and/or situational factors?

2) Which of the approaches described by the authors is best for pain control?

26/CLINICAL APPLICATION OF BIOFEEDBACK TECHNIQUES FOR THE ELDERLY

Amos Zeichner, PhD
Judith A. Boczkowski, PhD

Editor's Introduction

Because elders have increased sensitivity to many medications, and because polypharmacology means that there are compound risks for harmful interactions, nonpharmacological approaches must be pursued whenever possible. Biofeedback approaches offer the promise of decreasing reliance on purely pharmacological means.

Zeichner and Boczkowski review basic biofeedback applications (e.g., heartrate, muscle tension) and discuss applications for elders (stress, anxiety, cardiovascular, incontinence, arthritis, dermatitis, CVA).

CG previously reported on the use of biofeedback in the case of arthritis (v. 2, #3, pp. 39–46) and an alcoholic complaining of tension and insomnia (v. 1, #2, pp. 72–73).

A recent report published by the National Institute on Aging (National Institute on Aging, 1983) estimated that about 26 million Americans who are over the age of 65 account for 29% of the nation's health care costs, use 25% of prescription drugs, make 15% of all physician's office visits, account for 34% of all days in short-stay hospitals, and comprise 87% of nursing homes residents. Clearly, these figures represent the dire need of the elderly health service consumer to be helped in his/her fight against the all too often experienced decrements of the aging process. One major

Amos Zeichner is at the Psychology Department, University of Georgia, Athens, GA 30602. Judith A. Boczkowski is at the Psychology Department, University of Notre Dame, Notre Dame, IN 46556.

457

cause for the deterioration of the elderly's quality of life is the development and maintenance of chronic physical disorders in later life. Conditions such as incontinence, both urinary and fecal, hypertension, cardiac arrhythmia, arthritis, chronic pain, sleep disorders, eczematious dermatitis, and various physical impairments following stroke, are only some of the maladies requiring specific attention in the elderly.

The disorders listed above clearly are not exclusively "disorders of old age." All these conditions are diagnosed in all ages commonly with the exclusion of the very young. In all cases, medical interventions such as medication, physical therapy, or surgery would be considered and undertaken, generally with a reasonable degree of success. However, special considerations are indicated when the patient is in his/her later years and, as is often the case, in frail health. As the statistics mentioned above suggest, the elderly patient will, in all likelihood, be on some medication regimen. The use of further medication to combat yet another ailment may create the problem of hazardous drug interaction or will result in a situation where one drug will render the other ineffective. Relatedly, as the complexity of the regimen increases, the level of medication compliance in the elderly decreases. Further, it is widely accepted that the elderly person is a poor surgery risk. A suppressed immune system or the presence of other risk factors may eliminate surgery as an option. Therefore, physicians would elect not to go the surgical route with an older patient when other options are available.

Psychologically based interventions have emerged over the past three decades as useful adjuncts to medical regimens or, in some cases, as separately used therapeutic approaches. Among the psychological interventions used with young and old patients suffering from physical disorders are progressive muscle relaxation (Alexander, Cropp, & Chai, 1979), autogenic training (Keefe, Surwit, & Pilon, 1980), hypnosis (Melzack & Perry, 1975), biofeedback (Gannon & Sternbach, 1971), cognitive retraining (Ben-Yishay & Diller, 1973), contingency management (Fordyce, Fowler, Lehmann, DeLateur, Sand, & Trieschmann, 1973) stress management (Roskies, 1983), and systematic desensitization (Moore, 1965). All these techniques have been used with varying degrees of success. The purpose of this paper is to address one of these approaches, specifically biofeedback, that has been used in the treatment of the elderly. Prior to discussing biofeedback applications specific to the elderly, a cursory review of general biofeedback application is presented. Methodological problems and recommendations are discussed in the conclusions.

GENERAL BIOFEEDBACK APPLICATIONS

The most widely accepted definition of biofeedback is a technique by which an individual is presented with auditory and/or visual information regarding ongoing internal physiological events. The technique is used to teach a person to manipulate these usually involuntary events by means of mediating cognitive processes (Basmajian, 1979). Systematic clinical use of biofeedback as an intervention began with Marinacci and Horande (1960) who used EMG feedback to retrain neuromuscular control in patients with neurological dysfunctions. Stroke patients were treated with EMG feedback to relearn how to flex affected extremities (Andrews, 1964). The use of EMG biofeedback with stroke patients and resulting neuromuscular problems, a condition quite prevalent in older populations, became widespread in the 1970s (Brudny, Grynbaum, & Korein, 1973; Basmajian, Kukulka, Narayan, & Takebe, 1975; Johnson & Garton, 1973).

Before long, it became apparent to researchers and clinicians alike that the EMG feedback technique can be applied in two general approaches. As in the cases cited above, patients are given feedback regarding muscle activity in a symptom-specific muscle group with the goal of effecting change in that muscle group (e.g., reduce pain, increase control). A second approach borrows from the general relaxation training approaches developed by Jacobson (1942) and Benson, Beary, and Carol (1974) applying the biofeedback technique as a nonspecific intervention (i.e., symptom-irrelevant site) to effect a general relaxation response and a reduction of autonomic arousal in the patient. In the treatment of tension headaches, for example, EMG feedback was initially used to induce a general body relaxation for pain relief (Budzynski, Stoyva, Adler, & Mullaney, 1973). Further, EMG feedback is extensively used for the treatment of anxiety (Gatchel, 1982).

Other clinical biofeedback techniques that have been developed include peripheral blood flow, skin temperature, EEG, heart rate, blood pressure, gastric motility, respiration, electrodermal response, sphincter activity, and others. Peripheral blood flow and skin temperature feedback is administered with the goal of increasing or decreasing blood flow in a specific peripheral site. Skin temperature is conceptualized as an indirect index of the amount of blood flow in a given region at a given time. Both these feedback modalities are used, among others, in the treatment of migraine headache (Adams, Feuerstein, & Fowler, 1980). EEG feedback, where the patient is receiving feedback of various brain wave patterns has been successfully used with patients suffering from epilepsy (Lubar, 1982) and from stress and anxiety (Papsdorf, Ghannam, Kuzma, & Jamieson, 1979). Heart rate and blood pressure feedback is utilized, among other techniques, in work with healthy individuals who are at risk for developing cardiovascular disease and with cardiac patients who suffer from angina pectoris, cardiac arrhythmia (Blecker & Engel, 1973), or those who evidence hypertension (Elder & Eustis, 1975). The common goal in these treatments is to teach patients to control their blood pressure and heart rate and to maintain these indices within normal ranges. Incontinent patients with difficulties maintaining sufficient sphincter control are helped with feedback of the sphincteric response at the rectal and bladder sphincters (Cerulli, Nikoomanesh, & Schuster, 1976; Schuster, 1979). Similarly, patients with reflex esophagitis receive feedback of their gastrointestinal motility and lower esophageal sphincter activity (Schuster, 1979). Feedback of the electrodermal response is used in the assessment and treatment of patients in phobic and anxiety states with the goal of teaching the patients to reduce the level of their general autonomic arousal (Lader, 1967).

As is evident from the cited literature, numerous biofeedback techniques have permeated equally numerous types of patient populations. Although the biofeedback techniques have a common goal (i.e., to teach patients to control specific bodily processes), they differ significantly from each other in application methodology. The instrumentation used in biofeedback interventions for the elderly are reviewed next.

APPLICATIONS FOR THE ELDERLY

A careful review of the biofeedback literature and the published clinical data pertinent to the treatment of the elderly reveals the surprising fact that despite the pervasiveness of the use of biofeedback in the general population, very little is written about the use of this intervention with the elderly. Two types of pertinent published material exist; one consists of reports regarding the use of a biofeedback technique for a specific disorder or complaint where some of (or all) the patients are elderly, the other includes reports of biofeedback techniques specifically used with an elderly patient or population. Consequently, to make the most of the literature, the clinician interested in the use of biofeedback with the elderly should carefully examine the characteristics of the subjects discussed in various reports. Clinical conditions in which biofeedback treatment was used with the elderly are discussed below.

Stress and Anxiety

Sources of stress and anxiety in the life of the aging adult abound. Difficulty to accept the onset of old age, poor adjustment to retirement, onset of various physical dysfunctions, loss of spouse, and adjustment to new environments (e.g., move to a nursing home) are only a few examples of likely stressors. One biofeedback technique that has been used to ameliorate stress and anxiety conditions is training in EEG alpha activity. When a person is relaxed but not drowsy, the cortex emits a brain wave that, when graphically displayed, appears to oscillate relatively smoothly at a frequency commonly between 8Hz and 13 Hz. The recording of this "alpha rhythm" is done by a pen and chart oscillograph (e.g., the polygraph series 7, Grass Instruments, Quincy, Massachusetts) that is fitted with a auditory feedback signal device. Two small silver/silver chloride electrodes that are attached to the scalp immediately over the occipital lobes provide the EEG alpha signal. Commonly, a tone is presented to the patients contingent on the production of a brain-wave pattern in a selected frequency range.

In a study of 36 subjects between the ages of 65 and 75 years, Brannon (1976) established the effects of EEG alpha activity feedback on self-reported anxiety, level of autonomic arousal (via basal skin resistance), and functioning on a cognitive task. Three groups of subjects received tone feedback contingent of alpha rhythm, fake feedback (i.e., noncontingent tones), or feedback plus specific instructions how to relax and achieve alpha waves. Only the group that received feedback with instructions evidenced an increase in alpha activity over the treatment period, a reduction in self-reported anxiety and autonomic arousal, and an increase in cognitive test scores. Evidently, specific instructions were a crucial ingredient in the effectiveness of biofeedback in this case.

Another study (West, 1978) investigated the effects of EMG biofeedback plus muscle relaxation and relaxation alone on psychophysical manifestations of stress in the elderly (e.g., depression, anger, fatigue, headaches, sleep disturbances, pains, blood pressure). Forty-one volunteer residents of a nursing and retirement home (mean age, 80.6 years) received a six-week relaxation or biofeedback plus relaxation treatment program. Results indicated that both treatment groups improved their psychophysical status with the biofeedback plus relaxation group evidencing a greater improvement in anger, depression, confusion, and headaches. No other differential intervention effects were reported in this study. Similarly, in a case study of a 64-year-old woman (Tauber, 1983) frontalis EMG and GSR feedback were used to treat insomnia, neck pain, and bruxism. All symptoms were 90% reduced after a series of seven feedback plus relaxation sessions.

To combat depressive and psychophysiological symptomatology in older adults, Nadler (1978) tested a biofeedback and relaxation program. The intervention consisted of hand temperature feedback administered in conjunction with relaxation training. The techniques' goal was to induce a general state of relaxation and facilitate peripheral vasodilation thought to increase a sense of well-being and decrease physical symptomatology. The participants who were between the ages of 61 and 85 years received 10 training sessions over a five-week period. After learning to successfully relax and increase hand temperature (increases ranged 0.8–4.8 degrees Fahrenheit), participants evidenced improvement on physiological symptomatology and sense of well-being as assessed via questionnaires. A statistically nonsignificant decrease in depressive symptoms was also noted. Although these results seem to reflect the efficacy of temperature biofeedback in the treatment of depressive and physical symptoms, clearly, the concomitant use of relaxation and questionnaire assessment of dependent measures make drawing of unequivocal conclusions impossible.

Cardiac Arrhythmia

Cardiac arrhythmia is a condition of dysfunctional electrical impulse formation or conductance in the heart muscle. The clinical concomitants of this condition include abnormally slow or fast heart rate, arrhythmical heart muscle contractions, and disordered contractions of the heart chambers. The most common arrhythmia is premature ventricular contraction (PVC) which carries an expected death rate of 8 per 1000 or 43 per 1000 when the patient also has cardiovascular heart disease (Singer & Levinson, 1976). Although this condition can occur at any age, its occurrence frequency increases after the age of 50 (Corday & Irving, 1962). Emotional disorders such as acute anxiety, anger, or fear are thought to contribute to the development of cardiac arrhythmias via enhanced sympathetic activity.

Weiss and Engel (1971) report a series of case studies in which operant conditioning was used in the treatment of PVC in older adults. The program's goal was to teach patients to control their heart rate. The heart rate signal was monitored via a Beckman-Offner cardiotachometer and fed into a feedback device that consisted of three colored light bulbs. A lit red light indicated to the patient that his heart rate was too fast and was to be slowed down; a green light indicated the reverse; a yellow light was the reinforcer indicating that the desired heart rate was being maintained. The treated patients included individuals aged 52, 68, 73, and 60 years with medical histories of myocardial infarctions, congestive heart failure, and current PVC. Each patient received approximately 40–50 eighty-minute conditioning sessions during which he learned to increase and decrease his heart rate. Weiss and Engel report that patients who learned to control their heart rate also succeeded in controlling their PVCs. The diminished PVC rate generalized to ward and home situations. However, severe rates of PVCs, difficulty to produce mental imagery to aid in cardiac control, and a low level of motivation are some of the factors that may limit the effectiveness of this intervention.

It would seem important to reiterate at this point that other biofeedback techniques have been used to diminish cardiovascular disease risk. For example, Engel and colleagues (Engel, Gaardner, & Glasgow, 1981; Engel, Glasgow, & Gaardner, 1983) have used systolic blood pressure feedback in the treatment of essential hypertension. However, since treated were patients with a mean age of 49 years (with no standard deviation given), these studies will not be reviewed here.

Fecal and Urinary Incontinence

Incontinence is one of the most prevalent disabilities that plague residents of nursing homes. Approximately 55% of this population evidence chronic urinary incontinence, while 25% are fecally incontinent. Understandably, these disabilities cause despondency and social withdrawal in the afflicted. Ehrman (1983) notes that several factors are likely to increase the likelihood of incontinence. These

include: physical disability hindering sphincteric control, senile dementia causing, among others, to disattend to bowel and bladder cues
and disregard for social consequences of incontinence, and possible
psychological mediating factors, such as anxiety and depression,
that may be linked to the disorder. It should be noted, however, that
incontinence is not an ailment restricted to the elderly.

Engel (1979) reports on the use of biofeedback with the incontinent ranging in age from 6 to 96 with varied histories of fecal incontinence. The diagnosed problems are defined as low or nonexistent
contraction of the internal and external anal sphincters in response
to a distension of the rectum resulting from stool movement. The
goal of treatment is to restore continence in the patients via learning
to coordinate sphincteric contraction.

The biofeedback instrument consists of three balloons that are inserted into the patient's anus. One balloon is inserted into the rectum
(to stimulate stool pressure), one to the internal sphincter, and one
to the external sphincter. The air pressure in the blood activates a
pen and chart recorder that provides the visual feedback to the patient. During few biofeedback sessions that are each comprised of
approximately 50 trials, the patient is able to successfully learn how
to respond to a brief distension of his/her rectum by relaxing the internal sphincter and concomitantly with constricting the external
sphincter. Alternating biofeedback trials with trials where the patient is not given any external cues is an important step in the technique as the patient has to learn to respond to internal cues alone. To
date, clinics reporting on the use of this technique have described
commendable rates of success (Cerulli, Nikoomanesh, & Schuster,
1979; Engel, Nikoomanesh, & Schuster, 1974).

The treatment of urinary incontinence uses similar principles to
those applied in fecal incontinence (Cardozo, Stanton, Hafner, &
Allan, 1978). The bladder of the incontinent patient is catheterized
and filled with water. Muscle contraction sensing devices (strain
gauges) are providing feedback of bladder and sphincter muscle activity.[1] The patient has to learn how to tolerate large quantities of
water in his/her bladder (300–350 ml). Success rates of this technique have reached 75% reduction in incontinence incidents in 80%
of the treated patients (Ehrman, 1983).

Rheumatoid Arthritis

Approximately five million Americans are affected by rheumatoid arthritis, a chronic condition of pain and disability of unknown

etiology and precipitating cause (Arthritis Foundation, 1976). While at least half the patient population suffering from arthritis are age 50 or older, the diminishing level of immunocompetence occurring at old age is thought to be associated with the accelerated course of rheumatoid arthritis in the elderly. Whereas the common treatment for arthritis are antiinflammatory, some undesirable side effects such as ulcers, cataracts, and kidney damage have motivated clinicians to search for other interventions.

In a study of EMG activity in muscles next to arthritic joints, Wasserman and colleagues (1968) noted abnormally elevated activity he thought to be indicative of muscle contractions aimed at immobilizing the painful joint. These contractions can also reduce the blood supply to the affected area and produce irritants to nerve endings at the joint site. Consequently, hand temperature feedback to increase blood flow in arthritic hands (Denver, Laveault, Girard, Lacourciene, Latulippe, Grove, Prive, & Dorion, 1979) and joint temperature as a concomitant index of pain reduction (Varni, 1981) are new techniques recently used with arthritics.

In a case study of an 80-year-old woman with a 50-year history of arthritic pain (Boczkowski, 1984) blood volume pulse (BVP) and EMG feedback were used in the treatment of pain. Auditory feedback was given contingent on a decrease in muscle contraction for the EMG condition or an increase in dilation for the BVP condition. Six EMG feedback sessions over a four-week period were followed by eight BVP feedback sessions over a four-week period. Home exercises were assigned and dependent measures were taken at six and 12 months follow-up contacts. While the patient learned to reduce her hand EMG activity by 42% during sessions, no control over BVP was noted. At end of EMG training, the patient evidenced a 71% reduction in pain occurrences, a 50% reduction in medication intake, and a slight improvement of grip strength in the affected joints.

Another study (Noda, 1978) investigated the effects of EMG and temperature feedback training in the treatment of rheumatoid arthritic patients aged 45 to 68 years. Patients received either EMG or temperature feedback or both these techniques combined via electrodes and thermistors placed on the cervical muscle. Treatment consisted of eight biweekly sessions each with 12 two-minute training periods. Results indicated that only the patients receiving the combined feedback treatment were able to increase their grip strength. Most patients in the single feedback groups failed to learn to control EMG or temperature.

The studies reporting on the use of biofeedback in the treatment of the arthritic to date seem to suggest that a moderate degree of success can be expected from the intervention. However, it would also seem that the paucity of knowledge regarding the mechanism of arthritis interacts with the yet to be identified active ingredient of biofeedback. This results in only partial symptomatic relief in some of the treated patients.

Eczematous Dermatitis

Symptoms of dermatitis have been associated with reduced peripheral blood supply in the affected areas of the skin. This condition can be expected to occur when the patient evidences peripheral vasoconstriction mediated by the sympathetic branch of the autonomous nervous system under conditions of chronic stress.

To relieve the condition of diminished blood flow in the skin, areas affected by dermatitis hand warming and temperature feedback have been applied successfully. Manuso (1977) reports a case study of a 60-year-old female with a six-year history of chronic eczematous dermatitis of the hands. Skin dryness, lesions, and discoloration were some of the symptoms she evidenced. Although no organic precipitant was identified she was initially treated with antihistamines, corticosteroids, vitamins, and tranquilizers. None of these treatments was effective. Behavioral treatment initiated at that point consisted of twice daily 15-minute relaxation exercises as well as weekly biofeedback sessions designed to teach the patient to increase hand temperature via digital temperature feedback. Feedback was given in the form of auditory signals presented at a frequency contingent on hand temperature. Results indicated that during the 17-week program the patient successfully learned to raise her hand temperature. The dermatitis progressively remitted, skin dryness and scaling became minimal, and lesions disappeared. At six months follow-up the patient evidenced a dermatitis-free state.

Neuromuscular Disorders

Estimates of neurological dysfunction cases in the U.S. put the number at over 10 million (National Institutes of Health, 1976). With a yearly incidence of 400,000, stroke becomes one of the major causes for chronic neuromuscular dysfunctions. To aid in the muscular rehabilitation of stroke patients, EMG feedback is emerging as one of the most promising and least invasive, yet inexpensive, interventions (Brudny, 1982). Although individuals at all ages can experience a cerebrovascular accident (CVA), the population segment most likely to be at high risk are the elderly.

EMG feedback has been used with CVA patients among the elderly in an attempt to improve several neuromuscular dysfunctions such as foot drop, ankle dorsiflexion, wrist extension, and hand grasp. Basmajian and his colleagues undertook extensive treatment and experimentation with EMG biofeedback in the treatment of post-stroke patients (Basmajian, Kukulka, Narayan, & Takebe, 1975; Basmajian, Regenos, & Baker, 1977). Their patients experienced a CVA at least three months prior to treatment and evidenced a residual foot dorsiflexion paresis. Patients were between 30 and 63 years of age. Patients who received biofeedback training also received traditional physical therapy. EMG feedback training consisted of 20-minute training sessions in which the patients received auditory and visual EMG feedback of their ankle muscle activity during flexion. The patient was to increase his/her EMG activity by increasing the demand for feedback production (by adjusting the feedback equipment's threshold). Results indicated marked improvements in gait, foot drop, and muscle strength in the previously paretic ankle. These improvements were maintained at three month follow-up. Interestingly, the effectiveness of the treatment did not appear to be related to the patients' age.

Treatment of a hemiplegic patient with EMG biofeedback is reported by Nafpliotis (1976). A 61-year-old male suffered a CVA which resulted in right hemiplegia and mild aphasia where the patient lost the functional use of his upper and lower limbs. EMG feedback sessions lasting two and one-half months, were administered twice weekly for one and one-half hours, utilized a visual feedback device (i.e., voltmeter) that recorded the EMG. Following the treatment regimen, muscle control proved functional for walking, handwriting, and daily self-care activities.

EMG feedback was also used with hemiparetic stroke patients who required retraining of the wrist extensors and biceps muscles (Mroczek, Halpern, & McHugh, 1978). Patients' age ranged 50 to 75. Whereas half the patients received physical therapy followed by EMG biofeedback, the remaining patients received treatment in the reversed order. Volume-modulated auditory feedback was given via a loudspeaker and visual feedback was given by displaying a rising and falling dot on a 19″ oscilloscope screen. Although results showed increased EMG activity in affected muscles, no significant functional use increase was noted. No significant efficacy differences were found between the two treatment approaches.

Finally, the use of EMG biofeedback in the treatment of stroke patients raises the question to what degree do specific patient characteristics (e.g., sex, age, hemiparetic side) play a role in the effectiveness of the intervention. In an attempt to partially answer this question, Wolf, Baker, and Kelly (1979) treated 48 upper and 44 lower extremities of 52 stroke patients using EMG biofeedback by similar procedures to those described above. Age, sex hemiparetic side, duration of stroke or previous rehabilitation, and number of biofeedback training sessions had no relationship to treatment outcome. Lower extremities responded more favorably to treatment than upper limbs. However, the authors cite the presence of proprioceptive impairment, aphasia, and low motivational level as factors that further diminished success with upper extremities. Clearly, these factors, among others, are to be considered prior to treatment selection for this patient population.

CONCLUSIONS

This review attempted to selectively present studies reporting on the use of biofeedback techniques with the elderly and to provide the interested clinician with an updated appraisal of the techniques' efficacy. Several issues are raised by the state of the art. Biofeedback appears to be a most welcome addition to the intervention arsenal of the clinician. As mentioned earlier, numerous conditions exist when the elderly patient cannot benefit from the more traditional medical interventions. Not only, however, are the contraindications of a medical nature. Often there is a reluctance on the part of the patient to be treated by invasive and unpleasant methods. Biofeedback presents a desirable and, at times, a more effective alternative.

In spite of the encouraging results of the interventions reported in this review, the degree of biofeedback's efficacy as a treatment for the elderly remains unclear. Although most studies report a general level of effectiveness for the utilized techniques, the success rate is not always uniform. In every sample of patients one can find cases where self-control over physiological processes was not achieved. Furthermore, several studies comparing biofeedback to other interventions reported no significant efficacy differences among the different approaches. This raises the question whether any of the elderly have specific difficulties mastering self-control skills thereby rendering biofeedback effective only for a select group among older adults.

Physiological and psychological changes associated with the aging process ought to be considered by the clinician as they may mediate the outcome of the biofeedback application. Decrements in visual and auditory acuity may cause direct interference. Slowing of perceptual speed may interfere with the patient's processing of biofeedback information (Walsh, Till, & Williams, 1978). Diminishing level of energy in some older adults can hamper the progress and success of the rather demanding and numerous biofeedback training sessions. Further, specific physical conditions such as cardiopulmonary insufficiency may interfere with biofeedback via their contribution to the deterioration of cognitive functioning in the elderly (Hertzog, Schaie, & Gribbin, 1978; Libow, 1977). Also, the conditioning of physiological responses to specific stimuli (e.g., environmental cues) aimed at generalizing the effects of biofeedback proves to be increasingly difficult with old age (Botwinick & Kornetzky, 1960).

With old age the use of prescription drugs increases. Many elderly persons have been known to either abuse medications or suffer from the adverse effects of polypharmacy, or interactive effects of drugs. This condition has been reported to cause behavioral destabilization and impaired functioning in the patient. Depression and pessimism, whether due to drug action or adjustment difficulty to the aging process, will interfere with the learning process required in the biofeedback intervention. Finally, the high rate of noncompliance evidenced by the elderly (Boczkowski & Zeichner, in press) may yet prove to be an additional factor in the limitation of this intervention.

Regardless of its limitations, biofeedback is an intervention that has helped many older adults to improve their lot. The advantages and promise that biofeedback holds for this population will continue to enlarge the circle of clinicians offering it to their clients. This situation calls for a much needed improvement in the reports on the use of the technique with the elderly. Since it is patently clear that no uniformity can be achieved in the instrumentation, instruction, and procedures used in the application of biofeedback to a given disorder, professionals should work toward standardizing their reporting. Published studies that do not report information such as patient age and physical condition, transducer placement, monitored physiological values, feedback modality, or clear outcome measures, stand the risk of contributing little to the accumulating knowledge. Effective communication among clinicians administering biofeedback to the elderly would help in utilizing the technique to its fullest potential.

NOTE

1. A video-taped demonstration of a behavioral analysis of incontinence, biofeedback procedure, and instruction to the client how to practice self-control skills can be obtained by writing to Dr. Kathryn L. Burgio, Gerontology Research Center, Baltimore City Hospitals, 4940 Eastern Ave., Baltimore, MD 21224.

REFERENCES

Adams, H. E., Feuerstein, M., & Fowler, J. L. (1980). The migraine headache: A review of parameters, theories, and interventions. *Psychological Bulletin, 87,* 217–237.

Adrian, E. D., & Bronk, D. W. (1929). The discharge of impulses in motor nerve fibers. Part II. The frequency of discharge in reflex and voluntary contractions. *Journal of Physiology, 67,* 119–151.

Alexander, A. B., Cropp, G. J. A., & Chai, H. (1979). The effects of relaxation training on pulmonary mechanisms in children with asthma. *Journal of Applied Behavior Analysis, 12,* 27–35.

Andrews, J. M. (1964). Neuromuscular re-education of hemiplegic with aid of electromyograph. *Archives of Physical and Medical Rehabilitation, 45,* 530–532.

Arthritis Foundation. (1976). *Arthritis: The basic facts.* New York.

Basmajian, J. V. (1979). Introduction: Principles and background. In. J. V. Basmajian (Ed.), *Biofeedback: Principles and practice for clinicians.* Baltimore: The Williams & Wilkins Co.

Basmajian, J. V., Kukulka, C. G., Narayan, M. G., & Takebe, K. (1975). Biofeedback treatment of foot-drop after stroke compared with standard rehabilitation technique: Effects on voluntary control and strength. *Archives of Physical Medicine and Rehabilitation, 56,* 231–236.

Basmajian, J. V., Regenos, E. M., & Baker, M. P. (1977). Rehabilitating stroke patients with biofeedback. *Geriatrics, 32,* 85–88.

Benson, H., Beary, J. B., & Carol, M. (1974). The relaxation response. *Psychiatry, 37,* 37–46.

Ben-Yishay, Y., & Diller, L. (1973). Changing of atmospheric environment to improve mental and behavioral function: Application in treatment of senescence. *New York State Journal of Medicine, 73,* 2877–2880.

Blecker, E. R., & Engel, B. T. (1973). Learned control of ventricular rate in patients with atreal fibrillation. *Psychosomatic Medicine, 35,* 161–175.

Boczkowski, J. A. (1984). Biofeedback training for the treatment of chronic pain in an elderly arthritic female. *Clinical Gerontologist, 2,* 39–46.

Boczkowski, J. A., & Zeichner, A. (in press). Medication compliance and the elderly. *Clinical Gerontologist.*

Botwinick, J., & Kornetzky, C. (1960). Age differences in the acquisition and extinction of the GSR. *Journal of Gerontology, 15*, 83–84.

Brannon, L. J. (1976). The effects of biofeedback training of EEG alpha activity on the psychological functioning of the elderly (Doctoral dissertation, Pennsylvania State University, 1976). *Dissertation Abstracts International, 37*, 5875B.

Brudny, J. (1982). Biofeedback in chronic neurological cases: Therapeutic electromyography. In L. White & B. Tursky (Eds.), *Clinical biofeedback: Efficacy and mechanisms*. New York: The Guilford Press.

Brudny, J., Grynbaum, B. B., & Korein, J. (1973). Spasmodic torticollis: Treatment by feedback display of EMG. *Archives of Physical and Medical Rehabilitation, 55*, 403–408.

Budzynski, T. H., Stoyva, J. M., Adler, C. S., & Mullaney, D. J. (1973). EMG biofeedback and tension headache: A controlled outcome study. *Psychosomatic Medicine, 35*, 484–496.

Cardozo, L., Stanton, S. L., Hafner, J., & Allan, V. (1978). Biofeedback in the treatment of detrusor instability. *British Journal of Urology, 50*, 250–254.

Cerulli, M., Nikoomanesh, P., & Schuster, M. M. (1976). Progress in biofeedback treatment of fecal incontinence. *Gastroenterology, 70*, 869.

Cerulli, M., Nikoomanesh, P., & Schuster, M. M. (1979). Progress in biofeedback conditioning for fecal incontinence. *Gastroenterology, 76*, 742–746.

Corday, E., & Irving, D. W. (1962). *Disturbance of heart rate, rhythm, and conduction*. Philadelphia: W. B. Saunders Co.

Denver, D. R., Laveault, D., Girard, F., Lacourciere, Y., Latulippe, L., Grove, R. N., Prive, M., & Dorion, N. (1979). Behavioral medicine: Biobehavioral effects of short-term thermal biofeedback and relaxation in rheumatoid arthritic patients. *Biofeedback and Self Regulation, 4*, 245–246.

Ehrman, J. S. (1983). Use of biofeedback to treat incontinence. *Journal of the American Geriatric Society, 31*, 182–184.

Elder, S. T., & Eustis, N. K. (1975). Instrumental blood pressure conditioning in outpatients essential hypertensives. *Behavior Research and Therapy, 13*, 185–188.

Engel, B. T. (1979). *Using biofeedback with the elderly*. Washington, D.C.: National Institutes of Health, Publication No. 79-1404.

Engel, B. T., Gaardner, K. R., & Glasgow, M. S. (1981). Behavioral treatment of high blood pressure: I. Analysis of intra- and interdaily variations of blood pressure during one-month baseline period. *Psychosomatic Medicine, 43*, 255–270.

Engel, B. T., Glasgow, M. S., & Gaardner, K. R. (1983). Behavioral treatment of high blood pressure: III. Follow-up results and treatment recommendations. *Psychosomatic Medicine, 45*, 23–29.

Engel, B. T., Nikoomanesh, P., & Schuster, M. M. (1974). Operant conditioning of recto-sphincteric responses in the treatment of fecal incontinence. *The New England Journal of Medicine, 290*, 646–649.

Fordyce, W. E., Fowler, R. S., Lehmann, J. F., DeLateur, B., Sand, P. L., & Treischmann, R. (1973). Operant conditioning in the treatment of chronic pain. *Archives of Physical Medicine and Rehabilitation, 54*, 399–408.

Gannon, L., & Sternbach, R. A. (1971). Alpha enhancement as a treatment for pain: A case study. *Journal of Behavior Therapy and Experimental Psychiatry, 2*, 209–213.

Gatchel, R. J. (1982). EMG biofeedback in anxiety reduction. In L. White & B. Tursky (Eds.), *Clinical biofeedback: Efficacy and mechanisms*. New York: The Guilford Press.

Hertzog, C., Schaie, K. W., & Gribbin, K. (1978). Cardiovascular disease and changes in intellectual functioning from middle to old age. *Journal of Gerontology, 33*, 872–883.

Jacobson, E. (1942). *Progressive relaxation*. Chicago: University of Chicago Press.

Johnson, H. E., & Garton, W. H. (1973). Muscle re-education in hemiplegia by use of electromyographic device. *Archives of Physical Medicine, 54*, 320–322.

Keefe, F. J., Surwit, R. S., & Pilon, R. N. (1979). A one year follow-up of Raynaud's patients treated with behavior therapy techniques. *Journal of Behavioral Medicine, 2,* 385–391.

Lader, M. H. (1967). Palmar skin conductance measures in anxiety and phobic states. *Journal of Psychosomatic Research, 11,* 271.

Libow, L. S. (1977). Senile dementia and "pseudosenility": Clinical diagnosis. In C. Eisdorfer & R. O. Friedel (Eds.), *Cognitive and emotional disturbance in the elderly: Clinical issue.* Chicago: Year Book Medical Publishers.

Lubar, J. F. (1982). EEG operant conditioning in severe epileptics: Controlled multidimensional studies. In L. White & B. Tursky (Eds.), *Clinical biofeedback: Efficacy and mechanisms.* New York: The Guilford Press.

Manuso, J. J. (1977). The use of biofeedback-assisted hand warming in the treatment of chronic eczematous dermatitis of the hands: A case study. *Journal of Behavior Therapy and Experimental Psychiatry, 8,* 445–446.

Marinacci, A. A., & Horande, M. (1960). Electromyogram in neuromuscular re-education. *Bulletin of the Los Angeles Neurological Society, 25,* 57–71.

Martin, I., & Venables, P. H. (Eds.). (1980). *Techniques in Psychophysiology.* New York: Wiley & Sons.

Melzack, R., & Perry, C. (1975). Self-regulation of pain: The use of alpha-feedback and hypnotictraining for the control of chronic pain. *Experimental Neurology, 46,* 452–464.

Moore, N. (1965). Behavior therapy in bronchial asthma: A controlled study. *Journal of Psychosomatic Research, 9,* 257–276.

Mroczek, N., Halpern, D., & McHugh, R. (1978). Electromyographic feedback and physical therapy in neuromuscular retraining in hemiplegia. *Archives of Physical Medicine and Rehabilitation, 59,* 258–267.

Nadler, D. B. (1978). Temperature biofeedback and relaxation training for older adults (Doctoral dissertation, California School of Professional Psychology, 1979). *Dissertation Abstracts International, 39,* 3532B.

Nafpliotis, H. (1976). Electromyographic feedback to improve ankle dorsiflexion, wrist extension, and hand grasp. *Physical Therapy, 36,* 821–824.

National Institute on Aging. (1983). *Special Report on Aging.* Washington, D.C. NIH Publication No. 83-2489.

National Institutes of Health. (1976). *Neurological and communicative disorders.* Washington, D.C. NIH Publication No. 77-152.

Noda, H. H. (1978). An exploratory study of the effects of EMG and temperature biofeedback on rheumatoid arthritis (Doctoral dissertation, California School of Professional Psychology, 1978). *Dissertation Abstracts International, 39,* 3532B.

Papsdorf, J. D., Ghannam, J., Kuzma, T., & Jamieson, J. L. (1979). Conjugate lateral eye movements and stress: Implications for EEG biofeedback training. In N. Birbaumer & H. D. Kimmel (Eds.), *Biofeedback and self regulation.* Hillsdale, NJ: Lawrence Earlbaum Assoc.

Roskies, E. (1983). Stress management for Type A individuals. In D. Meichenbaum & M.E. Jaremko (Eds.), *Stress reduction and prevention.* New York: Plenum.

Schuster, M. M. (1979). Biofeedback control of gastrointestinal motility. In J. V. Basmajian (Ed.), *Biofeedback: Principles and practice for clinicians.* Baltimore: The Williams & Wilkins Co.

Singer, R. B., & Levinson, L. (Eds.). (1976). *Medical risks: Patterns of mortality and survival.* Lexington, Massachusetts: D. C. Heath & Co.

Tauber, L. (1983). Biofeedback as an adjunct in treating elders. *Clinical Gerontologist, 1,* 72–73.

Varni, J. W. (1981). Self-regulation techniques in the management of chronic arthritic pain in hemophilia. *Behavior Therapy, 12,* 184–194.

Walsh, D., Till, R., & Williams, M. (1978). Age and differences in peripheral perceptual processing: A monoptic backward masking investigation. *Journal of Experimental Psychology: Human Perception and Performance, 4,* 232–243.

Wasserman, R. R., Oester, Y. T., Oryshkevich, R. S., Montgomery, M. M., Poske, R. M.,

& Ruksha, A. (1968). Electromyographic, electrodiagnostic, and motor nerve conduction observation in patients with rheumatoid arthritis. *Archives of Physical Medicine and Rehabilitation, 9,* 90–95.

Weiss, M. D. (1973). *Biomedical instrumentation.* Philadelphia: Chilton Book Co.

Weiss, T., & Engel, B. T. (1971). Operant conditioning of heart rate in patients with premature ventricular contractions. *Psychosomatic Medicine, 33,* 301–321.

West, H. L. (1978). The differential effects of biofeedback/relaxation training on elderly people (Doctoral dissertation, North Texas State University, 1978). *Dissertation Abstracts International, 39,* 1523B.

Wolf, S. L., Baker, M. P., & Kelly, J. L. (1979). EMG biofeedback in stroke: Effect of patient characteristics. *Archives of Physical Medicine and Rehabilitation, 60,* 96–102.

Questions

1) Which biofeedback procedures might be appropriate for a patient complaining of chronic pain?

2) Are biofeedback procedures compatible with more traditional forms of psychotherapy?

27/SUICIDE IN THE ELDERLY
Assessment and Intervention

Donald I. Templer, PhD
Gordon G. Cappelletty, MA

Editor's Introduction

Depression is frequently cited as the primary cause of suicide. Elder males have the highest suicide rates of any age group in America. The male/female disparity increases in later life. A similar trend is reported in white/black rates.

Templer and Cappelletty review these facts and suggest some explanations. A major finding is that elder attempts are more likely to be lethal, so the suicidal elder must be taken seriously. Persons at risk are the unmarried (especially the recently widowed), the involuntarily retired, the physically ill, alcohol abusers, inner city isolates, and white males. Of particular importance is the fact that geriatric suicides are more traceable to an accumulation of negative events and circumstances than to one specific precipitant.

The authors review the roles of medication, ECT, and psychotherapy in the management of suicidal risk.

INTRODUCTION

The original intention of this review was to focus upon the more definitive and rigorous research conducted in the 1970s and 1980s regarding the assessment of and intervention into suicidal elders. However, because so much of the literature is of a clinical impressionistic nature, there is a focus upon what is not known as well as

Donald I. Templer and Gordon G. Cappelletty are affiliated with the California School of Professional Psychology, Fresno.

475

upon that which is known in this field. Also, digression into the nature and demography of suicide in the elderly was undertaken in order to provide a more comprehensive perspective. It is difficult to diagnose and treat problems about which one knows very little, particularly regarding the life threatening behavior of suicidal acts committed by the elderly.

INCIDENCE AND DEMOGRAPHY
OF SUICIDE IN THE ELDERLY

It has been clearly established that the suicide rate is the highest in the elderly population, especially among elderly white males. Although persons over the age of 65 comprise only approximately 10% of the population, they constitute about one-fifth to one-quarter of all successful suicides (Bock, 1972; Butler & Lewis, 1973; Grollman, 1971; Rachlis, 1970; Resnick & Cantor, 1970; Seiden, 1981).

One can better understand the etiology of both medical and psychological problems by investigating what sort of persons are more prone to the condition under consideration. Regarding the suicide rate in the United States, we will present incidence rates for our tentative generalization that the demographic trends in suicide become more pronounced with old age.

Gender

The suicide rate for males continues to rise with age, even into the 70s and 80s (Botwinick, 1973). With females, on the other hand, there is a slight decrease in the rate of suicide beginning in the 50s. For persons in their 20s, the male rate is about twice that of the female suicide rate. In the 70s, the suicide rate is approximately six times as great for males as for females. By age 85, the male rate climbs to more than 10 times the female rate (Miller, 1976; Rachlis, 1970).

Suicidologists have known for many years that although women *attempt* suicide more often than men, men are more *successful* in their attempts (Bromley, 1966; Burvill, 1972). To date there is no truly satisfactory explanation for the difference between male and female rates. Depression, the mental disorder most commonly associated with suicide in old age, occurs as frequently among women as it does among men (Miller, 1976). While most of the research into this sex difference has been done with younger suicides, one study has speculated that the impact of retirement and physical decline is more devastating to the self-esteem of men than women (Busse & Pfeiffer, 1969).

Black versus White Rates

Black men and white men do not differ remarkably in terms of suicide rate during youth. In mid-life, however, the rate of suicide among white men is approximately twice that for black men. In old age, the white male has several times the risk of committing suicide as the black male. While the rate for white males steadily increases with age, the rate for black males decreases past age 50 until by age 60 it is not much higher than the rate for black women. The white male rate continues to increase dramatically into advanced old age where the rate may be as much as 10 or 20 times as high as for black males, depending upon the year for which statistics were compiled. The ratio of white female to black female suicides changes in a much less dramatic fashion as a function of age, and the elderly white female rate is not dramatically higher than the black female rate.

The reasons for the grossly higher rates for white than for black elderly men are not clear. However, several plausible explanations have been given. Seiden (1981) neatly placed these explanations into six categories. The "differential life expectancy" explanation states that because blacks have a "tougher" and shorter life, those who are "susceptible" to suicide may die young. The "deviant burnout" hypothesis states that blacks who are frustrated with and angry about their status, and have deviant life styles experience the "calming effects of the passing years." The "screening out of the violence prone" explanation is based upon the high homicide and incarceration rate among blacks, and claims that the more violent blacks (and hence, more suicide susceptible) have either been killed or incarcerated prior to reaching old age. The fourth explanation looks at the "role and status of the elderly." According to this explanation, blacks accord more respect and status to their elderly and allow them more social participation than do whites. The "traditional values" hypothesis is similar to the previous explanation, and deals with the values blacks place upon religion, family, and the serious contemplation of suicide as an alternative to a miserable life. The final explanation is the "age specific motives" hypothesis. This explanation claims that the loss of status and income that come with age are not as great for blacks because they were at a lower level than in the white population.

Robins, West, and Murphy (1976) formulated ten hypotheses regarding the lower suicide rates of elderly blacks compared to elderly white men. They tested these hypotheses with elderly men in the community and found that the following six hypotheses were borne out:

1. Older white men have more frequent and severe depression than blacks.
2. Alcoholism is more common in older whites than in older blacks.
3. Whites are less religious and less disapproving of suicide than blacks.
4. Whites are more likely to personally know a suicide.
5. Growing old is considered less reason for personal pride and homage from others by whites than blacks.
6. Older whites may be less likely to be in intact marital relationships than blacks.

Even though elderly blacks are less likely to attempt suicide than elderly whites, the matter of elderly blacks who are suicidal is worthy of attention. Hendin (1969) maintained that because of the strong emphasis upon religious values and compliance in the upbringing of older blacks, the suicidal black male is more apt to think of himself as a moral failure. This is in contrast to the white older person who thinks of himself as a failure with respect to achievement.

A Cross-Cultural Conceptualization

A very interesting study tested the theoretical position that dependence in a nation can create serious social and economic problems (Lester, 1973). Lester calculated 2 ratios for 31 different countries: (a) the ratio comparing the number of people under 15 to those 15 to 64 years of age, and (b) the ratio comparing the number of the number of people over 65 to those 15 to 64 years of age. The first ratio had a correlation of .56 with homicide rate and −.55 with the suicide rate. The second ratio had a correlation of −.64 with the homicide rate, and .52 with the suicide rate. Lester has suggested that in a society in which the adults suffer frustration from social and economic stresses caused by large numbers of young dependents, the latter are attacked. However, if economic and social stresses are a function of a large number of old dependents, aggression is turned inward in the form of suicide.

RELATIONSHIP BETWEEN AGE AND DEPRESSION

The positive association of suicide with depression cannot be contested. Because of this relationship and the declining health, abilities, status, and avenues for pleasure in the elderly it is often assumed that the prevalence of depression is greater in older persons than in the young. However, the evidence is not all that clear. Some studies have reported a positive association between age and depression (Aaronson, 1964; Britton & Savage, 1965; Calder & Hokanson, 1959; Colligan, Osborne, Swenson, & Offord, 1983; Gurin, Veroff, & Fell, 1960; Gynther & Shimkunas, 1966; Kornetsky, 1958; Leon, Gillum, Gillum, & Gouze, 1979; Swenson, 1961; Whitmyre & Cohen, 1973), some a negative relationship (Comstock & Helsing, 1976; Radloff, 1975), and some no relationship or an ambiguous one (Canter, Day, Imboden, & Cluff, 1964; Hardyck, 1964; Thumin, 1969; Swenson, Pearson, & Osborne, 1973; Weis & Russakoff, 1977).

Sampling and methodology more generally probably account for the conflictual findings presented above. The present authors suspect that the different instruments for measuring depression play a strong role in the confusing perspective that emerges. It is doubtful if all elements of the traditional depression syndrome that the depression scales assess are applicable to the elderly. Does diminished energy necessarily mean depression in an 80-year-old? Does a reduced sex drive necessarily imply depression in a 90-year-old? To prevent suicide in any population, it is important to appropriately assess depression in that population.

It is probable that most of the standard scales used in measuring depression are less than ideally suited to the elderly. In one study, the elderly obtained a significantly higher overall mean on the Beck Depression Inventory, but the older sample did not differ significantly from the younger when the last six items pertaining to somatic functioning were eliminated (Zemore & Eames, 1979). One instrument that shows promise for assessing depression in older persons is the Geriatric Depression Scale (Brink, 1984; Brink, Yesavage, Lum, Heersema, Adey, & Rose, 1982; Yesavage, Brink, Rose, Lum, Huang, Adey, & Leirer, 1983). This scale was developed specifically for the geriatric population, and has taken into account the normal physiological and psychological changes which occur with age. A decrease in appetite and in the total amount of sleep needed, for example, are indicative of depression in younger persons but reflect the normal processes of advancing age.

LETHALITY AND NATURE OF SUICIDAL ACTS IN THE ELDERLY

There can be little doubt about the fact that suicidal methods in the elderly are more lethal than in younger people (Butler & Lewis, 1973; Miller, 1976). The elderly are less likely than younger persons to attempt suicide (Grollman, 1971). But when the elderly do make an attempt, it is more likely to be successful than a younger person's attempt. Elderly persons are also less likely to utilize suicidal gestures as a manipulative ploy or a cry for help (Butler & Lewis, 1973). A number of studies have shown that elderly persons are much less likely to be rescued from a suicide attempt (Rachlis, 1970; Resnick & Canter, 1970; Seiden, 1974). In addition, the elderly utilize suicide prevention services to a proportionately much lesser degree than younger persons (Rachlis, 1970). However, those that do call a suicide "hot line" feel lonely and are often angry for having been abandoned by family and friends (Fareberow & Moriwaki, 1975).

The implications of the above findings are very clear. The suicidal elderly person is to be taken extremely seriously. It is unlikely that a clinician will get a "second chance" with one of these clients.

CIRCUMSTANCES INCREASING THE PROBABILITY OF SUICIDE

Elderly persons who are widowed are apparently more likely to commit suicide than those whose spouses are living (Renwick & Cantor, 1970). It has also been noted that elderly persons who have been involuntarily retired contemplate suicide more often than those for whom retirement was voluntary (Peretti & Wilson, 1978). Poor health, living alone, abuse of alcohol, and residence in deteriorating sections of a large city are also related to suicide in the elderly (Miller, 1976).

Regarding the common sense finding, consistently reported in the literature, of the positive relationship between poor health and suicide risk in older persons, it is noteworthy that one study reported that 35% of hospitalized cardiac patients expressed a wish for death (Dovenmuehle & Verwoerdt, 1962). It is apparent that suicide in the suffering elderly is a matter laden with many value judgements. These value judgements are discussed by Schneidman (1973) in the context of all significant others involved, and in terms of Weisman and Kastenbaum's (1968) conceptualization of an "appropriate death." The recommendation of Cutter (1984) seems as reasonable as it is straightforward:

> Allowing nature to take its course is not equivalent to clinical suicide but merely another life affirming choice that can come out of existing relations and life styles of the people involved. The search for death with dignity can be supported by health professionals. The impulsive, and distress motivated impulse to engage in solitary, secretive self injury requires professional intervention. (p. 68)

Without going into a discussion of the moral and ethical implications of suicide for sick or seriously disabled elderly persons, it is the current authors' opinion that people dealing with depressed and suicidal elders need to become aware of their own values regarding this issue.

In contrast to younger persons, older adults are less likely to have their suicidal act precipitated by a specific, emotionally upsetting event. The suicidal act of an elderly person is more likely to result from the accumulation of events and circumstance over a prolonged period of time (Miller, 1976). The suicidal elder will appear more rational and less emotional than a younger person regarding the decision to take his or her own life.

INTERVENTION WITH THE SUICIDAL ELDER

It should be clear at this point that since the elderly have a higher suicide rate, use much more lethal methods, are less likely to communicate their suicidal intentions, and more often feel the effects of adverse circumstances such as poor health and financial difficulties that are not likely to improve significantly, intervention must be undertaken with resolve, vigor, and persistence.

Intervention with antidepressant drugs and electroconvulsive therapy (ECT) are of demonstrated benefit in the treatment of depression for persons of all ages. However, the side effects and risks of these treatments are of much greater concern with the elderly client than with the young. Cardiovascular problems must certainly be taken into account in the consideration of both antidepressants and ECT in the elderly. Elderly persons metabolize drugs much differently than younger persons, are often concurrently administered a virtual pharmacopia of medications by different physicians for multiple physical complaints, and often experience more side effects from the medications they receive. Particularly with ECT, complications which can result in death are much more common in the elderly and this potential must be carefully considered in the development of an effective treatment plan. Furthermore, research with patients who have received ECT, as well as experimental research with animals converge to the generalization that brain pathology is more likely to result in the elderly (Templer & Veleber, 1982). As with any course of treatment, the potential risks of both antidepressant medications and ECT must be weighed against the potential benefits.

Psychotherapy is not a path guaranteed to be paved with gold. Traditionally, older persons have been regarded as less amenable to insight-oriented therapy. However, the present authors are not convinced that insight-oriented therapy is as effective a treatment for depression in persons of any age as its proponents believe it to be. The declining cognitive abilities of the elderly is a factor that is certainly not facilitative of psychotherapeutic progress. On the other hand, it should be borne in mind that only about 5% of elderly persons may be regarded as senile (Butler, 1974). Perhaps a balanced perspective would be to remain cognizant of possible deficits in an elderly client, but not to jump to conclusions regarding an elderly person's mental faculties simply because of age. The reluctance of psychotherapists to work with the elderly has been discussed and is itself a phenomenon of interest and concern, although not central to the intentions of this review (Garfinkel, 1975; Knight, 1978; Levy, Derogatis, Gallagher, & Gatz, 1980; Sparacino, 1978).

Case studies have been reported which show the efficacy of certain interventions with elderly persons at risk for suicidal behavior. Brink (1977) presented the case of a 64-year-old Mexican widow with suicidal thoughts. External constraints necessitated that psychotherapy be completed within 15 days. The focus was not on establishing transference or personality reconstruction, but on identifying problems and promptly formulating practical solutions. The therapy appeared to have been beneficial with this woman.

Mehta, Mathew, and Mehta (1978) reported a case involving an elderly couple with multiple health problems. This couple had made a suicide pact with one another. During a three-week hospitalization, they were treated with psychotherapy and amitryptaline and then followed closely after discharge. Again, this intervention appeared to have been beneficial as the couple reported less dysphoria after discharge from the hospital.

Case studies such as these generate guarded optimism in addition to offering practical intervention strategies and techniques when dealing with suicidal elderly. Controlled research into the efficacy of psychotherapy with the elderly is needed, however, before a more definitive perspective on intervention can be obtained.

The dearth of controlled research upon the efficacy of psychotherapy with depressed older persons has been commented upon by previous authors (Levy, Derogatis, Gallagher, & Gatz, 1980; Mintz, Steuer, & Jarvik, 1981). An exception is the good study by Gallagher and Thompson (1983) who found that the nonendogenously depressed older person exhibited significantly greater improvement with psychotherapy than the endogenously depressed older person. However, since control subjects receiving no psychotherapy were not employed, one cannot be certain whether the greater improvement of the nonendogenously depressed persons was a function of effects of psychotherapy or a function of some other factor such as spontaneous remission. Furthermore, even if the study did permit a definitive generalization regarding psychotherapeutic efficacy in the treatment of depression, further research upon how this efficacy impacts upon short-term and long-term suicide prevention would be needed.

In addition to psychotherapeutic intervention, general strategies of psychosocial intervention have been recommended as well. Resnick and Cantor (1970) maintain that the first step is that of establishing trust and "taking action" even if that action is no more than a promise for help. "Involving others" is another strategy viewed by Resnick and Cantor as very important in the treatment of suicidal elders, and ranges from the involvement of friends and relatives to the "buddy system" of calls and visits.

Leviton (1973) has suggested that broadly conceptualized sexuality which includes not only sexual relationships but attention to personal appearance, physical fitness, and social relationships, could be a deterrent to suicide among the elderly. Rachlis (1970) has recommended using senior citizen centers for identifying suicidal older persons and initiating appropriate intervention. Such strategies, as with the case reports, are interesting and quite probably helpful, but must be buttressed by well-controlled research before they can be used with confidence.

CONCLUSION

The suicide rate of the elderly, especially that of white males, is extremely high, and their suicidal acts are often quite lethal. Suicide in this population often occurs in the context of physical and psychological problems, social isolation, involuntary retirement, and the death of a spouse. Assessment of and intervention with the suicidal elderly are areas which need much more research in order to establish the validity and efficacy of current practices.

On the basis of the research reviewed, it certainly appears that suicidal indications in the elderly are to be taken most seriously and treated in a vigorous broad spectrum approach. Psychological, physical, and interpersonal factors need to be considered in any intervention aimed at the suicidal elderly. In addition to the traditional approaches of medication, ECT, and psychotherapy in the treatment of depression, work may need to be done to reduce the social isolation of elderly persons as well. Since the suicidal elderly person will seldom come to us, we must reach out to them in a persistent and sustained manner.

Finally, the need to rule out medical causes for depression before optimal intervention planning is especially important with the elderly. A number of physical illnesses that can cause depression are more common in old age. Furthermore, some of the drugs that are frequently prescribed for the elderly, such as antihypertensive and cardiac medications and sedatives, can cause depressive symptomatology and a simple change in medications may be all that is needed.

REFERENCES

Aaronson, B. S. (1964). Aging, personality change, and psychiatric diagnosis. *Journal of Gerontology, 19,* 144-148.

Bock, E. W. (1972). Aging and suicide: The significance of marital, kinship, and alternative relations. *Family Coordinator, 21,* 71-79.

Botwinick, J. (1973). *Aging and behavior.* New York: Springer.

Brink, T. L. (1977). Brief psychotherapy: A case report illustrating its potential effectiveness. *Journal of the American Geriatric Society, 25,* 273-276.

Brink, T. L. (1984). Limitations of the GDS in cases of pseudodementia. *Clinical Gerontologist, 2,* 60-61.

Brink, T. L., Yesavage, J. A., Lum, O., Heersema, P. H., Adey, M., & Rose, T. L. (1982). Screening test for geriatric depression. *Clinical Gerontologist, 1,* 37-43.

Britton, P. G., & Savage, R. D. (1966). The MMPI and the aged—Some normative data from a community sample. *British Journal of Psychiatry, 112,* 941-943.

Bromley, D. B. (1966). *The psychology of human ageing.* Baltimore: Penguin Press.

Burvill, P. W. (1972). Recent decreased ratio of male:female suicide rates. *International Journal of Social Psychiatry, 18,* 137-139.

Busse, E. W., & Pfeiffer, E. (1969). Functional psychiatric disorder in old age. In E. Busse & E. Pfeiffer (Eds.), *Behavior and adaptation in late life.* Boston: Little, Brown.

Butler, R. N. (1974). Successful aging and the role of the life review. *Journal of the American Geriatric Society, 22,* 529-535.

Butler, R., & Lewis, M. (1973). *Aging and mental health.* St. Louis: Mosby.

Calden, G., & Hokanson, J. E. (1959). The influence of age on MMPI responses. *Journal of Clinical Psychology, 15,* 194-195.

Canter, A., Day, C., Imboden, J., & Cluff, L. (1962). The influence of age and health status on the MMPI scores of a normal population. *Journal of Clinical Psychology, 18,* 71-73.

Colligan, R. C., Osborne, D., Swenson, W. M., & Offord, K. P. (1983). *The MMPI: A contemporary normative study.* New York: Praeger Scientific.

Comstock, G. W., & Helsing, K. J. (1976). Symptoms of depression in two communities. *Psychological Medicine, 6,* 551-563.

Cutter, F. (1984). Suicidal elders: Recognition and management. *Clinical Gerontologist, 2,* 66-68.

Dovenmuehle, R. H., & Verwoerdt, A. (1962). Physical illness and depressive symptomatology. I. Incidence of depressive symptoms in hospitalized cardiac patients. *Journal of the American Geriatric Society, 10,* 932-947.

Fareberow, N. L., & Moriwaki, S. Y. (1975). Self-destructive crises in the older person. *The Gerontologist,* 333-337.

Gallagher, D. E. & Thompson, L. W. (1983). Effectiveness of psychotherapy for both endogenous and nonendogenous depression in older adult outpatients. *Journal of Gerontology, 38,* 707-712.

Garfinkel, A. (1975). The reluctant therapist. *Gerontologist, 15,* 138-141.

Gurin, G., Veroff, J., & Feld, S. (1960). *Americans view their mental health: A nationwide interview survey.* New York: Basic Books.

Grollman, E. (1971). *Suicide: Prevention, intervention, and postvention.* Boston: Beacon Press.

Gynther, M. D., & Shimkunas, A. M. (1966). Age and MMPI performance. *Journal of Consulting Psychology, 30,* 118-121.

Hardyck, C. D. (1964). Sex differences in personality changes with age. *Journal of Gerontology, 19,* 78-82.

Hendin, H. (1969). Black suicide. *Archives of General Psychiatry, 21,* 407-422.

Knight, R. (1978). Psychotherapy and behavior change with the non-institutionalized aged. *International Journal of Aging and Human Development, 9,* 221-236.

Kornetsky, C. (1958). Minnesota Multiphasic Personality Inventory: Results obtained from a population of aged men. In J. E. Birren, R. N. Butler, S. W. Greenhouse, L. Sokoloff, & M. R. Yarrow (Eds.), *Human aging I: A biological and behavioral study.* Bethesda, MD: U.S. Dept. of Health, Education, & Welfare, NIMH.

Leon, G. R., Gillum, B., Gillum, R., & Gouze, M. (1979). Personality stability and change over a 30-year period—Middle age to old age. *Journal of Consulting and Clinical Psychology, 47,* 517-524.

Lester, D. (1973). Suicide, homicide, and age dependency ratios. *International Journal of Aging and Human Development, 4,* 127-145.

Leviton, D. (1973). The significance of sexuality as a deterrent to suicide among the aged. *Omega, 4,* 163-174.

Levy, S. M., Derogatis, L. R., Gallagher, D., & Gatz, M. (1980). Intervention with older adults and the evaluation of outcome. In L. W. Poon (Ed.), *Aging in the 1980s: Psychological issues.* Washington, D.C.: American Psychological Association.

Mehta, D., Mathew, P., & Mehta, S. (1978). Suicide pact in a depressed elderly couple: Case report. *Journal of the American Geriatric Society, 26,* 136-138.

Mintz, J., Steuer, J., & Jarvik, L. (1981). Psychotherapy with depressed elderly patients: Research considerations. *Journal of Consulting and Clinical Psychology, 49,* 542-548.

Miller, M. (1976). Suicide among older men. *Dissertation Abstracts International, 36.*

Peretti, P. O., & Wilson, C. (1978). Contemplated suicide among voluntary and involuntary retirees. *Omega, 9,* 193-201.

Rachlis, D. (1970). Suicide and loss adjustment in the aging. *Bulletin of Suicidology, 1,* 23-26.

Radloff, L. (1975). Sex differences in depression: The effects of occupation and marital status. *Sex Roles, 1,* 249-265.

Resnick, J. L. P., & Cantor, J. M. (1970). Suicide and aging. *Journal of American Geriatric Society, 18,* 152-158.

Robins, L. N., West, P. A., & Murphy, G. E. (1977). Suicide and depression in older men: A study testing ten hypotheses regarding the high rate in whites. *Social Psychiatry, 12,* 127-137.

Seiden, R. H. (1974). Suicide: Preventable death. *Public affairs report* (Bulletin of the Institute of Government Studies, University of California at Berkeley), *15,* 1-5.

Seiden, R. H. (1981). Mellowing with age: Factors influencing the nonwhite suicide rate. *International Journal of Aging and Human Development, 13,* 265-284.

Schneidman, E. (1973). Suicide in the aged. In R. H. Davis & M. Neiswender (Eds.), *Dealing with death.* Los Angeles: Andrus Gerontology Center.

Sparacino, J. (1978). Individual psychotherapy with the aged: A selective review. *International Journal of Aging and Human Development, 9,* 197-220.

Swenson, W. M. (1961). Structural personality testing in the aged: An MMPI study of the gerontic populations. *Journal of Clinical Psychology, 17,* 302-304.

Swenson, W. M., Pearson, J. S., & Osborne, D. (1973). *An MMPI source book: Basic item, scale, and pattern data on 50,000 medical patients.* Minneapolis: University of Minnesota Press.

Templer, D. I., & Veleber, D. M. (1982). Can ECT permanently harm the brain? *Clinical Neuropsychology, 4,* 62-66.

Thumin, F. (1969). MMPI scores as related to age, education, and intelligence among male job applicants. *Journal of Applied Psychology, 53,* 404-407.

Weis, R. W., & Russakoff, S. (1977). Relationship of MMPI scores of drug-abusers to personal variables and type of treatment program. *Journal of Psychology, 96,* 25-29.

Weisman, A., & Kastenbaum, R. (1968). *The psychological autopsy: A study of the terminal phase of life.* New York: Basic Books.

Whitmyre, J. W., & Cohen, D. (1973). Personality characteristics of psychiatric hospitalized veterans of three age ranges. *Newsletter for Research in Mental Health and Behavioral Sciences, 15,* 12-15.

Yesavage, J. A., Brink, T., Rose, T. L., Lum, O., Huang, V., Adey, M., & Leirer, V. O.

(1983). Development and validation of a geriatric depression screening scale: A preliminary report. *Journal of Psychiatric Research, 17*, 37–49.

Zemore, R., & Eames, N. (1979). Psychic and somatic symptoms of depression among young adults, institutionalized aged and noninstitutionalized aged. *Journal of Gerontology, 34*, 716–722.

Questions

1) What techniques, other than demographic data, are there for the assessment of suicidal risk?

2) The assessment and management of suicidal risk in later life is a controversial topic. Would most geriatric psychotherapists agree with Templer and Cappelletty about the limited role of insight?

3) Do most geriatric psychiatrists agree with Templer and Cappelletty about the dangers of ECT?

28/DRUG EFFECTS IN ALZHEIMER'S DISEASE

Thomas Crook, PhD

Editor's Introduction

The role of medication in the treatment of geriatric depression has been discussed in several previous issues of *CG.* Tricyclics were covered by a review article (v. 2, #1, pp. 3–29). Other medications covered have been lithium (v. 3, #1, pp. 47–60), propranolol (v. 3, #3, pp. 36–39), maprotiline (v. 1, #4, pp. 71–73). The issue of side effects was raised in one article (v. 1, #4, pp. 3–18) and several clinical comments (v. 3, #4, pp. 67–77).

Nearly a million and a half Americans suffer from dementia, and the number is growing. Crook reviews the search for a miracle drug to cure, prevent, or arrest dementia. As recently as two decades ago, a vascular etiology was assumed, and this led to vasodilators, anticoagulants, and hyperbaric oxygenation chambers. The unimpressive results wrought by such treatments led to a rethinking of dementia, and the conclusion that the neurological degeneration seen in Alzheimer's disease characterized most cases of senile dementia.

Crook then focuses on state-of-the-art "antisenility" medications, their utility, and side effects. Dihydroergotoxine (Hydergine) has had a modest, but statistically significant and replicable impact on a broad range of clinical symptoms, though this may be due to more of a mood elevation than to cognitive amelioration. Longer trials and higher dosages may be warranted. The utility of vasodilators and stimulants is even more limited, and probably confined to secondary symptoms such as mood. The author has a cau-

Thomas Crook is affiliated with the Center for Studies of the Mental Health of the Aging, National Institute of Mental Health, 5600 Fishers Lane, Rockville, MD 20857.

tionary note in the use of antipsychotics with dementia patients.

Crook then discusses some relatively experimental drugs. The cholinomimetic compounds presume that Alzheimer's disease impairs memory function by means of a depletion of choline. The studies on physostigmine, lecithin, THA, and muscarinic agonists are encouraging, as are those with the nootropic, piracetam. "Small but reliable changes can be produced in a disease previously thought to be marked by inexorable deterioration."

Other studies are being performed with neuropeptides (e.g., vasopressin), rhealogic agents, and chelators, but research on these has been inadequate.

Alzheimer's disease (AD) may be the most tragic and dehumanizing disorder of late life. In AD one literally "loses one's mind," being reduced from the unique product of decades of personal experience to a drifting, vegetative state in which the children and spouse to whom a lifetime was devoted become unrecognizable and, eventually, even the abilities to move about and utter interpretable sounds are lost. Nearly one and one-half million Americans are now incapacitated as a result of AD and that number will double within the next fifty years as the rapid and unprecedented growth of the elderly population continues.

The search for effective pharmacologic treatments for the symptoms of AD and other age-related disorders was underway well before the journey of Ponce de Leon to the new world in 1513. Only in recent years, however, have attempts to treat late-life dementing disorders been based on sound empirical data rather than on assumptions about disease processes. It is noteworthy that in the late 1700s Benjamin Rush, the first American psychiatrist and signer of the Declaration of Independence, reasoned that mental disorders were caused by sludging of the blood within the brain and developed the "gyrating chair" in which patients were spun in a circular motion to improve blood flow and, hence, facilitate mental function. Until scarcely more than a decade ago, some two hundred years after Dr. Rush's experiments, most treatment strategies for AD and related disorders were still based on a presumed vascular etiology. Although the gyrating chair had been replaced by vasodilators, anticoagulants, and other drugs, as well as such creative techniques as hyperbaric oxygenation, assumptions about the etiology of dementia remained virtually unchanged. Of course the causes of AD are still unknown but several rational treatment strategies have emerged during recent years based on specific neurochemical deficits demonstrated in AD or on behavioral drug effects discovered in animal models relevant to the disorder.

This paper reviews drugs currently prescribed in the United States for the treatment of AD and considers a broad range of investigational drugs recently studied or currently under study in AD. Particular emphasis will be placed on recent trials with cholinergic compounds, neuropeptides, and "nootropic" drugs.

CURRENT PHARMACOLOGIC TREATMENTS

The drugs currently marketed for the treatment of age-related cognitive symptoms such as those seen in AD are listed in Table 1. Of these, by far the most widely prescribed is dihydroergotoxine. This compound is a combination of three ergot alkaloids in their dihydrogenated forms. Dihydroergotoxine has been studied in more than 33 double-blind, clinical trials in aged patients with complaints of memory impairment. Most of the trials were undertaken prior to the development of current diagnostic criteria and samples were probably composed of both AD and multi-infarct dementia (MID) patients as well as patients with other specific organic disorders and with depression. In such studies, dihydroergotoxine has consistently been shown to exert a quite modest but statistically significant effect on a broad range of clinical symptoms assessed through patient

TABLE 1

Drugs Currently Prescribed in the United States
to Treat Cognitive Impairments in the Elderly

dihydroergotoxine

Vasodilators
    papaverine
    isoxsuprine
    cyclandelate

"Stimulants"
    methylphenidate
    pentylenetetrazol

procaine GH3 (in Nevada)

report and clinical observation (Yesavage, Tinklenberg, Hollister, & Berger, 1979; Hollister & Yesavage, in press). However, where patient performance has been measured directly, using psychological tests or mental status exams, drug effects have generally not been apparent (McDonald, 1982). It thus appears that the drug exerts a mild activating or mood-elevating effect rather than a direct effect on memory or cognitive processes (Crook, 1983). Nevertheless, dihydroergotoxine may produce overall clinical improvement in some AD and MID patients and, given the absence of reasonable alternatives, a trial of the drug in individual patients may be warranted. Two recent studies (Yesavage, Hollister, & Burian, 1979; Yoshikawa et al., 1983) suggest that a daily dose of 6 mg rather than the standard 3 mg dose may be more efficacious. Also, it has been argued that an extended trial of 6 months is warranted (Hollister & Yesavage, in press).

Aside from the question of diminishing established symptoms, it has been argued that dihydroergotoxine is effective in preventing cognitive deterioration in normal or mildly impaired elderly persons (Kugler et al., 1978; Spiegel, Huber & Lobule, in press). Of course, a great deal more evidence will be required to establish any such prophylactic effect.

Evidence of clinical efficacy for the three vasodilators listed in Table 1 is extremely limited in either AD or MID (Yesavage et al., 1979). In the case of papaverine, for example, five direct comparisons with dihydroergotoxine favor the latter drug despite its quite modest therapeutic effects. Clinical studies recently undertaken with these "desi" drugs are currently being examined by the Federal Food and Drug Administration and their future in the marketplace is uncertain.

The two stimulants listed in Table 1 are currently approved for multiple indications, including the treatment of selected symptoms associated with senile dementia. In general, the utility of stimulants in AD or MID is extremely limited (Crook, 1979; Loew & Singer, 1983). Methylphenidate does not appear to directly improve memory or other cognitive processes (Crook, Ferris, Sathananthan, Raskin, & Gershon, 1977), but the drug may be of some limited value in treating secondary symptoms of dementia seen in some patients such as fatigue, motor retardation, or depressed mood (Branconnier & Cole, 1980). In the case of pentylenetetrazol, or the many compounds containing pentylenetetrazol and nicotinic acid, there appears to be no sound evidence of efficacy.

The last drug listed in Table 1, a procaine formulation marketed as Gerovital or GH3, is not approved by the Federal Food and Drug Administration for the treatment of primary or secondary symptoms of dementia but is sold within the state of Nevada. The drug appears to have no direct effect on cognition but it is a relatively weak mono-amine oxidase inhibitor and may have mild mood-elevating effects (Jarvik & Milne, 1975; Ostfeld, Smith, & Stotsky, 1977).

In addition to the drugs listed in Table 1, compounds marketed for other indications, such as anticoagulants, have been studied in AD but no satisfactory evidence of efficacy has emerged.

Thus, it would appear that compounds currently available to the clinician for treating the primary symptoms of senile dementia are of quite limited utility. It is important to emphasize, however, that, in a sense, many major psychotropic agents on the market could be described as antidementia drugs. For example, neuroleptics are used to treat a broad range of dyssocial and psychotic symptoms that may accompany the disorder; antidepressants are widely used to treat affective symptoms that accompany, and may even mimic, senile dementia; and sedative-hypnotics are used to treat the sleep disorders that predictably occur in dementia patients.

The place of neuroleptics in the treatment of dementia patients is particularly important. Despite the widespread use of these drugs in severely impaired dementia patients, remarkably little is known about their optimal use in that population. It is clear that many generalizations from research in young adult schizophrenics are hazardous. For example, neuroleptic dosage requirements in demented elderly patients are frequently far lower than in younger psychotic patients (Davis, 1981). Although a great deal more clinical research with neuroleptics in elderly dementia patients is needed, and it is clear that these drugs will not cure senile dementia, they remain extremely important management tools that may delay, and in some cases prevent, institutionalization.

INVESTIGATIONAL DRUGS

Cholinomimetic Compounds

A number of strategies have been employed in the search for an effective treatment for AD (Crook & Gershon, 1981). Clearly, the most systematic research has followed the cholinergic hypothesis of geriatric memory dysfunction. The principal cholinomimetic drugs or drug combinations studied to date are identified in Table 2.

The most thoroughly studied of these compounds are the acetylcholine precursors choline and lecithin. More than 20 controlled clinical trials have been conducted with these compounds in patients with presumed AD. As a result of these trials it now appears reasonable to conclude that precursor therapy is not an effective treatment in AD (Rosenberg, Greenwald, & Davis, 1983). There is one recent study (Little, Chuaqui-Kidd, & Levy, 1984) arguing that long-term lecithin administration exerts a therapeutic effect in a subgroup of AD patients, but the study is clearly open to methodologic criticism.

Trials with acetylocholinesterase inhibitors, physostigmine and tetrahydroaminoacridine (THA), and with muscarinic agonists such as arecoline and RS86 are somewhat more encouraging. Briefly, studies with physostigmine, alone (Davis, et al., 1983) and in combination with lecithin (Thal, Fuld, Masur, & Sharpless, 1983; Thal, Masur, Sharpless, Fuld, & Davies, 1984), have shown clinically modest but quite clear drug effects on selected cognitive measures in some AD patients. Similar changes have also been reported with another cholinesterase inhibitor, tetrahydroaminoacridine (Summers, Viesselman, & Marsh, 1981), and with the muscarinic agonist arecoline (Christie, Shering, Ferguson, & Glenn, 1981). Prelim-

TABLE 2

Cholinomimetics

Acetylcholine Precursors
    choline chloride
    lecithin (phosphatidylcholine)

Acetycholinesterase Inhibitors
    physostigmine
    tetrahydroaminoacridine (THA)

Agonists
    arecoline
    RS-86
    bethanecol

Combination Treatments
    lecithin plus piracetam
    lecithin plus physostigmine

inary reports of subjective improvement in confirmed AD patients have also come from Dr. Robert Harbaugh and colleagues at Dartmouth University where the muscarinic agonist bethanecol has been administered by intracranial infusion delivered through an implantable pump (Harbaugh, Roberts, Coombs, Saunders, & Reeder, 1984).

Studies have also been conducted in both humans and animals in which lecithin was combined with the much-studied "nootropic" compound piracetam. The combination treatment was found more effective than treatment with either compound alone in facilitating retention in aged rats (Bartus, Dean, Sherman, Friedman, & Baer, 1981) and preliminary analyses of ongoing controlled studies in humans suggest that modest improvement may occur in some AD patients on specific measures (Ferris et al., 1982; Growdon, Corkin, & Huff, 1984).

In general, the cholinergic agents studied to date have clearly not been established as clinically effective therapeutic agents in AD. However, studies with cholinesterase inhibitors, muscarinic agonists, and combined therapies demonstrate that small but reliable changes can be produced in a disease previously thought to be marked by inexorable deterioration.

Neuropeptides

Several neuropeptides have been shown to exert significant effects on learning and memory in animal models. On the basis of these findings, clinical trials with neuropeptides related to adrenocortotrophic hormone (ACTH) and vasopressin (VP) have been undertaken in patients with presumed AD, as well as in normals and persons suffering from other forms of cognitive impairment. The principal ACTH and VP compounds studied are listed in Table 3, together with the opiate antagonist naloxone—a compound also recently studied in AD.

In general, clinical studies with ACTH and VP peptides have been disappointing, although clinical effects have been reported and the search continues for more effective compounds (Berger & Tinklenberg, 1981; Tinklenberg, Thornton, & Yesavage, in press). It appears that the principal effects of the ACTH peptides are on mood and attention, rather than on learning and memory, and, thus, drug effects may resemble those seen with dihydroergotoxine and other "geriatric drugs" (Pigache, in press). Similarly, VP peptides ap-

TABLE 3

Neuropeptides

ACTH 4-10

ORG 2766 (ACTH 4-9 analog)

vasopressin

lysine vasopressin (LVP)

1-desamino-8-d-arginine vasopressin (DDAVP)

desglycinamide-arginine vasopressin (DGAVP)

naloxone, naltrexone

pear to produce non-specific CNS stimulation, rather than direct improvement of memory or other cognitive functions impaired in AD (Tinklenberg et al., in press). Whatever the mechanism, the magnitude of clinical change observed in clinical studies of ACTH and VP peptides in AD has been generally quite modest.

A recent study that generated considerable interest (Reisberg et al., 1983) suggested that the narcotic antagonist naloxone may be of clinical value in treating AD. Other evidence (Blass et al., 1983) questions the utility of the drug and, at present, several well-controlled studies are underway to determine whether the drug, or the oral analog naltrexone, is clinically effective in AD. Evidence from animal studies suggests that, like the ACTH and VP peptides, the primary effects of the drug may be on attentional processes rather than learning and memory (Arnsten, 1984).

Vascular and Rhealogic Agents

As discussed in the previous section on marketed drugs, the evidence to support use of the established vasodilators in AD is, at best, tenuous (Yesavage et al., 1979). The use of these compounds grew out of the hypothesis that dementia results from cerebral arteriosclerosis, reduced blood flow, and consequent cerebral ischemia. Of course, it is now clear that this is not the cause of AD and even in the case of vascular dementias, vasodilator therapy may be problematic since it may actually reduce blood flow to ischemic areas (Cook & James, 1981). Thus, there is little current research interest in vasodilator therapy in AD.

In contrast to the direct-acting vasodilators, the compounds listed in Table 4 have more complex metabolic or rhealogic effects and have been studied, or are under study, in patients with presumed AD or in samples that include AD patients. In general, these drugs may produce quite modest effects in some patients on psychiatric ratings of alertness, depression, and confusion, but there is no sound evidence of objective changes in memory or other cognitive variables. Of primary research interest at present are selected calcium channel blockers, particularly nimodopine, which have diverse metabolic effects and have not yet been adequately tested in either vascular dementias or AD.

Other Investigational Drugs of Interest

Several of the many other investigational drugs of interest are listed in Table 5. Among the compounds listed, those that have received by far the most attention are the so-called "nootropic agents"—piracetam and its analogs and CI-911. These drugs have clear behavioral effects in animal learning paradigms but do not produce the side effects seen with other psychoactive drugs. Piracetam, the prototype nootropic compound, is an analog of gamma amino-

TABLE 4

Vasoular and Rhealogic Agents

nylidrin

pentoxifylline

suloctodil

naftidrofuryl

vincamine, apovincamine, vinconate

calcium channel blockers (nimodipine)

TABLE 5

Other Investigational Drugs
of Interest

piracetam and analogs (aniracetam, oxiracetam, pramiracetam)

CI-911

4-amino-pyradine, 3, 4-diaminepyradine

Active Lipid

centrophenoxine

aluminum chelators

alapractolate

butyric acid (GABA) that has clear effects on brain metabolism, facilitates performance on measures of learning and retention in rats, and protects against hypoxia-induced memory impairment in animals (Giurgea, 1976). Controlled clinical studies in AD and other age-related cognitive disorders have been equivocal and suggest no clear pattern of cognitive improvement (Ferris et al., 1982). As noted previously, a combination treatment of piracetam plus lecithin was found more effective than either drug alone in facilitating retention in aged rats (Bartus, Dean, Sherman, Friedman, & Baer, 1981) and preliminary analyses of ongoing clinical studies (Ferris, 1981; Growdon et al., 1984) suggest that some patients with AD may also show response to this treatment. However, any effects are likely to be subtle.

Positive reports have appeared concerning the efficacy of the newer piracetam analogs in AD (Branconnier et al., 1983; Itil, Menon, Bozak, & Songar, 1982) and multicenter studies with several of these drugs, as well as with CI-911, are currently underway. Any conclusion as to whether these drugs represent significant improvements over the quite modest effects of piracetam must await the outcome of these studies. A dramatic therapeutic advance appears unlikely.

Among other experimental drugs of interest in AD are 4-aminopyradine and 3, 4-diaminepyradine, compounds with multiple pharmacologic effects that facilitate oxidative metabolism (Gibson &

Peterson, 1983); Active Lipid, a compound designed to fluidize cell membranes (Lyte & Shinitsky, 1984); centrophenoxine, a stimulant also thought to deplete age-related lipofuscin accumulation (Nandy, 1981); aluminum chelators such as desferrioxamine (DeBoni & McLachlan, 1981); and alaproclate, a 5-HT reuptake inhibitor (Carlsson, 1981).

In view of the emerging neurochemical evidence that AD involves multiple neurotransmitter systems (Bondareff, Mountjoy, & Roth, 1982; Bowen, 1983), it may be that therapeutic strategies involving combination treatments or even an individualized "cocktail" approach (Carlsson, 1981) will be necessary to develop effective treatments for what may be the most tragic and dehumanizing of all mental disorders.

Although clearly effective drugs have not yet been developed for treating the primary symptoms of AD, dramatic progress has been made in recent years in uncovering the neurochemical deficits in the disorder and, hence, in developing rational treatment strategies. If the pace of this progress continues, we may see the development of a truly effective compound for treating AD in the not too distant future. Such a drug would be of inestimable medical and social value.

REFERENCES

Arnsten, A. F. T. (1984). Behavioral effects of naloxone in animals and humans: Potential for treatment of aging disorders. In R. J. Wurtman, S. H. Corkin, & J. H. Growdon (Eds.), *Alzheimer's disease: Advances in basic research and therapies.* Cambridge, MA: Center for Brain Sciences and Metabolism Charitable Trust.

Bartus, R. T., Dean, R. L., Sherman, K. A., Friedman, E., & Baer, B. (1981). Profound effects of combining choline and piracetam on memory. *Neurobiology of Aging, 2,* 105–111.

Berger, P. A., & Tinklenberg, J. R. (1981). Neuropeptides and senile dementia. In T. Crook & S. Gershon (Eds.), *Strategies for the development of an effective treatment for senile dementia.* New Canaan, CT: Mark Powley Associates.

Blass, J., Reding, M. J., Drachman, D., Mitchell, A., Glosser, G., Katzman, R., Thal, L. J., Grenell, S., Spar, J. E., Larue, A., & Liston, E. (1983). Cholinesterase inhibitors and opiate antagonists in patients with Alzheimer's disease. *New England Journal of Medicine, 309,* 555–556.

Bondareff, W., Mountjoy, L. Q., & Roth, M. (1982). Loss of neurons of origin of the adrenergic projection to cerebral cortex (nucleus locus coeruleus) in senile dementia. *Neurology, 32,* 164–168.

Bowen, D. (1983). Biochemical assessment of neurotransmitter and metabolic dysfunction and cerebral atrophy in Alzheimer's disease. In R. Katzman (Ed.), *Biological Aspects of Alzheimer's Disease.* Cold Spring Harbor, NY: Banbury Report 15.

Branconnier, R. J., & Cole, J. O. (1980). The therapeutic role of methylphenidate in senile organic brain syndrome. In J. O. Cole & J. E. Barrett (Eds.), *Psychopathology in the Aged.* New York: Raven Press.

Branconnier, R. J., Cole, J. O., Dessaim, E. C., Spera, K. F., Ghazrinian, S., & DeVitt, D. (1983). The therapeutic efficacy of pramiracetam in Alzheimer's disease: Preliminary observations. *Psychopharmacology Bulletin, 19,* 726–730.

Carlsson, A. (1981). Aging and brain neurotransmitters. In T. Crook & S. Gershon (Eds.), *Strategies for the development of an effective treatment for senile dementia.* New Canaan, CT: Mark Powley Associates.

Christie, J. E., Shering, A., Ferguson, J., & Glenn, A. I. M. (1981). Physostigmine and arecoline: Effects of intravenous infusions in Alzheimer presenile dementia. *British Journal of Psychiatry, 138,* 46–50.

Cook, P., & James, I. (1981). Cerebral vasodilators. *New England Journal of Medicine, 305,* 1508–1513.

Crook, T. (1979). Central-nervous-system stimulants: Appraisal of use in geropsychiatric patients. *Journal of the American Geriatric Society, 27,* 476–477.

Crook, T. (1983). Hydergine and the vasodilators: Are they useful in geriatric psychiatry? Paper presented at the annual Brookdale Symposium on Geriatric Medicine, Mt. Sinai School of Medicine, New York, December.

Crook, T., & Gershon, S. (Eds.) (1981). *Strategies for the development of an effective treatment for senile dementia.* New Canaan, CT: Mark Powley Associates.

Crook, T., Ferris, S., Sathananthan, G., Raskin, A., & Gershon, S. (1977). The effect of methyphenidate on test performance in the cognitively impaired aged. *Psychopharmacology, 52,* 251–255.

Davis, J. M. (1981). Antipsychotic drugs. In T. Crook & G. Cohen (Eds.), *Physicians handbook on psychotherapeutic drug use in the aged.* New Canaan, CT: Mark Powley Associates.

Davis, K. L., Mohs, R. C., Rosen, W. G., Greenwald, B. S., Levy, M. I., & Horvath, T. B. (1983). Memory enhancement with oral physostigmine in Alzheimer's Disease. *New England Journal of Medicine, 308,* 721–723.

DeBoni, V., & McLachlan, D. R. C. (1981). Biochemical aspects of SDAT and aluminum as a neurotoxic agent. In T. Crook & S. Gershon (Eds.), *Strategies for the development of an effective treatment for senile dementia.* New Canaan, CT: Mark Powley Associates.

Ferris, S. H. (1981). Empirical studies in senile dementia with central nervous system stimulants and metabolic enhancers. In T. Crook & S. Gershon (Eds.), *Strategies for the development of an effective treatment for senile dementia.* New Canaan, CT: Mark Powley Associates.

Ferris, S. H., Reisberg, B., Crook, T., Friedman, E., Schneck, M., Mir, P., Sherman, K. A., Corwin, J., Gershon, S., & Bartus, R. T. (1982). Pharmacologic treatment of senile dementia: Choline, L-DOPA, piracetam, and choline plus piracetam. In S. Corkin, K. L. Davis, J. H. Growdon, E. Usdin, & R. J. Wurtman (Eds.), *Alzheimer's disease: A report of progress.* New York: Raven Press.

Gibson, G. E., & Peterson, C. (1983). Pharmacologic models of age-related cognitive impairments. In T. Crook, S. Ferris, & R. Bartus (Eds.), *Assessment in Geriatric Psychopharmacology.* New Canaan, CT: Mark Powley Associates.

Giurgea, C. (1976). Piracetam: Nootropic pharmacology of neurointegrative activity. *Current Developments in Psychopharmacology, 3,* 221–276.

Growdon, J. H., Corkin, S., & Huff, F. J. (1984). Alzheimer's disease: Treatment with nootropic drugs. In R. J. Wurtman, S. H. Corkin, & J. H. Growdon (Eds.), *Alzheimer's disease: Advances in basic research and therapies.* Cambridge, MA: Center for Brain Sciences and Metabolism Charitable Trust.

Harbaugh, R. E., Roberts, D. W., Coombs, D. W., Saunders, R. L., & Reeder, T. M. (1984). Preliminary report: Intracranial cholinergic drug infusion in patients with Alzheimer's disease. *Neurosurgery, 15*(4), 514–518.

Hollister, L. E., & Yesavage, J. (in press). Co-Dergocrine for senile dementias: After thirty years many unanswered questions. *Annals of Internal Medicine.*

Itil, T. M., Menon, G. N., Bozak, M., & Songar, A. (1982). The effects of oxiracetam (ISF 2522) in patients with organic brain syndrome (a double-blind controlled study with piracetam). *Drug Development Research, 2,* 447–461.

Jarvik, L. F., & Milne, J. F. (1975). Gerovital-H3: A review of the literature. In S. Gershon & A. Raskin (Eds.), *Genesis and treatment of psychologic disorders in the elderly.* New York: Raven Press.

Kugler, J., Oswald, W. D., Herzfeld, U., Seud, R., Pingel, J., & Welzel, D. (1978). Long-term treatment of the symptoms of senile cerebral insufficiency: A prospective study of hydergine. *Dtsch. Med. Woechenschr., 103,* 456–462.

Little, A., Chuaqui-Kidd, P., & Levy, R. (1984). Early results from a double-blind, placebo-controlled trial of high dose lecithin in Alzheimer's disease: Psychometric test performance, plasma choline levels and the effects of drug compliance. In R. J. Wurtman, S. H. Corkin, & J. H. Growdon (Eds.), *Alzheimer's disease: Advances in basic research and therapies.* Cambridge, MA: Center for Brain Sciences and Metabolism Charitable Trust.

Loew, D. M., & Singer, J. M. (1983). Stimulants and senility. In I. Creese (Ed.), *Stimulants: Neurochemical, behavioral, and clinical perspectives.* New York: Raven Press.

Lyte, M., & Shinitzky, M. (1984). Possible reversal of tissue aging by a lipid diet. In R. J. Wurtman, S. H. Corkin, & J. H. Growdon (Eds.), *Alzheimer's disease: Advances in basic research and therapies.* Cambridge, MA: Center for Brain Sciences and Metabolism Charitable Trust.

McDonald, R. J. (1982). Drug treatment of senile dementia. In D. Wheatly (Ed.), *Psychopharmacology of old age.* London: Oxford University Press.

Nandy, K. (1981). Lipofuscin pigment and immunological factors in the pathogenesis and treatment of senile dementia. In T. Crook & S. Gershon (Eds.), *Strategies for the development of an effective treatment for senile dementia.* New Canaan, CT: Mark Powley Associates.

Ostfeld, A., Smith, C. M., & Stotsky, B. A. (1977). The systemic use of procaine in the treatment of the elderly: A review. *Journal of the American Geriatric Society, 25,* 1–19.

Pigache, R. M. (in press). The human psychopharmacology of peptides related to ACTH and alpha-MSH. In L. Gram, E. Usdin, S. Dahl, & P. Kragh-Sorensen (Eds.), *Clinical Pharmacology and Psychiatry.* New York: Macmillan.

Reisberg, B., Ferris, S. H., Anand, R., Mir, P., Geiber, V., DeLeon, M. J., & Roberts, E. (1983). Effects of naloxone in senile dementia: A double-blind trial. *New England Journal of Medicine, 308,* 721–722.

Rosenberg, G. S., Greenwald, B., & Davis, K. (1983). Pharmacologic treatment of Alzheimer's disease: An overview. In B. Reisberg (Ed.), *Alzheimer's disease: The standard reference.* New York: The Free Press.

Spiegel, R. Huber, F., & Lobule, S. (in press). A controlled long-term study with ergoloid mesylates (Hydergine) in healthy, elderly volunteers. Results after 2 years. *Journal of the American Geriatric Society.*

Summers, W. K., Viesselman, J. O., & Marsh, G. M. (1981). Use of THA in treatment of Alzheimer-like dementia: Pilot study in twelve patients. *Biology of Psychiatry, 16,* 145–153.

Thal, L. J., Masur, D. M., Sharpless, N. S., Fuld, P. A., & Davies, P. (1984). Acute and chronic effects of oral physostigmine and lecithin in Alzheimer's disease. In R. J. Wurtman, S. H. Corkin, & J. H. Growdon (Eds.), *Alzheimer's disease: Advances in basic research and therapies.* Cambridge, MA: Center for Brain Sciences and Metabolism Charitable Trust.

Tinklenberg, J. R., Thornton, J. E., & Yesavage, J. A. (in press). *Clinical Geriatric Psychopharmacology and Neuropeptides.*

Yesavage, J. A., Tinklenberg, J. R., Hollister, L. E., & Berger, P. A. (1979). Vasodilators in senile dementia: A review of the literature. *Archives of General Psychiatry, 36,* 220–223.

Yesavage, J. A., Hollister, L. E., & Burian, E. (1979). Dihydroergotoxine: 6-mg versus

3-mg dosage in the treatment of senile dementia. Preliminary report. *Journal of the American Geriatric Society, 27,* 80–82.

Yoshikawa, M., Hirai, S., Aizawa, T., Kuroiwa, Y., Goto, F., Sofue, I., Toyokura, Y., Yamamura, H., & Iwasaki, Y. (1983). A dose-response study with dihydroergotoxine mesylate in cerebrovascular disturbances. *Journal of the American Geriatric Society, 31,* 1–7.

Questions

1) Does the development of these drugs portend an end to the need for psychotherapy with dementia patients?

2) Discuss the relationship between these drugs and techniques for assessment of dementia and depression.

29/SOME ETHICAL ISSUES IN DEMENTIA CARE

Peter V. Rabins, MD
Nancy L. Mace, MA

Editor's Introduction

The authors of this chapter are also the authors of one of the finest books on how to care for a dementia patient in the home. (*The 36-Hour Day* was reviewed in *CG*, v. 1, #3, p. 103.)

In this chapter Rabins and Mace reflect upon the fact that since dementia makes an individual less capable of making his/her own decisions, the caregiver must usurp autonomy and perhaps even limit the patient's freedom. Related issues are the professional commitment to beneficence and non-maleficence as well as the legal principle of incompetency.

Four cases illustrate the ethical dilemmas posed by dementia, death, and disability. The authors advise that dementia, in and of itself, does not necessarily entail mental incompetence. The expressed wishes of the patient should be considered. Family issues are also reviewed.

By definition, the dementing illnesses impair an individual's intellectual functioning. However, they do not necessarily impair judgement or the ability to make decisions about the future. Because of this seeming contradiction the dementing illnesses can present ethical, moral, and legal dilemmas. These can range from whether a person should be allowed to change a will, drive a car, or go for a

Peter V. Rabins and Nancy L. Mace are affiliated with the T. Rowe and Eleanor Price Teaching Service, Department of Psychiatry and Behavioral Sciences, Johns Hopkins University School of Medicine. Melinda Fitting, PhD and Peter Dans, MD provided helpful reviews of earlier drafts.

Send correspondence and reprint requests to: Peter Rabins, MD, Meyer 279, 600 N. Wolfe Street, Baltimore, MD 21205.

503

walk by herself to whether she can decide to forego an operation. This article will examine some of these dilemmas from the perspective of the professional care provider. It will briefly discuss the ethical, moral, and legal principles involved and will discuss four actual but disguised cases to illustrate the conflicts that can arise. It will also suggest potential solutions. It will not discuss questions about allocation of resources. It will separate principles into moral (societal), ethical (professional), and legal categories although this breakdown is controversial.

MORAL ISSUES

Autonomy, the right of an adult to fully determine his destiny, is a basic societal moral stricture. American society has chosen not to deprive an individual of her autonomy unless her behavior is dangerous or, in the case of guardianship, the ill person clearly cannot care for herself. Restrictions on individual autonomy have been codified in law and clarified by legal decisions which will be discussed below. Not all cultures or societies place the rights of the individual at the apex of moral values, but this is a general western value especially supported by law in the United States.

ETHICAL ISSUES

The helping professions have ethical guidelines which reflect society's moral beliefs. They may be codified in such things as the Hippocratic Oath or in specific documents of a professional association. In their broadest context, they reflect several ideas. *Beneficence*, the goal of helping the distressed, underlies all the helping professions. A related doctrine, which has probably been most clearly expressed in the medical professions, is, to do no harm. This has been called *nonmaleficence*. These two ethical principles—to do no harm and to relieve suffering—sometimes conflict. Indeed, most interventions have some risks associated with them. The clinician must inform the patient and family of the risks but not frighten them by being overly explicit. The choice to accept or reject the risks is theirs.

LEGAL PRINCIPLES

When an individual reaches the age of majority (adulthood) she is automatically assumed to be fully competent and autonomous. The lack of competency, i.e., *incompetency*, must be legally determined. Then and only then can the individual's autonomy be limited.

Surprisingly, the guidelines for determining lack of competency are far from clear. They usually involve a determination that an individual is unable to make judgements in her best interest. Since individuals can make bad decisions or decisions that others disagree with, incompetency decisions are fraught with conflict. Roth, Meisel, and Lidz (1977) have suggested the following criteria by which a person's competency might be judged. These are (1) whether the person evidences a choice; (2) whether the choice is a reasonable one; (3) whether the choice is based upon rational reasons; (4) whether the person has the ability to understand the information vital to the decision-making process; and (5) whether the person has an actual understanding of that information. An examination of these criteria shows why arguments about competency can be complex. How does one decide whether any choice is reasonable? How does an authority decide what specific information is needed to go into making a decision, and furthermore, how does he decide whether the person in question actually "understands" that information? Decisions about incompetency demand judgements by the deciding legal authority but input from professionals is almost always sought. As will be discussed below, we do not believe the court need be involved in many cases of dementia, even where severe impairment is present.

These moral, ethical, and legal principles do not exist in a vacuum. In fact they often conflict. The health professional can play a key role in helping those under their care to consider the various pressures of these conflicts, to assure that harm is minimized, and to help resolve differences. The four cases below illustrate these conflicts and suggest that an understanding of the principles involved can aid in resolving them.

CASE EXAMPLES

Case 1

Mrs. A. was a 71-year-old woman referred to a church social work agency by concerned neighbors. She had no known family. She had become increasingly forgetful over the past several years and had become lost in her neighborhood on two occasions. When the social worker visited Mrs. A. at home and expressed the neighbor's concern, they discussed the fact that Mrs. A. had been feeling confused in recent months. The social worker found Mrs. A. to be a healthy appearing woman who repeated herself frequently during the interview and was noticeably forgetful. However, she had food in the kitchen, was not evidently undernourished, and had kept the house orderly. Mrs. A. agreed to a medical evaluation of her memory difficulties and the social worker set up an appointment. However, the appointment was not kept. When Mrs. A. was recontacted by the social worker, she stated that she did not need such an evaluation and refused it. The social worker made two subsequent visits at which Mrs. A. again refused medical attention.

The social worker was concerned about Mrs. A.'s becoming lost, her ability to shop for her food, and her ability to obtain help in an emergency. However, after talking with the neighbors and the patient she found no specific evidence that Mrs. A. had been in any dangerous situations other than getting lost. Several of the neighbors helped her with shopping but she prepared her own meals. The social worker did not believe it was in the woman's best interest to continue living alone in a totally unsupervised setting and discussed alternative living situations with her, but Mrs. A. adamantly refused to move.

In this case example the practitioner was faced with a person suffering some cognitive decline who refused medical intervention and relocation to a more sheltered living situation. Because she found no evidence that the client was a danger to herself, the social worker chose to continue making home visits. She was subsequently able to establish a relationship with the client and able to periodically reassess the situation. She decided that if instances of dangerous behaviors arose she would then attempt to make changes through the legal system if Mrs. A. continued to refuse care. Six months after the contact the situation remains unchanged.

This example identifies several issues. First, it illustrates that conflict can arise between the concept of individual autonomy and the practitioner's goal of helping the person (i.e., beneficence). In the example, the social worker acceded to the client because she was meeting her own needs and because there was no evidence of danger. The patient's autonomy was thus upheld. However, a second element, that of compromise was also initiated. The social worker was able to maintain continued contact with the client and thus some vigilance. She was able to act beneficently although not to the extent she would have liked. This case also demonstrates that cognitive impairment does not always lead to significant behavioral abnormalities. Judgements of danger are difficult but understanding the characteristics of the specific dementing illness from which the patient suffers aids in deciding what the patient can still do safely. Determining how deficits are reflected in impaired day-to-day function is equally important. The next case further illustrates this point.

Case 2

Mrs. B. was a 68-year-old woman who had been independent all her adult life. For several years her memory had been deteriorating and she was significantly forgetful. She had stopped driving and therefore had no way to shop. Her children had been shopping for her or taking her shopping but her daughter was returning to work and this would no longer be possible. Her family now felt she was unable to live alone any longer. A medical evaluation demonstrated that her health was good and revealed no treatable cause of her thinking impairment. A cognitive assessment found impaired memory and loss of abilities to carry out complex tasks. The family felt that nursing home placement might be best. This was a source of great distress to the patient and she refused to move. A standoff ensued in which the patient refused placement and the children demanded it. She clearly understood the dangers of living alone, including the fact that she might forget to turn off the stove (and thus start a fire) and that she could no longer shop for food. The family felt she was a hazard to herself and to others in her apartment building and consulted a social services agency. The social worker suggested a daytime companion who could cook and shop for Mrs. B. After initially resisting, Mrs. B. accepted this compromise but she continues to complain about it.

As in case 1, Mrs. B. is relatively functional. However, unlike case 1, this person is in some danger: she cannot obtain food or cook for herself. What if a compromise could not have been worked out?

We believe the presence of probable danger supports the need for more direct intervention. When harm is likely, beneficence takes precedence over autonomy. Ultimately this might lead to legal action but this should be a last resort and is rarely necessary in our experience. In the example some autonomy was maintained but the presence of a caretaker in the house certainly limited it.

Here again, compromise led to a solution in which the patient's autonomy could be partially supported. This is not always possible but health care providers can often see alternatives which partially meet the conflicting goals of the people and principles involved. In some situations there can be no compromise. It is in such instances that turning to the legal system is the appropriate recourse. If imminent danger exists we believe that the health practitioner has an ethical obligation to intervene to save life or to provide a stabilizing intervention until a legal decision can be made.

Case 3

A 78-year-old man who had no family had been in a nursing home for several years. During his stay in the nursing home his condition deteriorated markedly. While he was still able to walk with assistance and to feed himself with his hands, he could no longer express himself verbally. For several days he had become increasingly agitated and more negative than usual. Physical examination suggested pneumonia as a possible cause of the recent deterioration. A decision then had to be made about evaluation and treatment of the pneumonia.

This example raises questions about life saving interventions in a severely ill patient. In this example a decision to intervene had to be made quickly because delaying the decision would likely have led to death. Had the patient been competent, his wishes would have been sought and his autonomy upheld. In this example, however, the patient could not communicate, thus there was no direct way to know his wishes or determine competency.

If the patient had had an available and responsible family member they should have been contacted, and their wishes considered and followed unless the practitioner believed that motives other than the best interest of the patient were intended. In the case of the latter, a judicial decision should probably be sought.

The clinician also needed to consider the ability of the acute treatment to restore the patient to a functional level. If the treatment could have done so then the principle of beneficence would suggest its initiation.

Questions about withholding a life-saving medical intervention arise in several different circumstances. At times the patient has the cognitive and emotional ability to participate in the decision. When this is the case the discussions should ideally take place prior to the appearance of the life-threatening condition. However, whether or not previous discussions have taken place, involvement of the person is appropriate *if* he has the ability to participate. This preserves the person's autonomy. In the case of dementia, a decision must first be made as to whether the person truly has the autonomy (i.e., the competency) to make such decisions. The difficulties in establishing incompetency are noted above.

Is a legal determination *necessary* when the patient cannot participate? We do not believe so. Decisions about such matters are presently often made without the involvement of the legal system. We would suggest involvement of the court only when significant conflict exists or no family is available. Several legal precedents have supported this view.

In Superintendent of Belchertown State School vs. Saikewicz (Annas, 1979), the court was asked by the institution caring for an elderly mentally retarded man with no family whether it should treat a newly developed leukemia. The court determined that it rather than the patient's physicians should decide whether treatment could be withheld because the patient himself could not participate in the decision and because his underlying mental retardation was life long. In re Dinnerstein (Langone, 1981), on the other hand, the court ruled that the family could decide if resuscitation should be withheld in the event of a catastrophic illness in a 70-year-old woman with progressive Alzheimer's disease. The court stated that their desire to withdraw the life-sustaining respirator would be withdrawing active treatment of an acute problem but would not bring the patient any improvement in her underlying disorder. These two cases support the legal principle that an active treatment can be withheld in consultation with the family if it is unlikely to lead to improvement in a severely ill patient.

We believe that the decision to withhold a treatment must be made on a case-to-case basis and that it should rest, in part, on possible gains that the ill person himself might make. When the patient's autonomy cannot be preserved by involving him in the decision, beneficence must be considered. Active treatment should be instituted if significant improvement in functioning can result. If the potential gains from treatment are not expected to bring significant improvement, the family's wish should take precedence. If there is no family or guardian who had a relationship prior to the onset of the disorder, we believe active treatment should be pursued.

Similar guidelines have been developed to guide institution of cardio-pulmonary resuscitation (CPR) in severely ill individuals who have suffered a cardiac arrest. Rabkin et al. (1976) suggest that CPR be withheld if the answers to the following 3 questions are "Yes": (1) is the underlying disease irreversible? (2) is the patient's current physiological status beyond improvement? (3) is death imminent? We would suggest that similar guidelines be used to decide when withholding acute treatment of a demented person is an option. The following should be answered yes: (1) Is the impairment severe? (2) is it unlikely that the patient will improve significantly if a therapy is initiated? (3) Is death imminent? Identifying these are crucial questions may help families clarify the issues underlying this difficult decision to withhold treatment.

Case 4

Mr. D., a 63-year-old man who had suffered Alzheimer's disease for at least 6 years, was placed in a nursing home by his family because they could no longer provide care at the level at which he required it. He was unable to ambulate and had been incontinent for more than one year. He had no intelligible speech but did appear to brighten up considerably when visited by his family. After being in the nursing home for four months he began having difficulty swallowing. One month later he stopped eating. Attempts by the staff to feed him met with marked resistance. He pushed nursing aides away at times and at other times did not swallow what was in his mouth. He began losing weight and became cachetic. Two months later he would/could not chew or swallow any food. A meeting was held with the family, the director of nursing, and the physician regarding placement of a nasogastric tube. They discussed the fact that no structural reason for an inability to swallow had been found and that Mr. D. would soon die if an alternative means of feeding him was not initiated.

Feeding difficulties are common in the late stages of many dementing illnesses. There are several potential causes. They can arise as sequelae of the neurologic disorder itself if the brain centers involved in feeding, chewing and/or swallowing are affected. They can also result if the musculature involved becomes ineffective. Psychiatric disorders can also lead to refusal to eat. Depressed patients may feel they should not eat because they are bad or cannot eat because they mistakenly believe they have cancer. Paranoid patients may believe their food is being poisoned and not eat.

Therefore, the first step in deciding about how to intervene in instances of life-threatening behavior (here eating refusal) is to properly diagnose why the patient is acting in a dangerous manner. If a potentially treatable condition is a likely or possible cause of the behavior then we believe the decision should be made to treat the underlying psychiatric or medical disorder; that is, beneficence should be followed if treatment and reversibility exist. In the current example no treatable cause was found and the patient would have required feeding through a nasogastric tube or gastrostomy for the rest of his life. This case differs from case 3 in that the intervention is not time limited. It shares in common the fact that withholding the intervention will likely lead to starvation and death.

When the patient is unable to participate in the discussion, we do not believe the motive of wanting to die as an explanation for food refusal/not eating can be invoked. Without the patient's *explicit* input that he does not want to eat, we believe no intention can be ascribed to the behavior.

In the present example the family and the health care system are left totally with the decision, a decision as to what is best for the patient and for the family. The emotional cost of prolonged suffering to the family and the financial cost to the family and society are sometimes as involved in the decision and we believe an open discussion of all issues is best.

Courts have supported the principle of allowing withdrawal of an already established treatment when no chance of recovery exists. The case of In re Quinlan (Annas, 1979) is a well known example in which the court decided that the family could decide whether to continue a life saving intervention (respirator support) since the patient was unable to.

Withholding an intervention to feed a patient differs from withdrawing respirator support. The patient on a respirator is not usually awake and is unlikely to suffer discomfort. Starvation in an awake person, on the other hand could, be a prolonged uncomfortable state. Moreover, feeding an ill and helpless person is a moral precept strongly ingrained in societal mores. We do believe that the ultimate decision should rest with the family if the patient cannot contribute. Choosing to withhold feeding should be an alternative although we personally do not favor doing so. Lynn and Childress (1983) have recently reviewed the issues involved in the withholding and withdrawal of food and water.

CONCLUSION

These case examples illustrate some difficult decisions that can arise during the care of cognitively impaired individuals. The ill person's wishes must be considered if he is competent. Judgment about competency must rest on the understanding of the effects of the dementia on behavior and judgement, not on the fact that dementia is present. If the patient cannot participate we believe previously expressed wishes should be considered. If family is available and if selfish motives are not major determinants, their wishes should be followed. When a decision is made to withhold treatment, it should be done only after careful deliberation and should be made only when the potential for recovery is low. Finally, health care practitioners should keep in mind that family members often need emotional support during the deliberation over the delicate issues and after a difficult decision has been made.

REFERENCES

Annas, G. J. (1979). Reconciling Quinlan and Saikewicz: Decision making for the terminally ill incompetent. *American Journal of Law and Medicine, 4:* 367–396.
Langone, J. (1981). *Thorny issues.* Boston: Little, Brown and Co.
Lynn, J., & Childress, J. F. (1983). Must patients always be given food and water? *Hastings Center Report, 13,* 17–21.
Rabkin, M. T., Gillerman, G., & Rice, N. R. (1976). Orders not to resuscitate. *New England Journal of Medicine, 295,* 364–366.
Roth, L. H., Meisel, A., & Lidz, C. W. (1977). Tests of competency to consent to treatment. *American Journal of Psychiatry, 134,* 279–284.

Questions

1) Discuss a dementia case you are familiar with, and consider the ethical dimensions posed by Rabins and Mace.

2) How does the presence of depression or paranoia distort the patient's ability to express his/her wishes?

Index